ROTHMAN'
RUGBY LE
YEARBOOK

Raymond Fletcher
and David Howes

ROTHMANS

HEADLINE

First published in 1996
by HEADLINE BOOK PUBLISHING LTD

10 9 8 7 6 5 4 3 2 1

COVER PHOTOGRAPHS

Front Cover: Great Britain winger Jason Robinson touches down at Wembley against Australia in the opening encounter of the 1995 Halifax Centenary World Cup. *Photographer:* Clive Brunskill, of the Allsport Photographic Agency.

Back Cover: World record signing Paul Newlove in action on his debut for St. Helens against Workington Town in November 1995, three days after his £500,000-rated transfer from Bradford Bulls. *Photographer:* Andrew Varley, of the Varley-Wilkinson Agency.

ACKNOWLEDGEMENTS

The compilers would like to acknowledge the assistance of the Rugby League Record Keepers' Club, club secretaries and individuals in providing material as a further source of reference for accuracy.

PHOTOGRAPHERS

Modern day domestic photographs in this *Rothmans Rugby League Yearbook* are mainly from the files of the *Rugby Leaguer* – with acknowledgement to Chief Photographer Gerald Webster and his staff – and freelance photographer Andrew Varley, of the Leeds-based Varley-Wilkinson Agency.

British Library Cataloguing in Publication Data
Rothmans Rugby League Yearbook – 1996
1. Rugby football – Great Britain –
Periodicals
793.33.3.0941 GV945.9.G7

ISBN 0 7472 7767 2

Typeset by Wearset, Boldon, Tyne and Wear

Reproduced, printed and bound in Great Britain by
The Bath Press, Avon

HEADLINE BOOK PUBLISHING LTD
A division of Hodder Headline PLC
338 Euston Road
London NW1 3BH

Rothmans Rugby League Yearbook 1996

CONTENTS

CONTENTS

EDITORIAL PREFACE

It says much for their faith in the future of Rugby League that Headline publishers were keen to bring out an edition in time for the launch of the new Super League and summer rugby era. And we thought we were going to have a year to prepare for the next edition!

It has meant an all-out effort, but hope we have maintained the high standards we always set ourselves. Unfortunately, the circumstances have brought a reduction in pages to a still hefty 320 and resulted in some regular features being abbreviated.

We are again indebted to those who have supplied data for cross-checking purposes, including the Record Keepers' Club and a number of individual compilers. Thanks also to the Rugby Football League and their staff for taking the time, in a particularly busy period for them, to supply official statistics.

Ian Marshall has again been an important link at Headline, while Celia Kent's occasional gentle nudge has kept us on our toes. The yearbook has also become part of the game's North East expansion with Wearset, based in South Tyneside, taking over the typesetting and we have been impressed with their enthusiasm and efficiency.

Thanks finally, and always, to our wives for putting up with our battle against deadlines and cursing of a new computer with a mind of its own.

● **Facts and figures in this *Rothmans Rugby League Yearbook* as at 1 February 1996. It should be noted that for record purposes the 1995-96 season ended with the last of the league matches on 21 January and did not include the Silk Cut Challenge Cup which became part of the 1996 season.**

RAYMOND FLETCHER

DAVID HOWES

SUPER LEAGUE

Rarely can two eras of sport have been so dramatically linked as those which saw Rugby League's Centenary Season being followed by the first Super League and summer rugby campaign. One hundred years of playing in winter and many of the game's well-loved traditions now make way for what administrators believe will be a bright, new era for Rugby League. With a top Super League of just 12 clubs, quality has finally been put ahead of quantity and matches will be played in much better conditions for both players and spectators. The inclusion of Paris in the European Super League should also give impetus to plans to expand the game worldwide.

But many of the game's most loyal followers have still to be convinced that the revolutionary changes will be for the better and feel that much has already been lost as old values were cast aside in the race to go up-market. Many team strips have lost all sense of identity and tradition, while even club names have become trendier with the additional titles of Bears, Hawks, Centurions and the like.

The game itself is also changing with most of the rule changes aimed at increasingly faster play. They have brought a big increase in the number of high-scoring matches, reaching a peak last season with Castleford's 50-44 win at London Broncos.

Perhaps it is the pace at which the old game is changing that has upset so many. For the moves toward Super League and all it means began only in April 1995 when the League accepted News Corporation's £87m. It was part of News boss Rupert Murdoch's battle plan to gain control of televised Australian Rugby League, but the British League saw it only as a way of reviving a game that was in serious financial trouble.

Whatever the reasons or motives for the revolution, it has taken place and Super League is now a fact of Rugby League life. The *Rothmans Rugby League Yearbook* acknowledges that and records what the first season has in store.

THE CLUBS
European Super League: Bradford Bulls, Castleford, Halifax, Leeds, London Broncos, Oldham Bears, Paris St. Germain, St. Helens, Sheffield Eagles, Warrington, Wigan, Workington Town
Division One: Batley, Dewsbury, Featherstone Rovers, Huddersfield, Hull, Keighley Cougars, Rochdale Hornets, Salford Reds, Wakefield Trinity, Whitehaven, Widnes
Division Two: Barrow Braves, Bramley, Carlisle, Chorley Chieftains, Doncaster Dragons, Highfield, Hull Kingston Rovers, Hunslet Hawks, Leigh Centurions, Swinton, York

THE SEASON
The first Super League matches were to be staged on the weekend beginning Friday 29 March 1996 with Paris St. Germain and Sheffield Eagles set to launch the new era in France.

Each club will play the others in its division home and away, with the last matches being played on the weekend of 25 August.

Promotion and relegation will be one up–one down between the top two divisions with two up–two down between the First and Second.

BSkyB will televise live a Super League match every Friday and Saturday evening throughout the season. The choice of other match days vary from club to club over Friday, Saturday and Sunday with kick-off times between afternoon and early evening.

Most clubs are aiming to provide pre-match family entertainment, including curtain-raisers between Academy teams.

Super League executive Mal Meninga, former skipper of Australia, shows off the Super League logo during a promotional visit to Headingley, Leeds.

Super League will be sponsored by Stones Bitter in a £1.75m three-year deal.

The final of the 1996 Silk Cut Challenge Cup, which began in January, will be staged as usual at Wembley on 27 April.

The European International Championship, involving England, France and Wales, will be staged on Wednesday evenings in June.

THE PREMIERSHIPS

The 1996 Super League champions will play the fourth-placed club with the runners-up taking on the club that finishes third, the higher placed club having home advantage each time. Both games will take place on Sunday 1 September and the winners will contest the final at Old Trafford, Manchester, a week later.

There will also be a Divisional Premiership with the finalists meeting as the first part of the now traditional double-header at Old Trafford. The Divisional Premiership play-offs will involve the First Division champions entertaining the Second Division title holders, with the winners meeting the victors of a clash between the First Division second and third placed clubs, with the former having home advantage.

WORLD CLUB CHAMPIONSHIP

The climax of the Super League season was to be the World Club Championship, but the legal battle between Australian RL and News Corporation put the prospects of it being launched in 1996 in doubt.

It was still expected, however, that the Championship would be a major part of future Super League seasons on the following lines:

The eight-team tournament will involve the top four clubs in the European Super League and the top four in the Australasian Super League.

In Europe, Super League's top team will play Australasia's fourth placed club, while the

European runners-up face the club finishing third Down Under.

In Australia, the winners of the Australasian Super League title will take on the team that finishes fourth in Europe, leaving the runners-up to face the third placed European club.

The winners of the European double-header will go forward to the World Club Championship semi-final to be played in England. There will be similar play-off games in Australia.

The first Super League World Club Championship final was scheduled for Australia, but future finals could be played anywhere in the world.

MEMORIES

1995-96 HEADLINES
Behind the scoring feats and records of the 1995-96 season were a number of stories which made the headlines:

THE CENTENARY SEASON
Early plans to celebrate the game's Centenary Season fell flat with a number of proposed events cancelled. The biggest disappointment was the calling off of a planned Founders' Day including a carnival parade at Huddersfield, the game's birthplace, on 28 August.

The decision to have an interim season before switching over to summer rugby also faced criticism as it meant each club cramming 20 League matches plus the Regal Trophy in less than five months. And it included a month's break to take in the Centenary World Cup, which turned out to be a huge success after early fears of it being a flop.

FRAMING THE FUTURE
Two days after the last matches of the game's Centenary Season the League's Board of Directors presented their up-dated *Framing of the Future (Minimum Standards Guideline Details)* report. Chief Executive Maurice Lindsay told a press conference on 23 January that it was "The bible for future progress of our sport and, as such, its importance cannot be overestimated."

He emphasised that clubs must be prepared to abide by the stricture of the contents for they provided the key to the distribution of Rupert Murdoch's News Corporation funds throughout the game. It was Murdoch's £87m that had launched plans for Super League almost a year earlier.

Although the 51-page document's far-reaching proposals had to be voted on by the full RL Council on 7 February (after this yearbook went to press) most were expected to be given the go-ahead.

The proposals, which are reduced in some instances for non-Super League clubs, included:

● Grounds to have minimum capacity of 10,000 (6,000 under cover) with at least 2,500 seated.
● Clubs must appoint a Chief Executive, Financial Controller, Football Manager, Media/Marketing Manager, Commercial Manager and Academy Youth Development Manager by 1 April.
● 50 per cent of the News Corporation money must go on facility development, until the minimum standards for grounds are met.
● A salary cap of 40 per cent of total income to be installed on 1 January 1997, to include benefits in kind to players.

At the same press conference it was announced that the Board of Directors had made other important decisions, which included:

● A voting structure change to give Super League clubs four votes, First Division clubs two and Second Division one.
● Chorley Chieftains and Highfield warned that unless they improved they could be relegated to the National Conference League. Doncaster Dragons told they would not get full membership until they improved.
● The overseas quota to be increased from three to five players for all countries, including emerging nations who had previously been excluded. London Broncos, however, would continue to be exempt from any restrictions. Other clubs signing more than three overseas players will have to pay up to £15,000 into the RFL Development Fund.
● Referees to be assisted with TV replays of debatable try decisions in matches being covered by Sky TV.

IN LEAGUE WITH UNION
Rugby Union's revolutionary decision to go professional also had far-reaching consequences for Rugby League. With supreme irony, the major U-turn came during Rugby League's Centenary Season which marked the Northern Union's breakaway from the English RU over broken-time payments to players.

Now after 100 years of ostracising all things Rugby League, the Rugby Union was prepared to accept a virtual free interchange of players between the two codes and sanction other ventures that would have been unthinkable even a year ago.

Former Welsh RU international Jonathan Davies became the first professional league player to officially return to Rugby Union when he left Warrington for Cardiff on 31 October in a reported £100,000 transfer deal.

A few other players made a similar return to Rugby Union and others planned to play both codes by taking advantage of Rugby League's switch to playing in summer. John Devereux appeared to be the first to make a definite move to play all the year, when Widnes agreed to rent him out to Sale RU.

Further indications of the amazing bridge-building between the codes came when Wigan accepted an invitation to the Middlesex Sevens and agreed to face Bath RU in two challenge matches.

Wigan and neighbours Orrell RU were also planning joint arrangements, while Leeds RU agreed to move in with Leeds RL at Headingley.

The breaking down of barriers inevitably led to speculation that the two codes would eventually merge to form one game of rugby and after the unbelievable events of the past 12 months that could not be ruled out.

RULE CHANGES

The sudden introduction of new rules four months into the Centenary Season was criticised for its timing but brought general acceptance that they would speed up the game even more.

Instigated by Greg McCallum, the Referees' Coaching Director, the rules which came into force from 11 December were:
● No striking for the ball at the play-the-ball by the tackling team's acting half back.
● The ball must always be played backwards at the play-the-ball.

● All scrums to be at least 20 metres in from the touchline, instead of 10 metres.
● The scoring team to restart play by kicking off from the centre spot.

The reasoning behind the play-the-ball changes was to simplify the rule around an area that often caused problems of interpretation for referees.

Having all scrums at least 20 metres in from touch was intended to encourage more blind-side play.

The decision to make the scoring team restart play was to give the opposition the chance to strike back immediately after conceding points. There had been growing concern that a scoring side could get a "roll on" by receiving the ball again each time they scored.

Although the rule changes were said to be for an experimental period, they were soon adapted by the Super League International Board.

The season had also begun with a change which doubled the number of substitutes to four players per squad, who could only be used once. But this was to apply only to Stones Bitter Centenary Championship matches.

All other club matches, including cup ties, were to have two substitutes per squad but allowing up to four changes.

It was also decided to introduce action replays in televised Super League matches to assist referees over debatable decisions. Referees would be linked with an official in the stand studying the action in slow-motion replays.

NEWLOVE GOES IN RECORD DEAL

Paul Newlove was transferred from Bradford Bulls to St. Helens in a record £500,000 deal on 29 November. St. Helens paid £250,000 in cash and parted with Paul Loughlin, Sonny Nickle and Bernard Dwyer in exchange for the Great Britain Test centre.

The overall value exceeded the £440,000 Wigan paid Widnes for Martin Offiah in January 1992, which remains the record cash-only transfer. (Also see TRANSFERS chapter.)

JUNE

Oldham hooker David Stephenson banned for two years by the League for using steroids . . . . Castleford prop Dean Sampson joins Parramatta for a summer stint . . . . Hull sign Doncaster duo Terry Manning and Alex Green . . . . Oldham introduce their own drug-testing programme . . . . Widnes lose court case and sign the Super League contract . . . . Featherstone Rovers recruit former Doncaster forward Simon Tuffs . . . . Western Samoan Lukeni Savelio joins Salford . . . . Bradford Northern part company with coach Peter Fox . . . . Wales's World Cup preparation tour of America devalued by the withdrawal of several key players . . . . Hull forward Jon Sharp joins Featherstone Rovers . . . . Sheffield Eagles capture Halifax hooker John Lawless . . . . Wales beat an American XIII 66-10 in Philadelphia . . . . Bradford Northern winger David Myers joins Western Suburbs on a summer contract . . . . Swinton sign St. Helens duo Peter Cannon and Jason Roach in a £30,000 deal . . . . Sheffield Eagles pair Ryan Sheridan and Richard Chapman jailed for four months for taking part in a motorway speed chase . . . . Renamed Bradford Bulls appoint Australian Brian Smith as coach . . . . The League accuse Australian counterparts of dirty-tricks campaign by offering signing-on deals to contracted players . . . . St. Helens offer eight players, including Welsh international Jonathan Griffiths . . . . Warrington coach Brian Johnson rejects an offer from hometown Illawarra . . . . St. Helens and Newcastle Knights row over insurance cover and return date for Saints forward Chris Joynt . . . . London Broncos recruit Terry Matterson from Brisbane Broncos . . . . Dewsbury forward Andy Fisher moves to Hull . . . . Wales run in 18 tries in 92-4 defeat of an American XIII in Philadelphia . . . . Leigh exchange teenage half back Sheldon Hannon for Salford's £25,000-rated Shaun Brown . . . .

Wigan, Leeds and Sheffield Eagles join the chase for New Zealand RU wing star Jonah Lomu . . . . Welsh international Paul Kennett listed at £25,000 at top of Swinton's summer sale . . . . Keighley Cougars sign Wigan hooker Phil Cantillon for £25,000 . . . . Warrington announce plans for a 17,000-capacity stadium near their current Wilderspool home . . . . Dewsbury release coach Tony Fisher for three months to help prepare South Africa for the Centenary World Cup . . . . Hull offer hooker Mike Dixon at £35,000 . . . . Doug Laughton resigns as coach of Leeds only hours after the club announce the appointment of New Zealander Dean Bell as his assistant . . . . All Black winger Jonah Lomu rejects Rugby League offers and stays in RU code . . . . Winger Paul Sterling priced at £100,000 by Hull . . . . England RU scrum half Dewi Morris turns down approach from Workington Town . . . . Leeds appoint former New Zealand loose forward Hugh McGahan as team manager . . . . The Rugby League Council decides to maintain the overseas quota at three after demands for a reduction to two . . . . Widnes receive transfer demands from Emosi Koloto, Darren Wright, Paul Hulme and David Hulme . . . . Sheffield Eagles' Great Britain Under-21 skipper Alex Thompson signs a two-year contract with Newcastle Knights . . . . Bradford Bulls sign winger Jon Scales from Leeds and offer a winter contract to South Queensland Crushers utility back St. John Ellis, formerly with Castleford . . . . Australian forward Darren Fritz to rejoin Wakefield Trinity after a two-year absence . . . . Bramley to share Leeds RU's ground.

JULY

Halifax sign winger Abi Ekoku from London Broncos . . . . Castleford's Great Britain Under-21 forward Andy Hay moves to Sheffield Eagles . . . . Bradford Bulls recruit Widnes prop Andy Ireland . . . . London Broncos duo Mark Johnson and Logan Campbell join Workington Town . . . . Hull sign winger Leigh Deakin from

York .... Wakefield Trinity centre Adrian Flynn moves to Castleford .... Keighley Cougars recruit Salford utility back Jason Critchley in part-exchange for Neil Kenyon .... Hull K.R. pay St. Helens £15,000 for prop Andy Dannatt .... A special meeting of the League votes for one-up/one-down for the Super League and two-up/two-down for the First Division .... Workington Town coach Peter Walsh walks out to take up assistant coach role at Illawarra .... Hull sack former Great Britain winger Paul Eastwood after criticising the club .... Keighley Cougars coach Phil Larder put in charge of England for the Centenary World Cup, assisted by Castleford's John Joyner and Oldham's Andy Goodway .... Kath Hetherington becomes first woman president of the Rugby Football League .... The League decide to trial the use of four substitutes in Centenary Championship matches .... Highfield appoint Tommy Frodsham as coach to replace Chris Arkwright .... Leeds re-open bidding for Jonah Lomu with a £2.5m offer .... Free transfer Shane Cooper moves from St. Helens to neighbours Widnes .... Hull loose forward Dean Busby joins St. Helens .... Swinton recruit Neil Measures from Leigh .... England name a 40-man squad for the Centenary World Cup, including Wigan teenager Kris Radlinski but omitting Leeds captain Garry Schofield .... Wakefield Trinity's Daio Powell charged with unlawful killing outside a Perth, Australia, nightclub .... Keighley Cougars withdraw a threat of legal action over exclusion from the Super League .... Salford sign Dewsbury threequarter Darren Rogers .... Oldham offer Kiwi loose forward Mike Kuiti at £30,000 .... Workington Town sign Frenchman David Fraisse from Bradford Bulls .... Wakefield Trinity recruit Western Suburbs utility back Steve Georgallis for the Centenary campaign .... Mark Elia leaves St. Helens to join French club Albi as player-coach .... Workington Town appoint Phil McKenzie and Billy McGinty as joint player-coaches .... Hull K.R. sign Sam Stewart from London Broncos .... Halifax recruit Western Samoan full back Michael Umaga .... Wakefield Trinity pay Oldham £20,000 for Mike Kuiti .... Castleford sign Andrew Schick from the Brisbane Redcliffe club .... Keighley Cougars winger Johnny Walker moves to Batley .... Halifax list Craig Turner at £20,000 .... Hunslet sign Steve Durham from Wakefield Trinity and Jason Viller from Rochdale Hornets .... Steve Ball becomes Hull's first full-time chief executive.

AUGUST

Newly formed Doncaster Dragons, based at Stainforth, admitted into the Centenary Second Division .... Doug Laughton appointed team manager at Widnes .... Tony Myler quits as coach of Widnes .... Loose forward Les Holliday leaves Dewsbury for a second spell at Swinton .... Castleford recruit former Doncaster hooker Colin Maskill .... Wigan lift the Charity Shield by beating Leeds 45-20 in Dublin .... Wigan reject a £100,000 bid from Western Reds for Barrie-Jon Mather .... A League Tribunal rules that John Schuster is registered with Halifax despite signing for Salford .... Huddersfield sign Gus O'Donnell on loan from St. Helens .... Doncaster Dragons appoint Peter Astbury as coach .... Salford sign Western Samoan RU World Cup star Fata Sini .... Warrington ask £75,000 for Gary Tees and £65,000 for Dave Elliott .... Widnes list Emosi Koloto at £50,000 .... The League announce a winner-takes-all prize of £75,000 for the Centenary Champions plus perpetual retention of the Championship Trophy .... Huddersfield sign Salford forward Bob Marsden for £20,000 .... League Tribunal orders St. Helens to pay Hull £80,000 for Dean Busby, plus £20,000 for a Great Britain appearance and 20 per cent of any future transfer profit .... Bramley sign Hull K.R.'s Kenny Hill .... Fiji RU centre Carlos Hassan joins Bradford Bulls .... Halifax full back Steve Hampson moves to

Salford .... Oldham sign Western Samoan Afi Leulai .... Wigan release Frano Botica .... Wakefield Trinity sign veteran full back Keith Mumby from Bradford Bulls .... Wakefield Trinity prop Mark Sheals is transferred to Swinton .... Kurt Sorensen moves from Whitehaven to take over as coach of Workington Town .... Salford offer Gary Tyrer at £10,000 .... League headquarters moved from Chapeltown Road to Red Hall, Leeds .... Paul Eastwood, axed by Hull, joins neighbours Hull K.R. .... Huddersfield offer Phil Hellewell at £15,000 .... Prop Gary Rose listed at £35,000 by Hull .... Andy Platt bids for an England place in the Centenary World Cup by joining Widnes for the winter campaign .... Bradford Bulls recruit second row Warren Jowitt from Hunslet Hawks .... Parramatta's Brett Plowman joins Widnes .... Sheffield Eagles sign Frenchman Frederic Banquet from Featherstone Rovers.

SEPTEMBER

St. Helens full back David Lyon joins Sheffield Eagles on loan .... Whitehaven appoint New Zealand Junior Kiwis coach Stanley Martin as coach .... Dewsbury sign ex-Bradford utility back Dave Watson on a match-by-match basis .... Salford ask £10,000 each for Phil Swift and Darren Betts .... Wakefield Trinity sign Cavill Heugh on loan from London Broncos .... St. Helens pay Widnes £85,000 for utility back Karle Hammond .... Hull hand over £50,000 to Halifax for loose forward Gary Divorty .... Wigan ask £120,000 for Great Britain prop Barrie McDermott .... The League increase the ban for use of steroids from two to four years .... The League confirm soccer club Newcastle United's desire to enter a Super League team in 1997 .... Western Samoa RU star Shem Tatupu joins Wigan .... League consider organising some other Centenary celebrations after cancelling Founders' Day Parade in Huddersfield .... Leeds and Western Samoa forward Esene Faimalo ruled out of World Cup with eye injury .... Wigan's Barrie McDermott moves to Leeds for £100,000 .... Castleford sign Brendon Tuuta from Featherstone Rovers .... Halifax recruit Western Samoan centre Fereti Tuilagi .... Salford sign Peter Edwards from Auckland Warriors .... League Tribunal orders Salford to pay Dewsbury £30,000 for Darren Rogers plus £5,000 after 15 first-team matches .... Warrington recruit scrum half Mike Ford from South Queensland Crushers .... Featherstone Rovers sign Richard Slater from Wakefield Trinity .... Widnes utility back Sean Alvarez moves to Rochdale Hornets .... St. George centre Graeme Bradley signs for Bradford Bulls .... Wigan assistant coach Joe Lydon turns down the coaching role at Super League club Paris St. Germain .... Scrum half Mark Aston rejoins Sheffield Eagles in a £70,000 deal .... Warrington list Chris Rudd at £35,000 .... York pay £10,000 for Bramley's Andy Marson .... Dewsbury recruit six South African players .... Doncaster Dragons sack coach Peter Astbury and assistant Andy Gascoigne .... Bradford Bulls make Paul Newlove available .... Doncaster Dragons appoint Peter Regan as coach .... Castleford sign Frano Botica from Auckland Warriors .... London and Brisbane Broncos both discard problem player Julian O'Neill .... Chorley sign St. Helens half back Gus O'Donnell .... Sheffield Eagles recruit Danny McAllister from South Queensland Crushers .... Brendon Tuuta acquitted of assault following Featherstone's match at Workington Town in February .... Leeds bring in Texan strength trainer Edgar Curtis in advisory capacity .... Diana Ross to be star entertainer at World Cup opening ceremony.

OCTOBER

Rugby League Centenary stamps issued .... England beat Australia at Wembley in opening match of Halifax Rugby League Centenary World Cup .... Leeds captain Garry Schofield faces disrepute charge after accusing League Chief Executive Maurice Lindsay of interfering

13

in England team selection to keep him out of World Cup squad . . . . Warrington's Gary Tees and Paul Darbyshire sign for Australian club Western Suburbs . . . . Wigan centre Gary Connolly out of early World Cup matches with pneumonia . . . . Australian Test winger Wendell Sailor decides not to join London Broncos . . . . Former Sheffield Eagles coach Bill Gardner to rejoin coaching staff for a month . . . . Cardiff RU officials meet Warrington counterparts to discuss return of Jonathan Davies to Welsh RU . . . . Plan for first professional club in Scotland – Border Reivers . . . . Bradford Bulls sign Carlisle forward Simon Knox . . . . Peter Rush quits as Rochdale Hornets chairman and director, replaced by Ray Taylor . . . . South Africa seeking to replace Tony Fisher as coach . . . . Emerging Nations World Cup tournament starts with double-header at Featherstone . . . . Three World Cup players banned after failing drugs test – Pierre Grobbelaar (South Africa), Stephan Millet (France) and Syd Eru (New Zealand) . . . . Sheffield Eagles sign three Fijian World Cup stars – Waisale Sovatabua, Joe Dakuitoga and Malakai Yasa . . . . Leigh sign Tonga's Jimmy Veikoso . . . . England winger Shaun Edwards ruled out of World Cup by a knee injury infection after one match . . . . Rugby League Chief Executive Maurice Lindsay criticises BBC for not giving greater coverage to World Cup . . . . International Board meeting in London makes no move to resolve Super League-Australian RL dispute . . . . Chorley sign centre Mike Stewart from Rochdale Hornets and Chorley RU captain Mike Bramwell . . . . Warrington's Jonathan Davies becomes first professional Rugby League player to return to Rugby Union since the 13-a-side code went professional . . . . Keighley Cougars hit financial crisis . . . . Australian Peter Regan replaces Peter Astbury and Andy Gascoigne as Doncaster's coach . . . . New Zealander Stan Martin takes over as Whitehaven coach . . . . Wakefield Trinity may move to new £200 million centre of excellence

proposed for former Sharlston Colliery site . . . . Garry Schofield severely reprimanded for bringing the game into disrepute by accusing League Chief Executive Maurice Lindsay of vetoing his England selection . . . . Hunslet sign Tim Sharp from York . . . . Workington Town sign Tongans Peri Amato and Taukolo Tonga . . . . Bradford Bulls sign Australian utility player Alan Wilson from St. George . . . . International Board investigate Australian coach Bob Fulton's criticism of controller of referees Greg McCallum after World Cup semi-final and take no action . . . . Bradford Bulls forward Paul Dixon joins Sheffield Eagles . . . . Featherstone Rovers sign New Zealand international forward Simon Angell . . . . Cook Islands beat Ireland 22-6 at Bury in first Emerging Nations World Cup final . . . . New Zealand RL president Graham Carden rebukes BARLA chief Maurice Oldroyd over links with Australian RL . . . . Australia beat England 16-8 in World Cup final at Wembley . . . . Huddersfield sack George Fairbairn as coach . . . . Paris seek Andy Goodway as coach . . . . Phil Ford angry over £30,000 transfer fee placed on him by Salford . . . . Former Junior Kiwi Damien Mackie joins Featherstone Rovers . . . . Former coach Dave Cox dies of leukaemia in Australia . . . . Wakefield Trinity sign full back Andrew Leeds from Australian club Western Suburbs . . . . League president Kath Hetherington joins attack on BARLA'S Australian RL links . . . . Leeds centre Kevin Iro retires from New Zealand international scene.

NOVEMBER

London Broncos play first of four "home" matches at the Harlequins RU ground, The Stoop, losing 34-50 to St. Helens . . . . Sheffield Eagles sign French international back Jean-Marc Garcia . . . . Bradford Bulls capture Dewsbury full back Nathan Graham . . . . Broadcaster Stuart Pyke quits as St. Helens director . . . . Former Australian Test captain Mal Meninga is chief guest at Super League launch at Headingley . . . . League Chief

Executive Maurice Lindsay says the Ashes trophy will never be competed for again, adding "the Ashes are for cricket" .... Former Australian Test forward Peter Tunks appointed Wakefield Trinity chief executive .... Bradford Bulls coach Brian Smith appointed their chief executive .... Cook Islands half back Ali Davys signs for Salford .... The remainder of Hull's famous Threepenny Stand demolished to make way for new structure .... Wigan sign outstanding Yorkshire junior Lee Gilmour from Dewsbury Moor .... Wigan invited to play in Middlesex RU Sevens .... The Rugby Football League appoint Mark Newton as director of marketing and Tony Gale as internal audit executive .... Sir John Hall still hopes to have a Newcastle club in the 1997 Super League .... Dewsbury crisis over £330,000 tax debt .... Warrington's Iestyn Harris named the John Smith's International Player of the Year .... Bradford Bulls' Deryck Fox returns to Featherstone Rovers along with Roy Powell in exchange for Matt Calland .... Barrie-Jon Mather quits Wigan after failing to command first team place .... Warrington's Greg Mackey returning to Australia .... Former St. George centre Rod Hill joins York .... Doncaster play their first home match at Regal Meadow Court Stadium, Stainforth, and beat York 31-8 .... Phil Windley quits as Hull coach after hearing that the club are showing an interest in overseas coaches, including Australian Phil Sigsworth .... Salford list Mike Gregory at £15,000 after dispute with coach Andy Gregory .... St. Helens list Bernard Dwyer at £95,000 after he asks for a move .... French international Frederic Banquet leaves Sheffield Eagles for Wakefield Trinity .... Bradford Bulls to pay amateur clubs £500 each time they sign one of their players .... Warrington sign Fijian centre Manoa Thompson from Auckland Warriors .... South Africa Rugby League end alignment with the British RFL .... London Broncos announce one-year deal to play home matches at Charlton Athletic soccer ground .... Hunslet

Hawks sign Tongan international Des Maea from Auckland Warriors .... Graham Heptinstall resigns as Doncaster chief executive .... Rochdale Hornets sign Adam Greenwood from Bradford Bulls and take Jason Green on loan from Widnes .... Oldham coach Andy Goodway signs new two-year contract to end speculation that he was to take over at new Paris club .... Halifax list Martin Ketteridge at £25,000 after he requested a move .... Carlisle sign New Zealander Richard Henera .... Hunslet Hawks celebrate first match at the new South Leeds Stadium with 37-10 defeat of Leigh Centurions .... League chairman Rodney Walker predicts club mergers in future .... Warrington assistant coach Clive Griffiths withdraws from Wales RU coach shortlist .... Halifax transfer list Mark Preston at £70,000 after the winger decides against playing full time .... Super League clubs reject breakaway moves .... Leeds transfer list Richie Eyres at £95,000 .... Oldham seek compensation from Orrell RU after Nigel Heslop returns to play for his old club .... Warrington sign Tongans Mateaki Mafi and Salesi Finau .... Darryl Van de Velde appointed Huddersfield coach .... St. Helens sign Paul Newlove from Bradford Bulls in world record £500,000 deal – paying £250,000 and exchanging Paul Loughlin, Bernard Dwyer and Sonny Nickle .... Leeds Metropolitan University survey into racism in Rugby League reveals it is only a small problem .... Barrie-Jon Mather set to prolong dispute with Wigan by joining Australian club Perth Western Reds .... Former player Brian Noble appointed a full-time coach at Bradford Bulls .... Dewsbury sign former Doncaster half back Barry Eaton as a free agent .... Whitehaven take Wigan reserve winger Darren Williams on loan .... Warrington forward Bruce McGuire to return to Australia .... Batley list Simon Wilson at £10,000 after he asked for a transfer.

DECEMBER

Wigan and Bath have preliminary talks about meeting in League-Union challenge matches

.... Bradford Bulls sign Australian forward Jeremy Donougher from South Sydney .... Swinton capture Tongan World Cup players Willie Wolfgramm and Talite Liava'a .... St. Helens dismiss reports that Scott Gibbs is set to return to Rugby Union .... Adrian Hadley threatens to quit Widnes over contract dispute .... Hull reject Bradford Bulls' offer for Steve McNamara and Richard Gay .... Oldham sign Ireland's Emerging Nations World Cup forward Tony Nuttall .... Halifax's transfer-listed winger Mark Preston considering playing for his old RU club Fylde during the winter .... Experimental rule changes announced – scoring teams to restart play, scrums to be 20 metres from touch, ball must be played backwards at play-the-ball with no striking for it by opposition .... Leeds and Wigan confirm interest in New Zealand RU international half back Junior Tonu .... Workington Town drop interest in former England RU scrum half Dewi Morris .... Leigh full back Steve Wynne retires with recurring shoulder injury .... Rugby Union to allow the immediate return of former players who switched to Rugby League – but only for non-competitive matches this season .... Hunslet sign Simon Wilson from Batley .... Wigan consider staging Orrell RU matches at Central Park .... Super League authorities block Barrie-Jon Mather's hopes of leaving Wigan for Perth Western Reds .... Finalists England and Australia set to receive £1 million each from Halifax Rugby League Centenary World Cup .... League reject move to scrap overseas quota .... Leo Casey and Owen Simpson among nine Featherstone Rovers players put on transfer list .... John Dorahy rules himself out of the running for Hull coaching job .... Hull drop Maea David after he signs for Australian club Illawarra .... Warrington reject Kevin Ellis's move to return .... Aberavon RU club inquire about entering a team in Division Two next season .... Leeds deny making record bid for Warrington's Iestyn Harris .... Oldham to add Bears to title .... League delay decision on re-admitting Blackpool Gladiators to Division Two .... Chorley bid for Hull's Tim Street .... Halifax sign Junior Kiwi Martin Moana .... Oldham fined £4,000, suspended for 12 months, for fielding weakened team against Warrington in August .... Martin Offiah outjumps world champion Jonathan Edwards on BBC-TV Sports Personality of the Year competition .... Keighley Cougars given financial lifeline by consortium of Yorkshire businessmen plus a £50,000 loan from the League .... Hull Kingston Rovers sign Papua New Guinea internationals Stanley Gene and John Okul .... Bradford Bulls sign young Leeds international Paul Cook in exchange for Carl Hall and an undisclosed sum of cash .... Warrington sign Paul Barrow from Swinton .... Moldovan forward Vyacheslav Sapega not retained after trials with Oldham reserves .... St. Helens scrum half Bobbie Goulding banned for three matches after being cited by Halifax for high tackle on John Fieldhouse, but it was not proven that the foul caused the prop's broken jaw .... Michel Mazaré appointed coach of Paris Super League club .... Plan for new format for the RL Challenge Cup proposed by Halifax Chief Executive .... Va'aiga Tuigamala signs two-year extension to contract, keeping him at Wigan until 1999 .... Bradford Bulls rebuilding continues with the signing of Dewsbury's David Longo in exchange for Craig Moore and Shaun Austerfield .... Keighley Cougars take Dewsbury's Paul Delaney on loan .... Salford reject Leeds move for Under-21 international centre Nathan McAvoy after being offered Alan Tait, Richie Eyres and Harvey Howard plus cash in exchange .... Warrington ban Iestyn Harris from playing Rugby Union during close season .... League study implications of European Court ruling that threatens transfer system .... Wigan coach Graeme West apologises to Widnes for suggesting they narrowed pitch before Regal Trophy tie .... Dewsbury half back Mark Conway retires .... Greg Mackey plays last match for Warrington before returning to Australia .... League Chief

Executive Maurice Lindsay appointed first chairman of World Super League International Board .... Rochdale Hornets forward Tony Hilton suspended for three months for taking banned ephedrine drug, which is used in cough mixtures .... International Super League Board adopt new play-the-ball and kick-off rules being tried out in England .... League deny report that Rupert Murdoch's News Corp could veto transfers .... Halifax list Great Britain Under-21 hooker Paul Rowley at £250,000 .... Batley reject Leeds bid for £110,000-rated Australian scrum half Glen Tomlinson .... Hull appoint former Australian Test player Phil Sigsworth as coach .... Widnes's £8m redevelopment of Naughton Park given go-ahead .... Oldham's Mike Edwards makes surprise signing for Swinton after loan spell with Leigh Centurions .... St. Helens and Wigan seek League permission to continue traditional Boxing Day meetings .... All but two Boxing Day matches postponed because of frost .... Leigh sign Steve Lay from Halifax for £12,000 .... St. John Ellis moves from Bradford Bulls to Halifax .... Halifax coach Steve Simms calls for remaining Stones Bitter Centenary Championship matches to be cancelled because of fixture pile-up .... Bradford Bulls centre Matt Calland banned for rest of League season after being sent off for third time during present campaign .... League order club officials to stop criticising fixture pile-up .... Wigan and England captain Shaun Edwards awarded OBE in New Year Honours.

JANUARY

Gavin Allen to join London Broncos instead of new Australian club Adelaide Rams .... Swinton appoint coach Tony Barrow chief executive .... Former Leeds coach Doug Laughton accepts out-of-court settlement over his claim of constructive dismissal .... Brian Johnson quits as Warrington coach after club record 80-0 defeat at St. Helens in Regal Trophy semi-final – assistant Clive Griffiths

takes over at least until end of League season .... St. Helens fined £10,000 – half suspended until end of year – for fielding weakened team at Wigan on Boxing Day when they lost 58-4 .... Peter Roe quits as Barrow coach .... Former Australian Test forward Les Davidson returning to Warrington after seven years .... Dave Callaghan starts work as the League's first broadcast manager .... Castleford sign Hull's international full back Richard Gay for reported £100,000 .... Salford crowned First Division champions while Hull Kingston Rovers lift the Second Division title .... Wakefield Trinity appoint Australian Mitch Brennan as coaching director and marketing manager .... David Peacock departs as League's finance executive .... American Gladiators champion Wesley "Two Scoops" Berry to have trials with Keighley Cougars .... Peter Roe appointed Swinton coach .... Wales named BBC Wales Sports Team of 1995 .... Dewsbury players to go full-time .... Wigan win Regal Trophy for record-extending eighth time after classic encounter with St. Helens .... Thatto Heath and West Hull knock out professionals in Silk Cut Challenge Cup third round .... Wigan clinch record-extending seventh successive Stones Bitter Championship .... Wigan referee John Connolly stands down after making crucial error in Halifax-Warrington match .... Wigan to compete in Rugby Union's Middlesex Sevens .... Coach Eric Hughes departs St. Helens after learning his contract is not to be renewed and Australian Shaun McRae is already lined up as a replacement .... Halifax protest over Wigan's inclusion in Middlesex Sevens causing postponement of Super League match .... 100 years of winter Rugby League ends on a typical wet, freezing Sunday afternoon .... Bradford Bulls sign £100,000-plus rated Australian scrum half Glen Tomlinson from Batley in exchange for Roger Simpson, David Turpin and Phil Hardwick .... John Myler quits as St. Helens Academy coach in protest over Eric Hughes' departure .... Australian

Test forward Les Davidson not returning to Warrington because he is contracted to Australian Super League .... Warrington appoint John Dorahy as coach and Alex Murphy as football executive .... Widnes rent John Devereux to Sale Rugby Union as the first player to play both codes throughout the year .... The League announce several proposals put forward by their Board of Directors in *Framing of the Future* report .... Board of Directors recommend TV action replays to assist referees in televised Super League matches; overseas quota increased to five; Chorley Chieftains and Highfield warned they must improve or be relegated to National Conference League .... Doncaster Dragons fail to win full membership of the League .... Oceania squad to tour Britain in October .... BARLA suspend dialogue with the League after the professional body move to take over National Conference League .... Mike Nicholas heads move to field Welsh club in Division Two .... Northampton Knights seek entry .... Phil Larder appointed coach of Great Britain, with Clive Griffiths and Gary Hetherington as assistants .... Plans for Challenge Cup to precede Super League each season .... St. Helens confirm Shaun McRae as coach .... London Broncos sack coach Gary Grienke .... Barrie-Jon Mather fails in

High Court move to gain release from Wigan .... Salford release Phil Ford to return to Welsh RU with Rumney .... Wigan admit not having passed on World Cup match receipts but deny cash crisis .... Bath RU and Wigan agree to May dates for cross-code clashes .... Wigan's Shaun Edwards wins appeal against one-match ban to make 43rd successive Challenge Cup appearance .... Snow wipes out all but four of Silk Cut Challenge Cup fourth round ties .... West Hull beat York to become first amateur club to knock out two professionals from Challenge Cup in same season .... York put entire squad of 31 players on transfer list .... Castleford forward Tony Morrison rejoins Swinton .... Great Britain v. France Under-21 international postponed because of Silk Cut Challenge Cup backlog .... Leeds RU sign five-year deal to play home matches at Headingley with other closer ties planned .... London Broncos appoint Tony Currie as new coach .... Jim Crellin replaces Tommy Frodsham as Highfield's team manager with Alex Melling the new player-coach .... Paris allay fears that they are not ready for Super League by announcing international-packed squad .... Workington Town and Featherstone Rovers each receive £250,000 grant from Sports Ground Initiative Trust; Leigh get £150,000.

Leeds threequarter Francis Cummins, scorer of 14 tries and 16 goals in 22 Centenary season appearances.

CLUBS

The following is a focus on last season's 33 professional Rugby League clubs, the section providing each club with a profile and an analysis of their 1995-96 campaign on a match-by-match basis with a summary for each first team player.

KEY

In the individual club profiles the following headings are featured:

First season refers to when the club gained senior league status. In some instances clubs have disbanded and re-formed, sometimes under different titles. For record purposes these changes are ignored except where there has been a break of more than one full season.

Honours. Until they were scrapped in 1970, the Yorkshire and Lancashire Leagues were among the honours in the professional game. Before 1903 they operated under the title of the Lancashire and Yorkshire Senior Competitions. Winners of these competitions are included under the Lancashire and Yorkshire League Champions. The pre-1903 Yorkshire Senior Competition should not be confused with the league operating for A-teams in Yorkshire which had the same title.

Regal Trophy is the current title for the John Player/Player's No. 6 Trophy competition.

Coaches. The clubs' individual coaching register is from the start of the 1974-75 season.

Attendances. Crowds in brackets are at neutral venues.

Appearances. Players' totals are based on official teamsheets submitted to the League after each first team match. + indicates playing substitute appearance.

Great Britain Register. The figure in brackets after a player's name is the number of Great Britain appearances he made while serving the club under whose entry he is listed, and the number after the + sign indicates playing substitute. This is followed by the time-span between his first and last British cap at that club.

Signings Register. * Indicates where clubs have agreed to a player being signed 'on loan', a temporary transfer, the Rugby Football League prohibiting a subsequent transfer within 28 days. Where a player on loan has not been retained, his return to his original club is also marked *.

Date of Birth. The dates are supplied in good faith by the Rugby Football League from their registration of players. This also applies to dates of signing and previous club.

In the match-by-match review for each club the following abbreviations are used:

SBC	—	Stones Bitter Centenary Championship	A	—	Away
FD	—	First Division	W	—	Won
SD	—	Second Division	L	—	Lost
RT	—	Regal Trophy	D	—	Drawn
P	—	Preliminary Round	dg	—	Drop goal
H	—	Home	Pr	—	Probationer

BARROW BRAVES

Ground: Craven Park (01229-820273)
First Season: 1900-01. Added Braves to title in 1995-96
Nickname: Braves
Chairman: Alan Winward
Secretary: Karen Heighton
Honours: **Division Two** Champions, 1975-76, 1983-84
Challenge Cup Winners, 1954-55
Beaten finalists, 1937-38, 1950-51, 1956-57, 1966-67
Regal Trophy Beaten finalists, 1980-81
Lancashire Cup Winners, 1954-55, 1983-84
Beaten finalists, 1937-38

RECORDS

Match
Goals: 17 by Darren Carter v. Nottingham C., 27 Nov 1994
Tries: 6 by Val Cumberbatch v. Batley, 21 Nov 1936
Jim Thornburrow v. Maryport, 19 Feb 1938
Frank Castle v. York, 29 Sep 1951
Steve Rowan at Nottingham C., 15 Nov 1992
Points: 42 by Darren Carter v. Nottingham C., 27 Nov 1994

Season
Goals: 135 by Joe Ball, 1956-57
Tries: 50 by Jim Lewthwaite, 1956-57
Points: 305 by Ian Ball, 1979-80

Career
Goals: 741 by Willie Horne, 1943-58
Tries: 352 by Jim Lewthwaite, 1943-57
Points: 1,818 by Willie Horne, 1943-58
Appearances: 500 by Jim Lewthwaite, 1943-57
Highest score: 138-0 v. Nottingham C., 27 Nov 1994
Highest against: 90-0 at Leeds, 11 Feb 1990
Attendance: 21,651 v. Salford (League), 15 Apr 1938

COACHING REGISTER
● **Since 1974-75**

Frank Foster	May 73 - Apr 83
Tommy Dawes	May 83 - Feb 85
Tommy Bishop	Feb 85 - Apr 85
Ivor Kelland	May 85 - Feb 87
Dennis Jackson	Feb 87 - Nov 87
Rod Reddy	Nov 87 - Nov 89
Dennis Jackson	Nov 89 - Apr 90
Steve Norton	May 90 - Feb 91
Paul Kavanagh	Feb 91 - July 92
Geoff Worrall	July 92 - Apr 93
Denis Ramsdale	May 93 - Sep 94
Peter Roe	Sep 94 - Jan 96

GREAT BRITAIN REGISTER
(19 players)

Bill Burgess	(16)	1924-29
Bill Burgess	(13)	1962-68
David Cairns	(2)	1984
Chris Camilleri	(2)	1980
Charlie Carr	(7)	1924-26
Frank Castle	(4)	1952-54
Roy Francis	(1)	1947
Harry Gifford	(2)	1908
Dennis Goodwin	(5)	1957-58
Jack Grundy	(12)	1955-57
Phil Hogan	(4+1)	1977-78
Willie Horne	(8)	1946-52
Phil Jackson	(27)	1954-58
Joe Jones	(1)	1946
Bryn Knowelden	(1)	1946
Eddie Szymala	(1+1)	1981
Ted Toohey	(3)	1952
Alec Troup	(2)	1936
Jack Woods	(1)	1933

1995-96 REGISTRATION DATE

Signed	Player	Club From
4.8.95	McDermott, Brett	Roose ARL
8.8.95	Chelton, Gavin	–
21.8.95	Clarke, Darren	Roose ARL
24.8.95	Walsh, Timothy	–
15.9.95	*Why, Adrian	London B.
15.9.95	Hughes, Alan	Askam ARL
27.10.95	Robinson, Glyn	Millom ARL
3.11.95	Brown, John	Kirby Lonsdale RU
10.1.96	Devereux, Roy	–

BARROW BRAVES 1995-96 PLAYERS' SUMMARY

	Date of birth	App	T	G	D	Pts	Previous club	Signed
Ashcroft, Steve	29.12.69	19+1	1	0	0	4	Chorley B.	11.3.94
Atkinson, Phil	25.9.74	13+1	2	29	2	68	Ulverston ARL	24.6.93
Barber, Glen	29.1.73	2+1	1	0	0	4	Australia	8.8.95
Bent, Peers	28.12.70	1+1	0	0	0	0	Blackpool G.	22.6.93
Brown, John	11.4.71	1+1	0	0	0	0	Kirby Lonsdale RU	3.11.95
Chelton, Gavin		8+2	0	0	0	0		8.8.95
Clarke, Darren	14.5.70	0+2	0	0	0	0	Roose ARL	21.8.95
Clayton, Richard	24.2.70	2+1	0	0	0	0	Chorley	9.3.95
Creary, Richard	21.6.69	6	0	0	0	0	Askam ARL	12.8.93
Everett, Phil	23.4.76	16	3	0	0	12	Barrow I. ARL	24.5.93
Green, Mark	23.7.78	0+1	0	0	0	0	Roose ARL	6.5.94
Hannah, Chris	22.11.71	8+2	1	0	0	4	Keighley C.	4.12.94
Hansen, Sam	23.7.68	16	2	0	0	8	Tonga	4.10.93
Howarth, Stuart	2.9.74	7	1	0	1	5	Ulverston ARL	10.8.93
John, Martin	16.2.76	4+8	2	0	0	8	Ulverston ARL	24.5.93
Kerr, Gareth	17.1.76	9	4	0	0	16	Walney ARL	24.5.93
Little, Duane		0+1	0	0	0	0		
Luxon, Jeff	2.6.71	9	2	0	0	8		
Masters, Jacob		0+1	0	0	0	0		
McDermott, Brett	10.9.78	3	0	0	0	0	Roose ARL	4.8.95
Milburn, Peter	16.12.75	2	0	0	0	0	Roose ARL	19.2.93
Morrow, Shaun	31.12.63	16	3	0	0	12	Walney ARL	3.7.91
Neale, Steve	24.4.68	1+3	0	0	0	0	Holker Pioneers ARL	24.6.93
Quayle, Stuart	22.4.68	7+6	0	0	0	0	Walney ARL	11.8.94
Robinson, Glyn	15.1.71	3+1	1	0	0	4	Millom ARL	27.10.95
Robinson, Roy	18.1.65	17	10	0	0	40	Millom ARL	10.8.92
Shaw, Neil	29.9.68	15	2	29	4	70	Barrow I. ARL	8.1.88
Slater, Ben	5.9.76	12+1	0	0	2	2	Roose ARL	19.8.84
Smith, Jamie	2.10.76	15	3	0	0	12	Roose ARL	16.6.93
Spenceley, Gary	5.2.67	13	7	0	0	28	Roose ARL	15.4.95
Stewart, Troy	30.6.72	1	0	0	0	0		
Trainor, Pat	8.4.64	18	5	0	0	20	Walney ARL	20.10.87
Walsh, Tim	14.3.68	10+1	5	0	0	20		24.8.95
Whalley, Andy	4.3.75	9+2	4	0	0	16	Ulverston ARL	10.8.93
Why, Adrian	14.6.67	2+4	0	0	0	0	London B.	15.9.95
Wilson, Darren	7.3.73	20	4	0	0	16		14.4.95
Trialist		1	0	0	0	0		
TOTALS								
37 players			63	58	9	377		

BARROW BRAVES 1995-96 MATCH ANALYSIS

Date	Com-petition	H/A	Opponents	Rlt	Score	Tries	Goals	Atten-dance	Referee
20.8.95	SD	H	Highfield	W	64-10	Spenceley (3), R. Robinson (2), Whalley (2), Barber, Ashcroft, Trainor, Howarth	Atkinson (10)	747	Atkin
27.8.95	SD	H	Carlisle	W	21-20	Atkinson, Wilson, Kerr	Atkinson (4), Howarth (dg)	948	Ganson
30.8.95	SD	A	Swinton	L	8-42	Shaw	Shaw (2)	–	–
3.9.95	SD	A	Chorley	L	12-15	Whalley, Trainor	Atkinson (2)	–	–
10.9.95	SD	H	Hull K.R.	L	9-27	R. Robinson	Shaw (2,dg)	849	Owram
17.9.95	SD	A	Leigh C.	L	8-28	R. Robinson (2)	–	–	–
24.9.95	SD	H	York	W	36-6	Smith (2), Kerr, Morrow, Trainor	Shaw (8)	728	Redfearn
1.10.95	RT(1)	H	Park Amateurs	W	29-11	R. Robinson (3), Kerr, Smith, Trainor	Shaw (2,dg)	520	Kirkpatrick
1.11.95	SD	A	Bramley	L	20-26	Hannah, R. Robinson, Whalley, Wilson	Shaw (2)	–	–
5.11.95	SD	H	Doncaster D.	L	21-22	Spenceley (2), Everett, Kerr	Shaw (2,dg)	705	Redfearn
12.11.95	RT(2)	A	Dewsbury	L	6-17	Everett	Shaw	–	–
15.11.95	SD	H	Swinton	L	3-6	–	Shaw, Slater (dg)	474	Atkin
19.11.95	SD	A	Hull K.R.	L	7-48	Shaw	Shaw, Slater (dg)	–	–
29.11.95	SD	A	Highfield	W	44-16	Walsh (4), Luxon, R. Robinson, G. Robinson, Spenceley	Shaw (6)	–	–
6.12.95	SD	A	Hunslet H.	L	5-17	Wilson	Shaw (dg)	–	–
10.12.95	SD	H	Leigh C.	L	8-22	Luxon	Shaw (2)	650	Burke
13.12.95	SD	H	Hunslet H.	L	16-28	Hansen, Walsh, John	Atkinson (2)	442	Atkin
17.12.95	SD	A	York	L	6-42	Morrow	Atkinson	–	–
7.1.96	SD	H	Bramley	L	8-28	Trainor	Atkinson (2)	586	Grimshaw
10.1.96	SD	A	Carlisle	L	6-48	Wilson	Atkinson	–	–
17.1.96	SD	H	Chorley C.	W	23-16	Everett, Hansen, John, Morrow	Atkinson (3,dg)	540	Grimshaw
21.1.96	SD	A	Doncaster D.	W	17-16	Atkinson, Spenceley	Atkinson (4,dg)	–	–

Barrow winger Bill Burgess Jnr., capped 13 times for Great Britain.

Twelve caps in a three-year Great Britain career for Barrow's Jack Grundy.

23

BATLEY

Highest score: 78-22 v. Leigh, 26 Mar 1995
Highest against: 78-9 at Wakefield T.,
26 Aug 1967
Attendance: 23,989 v. Leeds (RL Cup), 14 Mar 1925

Ground:	Mount Pleasant (01924-470062)
First Season:	1895-96
Nickname:	Gallant Youths
Chairman:	Ron Earnshaw
Secretary:	Richard Illingworth
Honours:	**Championship** Winners, 1923-24
	Challenge Cup Winners, 1896-97,
	1897-98, 1900-01
	Yorkshire Cup Winners, 1912-13
	Beaten finalists, 1909-10, 1922-23,
	1924-25, 1952-53
	Yorkshire League Winners,
	1898-99, 1923-24

RECORDS
Match

Goals:	13 by Simon Wilson v. Leigh, 26 March 1995
Tries:	5 by Joe Oakland v. Bramley, 19 Dec 1908
	Tommy Brannan v. Swinton, 17 Jan 1920
	Jim Wale v. Bramley, 4 Dec 1926
	Jim Wale v. Cottingham, 12 Feb 1927
	Tommy Oldroyd at Highfield, 6 Mar 1994
Points:	30 by Simon Wilson v. Leigh, 26 Mar 1995

Season

Goals:	127 by Simon Wilson, 1994-95
Tries:	29 by Jack Tindall, 1912-13
Points:	300 by Simon Wilson, 1994-95

Career

Goals:	463 by Wharton "Wattie" Davies, 1897-1912
Tries:	123 by Wharton "Wattie" Davies, 1897-1912
Points:	1,297 by Wharton "Wattie" Davies, 1897-1912
Appearances:	421 by Wharton "Wattie" Davies, 1897-1912

COACHING REGISTER
● **Since 1974-75**

Don Fox	Nov 72 - Oct 74
Alan Hepworth	Nov 74 - Apr 75
Dave Cox	May 75 - June 75
Trevor Walker	June 75 - June 77
Albert Fearnley	June 77 - Oct 77
Dave Stockwell	Oct 77 - June 79
★ Tommy Smales	June 79 - Oct 81
Trevor Lowe	Oct 81 - May 82
Terry Crook	June 82 - Nov 84
George Pieniazek	Nov 84 - Nov 85
Brian Lockwood	Nov 85 - May 87
Paul Daley	July 87 - Apr 90
Keith Rayne	May 90 - Apr 91
David Ward	May 91 - Oct 94
Jeff Grayshon	Oct 94 -
★ *Ex-forward*	

GREAT BRITAIN REGISTER
(4 players)

Norman Field	(1)	1963
Frank Gallagher	(8)	1924-26
Carl Gibson	(+1)	1985
Joe Oliver	(4)	1928

1995-96 REGISTRATION DATE

Signed	Player	Club From
12.6.95	McCabe, Iain	–
16.6.95	Jackson, Simon	St. John Fisher ARL
19.6.95	Sheard, Paul	–
28.6.95	Hartley, Neil	–
28.6.95	Holmes, Phil	–
18.7.95	Heron, David	Bradford B.
21.7.95	Jackson, David	Worthing RU
23.7.95	Chapman, Mark	–
7.8.95	Barnett, Gary	Bramley
11.8.95	*Hardwick, Phil	Bradford B.
11.8.95	Sharp, Tim	York
11.9.95	Conway, Stephen	–
13.9.95	Wood, Jason	Featherstone R.
18.9.95	Walker, John	Keighley C.
3.10.95	Barron, Richard	–
3.10.95	Gibbon, Chris	–
3.10.95	Grogan, Leigh	–
3.10.95	Slack, Dean	Batley Boys ARL
3.10.95	Stevens, Craig	Batley Boys ARL
3.10.95	Weston, Lee	–

BATLEY 1995-96 PLAYERS' SUMMARY

	Date of birth	App	T	G	D	Pts	Previous club	Signed
Bailey, Mark	30.9.70	0+1	0	0	0	0	Ovenden ARL	12.4.95
Bargate, Lee	12.9.71	4	1	0	0	4	Middleton ARL	27.6.90
Barnett, Gary	25.3.71	8+4	3	0	0	12	Bramley	7.8.95
Cass, Mark	17.11.71	22	3	0	0	12	Hull	29.2.92
Chapman, Mark	25.3.71	13+1	0	7	0	14		23.7.95
Child, Darren	30.10.66	17+1	0	0	0	0	Morley RU	13.9.90
Gilfillan, John	11.3.65	17	4	0	0	16	Salford	16.12.94
Green, Mark	13.3.72	12+3	1	0	0	4		13.3.95
Harrison, Paul	24.9.70	19+2	7	0	0	28	Hull	19.7.94
Heron, David	1.3.58	17+2	5	0	0	20	Bradford N.	18.7.95
Heron, Wayne	5.5.61	0+2	0	0	0	0	Bradford N.	22.2.90
McWilliams, Chris	1.6.69	7+4	0	0	0	0	Ovenden ARL	1.8.94
Middleton, Graham	2.11.70	13+3	2	0	0	8	Leeds	1.7.93
Mirfin, Phil	20.11.68	10+10	3	0	0	12	Castleford	
Moverley, Robert	18.1.69	0+1	0	0	0	0	Stanningley ARL	21.8.94
Moxon, Darren	17.9.70	21	5	0	0	20	Bradford N.	11.12.92
Parkinson, Andrew	8.7.65	18	2	24	0	56	Dewsbury	2.1.90
Redick, Paul	22.1.67	3	1	0	0	4	Shaws ARL	6.7.90
Scott, Mark	30.1.65	3	0	0	0	0	Batley Boys ARL	9.5.84
Thornton, Gary	9.3.63	21	1	0	0	4	Wakefield T.	24.8.90
Tomlinson, Glen	18.3.70	18	10	0	0	40	Australia	29.8.91
Walker, John	27.12.68	19	6	0	0	24	Keighley C.	18.9.95
Walker, Steve	8.11.69	1	1	0	0	4	Dudley Hill ARL	17.12.92
Walton, Tony	20.12.63	17+1	3	0	0	12	Doncaster	1.10.93
Wilson, Simon	22.10.67	6+6	3	19	1	51	Batley Boys ARL	16.11.84
TOTALS								
25 players			61	50	1	345		

BATLEY 1995-96 MATCH ANALYSIS

Date	Com-petition	H/A	Opponents	Rlt	Score	Tries	Goals	Atten-dance	Referee
20.8.95	FD	A	Rochdale H.	L	14-21	Barnett, D. Heron	Wilson (3)	–	–
23.8.95	FD	H	Hull	L	8-30	–	Wilson (4)	1176	Burke
27.8.95	FD	A	Dewsbury	L	18-28	Middleton, Moxon, J. Walker	Wilson (3)	–	–
3.9.95	FD	H	Wakefield T.	W	18-11	Harrison, D. Heron, Wilson	Wilson (3)	1206	Oddy
10.9.95	FD	A	Salford R.	L	24-52	Moxon, Thornton, Tomlinson, Wilson, J. Walker	Wilson (2)	–	–
17.9.95	FD	H	Whitehaven	W	20-6	Mirfin (2), D. Heron, Tomlinson	Wilson, Chapman	929	Cross
20.9.95	FD	A	Widnes	L	10-34	Gilfillan	Chapman (3)	–	–
24.9.95	FD	H	Featherstone R.	W	26-14	Tomlinson (3), Harrison (2)	Wilson (2), Chapman	1456	Nicholson
1.11.95	FD	H	Keighley C.	L	14-21	J. Walker (2), Moxon	Wilson	3018	Cross
5.11.95	FD	A	Huddersfield	L	8-57	Middleton, Wilson	–	–	–
12.11.95	RT(2)	H	Wakefield T.	W	21-14	Tomlinson (2), Harrison, D. Heron	Chapman (2), Wilson (dg)	1522	Morris
15.11.95	FD	A	Hull	L	8-42	Harrison, J. Walker	–	–	–
19.11.95	FD	H	Rochdale H.	W	34-10	Gilfillan (2), Walton (2), D. Heron, Tomlinson	Parkinson (5)	1008	Ganson
26.11.95	RT(3)	H	Warrington	L	22-35	Moxon, Tomlinson, Walton	Parkinson (5)	1754	Lee
29.11.95	FD	H	Salford R.	D	12-12	Barnett (2)	Parkinson (2)	884	Burke
3.12.95	FD	A	Whitehaven	L	10-20	Harrison (2)	Parkinson	–	–
13.12.95	FD	H	Widnes	L	18-22	Gilfillan, Mirfin, Parkinson	Parkinson (3)	785	Taberner
17.12.95	FD	A	Featherstone R.	L	14-44	Cass, Green, Parkinson	Parkinson	–	–
3.1.96	FD	H	Dewsbury	W	12-10	Bargate, J. Walker	Parkinson (2)	1270	Oddy
10.1.96	FD	A	Wakefield T.	L	14-24	Tomlinson, Moxon, Cass	Parkinson	–	–
14.1.96	FD	A	Keighley C.	L	8-14	Redick	Parkinson (2)	–	–
21.1.96	FD	H	Huddersfield	L	12-20	Cass, S. Walker	Parkinson (2)	1320	Shaw

25

BRADFORD BULLS

Ground: Odsal Stadium (01274-733899)
First Season: 1895-96 as "Bradford". Disbanded and became Bradford Northern in 1907-08. Disbanded during 1963-64 and re-formed for start of 1964-65. Retitled Bradford Bulls from the start of 1995-96
Nickname: Bulls
Chairman: Chris Caisley
Chief Exec: Brian Smith
Honours: **Championship** Beaten finalists, 1947-48, 1951-52
War Emergency League Championship winners, 1939-40, 1940-41, 1944-45
Beaten finalists, 1941-42
Division One Champions, 1903-04, 1979-80, 1980-81
Division Two Champions, 1973-74
Challenge Cup Winners, 1905-06, 1943-44, 1946-47, 1948-49
Beaten finalists, 1897-98, 1944-45, 1947-48, 1972-73
Regal Trophy Winners, 1974-75, 1979-80
Beaten finalists, 1990-91, 1992-93
Premiership Winners, 1977-78
Beaten finalists, 1978-79, 1979-80, 1989-90
Yorkshire Cup Winners, 1906-07, 1940-41, 1941-42, 1943-44, 1945-46, 1948-49, 1949-50, 1953-54, 1965-66, 1978-79, 1987-88, 1989-90
Beaten finalists, 1913-14, 1981-82, 1982-83, 1991-92
Yorkshire League Winners, 1899-1900, 1900-01, 1939-40, 1940-41, 1947-48

RECORDS

Match
Goals: 14 by Joe Phillips v. Batley, 6 Sep 1952
Tries: 7 by Jim Dechan v. Bramley, 13 Oct 1906
Points: 36 by John Woods v. Swinton, 13 Oct 1985

Season
Goals: 173 by Eddie Tees, 1971-72
Tries: 63 by Jack McLean, 1951-52
Points: 364 by Eddie Tees, 1971-72

Career
Goals: 779 by Keith Mumby, 1973-90 & 1992-93
Tries: 261 by Jack McLean, 1950-56
Points: 1,828 by Keith Mumby, 1973-90 & 1992-93
Appearances: 580+8 by Keith Mumby, 1973-90 & 1992-93

Highest score: 76-0 v. Leigh East, 17 Nov 1991
Highest against: 75-18 at Leeds, 14 Sep 1931
Attendance: 102,569 Warrington v. Halifax (RL Cup final replay), 5 May 1954
Home match: 69,429 v. Huddersfield (RL Cup), 14 Mar 1953

Keith Mumby, holder of the Bradford club records for most goals, points and appearances in a career.

COACHING REGISTER
● Since 1974-75

Ian Brooke	Jan 73 - Sep 75
Roy Francis	Oct 75 - Apr 77
Peter Fox	Apr 77 - May 85
Barry Seabourne	May 85 - Sep 89
Ron Willey	Oct 89 - Mar 90
David Hobbs	Mar 90 - Oct 91
Peter Fox	Oct 91 - June 95
Brian Smith	June 95 -

GREAT BRITAIN REGISTER
(33 players)

David Barends	(2)	1979
Eric Batten	(4)	1946-47
Ian Brooke	(5)	1966
Len Casey	(5)	1979
Gerald Cordle	(1)	1990
Willie Davies	(3)	1946-47
Karl Fairbank	(10+6)	1987-94
Tony Fisher	(8)	1970-78
Phil Ford	(7)	1987-88
Trevor Foster	(3)	1946-48
Deryck Fox	(1)	1992
Jeff Grayshon	(11)	1979-82
Ellery Hanley	(10+1)	1984-85
David Hobbs	(1+1)	1989
Dick Jasiewicz	(1)	1984
Jack Kitching	(1)	1946
Arthur Mann	(2)	1908
Keith Mumby	(11)	1982-84
Paul Newlove	(5+1)	1993-94
Brian Noble	(11)	1982-84
Terry Price	(1)	1970
Johnny Rae	(1)	1965
Bill Ramsey	(+1)	1974
Alan Rathbone	(4+1)	1982-85
Alan Redfearn	(1)	1979
David Redfearn	(6+1)	1972-74
Kelvin Skerrett	(8)	1989-90
Tommy Smales	(3)	1965
Bert Smith	(2)	1926
Jimmy Thompson	(1)	1978
Ken Traill	(8)	1950-54
Ernest Ward	(20)	1946-52
Frank Whitcombe	(2)	1946

1995-96 REGISTRATION DATE

Signed	Player	Club From
5.5.95	Walker, Matthew	Dewsbury Moor ARL
13.6.95	Simpson, Darren	–
21.6.95	Hodgkinson, Tom	St. Helens
8.8.95	Scales, Jonathan	Leeds
17.8.95	Tomlinson, Max	Doncaster
29.8.95	Ellis, St. John	Australia
31.8.95	Jowitt, Warren	Hunslet H.
5.9.95	Walker, James	–
10.9.95	Ireland, Andy	Widnes
12.9.95	Parker, Chris	Sharlston Rovers ARL
12.9.95	Rhodes, Tom	Bingley ARL
19.9.95	Hassan, Carlos	New Zealand RU
20.9.95	Poor, Antel	West Bowling ARL
23.10.95	Knox, Simon	Carlisle
30.10.95	Wilson, Alan	Australia
2.11.95	Graham, Nathan	Dewsbury
15.11.95	Calland, Matt	Featherstone R.
23.11.95	*Pickles, Stephen	Leeds
23.11.95	Robinson, Craig	Dudley Hill ARL
28.11.95	Dwyer, Bernard	St. Helens
28.11.95	Loughlin, Paul	St. Helens
28.11.95	Nickle, Sonny	St. Helens
13.12.95	Cook, Paul	Leeds
14.12.95	Longo, Davide	Dewsbury
19.12.95	Bradley, Graeme	Australia
29.12.95	*Hellewell, Phil	Huddersfield
29.12.95	Donougher, Jeremy	Australia

Australian centre Graeme Bradley, a December 1995 signing by Bradford Bulls.

27

BRADFORD BULLS 1995-96 PLAYERS' SUMMARY

	Date of birth	App	T	G	D	Pts	Previous club	Signed
Boothroyd, Alan		5+7	0	0	0	0		
Bourneville, Eugene	19.6.72	4+6	0	0	0	0	New Zealand	15.4.94
Bradley, Graeme	20.3.64	2+1	0	0	0	0	Australia	19.12.95
Calland, Matt	20.8.71	4	2	0	0	8	Featherstone R.	15.11.95
Christie, Gary	23.1.72	16	6	0	0	24	Wakefield T.	24.11.94
Cook, Paul	23.7.76	7	4	25	0	66	Leeds	13.12.95
Cordle, Gerald	29.9.60	5	1	0	0	4	Cardiff RU	12.7.89
Dixon, Paul	28.10.62	5+1	0	0	0	0	Leeds	1.8.93
Donohue, Jason	18.4.72	15+5	3	0	0	12	Leigh	18.8.94
Donougher, Jeremy	28.11.69	3+1	0	0	0	0	Australia	19.12.95
Dwyer, Bernard	20.4.67	5	0	0	0	0	St. Helens	28.11.95
Ellis, St. John	3.10.64	11+1	5	14	0	48	Australia	29.8.95
Fairbank, Karl	1.6.63	14+3	1	0	0	4	Elland ARL	24.7.86
Fox, Deryck	17.9.64	10	1	32	0	68	Featherstone R.	9.9.92
Graham, Nathan	23.11.71	9+3	0	0	0	0	Dewsbury	2.11.95
Hall, Carl	10.8.69	8+4	6	0	0	24	Doncaster	4.5.94
Hamer, Jon	23.2.66	10+5	0	0	0	0	Elland ARL	29.8.84
Hassan, Carlos	22.1.71	7+4	6	0	0	24	New Zealand RU	19.9.95
Hellewell, Phil	23.4.67	0+1	0	0	0	0	Huddersfield	29.12.95
Hodgkinson, Tommy	15.4.70	4+1	1	0	0	4	St. Helens	21.6.95
Ireland, Andy	6.12.71	13+3	1	0	0	4	Widnes	10.9.95
Jowitt, Warren	9.9.74	0+2	0	0	0	0	Hunslet H.	31.8.95
Knox, Simon	14.10.72	9+3	1	0	0	4	Carlisle	23.10.95
Longo, Davide	9.12.75	2+2	1	0	0	4	Dewsbury	14.12.95
Loughlin, Paul	28.7.66	7	3	1	0	14	St. Helens	28.11.95
McDermott, Brian	16.3.70	13+5	2	0	0	8	Eastmoor ARL	22.9.92
Medley, Paul	21.9.66	7+5	0	0	0	0	Halifax	31.8.89
Moore, Craig	24.10.74	2	0	0	0	0	Bradford Academy	25.4.93
Myers, David	31.7.71	3+1	0	0	0	0	Widnes	4.7.94
Newlove, Paul	10.8.71	6	6	0	0	24	Featherstone R.	13.7.93
Nickle, Sonny	4.5.69	7	4	0	0	16	St. Helens	28.11.95
Paul, Robbie	3.2.76	22	8	0	0	32	New Zealand	8.7.94
Pickles, Stephen	2.11.73	1	1	0	0	4	Leeds	23.11.95
Powell, Roy	30.4.65	6+3	2	0	0	8	Leeds	28.2.92
Robinson, Craig	23.5.72	1	0	0	0	0	Dudley Hill ARL	23.11.95
Scales, Jonathan	28.7.74	8+2	5	0	0	20	Leeds	8.8.95
Shaw, Graeme	13.6.75	1	1	0	0	4	Moldgreen ARL	29.6.94
Simpson, Darren	13.11.77	0+3	0	0	0	0		13.6.95
Simpson, Roger	27.8.67	9+1	5	0	0	20	Moldgreen ARL	17.1.85
Summers, Neil	10.10.68	14+2	5	0	0	20	Headingley RU	4.6.90
Tomlinson, Max	12.4.70	0+1	0	0	0	0	Doncaster	17.8.95
Turpin, David	21.1.73	4+3	0	0	0	0	Dudley Hill ARL	13.8.91
Wilson, Alan	25.9.67	7	0	0	0	0	Australia	30.10.95
Winterburn, Carl	8.9.70	0+1	0	0	0	0	Birkenshaw ARL	9.9.93
TOTALS								
44 players			81	72	0	468		

Representative appearances 1995-96
Newlove – England (4,4t).

BRADFORD BULLS 1995-96 MATCH ANALYSIS

Date	Com-petition	H/A	Opponents	Rlt	Score	Tries	Goals	Atten-dance	Referee
20.8.95	SBC	A	St. Helens	L	10-55	Hodgkinson, R. Simpson	Fox	–	–
23.8.95	SBC	H	Warrington	W	20-17	Summers (2), Hall, Scales	Fox (2)	4765	R. Connolly
27.8.95	SBC	A	Halifax	L	10-20	Newlove	Fox (3)	–	–
3.9.95	SBC	H	London B.	W	26-16	Ellis, Hall, Scales, Summers	Fox (5)	3674	Bates
10.9.95	SBC	A	Oldham B.	W	30-24	Scales, Newlove, Ellis, Paul, Christie, Powell	Fox (3)	–	–
17.9.95	SBC	H	Wigan	L	26-36	R. Simpson, Summers, Hall, Scales	Fox (5)	8819	Bates
22.9.95	SBC	A	Leeds	L	30-32	Shaw, Ireland, Cordle, Paul, Hall	Fox (5)	–	–
1.10.95	SBC	H	Sheffield E.	W	34-18	Newlove (3), Hall, Scales, Paul, Fox	Fox (3)	4291	Morris
1.11.95	SBC	H	Castleford	L	12-18	Paul (2)	Fox (2)	5089	J. Connolly
5.11.95	SBC	A	Workington T.	W	22-12	Newlove, Ellis, Christie, Powell	Fox (3)	–	–
12.11.95	RT(2)	H	Sheffield E.	W	22-0	Fairbank, Ellis, Paul	Ellis (5)	3353	Lee
17.11.95	SBC	H	St. Helens	L	18-32	R. Simpson, Hall, Hassan	Ellis (3)	3389	Smith
26.11.95	RT(3)	A	Leeds	L	28-42	Hassan (2), Knox, McDermott, Ellis, R. Simpson	Ellis (2)	–	–
1.12.95	SBC	H	Oldham B.	W	14-10	Nickle, Donohue	Ellis (3)	2787	Presley
10.12.95	SBC	A	London B.	L	24-27	R. Simpson, Christie, Nickle, McDermott, Calland	Loughlin, Ellis	–	–
17.12.95	SBC	H	Leeds	L	12-16	Paul, Nickle	Cook (2)	5546	Smith
20.12.95	SBC	A	Warrington	W	44-34	Hassan (3), Calland, Christie, Cook, Pickles	Cook (8)	–	–
1.1.96	SBC	H1	Halifax	L	18-22	Christie, Summers, Loughlin	Cook (3)	4539	Campbell
5.1.96	SBC	A	Sheffield E.	L	10-19	Cook, Donohue	Cook	–	–
12.1.96	SBC	A	Castleford	L	26-32	Loughlin (2), Longo, Nickle	Cook (5)	–	–
16.1.96	SBC	A	Wigan	L	18-32	Cook, Paul, Christie	Cook (3)	–	–
21.1.96	SBC	H	Workington T.	W	14-4	Donohue, Cook	Cook (3)	3036	Presley

1 At Huddersfield

Paul Loughlin, scorer of three tries and one goal in seven 1995-96 appearances for Bradford Bulls.

A Centenary season tally of four tries in seven games for Bradford Bulls for Sonny Nickle.

29

BRAMLEY

Ground: Clarence Field
First Season: 1896-97
Nickname: Villagers
Chairman: Jeff Wine
Secretary: Anthony Sugare
Honours: **BBC2 Floodlit Trophy** Winners, 1973-74

RECORDS
Match
Goals: 11 by Bernard Ward v. Doncaster, 1 Sep 1974
Dean Creasser v. Chorley, 17 Sep 1995
Tries: 7 by Joe Sedgewick v. Normanton, 16 Apr 1906
Points: 28 by Bernard Ward v. Doncaster, 1 Sep 1974

Season
Goals: 138 by Steve Carroll, 1991-92
Tries: 34 by Peter Lister, 1985-86
Points: 288 by Steve Carroll, 1991-92

Career
Goals: 926 by John Wilson, 1953-64
Tries: 140 by Peter Lister, 1982-91
Points: 1,903 by John Wilson, 1953-64
Appearances: 406+4 by John Wolford, 1962-76
Highest score: 74-0 v. Chorley, 17 Sep 1995
Highest against: 92-7 v. Australia, 9 Nov 1921
Attendance: 12,600 v. Leeds (League), 7 May 1947 — at Barley Mow
750 v. Hull K. R. (league) 10 Jan 1996 — at Clarence Field

COACHING REGISTER
● **Since 1974-75**

Arthur Keegan	May 73 - Sep 76
Peter Fox	Sep 76 - Apr 77
* Tommy Smales	May 77 - Dec 77
Les Pearce	Jan 78 - Oct 78
Don Robinson	Oct 78 - May 79
Dave Stockwell	June 79 - June 80
Keith Hepworth	June 80 - May 82
Maurice Bamford	May 82 - Oct 83
Peter Jarvis	Oct 83 - Apr 85
Ken Loxton	Apr 85 - Dec 85
Allan Agar	Dec 85 - Apr 87
Chris Forster	June 87 - Nov 87
Tony Fisher	Nov 87 - Feb 89
Barry Johnson	Mar 89 - Dec 90
John Kear	Dec 90 - Jan 91
Roy Dickinson	Jan 91 - Apr 92
Maurice Bamford	Apr 92 - Sep 93
Ray Ashton	Sep 93 -

* *Ex-forward*

1995-96 REGISTRATION DATE

Signed	Player	Club From
4.8.95	Hamilton, Dean	–
4.8.95	Minter, Steve	–
4.8.95	Smith, Ian	–
24.8.95	Hill, Ken	–
25.8.95	*Pickles, Damien	Huddersfield
28.9.95	Pitts, David	Stanningley ARL
30.10.95	Thornton, Wayne	–
14.11.95	*Currie, Eugene	Hunslet H.
6.12.95	Fella, Tony	Worth Village ARL
16.12.95	Bonsu, Andrew	Leeds Poly. ARL

John Kear, coach of Bramley for two months from December 1990.

BRAMLEY 1995-96 PLAYERS' SUMMARY

	Date of birth	App	T	G	D	Pts	Previous club	Signed
Agar, Andy	27.5.73	0+3	0	0	0	0	Pudsey ARL	4.6.91
Ashton, Ray	26.10.60	14+3	1	0	0	4	Workington T.	6.10.93
Beck, Alan		0+1	0	0	0	0		
Bell, Kevin	13.10.64	1	0	0	0	0	Wakefield R. ARL	2.7.91
Blankley, Dean	28.10.68	22	14	0	0	56	Castleford	2.11.90
Bonsu, Andrew	21.12.70	1	0	0	0	0	Leeds Poly. ARL	16.12.95
Creasser, Dean	18.8.70	17	2	47	0	102	Bison Sports ARL	17.12.91
Currie, Eugene	25.2.65	5	0	0	0	0	Hunslet H.	14.11.95
Fella, Tony	18.12.71	4+1	0	0	0	0	Worth Village ARL	6.12.95
Finnan, Andy	31.7.65	2	0	0	0	0	Brookhouse ARL	18.4.95
Fisher, Julian	4.10.70	4+1	0	0	0	0	Normanton ARL	15.12.92
Francis, Norman	2.10.64	12+1	5	0	0	20	Oldham	11.10.91
Freeman, Glen	9.4.72	14+3	0	0	0	0	Pudsey ARL	4.6.91
Freeman, Wayne	30.4.74	18+4	3	0	0	12	Pudsey ARL	27.8.91
Garrett, Paul	29.9.72	4	3	0	0	12	Saddleworth ARL	8.8.94
Greenwood, Barry	16.1.69	8	1	0	0	4	Saddleworth ARL	8.8.94
Hall, Dean	5.9.69	19+1	4	0	0	16	Dewsbury	15.8.93
Hall, Gary	11.1.68	21	1	0	0	4	Featherstone R.	30.8.91
Hamilton, Dean	12.3.73	1	1	0	0	4		4.8.95
Harrison, Mark	5.1.74	1+4	0	0	0	0		
Hill, Ken	20.9.68	16+1	1	0	1	5		24.8.95
Jewitt, Roy	26.2.72	12+1	3	0	0	12	Waterhead ARL	18.5.93
Keogh, David	7.11.76	0+1	0	0	0	0		
Long, Gordon	5.1.70	18	7	4	1	37	Westgate ARL	17.6.93
Marson, Andy	19.5.65	2	0	0	0	0	Hunslet	12.8.91
Minter, Steve	17.3.73	8+5	1	0	0	4		4.8.95
Pickles, Damien	2.12.70	20	13	10	0	72	Huddersfield	25.8.95
Pitts, Dave	19.10.71	1+1	0	0	0	0	Stanningley ARL	28.9.95
Quinlan, Brian	9.4.70	4	2	0	0	8	Oldham St. Annes ARL	22.7.94
Sharp, Ron	6.10.64	11+2	5	0	0	20		16.3.88
Smith, Ian	17.2.71	0+2	0	0	0	0		4.8.95
Smyth, Nicky		0+2	0	0	0	0		
Stead, Richard	22.3.70	18+3	8	0	0	32	Normanton ARL	15.12.92
Thornton, Wayne	31.8.66	8+3	0	0	0	0		30.10.95
Williams, Gareth	16.8.75	0+1	0	0	0	0		
TOTALS								
35 players			75	61	2	424		

BRAMLEY 1995-96 MATCH ANALYSIS

Date	Com-petition	H/A	Opponents	Rlt	Score	Tries	Goals	Atten-dance	Referee
20.8.95	SD	H	Swinton	L	16-30	Garrett, D. Hall, Hamilton, Quinlan	–	486	Asquith
23.8.95	SD	A	Doncaster D.	L	30-34	Garrett (2), Blankley, Long, Sharp	Long (3), Creasser (2)	–	–
27.8.95	SD	H	Hunslet H.	L	12-18	Blankley (2), Quinlan	–	562	Grimshaw
3.9.95	SD	A	Hull K.R.	L	12-51	D. Hall, Sharp	Creasser (2)	–	–
13.9.95	SD	A	Carlisle	L	12-22	Sharp	Creasser (4)	–	–
17.9.95	SD	H	Chorley	W	74-0	Pickles (5), W. Freeman (2), Blankley, Long, Francis, G. Hall, Minter, Stead	Creasser (11)	212	Presley
24.9.95	SD	A	Highfield	W	18-13	Francis (3), Stead	Creasser	–	–
1.10.95	RT(1)	H	Woolston R.	W	20-17	Pickles (2), Francis	Creasser (4)	350	Shaw
1.11.95	SD	H	Barrow B.	W	26-20	Blankley (3), Greenwood, Jewitt	Creasser, Long, Pickles	151	Asquith
5.11.95	SD	A	Leigh C.	W	20-14	Pickles (2), Blankley	Pickles (4)	–	–
12.11.95	RT(2)	H	Hunslet H.	L	4-22	–	Pickles (2)	650	Smith
15.11.95	SD	H	Doncaster D.	W	26-20	Long (2), Stead (2), Blankley	Pickles (3)	599	Shaw
26.11.95	SD	H	York	W	17-15	Pickles (2), Blankley	Creasser (2), Long (dg)	350	McGregor
29.11.95	SD	A	Swinton	L	7-28	Ashton	Creasser, Hill (dg)	–	–
3.12.95	SD	H	Carlisle	W	14-8	Blankley, Pickles	Creasser (3)	400	Taberner
10.12.95	SD	A	Chorley	D	20-20	Blankley, Sharp, Stead	Creasser (4)	–	–
13.12.95	SD	A	York	L	12-24	Blankley, Sharp	Creasser (2)	–	–
17.12.95	SD	H	Highfield	W	30-7	Jewitt (2), Creasser, D. Hall, Long, Pickles	Creasser (3)	250	Owram
7.1.96	SD	A	Barrow B.	W	28-8	Long (2), Creasser, W. Freeman, Stead	Creasser (4)	–	–
10.1.96	SD	H	Hull K.R.	L	4-40	Stead	–	750	Oddy
17.1.96	SD	A	Hunslet H.	L	16-24	D. Hall, Hill, Stead	Creasser (2)	–	–
21.1.96	SD	H	Leigh C.	L	6-38	Blankley	Creasser	700	McGregor

A pensive Ray Ashton, coach of Bramley since September 1993.

CARLISLE

Ground: Gillford Park (01228-401212)
First Season: 1981-82. Carlisle City entered the
League in 1928-29 but withdrew after
10 matches
Nickname: Border Raiders
Chairman: Alan Tucker
Secretary: Paul Scanlon-Wells

Hugh Waddell	Apr 94 - Dec 94
Paul Charlton	Dec 94 -

1995-96 REGISTRATION DATE

Signed	Player	Club From
1.9.95	Manihera, Tane	New Zealand
27.9.95	Rhodes, Stuart	Barrow B.

RECORDS

Match
Goals: 10 by Barry Vickers at Nottingham C.,
11 Mar 1990
Tries: 4 by Gary Peacham v. Workington T.,
25 Jan 1987
Kevin Pape v. Rochdale H.,
11 Feb 1987
Richard Henare v. Doncaster,
3 Jan 1996
Points: 24 by Barry Vickers at Nottingham C.,
11 Mar 1990

Season
Goals: 113 by Steve Ferres, 1981-82
Tries: 25 by Mick Morgan, 1981-82
Gary Peacham, 1984-85
Points: 242 by Steve Ferres, 1981-82

Career
Goals: 352 by Barry Vickers, 1988-92
Tries: 192 by Kevin Pape, 1984-94
Points: 768 by Kevin Pape, 1984-94
Appearances: 324 by Kevin Pape, 1984-94
Highest score: 70-0 v. Highfield, 23 Aug 1995
Highest against: 112-0 at St. Helens, 14 Sep 1986
Attendance: 5,903 v. Workington T. (League),
6 Sep 1981 — at Brunton Park;
2,042 v. Workington T. (RL Cup),
30 Jan 1994 — at Gillford Park

COACHING REGISTER
● **Since formation in 1981**

Allan Agar	May 81 - June 82
Mick Morgan	July 82 - Feb 83
John Atkinson	Feb 83 - Feb 86
Alan Kellett	Feb 86 - May 86
Roy Lester	June 86 - Nov 88
Tommy Dawes	Dec 88 - Jan 90
Cameron Bell	Feb 90 - Apr 94

Mick Morgan, coach of Carlisle for eight months from July 1982.

33

CARLISLE 1995-96 PLAYERS' SUMMARY

	Date of birth	App	T	G	D	Pts	Previous club	Signed
Armstrong, Derek	2.11.66	10+5	5	0	0	20	Hawick RU	20.4.92
Blake, Paul	17.11.70	1	0	0	0	0	Wigton RU	19.8.93
Brierley, Steve	30.3.61	21+1	0	0	0	0	Platform One ARL	22.8.83
Charlton, Gary	5.3.67	20	4	0	0	16	Whitehaven	27.11.90
Day, Glen		13+9	1	0	0	4		
Graham, George	19.1.66	20+1	4	0	0	16	Stirling County RU	22.10.91
Haile, Gary	30.8.68	3	3	0	0	12	Lowca ARL	1.2.95
Henare, Richard		6+1	10	0	0	40		
Holt, Darren	21.9.76	0+1	0	0	0	0		24.2.95
Kavanagh, Mike	5.2.71	24	3	2	1	17	Barrow	12.12.94
Knox, Simon	14.10.72	9	8	0	0	32	Hensingham ARL	1.12.91
Lynch, Matthew	6.12.69	24	9	0	0	36	Wigton RU	16.8.94
Manihera, Tane	6.8.74	15+1	9	0	0	36	New Zealand	1.9.95
Manning, Phil	23.2.62	21	10	0	0	40	Ayr RU	13.8.90
Meteer, Paul	11.2.70	6+1	0	0	0	0	Egremont ARL	6.1.95
Quayle, Barry	13.1.73	2+1	1	0	0	4	Frizington ARL	16.8.94
Rhodes, Stuart	16.1.72	24	13	0	0	52	Barrow B.	27.9.95
Richardson, Willie	6.10.60	24	6	96	0	216	Whitehaven	11.12.92
Rudd, Warren		10+5	0	0	0	0		
Ruddy, Gary	9.12.73	17	13	0	0	52	Barrow	26.1.95
Russell, Danny	24.12.69	20+1	12	0	0	48	Australia	23.8.93
Scott, Tony	17.5.62	0+1	0	0	0	0	Horse & Farrier ARL	9.4.84
Shackley, Mark		0+1	0	0	0	0		
Thurlow, Jason	18.12.69	21	9	0	0	36	Barrow	1.2.95
Williams, Barry	15.5.71	1+15	6	0	0	24	Broughton Red R.ARL	6.9.89
TOTALS								
25 players			126	98	1	701		

CARLISLE 1995-96 MATCH ANALYSIS

Date	Com-petition	H/A	Opponents	Rlt	Score	Tries	Goals	Atten-dance	Referee
20.8.95	SD	A	York	L	18-23	Richardson, Rhodes, Ruddy	Richardson (3)	–	–
23.8.95	SD	H	Highfield	W	70-0	D. Armstrong (3), Haile (3), Knox (3), Lynch (2), Ruddy, Kavanagh, Richardson	Richardson (7)	340	Taberner
27.8.95	SD	A	Barrow B.	L	20-21	Knox, Charlton, Graham	Richardson (4)	–	–
3.9.95	SD	H	Leigh C.	L	18-20	Knox, Ruddy, Rhodes	Richardson (3)	545	Shaw
10.9.95	SD	A	Chorley	W	28-17	Thurlow (2), Graham, Manning, Russell	Richardson (4)	–	–
13.9.95	SD	H	Bramley	W	22-12	Kavanagh, Ruddy, Williams	Richardson (5)	400	Redfearn
17.9.95	SD	A	Doncaster D.	W	30-12	Rhodes (2), Knox, Manning, Richardson	Richardson (5)	–	–
24.9.95	SD	H	Hunslet H.	W	26-14	Richardson, Knox, Manning, Russell	Richardson (5)	550	Owram
1.10.95	RT(1)	H	Doncaster D.	W	38-10	Manihera (2), Williams, Charlton, Knox, Richardson	Richardson (7)	435	Lee
1.11.95	SD	A	Hull K.R.	W	14-12	Manihera, Lynch	Richardson (3)	–	–
5.11.95	SD	H	Swinton	W	34-16	Thurlow (2), Manning, Russell, Lynch, Ruddy, Rhodes	Richardson (3)	550	McGregor
12.11.95	RT(2)	H	Castleford	W	19-18	Williams, Ruddy, Rhodes	Richardson (3), Kavanagh (dg)	850	Asquith
15.11.95	SD	A	Highfield	W	48-22	Ruddy (2), Williams, Russell, Manning, Kavanagh, Lynch, Rhodes	Richardson (8)	–	–
19.11.95	SD	H	Chorley	W	62-10	Manihera (2), Rhodes (2), Ruddy (2), D. Armstrong (2), Charlton, Thurlow, Russell	Richardson (9)	550	Atkin
26.11.95	RT(3)	A	Hunslet H.	W	22-17	Manihera, Thurlow, Russell, Williams	Richardson (3)	–	–
29.11.95	SD	H*	York	W	40-8	Ruddy (2), Rhodes, Manning, Williams, Manihera, Day, Richardson	Richardson (4)	571	Lee
3.12.95	SD	A	Bramley	L	8-14	Lynch, Ruddy	–	–	–
10.12.95	RT(QF)	A	Leeds	L	22-44	Graham (2), Manning (2)	Richardson (3)	–	–
17.12.95	SD	A	Hunslet H.	L	14-21	Manning, Russell, Rhodes	Richardson	–	–
3.1.96	SD	H*	Doncaster D.	W	42-4	Henare (4), Charlton, Manning, Rhodes, Thurlow	Richardson (3), Kavanagh (2)	450	Owram
7.1.96	SD	H	Hull K.R.	L	14-20	Lynch, Rhodes, Thurlow	Richardson	650	Ganson
10.1.96	SD	H*	Barrow B.	W	48-6	Henare (3), Russell (3), Manihera, Thurlow	Richardson (8)	350	Taberner
17.1.96	SD	A	Leigh C.	L	22-33	Henare (2), Lynch, Manihera, Quayle	Richardson	–	–
21.1.96	SD	A	Swinton	L	22-24	Russell (2), Henare, Lynch	Richardson (3)	–	–

* At Carlisle RU

35

CASTLEFORD

Ground: Wheldon Road (01977-552674)
First Season: 1926-27. There was also a Castleford team from 1896-97 to 1905-06 inclusive
Nickname: Tigers
Chairman: Phil Hindle
Secretary: Denise Cackett
Honours: **Championship** Beaten finalists, 1938-39, 1968-69
Challenge Cup Winners, 1934-35, 1968-69, 1969-70, 1985-86 Beaten finalists, 1991-92
Regal Trophy Winners, 1976-77, 1993-94
Premiership Beaten finalists, 1983-84, 1993-94
Yorkshire Cup Winners, 1977-78, 1981-82, 1986-87, 1990-91, 1991-92 Beaten finalists, 1948-49, 1950-51, 1968-69, 1971-72, 1983-84, 1985-86, 1987-88, 1988-89
Yorkshire League Winners, 1932-33, 1938-39, 1964-65
Eastern Division Championship Beaten finalists, 1963-64
Charity Shield Beaten finalists, 1986-87
BBC2 Floodlit Trophy Winners, 1965-66, 1966-67, 1967-68, 1976-77

RECORDS
Match
Goals: 17 by Geoff "Sammy" Lloyd v. Millom, 16 Sep 1973
Tries: 5 by Derek Foster v. Hunslet, 10 Nov 1972
John Joyner v. Millom, 16 Sep 1973
Steve Fenton v. Dewsbury, 27 Jan 1978
Ian French v. Hunslet, 9 Feb 1986
St. John Ellis at Whitehaven, 10 Dec 1989
Points: 43 by Geoff "Sammy" Lloyd v. Millom, 16 Sep 1973
Season
Goals: 158 by Geoff "Sammy" Lloyd, 1976-77

Tries: 40 by St. John Ellis, 1993-94
Points: 334 by Bob Beardmore, 1983-84
Career
Goals: 875 by Albert Lunn, 1951-63
Tries: 206 by Alan Hardisty, 1958-71
Points: 1,870 by Albert Lunn, 1951-63
Appearances: 585+28 by John Joyner, 1973-92
Highest score: 94-12 v. Huddersfield, 18 Sep 1988
Highest against: 62-12 at St. Helens, 16 Apr 1986
Attendance: 25,449 v. Hunslet (RL Cup), 9 Mar 1935

COACHING REGISTER
● **Since 1974-75**
  Dave Cox   Apr 74 - Nov 74
* Malcolm Reilly   Dec 74 - May 87
  Dave Sampson   May 87 - Apr 88
  Darryl Van de Velde   July 88 - May 93
  John Joyner   May 93 -
* *Shortly after his appointment Reilly returned to Australia to fulfil his contract before resuming at Castleford early the next season.*

John Joyner, appointed coach of Castleford in May 1993.

GREAT BRITAIN REGISTER
(28 players)

Arthur Atkinson	(11)	1929-36
Kevin Beardmore	(13+1)	1984-90
Bill Bryant	(4+1)	1964-67
Lee Crooks	(5)	1992-94
Jim Croston	(1)	1937
Bernard Cunniffe	(1)	1937
Billy Davies	(1)	1933
Derek Edwards	(3+2)	1968-71
St. John Ellis	(+3)	1991-94
Keith England	(6+5)	1987-91
Mike Ford	(+2)	1993
Alan Hardisty	(12)	1964-70
Dennis Hartley	(9)	1968-70
Keith Hepworth	(11)	1967-70
Shaun Irwin	(+4)	1990
John Joyner	(14+2)	1978-84
Brian Lockwood	(7)	1972-74
Tony Marchant	(3)	1986
Roger Millward	(1)	1966
Steve Norton	(2+1)	1974
David Plange	(1)	1988
Malcolm Reilly	(9)	1970
Peter Small	(1)	1962
Graham Steadman	(9+1)	1990-94
Gary Stephens	(5)	1979
Doug Walton	(1)	1965
Johnny Ward	(3)	1963-64
Kevin Ward	(14)	1984-89

Castleford winger Simon Middleton, four touchdowns in 12 Centenary season appearances.

1995-96 REGISTRATION DATE

Signed	Player	Club From
12.7.95	Hargrave, Spencer	Kippax ARL
25.7.95	Flynn, Adrian	Wakefield T.
10.8.95	Maskill, Colin	Doncaster
15.8.95	Schick, Andrew	Australia
16.8.95	Marchant, Tony	Dewsbury
17.8.95	Agar, Jonathan	–
31.8.95	*Reynolds, Simon	Huddersfield
12.9.95	Tuuta, Brendon	Featherstone R.
23.9.95	Wells, Jon	Sharlston R. ARL
28.9.95	Furness, David	–
9.10.95	Kear, Mark	Panthers ARL
15.10.95	Allen, Chris	–
5.11.95	Horner, Andrew	–
24.11.95	Botica, Frano	Wigan
31.12.95	Dobson, Gareth	New Sharlston Rovers ARL

37

CASTLEFORD 1995-96 PLAYERS' SUMMARY

	Date of birth	App	T	G	D	Pts	Previous club	Signed
Coventry, James	9.2.77	12+4	6	0	0	24	Castleford Academy	9.2.94
Crooks, Lee	18.9.63	14+1	0	38	0	76	Leeds	8.1.90
Darley, Paul	26.1.74	6+1	0	2	0	4	Kippax Welfare ARL	18.9.92
Eden, Phil	13.12.63	0+4	0	0	0	0	Wakefield T.	12.10.94
Flowers, Jason	30.1.75	14+1	7	0	0	28	Redhill ARL	12.5.93
Flowers, Stuart	18.4.71	4+7	0	0	0	0	Fryston ARL	17.1.94
Flynn, Adrian	9.9.74	18	10	0	0	40	Wakefield T.	25.7.95
Furness, David	20.6.72	3	3	0	0	12		28.9.95
Goddard, Richard	28.4.74	12+1	3	21	0	54	Wakefield T.	17.7.94
Harland, Lee	4.9.73	15+2	3	0	0	12	Halifax	17.2.95
Hill, Andy	16.12.76	2+2	0	0	0	0	Kippax ARL	1.7.94
Marchant, Tony	22.12.62	8+1	3	0	0	12	Dewsbury	16.8.95
Maskill, Colin	15.3.64	15+1	6	7	0	38	Doncaster	10.8.95
Middleton, Simon	2.2.66	12	4	0	0	16	Knottingley RU	20.4.91
Nikau, Tawera	1.1.67	16	3	0	0	12	Ryedale-York	19.8.91
Palmer, Craig	3.1.71	1+1	0	0	0	0	Featherstone ARL	20.1.95
Price, Simon	15.11.73	3	0	0	0	0	East Leeds ARL	14.9.91
Richardson, Shaun		0+3	0	0	0	0		
Sampson, Dean	27.6.67	13+3	1	0	0	4	Stanley R. ARL	1.9.86
Schick, Andrew	27.5.70	10+7	5	0	0	20	Australia	15.8.95
Smales, Ian	26.9.68	9+7	1	0	0	4	Featherstone R.	21.8.93
Smith, Chris	31.10.75	18+1	6	0	0	24	Redhill ARL	28.1.92
Smith, Tony	16.7.70	18+1	9	0	0	36	Wheldale ARL	25.1.88
Steadman, Graham	8.12.61	15+1	8	5	0	42	Featherstone R.	23.8.89
Stephens, Gareth	15.4.74	14+2	0	0	0	0	Leeds	11.7.94
Sykes, Nathan	8.9.74	15+5	2	0	0	8	Moldgreen ARL	14.9.91
Tonks, Ian	13.2.76	1	0	0	0	0	Redhill ARL	13.2.93
Tuuta, Brendon	29.4.65	5+4	0	0	0	0	Featherstone R.	12.9.95
TOTALS								
28 players			80	73	0	466		

Representative appearances 1995-96
Sampson – England (1+2,1t);
Smith, T. – England (3+1,2t).

CASTLEFORD 1995-96 MATCH ANALYSIS

Date	Com-petition	H/A	Opponents	Rlt	Score	Tries	Goals	Atten-dance	Referee
20.8.95	SBC	H	Oldham B.	W	28-22	T. Smith (2), J. Flowers, Middleton	Crooks (4), Darley (2)	4341	Kirkpatrick
25.8.95	SBC	H	Leeds	W	22-18	J. Flowers (2), Maskill (2), Middleton	Crooks	5695	Cummings
3.9.95	SBC	A	Sheffield E.	L	26-36	Coventry (2), Sykes, J. Flowers	Crooks (5)	–	–
6.9.95	SBC	H	Workington T.	W	32-24	C. Smith (2), Coventry, Marchant, Maskill	Crooks (5), Maskill	3287	R. Connolly
13.9.95	SBC	A	Wigan	L	8-40	Harland	Crooks, Maskill	–	–
17.9.95	SBC	A	St. Helens	L	18-35	Steadman, Nikau, J. Flowers	Crooks (2), Steadman	–	–
24.9.95	SBC	H	Warrington	W	34-25	Marchant (2), Flynn, Steadman, Harland, Maskill, T. Smith	Steadman (2), Maskill	4336	Campbell
29.9.95	SBC	A	Halifax	L	10-19	C. Smith	Goddard (3)	–	–
1.11.95	SBC	A	Bradford B.	W	18-12	T. Smith, Nikau, Goddard	Goddard (3)	–	–
5.11.95	SBC	H	London B.	L	8-37	Middleton, Coventry	–	4099	Kirkpatrick
12.11.95	RT(2)	A	Carlisle	L	18-19	J. Flowers, Nikau, C. Smith	Maskill (3)	–	–
15.11.95	SBC	H	Wigan	L	20-42	Steadman (2), Flynn, Maskill	Maskill, Steadman	5657	Cummings
19.11.95	SBC	A	Oldham B.	L	20-25	T. Smith, Middleton, Flynn	Crooks (4)	–	–
29.11.95	SBC	A	Workington T.	W	22-16	J. Flowers, Maskill, Flynn, Goddard	Crooks (3)	–	–
15.12.95	SBC	A	Warrington	L	20-31	C. Smith, Flynn, Schick	Crooks (4)	–	–
20.12.95	SBC	H	St. Helens	W	26-18	T. Smith (2), Goddard, C. Smith, Steadman	Crooks (3)	3567	J. Connolly
26.12.95	SBC	A	Leeds	L	16-28	Coventry, Flynn, Harland	Crooks, Steadman	–	–
1.1.96	SBC	H	Sheffield E.	L	12-42	Steadman (2)	Crooks (2)	3472	Kirkpatrick
7.1.96	SBC	H	Halifax	D	26-26	Flynn (2), Furness, Smales	Crooks (3), Goddard (2)	3478	R. Connolly
12.1.96	SBC	H	Bradford B.	W	32-26	Flynn (2), Schick, T. Smith, Steadman	Goddard (6)	2794	Cummings
21.1.96	SBC	A	London B.	W	50-44	Furness (2), Schick (3), Coventry, Sampson, T. Smith, Sykes	Goddard (7)	–	–

Castleford loose forward Tawera Nikau, who scored three tries in 16 games after a summer stint with Australian club Cronulla.

CHORLEY CHIEFTAINS

Highest score: 92-0 v. Nottingham C., 1 Oct 1995
Highest against: 78-6 at Keighley C., 21 Feb 1993
Attendance: 2,851 v. Oldham (League),
21 Jan 1990 - at Victory Park
5,026 v. Wigan (Lancs Cup),
15 Sep 1989 - at Leigh

Ground:	Victory Park (01257-232116)
First Season:	1989-90 as Chorley. Became Chorley Borough in 1991-92. Not to be confused with the Chorley Borough who succeeded Springfield/Blackpool Borough in 1988-89. Demoted to the National Conference League for 1993-94 and regained senior status in 1995-96 when they became Chorley Chieftains.
Nickname:	Chieftains
Chairman:	Lindsay Hoyle
Chief Executive:	Mike Greenhalgh

RECORDS

Match

Goals:	10 by Mike Smith v. Nottingham C., 1 Oct 1995
Tries:	4 by Martin Holden v. Nottingham C., 1 Oct 1995
Points:	24 by Mike Smith v. Nottingham C., 1 Oct 1995

Season

Goals:	73 by Mike Smith, 1989-90
Tries:	10 by David Bacon, 1989-90 Joe Walsh, 1992-93 Martin Holden, 1995-96

Career

Goals:	282 by Mike Smith, 1989-
Tries:	No player has scored 20 or more
Points:	583 by Mike Smith, 1989-
Appearances:	123+2 by Mike Smith, 1989-

COACHING REGISTER
● **Since formation in 1989**

Stan Gittins	June 89 - Apr 90
Bob Eccles	May 90 - Sep 91
John Taylor	Sep 91 - Jan 93
Carl Briscoe	Jan 93 - May 93
Bob Eccles	Aug 95 -

1995-96 REGISTRATION DATE

Signed	Player	Club From
3.8.95	Briscoe, Neil	–
3.8.95	Holden, Martin	–
3.8.95	Melling, Steve	–
3.8.95	Melling, Sean	–
3.8.95	Moore, Stuart	–
3.8.95	Tatlock, Sonny	Adlington ARL
3.8.95	Walker, Paul	–
3.8.95	Walker, Michael	Adlington ARL
17.8.95	Borowski, Nigel	–
17.8.95	Bretherton, Chris	–
18.8.95	*Honey, Chris	Barrow B.
18.8.95	Robinson, Gary	Hindley ARL
18.8.95	Ruane, Andy	–
25.8.95	Parker, Carl	Adlington ARL
25.8.95	Shaw, David	–
26.8.95	Grant, Carl	–
29.9.95	Bramwell, Michael	Chorley RU
8.12.95	Costello, John	Leigh C.

CHORLEY CHIEFTAINS 1995-96 PLAYERS' SUMMARY

	Date of birth	App	T	G	D	Pts	Previous club	Signed
Barnes, David	21.10.73	1+6	1	0	0	4		
Barr, Brendan	26.9.70	22	2	0	0	8	Wigan	23.9.94
Bimson, Jeff	15.1.67	13	2	0	0	8		
Borowski, Nigel	8.10.70	4	2	0	0	8	Milford ARL	17.9.94
Bramwell, Mike	30.1.70	15	6	0	0	24	Chorley RU	29.9.95
Bretherton, Chris	14.9.68	6	2		0	8		17.8.95
Briscoe, Carl	22.2.62	16+4	2	0	0	8	Blackpool B.	31.7.89
Briscoe, Neil	17.7.67	4+8	1	0	0	4		3.8.95
Clayton, Richard	24.2.70	9	2	0	0	8		
Costello, John	10.3.70	6	1	0	0	4	Leigh C.	8.12.95

	Date of birth	App	T	G	D	Pts	Previous club	Signed
Danawe, Billy		13+1	5	0	0	20		
Eccles, Bob	10.7.57	0+2	0	0	0	0		
Fell, David	25.4.66	5	3	0	0	12		
Fletcher, Damien		7+1	2	0	0	8		
Grant, Carl	19.11.72	1	0	0	0	0		26.8.95
Holden, Martin	23.6.69	16	10	12	1	65		3.8.95
Honey, Chris	25.1.68	20	3	0	0	12	Barrow B.	19.8.95
Marsh, Ian	15.4.66	7+2	4	0	0	16	Blackpool G.	25.12.92
Maskery, Mark	4.10.66	0+2	0	0	0	0	Huddersfield	24.12.92
Melling, Sean	3.2.66	17	7	0	0	28	Wigan St Patricks ARL	17.9.94
Melling, Steve	9.11.64	9	1	0	0	4	Wigan St Patricks ARL	17.9.94
O'Donnell, Gus	11.12.70	5	1	1	1	7		
Parker, Carl	25.12.74	13+4	5	0	0	20	Adlington ARL	25.8.95
Robinson, Gary	15.11.72	7+2	2	0	0	8	Hindley ARL	18.8.95
Robinson, Jeff	9.9.71	2+1	1	0	0	4		
Ruane, Andy	6.9.62	21	1	7	5	23		18.8.95
Ruane, Denis	10.4.69	2+2	0	0	0	0		
Shaw, Dave	12.8.68	1	1	0	0	4		25.8.95
Smith, Mike	24.11.67	14	2	45	1	99	Springfield B.	31.7.89
Stewart, Mike	16.1.66	12	2	0	0	8		
Tatlock, Sonny	7.8.78	0+1	0	0	0	0	Adlington ARL	3.8.95
Walker, Paul	18.4.68	3	0	0	0	0	Adlington ARL	17.9.94
Walsh, Joe	8.1.68	15+2	1	0	0	4	Salford	16.8.92
TOTALS								
33 players			72	65	8	426		

CHORLEY CHIEFTAINS 1995-96 MATCH ANALYSIS

Date	Com-petition	H/A	Opponents	Rlt	Score	Tries	Goals	Atten-dance	Referee
20.8.95	SD	A	Leigh C.	L	12-36	Steve Melling, Borowski	Smith (2)	–	–
27.8.95	SD	A	Highfield	W	25-21	C. Briscoe (2), Shaw	Smith (6), Holden (dg)	–	–
3.9.95	SD	H	Barrow B.	W	15-12	Bimson, Holden	Smith (3,dg)	550	Owram
10.9.95	SD	H	Carlisle	L	17-28	Sean Melling, Borowski	Smith (4), A. Ruane (dg)	410	Oddy
13.9.95	SD	H	York	L	8-27	Honey	Smith (2)	320	Lee
17.9.95	SD	A	Bramley	L	0-74	–	–	–	–
24.9.95	SD	H	Doncaster D.	W	35-18	Parker (2), Holden, Smith, Bramwell, Walsh	Smith (5), A. Ruane (dg)	575	Ganson
1.10.95	RT(1)	H	Nottingham C.	W	92-0	Holden (4), Sean Melling (3), Bretherton (2), Bramwell (2), Barr (2), Fletcher (2), Barnes, Smith, Parker	Smith (10)	425	Ganson
5.11.95	SD	H	Hull K.R.	L	9-48	Danawe, Holden	A. Ruane (dg)	1050	Shaw
12.11.95	RT(2)	H	Warrington	L	10-68	O'Donnell, J. Robinson	O'Donnell	1236	Presley
19.11.95	SD	A	Carlisle	L	10-62	Danawe, Stewart	A. Ruane	–	–
26.11.95	SD	A	Swinton	L	16-18	Bramwell (2), Clayton, Parker	–	–	–
29.11.95	SD	H	Leigh C.	L	17-29	Danawe, Stewart, G. Robinson	Holden (2), O'Donnell (dg)	650	Nicholson
3.12.95	SD	A	York	L	14-18	G. Robinson, Sean Melling	Holden (3)	–	–
10.12.95	SD	H	Bramley	D	20-20	Holden, Honey, Danawe	Holden (4)	310	Shaw
13.12.95	SD	H	Swinton	L	16-18	N. Briscoe, Honey, Holden	Holden (2)	350	McGregor
17.12.95	SD	A	Doncaster D.	W	21-12	Sean Melling, A. Ruane, Marsh	A. Ruane (3,dg), Holden	–	–
3.1.96	SD	A	Hunslet H.	L	14-38	Bimson, Fell	A. Ruane (3)	–	–
7.1.96	SD	H	Hunslet H.	L	8-34	Parker	Smith (2)	450	Owram
9.1.96	SD	H	Highfield	W	40-14	Marsh (2), Fell, Bramwell, Costello, Danawe, Holden	Smith (6)	350	Asquith
17.1.96	SD	A	Barrow B.	L	21-23	Fell, Marsh, Sean Melling	Smith (4), A. Ruane (dg)	–	Grimshaw
21.1.96	SD	A	Hull K.R.	L	6-58	Clayton	Smith	–	–

41

DEWSBURY

Highest score: 90-5 at Blackpool G., 4 Apr 1993
Highest against: 82-0 at Widnes, 30 Nov 1986
Attendance: 26,584 v. Halifax (Yorks Cup),
30 Oct 1920 — at Old Crown Flatt

Ground:	New Crown Flatt, Owl Lane (01924-465489)
First Season:	1901–02
Chairman:	Ken Davies
Secretary:	Matthew Kemp
Honours:	**Championship** Winners, 1972-73

Beaten finalists, 1946-47
War Emergency League
Winners, 1941-42 (1942-43 won final
but championship declared null and
void because Dewsbury played an
ineligible player.)
Beaten finalists, 1943-44
Division Two Champions, 1904-05
Challenge Cup Winners, 1911-12,
1942-43
Beaten finalists, 1928-29
Yorkshire Cup Winners, 1925-26,
1927-28, 1942-43
Beaten finalists, 1918-19, 1921-22,
1940-41, 1972-73
Yorkshire League Winners,
1946-47
BBC2 Floodlit Trophy Beaten
finalists, 1975-76

RECORDS

Match

Goals:	13 by Greg Pearce at Blackpool G., 4 Apr 1993
Tries:	8 by Dai Thomas v. Liverpool C., 13 Apr 1907
Points:	32 by Les Holliday v. Barrow, 11 Sep 1994

Season

Goals:	145 by Nigel Stephenson, 1972-73
Tries:	40 by Dai Thomas, 1906-07
Points:	368 by Nigel Stephenson, 1972-73

Career

Goals:	863 by Nigel Stephenson, 1967-78 & 1984-86
Tries:	144 by Joe Lyman, 1913-31
Points:	2,082 by Nigel Stephenson, 1967-78 & 1984-86
Appearances:	454 by Joe Lyman, 1913-31

COACHING REGISTER
● **Since 1974-75**

Maurice Bamford	June 74 - Oct 74
Alan Hardisty	Oct 74 - June 75
Dave Cox	June 75 - July 77
Ron Hill	July 77 - Dec 77
Lewis Jones	Dec 77 - Apr 78
Jeff Grayshon	May 78 - Oct 78
Alan Lockwood	Oct 78 - Oct 80
Bernard Watson	Oct 80 - Oct 82
Ray Abbey	Nov 82 - Apr 83
* Tommy Smales	May 83 - Feb 84
Jack Addy	Feb 84 - Jan 87
Dave Busfield	Jan 87 - Apr 87
Terry Crook	Apr 87 - Dec 88
Maurice Bamford	Dec 88 - Dec 90
Jack Addy	Dec 90 - Aug 93
Norman Smith	Aug 93 - Apr 95
Tony Fisher	Apr 95 -

* *Ex-forward*

Dewsbury forward Neil Kelly, a sole appearance in the 1995-96 season.

GREAT BRITAIN REGISTER
(6 players)

Alan Bates	(2+2)	1974
Frank Gallagher	(4)	1920-21
Jim Ledgard	(2)	1947
Roy Pollard	(1)	1950
Mick Stephenson	(5+1)	1971-72
Harry Street	(4)	1950

1995-96 REGISTRATION DATE

Signed	Player	Club From
7.7.95	Robinson, Chris	Bradford University
1.8.95	Darkes, Richard	Bradford B.
4.8.95	Lord, Paul	Swinton
16.8.95	Farrar, Mark	–
16.8.95	McAllister, Terry	Castleford
12.9.95	*Timson, Andrew	Bramley
18.9.95	Booyson, Jaco	South Africa
18.9.95	Boshoff, Willem	South Africa
18.9.95	van Deventer, Kobus	South Africa
18.9.95	Fourie, Tim	South Africa
18.9.95	Watts, Gideon	South Africa
27.9.95	Riley, Scott	Hunslet Boys ARL
6.10.95	Hird, Gavin	–
12.10.95	Carr, Richard	Redhill ARL
16.10.95	Coombe, Guy	South Africa
16.10.95	van Wyk, Pierre	South Africa
19.10.95	Jowitt, Robin	–
27.10.95	Bramald, Matthew	Westgate Redoubt ARL
31.10.95	*Pratt, Gareth	Rochdale H.
1.11.95	Lingard, Glynn	Featherstone R.
1.11.95	*Race, Wayne	Keighley C.
9.11.95	Bates, Gareth	Dewsbury North
2.12.95	Eaton, Barry	Wakefield T.
6.12.95	Donnelly, Scott	Australia
8.12.95	Gumbs, Hugh	Doncaster D.
14.12.95	Austerfield, Shaun	Bradford B.
14.12.95	Mitchell, Patrick	Oldham B.
14.12.95	Moore, Craig	Bradford B.
23.12.95	*O'Keefe, Paul	Rochdale H.
4.1.96	Brown, Chris	Oulton ARL

DEWSBURY 1995-96 MATCH ANALYSIS

Date	Com-petition	H/A	Opponents	Rlt	Score	Tries	Goals	Atten-dance	Referee
20.8.95	FD	A	Widnes	L	6-48	Longo	Conway	–	–
23.8.95	FD	A	Featherstone R.	L	10-18	Longo	Conway (3)	–	–
27.8.95	FD	H	Batley	W	28-18	Conway, Longo, Haigh, North	Conway (6)	1544	Nicholson
3.9.95	FD	A	Huddersfield	L	18-37	Longo (2), Crook	Woodcock (3)	–	–
10.9.95	FD	A	Keighley C.	L	5-44	Dickinson	Woodcock (dg)	–	–
17.9.95	FD	A	Rochdale H.	L	16-26	Farrar (2), Conway	Conway (2)	–	–
20.9.95	FD	H*	Hull	L	10-46	Cocks, Lord	Woodcock	1058	Asquith
1.10.95	FD	A	Wakefield T.	L	24-34	Conway (2), Lord, Johnston	Conway (4)	–	–
1.11.95	FD	A	Whitehaven	L	8-35	Booyson	Agar (2)	–	–
5.11.95	FD	H	Salford R.	L	8-23	Pratt, Race	–	1640	Cross
12.11.95	RT(2)	H	Barrow B.	W	17-6	Race, Jordan	van Deventer (4,dg)	662	Taberner
15.11.95	FD	H	Featherstone R.	L	22-23	Conway, Longo, Gittins	van Deventer (5)	1108	Nicholson
19.11.95	FD	H	Widnes	L	2-34	–	van Deventer	1045	Asquith
26.11.95	RT(3)	H	Rochdale H.	L	14-26	Bramald, G. Bell	Conway (3)	927	Bates
29.11.95	FD	H	Keighley C.	L	6-28	Bramald	Conway	2221	Gilmour
3.12.95	FD	H	Rochdale H.	L	16-21	Conway (2), North	Conway (2)	855	Gilmour
10.12.95	FD	A	Hull	L	14-58	North, G. Bell, Coombe	Conway	–	–
31.12.95	FD	H	Huddersfield	W	22-10	Austerfield (2), Bramald (2)	Eaton (3)	961	Burke
3.1.96	FD	A	Batley	L	10-12	Bramald, Eaton	Eaton	–	–
7.1.96	FD	H	Wakefield T.	L	14-16	Eaton (2)	Eaton (3)	1900	Nicholson
14.1.96	FD	H	Whitehaven	L	4-20	Fourie	–	908	Asquith
21.1.96	FD	A	Salford	L	18-46	Bramald, Eaton, Haigh	Eaton (3)	–	–

* At Batley

DEWSBURY 1995-96 PLAYERS' SUMMARY

	Date of birth	App	T	G	D	Pts	Previous club	Signed
Agar, Richard	20.1.72	3	0	2	0	4	Travellers Saints ARL	26.8.93
Austerfield, Shaun	11.9.75	4	2	0	0	8	Bradford B.	14.12.95
Bates, Gareth	21.3.73	2	0	0	0	0	Dewsbury North ARL	9.11.95
Bates, Ian	2.3.68	11	0	0	0	0	Rochdale H.	8.8.94
Bell, Glen	26.3.65	12+5	2	0	0	8	New Zealand	10.8.91
Booyson, Jaco	27.3.67	8	1	0	0	4	South Africa	18.9.95
Bramald, Matthew	6.2.73	10	6	0	0	24	Westgate Redoubt ARL	27.10.95
Cocks, Mark	12.5.74	4	1	0	0	4	Redhill ARL	17.6.91
Conway, Mark	31.1.64	11+1	7	23	0	74	Wakefield T.	22.6.93
Coombe, Guy	26.7.72	7	1	0	0	4	South Africa	16.10.95
Cornforth, Phil	16.11.69	1+1	0	0	0	0	Bradford N.	1.6.92
Crook, Paul	12.2.74	11+2	1	0	0	4	Stanley Rangers ARL	31.5.91
Crouthers, Kevin	3.1.76	5+1	0	0	0	0	Stanley Rangers ARL	25.7.94
Darkes, Richard	5.10.68	8	0	0	0	0	Bradford B.	1.8.95
Dickinson, Andy	26.8.61	2+1	1	0	0	4	Huddersfield	1.7.90
Donnelly, Scott	19.8.74	2	0	0	0	0	Australia	6.12.95
Eaton, Barry	30.9.73	6	4	10	0	36	Wakefield T.	2.12.95
Farrar, Mark	27.7.68	3+1	2	0	0	8	Doncaster	16.8.95
Firth, Jason	16.6.77	0+1	0	0	0	0	Thornhill ARL	18.3.95
Fourie, Tim	12.3.68	11	1	0	0	4	South Africa	18.9.95
Gittins, Jimmy	1.1.74	7+1	1	0	0	4	Stanley Rangers ARL	31.5.91
Graham, Nathan	23.11.71	1	0	0	0	0	Dewsbury Colts	23.11.89
Haigh, Mark	24.1.70	13+1	2	0	0	8	Hanging Heaton ARL	26.7.89
Johnston, Lyndon	24.1.69	8	1	0	0	4	Ossett Trinity ARL	3.1.95
Jordan, Trent	31.7.69	7+1	1	0	0	4	Highfield	2.3.94
Kelly, Neil	10.5.62	0+1	0	0	0	0	Wakefield T.	31.10.88
Lingard, Glynn	1.1.69	12+1	0	0	0	0	Featherstone R.	1.11.95
Longo, Davide	9.12.75	13+2	6	0	0	24	Stanley R. ARL	1.7.93
Lord, Paul	22.12.67	11	2	0	0	8	Swinton	4.8.95
McAllister, Terry	29.9.71	9+9	0	0	0	0	Castleford	16.8.95
McKelvie, Danny	10.10.69	5+4	0	0	0	0	Ryedale-York	29.10.94
Mitchell, Patrick	26.1.73	1	0	0	0	0	Oldham	14.12.95
Moore, Craig	24.10.74	3	0	0	0	0	Bradford B.	14.12.95
North, Chris	6.1.76	16	3	0	0	12	Stanley ARL	27.4.94
O'Keefe, Paul	28.6.71	4	0	0	0	0	Rochdale H.	23.12.95
Osborne, Jason	18.3.70	1	0	0	0	0		
Pratt, Gareth	23.8.69	5+3	1	0	0	4	Rochdale H.	31.10.95
Race, Wayne	17.4.66	5	2	0	0	8	Keighley C.	1.11.95
Turner, Robert	14.3.69	8	0	0	0	0	Doncaster	3.4.95
van Deventer, Kobus	19.6.67	6+1	0	10	1	21	South Africa	18.9.95
van Wyk, Pierre	4.8.73	1	0	0	0	0	South Africa	16.10.95
Wilkinson, Shaun	23.9.68	2+1	0	0	0	0		
Williams, Shane	20.10.71	12+2	0	0	0	0	Dewsbury C. ARL	1.6.92
Wood, Danny	8.10.77	1	0	0	0	0	Hunslet Boys ARL	1.12.94
Woodcock, Robert	9.10.74	3+1	0	4	1	9	Eastmoor ARL	1.3.93
Worthy, Paul	14.5.68	11	0	0	0	0	Leeds	21.5.91
TOTALS								
46 players			48	49	2	292		

44

DONCASTER DRAGONS

Ground: Meadow Court
First Season: 1951-52. Added Dragons to title
              after reforming for 1995-96 season
Nickname: Dragons
Chairman: David Prime
Chief Exec.   Graham Heptinstall

RECORDS
Match
Goals: 12 by Tony Zelei v. Nottingham C.,
            1 Sep 1991
            Robert Turner v. Highfield,
            20 Mar 1994
Tries: 5 by Carl Hall v. Mysons, 31 Oct 1993
Points: 32 by Tony Zelei v. Nottingham C.,
            1 Sep 1991

Season
Goals: 123 by Robert Turner, 1993-94
Tries: 21 by Mark Roache, 1989-90
Points: 272 by Robert Turner, 1993-94

Career
Goals: 850 by David Noble, 1976-77, 1980-89
            & 1992
Tries: 105 by Mark Roache, 1985-
Points: 1,751 by David Noble, 1976-77, 1980-89
            & 1992
Appearances: 305+15 by David Noble, 1976-77,
            1980-89 & 1992
Highest score: 96-0 v. Highfield, 20 Mar 1994
Highest against: 75-3 v. Leigh, 28 Mar 1976
Attendance: 10,000 v. Bradford N. (RL Cup), 16
            Feb 1952 — at York Road Stadium;
            1,240 v. York (league) 19 Nov 1995 —
            at Meadow Court

COACHING REGISTER
● **Since 1974-75**

Ted Strawbridge	Feb 73 - Apr 75
Derek Edwards	July 75 - Nov 76
Don Robson	Nov 76 - Sep 77
Trevor Lowe	Sep 77 - Apr 79
* Tommy Smales	Feb 78 - Apr 79
Billy Yates	Apr 79 - May 79
Don Vines	Sep 79 - Jan 80
Bill Kenny	June 80 - May 81
Alan Rhodes	Aug 81 - Mar 83
Clive Sullivan	Mar 83 - May 84
John Sheridan	June 84 - Nov 87
Graham Heptinstall	Nov 87 - Jan 88
John Sheridan	Jan 88 - Apr 89
Dave Sampson	May 89 - Jan 92
Geoff Morris	Jan 92 - Nov 92
Tony Fisher	Nov 92 - Dec 94
Ian Brooke	Dec 94 - Apr 95
Peter Astbury Andy Gascoigne	} July 95 - Sep 95
Peter Regan	Sep 95 -

* *Ex-forward, who shared the coaching post with Trevor Lowe for just over a year.*

1995-96 REGISTRATION DATE

Signed	Player	Club From
30.1.95	*Goulbourne, Alex	Featherstone R.
17.8.95	*Connell, Phil	York
17.8.95	*Gascoigne, Andy	York
17.8.95	*Lee, David	Dewsbury
18.8.95	Gumbs, Hugh	Oldham
18.8.95	Lidbury, Steve	Lock Lane ARL
18.8.95	Norman, Stephen	Kippax ARL
19.8.95	Heptinstall, Jason	York
19.8.95	Hewitt, Richard	–
21.8.95	*Carroll, Steve	Bramley
21.8.95	*Harrison, Mark	Leeds
31.8.95	*Timmins, Jason	Wakefield T.
31.8.95	*Webster, Mark	Wakefield T.
26.10.95	McCone, Stewart	–
26.10.95	Pollinger, Darren	Australia
31.10.95	*Ellis, Mark	Featherstone R.
31.10.95	*Randall, Carl	Sheffield E.
7.11.95	Mycock, Shaun	–
14.11.95	Merrick, David	Featherstone R.
15.11.95	*Summers, James	Sheffield E.
1.12.95	*Bradbrook, Neil	Featherstone R.
4.12.95	Levien, Matthew	Hunslet H.
8.12.95	*Griffiths, Mark	Wigan
30.12.95	Penny, Jason	New Zealand
3.1.96	Lake, Ernest	Moorends ARL
12.1.96	Morgan, Gavin	Sheffield E.

DONCASTER DRAGONS 1995-96 PLAYERS' SUMMARY

	Date of birth	App	T	G	D	Pts	Previous club	Signed
Barron, Neil	30.9.66	14	1	0	0	4		18.8.95
Beardsmore, Paul	5.5.70	1+2	0	0	0	0		8.7.87
Bradbrook, Neil	6.1.72	6+1	1	0	0	4	Featherstone R.	1.12.95
Busby, Lance	1.2.73	5	0	0	0	0		
Carroll, Steve	9.11.60	4	0	12	0	24	Bramley	6.12.92
Cartwright, Phil	14.1.61	4	0	0	0	0		
Chappell, Tony	9.10.64	21	12	41	3	133		
Collins, Simon	23.4.67	2+1	0	0	0	0		
Connell, Phil	14.11.69	17+1	2	0	0	8	York	17.8.95
Davidson, Jason	2.10.73	8+2	3	0	0	12		
Ellis, Mark	23.5.67	3	0	0	0	0	Featherstone R.	31.10.95
Fletcher, Ian	4.3.65	17+1	2	0	0	8	York	28.3.89
French, Michael	20.1.72	2	0	0	0	0		
Gascoigne, Andy	2.4.62	5+1	5	0	0	20	York	17.8.95
Goggins, Mick	1.2.72	2+1	0	0	0	0		
Goulbourne, Alex	20.7.74	12	3	0	0	12	Featherstone R.	30.1.95
Griffiths, Mark	12.11.74	2+1	0	0	0	0	Wigan	8.12.95
Gumbs, Hugh	4.9.69	1+1	0	0	0	0	Oldham	18.8.95
Harrison, Mark	5.1.74	2+3	0	0	0	0	Leeds	21.8.95
Heptinstall, Jason	3.12.69	18+1	2	0	0	8	York	19.8.95
Hewitt, Richard	7.10.74	7+3	6	0	0	24		18.8.95
Hudson, Justin	3.12.72	2	0	0	0	0		21.7.93
Lee, David	7.3.71	1	0	0	0	0	Dewsbury	17.8.95
Levien, Matt	27.6.70	4	0	0	0	0	Hunslet H.	4.12.95
Lidbury, Steve	12.3.66	20+1	7	0	0	28	Lock Lane ARL	18.8.95
McCone, Stewart	17.12.71	1	0	0	0	0		26.10.95
Merrick, Dave	25.2.76	4+1	2	0	0	8	Featherstone R.	14.11.95
Morgan, Darren	22.1.76	0+1	0	0	0	0		
Morgan, Gavin	1.6.76	2	0	0	0	0	Sheffield E.	12.1.96
Morgan, John	2.4.64	6	0	0	0	0		
Mycock, Shaun	12.5.74	7	3	0	0	12		7.11.95
Norman, Steve	15.9.69	2+1	0	0	0	0	Kippax ARL	18.8.95
Pennant, Audley	26.2.63	7	1	0	0	4	Bradford N.	24.9.85
Penny, Jason	19.11.71	1	0	0	0	0	New Zealand	5.9.95
Pollinger, Darren	8.9.70	1+3	2	0	1	9	Australia	26.10.95
Punchard, Richard	10.5.68	6+1	1	0	0	4		
Randall, Carl	22.12.71	8	4	0	0	16	Sheffield E.	31.10.95
Reeves, Mark	14.1.70	0+1	0	0	0	0		
Roache, Mark	24.11.62	14+1	1	0	0	4	Castleford	2.9.85
Roadknight, John	3.11.73	2	0	0	0	0		
Roberts, Howard	3.5.63	13+1	4	0	0	16		

(continued)

	Date of birth	App	T	G	D	Pts	Previous club	Signed
Stewart, Ian	7.11.61	4	0	0	0	0		
Sullivan, Scott	25.10.73	2	0	0	0	0		
Summers, James	25.3.73	5	0	0	0	0	Sheffield E.	15.11.95
Timmins, Jason	2.12.69	2	0	0	0	0	Wakefield T.	31.8.95
Timson, Andy	13.4.61	3	0	0	0	0		
Tomlinson, Paul	1.2.64	0+1	0	0	0	0		
Webster, Mark	23.6.70	1+1	0	0	0	0	Wakefield T.	31.8.95
Westwood, Dave		0+1	0	0	0	0		
Wright, Darren		2+1	0	0	0	0		
TOTALS								
50 players			62	53	4	358		

DONCASTER DRAGONS 1995-96 MATCH ANALYSIS

Date	Com-petition	H/A	Opponents	Rlt	Score	Tries	Goals	Atten-dance	Referee
20.8.95	SD	H1	Hull K.R.	L	24-50	Lidbury (2), Gascoigne, Heptinstall, Punchard	Carroll (2)	1683	Presley
23.8.95	SD	H1	Bramley	W	34-30	Chappell (2), Barron, Roberts, Gascoigne	Carroll (7)	1252	Shaw
3.9.95	SD	A	Hunslet H.	L	16-37	Gascoigne, Chappell, Connell	Carroll (2)	–	–
10.9.95	SD	A	York	L	18-20	Gascoigne, Fletcher, Pennant	Chappell (2), Carroll	–	–
13.9.95	SD	A	Swinton	L	0-58	–	–	–	–
17.9.95	SD	H1	Carlisle	L	12-30	Gascoigne, Roberts	Chappell (2)	1022	Atkin
24.9.95	SD	A	Chorley	L	18-35	Chappell (2), Roberts	Chappell (3)	–	–
1.10.95	RT(1)	A	Carlisle	L	10-38	Fletcher, Hewitt	Chappell	–	–
1.11.95	SD	H1	Highfield	W	24-17	Goulbourne, Pollinger, Randall	Chappell (5,2dg)	900	Taberner
5.11.95	SD	A	Barrow B.	W	22-21	Chappell (2), Gouldbourne, Roache	Chappell (3)	–	–
15.11.95	SD	A	Bramley	L	20-26	Goulbourne, Randall, Mycock	Chappell (4)	–	–
19.11.95	SD	H	York	W	31-8	Lidbury (2), Roberts, Pollinger, Chappell	Chappell (5), Pollinger (dg)	1240	Oddy
26.11.95	SD	H	Leigh C.	L	12-38	Chappell, Mycock	Chappell (2)	1174	Atkin
29.11.95	SD	A	Hull K.R.	L	4-56	Chappell	–	–	–
3.12.95	SD	H	Swinton	L	12-34	Randall, Davidson	Chappell (2)	829	Shaw
13.12.95	SD	A	Leigh C.	L	16-42	Hewitt, Mycock, Bradbrook	Chappell (2)	–	–
17.12.95	SD	H	Chorley	L	12-21	Hewitt, Merrick	Chappell (2)	885	Cross
3.1.96	SD	A	Carlisle	L	4-42	Lidbury	–	–	–
7.1.96	SD	A	Highfield	W	41-28	Davidson (2), Hewitt (2), Lidbury, Heptinstall, Merrick, Randall	Chappell (4,dg)	–	–
10.1.96	SD	H2	Hunslet H.	L	12-36	Chappell, Lidbury	Chappell (2)	545	Presley
21.1.96	SD	H	Barrow	L	16-17	Chappell, Connell, Hewitt	Chappell (2)	730	Atkin

1 At Doncaster R. FC;
2 At Featherstone

FEATHERSTONE ROVERS

Ground:	Post Office Road (01977-702386)
First Season:	1921-22
Nickname:	Colliers
Chairman:	Steve Wagner
Secretary:	Robin Hays
Honours:	**Championship** Beaten finalists, 1927-28
	Division One Champions, 1976-77
	Division Two Champions, 1979-80, 1992-93
	Challenge Cup Winners, 1966-67, 1972-73, 1982-83
	Beaten finalists, 1951-52, 1973-74
	Second Division/Divisional Premiership Winners, 1992-93
	Beaten finalists, 1987-88
	Yorkshire Cup Winners, 1939-40, 1959-60
	Beaten finalists, 1928-29, 1963-64, 1966-67, 1969-70, 1970-71, 1976-77, 1977-78, 1989-90
	Captain Morgan Trophy Beaten finalists, 1973-74

RECORDS

Match

Goals:	13 by Mark Knapper v. Keighley, 17 Sep 1989
Tries:	6 by Mike Smith v. Doncaster, 13 Apr 1968
	Chris Bibb v. Keighley, 17 Sep 1989
Points:	40 by Martin Pearson v. Whitehaven, 26 Nov 1995

Season

Goals:	163 by Steve Quinn, 1979-80
Tries:	48 by Paul Newlove, 1992-93
Points:	391 by Martin Pearson, 1992-93

Career

Goals:	1,210 by Steve Quinn, 1975-88
Tries:	162 by Don Fox, 1953-66
Points:	2,654 by Steve Quinn, 1975-88
Appearances:	440 by Jim Denton, 1921-34

Highest score: 86-18 v. Keighley, 17 Sep 1989
Highest against: 70-2 at Halifax, 14 Apr 1941
Attendance: 17,531 v. St. Helens (RL Cup), 21 Mar 1959

COACHING REGISTER

● **Since 1974-75**

* Tommy Smales	July 74 - Sep 74
Keith Goulding	Sep 74 - Jan 76
† Tommy Smales	Feb 76 - May 76
Keith Cotton	June 76 - Dec 77
Keith Goulding	Dec 77 - May 78
Terry Clawson	July 78 - Nov 78
† Tommy Smales	Nov 78 - Apr 79
Paul Daley	May 79 - Jan 81
Vince Farrar	Feb 81 - Nov 82
Allan Agar	Dec 82 - Oct 85
George Pieniazek	Nov 85 - Nov 86
Paul Daley	Nov 86 - Apr 87
Peter Fox	May 87 - Oct 91
Allan Agar	Oct 91 - Aug 92
Steve Martin	Sep 92 - Oct 94
David Ward	Oct 94 -

* *Ex-forward*
† *Ex-scrum half*

GREAT BRITAIN REGISTER

(16 players)

Tommy Askin	(6)	1928
Chris Bibb	(1)	1990
John "Keith" Bridges	(3)	1974
Terry Clawson	(2)	1962
Malcolm Dixon	(2)	1962-64
Steve Evans	(5+3)	1979-80
Deryck Fox	(9+4)	1985-92
Don Fox	(1)	1963
David Hobbs	(7+1)	1984
Gary Jordan	(2)	1964-67
Steve Molloy	(1)	1994
Arnold Morgan	(4)	1968
Steve Nash	(16)	1971-74
Paul Newlove	(7+3)	1989-93
Peter Smith	(1+5)	1977-84
Jimmy Thompson	(19+1)	1970-77

1995-96 REGISTRATION DATE

Signed	Player	Club From
1.8.95	Rothwell, Andy	Doncaster
1.8.95	Sharp, Jon	Hull
11.8.95	Miller, Tony	–
16.8.95	Arundel, Stuart	–

17.8.95	Carolan, Patrick	Leeds	
17.8.95	Lingard, Glynn	Doncaster	
26.8.95	Millington, John	–	
26.8.95	Steel, Wayne	Eagle Hotel ARL	
28.8.95	Bickerton, Simon	Featherstone Jnrs. ARL	
1.9.95	*Flanagan, Neil	Huddersfield	
9.9.95	Clewlow, Stuart	–	
22.9.95	Coventry, Richard	Featherstone Jnrs. ARL	
28.9.95	Slater, Richard	Wakefield T.	
1.10.95	Booth, Craig	London B.	
31.10.95	Mackie, Damien	New Zealand	
7.11.95	Rombo, Eddie	Dewsbury	
15.11.95	Fox, Deryck	Bradford B.	
15.11.95	Powell, Roy	Bradford B.	
17.11.95	Angell, Simon	New Zealand	
20.12.95	Wray, Andrew	Featherstone Jnrs. ARL	

FEATHERSTONE ROVERS 1995-96 PLAYERS' SUMMARY

	Date of birth	App	T	G	D	Pts	Previous club	Signed
Angell, Simon	12.11.70	4+2	0	0	0	0	New Zealand	17.11.95
Arundel, Stuart	20.2.71	2	0	0	0	0		16.8.95
Aston, Mark	27.9.67	6	1	0	0	4	Sheffield E.	1.7.94
Bibb, Chris	3.6.68	12+2	2	0	0	8		
Calland, Matt	20.8.71	5	5	0	0	20	Rochdale H.	8.9.93
Casey, Leo	17.9.65	8+4	1	0	0	4	Oldham	26.7.90
Evans, Danny	15.10.74	1+2	0	0	0	0	Travellers ARL	1.8.92
Flanagan, Neil	11.6.70	1	0	0	0	0	Huddersfield	1.9.95
Fox, Deryck	17.9.64	9	1	0	0	4	Bradford B.	15.11.95
Gibson, Carl	23.4.63	18	5	0	0	20	Leeds	25.8.93
Gunn, Richard	25.2.67	6+10	1	0	0	4	Leeds	24.9.92
Heptinstall, Andy	28.4.76	3	2	0	0	8	Travellers Saints ARL	7.1.93
Hughes, Darren	19.6.74	0+2	0	0	0	0	Leeds	2.9.93
Jackson, Craig	25.10.73	6+1	1	0	0	4	Isberg Celtic ARL	30.9.93
Lingard, Glynn	1.1.69	1+2	0	0	0	0	Doncaster D.	17.8.95
Mackie, Damien	11.2.72	11	2	0	0	8	New Zealand	31.10.95
Miller, Tony	30.3.68	3+7	0	0	0	0		11.8.95
Molloy, Steve	11.3.69	18	4	0	0	16	Leeds	3.11.93
Naidole, Joe	23.12.67	15+2	4	0	0	16	Huddersfield	29.12.94
Newlove, Richard	18.7.78	1	1	0	0	4		6.3.95
Pearson, Martin	24.10.71	21	16	83	3	233	Travellers Saints ARL	16.11.88
Powell, Roy	30.4.65	9	1	0	0	4	Bradford B.	15.11.95
Rodger, Brett	16.1.69	10+1	3	0	0	12	New Zealand	3.1.95
Roebuck, Neil	4.10.69	16+1	1	0	0	4	Castleford	13.1.93
Rombo, Eddie	19.3.67	19	6	0	0	24	Dewsbury	7.11.95
Rothwell, Andy	5.9.67	5	2	0	0	8	Doncaster D.	1.8.95
Sharp, Jon	8.3.67	10	0	0	0	0	Hull	1.8.95
Simpson, Owen	12.9.65	16	4	0	0	16	Keighley	9.11.90
Sims, Jason	15.7.70	0+3	0	0	0	0	Redhill ARL	8.11.94
Slater, Richard	29.8.70	12	2	0	0	8	Wakefield T.	28.9.95
Southernwood, Graham	5.11.71	5	1	0	0	4	Castleford	17.2.94
Thompson, Alex	16.11.74	1	0	0	0	0	Travellers ARL	21.10.92
Tuffs, Simon	3.2.68	8	0	0	0	0	Doncaster	24.5.95
Tuuta, Brendon	29.4.65	2	0	0	0	0	Australia	14.9.90
Wilson, Warren	3.5.63	9+1	2	0	0	8	Halifax	17.11.94
TOTALS								
35 players			68	83	3	441		

FEATHERSTONE ROVERS 1995-96 MATCH ANALYSIS

Date	Competition	H/A	Opponents	Rlt	Score	Tries	Goals	Attendance	Referee
20.8.95	FD	A	Hull	W	26-20	Calland (2), Pearson (2)	Pearson (5)	–	–
23.8.95	FD	H	Dewsbury	W	18-10	Calland, Rombo, Casey	Pearson (3)	2364	Cross
27.8.95	FD	A	Wakefield T.	W	28-19	Calland (2), Pearson (2), Southernwood	Pearson (4)	–	–
3.9.95	FD	H	Salford R.	L	16-38	Bibb, Newlove	Pearson (4)	2407	Gilmour
10.9.95	FD	A	Whitehaven	W	27-18	Aston, Gibson, Rothwell, Pearson	Pearson (5,dg)	–	–
17.9.95	FD	H	Widnes	L	18-30	Gunn, Pearson	Pearson (5)	2118	Burke
24.9.95	FD	A	Batley	L	14-26	Molloy (2), Bibb	Pearson	–	–
1.10.95	FD	H	Huddersfield	L	10-22	Gibson, Rothwell	Pearson	2079	Cross
1.11.95	FD	H	Rochdale H.	L	16-24	Slater	Pearson (6)	1575	Burke
5.11.95	FD	A	Keighley C.	L	0-31	–		–	–
12.11.95	RT(2)	A	Huddersfield	L	21-22	Pearson (2), Gibson	Pearson (4,dg)	–	–
15.11.95	FD	A	Dewsbury	W	23-22	Simpson (2), Gibson	Pearson (5,dg)	–	–
19.11.95	FD	H	Hull	W	34-18	Molloy, Slater, Wilson, Simpson, Pearson	Pearson (7)	2422	Gilmour
26.11.95	FD	H	Whitehaven	W	60-10	Pearson (4), Molloy, Simpson, Jackson, Mackie, Rodger	Pearson (12)	1569	Grimshaw
3.12.95	FD	A	Widnes	W	16-14	Rombo, Powell	Pearson (4)	–	–
17.12.95	FD	H	Batley	W	44-14	Naidole (3), Roebuck, Rodger, Gibson, Rombo, Pearson	Pearson (6)	1720	Nicholson
1.1.96	FD	A	Salford R.	L	6-24	Pearson	Pearson	–	–
4.1.96	FD	H	Wakefield T.	W	8-4	Mackie	Pearson (2)	2334	Cross
7.1.96	FD	A	Huddersfield	L	10-34	Heptonstall, Rombo	Pearson	–	–
14.1.96	FD	A	Rochdale H.	L	16-39	Rombo (2), Heptinstall	Pearson (2)	–	–
21.1.96	FD	H	Keighley C.	W	30-14	Fox, Naidole, Wilson, Pearson, Rodger	Pearson (5)	2390	Cross

One try in nine Centenary season games for Deryck Fox on his return to Post Office Road.

Former Test forward Roy Powell, a November 1995 signing by Featherstone Rovers from Bradford Bulls.

HALIFAX

Ground: Thrum Hall (01422-361026)
First Season: 1895-96
Nickname: Thrum Hallers
Chairman: Chris Whiteley
Chief Exec. Nigel Wood
Honours: **Championship** Winners, 1906-07, 1964-65
Beaten finalists, 1952-53, 1953-54, 1955-56, 1965-66
War Emergency League Beaten finalists, 1942-43, 1944-45
Division One Champions, 1902-03, 1985-86
Challenge Cup Winners, 1902-03, 1903-04, 1930-31, 1938-39, 1986-87
Beaten finalists, 1920-21, 1940-41, 1941-42, 1948-49, 1953-54, 1955-56, 1987-88
Regal Trophy Winners, 1971-72
Beaten finalists, 1989-90
Premiership Trophy Beaten finalists, 1985-86
Second Division Premiership Beaten finalists, 1990-91
Yorkshire Cup Winners, 1908-09, 1944-45, 1954-55, 1955-56, 1963-64
Beaten finalists, 1905-06, 1907-08, 1941-42, 1979-80
Yorkshire League Winners, 1908-09, 1920-21, 1952-53, 1953-54, 1955-56, 1957-58
Eastern Division Championship Winners, 1963-64
Charity Shield Winners, 1986-87
Beaten finalists, 1987-88

RECORDS
Match
Goals: 14 by Bruce Burton at Hunslet, 27 Aug 1972
Tries: 8 by Keith Williams v. Dewsbury, 9 Nov 1957
Points: 32 by John Schuster at Doncaster, 9 Oct 1994

Season
Goals: 147 by Tysul Griffiths, 1955-56
Tries: 48 by Johnny Freeman, 1956-57
Points: 362 by John Schuster, 1994-95

Career
Goals: 1,028 by Ron James, 1960-72
Tries: 290 by Johnny Freeman, 1954-67
Points: 2,191 by Ron James, 1960-72
Appearances: 481 by Stan Kielty, 1946-58
Highest score: 82-8 v. Runcorn H., 14 Oct 1990
Highest against: 64-0 at Wigan, 7 Mar 1923
Attendance: 29,153 v. Wigan (RL Cup), 21 Mar 1959

COACHING REGISTER
● **Since 1974-75**

Derek Hallas	Aug 74 - Oct 74
Les Pearce	Oct 74 - Apr 76
Alan Kellett	May 76 - Apr 77
Jim Crellin	June 77 - Oct 77
Harry Fox	Oct 77 - Feb 78
Maurice Bamford	Feb 78 - May 80
Mick Blacker	June 80 - June 82
Ken Roberts	June 82 - Sep 82
Colin Dixon	Sep 82 - Nov 84
Chris Anderson	Nov 84 - May 88
Graham Eadie	May 88 - Aug 88
Ross Strudwick	Aug 88 - Feb 89
Alan Hardisty	Feb 89 - Apr 89
John Dorahy	June 89 - Aug 90
Peter Roe	Aug 90 - May 91
Roger Millward	May 91 - Dec 92
Malcolm Reilly	Jan 93 - Sep 94
Steve Simms	Sep 94 -

Malcolm Reilly, coach of Halifax for 21 months from January 1993.

GREAT BRITAIN REGISTER
(32 players)

Alvin Ackerley	(2)	1952-58
Arthur Bassett	(2)	1946
Jack Beames	(2)	1921
Nat Bentham	(2)	1929
John Bentley	(1)	1994
Harry Beverley	(2)	1937
Oliver Burgham	(1)	1911
Arthur Daniels	(3)	1952-55
Will Davies	(1)	1911
Colin Dixon	(1)	1968
Paul Dixon	(3+3)	1987-88
Percy Eccles	(1)	1907
Terry Fogerty	(+1)	1966
Tony Halmshaw	(1)	1971
Karl Harrison	(8+3)	1991-94
Michael Jackson	(+2)	1993
Neil James	(1)	1986
Robbie Lloyd	(1)	1920
Alf Milnes	(2)	1920
Stuart Prosser	(1)	1914
Dai Rees	(1)	1926
Charlie Renilson	(7+1)	1965-68
Joe Riley	(1)	1910
Ken Roberts	(10)	1963-66
Asa Robinson	(3)	1907-08
Derrick Schofield	(1)	1955
John Shaw	(5)	1960-62
Cyril Stacey	(1)	1920
John Thorley	(4)	1954
Jack Wilkinson	(6)	1954-55
Frank Williams	(2)	1914
David Willicombe	(1)	1974

1995-96 REGISTRATION DATE

Signed	Player	Club From
5.7.95	Ekoku, Abi	London B.
5.7.95	Marns, Oliver	–
10.7.95	Campbell, Elliot	Milford ARL
18.7.95	James, Andrew	–
7.8.95	Briggs, Carl	Sheffield E.
7.8.95	Hoey, Chris	Ovenden ARL
8.8.95	Amone, Asa	Tonga
10.8.95	Umaga, Mike	New Zealand
11.8.95	*Hutchinson, Rob	Hull K.R.
14.8.95	Rika, Craig	–
24.8.95	*Greenwood, Brandon	Hull
8.9.95	Everett, Richard	–
14.9.95	Knowles, Lee	New Sharlston ARL
22.9.95	Tuilagi, Fereti	W. Samoa RU
23.9.95	Taylor, Lee	New Sharlston ARL
28.9.95	Seal, Daniel	Greetland ARL
8.10.95	Chester, Chris	New Sharlston ARL
16.10.95	Haigh, Neil	–
19.12.95	Moana, Martin	New Zealand
22.12.95	Ellis, St. John	Bradford B.
26.12.95	Hobson, Andy	New Sharlston ARL
27.12.95	McGuire, James	–

Halifax hooker Paul Rowley listed at £250,000 during the 1995-96 season

HALIFAX 1995-96 PLAYERS' SUMMARY

	Date of birth	App	T	G	D	Pts	Previous club	Signed
Amone, Asa	8.1.66	17+1	2	6	0	20	Tonga RU	16.8.95
Anderson, Grant	21.2.69	12+1	2	0	0	8	Castleford	1.7.94
Anderson, Paul	25.10.71	0+3	0	0	0	0	Leeds	16.9.93
Baldwin, Simon	31.3.75	15+4	9	0	0	36	Leigh	24.10.94
Bentley, John	5.9.66	12	10	0	0	40	Leeds	21.8.92
Briggs, Carl	27.9.74	11+7	4	0	9	25	Sheffield E.	7.8.95
Chester, Chris	8.10.78	4+1	2	0	0	8	New Sharlston ARL	8.10.95
Dean, Craig	20.10.76	13+4	6	0	0	24	Leigh East ARL	1.7.93
Divorty, Gary	28.1.66	1+3	0	0	0	0	Leeds	21.8.92
Ekoku, Abi	13.4.66	9+4	4	0	0	16	London B.	5.7.95
Ellis, St. John	3.10.64	5	0	0	0	0	Bradford B.	22.12.95
Fieldhouse, John	28.6.62	9+4	0	0	0	0	Oldham	17.10.91
Gillespie, Carl	25.7.70	14+9	5	0	0	20	Old Crossleyans RU	22.12.94
Harrison, Karl	20.2.64	17	1	0	0	4	Hull	8.8.91
Highton, Paul	10.11.76	9+7	3	0	0	12	Waterhead ARL	2.8.93
Hutchinson, Rob	20.9.68	1	0	0	0	0	Hull K.R.	11.8.95
Jackson, Michael	11.10.69	15+4	3	0	0	12	Wakefield T.	13.7.93
Jackson, Wayne	19.9.67	10+6	0	0	0	0	Doncaster	1.5.95
James, Andy	30.11.75	0+2	0	0	0	0	Halifax Academy	18.7.95
Ketteridge, Martin	2.10.64	9+3	0	3	0	6	Castleford	16.2.95
Marshall, Richard	9.10.75	0+1	0	0	0	0	St. Helens Academy	14.6.93
Moana, Martin	13.8.73	3+1	1	0	0	4	New Zealand	14.12.95
Moriarty, Paul	16.7.64	9+1	2	0	0	8	Widnes	7.7.94
Munro, Damian	6.10.76	8	5	0	0	20	Waterhead ARL	20.12.94
Parker, Wayne	2.4.67	14	5	0	1	21	Hull K.R.	4.8.94
Perrett, Mark	18.7.73	7+8	3	0	0	12	Ovenden ARL	18.9.91
Preston, Mark	3.4.67	7+2	1	0	0	4	Wigan	11.6.91
Rowley, Paul	12.3.75	18+1	4	0	0	16	Leigh	8.11.94
Schuster, John	17.1.64	12	4	48	0	112	Australia	22.8.93
Slicker, Michael	16.8.78	1+2	0	0	0	0	Leigh East ARL	5.10.94
Southernwood, Roy	23.6.68	5+1	0	0	0	0	Castleford	24.8.90
Tuilagi, Fereti	9.6.71	11	3	0	0	12	Western Samoa RU	20.9.95
Turner, Craig	10.3.73	0+1	0	0	0	0	Siddal ARL	17.1.92
Umaga, Mike	19.2.66	21	10	18	0	76	Western Samoa RU	10.8.95
TOTALS								
34 players			89	75	10	516		

Representative appearances 1995-96

Amone – Tonga (2,6g);
Bentley – England (3,1t);
Harrison – England (4);
Moriarty – Wales (3);
Perrett – Wales (1);
Schuster – Wales (1);
Western Samoa (2,11g).

HALIFAX 1995-96 MATCH ANALYSIS

Date	Com-petition	H/A	Opponents	Rlt	Score	Tries	Goals	Atten-dance	Referee
23.8.95	SBC	H	London B.	W	50-12	Schuster (2), Bentley, Baldwin, Preston, Briggs, Umaga, Parker	Schuster (8), Briggs (2dg)	4046	Smith
27.8.95	SBC	H	Bradford B.	W	20-10	Bentley, Baldwin, Gillespie	Schuster (4)	6156	R. Connolly
1.9.95	SBC	A	Oldham B.	W	21-4	Rowley (2), Moriarty	Schuster (4), Briggs (dg)	–	–
6.9.95	SBC	H	Wigan	L	13-48	M. Jackson, Briggs	Schuster (2), Briggs (dg)	7776	Campbell
10.9.95	SBC	A	Leeds	L	27-60	Ekoku (2), Bentley, Baldwin, Briggs	Schuster (3), Briggs (dg)	–	–
17.9.95	SBC	H	Sheffield E.	W	28-6	Bentley (4), Umaga	Schuster (3), Briggs (2dg)	3528	Kirkpatrick
24.9.95	SBC	A	Workington T.	W	24-17	Ekoku (2), Highton, Moriarty, Bentley	Umaga (2)	–	–
29.9.95	SBC	H	Castleford	W	19-10	Parker, Gillespie, Harrison	Umaga (3), Briggs (dg)	3891	Bates
1.11.95	SBC	A	Warrington	W	16-14	Umaga, Parker	Schuster (4)	–	–
5.11.95	SBC	A	St. Helens	L	20-58	Umaga, Gillespie, Tuilagi	Schuster (4)	–	–
12.11.95	RT(2)	H	Swinton	W	20-18	Schuster, Highton, Perrett	Schuster (4)	2994	Cross
15.11.95	SBC	A	London B.	L	27-38	Umaga, Gillespie, Dean, Perrett	Schuster (5), Briggs (dg)	–	–
25.11.95	RT(3)	A	London B.	W	22-18	Bentley (2), Tuilagi, Schuster	Schuster (3)	–	–
3.12.95	SBC	H	Leeds	W	29-10	Dean (2), Parker (2), M. Jackson	Schuster (4), Parker (dg)	6000	J. Connolly
10.12.95	RT(QF)	A	St. Helens	L	18-46	Umaga (2), Baldwin	Amone (3)	–	–
13.12.95	SBC	A	Wigan	L	18-32	Baldwin (2), Tuilagi, Munro	Amone	–	–
17.12.95	SBC	H	Workington T.	W	26-12	Anderson (2), Dean, Amone, Rowley, Baldwin	Ketteridge	3000	R. Connolly
20.12.95	SBC	A	Sheffield E.	L	14-38	Briggs, M. Jackson, Munro	Amone	–	–
1.1.96	SBC	A1	Bradford B.	W	22-18	Baldwin, Dean, Munro, Umaga	Umaga (2), Ketteridge	–	–
4.1.96	SBC	H	Oldham B.	L	4-12	–	Umaga (2)	4155	Bates
7.1.96	SBC	A	Castleford	D	26-26	Amone, Chester, Gillespie, Munro, Perrett	Amone, Umaga, Ketteridge	–	–
14.1.96	SBC	H	Warrington	W	20-14	Chester, Munro, Rowley	Umaga (4)	3445	J. Connolly
21.1.96	SBC	H	St. Helens	W	32-24	Umaga (2), Baldwin, Dean, Highton, Moana	Umaga (4)	4574	Cummings

1 At Huddersfield

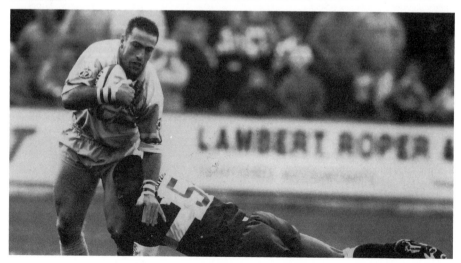

Halifax winger John Bentley, scorer of one try in three 1995 Centenary World Cup games for England.

HIGHFIELD

Ground: Hope Street
First Season: 1922-23 as Wigan Highfield. Became London Highfield in 1933-34. Became Liverpool Stanley in 1934-35 and changed to Liverpool City in 1951-52. Became Huyton in 1968-69 and changed to Runcorn Highfield in 1984-85. Became Highfield in 1991-92.
Chairman: Geoff Fletcher
Secretary: Brian Morris
Honours: **Lancashire League** Winners, 1935-36

RECORDS

Match
Goals: 11 by Peter Wood v. Batley, 21 Oct 1984
Tries: 5 by John Maloney v. Bramley, 25 Apr 1931
Points: 30 by Norman Barrow v. Keighley, 31 Mar 1991

Season
Goals: 126 by Peter Wood, 1984-85
Tries: 28 by John Maloney, 1930-31
Points: 240 by Peter Wood, 1984-85

Career
Goals: 304 by Wilf Hunt, 1955-66
Tries: 204 by John Maloney, 1926-45
Points: 731 by Wilf Hunt, 1955-66
Appearances: 413 by John Maloney, 1926-45
Highest score: 59-11 v. Bramley, 4 May 1934
Highest against: 104-4 v. Keighley C, 23 Apr 1995 (home game at Rochdale)
Attendance: 18,000 v. Wigan (League), 2 Sep 1922 — at Tunstall Lane, Pemberton
1,071 v. Huddersfield (league) 2 Oct 1994 — at Hope Street

COACHING REGISTER

● **Since 1974-75**

Terry Gorman	Aug 74 - May 77
Geoff Fletcher	Aug 77 - June 86
Frank Wilson	July 86 - Nov 86
Arthur Daley } Paul Woods }	Nov 86 - Apr 87
Bill Ashurst	Apr 87 - Jan 89
John Cogger	Jan 89 - Feb 89
Geoff Fletcher	Feb 89 - Apr 89
Dave Chisnall	June 89 - Oct 90
Alan Bishop	Oct 90 - Apr 91
Chris Arkwright	Apr 91 - Aug 91
Willie Johnson	Aug 91 - Apr 93
Mike Peers	Apr 93 - Sep 94
Chris Arkwright	Sep 94 - July 95
Tommy Frodsham	July 95 - Jan 96
Jim Crellin	Jan 96 -

GREAT BRITAIN REGISTER

(4 players)

Ray Ashby	(1)	1964
Billy Belshaw	(6)	1936-37
Nat Bentham	(6)	1928
Harry Woods	(5)	1936

1995-96 REGISTRATION DATE

Signed	Player	Club From
8.8.95	Barrow, Simon	Parkside ARL
8.8.95	Howden, Ben	Orrell St. James ARL
8.8.95	Lloyd, David	Parkside ARL
10.8.95	Chisnall, Ian	Parkside Golborne ARL
17.8.95	Byron, Graham	–
17.8.95	Chisnall, Darren	Hare & Hounds ARL
17.8.95	Chisnall, Phil	Pilkington Recs ARL
17.8.95	Derbyshire, Peter	Hare & Hounds
17.8.95	dal Ferro, Alastair	Thatto Heath ARL
17.8.95	Lawrenson, Jason	Hare & Hounds ARL
17.8.95	Lyon, Neil	Oldham Academy
17.8.95	McTomney, Anthony	–
17.8.95	Reid, Nicholas	–
17.8.95	Roberts, Paul	Swinton
17.8.95	Robinson, Tom	Blackheath ARL
17.8.95	Taylor, Mark	Sefton RU
18.8.95	Lever, David	Leigh C.
20.8.95	Bacon, Michael	Warrington
20.8.95	*Holden, Graham	Widnes
22.8.95	Frodsham, Tommy	–

23.8.95	*Fanning, Sean	Leigh C.		27.9.95	Dainty, Mark	–
23.8.95	Spruce, Kieron	–		1.11.95	*Measures, Neil	Leigh C.
25.8.95	Litherland, David	Halifax		11.11.95	Brown, Mark	Orrell St. James ARL
26.8.95	Pennington, Anthony	Haresfinch ARL		11.11.95	Gavin, Paul	Blackbrook ARL
				11.11.95	Hale, Chris	RU
8.9.95	Tunstall, Keith	Protico ARL		11.11.95	Maiden, Daniel	Highfield Academy
12.9.95	*Earner, Adrian	Swinton		29.11.95	Heaton, Billy	Leigh C.
15.9.95	Holden, Garry	Pilkington Recs ARL		9.12.95	Dooney, Gary	Parkside ARL
21.9.95	Binns, Paul	Orrell St. James ARL		9.12.95	Flynn, Karl	Parr Hare & Hounds ARL
22.9.95	*Best, Brian	Swinton				
23.9.95	Callaghan, Ian	Blackbrook ARL		16.1.96	Wade, Neil	–

HIGHFIELD 1995-96 PLAYERS' SUMMARY

	Date of birth	App	T	G	D	Pts	Previous club	Signed
Ashall, Barry	1.9.71	1	0	0	0	0	Swinton	27.8.93
Barber, Darren		1	0	0	0	0		
Barrow, Simon	14.4.77	1+1	0	0	0	0	Parkside ARL	8.8.95
Binns, Paul	31.3.70	8+2	1	0	0	4	Orrell St. James ARL	21.9.95
Bridge, Alan		1	0	0	0	0		
Bridge, Russell	8.10.64	17	3	0	0	12	Leigh	4.8.95
Brown, Mark	7.4.72	2	1	0	0	4	Orrell St. James ARL	11.11.95
Callaghan, Ian	21.12.71	5	3	4	1	21	Blackbrook ARL	23.9.95
Chambers, Steve		1	0	0	0	0		
Chisnall, Darren	22.9.69	7+5	0	0	0	0	Hare & Hounds ARL	17.8.95
Chisnall, Ian	21.1.77	5+1	1	0	0	4	Parkside Golb'ne ARL	10.8.95
Crehan, Andy	27.11.67	5	0	0	0	0	Swinton	3.2.94
Dainty, Mark	8.11.62	1	0	0	0	0		27.9.95
dal Ferro, Alastair	16.12.70	1+3	0	0	0	0	Thatto Heath ARL	17.8.95
dal Ferro, Giasone	16.12.70	5	0	0	0	0		26.8.95
Derbyshire, Peter	6.12.72	3	0	0	0	0	Hare & Hounds ARL	17.8.95
Dooney, Gary	7.2.68	14	1	0	0	4	Parkside ARL	9.12.95
Drinkwater, Matt	18.4.75	8+4	1	0	0	4	Woolston ARL	16.8.93
Earner, Adrian	19.11.66	4	0	0	0	0	Swinton	12.9.95
Fanning, Sean	16.6.62	15	7	36	0	100	Leigh C.	23.8.95
Flynn, Karl	28.4.75	5	0	0	0	0	Hare & Hounds ARL	9.12.95
Frodsham, Tommy	12.1.61	15+2	4	0	0	16		22.8.95
Gavin, Paul	26.1.73	6+2	2	0	0	8	Blackbrook ARL	11.11.95
Hale, Chris	23.9.67	2+3	0	0	0	0	RU	11.11.95
Hart, Wayne		1	0	0	0	0		
Heaton, Billy	31.1.74	3	0	0	0	0	Leigh C.	29.11.95
Holden, Garry	22.9.71	14	3	0	2	14	Pilkington Recs ARL	15.9.95
Holden, Graham	3.1.74	7	2	0	0	8	Widnes	20.8.95
Howden, Ben		2+2	0	0	0	0	Orrell St. James ARL	8.8.95
Johnson, Kevin	4.4.72	14+1	4	2	1	21	Leigh	
Kelly, Paul.		1	0	0	0	0		
Lawrenson, Jason	18.3.71	13+2	1	0	0	4	Hare & Hounds ARL	17.8.95

(continued)

	Date of birth	App	T	G	D	Pts	Previous club	Signed
Lever, Dave	2.2.70	17	2	0	0	8	Leigh C.	18.8.95
Leyland, James		0+1	0	0	0	0		
Litherland, Roy	1.11.70	6	2	0	0	8	Halifax	25.8.95
Lloyd, David	6.1.77	3+1	1	0	0	4	Parkside ARL	8.8.95
Lyon, Neil	11.1.76	0+1	0	0	0	0	Oldham Academy	17.8.95
Maiden, Daniel	16.3.77	0+1	0	0	0	0	Highfield Academy	11.11.95
Measures, Neil	11.1.71	6+1	0	0	0	0	Leigh C.	1.11.95
Morris, Graham		1	0	0	0	0		
Pennington, Tony	26.1.67	17	3	8	1	29	Haresfinch ARL	26.8.95
Pitman, Dave	9.1.72	4	1	0	0	4	Crosfields ARL	10.3.95
Reid, Nick	2.5.73	1+1	0	0	0	0		17.8.95
Rippon, Andy	10.2.65	4	0	0	0	0	Swinton	
Roberts, Paul	19.11.72	6	1	0	0	4	Swinton	17.8.95
Robinson, Tom	19.2.70	1	0	0	0	0	Blackheath ARL	17.8.95
Smith, Seb	26.5.72	2+1	2	0	0	8	RU	5.2.95
Spruce, Kieron	14.1.78	2+2	0	0	0	0		23.8.95
Taylor, Mark	7.2.72	1+3	0	0	0	0	Sefton RU	17.8.95
Tunstall, Keith	19.9.71	2	0	0	0	0	Protico ARL	8.9.95
Wade, Neil	15.4.73	19	2	0	0	8		28.9.95
Williams, Andrew		1	0	0	0	0		
Trialists (3)		5	0	0	0	0		

TOTALS

55 players | | | 48 | 50 | 5 | 297

HIGHFIELD 1995-96 MATCH ANALYSIS

Date	Competition	H/A	Opponents	Rlt	Score	Tries	Goals	Attendance	Referee
20.8.95	SD	A	Barrow B.	L	10-64	Drinkwater, Smith	K. Johnson	–	–
23.8.95	SD	A	Carlisle	L	0-70	–	–	–	–
27.8.95	SD	H	Chorley	L	21-25	Smith, Litherland, Roberts	Pennington (4,dg)	302	Shaw
10.9.95	SD	H	Swinton	L	2-66	–	Pennington	468	Ganson
13.9.95	SD	H	Leigh C.	L	5-66	–	Pennington, (2) K. Johnson (dg)	570	Asquith
17.9.95	SD	A	York	L	14-74	R. Bridge, Pitman, Wade	Pennington	–	–
24.9.95	SD	H	Bramley	L	13-18	Pennington	Callaghan (4), Garry Holden (dg)	328	Cross
1.10.95	RT(1)	H	Hemel Hempstead	W	48-18	Fanning (2), Lawrenson, Graham Holden, Garry Holden, Lever, Binns, Frodsham, K. Johnson	Fanning (5), K. Johnson	220	Atkin
1.11.95	SD	A	Doncaster D.	L	17-24	Fanning (2), Wade	Fanning (2), Garry Holden (dg)	–	–
5.11.95	SD	H	Hunslet H.	L	12-28	R. Bridge, Brown	Fanning (2)	329	Oddy
12.11.95	RT(2)	A	London B.	L	0-82	–	–	–	–
15.11.95	SD	H	Carlisle	L	22-48	Pennington, Fanning, Garry Holden	Fanning (5)	171	Grimshaw
19.11.95	SD	A	Swinton	L	8-52	Pennington	Fanning (2)	–	–
26.11.95	SD	A	Hull K.R.	L	6-60	Garry Holden	Fanning	–	–
29.11.95	SD	H	Barrow B.	L	16-44	Callaghan, Frodsham	Fanning (4)	381	Owram
3.12.95	SD	A	Leigh C.	L	16-54	K. Johnson, R. Bridge, Fanning	Fanning (2)	–	–
10.12.95	SD	H	York	D	24-24	K. Johnson (2), Callaghan, Frodsham	Fanning (4)	150	Lee
13.12.95	SD	H	Hull K.R.	L	14-54	Gavin (2), Callaghan	Fanning	270	Grimshaw
17.12.95	SD	A	Bramley	L	7-30	Fanning	Fanning, Callaghan (dg)	–	–
7.1.96	SD	H	Doncaster D.	L	28-41	Dooney, Frodsham, Litherland, Graham Holden, Lloyd	Fanning (4)	413	Burke
9.1.96	SD	A	Chorley	L	14-40	I. Chisnall, Lever	Fanning (3)	–	–
21.1.96	SD	A	Hunslet H.	L	0-82	–	–	–	–

HUDDERSFIELD

Ground: Alfred McAlpine Stadium
(01484-530710)

First Season: 1895-96; added Barracudas to title
from 1984-85 to 1987-88 inclusive

Nickname: Fartowners

Chairman: Ken Davies

General
  Manager: Les Coulter

Honours: **Championship** Winners, 1911-12,
1912-13, 1914-15, 1928-29, 1929-30,
1948-49, 1961-62
Beaten finalists, 1913-14, 1919-20,
1922-23, 1931-32, 1945-46, 1949-50
Division Two Champions, 1974-75
Division Three Champions, 1991-92
Challenge Cup Winners, 1912-13,
1914-15, 1919-20, 1932-33, 1944-45,
1952-53
Beaten finalists, 1934-35, 1961-62
Second Division Premiership
Beaten finalists, 1994-95
Yorkshire Cup Winners, 1909-10,
1911-12, 1913-14, 1914-15, 1918-19,
1919-20, 1926-27, 1931-32, 1938-39,
1950-51, 1952-53, 1957-58
Beaten finalists, 1910-11, 1923-24,
1925-26, 1930-31, 1937-38, 1942-43,
1949-50, 1960-61
Yorkshire League Winners,
1911-12, 1912-13, 1913-14, 1914-15,
1919-20, 1921-22, 1928-29, 1929-30,
1948-49, 1949-50, 1951-52
Eastern Division Beaten finalists,
1962-63

RECORDS
Match

Goals: 18 by Major Holland v. Swinton Park,
28 Feb 1914

Tries: 10 by Lionel Cooper v. Keighley,
17 Nov 1951

Points: 39 by Major Holland v. Swinton Park,
28 Feb 1914

Season

Goals: 147 by Ben Gronow, 1919-20

Tries: 80 by Albert Rosenfeld, 1913-14

Points: 332 by Pat Devery, 1952-53

Career

Goals: 958 by Frank Dyson, 1950-63

Tries: 420 by Lionel Cooper, 1947-55

Points: 2,072 by Frank Dyson, 1950-63

Appearances: 485 by Doug Clark, 1909-29

Highest score: 142-4 v. Blackpool G., 26 Nov 1994

Highest against: 94-12 at Castleford, 18 Sep 1988

Attendance: 32,912 v. Wigan (League),
4 Mar 1950 — at Fartown,
9,348 v. Halifax (RL Cup),
12 Feb 1995 — at Alfred McAlpine
Stadium

COACHING REGISTER
● **Since 1974-75**

Brian Smith	Jan 73 - Mar 76
Keith Goulding	Mar 76 - Dec 76
Bob Tomlinson	Jan 77 - May 77
Neil Fox	June 77 - Feb 78
* Roy Francis	—
Keith Goulding	May 78 - July 79
Ian Brooke	July 79 - Mar 80
Maurice Bamford	May 80 - May 81
Les Sheard	June 81 - Nov 82
Dave Mortimer	Nov 82 - Aug 83
Mel Bedford	Aug 83 - Nov 83
Brian Lockwood	Nov 83 - Feb 85
Chris Forster	Feb 85 - Dec 86
Jack Addy	Jan 87 - Mar 88
Allen Jones ⎫ Neil Whittaker ⎭	Mar 88 - Nov 88
Nigel Stephenson	Nov 88 - Mar 90
Barry Seabourne	Mar 90 - Feb 91
Mick Blacker ⎫ Francis Jarvis ⎭	Feb 91 - Sep 91
Alex Murphy	Sep 91 - Apr 94
George Fairbairn	June 94 - Oct 95
Darryl Van de Velde	Dec 95 -

* *Although Roy Francis was appointed he was unable to take over and Dave Heppleston stood in until the next appointment.*

GREAT BRITAIN REGISTER
(24 players)

Player		Years
Jim Bowden	(3)	1954
Ken Bowman	(3)	1962-63
Brian Briggs	(1)	1954
Stan Brogden	(9)	1929-33
Jack Chilcott	(3)	1914
Doug Clark	(11)	1911-20
Don Close	(1)	1967
Dick Cracknell	(2)	1951
Jim Davies	(2)	1911
Frank Dyson	(1)	1959
Ben Gronow	(7)	1911-20
Fred Longstaff	(2)	1914
Ken Loxton	(1)	1971
Stan Moorhouse	(2)	1914
Bob Nicholson	(3)	1946-48
Johnny Rogers	(7)	1914-21
Ken Senior	(2)	1965-67
Tommy Smales	(5)	1962-64
Mick Sullivan	(16)	1954-57
Gwyn Thomas	(8)	1920-21
Dave Valentine	(15)	1948-54
Rob Valentine	(1)	1967
Harold Wagstaff	(12)	1911-21
Harold Young	(1)	1929

1995-96 REGISTRATION DATE

Signed	Player	Club From
4.8.95	Salmon, Robert	–
9.8.95	Bunyan, James	Milford ARL
11.8.95	*O'Donnell, Gus	St. Helens
13.8.95	Moore, Adrian	Dewsbury Moor ARL
17.8.95	Higgins, John	–
17.8.95	Hirst, Andrew	–
17.8.95	Simpson, Anthony	Sheffield E.
18.8.95	Farrell, Andrew	–
19.8.95	Adams, Guy	–
30.8.95	Marsden, Robert	Salford
4.9.95	Toole, Adrian	Australia
14.9.95	Adams, Marcel	–
15.9.95	Delrose, Darrel	–
15.9.95	James, Sean	Moldgreen ARL
16.11.95	Burns, Mark	Lindley Swifts ARL
21.12.95	*Senior, Lee	Featherstone R.
29.12.95	Boothroyd, Alan	Bradford B.
2.1.96	*Wilson, Alan	Bradford B.

Winger Mick Sullivan, capped 16 times while serving Huddersfield.

HUDDERSFIELD 1995-96 PLAYERS' SUMMARY

	Date of birth	App	T	G	D	Pts	Previous club	Signed
Austin, Greg	14.6.63	15	12	0	0	48	Salford	18.8.94
Barnett, Steve	8.10.68	2	0	0	0	0	Bradford N.	22.9.92
Barton, Ben	4.12.74	9	1	0	0	4		1.7.93
Booth, Steve	18.9.76	6+4	4	0	0	16	Oulton ARL	4.4.95
Boothroyd, Alan	19.6.66	0+2	0	0	0	0	Bradford B.	29.12.95
Bruce, Jonathan	30.10.71	6+5	0	0	0	0	Dudley Hill ARL	19.7.94
Bunyan, James	2.11.77	1+1	0	0	0	0	Milford ARL	9.8.95
Coulter, Gary	12.7.69	12+2	2	0	0	8	Doncaster	17.1.92
Hanger, Dean	24.2.70	16	7	0	0	28	Leigh	19.8.94
Kebbie, Brimah	21.9.65	12	6	0	0	24	Bradford N.	29.7.94
Kerry, Steve	10.3.66	13+1	4	5	3	29	Oldham	7.10.94
Marsden, Bob	28.2.66	20+2	2	0	0	8	Salford	30.8.95
Milner, Lee	26.2.77	3+3	2	0	0	8	Huddersfield Academy	8.8.94
Moore, Johnny	8.7.74	9	1	4	0	12	Park Amateurs ARL	15.8.92
Morris, Nigel	2.10.74	1+1	0	0	0	0	Thatto Heath ARL	17.6.93
O'Donnell, Gus	11.12.70	3+2	0	0	0	0	St. Helens	11.8.95
Pearce, Greg	2.9.67	16+3	1	59	0	122	Halifax	15.9.93
Pearson, Richard	9.10.74	8+2	3	0	0	12	Ovenden ARL	31.10.91
Pucill, Andy	19.11.67	15+1	1	0	0	4	Swinton	21.8.92
Reynolds, Simon	10.3.73	5	1	0	0	4	Moldgreen ARL	27.8.93
Richards, Basil	9.7.65	17+1	2	0	0	8	Warrington	27.8.93
Salmon, Robert	10.12.69	1	0	0	0	0		4.8.95
Senior, Lee	27.8.74	3	1	1	0	6	Featherstone R.	21.12.95
Sewell, Andy		0+1	0	0	0	0		
Shelford, Darrall	29.7.62	21	3	0	0	12	Bradford N.	11.8.94
Simpson, Anthony	12.3.69	3	0	0	0	0	Sheffield E.	17.8.95
Slater, Lee	8.9.74	2+1	0	0	0	0	Ovenden ARL	12.8.92
Smith, Dave		0+2	0	0	0	0		
St. Hilaire, Lee	15.2.67	19	4	0	0	16	Huddersfield Acad.	30.12.92
St. Hilaire, Marcus	26.1.77	7	4	0	0	16	Moldgreen ARL	31.7.94
Taylor, Mick	11.9.61	4+9	0	0	0	0	Bradford N.	7.9.94
Thomas, Ian	6.11.64	7+1	5	0	0	20	Hudd'd Supp. ARL	3.6.83
Thornton, Danny		1	0	0	0	0		
Toole, Adrian	12.6.65	16	2	0	0	8	Australia	31.8.95
Ventola, Roy		11	1	0	0	4		
Wilson, Alan	25.9.67	1	0	0	0	0	Bradford B.	2.1.96
TOTALS								
36 players			69	69	3	417		

HUDDERSFIELD 1995-96 MATCH ANALYSIS

Date	Competition	H/A	Opponents	Rlt	Score	Tries	Goals	Attendance	Referee
20.8.95	FD	H	Keighley C.	L	26-36	Shelford (3), Pearson	Pearce (4), Kerry	4739	Nicholson
23.8.95	FD	H	Rochdale H.	L	12-27	Pearson, Kebbie	Pearce (2)	1772	Atkin
27.8.95	FD	A	Hull	L	10-37	Austin, Thomas	Pearce	–	–
3.9.95	FD	H	Dewsbury	W	37-18	Thomas (3), Kerry (2), Kebbie	Pearce (6), Kerry (dg)	2221	Burke
10.9.95	FD	A	Wakefield T.	L	22-26	Hanger (2), Coulter, Moore	Pearce (3)	–	–
17.9.95	FD	H	Salford R.	L	20-48	Toole (2), Kebbie	Kerry (4)	2803	Nicholson
20.9.95	FD	A	Whitehaven	L	14-21	Hanger, L. St. Hilaire	Pearce (3)	–	–
23.9.95	FD	H	Widnes	L	29-34	M. St. Hilaire (2), Austin (2), Ventola	Pearce (4), Kerry (dg)	2055	Asquith
1.10.95	FD	A	Featherstone R.	W	22-10	Milner, Marsden, Hanger, M. St. Hilaire	Pearce (3)	–	–
5.11.95	FD	H	Batley	W	57-8	Hanger (2), Austin (2), Kerry, L. St. Hilaire, Barton, Richards, Pearce	Pearce (10), Kerry (dg)	2389	Taberner
12.11.95	RT(2)	H	Featherstone R.	W	22-21	L. St. Hilaire, Kebbie, Austin	Pearce (5)	2337	Nicholson
15.11.95	FD	A	Rochdale H.	L	8-20	Booth	Pearce (2)	–	–
19.11.95	FD	A	Keighley C.	L	6-40	Booth	Moore	–	–
26.11.95	RT(3)	H	Wigan	L	0-32	–	–	6026	Cummings
29.11.95	FD	H	Wakefield T.	L	14-22	Booth, Pearson	Moore (2), Pearce	2062	Ganson
3.12.95	FD	A	Salford R.	L	12-31	Marsden, Pucill	Pearce (2)	–	–
10.12.95	FD	H	Whitehaven	L	14-26	Austin, Richards	Pearce (2), Moore	1711	Asquith
17.12.95	FD	A	Widnes	W	18-14	Austin (2), Thomas	Pearce (3)	–	–
24.12.95	FD	H	Hull	L	10-23	Coulter, L. St. Hilaire	Pearce	2435	Ganson
31.12.95	FD	A	Dewsbury	L	10-22	Austin, Reynolds	Senior	–	–
7.1.96	FD	H	Featherstone R.	W	34-10	Austin (2), Booth, Kerry, L. Senior, M. St. Hilaire	Pearce (5)	2089	Taberner
21.1.96	FD	A	Batley	W	20-12	Kebbie (2), Hanger, Milner	Pearce (2)	–	–

Brian Lockwood, coach of Huddersfield from November 1983 to February 1985.

A one-year stint as Huddersfield coach for Barry Seabourne from March 1990 to February 1991.

HULL

Ground: The Boulevard (01482-329040)
First Season: 1895-96
Nickname: Airlie Birds
Chairman: Alan Mason
Chief Exec: Stephen Ball
Honours: **Championship** Winners, 1919-20, 1920-21, 1935-36, 1955-56, 1957-58
Beaten finalists, 1956-57
Division One Champions, 1982-83
Division Two Champions, 1976-77, 1978-79
Challenge Cup Winners, 1913-14, 1981-82
Beaten finalists, 1907-08, 1908-09, 1909-10, 1921-22, 1922-23, 1958-59, 1959-60, 1979-80, 1982-83, 1984-85
Regal Trophy Winners, 1981-82
Beaten finalists, 1975-76, 1984-85
Premiership Winners, 1990-91
Beaten finalists, 1980-81, 1981-82, 1982-83, 1988-89
Yorkshire Cup Winners, 1923-24, 1969-70, 1982-83, 1983-84, 1984-85
Beaten finalists, 1912-13, 1914-15, 1920-21, 1927-28, 1938-39, 1946-47, 1953-54, 1954-55, 1955-56, 1959-60, 1967-68, 1986-87
Yorkshire League Winners, 1918-19, 1922-23, 1926-27, 1935-36
Charity Shield Beaten finalists, 1991-92
BBC2 Floodlit Trophy Winners, 1979-80

RECORDS
Match
Goals: 14 by Jim Kennedy v. Rochdale H., 7 Apr 1921
Geoff "Sammy" Lloyd v. Oldham, 10 Sep 1978
Tries: 7 by Clive Sullivan at Doncaster, 15 Apr 1968
Points: 36 by Jim Kennedy v. Keighley, 29 Jan 1921

Season
Goals: 170 by Geoff "Sammy" Lloyd, 1978-79
Tries: 52 by Jack Harrison, 1914-15
Points: 369 by Geoff "Sammy" Lloyd, 1978-79

Career
Goals: 687 by Joe Oliver, 1928-37 & 1943-45
Tries: 250 by Clive Sullivan, 1961-74 & 1981-85
Points: 1,842 by Joe Oliver, 1928-37 & 1943-45
Appearances: 501 by Edward Rogers, 1906-25
Highest score: 86-0 v. Elland, 1 Apr 1899
Highest against: 66-16 at Wigan, 23 Apr 1995
Attendance: 28,798 v. Leeds (RL Cup), 7 Mar 1936

COACHING REGISTER
● **Since 1974-75**

David Doyle-Davidson	May 74 - Dec 77
Arthur Bunting	Jan 78 - Dec 85
Kenny Foulkes	Dec 85 - May 86
Len Casey	June 86 - Mar 88
Tony Dean ⎫	
Keith Hepworth ⎭	Mar 88 - Apr 88
* Brian Smith	July 88 - Jan 91
* Noel Cleal	Sep 90 - Apr 92
Royce Simmons	May 92 - Apr 94
Tony Gordon	May 94 - Dec 94
Russ Walker/Phil Windley	Dec 94 - May 95
Phil Windley	May 95 - Nov 95
Phil Sigsworth	Jan 96 -

* *Joint coaches Sep 90 - Jan 91.*

Clive Sullivan, holder of the Hull record for most tries in a match.

GREAT BRITAIN REGISTER

(35 players)

Billy Batten	(1)	1921
Harold Bowman	(8)	1924-29
Frank Boylen	(1)	1908
Robin Coverdale	(4)	1954
Mick Crane	(1)	1982
Lee Crooks	(11+2)	1982-87
Andy Dannatt	(3)	1985-91
Gary Divorty	(2)	1985
Bill Drake	(1)	1962
Jim Drake	(1)	1960
Paul Eastwood	(13)	1990-92
Steve Evans	(2)	1982
Vince Farrar	(1)	1978
Dick Gemmell	(2)	1968-69
Emlyn Gwynne	(3)	1928-29
Tommy Harris	(25)	1954-60
Karl Harrison	(3)	1990
Mick Harrison	(7)	1967-73
Billy Holder	(1)	1907
Lee Jackson	(11)	1990-92
Mark Jones	(+1)	1992
Arthur Keegan	(9)	1966-69
Steve McNamara	(+2)	1992-93
Edgar Morgan	(2)	1921
Steve Norton	(9)	1978-82
Wayne Proctor	(+1)	1984
Paul Rose	(1)	1982
Garry Schofield	(15)	1984-87
Trevor Skerrett	(6)	1980-82
Billy Stone	(8)	1920-21
Clive Sullivan	(17)	1967-73
Bob Taylor	(2)	1921-26
Harry Taylor	(3)	1907
David Topliss	(1)	1982
Johnny Whiteley	(15)	1957-62

1995-96 REGISTRATION DATE

Signed	Player	Club From
28.6.95	Green, Alex	Doncaster
28.6.95	Manning, Terry	Doncaster
17.7.95	Deakin, Leigh	York
31.7.95	Fisher, Andy	Dewsbury
31.7.95	Parker, Paul	–
31.7.95	Wray, Samuel	–
13.8.95	Busby, David	West Hull ARL
13.8.95	Long, Matthew	Thornhill ARL
15.8.95	Pearson, Carl	Leeds
21.8.95	Cooper, David	–
8.9.95	Divorty, Gary	Halifax
2.12.95	Godfrey, Alex	New Earswick ARL
2.12.95	Godfrey, Matthew	New Earswick ARL
6.12.95	Day, James	Minedhead ARL

Loose forward Gary Divorty, an August 1995 return to the Boulevard.

HULL 1995-96 PLAYERS' SUMMARY

	Date of birth	App	T	G	D	Pts	Previous club	Signed
Aston, Jon	5.6.76	2+8	0	0	0	0	Hull K.R.	16.6.93
Buttle, Shane	4.1.72	1	0	0	0	0	Hull Dockers ARL	22.9.94
Cassidy, Jeremy "Jez"	30.3.74	10+6	3	0	0	12	Hull Academy	31.10.92
Craven, Steve	9.4.72	16+1	5	0	0	20	Ryedale-York	22.8.94
Danby, Rob	30.8.74	7+1	1	0	0	4	Hull Boys ARL	30.8.91
David, Maea		12	4	0	0	16	New Zealand	22.9.94
Divorty, Gary	28.1.66	17+1	3	0	2	14	Halifax	8.9.95
Dixon, Mike	6.4.71	7	1	0	0	4	East Park ARL	29.8.89
Duke, Gary	23.4.74	13	4	0	0	16	Hull Academy	8.6.92
Fisher, Andy	17.11.67	17+1	5	0	0	20	Dewsbury	31.7.95
Foster, Shane	30.8.76	4	3	0	0	12	Hull Academy	2.11.93
Gay, Richard	9.3.69	13	9	0	0	36	Hull Boys ARL	13.9.89
Gray, Kevin	10.12.75	2+4	1	0	0	4	Minehead ARL	1.7.92
Green, Alex	9.2.71	1	1	0	0	4	Doncaster	28.6.95
Hewitt, Mark	17.3.74	10	5	7	0	34	Hull Academy	9.3.93
Jackson, Anthony "Chico"	20.11.69	6+12	4	0	0	16	Greatfield ARL	8.7.88
Kitching, Chris	1.8.77	11	8	0	0	32	Hull Academy	1.8.94
Long, Matthew	24.5.74	3+2	1	0	0	4	Thornhill ARL	13.8.95
Manning, Terry	4.12.65	19+1	4	0	0	16	Doncaster	28.6.95
McKenzie, Leroy	2.9.69	13	6	0	0	24	Moseley RU	14.8.94
McNamara, Steve	18.9.71	22	10	100	1	241	Skirlaugh ARL	15.6.89
Nolan, Rob	2.10.68	10+1	0	0	0	0	Hull Colts	1.1.88
Richardson, Lee	29.10.68	2	0	0	0	0	Hull K.R.	22.9.94
Rose, Gary	25.7.65	0+1	0	0	0	0	Leeds	19.10.94
Sedman, Lance	24.8.76	0+1	0	0	0	0	Hull Boys ARL	3.4.93
Sterling, Paul	2.8.64	14	11	0	0	44	Bfd-Bingley RU	19.8.93
Street, Tim	29.6.68	22	1	0	0	4	Leigh	29.11.93
Vaikona, Tevita	18.8.74	16	15	0	0	60	New Zealand	1.7.94
Walker, Russ	1.9.62	0+1	0	0	0	0	Barrow	8.1.90
Wilson, Richard	5.2.75	0+2	0	0	0	0		
Windley, Johan	20.8.75	16	4	0	0	16	Isberg ARL	19.8.93
TOTALS								
31 players			109	107	3	653		

Representative appearances 1995-96
Vaikona – Tonga (2).

HULL 1995-96 MATCH ANALYSIS

Date	Competition	H/A	Opponents	Rlt	Score	Tries	Goals	Attendance	Referee
20.8.95	FD	H	Featherstone R.	L	20-26	Danby, Green	Hewitt (6)	3140	Oddy
23.8.95	FD	A	Batley	W	30-8	Duke, Fisher, Gay, McKenzie, McNamara	McNamara (5)	–	–
27.8.95	FD	H	Huddersfield	W	37-10	Gay, McKenzie, Foster, Manning, Vaikona, Windley	McNamara (6,dg)	2676	Presley
3.9.95	FD	A	Keighley C.	L	12-21	Foster (2)	McNamara (2)	–	–
10.9.95	FD	H	Rochdale H.	W	40-20	Gay, Cassidy (2), McKenzie, Windley, McNamara	McNamara (6)	2777	Burke
20.9.95	FD	A	Dewsbury	W	46-10	Hewitt (2), McNamara (2), Duke, Gay, McKenzie, Craven	McNamara (7)	–	–
24.9.95	FD	H	Wakefield T.	W	56-8	Gay (2), Divorty (2), Hewitt, Fisher, Vaikona, Windley, David	McNamara (9), Hewitt	3139	Lee
1.10.95	FD	A	Salford R.	L	22-38	Hewitt, Duke, Sterling, Jackson	McNamara (3)	–	–
1.11.95	FD	A	Widnes	L	26-29	Kitching (2), Sterling, Vaikona	McNamara (5)	–	–
5.11.95	FD	H	Whitehaven	W	36-18	Fisher (3), Gay, Manning, Vaikona	McNamara (6)	2343	Burke
12.11.95	RT(2)	H	York	W	56-18	David (3), Jackson, Kitching, Craven, Vaikona, Windley, Duke, McNamara	McNamara (8)	2411	R. Connolly
15.11.95	FD	H	Batley	W	42-8	McNamara (2), Vaikona (2), Kitching (2), Craven	McNamara (7)	2222	Lee
19.11.95	FD	A	Featherstone R.	L	18-34	Craven, Gay, McNamara	McNamara (3)	–	–
26.11.95	RT(3)	H	St. Helens	L	26-38	Vaikona (2), Divorty, Sterling	McNamara (5)	4180	Presley
29.11.95	FD	A	Rochdale H.	L	20-54	McKenzie, McNamara, Sterling, Street	McNamara (2)	–	–
10.12.95	FD	H	Dewsbury	W	58-14	Sterling (3), Kitching (2), McKenzie, Vaikona, Craven, Jackson, Long	McNamara (9)	1964	Nicholson
17.12.95	FD	A	Wakefield T.	L	4-34	Manning	–	–	–
24.12.95	FD	A	Huddersfield	W	23-10	McNamara, Cassidy, Dixon, Vaikona	McNamara (3), Divorty (dg)	–	–
1.1.96	FD	H	Keighley C.	W	20-12	Vaikona (2), Sterling (2)	McNamara (2)	3814	Asquith
7.1.96	FD	H	Salford R.	L	15-20	Jackson, Sterling	McNamara (3), Divorty (dg)	3206	Shaw
14.1.96	FD	H	Widnes	W	32-24	Vaikona (2), Hewitt, Manning, Sterling	McNamara (6)	3249	McGregor
21.1.96	FD	A	Whitehaven	L	14-22	Kitching, Gray	McNamara (3)	–	–

Hull full back Richard Gay, scorer of nine tries in 13 Centenary season games.

Hull skipper Steve McNamara, who tallied 241 points in the 1995-96 season.

HULL KINGSTON ROVERS

Ground: Craven Park (01482-74648)
First Season: 1899-1900
Nickname: Robins
Chairman: Barry Lilley
Secretary: Ron Turner
Honours: **Championship** Winners, 1922-23, 1924-25
Beaten finalists, 1920-21, 1967-68
Division One Champions, 1978-79, 1983-84, 1984-85
Division Two Champions, 1989-90
Division Two (3rd league) Champions, 1995-96
Challenge Cup Winners, 1979-80
Beaten finalists, 1904-05, 1924-25, 1963-64, 1980-81, 1985-86
Regal Trophy Winners, 1984-85
Beaten finalists, 1981-82, 1985-86
Premiership Winners, 1980-81, 1983-84
Beaten finalists, 1984-85
Second Division Premiership Beaten finalists, 1989-90
Yorkshire Cup Winners, 1920-21, 1929-30, 1966-67, 1967-68, 1971-72, 1974-75, 1985-86
Beaten finalists, 1906-07, 1911-12, 1933-34, 1962-63, 1975-76, 1980-81, 1984-85
Yorkshire League Winners, 1924-25, 1925-26
Eastern Division Championship Winners, 1962-63
Charity Shield Beaten finalists, 1985-86
BBC2 Floodlit Trophy Winners, 1977-78
Beaten finalists, 1979-80

RECORDS

Match

Goals: 14 by Alf Carmichael v. Merthyr Tydfil, 8 Oct 1910
Mike Fletcher v. Whitehaven, 18 Mar 1990
Colin Armstrong v. Nottingham C. (at Doncaster), 19 Aug 1990

Tries: 11 by George West v. Brookland R., 4 Mar 1905

Points: 53 by George West v. Brookland R., 4 Mar 1905

Season

Goals: 199 by Mike Fletcher, 1989-90
Tries: 45 by Gary Prohm, 1984-85
Points: 450 by Mike Fletcher, 1989-90

Career

Goals: 1,192 by Cyril Kellett, 1956-67
Tries: 207 by Roger Millward, 1966-80
Points: 2,489 by Cyril Kellett, 1956-67
Appearances: 481+8 by Mike Smith, 1974-91
Highest score: 100-6 v. Nottingham C. (at Doncaster), 19 Aug 1990
Highest against: 76-8 at Halifax, 20 Oct 1991
Attendance: 27,670 v. Hull (League), 3 Apr 1953 — at Boothferry Park, Hull C. AFC
8,557 v. Hull (League), 1 Jan 1991 — at New Craven Park

New Zealander Sam Stewart, a July 1995 capture by Hull K.R. from London Broncos.

COACHING REGISTER
- **Since 1974-75**

Arthur Bunting	Feb 72 - Nov 75
Harry Poole	Dec 75 - Mar 77
Roger Millward	Mar 77 - May 91
George Fairbairn	May 91 - May 94
Steve Crooks	May 94 -

GREAT BRITAIN REGISTER
(26 players)

David Bishop	(+1)	1990
Chris Burton	(8+1)	1982-87
Alan Burwell	(7+1)	1967-69
Len Casey	(7+2)	1977-83
Garry Clark	(3)	1984-85
Alec Dockar	(1)	1947
George Fairbairn	(3)	1981-82
Jack Feetham	(1)	1929
Peter Flanagan	(14)	1962-70
Frank Foster	(1)	1967
David Hall	(2)	1984
Paul Harkin	(+1)	1985
Steve Hartley	(3)	1980-81
Phil Hogan	(2+2)	1979
Roy Holdstock	(2)	1980
Bill Holliday	(8+1)	1964-67
David Laws	(1)	1986
Brian Lockwood	(1+1)	1978-79
Phil Lowe	(12)	1970-78
Roger Millward	(27+1)	1967-78
Harry Poole	(1)	1964
Paul Rose	(1+3)	1974-78
Mike Smith	(10+1)	1979-84
Brian Tyson	(3)	1963-67
David Watkinson	(12+1)	1979-86
Chris Young	(5)	1967-68

1995-96 REGISTRATION DATE

Signed	Player	Club From
30.7.95	Stewart, Sam	London B.
3.7.95	D'Arcy, Robert	West Hull ARL
16.8.95	Marsden, Lee	York
16.8.95	O'Brien, Richard	Featherstone R.
17.8.95	Dannatt, Andy	St. Helens
17.8.95	Moore, Peter	Hull
17.8.95	Rushton, Nick	Hull
24.8.95	Eastwood, Paul	Hull
1.9.95	Brown, Colin	Skirlaugh ARL
7.9.95	Hadi, Steve	–

Former St. Helens prop Andy Dannatt, an August 1995 recruit by Hull K.R.

67

HULL KINGSTON ROVERS 1995-96 PLAYERS' SUMMARY

	Date of birth	App	T	G	D	Pts	Previous club	Signed
Adams, Jonathan	20.4.76	2	0	0	0	0	Minehead ARL	
Atkins, Gary	12.10.66	19	18	0	1	73	Ryedale-York	8.2.93
Batty, Chris	16.5.76	3	0	0	0	0	Minehead ARL	1.9.94
Bibby, Mike	23.10.70	3+2	2	0	0	8	East Park ARL	28.8.93
Brown, Colin	17.6.71	11	4	0	1	17	Skirlaugh ARL	21.6.89
Brown, Gary	5.9.74	12+5	14	0	0	56	Embassy ARL	1.9.95
Chamberlain, Richard	1.4.73	7	4	0	0	16	Greatfield ARL	16.9.92
Charles, Chris	7.3.76	3+3	1	0	0	4	Hull Boys ARL	1.6.91
Charlesworth, Adam	8.6.73	7+1	2	0	0	8	Hull University ARL	2.2.94
Coult, Mick	14.10.69	1	0	0	0	0	Scunthorpe RU	8.6.93
Crane, Mike	11.2.71	13	9	0	0	36	West Hull ARL	13.10.93
D'Arcy, Robert	13.10.70	12	5	0	0	20	St. Helens	3.7.95
Dannatt, Andy	20.11.65	14+1	0	0	0	0	Hull	17.8.95
Dearlove, Andy	19.9.72	1	0	0	0	0	Hull	22.9.94
Eastwood, Paul	3.12.65	15	11	6	0	56	Hull K.R. Academy	24.8.95
Everitt, Christian "Bob"	15.4.75	5+2	4	0	0	16	Hull K.R. Colts	9.8.93
Fletcher, Mike	14.4.67	22	5	116	1	253	Eureka ARL	28.9.85
Fletcher, Paul	17.3.70	22	5	0	0	20		1.9.87
Hardy, Craig	24.8.73	10+2	0	0	0	0	Eureka ARL	11.12.92
Harrison, Chris	28.9.67	22	8	0	0	32	Hull K.R. Colts	23.9.91
Harrison, Des	10.10.64	11+4	2	0	0	8	ARL	16.4.85
Hoe, Sean	3.12.70	11	3	0	0	12	Crown Malet ARL	14.7.90
Leighton, Jamie	5.9.73	3+7	2	0	0	8	Sheffield E.	22.7.91
Lumb, Tim	19.2.70	3	1	0	1	5	Featherstone R.	10.3.95
O'Brien, Richard	25.10.71	1+9	4	0	0	16	Sheffield E.	16.8.95
Plange, David	24.7.65	20	28	0	0	112	Hull	8.8.94
Rushton, Nicky	10.12.71	1	0	0	0	0	Hull	17.8.95
Scott, Paul	7.10.74	6+1	2	0	0	8	Hull Academy	23.7.93
Stewart, Sam	5.12.62	21	4	0	0	16	London B.	30.7.95
Wardrobe, Neil	12.9.72	5+6	5	1	0	22	Beverley RU	30.9.92
Whittaker, Sam	11.1.77	0+1	1	0	0	4	Hull Boys ARL	1.7.93
TOTALS			144	123	4	826		

31 players

HULL KINGSTON ROVERS 1995-96 MATCH ANALYSIS

Date	Competition	H/A	Opponents	Rlt	Score	Tries	Goals	Attendance	Referee
20.8.95	SD	A	Doncaster D.	W	50-24	Plange (4), Atkins, Bibby, G. Brown, Chamberlain, Lumb	M. Fletcher (7)	–	–
22.8.95	SD	H	Leigh C.	W	33-24	Plange, Bibby, G. Brown, Chamberlain, P. Fletcher	M. Fletcher (6), Lumb (dg)	2073	Oddy
27.8.95	SD	A	York	L	14-27	D. Harrison, M. Fletcher	M. Fletcher (3)	–	–
3.9.95	SD	H	Bramley	W	51-12	M. Fletcher (2), Plange (2), Atkins, P. Fletcher, Everitt, Leighton	M. Fletcher (9), C. Brown (dg)	1691	Ganson
10.9.95	SD	A	Barrow B.	W	27-9	Atkins, P. Fletcher, Everitt, Stewart	M. Fletcher (4), Wardrobe, Atkins (dg)	–	–
12.9.95	SD	H	Hunslet H.	W	30-6	Everitt, C. Brown, Charlesworth, D'Arcy, C. Harrison	M. Fletcher (5)	1807	Nicholson
24.9.95	SD	A	Swinton	W	22-15	D'Arcy (2), C. Harrison, Charlesworth	M. Fletcher (3)	–	–
1.10.95	RT(1)	H	Blackpool G.	W	72-6	Plange (2), Atkins (2), D. Harrison, Everitt, Leighton, C. Brown, Stewart, C. Harrison, Hoe, Scott, Whittaker,	Eastwood (6), M. Fletcher (4)	1087	Asquith
1.11.95	SD	H	Carlisle	L	12-14	C. Brown, Eastwood	M. Fletcher (2)	1420	Owram
5.11.95	SD	A	Chorley	W	48-9	Plange (3), G. Brown (2), Eastwood (2), Crane	M. Fletcher (8)	–	–
12.11.95	RT(2)	H	Rochdale H.	L	10-14	C. Harrison, G. Brown	M. Fletcher	1548	Campbell
15.11.95	SD	A	Leigh C.	W	25-16	Crane (2), Wardrobe, P. Fletcher	M. Fletcher (4,dg)	–	–
19.11.95	SD	H	Barrow B.	W	48-7	Atkins (2), G. Brown (2), Eastwood (2), Plange, C. Harrison, Hoe	M. Fletcher (6)	1590	Taberner
26.11.95	SD	H	Highfield	W	60-6	Plange (3), G. Brown (2), M. Fletcher , C. Brown, C. Harrison, Hoe, Eastwood, O'Brien, Stewart	M. Fletcher (6)	1258	Redfearn
29.11.95	SD	H	Doncaster D.	W	56-4	Plange (2), Wardrobe (2), G. Brown, Chamberlain, P. Fletcher, C. Harrison, Crane, Stewart	M. Fletcher (8)	1509	McGregor
3.12.95	SD	A	Hunslet H.	W	28-8	Atkins, Wardrobe, D'Arcy, Eastwood, O'Brien	M. Fletcher (4)	–	–
13.12.95	SD	A	Highfield	W	54-14	Plange (3), Crane (2), O'Brien, Charles, Atkins, Chamberlain, Wardrobe,	M. Fletcher (7)	–	–
17.12.95	SD	H	Swinton	W	42-10	Atkins (4), G. Brown, Plange, C Harrison	M. Fletcher (7)	1671	Burke
2.1.96	SD	H	York	W	26-2	Atkins (2), O'Brien, Eastwood, Plange	M. Fletcher (3)	1557	McGregor
7.1.96	SD	A	Carlisle	W	20-14	Crane, Eastwood, M. Fletcher	M. Fletcher (4)	–	–
10.1.96	SD	A	Bramley	W	40-4	G. Brown (2), Crane (2), Atkins, Eastwood, Plange	M. Fletcher (6)	–	–
21.1.96	SD	H	Chorley C.	W	58-6	Plange (4), Atkins (2), G. Brown, Scott, D'Arcy, Eastwood	M. Fletcher (9)	1807	Redfearn

HUNSLET HAWKS

Highest score: 82-0 v. Highfield, 21 Jan 1996
Highest against: 76-8 v. Halifax, 27 Aug 1972
Attendance: 24,700 v. Wigan (RL Cup),
15 Mar 1924 — at Parkside;
2,350 v. Leigh C. (League)
17 Nov 1995 — at South Leeds
Stadium

Ground:	South Leeds Stadium
First Season:	1895-96. Disbanded at end of 1972-73. Re-formed as New Hunslet in 1973-74. Retitled Hunslet from start of 1979-80. Added Hawks to title in 1995-96
Nickname:	Hawks
Chairman:	Graham Liles
Chief Exec:	Nigel Bosworth
Honours:	**Championship** Winners, 1907-08, 1937-38

Beaten finalists, 1958-59
Division Two Champions, 1962-63, 1986-87
Challenge Cup Winners, 1907-08, 1933-34
Beaten finalists, 1898-99, 1964-65
Second Division Premiership
Beaten finalists, 1986-87
Yorkshire Cup Winners, 1905-06, 1907-08, 1962-63
Beaten finalists, 1908-09, 1929-30, 1931-32, 1944-45, 1956-57, 1965-66
Yorkshire League Winners, 1897-98, 1907-08, 1931-32

RECORDS

Match

Goals:	12 by Billy Langton v. Keighley, 18 Aug 1959
Tries:	7 by George Dennis v. Bradford N., 20 Jan 1934
Points:	30 by Simon Wilson v. Highfield, 21 Jan 1996

Season

Goals:	181 by Billy Langton, 1958-59
Tries:	34 by Alan Snowden, 1956-57
Points:	380 by Billy Langton, 1958-59

Career

Goals:	1,044 by Billy Langton, 1955-66
Tries:	154 by Fred Williamson, 1943-55
Points:	2,202 by Billy Langton, 1955-66
Appearances:	569+10 by Geoff Gunney, 1951-73
	572 by Jack Walkington, 1927-48

COACHING REGISTER

● **Since 1974-75**

Paul Daley	Apr 74 - Aug 78
Bill Ramsey	Aug 78 - Dec 79
Drew Broatch	Dec 79 - Apr 81
Paul Daley	Apr 81 - Nov 85
* Peter Jarvis	Nov 85 - Apr 88
* David Ward	July 86 - Apr 88
Nigel Stephenson	June 88 - Oct 88
Jack Austin }	Oct 88 - Jan 89
John Wolford }	
David Ward	Jan 89 - May 89
Graeme Jennings	Sep 89 - Apr 90
Paul Daley	May 90 - Dec 93
Steve Ferres	Jan 94 -

* *Joint coaches from July 1986.*

GREAT BRITAIN REGISTER

(23 players)

Billy Batten	(9)	1907-11
Harry Beverley	(4)	1936-37
Alf Burnell	(3)	1951-54
Hector Crowther	(1)	1929
Jack Evans	(4)	1951-52
Ken Eyre	(1)	1965
Brian Gabbitas	(1)	1959
Geoff Gunney	(11)	1954-65
Dennis Hartley	(2)	1964
John Higson	(2)	1908
Dai Jenkins	(1)	1929
Albert Jenkinson	(2)	1911
Bill Jukes	(6)	1908-10
Bernard Prior	(1)	1966
Bill Ramsey	(7)	1965-66
Brian Shaw	(5)	1956-60
Geoff Shelton	(7)	1964-66
Fred Smith	(9)	1910-14
Sam Smith	(4)	1954
Cecil Thompson	(2)	1951
Les White	(7)	1932-33
Dicky Williams	(3)	1954
Harry Wilson	(3)	1907

1995-96 REGISTRATION DATE

Signed	Player	Club From
12.7.95	Durham, Steve	Wakefield T.
21.7.95	Levien, Matthew	New Zealand
27.7.95	Rowse, Martin	–
11.8.95	Ballentyne, Darren	Middleton M. ARL
11.8.95	Richardson, Gary	–
11.8.95	Walker, James	–
11.8.95	Williamson, Leon	–
14.8.95	Hooton, Harry	Hunslet Parkside ARL
17.8.95	Zelei, Tony	–
18.8.95	McIntosh, Andrew	–
19.8.95	Barnett, Matthew	Hunslet Parkside ARL
24.8.95	Baker, Richard	East Leeds ARL
24.8.95	Viller, Jason	Rochdale H.
7.9.95	Lambert, Matthew	–
8.9.95	*Fraser, Paul	Bramley
15.9.95	Lynch, Gordon	–
19.10.95	Sharp, Tim	York
10.11.95	*Hanlan, Lee	Wakefield T.
23.11.95	Maea, Des	New Zealand
30.11.95	*Evans, Daniel	Featherstone R.
8.12.95	Wilson, Simon	Batley

HUNSLET HAWKS 1995-96 PLAYERS' SUMMARY

	Date of birth	App	T	G	D	Pts	Previous club	Signed
Baker, Richard	26.1.75	17	8	0	0	32	East Leeds ARL	24.8.95
Ballentyne, Darren	21.11.73	1+2	1	0	0	4	Middleton M. ARL	11.8.95
Boothroyd, Giles	17.3.69	8	2	0	0	8	Castleford	17.8.93
Brook, David	4.2.71	21+2	5	0	1	21	Middleton ARL	4.6.90
Close, David	7.5.66	20	5	22	7	71	Ryedale-York	5.4.94
Coyle, Michael	5.3.71	20	5	0	0	20	Middleton ARL	18.7.90
Creasser, David	18.6.65	0+1	0	0	0	0	Keighley C.	
Durham, Steve	12.10.63	2+1	0	0	0	0	Wakefield T.	12.7.95
Evans, Danny	15.10.74	0+4	0	0	0	0	Featherstone R.	30.11.95
Farrell, Carlton	23.6.66	4+3	3	0	0	12	Keighley C.	18.8.94
Grant, Bob	26.3.70	5+4	1	0	0	4		
Hanlan, Lee	6.10.71	10	2	0	1	9	Wakefield T.	10.11.95
Jowitt, Warren	9.9.74	2	1	0	0	4	Stanley R. ARL	6.9.93
Lambert, Matt	6.8.71	22	2	0	0	8		
Levien, Matt	27.6.70	9	1	0	0	4	New Zealand	21.7.95
Lee, Neil	23.8.75	3+6	1	0	0	4	Middleton ARL	1.2.94
Limb, Scott	15.6.73	13	5	0	0	20	Featherstone R.	25.3.94
Little, Peter	23.8.65	1	0	0	0	0		
Longstaff, Jason	8.2.71	1+3	0	0	0	0	Oulton ARL	26.1.94
Maea, Des	22.3.69	7+3	2	0	0	8	New Zealand	21.11.95
Pell, Richard	17.10.66	16+1	1	19	0	42	Doncaster	18.2.94
Pryce, Steve	12.5.69	21+1	4	0	0	16	Ryedale-York	2.8.94
Richardson, Gary	23.5.66	12+1	15	0	0	60		11.8.95
Ross, Chris	23.8.78	0+1	0	0	0	0		
Rowse, Martin	8.3.69	10+3	0	0	0	0	Doncaster	18.2.94
Sharp, Tim	20.2.70	14+1	2	0	0	8	York	19.10.95
Viller, Jason	29.10.71	22	18	0	0	72	Rochdale H.	24.3.95
Walker, Jim	22.11.73	2	2	0	0	8		11.8.95
Watson, Chris	9.9.67	7	0	0	0	0	Castleford	25.8.94
White, Paul	5.11.64	18+1	9	0	0	36	Ryedale-York	5.3.91
Williamson, Leon	22.8.74	2	0	0	0	0		11.8.95
Wilson, Simon	22.10.67	9	8	42	0	116	Batley	
Zelei, Tony	5.1.68	0+2	0	0	0	0		17.8.95
TOTALS								
33 players			103	83	9	587		

HUNSLET HAWKS 1995-96 MATCH ANALYSIS

Date	Com-petition	H/A	Opponents	Rlt	Score	Tries	Goals	Atten-dance	Referee
23.8.95	SD	A	York	W	21-10	Coyle, Jowitt, Limb	Close (4,dg)	–	–
27.8.95	SD	A	Bramley	W	18-12	Close, Viller	Close (4,2dg)	–	–
3.9.95	SD	H1	Doncaster D.	W	37-16	Close (2), Viller (2), Boothroyd, Pryce, White	Pell (4), Close (dg)	900	Taberner
10.9.95	SD	A	Leigh C.	L	12-20	Viller, Boothroyd	Pell (2)	–	–
12.9.95	SD	A	Hull K.R.	L	6-30	Levien	Pell	–	–
17.9.95	SD	A	Swinton	L	11-30	Limb	Pell (3), Close (dg)	–	–
24.9.95	SD	A	Carlisle	L	14-26	Richardson (2), Baker	Pell	–	–
1.10.95	RT(1)	H1	Ellenborough	W	34-24	Richardson (3), Viller (2), Baker	Pell (5)	247	Smith
5.11.95	SD	A	Highfield	W	28-12	Richardson (3), Baker, Lambert, Viller	Pell, Close	–	–
12.11.95	RT(2)	A	Bramley	W	22-4	Viller (2), Brook, Hanlan	Close (3)	–	–
19.11.95	SD	H	Leigh C.	W	37-10	Viller (2), Richardson (2), Pryce, Baker, Grant	Close (4), Hanlan (dg)	2350	Owram
26.11.95	RT(3)	H	Carlisle	L	17-22	Lee, Maea, Sharp	Close (2), Brook (dg)	1355	R. Connolly
3.12.95	SD	H	Hull K.R.	L	8-28	Viller	Pell (2)	875	Asquith
6.12.95	SD	H	Barrow B.	W	17-5	Coyle, Maea	Close (4,dg)	500	Shaw
10.12.95	SD	H	Swinton	W	20-10	Richardson (2), Wilson (2)	Wilson (2)	820	Cross
13.12.95	SD	A	Barrow B.	W	28-16	Coyle (2), Richardson (2), Wilson	Wilson (4)	–	–
17.12.95	SD	H	Carlisle	W	21-14	Richardson, Viller, Baker	Wilson (4), Close (dg)	798	Lee
19.12.95	SD	H	York	L	22-26	Coyle, Viller, Pryce, Farrell	Wilson (3)	560	Nicholson
3.1.96	SD	H	Chorley	W	38-14	Brook (2), Close, Farrell, Limb, Viller, White	Wilson (5)	600	Atkin
7.1.96	SD	A	Chorley	W	34-8	Baker, Close, Hanlan, Pryce, Viller, Wilson	Wilson (5)	–	–
10.1.96	SD	A	Doncaster D.	W	36-12	White (4), Baker, Pell, Wilson	Wilson (4)	–	–
17.1.96	SD	H	Bramley	W	24-16	Lambert, Limb, White, Wilson	Wilson (4)	678	Redfearn
21.1.96	SD	H	Highfield	W	82-0	Brook (2), Viller (2), Walker (2), White (2), Wilson (2), Baker, Farrell, Ballantyne, Limb, Sharp	Wilson (11)	624	Oddy

1 At McLaren Field, Bramley

Three Hunslet appearances for prop forward Steve Durham after his July 1995 transfer from Wakefield Trinity.

KEIGHLEY COUGARS

Highest score: 104-4 v. Highfield (away game at Rochdale), 23 Apr 1995
Highest against: 92-2 at Leigh, 30 Apr 1986
Attendance: 14,500 v. Halifax (RL Cup), 3 Mar 1951

Ground: Cougar Park (01535-602602), previously titled Lawkholme Park until the 1992-93 season.
First Season: 1901-02. Added Cougars to title at start of 1991-92.
Nickname: Cougars
Chairman: Mike O'Neill
Honours: **Division Two** Champions, 1902-03, 1994-95
Division Three Champions, 1992-93
Challenge Cup Beaten finalists, 1936-37
Second Division Premiership Winners, 1994-95
Yorkshire Cup Beaten finalists, 1943-44, 1951-52

COACHING REGISTER
● **Since 1974-75**

Alan Kellett	Jan 73 - May 75
Roy Sabine	Aug 75 - Oct 77
Barry Seabourne	Nov 77 - Mar 79
Albert Fearnley (Mgr)	Apr 79 - Aug 79
Alan Kellett	Apr 79 - Apr 80
Albert Fearnley	May 80 - Feb 81
Bakary Diabira	Feb 81 - Sep 82
Lee Greenwood	Sep 82 - Oct 83
Geoff Peggs	Nov 83 - Sep 85
Peter Roe	Sep 85 - July 86
Colin Dixon	July 86 - June 89
Les Coulter	July 89 - Apr 90
Tony Fisher	June 90 - Sep 91
Peter Roe	Sep 91 - Apr 94
Phil Larder	May 94 -

RECORDS
Match
Goals: 15 by John Wasyliw v. Nottingham C., 1 Nov 1992
Tries: 5 by Ike Jagger v. Castleford, 13 Jan 1906
Sam Stacey v. Liverpool C., 9 Mar 1907
Nick Pinkney v. Hunslet, 16 Oct 1994
Nick Pinkney v. Highfield (away game at Rochdale), 23 Apr 1995
Points: 36 by John Wasyliw v. Nottingham C., 31 Oct 1993

Season
Goals: 187 by John Wasyliw, 1992-93
Tries: 45 by Nick Pinkney, 1994-95
Points: 490 by John Wasyliw, 1992-93

Career
Goals: 967 by Brian Jefferson, 1965-77
Tries: 155 by Sam Stacey, 1904-20
Points: 2,116 by Brian Jefferson, 1965-77
Appearances: 372 by Hartley Tempest, 1902-15
David McGoun, 1925-38

Phil Larder, appointed coach of Keighley Cougars in May 1994.

73

GREAT BRITAIN REGISTER
(1 player)
Terry Hollindrake   (1)   1955

1995-96 REGISTRATION DATE

Signed	Player	Club From
30.6.95	Foster, Matthew	Doncaster
1.8.95	Cantillon, Phil	Wigan
1.8.95	Critchley, Jason	Salford
7.12.95	*Delaney, Paul	Dewsbury
19.12.95	Gwilliam, Jonathan	Blackbrook ARL

KEIGHLEY COUGARS 1995-96 PLAYERS' SUMMARY

	Date of birth	App	T	G	D	Pts	Previous club	Signed
Appleby, Darren	14.6.67	7	0	0	0	0	Featherstone ARL	18.9.92
Berry, Joe	7.5.74	1+8	0	0	0	0		2.9.93
Cantillon, Phil	2.6.76	10+7	5	0	0	20	Wigan	1.8.95
Cochrane, Gareth	18.9.74	9+1	1	0	0	4	Hull	4.8.94
Critchley, Jason	7.12.70	19	10	0	0	40	Salford	1.8.95
Delaney, Andy	11.9.74	3+3	0	0	0	0	Dewsbury Moor ARL	22.7.93
Dixon, Keith	16.9.66	9+3	5	3	1	27	Keighley Academy	28.8.84
Doorey, Grant	3.2.68	21	4	0	0	16	Australia	5.10.94
Eyres, Andy	1.10.68	18+1	9	0	0	36	Widnes	24.3.91
Fleary, Darren	2.12.72	10+3	1	0	0	4	Dewsbury	6.7.94
Foster, Matthew	10.6.76	9+5	5	0	0	20	Doncaster	30.6.95
Gateley, Ian	21.3.66	18	2	0	0	8	Australia	14.6.93
Hall, Steve	7.9.67	1+4	0	0	0	0	Dudley Hill ARL	13.7.91
Irving, Simon	22.3.67	20	9	81	0	198	Leeds	8.9.94
Larder, David	5.6.76	16+1	6	0	1	25	Sheffield E.	27.11.94
Pinkney, Nick	6.12.70	20	10	0	0	40	Ryedale-York	13.5.93
Powell, Daryl	21.7.65	7	1	0	0	4	Sheffield E.	4.4.95
Ramshaw, Jason	23.7.69	13	2	0	2	10	Halifax	27.7.92
Roberts, Robert	21.6.78	0+1	0	0	0	0	East Leeds ARL	17.11.94
Robinson, Chris	2.9.70	16	1	0	2	6	Halifax	1.7.94
Stoop, Andre	8.10.66	11	5	0	0	20	Wigan	16.8.94
Tupaea, Shane	24.12.63	10+2	0	0	0	0	Oldham	17.8.94
Wood, Martin	24.6.70	21	6	1	1	27	Scarborough P.	17.1.92
Wray, Simon	19.5.70	4+1	0	0	0	0	Morley RU	27.10.94
TOTALS								
24 players			82	85	6	505		

Representative appearances 1995-96
Pinkney – England (3,2t);
Powell – England (2)

KEIGHLEY COUGARS 1995-96 MATCH ANALYSIS

Date	Competition	H/A	Opponents	Rlt	Score	Tries	Goals	Attendance	Referee
20.8.95	FD	A	Huddersfield	W	36-26	Pinkney (2), Critchley, Larder, Ramshaw, Stoop	Irving (6)	–	–
27.8.95	FD	A	Rochdale H.	W	50-4	Critchley (3), Pinkney (2), Irving (2), Larder, Wood	Irving (7)	–	–
3.9.95	FD	H	Hull	W	21-12	Stoop (2), Pinkney	Irving (4), Robinson (dg)	4186	Nicholson
10.9.95	FD	H	Dewsbury	W	44-5	Irving , Critchley, Larder, Wood, Cochrane, Dixon, Doorey, Gately	Irving (6)	3611	Atkin
17.9.95	FD	H	Wakefield T.	W	30-8	Cantillon (3), Pinkney, Critchley	Irving (5)	4121	Asquith
20.9.95	FD	A	Salford R.	W	22-14	Pinkney, Ramshaw, Doorey, Irving	Irving (3)	–	–
24.9.95	FD	H	Whitehaven	W	58-8	Larder (3), Eyres (3), Wood (2), Irving (2)	Irving (9)	3720	Burke
1.10.95	FD	A	Widnes	D	16-16	Stoop, Eyres	Irving (3), Ramshaw (2dg)	–	–
1.11.95	FD	A	Batley	W	21-14	Pinkney, Gately, Cantillon	Irving (4), Wood (dg)	–	–
5.11.95	FD	H	Featherstone R.	W	31-0	Eyres, Dixon, Stoop, Irving	Irving (5), Dixon (2), Robinson (dg)	4172	Ganson
11.11.95	RT(2)	H	St. Helens	L	14-42	Eyres, Wood, Critchley	Dixon	3737	J. Connolly
19.11.95	FD	H	Huddersfield	W	40-6	Dixon (3), Eyres (2), Foster, Irving	Irving (6)	3766	Lee
29.11.95	FD	A	Dewsbury	W	28-6	Fleary, Powell, Doorey, Pinkney	Irving (6)	–	–
3.12.95	FD	A	Wakefield T.	L	4-16	Critchley	–	–	–
10.12.95	FD	H	Salford R.	L	6-34	Robinson		4812	Ganson
17.12.95	FD	A	Whitehaven	D	8-8	Doorey	Irving	–	–
1.1.96	FD	A	Hull	L	12-20	Eyres, Foster	Irving (2)	–	–
4.1.96	FD	H	Rochdale H.	W	24-4	Foster, Pinkney, Wood	Irving (5), Wood	2262	Shaw
7.1.96	FD	H	Widnes	L	12-16	Critchley, Foster	Irving (2)	3698	Smith
14.1.96	FD	H	Batley	W	14-8	Critchley, Irving	Irving (2), Dixon (dg), Larder (dg)	3524	Nicholson
21.1.96	FD	A	Featherstone R.	L	14-30	Cantillon, Foster	Irving (3)	–	–

Two tries in 18 Centenary season games for Keighley Cougars' Australian prop Ian Gateley.

75

LEEDS

Ground: Headingley (0113-278-6181)
First Season: 1895-96
Nickname: Loiners
Chairman: Dennis Greenwood
Chief Exec: Alf Davies
Honours: **Championship** Winners, 1960-61, 1968-69, 1971-72
Beaten finalists, 1914-15, 1928-29, 1929-30, 1930-31, 1937-38, 1969-70, 1972-73
League Leaders Trophy Winners, 1966-67, 1967-68, 1968-69, 1969-70, 1971-72
Challenge Cup Winners, 1909-10, 1922-23, 1931-32, 1935-36, 1940-41, 1941-42, 1956-57, 1967-68, 1976-77, 1977-78
Beaten finalists, 1942-43, 1946-47, 1970-71, 1971-72, 1993-94, 1994-95
Regal Trophy Winners, 1972-73, 1983-84
Beaten finalists, 1982-83, 1987-88, 1991-92
Premiership Winners, 1974-75, 1978-79
Beaten finalists, 1994-95
Yorkshire Cup Winners, 1921-22, 1928-29, 1930-31, 1932-33, 1934-35, 1935-36, 1937-38, 1958-59, 1968-69, 1970-71, 1972-73, 1973-74, 1975-76, 1976-77, 1979-80, 1980-81, 1988-89
Beaten finalists, 1919-20, 1947-48, 1961-62, 1964-65
Yorkshire League Winners, 1901-02, 1927-28, 1930-31, 1933-34, 1934-35, 1936-37, 1937-38, 1950-51, 1954-55, 1956-57, 1960-61, 1966-67, 1967-68, 1968-69, 1969-70
BBC2 Floodlit Trophy Winners, 1970-71
Charity Shield Beaten finalists, 1995-96

RECORDS

Match
Goals: 13 by Lewis Jones v. Blackpool B., 19 Aug 1957
Tries: 8 by Fred Webster v. Coventry, 12 Apr 1913
Eric Harris v. Bradford N., 14 Sep 1931
Points: 31 by Lewis Jones v. Bradford N., 22 Aug 1956

Season
Goals: 166 by Lewis Jones, 1956-57
Tries: 63 by Eric Harris, 1935-36
Points: 431 by Lewis Jones, 1956-57

Career
Goals: 1,244 by Lewis Jones, 1952-64
Tries: 391 by Eric Harris, 1930-39
Points: 2,920 by Lewis Jones, 1952-64
Appearances: 608+18 by John Holmes, 1968-89
Highest score: 102-0 v. Coventry, 12 Apr 1913
Highest against: 74-6 at Wigan, 10 May 1992
Attendance: 40,175 v. Bradford N. (League), 21 May 1947

COACHING REGISTER
● **Since 1974-75**

Roy Francis	June 74 - May 75
Syd Hynes	June 75 - Apr 81
Robin Dewhurst	June 81 - Oct 83
Maurice Bamford	Nov 83 - Feb 85
Malcolm Clift	Feb 85 - May 85
Peter Fox	May 85 - Dec 86
Maurice Bamford	Dec 86 - Apr 88
Malcolm Reilly	Aug 88 - Sep 89
David Ward	Sep 89 - May 91
Doug Laughton	May 91 - Sept 95
Dean Bell	Sep 95 -

GREAT BRITAIN REGISTER

(74 players)

Les Adams	(1)	1932
John Atkinson	(26)	1968-80
Jim Bacon	(11)	1920-26
Ray Batten	(3)	1969-73
John Bentley	(1)	1992
Jim Birch	(1)	1907
Stan Brogden	(7)	1936-37
Jim Brough	(5)	1928-36
Gordon Brown	(6)	1954-55
Mick Clark	(5)	1968
Terry Clawson	(3)	1972
David Creasser	(2+2)	1985-88
Lee Crooks	(1)	1989
Willie Davies	(2)	1914
Kevin Dick	(2)	1980
Roy Dickinson	(2)	1985
Paul Dixon	(8+1)	1990-92
Les Dyl	(11)	1974-82
Richard Eyres	(+2)	1993
Tony Fisher	(3)	1970-71
Phil Ford	(5)	1989
Dick Gemmel	(1)	1964
Carl Gibson	(10)	1990-91
Bobbie Goulding	(1)	1992
Jeff Grayshon	(2)	1985
Bob Haigh	(3+1)	1970-71
Derek Hallas	(2)	1961
Ellery Hanley	(2)	1992-93
Fred Harrison	(3)	1911
David Heron	(1+1)	1982
John Holmes	(14+6)	1971-82
Syd Hynes	(12+1)	1970-73
Billy Jarman	(2)	1914
David Jeanes	(3)	1972
Dai Jenkins	(1)	1947
Lewis Jones	(15)	1954-57
Ken Jubb	(2)	1937
John Lowe	(1)	1932
Paul Medley	(3+1)	1987-88
Steve Molloy	(1)	1993
Ike Owens	(4)	1946
Steve Pitchford	(4)	1977
Harry Poole	(2)	1966
Roy Powell	(13+6)	1985-91

Dai Prosser	(1)	1937
Keith Rayne	(4)	1984
Kevin Rayne	(1)	1986
Bev Risman	(5)	1968
Don Robinson	(5)	1956-60
David Rose	(4)	1954
Garry Schofield	(29+2)	1988-94
Barry Seabourne	(1)	1970
Brian Shaw	(1)	1961
Mick Shoebottom	(10+2)	1968-71
Barry Simms	(1)	1962
Alan Smith	(10)	1970-73
Stanley Smith	(10)	1929-33
David Stephenson	(4+1)	1988
Jeff Stevenson	(15)	1955-58
Squire Stockwell	(3)	1920-21
Alan Tait	(1+4)	1992-93
Abe Terry	(1)	1962
Arthur "Ginger" Thomas	(4)	1926-29
Phil Thomas	(1)	1907
Joe Thompson	(12)	1924-32
Andrew Turnbull	(1)	1951
Hugh Waddell	(1)	1989
Billy Ward	(1)	1910
David Ward	(12)	1977-82
Fred Webster	(3)	1910
Dicky Williams	(9)	1948-51
Harry Woods	(1)	1937
Geoff Wriglesworth	(5)	1965-66
Frank Young	(1)	1908

1995-96 REGISTRATION DATE

Signed	Player	Club From
16.6.95	Kemp, Tony	Castleford
1.8.95	Forshaw, Mike	Wakefield T.
25.8.95	Smith, Kris	–
14.9.95	McDermott, Barrie	Wigan
22.9.95	Robinson, Craig	Sharlston ARL
29.9.95	Rivett, Leroy	East Leeds ARL
6.10.95	Windas, Chris	Minehead ARL
19.10.95	Campbell, Mark	East Leeds ARL
28.11.95	Woodcock, Marc	Sharlston ARL
14.12.95	Hall, Carl	Bradford B.
20.12.95	McDonald, Ryan	Broughton Red Rose ARL
3.1.96	Wrench, David	–

LEEDS 1995-96 PLAYERS' SUMMARY

	Date of birth	App	T	G	D	Pts	Previous club	Signed
Cook, Paul	23.7.76	15+3	8	74	0	180		1.12.92
Cummins, Francis	12.10.76	16+6	14	16	0	88	St. John Fisher ARL	12.10.93
Eyres, Richard	7.12.66	2	1	0	0	4	Widnes	16.9.93
Faimalo, Esene	11.10.66	4+2	1	0	0	4	Widnes	1.7.94
Fallon, Jim	27.3.65	20	13	0	0	52	Bath RU	6.7.92
Field, Jamie	12.12.76	8+2	0	0	0	0	Leeds Academy	12.12.93
Forshaw, Mike	5.1.70	18+5	5	0	0	20	Wakefield T.	1.8.95
Fozzard, Nick	22.7.77	5+13	2	0	0	8	Shaw Cross ARL	27.7.93
Gibbons, Anthony	18.1.76	5+3	3	1	0	14	East Leeds ARL	10.8.93
Gibbons, David	18.1.76	7+4	1	0	0	4	East Leeds ARL	10.8.93
Golden, Marvin	21.12.76	11+2	3	0	0	12	Hunslet Parkside ARL	22.12.93
Hall, Carl	10.8.69	6	2	0	0	8	Bradford B.	14.12.95
Handley, Patrick "Paddy"	18.9.75	0+3	0	0	0	0		17.9.93
Harmon, Neil	9.1.69	23+1	7	0	0	28	Warrington	24.8.93
Hassan, Phil	18.8.74	4+1	0	0	0	0	St. Pauls ARL	10.8.93
Holroyd, Graham	25.10.75	9+1	2	12	0	32	Siddal ARL	24.9.92
Howard, Harvey	29.8.68	7+6	0	0	0	0	Widnes	4.1.94
Innes, Craig	10.9.69	20	14	0	0	56	New Zealand RU	4.1.92
Iro, Kevin	25.5.68	15	11	0	0	44	Australia	29.10.92
Kemp, Tony	18.1.68	16	3	0	0	12	Castleford	16.6.95
Lowes, James	11.10.69	23+2	3	0	0	12	Hunslet	30.9.92
Mann, George	31.7.65	23	6	0	0	24	St. Helens	15.7.94
McDermott, Barrie	22.7.72	9+6	0	0	0	0	Wigan	14.9.95
Mercer, Gary	22.6.66	13+2	1	0	0	4	Warrington	5.8.92
Morley, Adrian	10.5.77	10+6	2	0	0	8	Eccles ARL	10.5.94
Riley, John	30.10.75	0+1	0	0	0	0	Blackbrook ARL	30.3.94
Schofield, Garry	1.7.65	13+2	10	2	4	48	Hull	23.10.87
Schultz, Matthew	9.8.75	0+2	0	0	0	0	Hull ARL	9.8.92
Shaw, Mick	16.7.75	9+10	6	0	0	24	Elland ARL	3.3.93
Tait, Alan	2.7.64	13+3	9	0	0	36	Widnes	14.8.92
Vassilakopoulos, Marcus	19.9.76	1+1	0	0	0	0	Hull ARL	20.9.93
TOTALS								
31 players			127	105	4	722		

Representative appearances 1995-96
Cook – England (1+1);
Eyres – Wales (3);
Iro – New Zealand (1+2,1t);
Kemp – New Zealand (3,1t);
Mann – Tonga (2)

LEEDS 1995-96 MATCH ANALYSIS

Date	Competition	H/A	Opponents	Rlt	Score	Tries	Goals	Attendance	Referee
13.8.95	CS	N1	Wigan	L	20-45	Faimalo, Kemp, Forshaw	Cook (4)	(5716)	Smith
20.8.95	SBC	A	Sheffield E.	W	34-6	Cummins (3), D. Gibbons, Mercer, Tait, Cook	Cummins (3)	–	–
25.8.95	SBC	A	Castleford	L	18-22	Kemp, Forshaw, Iro	Cummins (3)	–	–
30.8.95	SBC	H	Warrington	W	40-6	Schofield (2), Cook (2), Forshaw, Tait, Lowes	Cook (6)	10,586	Campbell
3.9.95	SBC	H	St. Helens	W	36-24	Cook (2), Cummins, Forshaw, Schofield, Fallon, Fozzard	Cook (4)	12,047	Cummings
10.9.95	SBC	H	Halifax	W	60-27	Innes (3), Fallon (2), Cummins (2), Mann, Schofield	Cook (11), Schofield (2dg)	12,040	Smith
17.9.95	SBC	A	London B.	L	12-26	Fallon, Innes	Cook (2)	–	–
22.9.95	SBC	H	Bradford B.	W	32-30	Kemp, Forshaw, Lowes, Golden, Harmon	Cook (6)	10,828	Cummings
27.9.95	SBC	H	Workington T.	W	50-12	Iro (3), Shaw (2), Tait, Cummins, Morley, Innes	Cook (7)	8877	Kirkpatrick
1.10.95	SBC	A	Oldham B.	W	43-14	Tait, Iro, Schofield, Fallon, Innes, Harmon, Eyres	Cook (7), Schofield (dg)	–	–
3.11.95	SBC	H	Wigan	W	23-11	Tait, Schofield, Mann, Cook	Cook (3), Schofield (dg)	17,049	Smith
12.11.95	RT(2)	H	Salford R.	W	46-22	Fallon (4), Schofield (2), Tait, Iro, Innes	Cook (5)	7589	Cummings
15.11.95	SBC	A	Workington T.	W	16-10	Iro, Fallon, Harmon	Cook (2)	–	–
19.11.95	SBC	H	Sheffield E.	L	22-27	Harmon, Iro, Cummins, Cook	Holroyd (3)	11,581	Bates
26.11.95	RT(3)	H	Bradford B.	W	42-28	Innes (2), Mann, Shaw, Iro, Cummins	Cook (9)	10,093	J. Connolly
29.11.95	SBC	A	Warrington	L	14-47	Cummins, Tait	Cook (3)	–	–
3.12.95	SBC	A	Halifax	L	10-29	A. Gibbons, Cummins	Cook	–	–
10.12.95	RT(QT)	H	Carlisle	W	44-22	Iro (2), Shaw (2), Holroyd, A. Gibbons, Cummins, Cook, Innes	Cook (4)	5130	Morris
17.12.95	SBC	A	Bradford B.	W	16-12	Harmon (2), Holroyd	Holroyd, Cummins	–	–
19.12.95	SBC	H	London B.	W	30-12	Cummins, Lowes, Fallon, Mann, A. Gibbons	Cummins (5)	7044	R. Connolly
26.12.95	SBC	H	Castleford	W	28-16	Golden (2), Cummins, Fallon, Hall	Cummins (4)	18,000	Morris
1.1.96	SBC	A	St. Helens	W	20-14	Schofield, Innes, Hall, Shaw	Holroyd (2)	–	–
5.1.96	RT(SF)	A	Wigan	L	18-38	Mann (2), Harmon, Morley	Holroyd	–	–
10.1.96	SBC	H	Oldham B.	W	28-26	Fallon, Fozzard, Tait, Schofield	Holroyd (4), Schofield (2)	7893	Kirkpatrick
21.1.96	SBC	A	Wigan	L	20-34	Innes (3), Tait	A. Gibbons, Holroyd	–	–

N1 at Dublin

Leeds winger Jim Fallon, scorer of 13 tries in 20 Centenary season games.

Three tries in 13 appearances in 1995-96 for Leeds threequarter Marvin Golden.

LEIGH CENTURIONS

Ground: Hilton Park (01942-674437)
First Season: 1895-96. Added Centurions to title in 1995-96
Chairman: Mick Higgins
Secretary: Wendy Stott
Honours: **Championship** Winners, 1905-06
Division One Champions, 1981-82
Division Two Champions, 1977-78, 1985-86, 1988-89
Challenge Cup Winners, 1920-21, 1970-71
Lancashire Cup Winners, 1952-53, 1955-56, 1970-71, 1981-82
Beaten finalists, 1905-06, 1909-10, 1920-21, 1922-23, 1949-50, 1951-52, 1963-64, 1969-70
BBC2 Floodlit Trophy Winners, 1969-70, 1972-73
Beaten finalists, 1967-68, 1976-77

RECORDS
Match
Goals: 15 by Mick Stacey v. Doncaster, 28 Mar 1976
Tries: 6 by Jack Wood v. York, 4 Oct 1947
Points: 38 by John Woods v. Blackpool B., 11 Sep 1977
John Woods v. Ryedale-York, 12 Jan 1992

Season
Goals: 173 by Chris Johnson, 1985-86
Tries: 49 by Steve Halliwell, 1985-86
Points: 400 by Chris Johnson, 1985-86

Career
Goals: 1,043 by Jim Ledgard, 1948-58
Tries: 189 by Mick Martyn, 1954-67
Points: 2,492 by John Woods, 1976-85 & 1990-92
Appearances: 503 by Albert Worrall, 1921-35 & 1936-38
Highest score: 92-2 v. Keighley, 30 Apr 1986
Highest against: 94-4 at Workington T., 26 Feb 1995
Attendance: 31,324 v. St. Helens (RL Cup), 14 Mar 1953

COACHING REGISTER
● **Since 1974-75**

Eddie Cheetham	May 74 - Mar 75
Kevin Ashcroft	June 75 - Jan 77
Bill Kindon	Jan 77 - Apr 77
John Mantle	Apr 77 - Nov 78
Tom Grainey	Nov 78 - Dec 80
* Alex Murphy	Nov 80 - June 82
* Colin Clarke	June 82 - Dec 82
Peter Smethurst	Dec 82 - Apr 83
Tommy Bishop	June 83 - June 84
John Woods	June 84 - May 85
Alex Murphy	Feb 85 - Nov 85
Tommy Dickens	Nov 85 - Dec 86
Billy Benyon	Dec 86 - Mar 90
Alex Murphy	Mar 90 - Aug 91
Kevin Ashcroft	Sep 91 - June 92
Jim Crellin	June 92 - Sep 92
Steve Simms	Nov 92 - Sep 94
Denis Ramsdale	Sep 94 - Nov 94
Ian Lucas	Dec 94 -

* *From Dec 80 to June 82 Clarke was officially appointed coach and Murphy manager.*

Tommy Bishop, coach of Leigh for the 1983-84 season.

GREAT BRITAIN REGISTER
(19 players)

Kevin Ashcroft	(5)	1968-70
Joe Cartwright	(7)	1920-21
Dave Chisnall	(2)	1970
Joe Darwell	(5)	1924
Steve Donlan	(+2)	1984
Des Drummond	(22)	1980-86
Peter Foster	(3)	1955
Chris Johnson	(1)	1985
Frank Kitchen	(2)	1954
Jim Ledgard	(9)	1948-54
Gordon Lewis	(1)	1965
Mick Martyn	(2)	1958-59
Walter Mooney	(2)	1924
Stan Owen	(1)	1958
Charlie Pawsey	(7)	1952-54
Bill Robinson	(2)	1963
Joe Walsh	(1)	1971
Billy Winstanley	(2)	1910
John Woods	(7+3)	1979-83

1995-96 REGISTRATION DATE

Signed	Player	Club From
13.6.95	Tickle, Shaun	–
21.7.95	Perigo, John	Australia
1.8.95	Brown, Shaun	Salford
1.8.95	O'Neill, Paul	Salford
20.8.95	Hadcroft, Alan	Leigh East ARL
20.8.95	Patel, Srfraz	Leigh East ARL
24.8.95	Blackburn, Paul	Leigh M.W. ARL
24.8.95	Parkinson, Joe	Wigan St. Patricks ARL
7.9.95	Lewis, Gavin	Leigh Rangers ARL
7.9.95	*Mehan, Paul	Huddersfield
10.9.95	McGughan, Mark	Orrell St. James ARL
16.11.95	Grainey, Gary	Leigh M.W. ARL
24.11.95	*Edwards, Mike	Oldham
24.11.95	*Lay, Steve	Halifax
24.11.95	Veikoso, Jimmy	Australia
19.12.95	*Cain, Alex	Sheffield E.

Dave Chisnall, two 1970 caps for Great Britain while with Leigh.

Leigh legend John Woods, capped for Great Britain 10 times while at Hilton Park.

81

LEIGH CENTURIONS 1995-96 PLAYERS' SUMMARY

	Date of birth	App	T	G	D	Pts	Previous club	Signed
Ball, Rob	22.3.76	7+3	2	0	0	8	Leigh Academy	26.11.94
Bannister, Shaun	23.9.69	19	5	0	0	20	Wigan St. Patricks ARL	29.12.94
Blakeley, Mike	22.11.70	1+2	2	6	0	20	Leigh M.W. ARL	16.7.90
Brown, Shaun	19.10.69	3	0	0	0	0	Salford	1.8.95
Burgess, Barry	23.11.75	7+1	7	0	0	28		31.5.95
Cain, Alex	2.9.73	1+3	0	0	0	0	Sheffield E.	19.12.95
Cheetham, Andrew	25.1.75	16	12	0	0	48	Orrell St. James ARL	9.12.93
Costello, John	10.3.70	6+2	1	0	0	4	Leigh M. ARL	6.9.91
Daniel, Paul	16.3.74	4	0	0	0	0	Leigh M. ARL	18.8.93
Davies, Glyn	3.12.74	15+2	13	4	0	60	St. Helens	11.11.93
Edwards, Mike	14.4.74	4+1	6	0	0	24	Oldham B.	24.11.95
Fletcher, Tim	5.12.68	0+1	0	0	0	0		
Grainey, Gary	25.7.67	0+1	0	0	0	0	Leigh M.W. ARL	16.11.95
Hadcroft, Alan	31.3.77	10	2	0	0	8	Leigh East ARL	20.8.95
Hall, Darren	8.4.76	1+1	1	0	0	4	Leigh East ARL	10.1.95
Hill, David	4.9.68	15	4	0	0	16	Blackbrook ARL	5.10.88
Ingram, David	4.1.75	5+2	4	0	0	16	Leigh Academy	29.12.94
Jukes, Neil	23.5.76	9+3	4	0	0	16	Rosebridge ARL	31.3.94
Lay, Steve	28.3.68	4	1	0	0	4	Halifax	24.11.95
Liku, Tau'alupe	21.2.71	19	7	0	0	28	Tonga	22.4.94
Marsh, Paul	18.6.74	7+1	0	0	0	0	St. Helens	24.1.94
McGughan, Mark	30.6.70	9+2	0	0	0	0	Orrell St. James ARL	10.9.95
McLoughlin, Paul	27.3.75	5	2	0	0	8	Warrington Academy	5.8.94
O'Loughlin, Jason	29.11.70	18+2	6	0	0	24	St. Helens	12.8.94
Parkinson, Joe	12.3.69	3+2	0	0	0	0	Wigan St. Patricks ARL	24.8.95
Perigo, John	20.12.71	11+4	3	0	0	12	Australia	21.7.95
Riley, David	20.11.74	0+1	0	0	0	0	Wigan	21.3.95
Robinson, Jeff	9.9.71	4	2	0	1	9		
Sarsfield, Mark	22.3.71	3+1	1	0	0	4	Widnes	24.9.93
Stazicker, Gerrard "Ged"	2.1.68	19+1	5	0	0	20	Salford	30.3.95
Tuavao, Hamoni	26.9.68	3+1	0	0	0	0	Widnes St. Maries ARL	30.3.95
Veikoso, Jimmy	31.5.71	8	6	2	0	28	Tonga	8.11.95
Weall, Jerome	27.8.75	1	0	0	0	0	Wigan St. Patricks ARL	29.7.94
Wilkinson, Chris	2.3.65	19	5	74	7	175	Swinton	31.3.95
Wilson, Christian	13.8.75	7+2	2	0	0	8	Wigan St. Patricks ARL	23.1.95
Wynne, Steve	9.12.71	10	4	0	0	16	Salford	15.2.95
TOTALS								
36 players			107	86	8	608		

Representative appearances 1995-96
Liku – Tonga (+1,1t).

LEIGH CENTURIONS 1995-96 MATCH ANALYSIS

Date	Competition	H/A	Opponents	Rlt	Score	Tries	Goals	Attendance	Referee
20.8.95	SD	H	Chorley	W	36-12	Cheetham (2), Wynne (2), Costello, O'Loughlin, Blakeley	Blakeley (3), Davies	1190	Owram
22.8.95	SD	A	Hull K.R.	L	24-33	Liku (2), Wynne, McLoughlin	Blakeley (3), Davies	–	–
27.8.95	SD	H	Swinton	W	28-18	Davies (3), Liku, McLoughlin, Wynne	Wilkinson (2)	1505	Cross
3.9.95	SD	A	Carlisle	W	20-18	Ball, Bannister, Davies	Wilkinson (4)	–	–
10.9.95	SD	H	Hunslet	W	20-12	Cheetham, O'Loughlin, Davies	Wilkinson (3,2dg)	1355	Gilmour
13.9.95	SD	A	Highfield	W	66-5	Cheetham (2), Davies (2), Wilson (2), Hall, Stazicker, Jukes, Hill, O'Loughlin, Wilkinson	Wilkinson (9)	–	–
17.9.95	SD	H	Barrow B.	W	28-8	Hill, Jukes, Davies, Liku, Wilkinson	Wilkinson (4)	1358	Oddy
27.9.95	SD	A	York	W	20-18	Cheetham, Davies, Hill	Wilkinson (3,2dg)	–	–
30.9.95	RT(1)	H	St. Esteve	L	16-19	Davies, Liku	Wilkinson (3), Davies	1543	Cummings
5.11.95	SD	H	Bramley	L	14-20	Cheetham (2), O'Loughlin	Wilkinson	1536	Grimshaw
15.11.95	SD	H	Hull K.R.	L	16-25	Cheetham, Sarsfield, Wilkinson	Wilkinson (2)	1212	McGregor
19.11.95	SD	A	Hunslet H.	L	10-37	Robinson, Liku	Wilkinson	–	–
26.11.95	SD	A	Doncaster D.	W	38-12	Ball, Cheetham, Jukes, O'Loughlin, Edwards, Hadcroft, Perigo	Wilkinson (3), Veikoso (2)	–	–
29.11.95	SD	A	Chorley C.	W	29-17	Bannister, Edwards, Perigo, Cheetham	Wilkinson (6,dg)	–	–
3.12.95	SD	H	Highfield	W	54-16	Bannister (2), Edwards (2), Burgess (2), Veikoso, Hadcroft, Jukes, Blakeley	Wilkinson (7)	858	McGregor
10.12.95	SD	A	Barrow B.	W	22-8	Robinson, Edwards, Burgess	Wilkinson (4,dg), Robinson (dg)	–	–
13.12.95	SD	H	Doncaster D.	W	42-16	Davies (2), Liku, Bannister, Edwards, Burgess, Lay, Ingram, Wilkinson	Wilkinson (3)	770	Redfearn
3.1.96	SD	A	Swinton	W	18-8	Davies, Hill, Veikoso	Wilkinson (2), Davies	–	–
7.1.96	SD	H	York	W	36-24	Veikoso (3), Burgess, Ingram, Wilkinson	Wilkinson (6)	1177	Oddy
17.1.96	SD	H	Carlisle	W	33-22	Stazicker (2), Burgess, Perigo, Veikoso	Wilkinson (6, dg)	–	–
21.1.96	SD	A	Bramley	W	38-6	Ingram (2), Stazicker (2), Burgess, Cheetham, O'Loughlin	Wilkinson (5)	–	–

83

LONDON BRONCOS

Highest score: 82-0 v. Highfield, 12 Nov 1995
Highest against: 72-6 v. Whitehaven, 14 Sep 1986
Attendance: 15,013 v. Wakefield T. (RL Cup),
15 Feb 1981 — at Craven Cottage
1,465 v. Castleford (League),
21 Jan 1996 — at The Valley

Ground:	The Valley
First Season:	1980-81. Began as Fulham. Became London Crusaders at start of 1991-92 and changed to London Broncos in 1994-95
Nickname:	Broncos
Chairman:	Barry Maranta
Chief Exec:	Robbie Moore
Honours:	**Division Two** Champions, 1982-83 **Second Division Premiership** Beaten Finalists, 1993-94

RECORDS

Match

Goals: 11 by Steve Guyett v. Huddersfield, 23 Oct 1988
Greg Pearce v. Runcorn H., 26 Aug 1990

Tries: 4 by Mark Riley v. Highfield, 17 Oct 1993
Mark Johnson at Highfield, 1 Apr 1994
Scott Roskell at Bramley, 19 Mar 1995
Evan Cochrane at Sheffield E., 27 Sept 1995
Paul Hauff v. Workington T. 1 Oct 1995
Shane Vincent v. Highfield, 12 Nov 1995

Points: 24 by John Gallagher v. Bramley, 27 Mar 1994

Season

Goals: 159 by John Gallagher, 1993-94
Tries: 43 by Mark Johnson, 1993-94
Points: 384 by John Gallagher, 1993-94

Career

Goals: 309 by Steve Diamond, 1981-84
Tries: 74 by Hussein M'Barki, 1981-84 & 1988-91
Points: 691 by Steve Diamond, 1981-84
Appearances: 148+14 by Hussein M'Barki, 1981-84 & 1988-91

COACHING REGISTER

● **Since formation in 1980**

Reg Bowden	July 80 - June 84
Roy Lester	June 84 - Apr 86
Bill Goodwin	Apr 86 - May 88
* Bev Risman	May 88 - Feb 89
Phil Sullivan	Feb 89 - Mar 89
Bill Goodwin	Mar 89 - Apr 89
Ross Strudwick	June 89 - Feb 93
Tony Gordon	Feb 93 - May 94
Gary Grienke	May 94 - Jan 96
Tony Currie	Jan 96 -

* *Team manager*

GREAT BRITAIN REGISTER

(1 player)

John Dalgreen	(1)	1982

1995-96 REGISTRATION DATE

Signed	Player	Club From
10.7.95	Hogg, Darren	New Zealand
13.7.95	Vincent, Shane	Australia
4.8.95	Butt, Ikram	Featherstone R.
4.8.95	Dynevor, Leo	Australia
14.8.95	O'Neill, Julian	Australia
17.8.95	Bawden, Russell	Australia
31.8.95	Cochrane, Evan	Australia
1.9.95	Gill, Peter	Australia
1.9.95	McKenna, Chris	Australia
7.9.95	Mestrov, Tony	Australia
14.9.95	Walker, Ben	Australia
18.9.95	Hauff, Paul	Australia
18.9.95	Mills, Paul	Australia
22.9.95	Keating, Shaun	Australia
22.9.95	Meyer, Keiran	Australia
29.9.95	Matterson, Terry	Australia
25.11.95	Scourfield, John	St. Marys ARL
20.12.95	Paul, Junior	–
29.12.95	McRae, Duncan	Australia
31.12.95	Allen, Gavin	Australia
2.1.96	Francis, Mick	Australia

LONDON BRONCOS 1995-96 PLAYERS' SUMMARY

	Date of birth	App	T	G	D	Pts	Previous club	Signed
Bawden, Russell	24.7.73	11+8	2	0	0	8		21.7.95
Booth, Craig	28.10.70	1+1	0	2	0	4	Oldham	31.3.95
Bryant, Justin	21.12.71	6+6	1	0	0	4	Australia	14.8.95
Butt, Ikram	25.10.68	16	4	0	0	16	Featherstone R.	4.8.95
Carroll, Bernard	3.3.70	2+1	1	0	0	4	New Zealand	25.8.95
Cochrane, Evan	13.12.71	13	6	0	0	24	Australia	31.8.95
Dynevor, Leo	13.2.74	15+1	9	20	0	76	Australia	4.8.95
Evans, Dave	17.6.69	4	0	0	0	0	Doncaster	10.3.95
Felton, Neil	12.3.69	1	0	0	0	0		
Francis, Mick	7.2.74	3	0	0	0	0	Australia	2.1.96
Gill, Peter	14.12.64	14	1	0	0	4	Australia	1.9.95
Green, Craig	24.1.70	8+5	2	0	0	8		15.8.95
Hauff, Paul	9.5.70	13	13	0	0	52	Australia	13.7.95
Heugh, Cavill	31.8.62	2+1	0	0	0	0	Rochdale H.	21.7.93
Hogg, Darren	16.6.73	1	0	0	0	0	New Zealand	10.7.95
Keating, Shaun	8.7.70	7+1	1	0	0	4	Australia	8.7.95
Langer, Kevin	8.6.63	8+9	5	0	0	20	Australia	2.12.94
Matterson, Terry	4.3.67	12	3	21	0	54	Australia	14.7.95
McKenna, Chris	9.10.74	13	9	0	0	36	Australia	1.9.95
McRae, Duncan	27.9.74	2	3	0	0	12	Australia	29.12.95
Mestrov, Tony	11.3.70	16	4	0	0	16	Australia	13.7.95
Meyer, Keiran	7.12.71	5	1	0	0	4	Australia	21.7.95
Mills, Paul	17.4.74	1	0	0	0	0	Australia	18.9.95
O'Donnell, David	6.4.68	10+2	0	0	0	0		
O'Neill, Julian	14.10.72	3	0	13	1	27	Australia	14.8.95
Paul, Junior	23.12.71	1	0	0	0	0		20.12.95
Pitt, Darryl	31.5.66	2+17	1	1	0	6	Australia	7.12.89
Rea, Tony	25.7.66	10+1	5	0	0	20	Australia	19.12.94
Riley, Mark	16.6.67	10+4	8	0	0	32	Peckham ARL	6.10.92
Roskell, Scott	25.4.69	9+4	5	0	0	20	Australia	27.8.92
Rosolen, Steve	16.11.68	15+3	5	0	0	20	Australia	2.1.92
Scourfield, John	12.12.67	3	2	0	0	8	St. Marys ARL	25.11.95
Shaw, Darren	5.10.71	20+1	1	0	0	4	Australia	15.8.94
Smith, Chris	8.8.66	2+1	0	7	0	14	Twickenham RU	30.8.91
Stevens, Paul	7.10.74	5+4	1	0	0	4	Wigan	15.3.95
Vincent, Shane	3.3.73	7	5	4	0	28	Australia	13.7.95
Walker, Ben	3.9.76	15+1	6	5	3	37	Australia	12.7.95
Why, Adrian	14.6.67	0+2	0	0	0	0	Fulham ARL	3.9.91
TOTALS								
38 players			104	73	4	566		

LONDON BRONCOS 1995-96 MATCH ANALYSIS

Date	Com-petition	H/A	Opponents	Rlt	Score	Tries	Goals	Atten-dance	Referee
20.8.95	SBC	A	Warrington	L	6-46	Langer	Booth	–	–
23.8.95	SBC	A	Halifax	L	12-50	Bryant, Roskell	Booth, Pitt	–	–
3.9.95	SBC	A	Bradford B.	L	16-26	Bawden, Green, Vincent	Vincent (2)	–	–
10.9.95	SBC	A	Wigan	L	12-50	Roskell, Rosolen	Vincent (2)	–	–
17.9.95	SBC	H1	Leeds	W	26-12	Dynevor, McKenna, Butt	O'Neill (6,dg), Walker (dg)	4331	Smith
20.9.95	SBC	A	Oldham B.	L	8-19	Butt	O'Neill (2)	–	–
24.9.95	SBC	A	Sheffield E.	W	42-10	Cochrane (4), Hauff (2), Walker (2)	O'Neill (5)	–	–
1.10.95	SBC	H2	Workington T.	W	44-8	Hauff (4), Rosolen, Butt, Cochrane, Matterson	Matterson (6)	1238	Campbell
27.10.95	SBC	H3	Oldham B.	W	46-14	Riley (2), Walker (2), Meyer, Langer, Hauff, Cochrane, Dynevor	Matterson (4), Dynevor	1156	Jeffs (Aus)
1.11.95	SBC	H4	St. Helens	L	34-50	McKenna (3), Riley, Hauff, Matterson	Dynevor (5)	1561	Bates
5.11.95	SBC	A	Castleford	W	37-8	Dynevor (3), Green, McKenna, Riley, Matterson	Matterson (3), Dynevor, Walker (dg)	–	–
12.11.95	RT(2)	H2	Highfield	W	82-0	Vincent (4), Roskell (2), Rosolen (2), Riley (2), Scourfield (2), Langer, Pitt, Bawden	Smith (6), Walker (5)	512	Shaw
15.11.95	SBC	H4	Halifax	W	38-27	Dynevor (2), McKenna (2), Walker, Riley, Gill, Rea	Dynevor (3)	1625	J. Connolly
19.11.95	SBC	H4	Warrington	L	10-18	Dynevor, Rea	Matterson	2451	J. Connolly
25.11.95	RT(3)	H4	Halifax	L	18-22	Mestrov (2), Rea, McKenna	Matterson	800	Morris
3.12.95	SBC	H1	Wigan	L	10-42	Butt, Mestrov	Dynevor	8338	Cummings
10.12.95	SBC	H3	Bradford B.	W	27-24	McKenna, Walker, Hauff, Riley, Mestrov	Matterson (3), Walker (dg)	939	Kirkpatrick
17.12.95	SBC	H3	Sheffield E.	L	14-21	Hauff (2), Stevens	Matterson	761	Campbell
19.12.95	SBC	A	Leeds	L	12-30	Roskell, Hauff	Matterson (2)	–	–
7.1.96	SBC	A	Workington T.	L	10-32	Keating, Langer	Smith	–	–
17.1.96	SBC	A	St. Helens	L	18-48	Carroll, Langer, Rea	Dynevor (3)	–	–
21.1.96	SBC	H3	Castleford	L	44-50	McRae (3), Shaw, Dynevor, Hauff, Rea, Rosolen	Dynevor (6)	1465	Kirkpatrick

1 At Brentford FC;
2 At Barnet Copthal,
3 At The Valley,
4 At Harlequins RU

OLDHAM BEARS

Highest score: 70-10 v. Bramley, 12 Feb 1995
Highest against: 67-11 at Hull K.R., 24 Sep 1978
Attendance: 28,000 v. Huddersfield (League),
24 Feb 1912

Ground: Watersheddings (0161-624-4865)
First Season: 1895-96. Added Bears to title in
1995-96
Nickname: Bears
Chairman: Jim Quinn
Chief Exec: Jim Quinn
Honours: **Championship** Winners, 1909-10,
1910-11, 1956-57
Beaten finalists, 1906-07, 1907-08,
1908-09, 1921-22, 1954-55
Division One Champions, 1904-05
Division Two Champions, 1963-64,
1981-82, 1987-88
Challenge Cup Winners, 1898-99,
1924-25, 1926-27
Beaten finalists, 1906-07, 1911-12,
1923-24, 1925-26
**Second Division/Divisional
Premiership** Winners, 1987-88,
1989-90
Beaten finalists, 1991-92
Lancashire Cup Winners, 1907-08,
1910-11, 1913-14, 1919-20, 1924-25,
1933-34, 1956-57, 1957-58, 1958-59
Beaten finalists, 1908-09, 1911-12,
1918-19, 1921-22, 1954-55, 1966-67,
1968-69, 1986-87, 1989-90
Lancashire League Winners,
1897-98, 1900-01, 1907-08, 1909-10,
1921-22, 1956-57, 1957-58

RECORDS
Match
Goals: 14 by Bernard Ganley v. Liverpool C.,
4 Apr 1959
Tries: 7 by James Miller v. Barry, 31 Oct 1908
Points: 30 by Abe Johnson v. Widnes, 9 Apr 1928
Season
Goals: 200 by Bernard Ganley, 1957-58
Tries: 49 by R. Farrar, 1921-22
Points: 412 by Bernard Ganley, 1957-58
Career
Goals: 1,365 by Bernard Ganley, 1951-61
Tries: 173 by Alan Davies, 1950-61
Points: 2,775 by Bernard Ganley, 1951-61
Appearances: 626 by Joe Ferguson, 1899-1923

COACHING REGISTER
● **Since 1974-75**

Jim Challinor	Aug 74 - Dec 76
Terry Ramshaw	Jan 77 - Feb 77
Dave Cox	July 77 - Dec 78
Graham Starkey (Mgr)	Jan 79 - May 81
Bill Francis	June 79 - Dec 80
Frank Myler	May 81 - Apr 83
Peter Smethurst	Apr 83 - Feb 84
Frank Barrow	Feb 84 - Feb 84
Brian Gartland	Mar 84 - June 84
Frank Myler	June 84 - Apr 87
* Eric Fitzsimons	June 87 - Nov 88
* Mal Graham	June 87 - Apr 88
Tony Barrow	Nov 88 - Jan 91
John Fieldhouse	Jan 91 - Apr 91
Peter Tunks	Apr 91 - Feb 94
Bob Lindner	Feb 94 - Apr 94
Andy Goodway	May 94 -

* Joint coaches June 87 - Apr 88

Andy Goodway, appointed coach of Oldham in May 1994.

GREAT BRITAIN REGISTER
(40 players)

Albert Avery	(4)	1910-11
Charlie Bott	(1)	1966
Albert Brough	(2)	1924
Terry Clawson	(9)	1973-74
Alan Davies	(20)	1955-60
Evan Davies	(3)	1920
Terry Flanagan	(4)	1983-84
Des Foy	(3)	1984-85
Bernard Ganley	(3)	1957-58
Andy Goodway	(11)	1983-85
Billy Hall	(4)	1914
Herman Hilton	(7)	1920-21
David Hobbs	(2)	1987
Dave Holland	(4)	1914
Bob Irving	(8+3)	1967-72
Ken Jackson	(2)	1957
Ernest Knapman	(1)	1924
Syd Little	(10)	1956-58
Tom Llewellyn	(2)	1907
Jim Lomas	(2)	1911
Bill Longworth	(3)	1908
Les McIntyre	(1)	1963
Terry O'Grady	(5)	1954
Jack Oster	(1)	1929
Dave Parker	(2)	1964
Doug Phillips	(3)	1946
Frank Pitchford	(2)	1958-62
Tom Rees	(1)	1929
Sid Rix	(9)	1924-26
Bob Sloman	(5)	1928
Arthur Smith	(6)	1907-08
Ike Southward	(7)	1959-62
Les Thomas	(1)	1947
Derek Turner	(11)	1956-58
George Tyson	(4)	1907-08
Hugh Waddell	(4)	1988
Tommy White	(1)	1907
Charlie Winslade	(1)	1959
Alf Wood	(4)	1911-14
Mick Worrall	(3)	1984

1995-96 REGISTRATION DATE

Signed	Player	Club From
2.6.95	Atcheson, Paul	Wigan
12.7.95	Maloney, Francis	Warrington
12.7.95	Myler, Robert	Warrington
24.7.95	Deacon, Paul	Hindley ARL
3.8.95	Lowe, Robert	St. Judes ARL
8.8.95	Gildart, Ian	Wakefield T.
25.8.95	Wilde, Steve	Saddleworth ARL
6.10.95	Leuila, Peaufai "Afi"	Tonga
1.11.95	Vyacheslav, Sepega	Moldova
4.11.95	McIlwaine, Andrew	–
1.12.95	McNicholas, Joe	Spotland Rangers ARL
12.12.95	Jones, Ward	–
12.12.95	Melling, Neil	–
13.12.95	Barker, Craig	–
14.12.95	Crook, Paul	Dewsbury
22.12.95	Nuttall, Tony	–

Wales full back Paul Atcheson, a June 1995 signing by Oldham from Wigan.

OLDHAM BEARS 1995-96 PLAYERS' SUMMARY

	Date of birth	App	T	G	D	Pts	Previous club	Signed
Abram, Darren	27.9.67	20+1	12	0	0	48	Rochdale H.	19.2.93
Atcheson, Paul	17.5.73	17+1	5	0	0	20	Wigan	2.6.95
Belle, Adrian	23.11.70	7+4	2	0	0	8	Rochdale H.	22.10.93
Bradbury, David	16.3.72	7	2	0	0	8	Leigh M. ARL	15.8.91
Burns, Gary	10.2.72	4+4	1	0	0	4		20.12.93
Clarke, John	3.3.74	6+1	1	0	0	4	East Leeds ARL	1.5.93
Cowan, Jimmy	4.12.75	2+1	0	0	0	0		15.5.95
Crompton, Martin	29.9.69	19	4	0	0	16	Wigan	7.9.93
Crook, Paul	12.2.74	1+2	1	0	0	4	Dewsbury	14.12.95
Davidson, Paul	1.8.69	5+3	0	0	0	0	Widnes	29.7.94
Edwards, Mike	14.4.74	1+1	0	0	0	0		
Faimalo, Joe	28.7.70	5+2	0	0	0	0	New Zealand	2.9.94
Gartland, Steve	3.10.70	9	0	12	1	25	Rochdale H.	20.7.94
Gibson, Wally	5.4.67	19+1	6	0	0	24	Huddersfield	25.9.92
Gildart, Ian	14.10.69	8+3	0	0	0	0	Wakefield T.	8.8.95
Green, Iyan	21.4.72	9+5	1	0	0	4		25.8.93
Hill, Howard	16.1.75	14+2	4	0	0	16	Hensingham ARL	18.7.94
Irwin, Shaun	8.12.68	0+1	1	0	0	4	Castleford	11.8.93
Leuila, Peaufai "Afi"	24.10.69	9+2	6	0	0	24	Tonga	27.9.95
Lord, Gary	6.7.66	17	3	0	0	12	Halifax	1.7.94
Maloney, Francis	26.5.73	15+1	4	48	1	113	Warrington	12.7.95
McIlwaine, Andrew	26.3.73	0+2	0	0	0	0		4.11.95
McKinney, Chris	12.11.76	4+7	3	0	0	12	Hensingham ARL	10.8.94
Myler, Rob	4.3.70	4+3	1	0	0	4	Warrington	12.7.95
Neal, Mike	4.9.73	5+4	0	0	0	0	Wigan	6.3.95
Norman, Paul	25.3.74	1+4	1	0	0	4	Parkside ARL	25.9.92
Parr, Chris	31.5.71	6+6	0	0	0	0	Swinton	19.10.93
Ranson, Scott	20.9.67	10	4	0	0	16	Swinton	6.2.92
Richards, Craig	27.1.70	8+3	1	0	0	4	Bradford N.	
Sherratt, Ian	9.8.65	10+1	0	0	0	0	Salford	8.11.91
Temu, Jason	17.4.72	16+2	0	0	0	0	New Zealand	30.9.94
Topping, Paul	18.9.65	15+2	4	0	0	16	Leigh	27.9.93
TOTALS								
32 players			67	60	2	390		

Representative appearances 1995-96
Atcheson – Wales (+1)

OLDHAM BEARS 1995-96 MATCH ANALYSIS

Date	Competition	H/A	Opponents	Rlt	Score	Tries	Goals	Attendance	Referee
20.8.95	SBC	A	Castleford	L	22-28	Abram, Crompton, Lord, Ranson	Maloney (3)	–	–
23.8.95	SBC	H	St. Helens	L	18-44	Abram, Maloney	Maloney (5)	4316	Morris
27.8.95	SBC	A	Warrington	L	8-40	McKinney, Topping	–	–	–
1.9.95	SBC	H	Halifax	L	4-21	Abram	–	2938	R. Connolly
10.9.95	SBC	H	Bradford B.	L	24-30	Belle (2), Hill, Clarke	Maloney (4)	3222	Cummings
20.9.95	SBC	H	London B.	W	19-8	Abram (2), Atcheson	Maloney (3,dg)	3004	Campbell
24.9.95	SBC	A	Wigan	L	12-42	Ranson, Crompton	Gartland (2)	–	–
1.10.95	SBC	H	Leeds	L	14-43	Lord, Hill	Maloney (3)	3782	R. Connolly
27.10.95	SBC	A	London B.	L	14-46	Ranson, Gibson	Maloney (3)	–	–
1.11.95	SBC	H	Workington T.	W	30-26	Abram (2), Hill, Gibson, Leuila, Maloney	Maloney (2), Gartland	2091	Morris
5.11.95	SBC	A	Sheffield E.	L	18-36	Abram, Hill, Green	Gartland (3)	–	–
12.11.95	RT(2)	A	Widnes	L	8-32	Ranson	Gartland (2)	–	–
19.11.95	SBC	H	Castleford	W	25-20	Abram, McKinney, Topping, Gibson	Gartland (4,dg)	2620	R. Connolly
1.12.95	SBC	A	Bradford B.	L	10-14	Gibson, Myler	Maloney	–	–
13.12.95	SBC	A	St. Helens	L	22-32	Abram, Topping, Atcheson, Bradbury	Maloney (3)	–	–
17.12.95	SBC	H	Wigan	W	28-26	Leuila (2), Burns, Crompton, McKinney	Maloney (4)	3540	Bates
4.1.96	SBC	A	Halifax	W	12-4	Crook, Gibson	Maloney (2)	–	–
10.1.96	SBC	A	Leeds	L	26-28	Gibson, Leuila, Richards, Topping	Maloney (5)	–	–
14.1.96	SBC	A	Workington T.	W	20-12	Bradbury, Lord, Crompton, Maloney	Maloney (2)	–	–
17.1.96	SBC	H	Warrington	W	30-19	Atcheson, Abram, Leuila, Maloney, Norman	Maloney (5)	2975	Cummings
21.1.96	SBC	H	Sheffield E.	W	26-16	Atcheson (2), Abram, Irwin, Leuila	Maloney (3)	3391	Bates

David Bradbury, scorer of two tries in seven Centenary season games.

One try in a single game for Oldham's Shaun Irwin after return from a serious injury.

PARIS SAINT GERMAINE

Ground: Charlety Stadium
First Season: 1996
Chairman: Jacques Fouroux
Chief Exec: Tas Baitieri

COACHING REGISTER
Michel Mazare   Jan 96 -

PLAYING REGISTER
FULL BACKS
Laurent Lucchese   Bagdad Yaha
WINGERS
Pascal Bomati   John Dickson
Bernard Lacombe   Mikhail Piskunov
CENTRES
Frederic Banquet   Pierre Chamorin
David Despin   Eric Vergniol
HALF BACKS
Todd Brown   Patrick Entat
Fabien Devecchi   Pascal Fages
PROPS
Daniel Coote   Karl Jaavuo
Greg Kacala   Jason Sands
Federic Teixido
HOOKERS
Abderazake Elkaloulki Jacques Pech
Patrick Torreilles
BACK ROWERS
Darren Adams   Didier Cabestany
Glen Cannon   Lilian Herbert
Pascal Jampy   Regis Pastre-Courtine

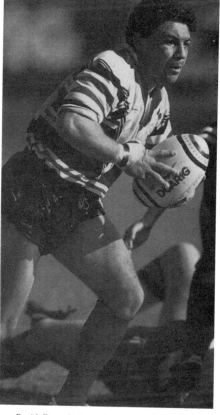

Patrick Entat, the former Hull and Leeds international scrum-half, who will be a key figure in the new Paris team.

ROCHDALE HORNETS

Highest score: 92-0 v. Runcorn H., 5 Nov 1989
Highest against: 79-2 at Hull, 7 Apr 1921
Attendance: 8,150 v. Oldham (Div. 2),
26 Dec 1989 — at Spotland
26,664 v. Oldham (RL Cup),
25 Mar 1922 — at Athletic Ground

Ground: Spotland (01706-48004)
First Season: 1895-96
Nickname: Hornets
Chairman: Ray Taylor
Secretary: Paul Reynolds
Honours: **Challenge Cup** Winners, 1921-22
                Regal Trophy Beaten finalists,
                1973-74
                Lancashire Cup Winners, 1911-12,
                1914-15, 1918-19
                Beaten finalists, 1912-13, 1919-20,
                1965-66, 1991-92
                Lancashire League Winners,
                1918-19
                BBC2 Floodlit Trophy Beaten
                finalists, 1971-72

RECORDS

Match
Goals: 14 by Steve Turner v. Runcorn H.,
            5 Nov 1989
Tries: 5 by Jack Corsi v. Barrow, 31 Dec 1921
            Jack Corsi v. Broughton Moor,
            25 Feb 1922
            Jack Williams v. St. Helens,
            4 Apr 1933
            Norman Brelsford v. Whitehaven,
            3 Sep 1972
Points: 32 by Steve Turner v. Runcorn H.,
            5 Nov 1989
            Steve Turner v. Blackpool G.,
            31 Oct 1993

Season
Goals: 150 by Martin Strett, 1994-95
Tries: 30 by Jack Williams, 1934-35
Points: 346 by Martin Strett, 1994-95

Career
Goals: 741 by Walter Gowers, 1922-46
Tries: 103 by Jack Williams, 1931-37
Points: 1,497 by Walter Gowers, 1922-46
Appearances: 456 by Walter Gowers, 1922-46

COACHING REGISTER
● **Since 1974-75**

Frank Myler	May 71 - Oct 74
Graham Starkey	Oct 74 - Nov 75
Henry Delooze	Nov 75 - Nov 76
Kel Coslett	Nov 76 - Aug 79
Paul Longstaff	Sep 79 - May 81
Terry Fogerty	May 81 - Jan 82
Dick Bonser	Jan 82 - May 82
Bill Kirkbride	June 82 - Sep 84
Charlie Birdsall	Sep 84 - Apr 86
Eric Fitzsimons	June 86 - June 87
Eric Hughes	June 87 - June 88
Jim Crellin	June 88 - June 89
Allan Agar	July 89 - Jan 91
Neil Holding	Jan 91 - Apr 91
Stan Gittins	Apr 91 - Jan 93
Peter Regan	Jan 93 - Oct 93
Steve Gibson	Oct 93 -

GREAT BRITAIN REGISTER
(8 players)

Johnnie Baxter	(1)	1907
Jack Bennett	(6)	1924
Joe Bowers	(1)	1920
Terry Fogerty	(1)	1974
Ernest Jones	(4)	1920
Malcolm Price	(2)	1967
Jack Robinson	(2)	1914
Tommy Woods	(2)	1911

1995-96 SIGNINGS REGISTER

Signed	Player	Club From
9.8.95	Poynton, Philip	St. Helens
27.10.95	Booth, Craig	–
27.10.95	*Flanagan, Neil	Huddersfield
20.11.95	Hayes, Ian	–
22.11.95	Greenwood, Adam	Bradford B.
24.11.95	*Green, Jason	Widnes
26.11.95	Rogers, Darrell	–
17.12.95	Agar, Richard	Dewsbury
7.1.96	Osbaldeston, Allan	Wigan St. Patricks ARL

ROCHDALE HORNETS 1995-96 PLAYERS' SUMMARY

	Date of birth	App	T	G	D	Pts	Previous club	Signed
Agar, Richard	20.1.72	5+4	0	3	1	7	Dewsbury	17.11.95
Alverez, Sean	28.3.69	6	1	1	0	6		
Atherton, Lee	1.11.74	1	0	0	0	0	Orrell St. James ARL	31.5.94
Booth, Craig	28.10.70	10	2	29	1	67		27.10.95
Churm, Chris	20.9.66	20+1	13	5	3	65	Oldham St. Annes ARL	1.4.94
Diggle, Craig	2.4.75	14	4	0	0	16	Mayfield ARL	13.8.93
England, Keith	27.2.64	17+3	3	0	0	12	Castleford	18.8.94
Fell, David	25.4.66	6+3	4	0	0	16	Salford	28.1.94
Flanagan, Neil	11.6.70	13+2	3	0	0	12	Huddersfield	27.10.95
Gibson, Steve	23.11.62	22	8	0	1	33	Salford	5.10.93
Grayshon, Paul	11.7.67	1+1	0	0	0	0	Bradford N.	21.9.94
Green, Jason	19.1.72	6	3	0	0	12	Widnes	24.11.95
Greenwood, Adam	26.5.67	9	1	0	0	4	Bradford B.	22.11.95
Higginson, Paul	5.6.68	5	1	0	0	4		
Hilton, Chris	15.1.76	8+1	1	0	0	4		
Hilton, Tony	11.7.71	3+7	0	0	0	0		
Kay, Martin	16.2.71	1	0	0	0	0	Oldham St. Annes ARL	20.8.90
Mannion, Kevin	31.8.78	4+2	0	0	0	0	Orrell St. James ARL	4.10.94
Marriott, Karl	21.11.69	18	8	0	0	32	Mayfield ARL	17.8.89
Mawdsley, Steve	7.10.67	6+7	1	0	0	4	Saddleworth ARL	21.7.94
Meadows, Mark	9.5.65	20	1	0	0	4	Leigh	7.2.95
Miller, Vincent	1.3.64	2	0	0	0	0	Fitton Hill ARL	7.1.94
O'Keefe, Paul	28.6.71	6	0	0	0	0		15.12.91
Pachniuk, Richard	24.3.71	22	9	0	0	36	Oldham	19.2.93
Pitt, Darren	14.5.71	15+1	2	0	0	8		12.8.93
Poynton, Phil	31.10.74	9	0	20	1	41	St. Helens	9.8.95
Ratu, Emon	30.10.65	6+6	2	0	0	8	Swinton	12.8.93
Reid, Wayne	15.12.69	20	2	0	0	8	Salford	18.8.94
Robey, Nick	6.9.77	1	0	0	0	0	Orrell St. James ARL	1.4.94
Ryan, Matt	5.5.71	13+1	1	0	0	4	Australia	22.8.95
Sharp, Henry	17.9.66	4	2	0	0	8	Halifax	9.12.94
Turner, Steve	5.12.61	6+7	0	7	0	14	Swinton	22.2.88
TOTALS								
32 players			72	65	7	425		

ROCHDALE HORNETS 1995-96 MATCH ANALYSIS

Date	Com-petition	H/A	Opponents	Rlt	Score	Tries	Goals	Atten-dance	Referee
20.8.95	FD	H	Batley	W	21-14	Churm, Sharp	Poynton (5), Churm (2dg), Gibson (dg)	1055	Cross
23.8.95	FD	A	Huddersfield	W	27-12	Sharp, Gibson, Diggle, Higginson	Poynton (5,dg)	–	–
27.8.95	FD	H	Keighley C.	L	4-50	Pachniuk	–	3038	Gilmour
10.9.95	FD	A	Hull	L	20-40	Churm, England, Reid	Poynton (4)	–	–
17.9.95	FD	H	Dewsbury	W	26-16	Marriott (2), Churm, Gibson, Pachniuk	Poynton (3)	1015	Lee
20.9.95	FD	A	Wakefield T.	L	6-28	Diggle	Poynton	–	–
24.9.95	FD	H	Salford R.	L	27-32	Churm, Reid, Fell, Pitt	Turner (3), Poynton (2), Churm (dg)	1639	Atkins
1.10.95	FD	A	Whitehaven	D	14-14	Pachniuk, Marriott, Ryan	Churm	–	–
1.11.95	FD	W	Featherstone R.	W	24-16	Pachniuk (2), Fell (2), Churm	Churm, Turner	–	–
5.11.95	FD	H	Widnes	L	14-34	Diggle, Alvarez, Flanagan	Alvarez	1476	Gilmour
12.11.95	RT(2)	A	Hull K.R.	W	14-10	Marriott, Churm, Ratu	Booth	–	–
15.11.95	FD	H	Huddersfield	W	20-8	England, Fell, Ratu	Booth (4)	1192	Cross
19.11.95	FD	A	Batley	L	10-34	Marriott	Turner (3)	–	–
26.11.95	RT(3)	A	Dewsbury	W	26-14	Pitt, J. Green, C. Hilton, Mawdsley, Meadows	Churm (3)	–	–
29.11.95	FD	H	Hull	W	54-20	Churm (3), Marriott (2), Gibson, Pachniuk, J. Green, Flanagan,	Booth (8), Agar	968	Asquith
3.12.95	FD	A	Dewsbury	W	21-16	Gibson, Pachniuk, Flanagan	Booth (4,dg)	–	–
10.12.95	RT(QT)	A	Warrington	L	20-38	Churm, Pachniuk, England	Booth (4)	–	–
13.12.95	FD	H	Wakefield T.	L	16-30	Churm (2), Booth	Booth (2)	838	Gilmour
17.12.95	FD	A	Salford R.	L	4-42	J. Green	–	–	–
4.1.96	FD	A	Keighley C.	L	4-24	Gibson	–	733	Cross
17.1.96	FD	H	Whitehaven	L	8-15	Gibson	Agar (2)	1026	R. Connolly
14.1.96	FD	H	Featherstone R.	W	39-16	Gibson (2), Booth, Churm, Diggle, Marriott, Pachniuk	Booth (5), Agar (dg)	–	–
21.1.96	FD	A	Widnes	L	6-22	Greenwood	Booth	–	–

ST. HELENS

Ground: Knowsley Road (01744-23697)
First Season: 1895-96
Nickname: Saints
Chairman: Eric Ashton
Chief Exec: David Howes
Honours: **Championship** Winners, 1931-32, 1952-53, 1958-59, 1965-66, 1969-70, 1970-71
Beaten finalists, 1964-65, 1966-67, 1971-72
League Leaders Trophy Winners, 1964-65, 1965-66
Club Championship (Merit Table) Beaten finalists, 1973-74
Division One Champions, 1974-75
Challenge Cup Winners, 1955-56, 1960-61, 1965-66, 1971-72, 1975-76
Beaten finalists, 1896-97, 1914-15, 1929-30, 1952-53, 1977-78, 1986-87, 1988-89, 1990-91
Regal Trophy Winners, 1987-88
Beaten finalists, 1995-96
Premiership Winners, 1975-76, 1976-77, 1984-85, 1992-93
Beaten finalists, 1974-75, 1987-88, 1991-92
Lancashire Cup Winners, 1926-27, 1953-54, 1960-61, 1961-62, 1962-63, 1963-64, 1964-65, 1967-68, 1968-69, 1984-85, 1991-92
Beaten finalists, 1932-33, 1952-53, 1956-57, 1958-59, 1959-60, 1970-71, 1982-83, 1992-93
Lancashire League Winners, 1929-30, 1931-32, 1952-53, 1959-60, 1964-65, 1965-66, 1966-67, 1968-69
Western Division Championship Winners, 1963-64
Charity Shield Winners, 1992-93
BBC2 Floodlit Trophy Winners, 1971-72, 1975-76
Beaten finalists, 1965-66, 1968-69, 1970-71, 1977-78, 1978-79

RECORDS
Match
Goals: 16 by Paul Loughlin v. Carlisle, 14 Sep 1986
Tries: 6 by Alf Ellaby v. Barrow, 5 Mar 1932
Steve Llewellyn v. Castleford, 3 Mar 1956
Steve Llewellyn v. Liverpool C., 20 Aug 1956
Tom Van Vollenhoven v. Wakefield T., 21 Dec 1957
Tom Van Vollenhoven v. Blackpool B., 23 Apr 1962
Frank Myler v. Maryport, 1 Sep 1969
Shane Cooper v. Hull, 17 Feb 1988
Points: 40 by Paul Loughlin v. Carlisle, 14 Sep 1986

Season
Goals: 214 by Kel Coslett, 1971-72
Tries: 62 by Tom Van Vollenhoven, 1958-59
Points: 452 by Kel Coslett, 1971-72

Career
Goals: 1,639 by Kel Coslett, 1961-76
Tries: 392 by Tom Van Vollenhoven, 1957-68
Points: 3,413 by Kel Coslett, 1961-76
Appearances: 519+12 by Kel Coslett, 1961-76
Highest score: 112-0 v. Carlisle, 14 Sep 1986
Highest against: 78-6 at Warrington, 12 Apr 1909
Attendance: 35,695 v. Wigan (League), 26 Dec 1949

COACHING REGISTER
● **Since 1974-75**

Eric Ashton	May 74 - May 80
Kel Coslett	June 80 - May 82
Billy Benyon	May 82 - Nov 85
Alex Murphy	Nov 85 - Jan 90
Mike McClennan	Feb 90 - Dec 93
Eric Hughes	Jan 94 - Jan 96
Shaun McRae	Jan 96 -

GREAT BRITAIN REGISTER
(54 players)

Chris Arkwright	(+2)	1985
Len Aston	(3)	1947
Billy Benyon	(5+1)	1971-72
Tommy Bishop	(15)	1966-69
Frank Carlton	(1)	1958
Eric Chisnall	(4)	1974
Gary Connolly	(7+3)	1991-93
Eddie Cunningham	(1)	1978
Rob Dagnall	(4)	1961-65
David Eckersley	(2+2)	1973-74
Alf Ellaby	(13)	1928-33
Les Fairclough	(6)	1926-29
John Fieldhouse	(1)	1986
Alec Fildes	(4)	1932
Alf Frodsham	(3)	1928-29
Peter Gorley	(2+1)	1980-81
Bobbie Goulding	(1+2)	1994
Doug Greenall	(6)	1951-54
Jonathan Griffiths	(1)	1992
Paul Groves	(1)	1987
Roy Haggerty	(2)	1987
Mervyn Hicks	(1)	1965
Neil Holding	(4)	1984
Dick Huddart	(12)	1959-63
Alan Hunte	(7)	1992-94
Les Jones	(1)	1971
Chris Joynt	(7+1)	1993-94
Tony Karalius	(4+1)	1971-72
Vince Karalius	(10)	1958-61
Ken Kelly	(2)	1972
Barry Ledger	(2)	1985-86
Paul Loughlin	(14+1)	1988-92
Stan McCormick	(1)	1948
Tom McKinney	(1)	1957
John Mantle	(13)	1966-73
Roy Mathias	(1)	1979
Glyn Moses	(9)	1955-57
Alex Murphy	(26)	1958-66
Frank Myler	(9)	1970
George Nicholls	(22)	1973-79
Sonny Nickle	(1+5)	1992-94
Harry Pinner	(5+1)	1980-86
Andy Platt	(4+3)	1985-88
Alan Prescott	(28)	1951-58
Austin Rhodes	(4)	1957-61
Jim Stott	(1)	1947
Anthony Sullivan	(1)	1991
Mick Sullivan	(10)	1961-62
Jim Tembey	(2)	1963-64
Abe Terry	(10)	1958-61
John Walsh	(4+1)	1972
Kevin Ward	(1+2)	1990-92
John Warlow	(3+1)	1964-68
Cliff Watson	(29+1)	1963-71

1995-96 REGISTRATION DATE

Signed	Player	Club From
18.8.95	Busby, Dean	Hull
18.8.95	Rigby, Daniel	Leigh Rangers ARL
7.9.95	Hammond, Karle	Widnes
28.11.95	Newlove, Paul	Bradford B.

St. Helens' Western Samoan packman Apollo Perelini, 10 tries in 20 Centenary season games.

ST. HELENS 1995-96 PLAYERS' SUMMARY

	Date of birth	App	T	G	D	Pts	Previous club	Signed
Anderson, Paul	2.4.77	1	0	0	0	0	St. Helens Academy	2.4.94
Arkwright, James	8.5.76	0+1	0	0	0	0	Leigh Miners ARL	1.7.93
Arnold, Danny	15.4.77	8+6	10	1	0	42	St. Helens Academy	15.4.94
Booth, Simon	9.12.71	7+2	3	0	0	12	Leigh	5.7.94
Busby, Dean	1.2.73	16+1	3	0	0	12	Hull	18.8.95
Capewell, Brian	21.10.77	0+2	0	3	0	6		28.12.94
Cunningham, Gareth	16.9.75	1+1	0	0	0	0	Blackpool Royals ARL	2.9.92
Cunningham, Keiron	28.10.76	23	7	0	0	28		28.10.93
Devine, Nick	13.8.76	1	0	0	0	0	Crosfields ARL	27.8.93
Dwyer, Bernard	20.4.67	8+3	0	0	0	0	Hare & Hounds ARL	22.5.84
Fogerty, Adam	6.3.69	13+2	6	0	0	24	Halifax	29.7.93
Gibbs, Scott	23.1.71	16	11	0	0	44	Swansea RU	18.4.94
Goulding, Bobbie	4.2.72	21	3	121	0	254	Widnes	27.7.94
Griffiths, Jonathan	23.8.64	0+1	0	0	0	0	Llanelli RU	22.5.89
Haigh, Andy	3.9.75	9+7	8	0	0	32	Crosfields ARL	10.8.93
Hammond, Karle	25.4.74	18+1	12	0	1	49	Widnes	7.9.95
Hayes, Joey	4.1.76	21	18	0	0	72		16.8.94
Joynt, Chris	7.12.71	15	7	0	0	28	Oldham	2.9.92
Leatham, Andy	30.3.77	6+3	1	0	0	4	Crosfields ARL	30.3.94
Loughlin, Paul	28.7.66	13	6	0	0	24	St. Helens Colts	8.8.83
Lyon, David	3.9.65	2+1	1	0	0	4	Warrington	23.9.92
Matautia, Vila	31.8.69	14+4	10	0	0	40	Doncaster	31.3.95
Mathison, Paul	15.11.75	0+3	0	0	0	0	St. Helens Academy	8.1.94
Morley, Chris	22.9.73	4+8	1	0	0	4	Woolston R. ARL	16.12.91
Newall, Chris	30.11.76	0+1	0	0	0	0	Wigan St Patricks ARL	1.12.93
Newlove, Paul	10.8.71	5	3	0	0	12	Bradford B.	28.11.95
Nickle, Sonny	4.5.69	5	1	0	0	4	Sheffield E.	3.7.91
Northey, Andy	17.2.72	16+7	9	0	0	36	Waterloo RU	19.12.94
O'Loughlin, Kevin	26.3.77	1+3	0	0	0	0		26.3.94
Perelini, Apollo	16.7.69	18+2	10	0	0	40	Western Samoa RU	3.6.94
Pickavance, Ian	20.9.68	13+5	4	0	0	16	Swinton	10.9.93
Prescott, Steve	26.12.73	21	8	15	0	62	Nutgrove ARL	3.11.92
Riley, Mike	20.11.70	3	0	0	0	0	Widnes Tigers ARL	5.1.90
Sheil, Richard	28.11.75	0+3	0	0	0	0	Blackbrook ARL	8.12.92
Sullivan, Anthony	23.11.68	15	20	0	0	80	Hull K.R.	29.4.91
Veivers, Phil	25.5.64	4+8	1	0	1	5	Australia	18.9.84
Walker, Martin	3.11.74	0+1	0	0	0	0	Leigh Miners ARL	7.12.93
Waring, Phil	5.3.75	7+7	5	0	0	20	Eccles ARL	7.12.93
TOTALS								
38 players			168	140	2	954		

Representative appearances 1995-96

Cunningham – Wales (+3); Gibbs – Wales (2); Goulding – England (4,1t,13g,1dg); Joynt – England (1+2,1t); Matautia – Western Samoa (2,3t); Perelini – Western Samoa (+2,1t); Sullivan – Wales (3,4t).

ST. HELENS 1995-96 MATCH ANALYSIS

Date	Com-petition	H/A	Opponents	Rlt	Score	Tries	Goals	Atten-dance	Referee
20.8.95	SBC	H	Bradford B.	W	55-10	Sullivan (3), Haigh, Hayes, Loughlin, Matautia, Nickle, Perelini	Goulding (8), Prescott, Veivers (dg)	7620	Campbell
23.8.95	SBC	A	Oldham B.	W	44-18	Hayes (2), Gibbs (2), Matautia, Perelini, Northey	Goulding (7), Prescott	–	–
28.8.95	SBC	H	Wigan	L	20-52	Prescott (2), Gibbs, K. Cunningham	Goulding (2)	14,054	Smith
3.9.95	SBC	A	Leeds	L	24-36	Sullivan (2), Matautia (2), Gibbs	Goulding (2)	–	–
10.9.95	SBC	A	Workington T.	W	66-22	Haigh (2), Waring (2), Pickavance (2), Busby, Joynt, Hayes, Loughlin, Matautia, Gibbs	Goulding (8), Prescott	–	–
13.9.95	SBC	H	Sheffield E.	W	62-20	Prescott (2), Waring (2), Hammond, Fogerty, Perelini, Matautia, Loughlin, Hayes	Goulding (11)	5082	Bates
17.9.95	SBC	H	Castleford	W	35-18	Joynt (2), Hammond, Sullivan, Loughlin, Perelini	Prescott (4), Goulding, Hammond (dg)	7400	R. Connolly
20.9.95	SBC	A	Warrington	L	16-28	Perelini, Arnold	Prescott (4)	–	–
1.11.95	SBC	A	London B.	W	50-34	Sullivan (3), Busby, Fogerty, Prescott, K. Cunningham, Loughlin, Goulding	Goulding (7)	–	–
5.11.95	SBC	H	Halifax	W	58-20	Sullivan (4), Hammond (2), Pickavance, Joynt, K. Cunningham, Matautia	Goulding (9)	7890	Campbell
11.11.95	RT(2)	A	Keighley C.	W	42-14	Gibbs (2), Joynt (2), Loughlin, Hayes, Sullivan, Goulding	Goulding (5)	–	–
17.11.95	SBC	A	Bradford B.	W	32-18	Hayes (2), Matautia, Prescott, Northey, Fogerty	Goulding (4)	–	–
26.11.95	RT(3)	A	Hull	W	38-26	Sullivan (2), Hayes (2), Perelini (2), Lyon	Goulding (5)	–	–
29.11.95	SBC	A	Sheffield E.	L	18-32	Fogerty, Hammond, Goulding	Goulding (3)	–	–
3.12.95	SBC	H	Workington T.	W	58-10	Sullivan (4), Fogerty (2), Newlove, Arnold, Hammond, Joynt, Northey	Goulding (7)	6906	R. Connolly
10.12.95	RT(QT)	H	Halifax	W	46-18	Hayes (2), Arnold (2), K. Cunningham, Northey, Gibbs, Perelini	Goulding (7)	7419	J. Connolly
13.12.95	SBC	H	Oldham B.	W	32-22	Hayes (3), Morley, Newlove, Arnold	Goulding (4)	5060	Presley
20.12.95	SBC	A	Castleford	L	18-26	Haigh, Matautia, Veivers, Leatham	Arnold	–	–
26.12.95	SBC	A	Wigan	L	4-58	Booth	–	–	–
1.1.96	SBC	H	Leeds	L	14-20	Hammond, Gibbs	Goulding (3)	6849	Morris
4.1.96	RT(SF)	H	Warrington	W	80-0	Northey (3), Arnold (2), Booth (2), Perelini (2), Busby, Gibbs, Hammond, Pickavance, Prescott	Goulding (12)	10,647	Smith
7.1.96	SBC	H	Warrington	W	54-14	Arnold (2), Hayes (2), K. Cunningham, Haigh, Hammond, Matautia	Goulding (8), Capewell (3)	5244	Campbell
13.1.96	RT(F)	N1	Wigan	L	16-25	K. Cunningham , Hayes, Newlove	Goulding (2)	(17,590)	Smith
17.1.96	SBC	H	London B.	W	48-18	Hammond (3), Northey (2), Arnold, Gibbs, Haigh, Prescott	Goulding (6)	5333	R. Connolly
21.1.96	SBC	A	Halifax	L	24-32	Haigh (2), Waring, K. Cunningham	Pescott (4)	–	–

N1 at Huddersfield

SALFORD REDS

Ground: The Willows (0161-737-6363)
First Season: 1896-97. Added Reds to title in
              1995-96
Nickname: Reds
Chairman: John Wilkinson
Chief Exec: Dave Tarry
Honours: **Championship** Winners, 1913-14,
              1932-33, 1936-37, 1938-39
              Beaten finalists, 1933-34
              Division One Champions, 1973-74,
              1975-76
              Division Two Champions, 1990-91
              Division One (2nd league)
              Champions, 1995-96
              Challenge Cup Winners, 1937-38
              Beaten finalists, 1899-1900, 1901-02,
              1902-03, 1905-06, 1938-39, 1968-69
              Regal Trophy Beaten finalists,
              1972-73
              Premiership Beaten finalists,
              1975-76
              Second Division Premiership
              Winners, 1990-91
              Lancashire Cup Winners, 1931-32,
              1934-35, 1935-36, 1936-37, 1972-73
              Beaten finalists, 1929-30, 1938-39,
              1973-74, 1974-75, 1975-76, 1988-89,
              1990-91
              Lancashire League Winners,
              1932-33, 1933-34, 1934-35, 1936-37,
              1938-39
              BBC2 Floodlit Trophy Winners,
              1974-75

RECORDS
Match
Goals: 13 by Gus Risman v. Bramley,
         5 Apr 1933
         Gus Risman v. Broughton R.,
         18 May 1940
         David Watkins v. Keighley,
         7 Jan 1972
         Steve Rule v. Doncaster,
         4 Sep 1981
Tries: 6 by Frank Miles v. Leeds, 5 Mar 1898
         Ernest Bone v. Goole, 29 Mar 1902

Points: Jack Hilton v. Leigh, 7 Oct 1939
         39 by Jim Lomas v. Liverpool C.,
         2 Feb 1907

Season
Goals: 221 by David Watkins, 1972-73
Tries: 46 by Keith Fielding, 1973-74
Points: 493 by David Watkins, 1972-73

Career
Goals: 1,241 by David Watkins, 1967-79
Tries: 297 by Maurice Richards, 1969-83
Points: 2,907 by David Watkins, 1967-79
Appearances: 496+2 by Maurice Richards, 1969-83
Highest score: 78-0 v. Liverpool C., 2 Feb 1907
Highest against: 70-6 at Wigan, 14 Mar 1993
Attendance: 26,470 v. Warrington (RL Cup),
         13 Feb 1937

COACHING REGISTER
● **Since 1974-75**
Les Bettinson   Dec 73 - Mar 77
Colin Dixon   Mar 77 - Jan 78
Stan McCormick   Feb 78 - Mar 78
Alex Murphy   May 78 - Nov 80
Kevin Ashcroft   Nov 80 - Mar 82
Alan McInnes   Mar 82 - May 82
Malcolm Aspey   May 82 - Oct 83
Mike Coulman   Oct 83 - May 84
Kevin Ashcroft   May 84 - Oct 89
Kevin Tamati   Oct 89 - July 93
Garry Jack   July 93 - Mar 95
Andy Gregory   Mar 95 -

Les Bettinson, coach of Salford from December 1973 to March 1977.

99

GREAT BRITAIN REGISTER
(28 players)

Bill Burgess	(1)	1969
Paul Charlton	(17+1)	1970-74
Mike Coulman	(2+1)	1971
George Curran	(6)	1946-48
Eddie Curzon	(1)	1910
Tom Danby	(3)	1950
Colin Dixon	(11+2)	1969-74
Alan Edwards	(7)	1936-37
Jack Feetham	(7)	1932-33
Keith Fielding	(3)	1974-77
Ken Gill	(5+2)	1974-77
Jack Gore	(1)	1926
Chris Hesketh	(21+2)	1970-74
Barney Hudson	(8)	1932-37
Emlyn Jenkins	(9)	1933-37
Jim Lomas	(5)	1908-10
Tom McKinney	(7)	1951-54
Alf Middleton	(1)	1929
Steve Nash	(8)	1977-82
Maurice Richards	(2)	1974
Gus Risman	(17)	1932-46
Jack Spencer	(1)	1907
Johnny Ward	(1)	1970
Silas Warwick	(2)	1907
Billy Watkins	(7)	1933-37
David Watkins	(2+4)	1971-74
Billy Williams	(2)	1929-32
Peter Williams	(1+1)	1989

1995-96 REGISTRATION DATE

Signed	Player	Club From
1.8.95	Hannan, Sheldon	Leigh C.
1.8.95	Kenyon, Neil	Keighley C.
10.8.95	Savelio, Lokeni	New Zealand
22.8.95	Hampson, Steve	Halifax
30.8.95	Knowles, Philip	Wigan
30.8.95	Napolitano, Carlo	Eccles ARL
11.9.95	Sini, Iefata	W. Samoa RU
14.9.95	Edwards, Peter	New Zealand
18.9.95	Rogers, Darren	Dewsbury
24.9.95	Daniel, Paul	Leigh C.
31.10.95	Myers, David	Bradford B.
22.11.95	Hudson, Lee	Leeds
24.11.95	Alker, Malcolm	Wigan St. Patricks ARL
30.11.95	Alexander, Neil	Salford Academy
8.12.95	*Appleby, Craig	Warrington
15.12.95	Davys, Alistair	Australia

Salford skipper David Young, who appeared in all three 1995 Centenary World Cup games for Wales.

SALFORD REDS 1995-96 PLAYERS' SUMMARY

	Date of birth	App	T	G	D	Pts	Previous club	Signed
Blakeley, Steve	17.10.72	17	9	93	0	222	Wigan	19.11.92
Blease, Ian	1.1.65	0+1	0	0	0	0	Folly Lane ARL	13.3.85
Burgess, Andy	1.4.70	0+4	0	0	0	0		1.4.87
Davys, Alistair "Ali"	1.7.70	0+2	1	0	0	4	Australia	11.11.95
Eccles, Cliff	4.9.67	21	7	0	0	28	Rochdale H.	19.8.94
Edwards, Peter	4.7.69	14+1	7	0	0	28	New Zealand	4.7.95
Forber, Paul	29.4.64	18+2	4	0	0	16	St. Helens	11.1.93
Ford, Phil	16.3.61	6	5	0	0	20	Leeds	28.8.92
Gregory, Andy	10.8.61	2+1	0	1	0	2	Leeds	16.11.93
Gregory, Mike	20.5.64	6+1	0	0	0	0	Warrington	2.8.94
Hampson, Steve	14.8.62	20	6	2	7	35	Halifax	22.8.95
Lee, Mark	27.3.68	21	3	0	0	12	St. Helens	8.1.90
Martin, Scott	29.12.74	19+1	5	0	0	20	Leigh	30.3.95
McAvoy, Nathan	31.12.76	21	17	0	0	68	Eccles ARL	8.2.94
Myers, David	31.7.71	2+5	0	0	0	0	Bradford B.	31.10.95
Naylor, Scott	2.2.72	20+1	8	0	0	32	Wigan	30.7.93
Panapa, Sam	14.5.62	20	14	0	0	56	Wigan	8.8.94
Randall, Craig	22.9.72	7+1	4	0	0	16	Leigh Miners ARL	21.5.91
Rogers, Darren	6.5.74	8+6	4	0	0	16	Dewsbury	18.9.95
Savelio, Lokeni	24.11.69	3+10	2	0	0	8	New Zealand	10.8.95
Sini, Iefata "Fata"	24.12.96	9	3	0	0	12	W. Samoa RU	23.8.95
Watson, Ian	27.10.76	5	0	18	4	40	Eccles ARL	11.9.94
Webster, Richard	9.7.68	13+4	7	0	0	28	Swansea RU	29.9.93
Young, David	26.7.67	21	5	0	0	20	Leeds	25.4.91
TOTALS								
24 players			111	114	11	683		

Representative appearances 1995-96
Panapa – Western Samoa (1+1);
Young – Wales (3)

Steve Hampson, who tallied 35 points in 20 Centenary season games for Salford Reds.

Darren Rogers, a September 1995 recruit by Salford Reds from Dewsbury.

101

SALFORD REDS 1995-96 MATCH ANALYSIS

Date	Competition	H/A	Opponents	Rlt	Score	Tries	Goals	Attendance	Referee
23.8.95	FD	A	Whitehaven	W	14-2	Webster, Eccles	Watson (2), A. Gregory	–	–
27.8.95	FD	H	Widnes	W	45-4	McAvoy (2), Randall (2), Eccles, Martin, Young, Webster	Watson (5,dg), Hampson	2886	Oddy
3.9.95	FD	A	Featherstone R.	W	38-16	Hampson (2), McAvoy (2), Eccles, Panapa, Rogers	Watson (4,dg), Hampson (dg)	–	–
10.9.95	FD	H	Batley	W	52-24	Panapa (2), Ford (2), Lee, Hampson, Webster, Eccles, Martin	Watson (7,2dg)	2455	Asquith
17.9.95	FD	A	Huddersfield	W	48-20	McAvoy (2), Panapa (2), Ford, Blakeley, Forber, Naylor	Blakeley (8)	–	–
20.9.95	FD	H	Keighley C.	L	14-22	McAvoy	Blakeley (5)	5194	Lee
24.9.95	FD	A	Rochdale H.	W	32-27	Edwards (2), Panapa, Rogers, Young	Blakeley (6)	–	–
1.10.95	FD	H	Hull	W	38-22	Ford (2), Panapa, Forber, Edwards, Blakeley	Blakeley (7)	2383	Burke
1.11.95	FD	H	Wakefield T.	W	40-12	McAvoy (2), Blakeley (2), Edwards, Panapa	Blakeley (8)	2029	Gilmour
5.11.95	FD	A	Dewsbury	W	23-8	Blakeley (2), Eccles	Blakeley (3), Hampson (1,3dg)	–	–
12.11.95	RT(2)	A	Leeds	L	22-46	Martin, Hampson, Forber, Blakeley	Blakeley (3)	–	–
14.11.95	FD	H	Whitehaven	W	58-18	Webster (3), Hampson (2), Eccles, McAvoy, Panapa, Forber, Sini	Blakeley (9)	1670	Asquith
29.11.95	FD	A	Batley	D	12-12	McAvoy, Panapa	Blakeley (2)	–	–
3.12.95	FD	H	Huddersfield	W	31-12	Sini (2), Lee, Young, McAvoy	Blakeley (5), Hampson (dg)	2044	Cross
10.12.95	FD	A	Keighley C.	W	34-6	Naylor, Lee, Panapa, Webster	Blakeley (8), Hampson (2dg)	–	–
17.12.95	FD	H	Rochdale H.	W	42-4	Naylor (2), Eccles, McAvoy, Randall, Martin, Young	Blakeley (7)	1933	Taberner
1.1.96	FD	H	Featherstone R.	W	24-6	Panapa (3), Naylor	Blakeley (4)	2326	Lee
4.1.96	FD	A	Widnes	L	22-24	Edwards, McAvoy, Randall, Rogers	Blakeley (3)	–	–
7.1.96	FD	A	Hull	W	20-15	Edwards (2), Naylor	Blakeley (4)	–	–
14.1.96	FD	A	Wakefield T.	W	28-6	Blakeley, McAvoy, Naylor, Savelio, Young	Blakeley (4)	–	–
21.1.96	FD	H	Dewsbury	W	46-18	McAvoy (2), Davys, Blakeley, Martin, Naylor, Rogers, Savelio	Blakeley (7)	3182	Lee

Five Salford Reds tries in six Centenary season games for Phil Ford before returning home to South Wales.

Former Swansea RU forward Richard Webster, scorer of seven tries in 17 games for Salford Reds in 1995-96.

SHEFFIELD EAGLES

Ground: Don Valley Stadium
(0114-261-0326)
First Season: 1984-85
Nickname: Eagles
Chairman: Gary Hetherington
Chief Exec: Gary Hetherington
Honours: **Division Two** Champions, 1991-92
Second Division/Divisional Premiership Winners, 1988-89, 1991-92
Yorkshire Cup Beaten finalists, 1992-93

RECORDS

Match

Goals: 12 by Roy Rafferty at Fulham, 21 Sep 1986
Mark Aston v. Keighley C., 25 Apr 1992
Tries: 5 by Daryl Powell at Mansfield M., 2 Jan 1989
Points: 32 by Roy Rafferty at Fulham, 21 Sep 1986

Season

Goals: 148 by Mark Aston, 1988-89
Tries: 30 by Iva Ropati, 1991-92
Points: 307 by Mark Aston, 1988-89

Career

Goals: 649 by Mark Aston, 1986-94 and 1995-
Tries: 114 by Daryl Powell, 1984-95
Points: 1,426 by Mark Aston, 1986-94 and 1995-
Appearances: 313+30 by Mark Gamson, 1984-
Highest score: 80-8 v. Wigan St. Patricks, 13 Nov 1988
Highest against: 80-2 v. Australia, 26 Oct 1994
Attendance: 7,984 v. Wakefield T. (Div. 1), 26 Sep 1990 — at Don Valley
8,636 v. Widnes (Div. 1), 8 Oct 1989 — at Bramall Lane, Sheffield U. FC

COACHING REGISTER

● **Since formation in 1984**

Alan Rhodes	Apr 84 - May 86
Gary Hetherington	July 86 - Apr 93
Bill Gardner	May 93 - Dec 93
Gary Hetherington	Dec 93 -

GREAT BRITAIN REGISTER

(3 players)

Mark Aston	(+1)	1991
Lee Jackson	(6)	1993-94
Daryl Powell	(19+9)	1990-94

1995-96 REGISTRATION DATE

Signed	Player	Club From
13.6.95	I'anson, Lee	–
20.6.95	Whakarau, Sonny	–
10.7.95	Hay, Andy	Castleford
13.7.95	Vincent, Jerome	France
22.8.95	*Hughes, Darren	Featherstone R.
1.9.95	Lawless, John	Halifax
1.9.95	*Lyon, David	St. Helens
6.9.95	Banquet, Frederic	Featherstone R.
20.9.95	Aston, Mark	Featherstone R.
26.9.95	McAllister, Daniel	Australia
10.10.95	Kaunaivalu, Malakai "Yasa, Malakai"	Fiji
10.10.95	Sovatabua, Waisale	Fiji
26.10.95	Garcia, Jean-Marc	France
30.10.95	Dakuitoga, Josaia	Australia
30.10.95	Dixon, Paul	Bradford B.

Paul Dixon, an October 1995 signing by Sheffield Eagles from Bradford Bulls.

103

SHEFFIELD EAGLES 1995-96 PLAYERS' SUMMARY

	Date of birth	App	T	G	D	Pts	Previous club	Signed
Armswood, Richard	20.1.75	0+1	0	0	0	0		20.12.93
Aston, Mark	27.9.67	8	1	25	2	56	Featherstone R.	20.9.95
Banquet, Frederic	24.3.76	5+1	1	13	0	30	Featherstone R.	6.9.95
Broadbent, Paul	24.5.68	16+3	1	0	0	4	Lock Lane ARL	26.10.87
Brier, Ben	6.10.70	0+1	0	0	0	0	Leicester RU	21.4.94
Carr, Paul	13.5.67	16+2	10	0	0	40	Hunslet	1.7.92
Chapman, Richard	5.9.75	1+1	0	0	0	0	Dewsbury Moor ARL	27.6.93
Cook, Michael	1.8.61	10+3	0	0	0	0	Hunslet Jnrs. ARL	28.2.87
Crowther, Matthew	6.5.74	1+2	0	0	0	0	Kippax ARL	11.9.91
Dakuitoga, Josaia "Joe"	25.9.65	9	1	0	0	4	Australia	10.10.95
Dixon, Paul	28.10.62	3+7	2	0	0	8	Bradford B.	30.10.95
Farrell, Anthony	17.1.69	7+2	2	0	0	8	Huddersfield	1.11.89
Gamson, Mark	17.8.65	13+4	1	0	0	4	Crigglestone ARL	27.7.84
Garcia, Jean-Marc	22.4.71	11	4	0	0	16	France	26.10.95
Glancy, John	14.4.62	4+3	0	0	0	0	Wakefield T.	25.7.94
Hay, Andy	5.11.73	14+2	6	0	0	24	Castleford	10.7.95
Hughes, Darren	19.6.74	5+1	3	0	0	12	Featherstone R.	22.8.95
Hughes, Ian	13.3.72	15+4	6	0	0	24	East Leeds ARL	1.7.91
Jackson, Lee	12.3.69	3	1	0	0	4	Hull	17.9.93
Laughton, Dale	10.10.70	1	0	0	0	0	Dodworth ARL	3.9.89
Lawford, Dean	9.5.77	11+3	1	2	1	9	Dewsbury Moor ARL	22.5.94
Lawless, Johnny	3.11.74	16+4	8	0	0	32	Halifax	1.9.95
Lyon, David	3.9.65	3+1	0	0	0	0	St. Helens	1.9.95
McAllister, Danny	21.12.74	10+2	1	0	0	4	Australia	26.9.95
Mycoe, David	1.5.72	9+2	1	31	1	67	Crigglestone ARL	31.7.89
Picksley, Richard	29.12.70	2	0	0	0	0	Lock Lane ARL	31.7.89
Price, Richard	26.6.70	9+8	4	0	0	16	Hull	19.3.91
Randall, Carl	22.12.71	1	0	0	0	0	Dodworth ARL	20.8.92
Senior, Keith	24.4.76	8+3	3	0	0	12	Sheffield E. Academy	1.9.94
Sheridan, Ryan	24.5.75	11+1	5	0	0	20	Dewsbury Moor ARL	10.7.91
Sodje, Bright	21.4.66	20	10	0	0	40	Hull K.R.	6.8.94
Sovatabua, Waisale	26.6.73	2+3	2	0	0	8	Fiji	10.10.95
Stott, Lynton	9.5.71	16+1	8	0	0	32	Halifax	19.12.92
Summerill, Darren	26.4.73	1	0	0	0	0	Rossington ARL	8.11.93
Turner, Darren	13.10.73	5+2	0	0	0	0	Leeds Academy	1.1.92
Vincent, Jerome		0+1	0	0	0	0	France	
Whakarau, Sonny	13.1.66	3+5	2	0	0	8	Doncaster	20.6.95
Yasa, Malakai Kaunaivalu	31.5.69	2+3	0	0	0	0	Fiji	10.10.95
Young, Andy	4.8.66	2+3	0	0	0	0	Eastmoor ARL	18.11.87
TOTALS								
39 players			84	71	4	482		

Representative appearances 1995-96
Banquet – France (2,2g);
Broadbent – England (1+1,2t);
Jackson – England (4).

SHEFFIELD EAGLES 1995-96 MATCH ANALYSIS

Date	Competition	H/A	Opponents	Rlt	Score	Tries	Goals	Attendance	Referee
20.8.95	SBC	H	Leeds	L	6-34	Price	Mycoe	4234	Bates
23.8.95	SBC	A	Wigan	L	20-52	Carr, Sheridan, Whakarau	Mycoe (4)	–	–
27.8.95	SBC	A	Workington T.	L	20-26	Mycoe, Sheridan, Broadbent, D. Hughes	Mycoe (2)	–	–
3.9.95	SBC	H	Castleford	W	36-26	Price (2), Carr, D. Hughes, I. Hughes, Jackson, Sodje	Banquet (4)	2504	Morris
8.9.95	SBC	H	Warrington	L	24-38	Banquet, Sodje, D. Hughes, Whakarau	Banquet (4)	4160	Campbell
13.9.95	SBC	A	St. Helens	L	20-62	Sodje, Lawford, Lawless	Banquet (4)	–	–
17.9.95	SBC	A	Halifax	L	6-28	Stott	Banquet	–	–
24.9.95	SBC	H	London B.	L	10-42	Sheridan	Aston (3)	3717	Smith
1.10.95	SBC	A	Bradford B.	L	18-34	Carr (2), Sodje, Senior	Aston	–	–
5.11.95	SBC	H	Oldham B.	W	36-18	Lawless (2), Hay (2), Senior, I. Hughes	Aston (6)	3987	Presley
12.11.95	RT(2)	A	Bradford B.	L	0-22	–	–	–	–
19.11.95	SBC	A	Leeds	W	27-22	Hay (2), Lawless, Dixon, Farrell	Aston (3,dg)	–	–
29.11.95	SBC	H	St. Helens	W	32-18	Carr (2), Stott, Farrell, Gamson	Aston (6)	1743	Morris
3.12.95	SBC	A	Warrington	W	33-8	Stott (2), Sodje, Aston, Sovatabua	Aston (6,dg)	–	–
8.12.95	SBC	H	Workington T.	W	34-8	Carr (2), Stott, Hay, Dakuitoga, Garcia	Mycoe (5)	2032	Campbell
17.12.95	SBC	A	London B.	W	21-14	Carr (2), I. Hughes (2)	Mycoe (2), Lawford (dg)	–	–
20.12.95	SBC	H	Halifax	W	38-14	Sodje (2), Lawless, Stott, Price, Garcia, Sovatabua	Mycoe (5)	1594	Kirkpatrick
1.1.96	SBC	A	Castleford	W	42-12	Lawless (2), Sodje (2), Garcia, Hay, McAllister, Stott	Mycoe (5)	–	–
5.1.96	SBC	H	Bradford B.	W	19-10	Dixon, I. Hughes, Sodje	Mycoe (3, dg))	2451	J. Connolly
19.1.96	SBC	H	Wigan	L	24-36	Sheridan (2), Stott, Lawless,	Mycoe (4)	4639	Cummings
21.1.96	SBC	A	Oldham B.	L	16-26	I. Hughes, Garcia, Senior	Lawford (2)	–	–

Nine 1995-96 appearances for Sheffield Eagles' loose forward Anthony Farrell.

One try in three Sheffield Centenary season games by hooker Lee Jackson.

105

SWINTON

Ground: Gigg Lane, Bury (0161-761-2328)
First Season: 1896-97
Nickname: Lions
Chairman: Malcolm White
General
  Manager: Tony Barrow
Honours: **Championship** Winners, 1926-27,
                1927-28, 1930-31, 1934-35
                Beaten finalists, 1924-25, 1932-33
                War Emergency League Beaten
                finalists, 1939-40
                Division One Champions, 1962-63,
                1963-64
                Division Two Champions, 1984-85
                Challenge Cup Winners,
                1899-1900, 1925-26, 1927-28
                Beaten finalists, 1926-27, 1931-32
                Second Division Premiership
                Winners, 1986-87
                Beaten finalists, 1988-89
                Lancashire Cup Winners, 1925-26,
                1927-28, 1939-40, 1969-70
                Beaten finalists, 1910-11, 1923-24,
                1931-32, 1960-61, 1961-62, 1962-63,
                1964-65, 1972-73
                Lancashire League Winners,
                1924-25, 1927-28, 1928-29, 1930-31,
                1960-61
                Lancashire War League Winners,
                1939-40
                Western Division Championship
                Beaten finalists, 1963-64
                BBC2 Floodlit Trophy Beaten
                finalists, 1966-67

RECORDS
Match
Goals: 12 by Ken Gowers v. Liverpool C.,
          3 Oct 1959
Tries: 5 by Morgan Bevan v. Morecambe,
          10 Sep 1898
          Billy Wallwork v. Widnes,
          15 Dec 1900
          Jack Evans v. Bradford N.,
          30 Sep 1922

Hector Halsall v. St. Helens,
24 Jan 1925
Dick Cracknell v. Whitehaven Rec.,
11 Feb 1928
Randall Lewis v. Keighley,
12 Jan 1946
John Stopford v. Bramley,
22 Dec 1962
Alan Buckley v. Salford, 8 Apr 1964
Joe Ropati v. Nottingham C.,
21 Jan 1990
Points: 29 by Bernard McMahon v. Dewsbury,
          15 Aug 1959

Season
Goals: 128 by Albert Blan, 1960-61
Tries: 42 by John Stopford, 1963-64
Points: 283 by Albert Blan, 1960-61

Career
Goals: 970 by Ken Gowers, 1954-73
Tries: 197 by Frank Evans, 1921-31
Points: 2,105 by Ken Gowers, 1954-73
Appearances: 593+8 by Ken Gowers, 1954-73
Highest score: 76-4 v. Pontefract, 8 Sep 1906
Highest against: 78-0 v. Wigan, 29 Sep 1992
Attendance: 26,891 v. Wigan (RL Cup),
          12 Feb 1964 (at Station Road)
          3,501 v. Wigan (Lancs Cup),
          29 Sep 1992 (at Gigg Lane)

COACHING REGISTER
● **Since 1974-75**

Austin Rhodes	June 74 - Nov 75
Bob Fleet	Nov 75 - Nov 76
John Stopford	Nov 76 - Apr 77
Terry Gorman	June 77 - Nov 78
Ken Halliwell	Nov 78 - Dec 79
Frank Myler	Jan 80 - May 81
Tom Grainey	May 81 - Oct 83
Jim Crellin	Nov 83 - May 86
Bill Holliday } Mike Peers }	June 86 - Oct 87
Frank Barrow	Oct 87 - June 89
Jim Crellin	July 89 - July 91
Chris O'Sullivan	July 91 - Dec 91
Tony Barrow	Jan 92 - Jan 96
Peter Roe	Jan 96 -

GREAT BRITAIN REGISTER
(15 players)

Tom Armitt	(8)	1933-37
Alan Buckley	(7)	1963-66
Fred Butters	(2)	1929
Billy Davies	(1)	1968
Bryn Evans	(10)	1926-33
Frank Evans	(4)	1924
Jack Evans	(3)	1926
Ken Gowers	(14)	1962-66
Hector Halsall	(1)	1929
Martin Hodgson	(16)	1929-37
Ron Morgan	(2)	1963
Billo Rees	(11)	1926-29
Dave Robinson	(12)	1965-67
John Stopford	(12)	1961-66
Joe Wright	(1)	1932

1995-96 REGISTRATION DATE

Signed	Player	Club From
12.6.95	Cannon, Peter	St. Helens
12.6.95	Roach, Jason	St. Helens
28.6.95	Birkett, Martin	Salford
25.7.95	Diamond, Chris	Blackbrook ARL
1.8.95	Stott, Roy	Blackbrook ARL
4.8.95	Holliday, Les	Dewsbury
9.8.95	Moran, Shaun	Wigan
16.8.95	Prior, James	Orrell St. James ARL
24.8.95	Sheals, Mark	Wakefield T.
30.8.95	Bibey, Barry	–
30.8.95	Else, Wesley	–
30.8.95	Flynn, Christian	–
30.8.95	McComas, David	–
30.8.95	Nicholson, Ken	–
12.9.95	*Fox, Kevin	Carlisle
13.11.95	Bolton, Mark	Swinton Academy
13.11.95	Myers, David	Swinton Academy
12.12.95	Twist, Michael	Oldham
20.12.95	Edwards, Mike	Oldham B.
5.1.96	Flannery, Danny	–

Peter Roe, appointed coach of Swinton in January 1996.

Swinton prop forward Mark Sheals, an August 1995 recruit from Wakefield Trinity.

SWINTON 1995-96 PLAYERS' SUMMARY

	Date of birth	App	T	G	D	Pts	Previous club	Signed
Ashcroft, Simon	27.6.70	22	20	0	0	80	Highfield	3.6.92
Barrow, Paul	20.10.74	16	9	0	0	36		15.3.93
Barrow, Tony	19.10.71	13+1	0	0	0	0	Oldham	6.2.92
Birkett, Martin	16.9.65	16+1	6	41	0	106	Salford R.	28.6.95
Bolton, Mark	12.8.77	1	1		0	4	Swinton Academy	13.11.95
Cannon, Peter	22.3.74	12	3	0	1	13	St. Helens	12.6.95
Chrimes, David	16.12.69	15+5	4	0	0	16	Oldham	13.1.95
Connor, Ian	21.3.70	11+6	4	0	0	16	St. Helens	22.1.95
Earner, Adrian	19.11.66	6+4	0	0	0	0	Leigh	3.11.92
Edwards, Mike	14.4.74	2+1	1	0	0	4	Oldham B.	20.12.95
Else, Wesley	27.5.77	1	1	3	0	10		30.8.95
Errington, Craig	17.8.72	2	1	0	0	4	Folly Lane ARL	8.9.92
Evans, Jim	14.6.72	9+1	5	4	0	28	Folly Lane ARL	17.5.94
Fox, Kevin	16.2.69	5	0	0	0	0	Carlisle	12.9.95
Gunning, John	30.3.69	19+1	3	19	0	50	Leigh	31.3.95
Hartill, David	19.4.74	1	0	0	0	0	Warrington	24.11.93
Holliday, Les	8.8.62	21	5	4	2	30	Dewsbury	4.8.95
Humphries, Tony	3.9.63	15+2	2	0	0	8	Rochdale H.	25.3.93
Liava, Talite	18.7.71	1	0	0	0	0		
Marsh, David	8.10.68	0+2	0	0	0	0	Widnes	20.5.93
McCabe, Carl	10.8.76	11	1	0	0	4	Nutgrove ARL	20.6.94
Moran, Shaune	15.9.73	0+2	0	0	0	0	Wigan	9.8.95
Price-Jones, Gavin	19.12.70	19	9	0	0	36	Australia	25.8.94
Roach, Jason	2.5.71	21	17	0	0	68	St. Helens	12.6.95
Sheals, Mark	26.11.66	10+2	1	0	0	4	Wakefield T.	24.8.95
Skeech, Ian	4.2.67	2+4	2	0	0	8	Newton-le-Willows RU	24.11.87
Tanner, David	29.9.65	12+9	5	5	0	30	Leigh	20.1.95
Welsby, Mark	7.7.70	22	7	0	0	28	Wigan	5.6.92
Wolfgramm, Willie	20.9.79	1	0	0	0	0		
TOTALS			107	76	3	583		
29 players								

SWINTON 1995-96 MATCH ANALYSIS

Date	Com-petition	H/A	Opponents	Rlt	Score	Tries	Goals	Atten-dance	Referee
20.8.95	SD	A	Bramley	W	30-16	P. Barrow (2), Ashcroft, McCabe, Tanner	Birkett (5)	–	–
27.8.95	SD	A	Leigh C.	L	18-28	Roach (2), Birkett	Birkett (3)	–	–
30.8.95	SD	H	Barrow B.	W	42-8	Ashcroft (2), Price-Jones (2), Welsby (2), Cannon, Roach	Birkett (4), Holliday	442	Burke
3.9.95	SD	H	York	W	18-10	P. Barrow, Roach, Ashcroft, Birkett	Birkett	714	Presley
10.9.95	SD	A	Highfield	W	66-2	Connor (3), Price-Jones (3), Chrimes (2), Roach (2), Ashcroft (2), P. Barrow, Welsby	Birkett (4), Tanner	–	–
13.9.95	SD	H	Doncaster D.	W	58-0	Ashcroft (3), P. Barrow (3), Tanner, Price-Jones, Chrimes, Gunning, Birkett	Birkett (7)	790	Gilmour
17.9.95	SD	H	Hunslet H.	W	30-11	Price-Jones (2), Welsby (2), Cannon	Birkett (4), Cannon (dg), Holliday (dg)	895	Redfearn
24.9.95	SD	H	Hull K.R.	L	15-22	Holliday, Errington, Ashcroft	Birkett, Holliday (dg)	1221	Taberner
1.10.95	RT(1)	H	West Hull	W	44-20	Humphries (2), Ashcroft (2), P. Barrow, Birkett, Roach, Connor	Birkett (6)	500	Nicholson
5.11.95	SD	A	Carlisle	L	16-34	Cannon, Holliday, Ashcroft	Birkett (2)	–	–
12.11.95	RT(2)	A	Halifax	L	18-20	Evans (2), Tanner	Birkett (3)	–	–
15.11.95	SD	A	Barrow B.	W	6-3	Ashcroft	Birkett	–	–
19.11.95	SD	H	Highfield	W	52-8	Roach (3), Ashcroft (3), Tanner, Price-Jones, Welsby, Evans	Tanner (4), Gunning (2)	510	Nicholson
26.11.95	SD	H	Chorley	W	18-16	Holliday, Ashcroft, Else	Else (3)	677	Oddy
29.11.95	SD	H	Bramley	W	28-7	Birkett (2), P. Barrow, Roach, Holliday	Gunning (4)	627	Cross
3.12.95	SD	A	Doncaster D.	W	34-12	Gunning (2), Ashcroft, Tanner, Roach, Chrimes	Gunning (5)	–	–
10.12.95	SD	A	Hunslet H.	L	10-20	Roach, Ashcroft	Gunning	–	–
13.12.95	SD	A	Chorley	W	18-16	Roach (2), Skeech	Gunning (3)	–	–
17.12.95	SD	A	Hull K.R.	L	10-42	Evans, Skeech	Gunning	–	–
3.1.96	SD	H	Leigh C.	L	8-18	Roach	Gunning (2)	935	Gilmour
10.1.96	SD	A	York	L	20-36	Holliday, Roach, Sheals	Holliday (3), Gunning	–	–
21.1.96	SD	H	Carlisle	W	24-22	Bolton, Edwards, Evans, Welsby	Evans (4)	759	Asquith

WAKEFIELD TRINITY

Ground: Belle Vue (01924-372445)
First Season: 1895-96
Nickname: Dreadnoughts
Chairman: Ted Richardson
Chief Exec: Peter Tunks
Honours: **Championship** Winners, 1966-67,
               1967-68
               Beaten finalists, 1959-60, 1961-62
               Division Two Champions, 1903-04
               Challenge Cup Winners, 1908-09,
               1945-46, 1959-60, 1961-62, 1962-63
               Beaten finalists, 1913-14, 1967-68,
               1978-79
               Regal Trophy Beaten finalists,
               1971-72
               Yorkshire Cup Winners, 1910-11,
               1924-25, 1946-47, 1947-48, 1951-52,
               1956-57, 1960-61, 1961-62, 1964-65,
               1992-93
               Beaten finalists, 1926-27, 1932-33,
               1934-35, 1936-37, 1939-40, 1945-46,
               1958-59, 1973-74, 1974-75, 1990-91
               Yorkshire League Winners,
               1909-10, 1910-11, 1945-46, 1958-59,
               1959-60, 1961-62, 1965-66

RECORDS
Match
Goals: 13 by Mark Conway v. Highfield,
          27 Oct 1992
Tries: 7 by Fred Smith v. Keighley,
          25 Apr 1959
          Keith Slater v. Hunslet, 6 Feb 1971
Points: 34 by Mark Conway v. Highfield,
          27 Oct 1992

Season
Goals: 163 by Neil Fox, 1961-62
Tries: 38 by Fred Smith, 1959-60
          David Smith, 1973-74
Points: 407 by Neil Fox, 1961-62

Career
Goals: 1,836 by Neil Fox, 1956-69 & 1970-74
Tries: 272 by Neil Fox, 1956-69 & 1970-74
Points: 4,488 by Neil Fox, 1956-69 & 1970-74
Appearances: 605 by Harry Wilkinson, 1930-49
Highest score: 90-12 v. Highfield, 27 Oct 1992
Highest against: 86-0 at Castleford, 17 Apr 1995
Attendance: 37,906 Leeds v. Huddersfield
          (RL Cup SF), 21 Mar 1936
          Home Match: 30,676 v.
          Huddersfield (RL Cup),
          26 Feb 1921

Mark Conway, holder of the Wakefield Trinity records for most goals and points in a match.

COACHING REGISTER
● **Since 1974-75**

Peter Fox	June 74 - May 76
Geoff Gunney	June 76 - Nov 76
Brian Lockwood	Nov 76 - Jan 78
Ian Brooke	Jan 78 - Jan 79
Bill Kirkbride	Jan 79 - Apr 80
Ray Batten	Apr 80 - May 81
Bill Ashurst	June 81 - Apr 82
Ray Batten	May 82 - July 83
Derek Turner	July 83 - Feb 84
Bob Haigh	Feb 84 - May 84
Geoff Wraith	May 84 - Oct 84
David Lamming	Oct 84 - Apr 85
Len Casey	Apr 85 - June 86
Tony Dean	June 86 - Dec 86
Trevor Bailey	Dec 86 - Apr 87
David Topliss	May 87 - Apr 94
David Hobbs	May 94 - Jan 95
Paul Harkin/	
Andy Kelly	Jan 95 -

GREAT BRITAIN REGISTER
(24 players)

Ian Brooke	(8)	1967-68
Neil Fox	(29)	1959-69
Bob Haigh	(2)	1968-70
Bill Horton	(14)	1928-33
Michael Jackson	(2+2)	1991-92
David Jeanes	(5)	1971-72
Berwyn Jones	(3)	1964-66
Herbert Kershaw	(2)	1910
Frank Mortimer	(2)	1956
Harry Murphy	(1)	1950
Tommy Newbould	(1)	1910
Jonty Parkin	(17)	1920-29
Charlie Pollard	(1)	1924
Ernest Pollard	(2)	1932
Harold Poynton	(3)	1962
Gary Price	(+1)	1991
Don Robinson	(5)	1954-55
Gerry Round	(8)	1959-62
Trevor Skerrett	(4)	1979
Stanley Smith	(1)	1929
David Topliss	(3)	1973-79
Derek Turner	(13)	1959-62
Don Vines	(3)	1959
Jack Wilkinson	(7)	1959-62

1995-96 REGISTRATION DATE

Signed	Player	Club From
25.7.95	Kuiti, Mike	Oldham
25.7.95	Wray, Jon	Castleford
15.8.95	Eaton, Barry	Doncaster
17.8.95	Vasey, Chris	–
6.9.95	Georgallis, Steve	Australia
6.9.95	*Hellewell, Phil	Huddersfield
8.9.95	*Heugh, Cavill	London B.
18.9.95	Davis, Brad	York
26.10.95	Grigg, Carl	Australia
8.11.95	Leeds, Andrew	Australia
14.11.95	*Summerill, Darren	Sheffield E.
14.11.95	*Whakarau, Sonny	Sheffield E.
17.11.95	*Banquet, Frederic	Sheffield E.
9.1.96	*Longstaff, Jason	Hunslet H.

Bob Haigh, capped twice for Great Britain while serving Wakefield Trinity.

WAKEFIELD TRINITY 1995-96 PLAYERS' SUMMARY

	Date of birth	App	T	G	D	Pts	Previous club	Signed
Allen, Kieran	21.11.75	5+3	2	1	0	10	Wakefield Academy	21.11.92
Banquet, Frederic	24.3.76	7+1	9	3	0	42	Sheffield E.	17.11.95
Barnard, Marcus	7.10.70	2	0	0	0	0		
Bastow, Andy	25.5.78	0+1	0	0	0	0		
Bell, Nigel	4.11.62	16	0	0	0	0	Eastmoor ARL	1.9.83
Brown, Paul	20.1.70	8	2	0	0	8	Walnut W. ARL	1.10.93
Child, Lee	28.9.74	2	0	0	0	0	Leeds	10.9.93
Clarkson, Michael	13.9.74	16+2	4	0	0	16	Stanley Rangers ARL	13.9.91
Conway, Billy	31.1.67	19	2	0	0	8	Wakefield Colts	30.8.84
Davis, Brad	13.3.68	7+1	4	1	0	18	York	18.9.95
Eaton, Barry	30.9.73	12+1	3	24	1	61	Doncaster	15.8.95
Flynn, Wayne	19.11.76	20+1	7	0	0	28	Dewsbury Moor ARL	14.7.93
Georgallis, Steve	17.6.68	17	5	0	0	20	Australia	31.8.95
Grigg, Carl	21.9.70	12	7	0	0	28	Australia	26.10.95
Hanlan, Lee	6.10.71	3	0	0	1	1	Batley	2.8.93
Hellewell, Phil	23.4.67	3+1	1	0	0	4	Huddersfield	6.9.95
Heugh, Cavill	31.8.62	4	1	0	0	4	London B.	8.8.95
Hicks, Paul	22.6.77	1+3	0	0	0	0	Normanton ARL	8.9.94
Hicks, Simon	30.8.73	3+2	0	0	0	0	Stanley Rangers ARL	13.5.92
Hirst, John	18.12.70	6+2	0	0	0	0	Stanley Rangers ARL	15.8.89
Knighton, Adam	18.9.73	10+1	5	0	0	20	Crigglestone ARL	8.4.92
Kuiti, Mike	18.3.63	19	2	0	0	8	Oldham	25.7.95
Leeds, Andrew	19.9.64	8	4	16	0	48	Australia	8.11.95
Luxford, Martin	5.3.77	1	0	0	0	0		
Marlow, Ian	18.1.63	8+5	1	0	0	4	Hull	3.9.93
McDonald, Wayne	3.9.75	11+3	3	0	0	12		10.5.93
McGowan, Steve	25.2.64	3	0	0	0	0	Bradford N.	24.11.94
Mosley, James	30.9.74	9+2	0	0	0	0	Moldgreen ARL	24.1.92
Mumby, Keith	21.2.57	1+2	0	0	0	0		
Slater, Richard	29.8.70	6	3	0	0	12	Normanton ARL	4.8.88
Stephenson, Francis	20.1.76	1	0	0	0	0	Dewsbury Moor ARL	14.7.93
Summerill, Darren	26.4.73	3+2	0	0	0	0	Sheffield E.	14.11.95
Thompson, John	3.5.59	1+3	0	0	0	0	Eastmoor ARL	1.7.78
Vasey, Chris	28.2.63	3+1	0	0	0	0		17.8.95
Whakarau, Sonny	13.1.66	10	1	0	0	4	Sheffield E.	14.11.95
Wilson, Andy	5.10.63	1	0	0	0	0	Queens Park ARL	8.11.88
Wray, Jon	19.5.70	15	1	0	0	4	Castleford	25.7.95
TOTALS 37 players			67	45	2	360		

112

WAKEFIELD TRINITY 1995-96 MATCH ANALYSIS

Date	Com-petition	H/A	Opponents	Rlt	Score	Tries	Goals	Atten-dance	Referee
20.8.95	FD	H	Whitehaven	L	14-44	Conway, Wray, Brown	Eaton	1732	Burke
23.8.95	FD	A	Widnes	L	10-24	Marlow	Eaton (3)	–	–
27.8.95	FD	H	Featherstone R.	L	19-28	Flynn, Slater, Eaton	Eaton (3,dg)	2402	Atkin
3.9.95	FD	A	Batley	L	11-18	Eaton	Eaton (3), Hanlan (dg)	–	–
10.9.95	FD	H	Huddersfield	W	26-22	Slater (2), Georgallis, Heugh, Knighton	Eaton (3)	1719	Presley
17.9.95	FD	A	Keighley C.	L	8-30	Flynn (2)	–	–	–
20.9.95	FD	H	Rochdale H.	W	28-6	Knighton (2), Georgallis (2), Flynn	Eaton (4)	1180	Cross
24.9.95	FD	A	Hull	L	8-56	Clarkson	Eaton (2)	–	–
1.10.95	FD	H	Dewsbury	W	34-24	Kuiti (2), Clarkson, Davis, Hellewell, Brown, Eaton	Eaton (3)	1835	Gilmour
1.11.95	FD	A	Salford R.	L	12-40	Knighton, Grigg	Leeds (2)	–	–
12.11.95	RT(2)	A	Batley	L	14-21	Flynn, Grigg	Leeds (3)	–	–
15.11.95	FD	H	Widnes	W	12-10	Clarkson, Grigg	Leeds (2)	1166	Smith
19.11.95	FD	A	Whitehaven	L	12-18	Leeds (2)	Eaton (2)	–	–
29.11.95	FD	A	Huddersfield	W	22-14	Banquet (2), Whakarau, Leeds, Grigg	Leeds	–	–
3.12.95	FD	H	Keighley C.	W	16-4	Banquet (2), Flynn	Leeds (2)	2203	Nicholson
13.12.95	FD	A	Rochdale H.	W	30-16	Banquet (4), McDonald, Grigg	Leeds (3)	–	–
17.12.95	FD	H	Hull	W	34-4	Leeds, Grigg, Flynn, Clarkson, Davis, Banquet, McDonald	Leeds (3)	1823	Ganson
4.1.96	FD	A	Featherstone R.	L	4-8	Knighton	–	–	–
7.1.96	FD	A	Dewsbury	W	16-14	Allen (2), Conway, Davis	–	–	–
10.1.96	FD	H	Batley	W	24-14	Davis, Georgallis, Grigg, McDonald	Banquet (3), Davis	1725	Gilmour
14.1.96	FD	H	Salford R.	L	6-28	Georgallis	Allen	2463	Gilmour

Wakefield Trinity utility forward Nigel Bell, who appeared 16 times in the 1995-96 season

Welsh International Ian Marlow, who figured in 13 Centenary season games.

WARRINGTON

Ground: Wilderspool (01925-35338)
First Season: 1895-96
Nickname: Wire
Chairman: Peter Higham
Chief Exec: Graham Armstrong
Honours: **Championship** Winners, 1947-48,
1953-54, 1954-55
Beaten finalists, 1925-26, 1934-35,
1936-37, 1948-49, 1950-51, 1960-61
League Leaders Trophy Winners,
1972-73
Club Championship (Merit Table)
Winners, 1973-74
Challenge Cup Winners, 1904-05,
1906-07, 1949-50, 1953-54, 1973-74
Beaten finalists, 1900-01, 1903-04,
1912-13, 1927-28, 1932-33, 1935-36,
1974-75, 1989-90
Regal Trophy Winners, 1973-74,
1977-78, 1980-81, 1990-91
Beaten finalists, 1978-79, 1986-87,
1994-95
Premiership Trophy Winners,
1985-86
Beaten finalists, 1976-77, 1986-87
Lancashire Cup Winners, 1921-22,
1929-30, 1932-33, 1937-38, 1959-60,
1965-66, 1980-81, 1982-83, 1989-90
Beaten finalists, 1906-07, 1948-49,
1950-51, 1967-68, 1985-86, 1987-88
Lancashire League Winners,
1937-38, 1947-48, 1948-49, 1950-51,
1953-54, 1954-55, 1955-56, 1967-68
BBC2 Floodlit Trophy Beaten
finalists, 1974-75
Captain Morgan Trophy Winners,
1973-74

RECORDS
Match
Goals: 14 by Harold Palin v. Liverpool C.,
13 Sep 1950
Tries: 7 by Brian Bevan v. Leigh, 29 Mar 1948
Brian Bevan v. Bramley,
22 Apr 1953
Points: 33 by George Thomas v. St. Helens,
12 Apr 1909

Season
Goals: 170 by Steve Hesford, 1978-79
Tries: 66 by Brian Bevan, 1952-53
Points: 363 by Harry Bath, 1952-53

Career
Goals: 1,159 by Steve Hesford, 1975-85
Tries: 740 by Brian Bevan, 1945-62
Points: 2,416 by Steve Hesford, 1975-85
Appearances: 620 by Brian Bevan, 1945-62
Highest score: 78-6 v. St. Helens, 12 Apr 1909
Highest against: 80-0 at St. Helens, 4 Jan 1996
Attendance: 34,304 v. Wigan (League),
22 Jan 1949

COACHING REGISTER
● **Since 1974-75**
Alex Murphy   May 71 - May 78
Billy Benyon   June 78 - Mar 82
Kevin Ashcroft   Mar 82 - May 84
Reg Bowden   June 84 - Mar 86
Tony Barrow   Mar 86 - Nov 88
Brian Johnson   Nov 88 - Jan 96
John Dorahy   Jan 96 -

Kevin Ashcroft, coach of Warrington for two years from March 1982.

GREAT BRITAIN REGISTER
(46 players)

Player		Years
Jack Arkwright	(6)	1936-37
Kevin Ashcroft	(+1)	1974
Willie Aspinall	(1)	1966
Allan Bateman	(1+2)	1992-94
Billy Belshaw	(2)	1937
Nat Bentham	(2)	1929
John Bevan	(6)	1974-78
Tom Blinkhorn	(1)	1929
Ernie Brooks	(3)	1908
Jim Challinor	(3)	1958-60
Neil Courtney	(+1)	1982
Billy Cunliffe	(11)	1920-26
Jonathan Davies	(4)	1993-94
George Dickenson	(1)	1908
Billy Dingsdale	(3)	1929-33
Des Drummond	(2)	1987-88
Ronnie Duane	(3)	1983-84
Bob Eccles	(1)	1982
Kevin Ellis	(+1)	1991
Jim Featherstone	(6)	1948-52
Mark Forster	(2)	1987
Eric Fraser	(16)	1958-61
Laurie Gilfedder	(5)	1962-63
Bobby Greenough	(1)	1960
Andy Gregory	(1)	1986
Mike Gregory	(19+1)	1987-90
Gerry Helme	(12)	1948-54
Keith Holden	(1)	1963
Albert Johnson	(6)	1946-47
Ken Kelly	(2)	1980-82
Tom McKinney	(3)	1955
Joe Miller	(6)	1933-36
Alex Murphy	(1)	1971
Albert Naughton	(2)	1954
Terry O'Grady	(1)	1961
Harold Palin	(2)	1947
Ken Parr	(1)	1968
Albert Pimblett	(3)	1948
Ray Price	(9)	1954-57
Bob Ryan	(5)	1950-52
Ron Ryder	(1)	1952
Frank Shugars	(1)	1910
George Skelhorne	(7)	1920-21
George Thomas	(1)	1907
Derek Whitehead	(3)	1971
John Woods	(+1)	1987

1995-96 REGISTRATION DATE

Signed	Player	Club From
3.7.95	Jones, Mark	Hull
24.7.95	Arnold, Stephen	Woolston R. ARL
4.8.95	Currier, Andy	Featherstone R.
16.8.95	Wingfield, Paul	–
31.8.95	Davies, Gareth	St. John Moores Univ.
14.9.95	Ford, Mike	Australia
17.9.95	Causey, Chris	Orrell St. James ARL
4.10.95	Stephens, Warren	Orrell St. James ARL
27.11.95	Thompson, Manoa	New Zealand
1.12.95	Carney, Martin	Orrell St. James ARL
14.12.95	Barrow, Paul	Swinton
14.12.95	Mafi, Mateaki	Tonga RU
18.12.95	Finau, Salesi	Australia

Scrum half Mike Ford, a September 1995 signing by Warrington from Australian outfit Queensland Crushers.

WARRINGTON 1995-96 PLAYERS' SUMMARY

	Date of birth	App	T	G	D	Pts	Previous club	Signed
Barrow, Paul	20.10.74	2+5	1	0	0	4	Swinton	14.12.95
Bennett, Andrew	23.7.73	4+6	2	0	0	8	Woolston R. ARL	10.8.90
Chambers, Gary	5.1.70	6+10	0	0	0	0	Kells ARL	15.2.88
Close, Graeme	8.5.77	0+3	0	0	0	0	Warrington Academy	8.5.94
Cullen, Paul	4.3.63	19	2	0	0	8	Crosfields ARL	25.11.80
Currier, Andy	8.4.66	15	6	0	0	24	Featherstone R.	4.8.95
Davies, Gareth	7.8.73	8	3	0	0	12	St. John Moores Univ.	31.8.95
Davies, Jonathan	24.10.62	7	4	29	3	77	Widnes	6.7.93
Eckersley, Chris	16.10.74	6+1	4	0	0	16	Warrington Academy	1.6.93
Finau, Salesi	5.5.73	4+1	0	0	0	0	Australia	7.12.95
Ford, Mike	18.11.65	11+2	3	1	1	15	Australia	14.9.95
Forster, Mark	25.11.64	18	10	0	0	40	Woolston R. ARL	27.11.81
Harris, Iestyn	25.6.76	22+1	11	55	2	156	Oldham St. Annes ARL	2.8.93
Hilton, Mark	31.3.75	19+3	1	0	0	4	Warrington Academy	13.8.92
Holden, Chris	5.11.76	0+1	0	0	0	0	Orrell St. James ARL	5.11.93
Hough, John	14.4.76	18	3	0	0	12		2.12.93
Jones, Mark	22.6.65	10+6	0	0	0	0	Hull	3.7.95
Kettlewell, Ronnie	10.10.72	3+1	0	0	0	0		24.5.95
King, David	6.9.67	6+7	1	0	0	4	Huddersfield	
Knott, Ian	2.10.76	7+4	4	1	0	18		10.10.93
Lee, Jason	16.1.71	6	3	0	0	12	Dudley Hill ARL	28.4.94
Mackey, Greg	20.10.61	11+4	2	0	6	14	Hull	18.8.92
Mafi, Mateaki	19.9.72	4+1	0	0	0	0	Tonga	7.12.95
McGuire, Bruce	31.1.62	9	0	0	0	0	Sheffield E.	17.6.94
Penny, Lee	24.9.74	21+3	16	0	0	64	Orrell St. James ARL	15.10.91
Roper, Jonathan	5.5.76	3	1	0	0	4	Hensingham ARL	5.5.93
Rudd, Chris	17.12.69	12+1	5	0	0	20	Kells ARL	15.2.88
Sculthorpe, Paul	22.9.77	16+4	7	0	0	28	Waterhead ARL	4.10.94
Shelford, Kelly	4.5.66	15	4	0	0	16	New Zealand	5.10.91
Sumner, Phil	14.6.71	7+1	0	0	0	0	Wigan St. Patricks ARL	8.7.88
Thompson, Manoa	11.6.68	8+1	2	0	0	8	New Zealand	27.11.95
Thursfield, John	22.10.69	6+4	0	0	0	0	ARL	9.9.86
Wainwright, Mike	25.2.75	9+2	5	0	0	20	Woolston R. ARL	9.5.92
Williams, Gerald	4.12.69	0+1	0	0	0	0		
TOTALS								
34 players			100	86	12	584		

Representative appearances 1995-96
Bateman – Wales (3);
J. Davies – Wales (3,10g,1dg);
Ellis – Wales (3,1t);
Harris – Wales (3,2t,1g,1dg);
Jones – Wales (+2).

WARRINGTON 1995-96 MATCH ANALYSIS

Date	Competition	H/A	Opponents	Rlt	Score	Tries	Goals	Attendance	Referee
20.8.95	SBC	H	London B.	W	46-6	Forster (3), Currier (2), J. Davies (2), Harris	J. Davies (7)	4031	Morris
23.8.95	SBC	A	Bradford B.	L	17-20	Sculthorpe, Wainwright, J. Davies	J. Davies (2,dg)	–	–
27.8.95	SBC	H	Oldham B.	W	40-8	Penny (2), King, Roper, Shelford, Harris, Wainwright	J. Davies (6)	4064	Morris
30.8.95	SBC	A	Leeds	L	6-40	Forster	J. Davies	–	–
3.9.95	SBC	A	Wigan	L	2-44	–	Harris	–	–
8.9.95	SBC	A	Sheffield E.	W	38-24	Lee (2), Mackey, Penny, Wainwright, Hough, Forster	Harris (4), Mackey (2dg)	–	–
15.9.95	SBC	H	Workington T.	L	14-16	Penny, Harris	J. Davies (3)	7714	Morris
20.9.95	SBC	H	St. Helens	W	28-16	Wainwright, Penny, Lee, G. Davies	J. Davies (5,dg), Mackey (dg)	6623	Cummings
24.9.95	SBC	A	Castleford	L	25-34	Sculthorpe (2), J. Davies	J. Davies (5,dg), Mackey (2dg)	–	–
1.11.95	SBC	H	Halifax	L	14-16	Cullen, Hough	Harris (3)	7179	Cummings
12.11.95	RT(2)	A	Chorley	W	68-10	Shelford (2), G. Davies (2), Eckersley (2), Ford, Hilton, Knott, Sculthorpe, Penny, Forster, Harris	Harris (8)	–	–
19.11.95	SBC	A	London B.	W	18-10	Penny, Sculthorpe, Forster	Harris (3)	–	–
26.11.95	RT(3)	A	Batley	W	35-22	Currier (2), Sculthorpe, Penny, Ford, Rudd	Harris (5), Mackey (dg)	–	–
29.11.95	SBC	H	Leeds	W	47-14	Penny (3), Harris (2), Wainwright, Mackey, Bennett	Harris (7,dg)	5460	Campbell
3.12.95	SBC	H	Sheffield E.	L	8-33	Rudd	Harris (2)	3496	Smith
10.12.95	RT(QT)	H	Rochdale H.	W	38-20	Currier (2), Sculthorpe, Cullen, Hough, Eckersley, Thompson	Harris (5)	2731	Bates
15.12.95	SBC	H	Castleford	W	31-20	Penny (2), Eckersley, Ford, Knott, Thompson	Harris (3), Ford (dg)	2229	J. Connolly
20.12.95	SBC	H	Bradford B.	L	34-44	Penny (2), Rudd (2), Knott, Harris	Harris (5)	3303	Cummings
1.1.96	SBC	H	Wigan	L	12-41	Barrow, Forster	Ford, Knott	5123	Presley
4.1.96	RT(SF)	A	St. Helens	L	0-80	–	–	–	–
7.1.96	SBC	A	St. Helens	L	14-54	Harris (2), Bennett	Harris	–	–
10.1.96	SBC	A	Workington T.	L	16-24	Forster, Shelford, Rudd	Harris (2)	–	–
14.1.96	SBC	A	Halifax	L	14-20	Forster, Penny	Harris (3)	–	–
17.1.96	SBC	A	Oldham	L	19-30	Harris (2), Knott	Harris (3,dg)	–	–

New Warrington captain Paul Cullen, scorer of two tries in 19 games in 1995-96.

Mark Jones who joined Warrington from Hull in July 1995.

117

WHITEHAVEN

Ground: Recreation Ground (01946-592869)
First Season: 1948-49
Nickname: Warriors
Chairman: Derek Mossop
Secretary: Bill Madine

RECORDS

Match
Goals: 13 by Lee Anderson at Highfield, 25 Jan 1995
Tries: 6 by Vince Gribbin v. Doncaster, 18 Nov 1984
Points: 30 by Lee Anderson at Highfield, 25 Jan 1995

Season
Goals: 141 by John McKeown, 1956-57
Tries: 34 by Mike Pechey, 1994-95
Points: 291 by John McKeown, 1956-57

Career
Goals: 1,050 by John McKeown, 1948-61
Tries: 148 by Bill Smith, 1950-62
Points: 2,133 by John McKeown, 1948-61
Appearances: 417 by John McKeown, 1948-61
Highest score: 86-6 at Highfield, 25 Jan 1995
Highest against: 92-10 at Hull K.R., 18 Mar 1990
Attendance: 18,500 v. Wakefield T. (RL Cup), 19 Mar 1960

COACHING REGISTER

● **Since 1974-75**

Jeff Bawden	May 72 - May 75
Ike Southward	Aug 75 - June 76
Bill Smith	Aug 76 - Oct 78
Ray Dutton	Oct 78 - Oct 79
Phil Kitchin	Oct 79 - Jan 82
Arnold Walker	Jan 82 - May 82
Tommy Dawes	June 82 - May 83
Frank Foster	June 83 - June 85
Phil Kitchin	June 85 - Oct 87
John McFarlane	Oct 87 - May 88
Barry Smith	July 88 - Sep 89
Eric Fitzsimons	Oct 89 - Mar 90
Norman Turley	June 90 - Apr 91
Jackie Davidson	May 91 - June 92
Gordon Cottier	June 92 - May 93
Kurt Sorensen	May 93 - Aug 95
Stan Martin	Oct 95 -

GREAT BRITAIN REGISTER

(5 players)

Player		Year
Vince Gribbin	(1)	1985
Bill Holliday	(1)	1964
Dick Huddart	(4)	1958
Phil Kitchin	(1)	1965
Arnold Walker	(1)	1980

1995-96 REGISTRATION DATE

Signed	Player	Club From
15.6.95	*Casey, Sean	St. Helens
15.6.95	*Fenlon, Tony	St. Helens
1.8.95	Brown, Thomas	Kells ARL
1.8.95	McNamara, Kevin	St. Bees ARL
1.8.95	*Murdoch, Gary	Carlisle
1.8.95	Round, Stephen	Hensingham ARL
18.8.95	Kenmare, Paul	Kells ARL
18.8.95	Kennedy, Martyn	Kells ARL
18.8.95	McFarlane, John	Frizington ARL
14.9.95	Hewer, Carl	Hensingham ARL
14.9.95	Morgan, Paul	Hensingham ARL
26.9.95	Edwards, Casino	New Zealand
26.9.95	Edwards, Shane	New Zealand
26.9.95	Kingham, Brett	New Zealand
29.9.95	*Walker, Scott	Widnes
6.11.95	Palmer, Glyn	Distington ARL
1.12.95	*Williams, Darren	Wigan
22.12.95	Rutherford, Lee	Kells ARL
2.1.96	Calvin, Graeme	Kells ARL

Ray Dutton appointed coach of Whitehaven in October 1978.

WHITEHAVEN 1995-96 PLAYERS' SUMMARY

	Date of birth	App	T	G	D	Pts	Previous club	Signed
Anderson, Lee	1.10.69	19	5	16	1	53	Kells ARL	1.10.94
Anderson, Scott	9.12.70	1+1	0	0	0	0	Wath Brow ARL	10.1.94
Atherton, Peter	29.12.70	2+4	0	0	0	0	St. Helens	7.10.94
Blaney, Gerrard "Ged"	17.6.65	0+1	0	0	0	0	Mirehouse ARL	8.1.89
Casey, Sean	9.12.71	12+4	5	0	0	20	St. Helens	15.6.95
Chambers, Craig	25.4.73	7+3	3	0	0	12	Kells ARL	6.8.93
Dover, Peter	9.12.65	6+2	2	0	0	8	Flimby ARL	1.7.89
Doyle (Edwards), Casino	23.2.75	14	2	0	0	8	New Zealand	26.9.95
Edwards, Shane	20.11.72	13	5	0	0	20	New Zealand	26.9.95
Fenlon, Anthony	2.2.72	10+2	4	16	0	48	St. Helens	15.6.95
Fisher, Billy	27.10.62	18+1	2	0	0	8	St. Benedicts RU	20.7.81
Gribbin, Vince	15.3.65	1+1	0	0	0	0	Hensingham ARL	23.7.82
Harrison, Mark	23.9.72	5+1	3	0	0	12		
Hetherington, Gary	5.7.65	13+4	0	0	0	0	Kells ARL	26.7.85
Hewer, Carl	21.2.76	6+1	0	0	1	1	Hensingham ARL	14.9.95
Kiddie, Lee	2.1.75	2	1	0	0	4	Kells ARL	18.9.93
Kingham, Brett	12.12.69	12	0	0	0	0	New Zealand	26.9.95
Lancaster, Paul	25.2.70	16+2	1	0	0	4	Egremont ARL	23.3.95
Lewthwaite, Graeme	5.7.72	8+3	1	0	0	4	Hensingham ARL	10.9.93
Maguire, Steve	12.8.63	16+2	1	20	1	45	Barrow	11.1.91
Morton, Graeme	15.1.73	6+1	1	0	0	4	Kells ARL	6.8.93
Murdoch, Gary	6.1.68	9	0	0	0	0	Carlisle	1.8.95
Palmer, Glyn	16.6.71	11	4	0	0	16	Distington ARL	6.11.95
Quirk, Les	6.3.65	12	6	0	0	24	St. Helens	4.7.94
Rooney, Ian	5.5.71	2	0	0	0	0	Wath Brow ARL	15.5.95
Rose, Graham		0+1	0	0	0	0		
Routledge, John	7.2.65	7	2	0	0	8	Egremont RU	24.8.90
Seeds, David	23.6.74	21	11	0	0	44	Kells ARL	7.9.93
Smith, Peter	13.8.66	17+1	2	0	0	8	Kells ARL	22.8.94
Walker, Scott	7.9.74	1+2	0	0	0	0	Widnes	29.9.95
Williams, Darren	27.4.74	6	5	0	0	20	Wigan	1.12.95
Wilson, Grant	25.7.75	0+2	0	0	0	0	Egremont ARL	18.5.94
TOTALS								
32 players			66	52	3	371		

119

WHITEHAVEN 1995-96 MATCH ANALYSIS

Date	Com-petition	H/A	Opponents	Rlt	Score	Tries	Goals	Atten-dance	Referee
20.8.95	FD	A	Wakefield T.	W	44-14	Anderson (2), Casey, Kiddie, Morton, Quirk, Smith	Fenlon (5), Anderson (3)	–	–
23.8.95	FD	H	Salford R.	L	2-14	–	Fenlon	1819	Presley
3.9.95	FD	A	Widnes	L	6-28	Fenlon	Fenlon	–	–
10.9.95	FD	H	Featherstone R.	L	18-27	Chambers (2), Fenlon	Fenlon (3)	1076	Lee
17.9.95	FD	A	Batley	L	6-20	Harrison	Fenlon	–	–
20.9.95	FD	H	Huddersfield	W	21-14	Fenlon, Chambers, Harrison, Dover	Anderson (2,dg)	1028	Oddy
24.9.95	FD	A	Keighley C.	L	8-58	Lewthwaite	Fenlon (2)	–	–
1.10.95	FD	H	Rochdale H.	D	14-14	Seeds (2), Harrison	Anderson	1032	Redfearn
1.11.95	FD	H	Dewsbury	W	35-8	Seeds (2), Edwards, Fisher, Smith, Casey, Anderson	Fenlon (3), Hewer (dg)	1003	Ganson
5.11.95	FD	A	Hull	L	18-36	Seeds, Edwards, Fisher	Anderson (3)	–	–
12.11.95	RT(2)	A	Wigan	L	26-68	Fenlon, Casey, Doyle, Palmer, Maguire	Anderson (3)	–	–
14.11.95	FD	A	Salford R.	L	18-58	Quirk (2), Lancaster, Dover	Maguire (3)	–	–
19.11.95	FD	H	Wakefield T.	W	18-12	Casey (2), Dover	Maguire (3)	1095	Cross
26.11.95	FD	A	Featherstone R.	L	10-60	Seeds, Doyle	Maguire	–	–
3.12.95	FD	H	Batley	W	20-10	Williams (2), Palmer	Anderson (4)	938	Burke
10.12.95	FD	A	Huddersfield	W	26-14	Routledge, Williams, Palmer, Seeds, Edwards	Maguire (3)	–	–
17.12.95	FD	H	Keighley C.	D	8-8	Edwards	Maguire (2)	1445	Shaw
7.1.96	FD	A	Rochdale H.	W	15-8	Williams, Quirk	Maguire (3,dg)	–	–
10.1.96	FD	H	Widnes	W	16-14	Anderson, Quirk, Seeds	Maguire (2)	1262	Ganson
14.1.96	FD	A	Dewsbury	W	20-4	Seeds (2), Anderson, Routledge	Maguire (2)	–	–
21.1.96	FD	H	Hull	W	22-14	Edwards, Palmer, Quirk, Seeds, Williams	Maguire	1352	Owram

WIDNES

Ground:	Naughton Park (0151-495-2250)
First Season:	1895-96
Nickname:	Chemics
Chairman:	Jim Mills
General Manager:	Frank Myler
Honours:	**Championship** Beaten finalists, 1935-36
	Division One Champions, 1977-78, 1987-88, 1988-89
	Challenge Cup Winners, 1929-30, 1936-37, 1963-64, 1974-75, 1978-79, 1980-81, 1983-84
	Beaten finalists, 1933-34, 1949-50, 1975-76, 1976-77, 1981-82, 1992-93
	Regal Trophy Winners, 1975-76, 1978-79, 1991-92
	Beaten finalists, 1974-75, 1977-78, 1979-80, 1983-84, 1988-89
	Premiership Winners, 1979-80, 1981-82, 1982-83, 1987-88, 1988-89, 1989-90
	Beaten finalists, 1977-78, 1990-91
	Lancashire Cup Winners, 1945-46, 1974-75, 1975-76, 1976-77, 1978-79, 1979-80, 1990-91
	Beaten finalists, 1928-29, 1939-40, 1955-56, 1971-72, 1981-82, 1983-84
	Lancashire League Winners, 1919-20
	Western Division Championship Beaten finalists, 1962-63
	Charity Shield Winners, 1988-89, 1989-90, 1990-91
	World Club Challenge Winners, 1989-90
	BBC2 Floodlit Trophy Winners, 1978-79
	Beaten finalists, 1972-73, 1973-74

RECORDS

Match

Goals: 11 by Robin Whitfield v. Oldham, 28 Oct 1965

Tries: 5 by Eddie Cunningham v. Doncaster, 15 Feb 1981
John Basnett at Hunslet, 17 Oct 1981
John Basnett v. Hull K.R., 2 Nov 1986
David Hulme v. Dewsbury, 30 Nov 1986
Andy Currier v. Featherstone R., 25 Sep 1988
Martin Offiah v. Warrington, 15 Mar 1989

Points: 34 by Andy Currier v. Featherstone R., 25 Sep 1988
Jonathan Davies v. Whitehaven, 26 Aug 1990

Season

Goals: 140 by Mick Burke, 1978-79
Tries: 58 by Martin Offiah, 1988-89
Points: 342 by Jonathan Davies, 1990-91

Career

Goals: 1,083 by Ray Dutton, 1966-78
Tries: 234 by Mal Aspey, 1964-80
Points: 2,195 by Ray Dutton, 1966-78
Appearances: 587+4 by Keith Elwell, 1970-86
Highest score: 82-0 v. Dewsbury, 30 Nov 1986
Highest against: 60-5 at Oldham, 9 Apr 1928
Attendance: 24,205 v. St. Helens (RL Cup), 16 Feb 1961

COACHING REGISTER

● **Since 1974-75**

Vince Karalius	Jan 72 - May 75
Frank Myler	May 75 - May 78
Doug Laughton	May 78 - Mar 83
Harry Dawson }Colin Tyrer }	Mar 83 - May 83
* Vince Karalius }Harry Dawson }	May 83 - May 84
Eric Hughes	June 84 - Jan 86
Doug Laughton	Jan 86 - May 91
Frank Myler	June 91 - May 92
Phil Larder	May 92 - May 94
Tony Myler	May 94 - Aug 95
Doug Laughton	Aug 95 -

* *Dawson quit as coach in March 1984 with Karalius continuing as team manager.*

121

GREAT BRITAIN REGISTER
(46 players)

Mick Adams	(11+2)	1979-84
John Basnett	(2)	1984-86
Keith Bentley	(1)	1980
Mick Burke	(14+1)	1980-86
Frank Collier	(1)	1964
Andy Currier	(2)	1989-93
Jonathan Davies	(8+1)	1990-93
John Devereux	(6+2)	1992-93
Ray Dutton	(6)	1970
Keith Elwell	(3)	1977-80
Richard Eyres	(3+4)	1989-93
John Fieldhouse	(6)	1985-86
Ray French	(4)	1968
Les Gorley	(4+1)	1980-82
Andy Gregory	(8+1)	1981-84
Ian Hare	(1)	1967
Fred Higgins	(6)	1950-51
Harold Higgins	(2)	1937
Les Holliday	(3)	1991-92
Eric Hughes	(8)	1978-82
David Hulme	(7+1)	1988-89
Paul Hulme	(3+5)	1988-92
Albert Johnson	(4)	1914-20
Vince Karalius	(2)	1963
George Kemel	(2)	1965
Doug Laughton	(4)	1973-79
Joe Lydon	(9+1)	1983-85
Tommy McCue	(6)	1936-46
Steve McCurrie	(1)	1993
Jim Measures	(2)	1963
Jim Mills	(6)	1974-79
Paul Moriarty	(1+1)	1991-94
Frank Myler	(14+1)	1960-67
Tony Myler	(14)	1983-86
George Nicholls	(7)	1971-72
Martin Offiah	(20)	1988-91
Dennis O'Neill	(2+1)	1971-72
Mike O'Neill	(3)	1982-83
Harry Pinner	(1)	1986
Glyn Shaw	(1)	1980
Nat Silcock	(12)	1932-37
Stuart Spruce	(1)	1993
Alan Tait	(9)	1989-92
John Warlow	(3)	1971
Darren Wright	(+1)	1988
Stuart Wright	(7)	1977-78

1995-96 REGISTRATION DATE

Signed	Player	Club From
22.6.95	Gartland, Paul	Swinton
22.6.95	Pechey, Mike	Whitehaven
24.7.95	Cooper, Shane	St. Helens
18.8.95	Moran, Mark	Simms Cross ARL
31.8.95	Ruane, Dennis	Simms Cross ARL
12.9.95	Plowman, Brett	Australia
28.10.95	Kilgannon, Eddie	Widnes Tigers ARL
24.11.95	Silcock, Mark	–

Shane Cooper, a July recruit by Widnes, having been given a free transfer by St. Helens.

WIDNES 1995-96 PLAYERS' SUMMARY

	Date of birth	App	T	G	D	Pts	Previous club	Signed
Ashton, Lee		1+1	3	0	0	12		
Blackwood, Mark	12.11.68	0+1	0	0	0	0	Kells ARL	1.2.93
Broadbent, Gary	31.10.76	11+3	0	0	0	0	Barrow ARL	20.3.93
Cassidy, Jim	28.7.72	1+6	2	0	0	8	Leigh	26.8.94
Collier, Andy	3.6.68	9+8	2	0	0	8	Leigh	20.7.94
Cooper, Shane	26.5.60	19	5	0	1	21	St. Helens	24.7.95
Devereux, John	30.3.66	22	14	0	0	56	Bridgend RU	10.10.89
Donno, John		2	0	0	0	0		
Gartland, Paul	2.11.72	22	7	9	0	46	Swinton	22.6.95
Green, Jason	19.1.72	2	0	0	0	0	Rochdale H.	18.9.94
Hadley, Adrian	1.3.63	7	3	33	0	78	Salford	4.8.92
Hansen, Liuaki "Lee"	23.7.68	20+2	1	0	0	4	Leigh	3.8.94
Harris, Paul	18.4.74	0+4	2	0	0	8	St. Maries ARL	13.8.92
Hulme, David	6.2.64	12	5	0	0	20	Halton H. ARL	4.8.80
Hulme, Paul	19.4.66	21	6	0	0	24	Halton H. ARL	5.7.83
Kelly, Chris	29.8.73	1+1	0	0	0	0		23.7.90
Makin, Craig	13.4.73	14+6	2	0	0	8	Orrell St. James ARL	10.1.92
McCurrie, Steve	2.7.73	23	12	0	0	48	Hensingham ARL	23.7.90
Myler, Danny		1	0	3	0	6		
Myler, Paul	11.11.72	4+2	0	0	0	0	Warrington	8.8.94
Pechey, Mike	16.12.68	14	3	0	0	12	Whitehaven	22.6.95
Platt, Andy		13	0	0	0	0		
Plowman, Brett	13.6.69	1+4	1	0	0	4	Australia	12.9.95
Ruane, David	24.9.63	14+1	2	0	0	8	Leigh	10.1.94
Smith, Peter	1.9.73	1+2	0	0	0	0	Widnes Tigers ARL	6.9.91
Spruce, Stuart	3.1.71	7	6	0	0	24	Widnes Tigers ARL	8.1.90
Thorniley, Tony	10.10.66	17	10	0	0	40	Warrington	19.7.94
Tyrer, Christian	19.12.73	18	2	45	1	99	Leigh Rangers ARL	23.7.90
Wright, Darren	17.1.68	22	7	0	0	28	Leigh Miners ARL	23.3.85
TOTALS								
29 players			95	90	2	562		

Representative appearances 1995-96
Devereux – Wales (3,1t);
Hadley – Wales (1+1);
Hansen – Tonga (2);
McCurrie – England (+1);
Platt – England (4)

WIDNES 1995-96 MATCH ANALYSIS

Date	Competition	H/A	Opponents	Rlt	Score	Tries	Goals	Attendance	Referee
20.8.95	FD	H	Dewsbury	W	48-6	Ashton (3), Hadley (2), Gartland, Harris, McCurrie, Pechey	Hadley (6)	2680	Gilmour
23.8.95	FD	H	Wakefield T.	W	24-10	Gartland, McCurrie, Devereux	Hadley (6)	2635	Nicholson
27.8.95	FD	A	Salford R.	L	4-45	Gartland	–	–	–
3.9.95	FD	H	Whitehaven	W	28-6	D. Hulme (3), Devereux, McCurrie	Hadley (4)	2934	Atkin
17.9.95	FD	A	Featherstone R.	W	30-18	Pechey, Devereux, Cooper, Wright	Hadley (7)	–	–
20.9.95	FD	H	Batley	W	34-10	D. Hulme (2), Plowman, Tyrer, Devereux, McCurrie	Hadley (5)	2669	Redfearn
23.9.95	FD	A	Huddersfield	W	34-29	Thorniley (2), Hadley, Devereux, Wright, P. Hulme	Hadley (5)	–	–
1.10.95	FD	H	Keighley C.	D	16-16	Gartland, McCurrie	Gartland (4)	5495	Presley
1.11.95	FD	H	Hull	W	29-26	Thorniley (2), Ruane, Spruce	Tyrer (5,dg), Gartland	2698	Lee
5.11.95	FD	A	Rochdale H.	W	34-14	Thorniley (2), Gartland (2), Cooper, Tyrer	Tyrer (5)	–	–
12.11.95	RT(2)	H	Oldham B.	W	32-8	McCurrie (2), Devereux (2), P. Hulme	Tyrer (6)	3472	Bates
15.11.95	FD	A	Wakefield T.	L	10-12	P. Hulme, Spruce	Tyrer	–	–
19.11.95	FD	A	Dewsbury	W	34-2	Spruce (2), McCurrie (2), Gartland, Devereux, Thorniley	Tyrer (3)	–	–
26.11.95	RT(3)	A	Workington T.	W	32-8	Spruce (2), Ruane, McCurrie, Thorniley	Tyrer (6)	–	–
3.12.95	FD	H	Featherstone R.	L	14-16	P. Hulme (2), Wright	Tyrer	2711	Ganson
9.12.95	RT(QF)	H	Wigan	L	23-28*	P. Hulme, Wright, Pechey	Tyrer (5), Cooper (dg)	3771	Smith
13.12.95	FD	A	Batley	W	22-18	Wright (2), Makin, Devereux	Tyrer (3)	–	–
17.12.95	FD	H	Huddersfield	L	14-18	Devereux, Cassidy, Hansen	Tyrer	2319	Oddy
4.1.96	FD	H	Salford R.	W	24-22	Devereux (2), McCurrie, Wright	Tyrer (4)	2795	Nicholson
7.1.96	FD	A	Keighley C.	W	16-12	Cooper, Thorniley	Tyrer (4)	–	–
10.1.96	FD	A	Whitehaven	L	14-16	Collier, Cooper, Makin	Tyrer	–	–
14.1.96	FD	A	Hull	L	24-32	Cassidy, Collier, Cooper, Thorniley	Gartland (4)	–	–
21.1.96	FD	H	Rochdale H.	W	22-6	Devereux (2), Harris, McCurrie	D. Myler (3)	2152	Taberner

* After 30 min. extra time. 16-16 normal time.

Widnes forward Steve McCurrie, who touched down 12 times in 23 Centenary season games.

Widnes full back Stuart Spruce, scorer of six tries in seven games in 1995-96.

WIGAN

Ground: Central Park (01942-231321)
First Season: 1895-96
Nickname: Riversiders
Chairman: Jack Robinson
Secretary: Mary Sharkey
Honours: **Championship** Winners, 1908-09,
1921-22, 1925-26, 1933-34, 1945-46,
1946-47, 1949-50, 1951-52, 1959-60
Beaten finalists, 1909-10, 1910-11,
1911-12, 1912-13, 1923-24, 1970-71
War Emergency League
Winners, 1943-44
Beaten finalists, 1940-41
League Leaders Trophy Winners,
1970-71
Division One Champions, 1986-87,
1989-90, 1990-91, 1991-92, 1992-93,
1993-94, 1994-95, 1995-96
(Centenary Champions)
Challenge Cup Winners, 1923-24,
1928-29, 1947-48, 1950-51, 1957-58,
1958-59, 1964-65, 1984-85, 1987-88,
1988-89, 1989-90, 1990-91, 1991-92,
1992-93, 1993-94, 1994-95
Beaten finalists, 1910-11, 1919-20,
1943-44, 1945-46, 1960-61, 1962-63,
1965-66, 1969-70, 1983-84
Regal Trophy Winners, 1982-83,
1985-86, 1986-87, 1988-89, 1989-90,
1992-93, 1994-95, 1995-96
Beaten finalists, 1993-94
Premiership Winners, 1986-87,
1991-92, 1993-94, 1994-95
Beaten finalists, 1992-93
Lancashire Cup Winners, 1905-06,
1908-09, 1909-10, 1912-13, 1922-23,
1928-29, 1938-39, 1946-47, 1947-48,
1948-49, 1949-50, 1950-51, 1951-52,
1966-67, 1971-72, 1973-74, 1985-86,
1986-87, 1987-88, 1988-89, 1992-93
Beaten finalists, 1913-14, 1914-15,
1925-26, 1927-28, 1930-31, 1934-35,
1935-36, 1936-37, 1945-46, 1953-54,
1957-58, 1977-78, 1980-81, 1984-85

Lancashire League Winners,
1901-02, 1908-09, 1910-11, 1911-12,
1912-13, 1913-14, 1914-15, 1920-21,
1922-23, 1923-24, 1925-26, 1945-46,
1946-47, 1949-50, 1951-52, 1958-59,
1961-62, 1969-70
Lancashire War League Winners,
1940-41
Charity Shield Winners, 1985-86,
1987-88, 1991-92, 1995-96
Beaten finalists, 1988-89, 1989-90,
1990-91, 1992-93
World Club Challenge Winners,
1987-88, 1991-92, 1993-94
Beaten finalists, 1992-93
BBC2 Floodlit Trophy Winners,
1968-69
Beaten finalists, 1969-70

RECORDS

Match

Goals: 22 by Jim Sullivan v. Flimby & Fothergill,
            14 Feb 1925
Tries: 10 by Martin Offiah v. Leeds,
            10 May 1992
            Shaun Edwards at Swinton,
            29 Sep 1992
Points: 44 by Jim Sullivan v. Flimby & Fothergill,
            14 Feb 1925

Season

Goals: 186 by Frano Botica, 1994-95
Tries: 62 by Johnny Ring, 1925-26
Points: 423 by Frano Botica, 1992-93

Career

Goals: 2,317 by Jim Sullivan, 1921-46
Tries: 478 by Billy Boston, 1953-68
Points: 4,883 by Jim Sullivan, 1921-46
Appearances: 774 by Jim Sullivan, 1921-46
Highest score: 116-0 v. Flimby & Fothergill,
            14 Feb 1925
Highest against: 58-3 at Leeds, 14 Oct 1972
Attendance: 47,747 v. St. Helens (League),
            27 Mar 1959

COACHING REGISTER

● **Since 1974-75**

Ted Toohey	May 74 - Jan 75
Joe Coan	Jan 75 - Sep 76
Vince Karalius	Sep 76 - Sep 79
Kel Coslett	Oct 79 - Apr 80

A rampaging Va'aiga Tuigamala in Centenary season action against Leeds at Headingley.

George Fairbairn	Apr 80 - May 81
Maurice Bamford	May 81 - May 82
Alex Murphy	June 82 - Aug 84
Colin Clarke ⎫	
Alan McInnes ⎭	Aug 84 - May 86
Graham Lowe	Aug 86 - June 89
John Monie	Sep 89 - May 93
John Dorahy	June 93 - May 94
Graeme West	May 94 -

GREAT BRITAIN REGISTER

(88 players)

Ray Ashby	(1)	1965
Ernest Ashcroft	(11)	1947-54
Eric Ashton	(26)	1957-63
Bill Ashurst	(3)	1971-72
Frank Barton	(1)	1951
John Barton	(2)	1960-61
Jack Bennett	(1)	1926
Denis Betts	(24+1)	1990-94
Dai Bevan	(1)	1952
Billy Blan	(3)	1951
Dave Bolton	(23)	1957-63
Billy Boston	(31)	1954-63
Tommy Bradshaw	(6)	1947-50
Frank Carlton	(1)	1962
Brian Case	(6+1)	1984-88
Mick Cassidy	(+2)	1994
Norman Cherrington	(1)	1960
Colin Clarke	(7)	1965-73
Phil Clarke	(15+1)	1990-94
Percy Coldrick	(4)	1914
Frank Collier	(1)	1963
Gary Connolly	(7)	1993-94
Neil Cowie	(1)	1993
Jack Cunliffe	(4)	1950-54
Martin Dermott	(11)	1990-93
Shaun Edwards	(32+4)	1985-94
Joe Egan	(14)	1946-50
Roy Evans	(4)	1961-62
George Fairbairn	(14)	1977-80
Andrew Farrell	(5)	1993-94
Terry Fogerty	(1)	1967
Phil Ford	(1)	1985
Bill Francis	(4)	1967-77
Danny Gardiner	(1)	1965
Ken Gee	(17)	1946-51
Henderson Gill	(14+1)	1981-88
Andy Goodway	(12)	1985-90
Bobbie Goulding	(5)	1990
John Gray	(5+3)	1974

Andy Gregory	(16)	1987-92
Steve Hampson	(11+1)	1987-92
Ellery Hanley	(23)	1985-91
Cliff Hill	(1)	1966
David Hill	(1)	1971
Jack Hilton	(4)	1950
Tommy Howley	(6)	1924
Bill Hudson	(1)	1948
Danny Hurcombe	(8)	1920-24
Bert Jenkins	(12)	1907-14
Keri Jones	(2)	1970
Roy Kinnear	(1)	1929
Nicky Kiss	(1)	1985
Doug Laughton	(11)	1970-71
Johnny Lawrenson	(3)	1948
Jim Leytham	(5)	1907-10
Ian Lucas	(1+1)	1991-92
Joe Lydon	(14+6)	1986-92
Barrie McDermott	(1+2)	1994
Billy McGinty	(4)	1992
Brian McTigue	(25)	1958-63
Barrie-Jon Mather	(+1)	1994
Joe Miller	(1)	1911
Jack Morley	(2)	1936-37
Martin Offiah	(13)	1992-94
Andy Platt	(17+1)	1989-93
Ian Potter	(7+1)	1985-86
Jack Price	(4)	1924
Dick Ramsdale	(8)	1910-14
Gordon Ratcliffe	(3)	1947-50
Johnny Ring	(2)	1924-26
Dave Robinson	(1)	1970
Jason Robinson	(4)	1993-94
Martin Ryan	(4)	1947-50
Billy Sayer	(7)	1961-63
Jim Sharrock	(4)	1910-11
Dick Silcock	(1)	1908
Nat Silcock	(3)	1954
Kelvin Skerrett	(6+2)	1992-93
David Stephenson	(5)	1982-87
Jim Sullivan	(25)	1924-33
Mick Sullivan	(19)	1957-60
Gwyn Thomas	(1)	1914
Johnny Thomas	(8)	1907-11
Shaun Wane	(2)	1985-86
Edward Ward	(3)	1946-47
Les White	(2)	1947
David Willicombe	(2)	1974
Billy Winstanley	(3)	1911

127

1995-96 REGISTRATION DATE

Signed	Player	Club From
12.6.95	Barrow, Stephen	Widnes
9.8.95	Cardiss, Darryl	Hunslet Boys ARL
22.8.95	Purtill, Kieron	Wigan St. Patricks ARL

25.8.95	Whitehead, Michael	Rosebridge ARL
16.9.95	Peters, Michael	–
22.9.95	Tatupu, Shem	Western Samoa
20.10.95	Gilmour, Lee	Dewsbury Moor ARL
25.11.95	Johnson, Paul	–

WIGAN 1995-96 PLAYERS' SUMMARY

	Date of birth	App	T	G	D	Pts	Previous club	Signed
Barrow, Steve	8.12.75	2+1	0	0	0	0	Widnes	12.6.95
Barrow, Warren	3.9.76	0+1	0	0	0	0	Orrell St. James ARL	3.9.93
Baynes, Neil	14.9.77	0+2	0	0	0	0	Wigan St. Judes ARL	14.9.94
Cardiss, Darryl	13.7.78	0+2	1	1	0	6	Hunslet Boys ARL	9.8.95
Cassidy, Mick	3.7.73	24+1	9	0	0	36	Wigan St. Judes ARL	24.5.90
Connolly, Gary	22.6.71	22	16	1	0	66	St. Helens	1.8.93
Cowie, Neil	16.1.67	17+4	4	0	0	16	Rochdale H.	3.9.91
Craig, Andrew	16.3.76	3+7	0	0	0	0	Wigan Academy	1.11.93
Dermott, Martin	25.9.67	3+10	0	0	0	0	Wigan St. Pats ARL	7.11.84
Edwards, Shaun	17.10.66	21	7	0	2	30	Wigan St. Pats ARL	18.10.83
Farrell, Andrew	30.5.75	14	6	85	0	194	Orrell St. James ARL	19.10.92
Hall, Martin	5.12.68	23+2	5	7	1	35	Rochdale H.	11.1.93
Haughton, Simon	10.11.75	20+3	10	0	0	40	Dudley Hill ARL	10.11.92
Johnson, Andrew	14.6.74	8+9	3	0	0	12	St. Patricks ARL	22.9.92
Johnson, Paul	25.11.78	0+1	0	0	0	0		25.11.95
Knowles, Matthew	2.9.75	0+5	0	0	0	0	Blackbrook ARL	3.10.92
Mather, Barrie-Jon	15.1.73	4+3	6	0	0	24	Arnold School	14.8.91
Murdock, Craig	24.10.73	4+10	1	0	0	4	Hensingham ARL	19.8.93
O'Connor, Terry	13.10.71	20+4	2	0	0	8	Salford	23.8.94
Offiah, Martin	29.12.66	23	26	0	0	104	Widnes	3.1.92
Paul, Henry	10.2.74	25+1	15	65	0	190	Auckland W. NZ	18.8.94
Quinnell, Scott	20.8.72	12+7	10	0	0	40	Llanelli RU	22.9.94
Radlinski, Kris	9.4.76	22+1	6	0	0	24	Wigan Academy	25.5.93
Robinson, Jason	30.7.74	24	18	0	0	72	Hunslet Parkside ARL	31.7.91
Skerrett, Kelvin	22.5.66	13+3	2	0	0	8	Bradford N.	13.8.90
Smyth, Rob	22.2.77	5+10	8	0	0	32	Rose Bridge ARL	22.2.94
Tallec, Gael	15.8.76	0+1	1	0	0	4	France	
Tatupu, Shem	18.2.68	0+1	0	0	0	0	W. Samoa	22.9.95
Tuigamala, Va'aiga	4.9.69	25+1	20	0	0	80	New Zealand RU	8.1.94
Wright, Nigel	8.11.73	4	5	0	1	21	Wakefield T.	
TOTALS 30 players			181	159	4	1,046		

Representative appearances 1995-96

Cassidy – England (2+2); Connolly – England (1); Cowie – Wales (+1); Edwards – England (1); Farrell – England (4,1t,7g); Hall – Wales (3); Haughton – England (1+3,2t); Mather – England (2); Offiah – England (3,2t); Paul – New Zealand (2+1); Quinnell – Wales (2); Radlinski – England (4+1,2t); Robinson – England (4,3t); Skerrett – Wales (3); Tallec – France (1); Tuigamala – Western Samoa (2,2t).

Charity Shield success for Wigan after the 45-20 win over Leeds in Dublin in August 1995.

WIGAN 1995-96 MATCH ANALYSIS

Date	Competition	H/A	Opponents	Rlt	Score	Tries	Goals	Attendance	Referee
13.8.95	CS	N1	Leeds	W	45-20	Wright (2), Haughton, Cassidy, Connolly, O'Connor, Farrell	Farrell (8), Wright (dg)	(5716)	Smith
18.8.95	SBC	A	Workington T.	W	48-6	Haughton (2), Robinson (2), Radlinski, Quinnell, Paul, Cassidy, Offiah	Farrell (6)	–	–
23.8.95	SBC	H	Sheffield E.	W	52-20	Wright (2), Tuigamala, Cowie, Connolly, Cassidy, Robinson, Offiah, Farrell	Farrell (8)	10,379	Kirkpatrick
28.8.95	SBC	A	St. Helens	W	52-20	Connolly (2), Robinson (2), Wright, Haughton, Offiah, Farrell	Farrell (10)	–	–
3.9.95	SBC	H	Warrington	W	44-2	Offiah (2), Haughton, Radlinski, Connolly, Edwards	Farrell (8), Paul (2)	13,700	Smith
6.9.95	SBC	A	Halifax	W	48-13	Cowie (2), Tuigamala (2), Hall, Mather, Paul, Offiah	Farrell (8)	–	–
10.9.95	SBC	H	London B.	W	50-12	Tuigamala (2), Connolly (2), Edwards, Mather, Cassidy, Haughton, Offiah	Farrell (5), Hall, Connolly	10,332	Kirkpatrick
13.9.95	SBC	H	Castleford	W	40-8	Mather, Tuigamala, Edwards, Paul, Cassidy, Offiah	Farrell (8)	12,151	Cummings
17.9.95	SBC	A	Bradford B.	W	36-26	Mather (2), Farrell (2), Connolly, Cassidy, Offiah	Farrell (4)	–	–
24.9.95	SBC	H	Oldham B.	W	42-12	Tallec, Smyth, Skerrett, Tuigamala, Paul, Robinson, Offiah	Farrell (7)	10,416	Morris
3.11.95	SBC	A	Leeds	L	11-23	Robinson, Offiah	Paul, Hall (dg)	–	–
12.11.95	RT(2)	H	Whitehaven	W	68-26	Offiah (5), Robinson (3), Quinnell (2), Mather, A. Johnson, Murdock	Paul (8)	6133	Kirkpatrick
15.11.95	SBC	A	Castleford	W	42-20	Paul (3), Cardiss, O'Connor, Tuigamala, Edwards, Hall	Paul (5)	–	–
19.11.95	SBC	H	Workington T.	W	44-20	Robinson (3), Connolly, Tuigamala, Edwards, Skerrett	Paul (8)	9851	Morris
26.11.95	RT(3)	A	Huddersfield	W	32-0	Connolly (2), Robinson, Offiah, Farrell	Farrell (6)	–	–
3.12.95	SBC	A	London B.	W	42-10	Offiah (4), Robinson, Radlinski, Connolly, Edwards	Farrell (5)	–	–
9.12.95	RT(QT)	A	Widnes	W	28-23*	Tuigamala (2), Smyth (2), Connolly, Quinnell	Farrell (2)	–	–
13.12.95	SBC	H	Halifax	W	32-18	Tuigamala (2), Paul, Hall, Connolly, A. Johnson	Paul (4)	8813	Cummings
17.12.95	SBC	A	Oldham B.	L	26-28	Quinnell (2), Offiah (2), Haughton	Paul (3)	–	–
26.12.95	SBC	H	St. Helens	W	58-4	Quinnell (4), Cassidy (2), Haughton (2), Robinson, Smyth	Hall (5), Paul (4)	19,526	Cummings
1.1.96	SBC	A	Warrington	W	41-12	Tuigamala (3), Smyth, Edwards, Haughton, Robinson	Paul (5), Hall, Edwards (dg)	–	–
6.1.96	RT(SF)	H	Leeds	W	38-18	Connolly (2), Paul, Hall, Robinson, Radlinski	Paul (7)	10,075	Cummings
13.1.96	RT(F)	N2	St. Helens	W	25-16	Paul (2), Radlinski, Tuigamala, Offiah	Paul (4), Edwards (dg)	(17,590)	Smith
16.1.96	SBC	H	Bradford B.	W	32-18	Smyth (2), Paul, Tuigamala, Cowie, Offiah	Paul (4)	11,385	Morris
19.1.96	SBC	A	Sheffield E.	W	36-24	Tuigamala (2), Cassidy, Offiah, Radlinski, Paul, Smyth	Paul (3), Cardiss	–	–
21.1.96	SBC	H	Leeds	W	34-20	Paul (2), A. Johnson, Hall, Offiah	Paul (7)	12,918	Smith

N1 at Dublin;
N2 at Huddersfield
* After 30 min. extra time. 16-16 normal time

WORKINGTON TOWN

Ground: Derwent Park (01900-603609)
First Season: 1945-46
Nickname: Town
Chairman: Kevan Gorge
Secretary: John Bell
Honours: **Championship** Winners, 1950-51
Beaten finalists, 1957-58
Division Two Champions, 1993-94
Challenge Cup Winners, 1951-52
Beaten finalists, 1954-55, 1957-58
Second Division/Divisional Premiership Winners 1993-94,
Beaten finalists, 1992-93
Lancashire Cup Winners, 1977-78
Beaten finalists, 1976-77, 1978-79, 1979-80
Western Division Championship Winners, 1962-63

RECORDS

Match

Goals: 13 by Dean Marwood v. Highfield, 1 Nov 1992
Dean Marwood v. Leigh, 26 Feb 1995
Tries: 7 by Ike Southward v. Blackpool B., 17 Sep 1955
Points: 42 by Dean Marwood v. Highfield, 1 Nov 1992
Dean Marwood v. Leigh, 26 Feb 1995

Season

Goals: 186 by Lyn Hopkins, 1981-82
Tries: 49 by Johnny Lawrenson, 1951-52
Points: 438 by Lyn Hopkins, 1981-82

Career

Goals: 809 by Iain MacCorquodale, 1972-80
Tries: 274 by Ike Southward, 1952-59 & 1960-68
Points: 1,800 by Iain MacCorquodale, 1972-80
Appearances: 415+4 Paul Charlton, 1961-69 & 1975-80

Highest score: 94-4 v. Leigh, 26 Feb 1995
Highest against: 68-0 at Wigan, 18 Jan 1987
68-6 at Leigh, 8 Mar 1992
Attendance: 17,741 v. Wigan (RL Cup), 3 Mar 1965 — at Derwent Park
20,403 v. St. Helens (RL Cup), 8 Mar 1952 — at Borough Park

COACHING REGISTER

● **Since 1974-75**

Ike Southward	Aug 73 - June 75
Paul Charlton	June 75 - June 76
Ike Southward	June 76 - Feb 78
Sol Roper	Feb 78 - Apr 80
Keith Irving	Aug 80 - Oct 80
Tommy Bishop	Nov 80 - June 82
Paul Charlton	July 82 - Dec 82
Dave Cox	Mar 83 - Mar 83
Harry Archer/Bill Smith	May 83 - June 84
Bill Smith	June 84 - Apr 85
Jackie Davidson	Apr 85 - Jan 86
Keith Davies	Feb 86 - Mar 87
Norman Turley	Mar 87 - Apr 88
Maurice Bamford	July 88 - Dec 88
Phil Kitchin	Dec 88 - May 90
Ray Ashton	June 90 - Dec 91
Dean Williams	Dec 91 - Apr 92
Peter Walsh	May 92 - July 95
Kurt Sorensen	Aug 95 -

GREAT BRITAIN REGISTER

(9 players)

Eddie Bowman	(4)	1977
Paul Charlton	(1)	1965
Brian Edgar	(11)	1958-66
Norman Herbert	(6)	1961-62
Vince McKeating	(2)	1951
Billy Martin	(1)	1962
Albert Pepperell	(2)	1950-51
Ike Southward	(4)	1958
George Wilson	(3)	1951

131

1995-96 REGISTRATION DATE

Signed	Player	Club From
29.6.95	Livett, Peter	–
24.7.95	Johnson, Mark	London B.
14.8.95	Fraisse, David	Bradford B.
16.8.95	Bibby, Dennis	Penrith ARL
7.9.95	Campbell, Logan	London B.
23.9.95	Armstrong, Craig	Westfield Hotel ARL
23.9.95	Crellin, Nicholas	Glasson Rangers ARL
23.9.95	Fisher, Craig	Glasson Rangers ARL
26.9.95	Roy, Neil	Warrington
19.10.95	Stamper, Mark	Hensingham ARL
24.10.95	Filipo, Lafaele	New Zealand
25.10.95	Palmada, Jason	New Zealand
21.11.95	Thompson, Graeme	Scottish Students

WORKINGTON TOWN 1995-96 PLAYERS' SUMMARY

	Date of birth	App	T	G	D	Pts	Previous club	Signed
Allen, John	16.6.72	2+3	1	0	0	4	Lowca ARL	1.5.95
Armstrong, Colin	26.1.63	16+2	0	2	0	4	Hull K.R.	3.10.90
Bethwaite, Mark	2.10.72	3+2	0	0	0	0	Glasson Rangers ARL	6.2.93
Burns, Paul	9.2.67	11+1	3	0	0	12	Barrow	16.8.92
Campbell, Logan	23.5.71	13	4	0	0	16	London B.	7.9.95
Carter, Darren	8.1.72	9+5	0	6	0	12	Millom ARL	31.10.92
Chilton, Lee	29.9.72	0+1	0	0	0	0		
Fawcett, Vince	13.11.70	16+1	8	0	0	32	Leeds	19.7.94
Filipo, Lafaele	24.10.65	6+2	0	0	0	0	New Zealand	24.10.95
Fraisse, David	20.12.68	16+3	5	0	1	21	Bradford B.	14.8.95
Gorley, Jonathan	21.7.71	5+3	2	0	0	8	Ellenborough R. ARL	24.8.93
Grima, Andrew	9.10.75	0+4	0	0	0	0	Workington T. Acad.	3.9.94
Holgate, Stephen	15.12.71	16+1	1	0	0	4	Hensingham ARL	14.7.94
Johnson, Mark	28.2.69	20	9	0	0	36	London B.	12.7.95
Keenan, Mark	11.11.75	5	0	0	0	0	Workington T. Acad.	3.9.94
Kitchin, Wayne	26.11.70	15+1	4	0	2	18	Kells ARL	26.9.89
Livett, Peter	13.2.71	16	4	0	0	16		29.6.95
Marwood, Dean	22.2.70	18+1	4	45	2	108	Barrow	23.12.91
McGinty, Billy	6.12.64	11+9	4	0	0	16	Wigan	1.7.94
McGuirk, Gary	26.9.71	1+5	0	0	0	0	Westfield Hotel ARL	18.6.90
McKenzie, Phil	13.6.63	8+1	0	0	0	0	Widnes	4.2.93
Moore, Jason	27.12.70	0+3	0	0	0	0	Ellenborough R. ARL	21.6.93
Palmada, Jason	25.2.69	11+1	3	0	0	12	New Zealand	25.10.95
Pape, Kevin	17.12.61	13+2	4	0	0	16	Carlisle	9.12.94
Penrice, Paul	27.2.66	8+12	2	0	0	8	Gt. Clifton ARL	30.7.87
Phillips, Rowland	28.7.65	22	2	0	0	8	Warrington	3.11.94
Riley, Peter	1.3.68	0+4	0	0	0	0	Gt. Clifton ARL	30.7.87
Roy, Neil	25.2.67	0+2	0	0	0	0	Warrington	26.9.95
Schubert, Gary	18.9.66	15+2	0	0	0	0	Carlisle	9.8.91
Smith, Leigh	1.9.75	4+1	0	0	0	0	Hensingham ARL	27.3.94
Wallace, Mark	21.2.78	6	1	0	0	4		
TOTALS 31 players			61	53	5	355		

Representative appearances 1995-96

Fraisse – France (1);
Johnson – South Africa (3);
Phillips – Wales (+3,1t).

WORKINGTON TOWN 1995-96 MATCH ANALYSIS

Date	Com-petition	H/A	Opponents	Rlt	Score	Tries	Goals	Atten-dance	Referee
18.8.95	SBC	H	Wigan	L	6-48	Burns	Marwood	5960	Cummings
27.8.95	SBC	H	Sheffield E.	W	26-20	Fraisse, Livett, McGinty, Pape	Marwood (5)	2828	Kirkpatrick
6.9.95	SBC	A	Castleford	L	24-32	Livett, Gorley, Johnson, Holgate	Marwood (4)	–	–
10.9.95	SBC	H	St. Helens	L	22-66	Livett, Pape, Gorley, Kitchin	Marwood (3)	3689	Morris
15.9.95	SBC	A	Warrington	W	16-14	Fraisse, Pape	Marwood (2,dg), Kitchin (2dg), Fraisse (dg)	–	–
24.9.95	SBC	H	Halifax	L	17-24	Fawcett (2), Fraisse	Marwood (2,dg)	3200	R. Connolly
27.9.95	SBC	A	Leeds	L	12-50	Fawcett, Pape, Marwood	–	–	–
1.10.95	SBC	A	London B.	L	8-44	Penrice, McGinty	–	–	–
1.11.95	SBC	A	Oldham B.	L	26-30	Campbell (2), Fawcett, Livett	Marwood (5)	–	–
5.11.95	SBC	H	Bradford B.	L	12-22	Campbell, Johnson	Marwood (2)	2852	R. Connolly
11.11.95	RT(2)	H	St. Esteve	W	30-14	Burns, Fraisse, Johnson, Kitchin, Fawcett, Phillips	Carter (3)	1376	McGregor
15.11.95	SBC	H	Leeds	L	10-16	Johnson	Carter (3)	2541	Presley
19.11.95	SBC	A	Wigan	L	20-44	Kitchin, Marwood, Palmada	Marwood (4)	–	–
26.11.95	RT(3)	H	Widnes	L	8-32	Johnson (2)	–	2500	Smith
29.11.95	SBC	H	Castleford	L	16-22	Burns, Fraisse	Marwood (4)	2157	Kirkpatrick
3.12.95	SBC	A	St. Helens	L	10-58	Fawcett (2)	Marwood	–	–
8.12.95	SBC	A	Sheffield E.	L	8-34	Kitchin, Phillips	–	–	–
17.12.95	SBC	A	Halifax	L	12-26	Johnson, McGinty	Armstrong (2)	–	–
7.1.96	SBC	H	London B.	W	32-10	Campbell, Allen, Johnson, Marwood, Palmada	Marwood (6)	2224	Lee
10.1.96	SBC	H	Warrington	W	24-16	Johnson, Penrice, McGinty, Palmada	Marwood (4)	2273	Morris
14.1.96	SBC	H	Oldham B.	L	12-20	Fawcett, Marwood	Marwood (2)	2891	Ganson
21.1.96	SBC	A	Bradford B.	L	4-14	Wallace	–	–	–

Eight tries in 17 Centenary season games for Workington Town threequarter Vince Fawcett.

Wales Centenary World Cup performer, Rowland Phillips who also appeared 22 times for Workington Town in the 1995-96 season.

133

YORK

Ground: Ryedale Stadium (01904-634636)
First Season: 1901-02 as York. Became
Ryedale-York at start of 1989-90.
Reverted to York at the start of
1995-96
Nickname: Wasps
Secretary: Ian Clough
Honours: **Division Two** Champions, 1980-81
Challenge Cup Beaten finalists,
1930-31
Yorkshire Cup Winners, 1922-23,
1933-34, 1936-37
Beaten finalists, 1935-36, 1957-58,
1978-79

RECORDS
Match
Goals: 12 by Gary Pearce at Nottingham C.,
4 Oct 1992
Tries: 7 by Brad Davis v. Highfield,
17 Sep 1995
Points: 28 by Gary Pearce at Nottingham C.,
4 Oct 1992
Brad Davis v. Highfield,
17 Sept 1995

Season
Goals: 146 by Vic Yorke, 1957-58
Tries: 35 by John Crossley, 1980-81
Points: 318 by Graham Steadman, 1984-85

Career
Goals: 1,060 by Vic Yorke, 1954-67
Tries: 167 by Peter Foster, 1955-67
Points: 2,159 by Vic Yorke, 1954-67
Appearances: 449 by Willie Hargreaves, 1952-65
Highest score: 84-0 at Nottingham C., 4 Oct 1992
Highest against: 75-3 at Warrington, 23 Sep 1950
Attendance: 14,689 v. Swinton (RL Cup),
10 Feb 1934 — at Clarence Street
4,977 v. Halifax (Div. 2),
5 Jan 1990 — at Ryedale Stadium

COACHING REGISTER
● **Since 1974-75**

Keith Goulding	Nov 73 - Sep 74
Gary Cooper	Dec 74 - Sep 76
Mal Dixon	Sep 76 - Dec 78
Paul Daley	Jan 79 - May 79
David Doyle-Davidson	July 79 - July 80
Bill Kirkbride	Aug 80 - Apr 82
Alan Hardisty	May 82 - Jan 83
Phil Lowe	Mar 83 - Mar 87
Danny Sheehan	Mar 87 - Apr 88
Gary Stephens	Apr 88 - June 91
Derek Foster	July 91 - Nov 92
Steve Crooks	Nov 92 - May 94
Roger Millward	June 94 - Dec 94
Stewart Horton	Jan 95 -

GREAT BRITAIN REGISTER
(7 players)

Edgar Dawson	(1)	1956
Harry Field	(3)	1936
Geoff Smith	(3)	1963-64
Jeff Stevenson	(4)	1959-60
Mick Sullivan	(1)	1963
Basil Watts	(5)	1954-55
Les White	(4)	1946

1995-96 REGISTRATION DATE

Signed	Player	Club From
1.7.95	Severs, David	–
18.7.95	Johnson, Michael	–
16.8.95	*Walker, Steve	Batley
18.8.95	*Hinchliffe, Andrew	Keighley C.
11.9.95	Forsyth, Craig	–
26.9.95	Marson, Andrew	Bramley
1.11.95	Hill, Rod	Australia
22.11.95	Walsh, Peter	Brotherton ARL
12.12.95	Morrell, Darren	Knottingley ARL

YORK 1995-96 PLAYERS' SUMMARY

	Date of birth	App	T	G	D	Pts	Previous club	Signed
Ball, Damian		10+4	7	6	0	40		
Cain, Mark	3.5.76	10	1	0	0	4	New Earswick ARL	17.4.95
Davies, Bryan	11.2.69	7+1	2	0	0	8	York All Blacks ARL	14.1.92
Davis, Brad	13.3.68	6	9	0	0	36	Huddersfield	9.8.94
Dobson, Steve	27.4.63	9	1	0	4	8	Sheffield E.	23.7.90
Forsyth, Craig		9+3	2	0	0	8		11.9.95
Gascoigne, Andy	2.4.62	5	1	0	0	4	Doncaster	30.6.94
Hayes, Richard	21.2.70	18+1	1	0	0	4	York All Blacks ARL	13.1.89
Hill, Rod		3+2	1	0	0	4	Australia	1.11.95
Hinchliffe, Andy		1	0	0	0	0	Keighley	18.8.95
Hopcutt, Chris	6.12.69	13	5	0	0	20	Scarborough P.	12.11.91
Jackson, Darryl	6.2.71	4+2	0	0	0	0	Nottingham C.	8.12.93
Judge, Chris	7.11.72	1	0	0	0	0	Heworth ARL	11.9.92
Johnson, Mick		19+1	3	0	0	12		18.7.95
Kettlestring, David	18.11.67	12	4	0	0	16	York All Blacks ARL	8.1.90
Laurence, Jason	23.1.70	13+1	12	0	0	48	Huddersfield	9.8.94
Marson, Andy		13	1	0	0	4	Bramley	26.9.95
Mawer, Keith	14.10.74	7+3	1	0	0	4	Acorn ARL	12.5.94
Morrell, Darren		0+4	0	0	0	0	Knothingley ARL	12.12.95
Mountain, Gary		3+1	1	0	0	4		1.4.95
Nicholson, Gavin	7.2.78	0+1	0	0	0	0	Oulton ARL	19.2.95
Pallister, Alan	4.12.70	17	6	0	0	24	York All Blacks ARL	1.11.90
Precious, Andrew	10.10.70	17+1	1	63	2	132		
Preston, Steve	22.12.75	3+1	0	0	0	0		13.1.95
Ramsden, Mick	13.11.71	17+3	4	0	0	16	York Civil Serv. ARL	1.6.91
Ramsey, Chris	8.9.71	0+1	0	0	0	0	Brotherton	26.12.94
Smirk, Terry	5.8.66	15+1	6	9	2	44	Hull	13.1.95
Smith, Dave	13.9.72	10+5	4	0	0	16		13.1.95
Thomas, Dean	10.5.66	18	2	0	0	8	L'pool St. Helens RU	26.8.93
Tichener, Lee	5.8.71	15+4	2	0	0	8	Bramley	1.7.93
Walker, Steve		6+1	0	0	0	0	Batley	16.8.95
Walsh, Peter		5+2	3	0	0	12	Brotherton ARL	22.11.95
TOTALS								
32 players			80	78	8	484		

YORK 1995-96 MATCH ANALYSIS

Date	Competition	H/A	Opponents	Rlt	Score	Tries	Goals	Attendance	Referee
20.8.95	SD	H	Carlisle	W	23-18	Pallister (2), Kettlestring, Ramsden	Ball (3), Dobson (dg)	571	Ganson
23.8.95	SD	H	Hunslet H.	L	10-21	–	Precious (2,dg), Ball (2), Smirk (dg)	728	Grimshaw
27.8.95	SD	H	Hull K.R.	W	27-14	Kettlestring, Precious, Davis, Johnson	Precious (5), Smirk (dg)	1055	Burke
3.9.95	SD	A	Swinton	L	10-18	Pallister, Davis	Precious	–	–
10.9.95	SD	H	Doncaster D.	W	20-18	Thomas (2), Smith	Precious (4)	1077	Cross
13.9.95	SD	A	Chorley	W	27-8	Davies, Kettlestring, Pallister, Ball	Precious (5), Dobson (dg)	–	–
17.9.95	SD	H	Highfield	W	74-14	Davis (7), Ball (2), Dobson, Ramsden, Davies, Forsyth, Hayes	Precious (8), Ball	564	Gilmour
24.9.95	SD	A	Barrow B.	L	6-36	Ramsden	Precious	–	–
27.9.95	SD	H	Leigh C.	L	18-20	Ramsden, Hopcutt	Precious (4,dg), Dobson (dg)	543	Grimshaw
30.9.95	RT(1)	H	Pia Xlll	W	24-22	Ball, Tichener, Laurence	Precious (6)	531	J. Connolly
12.11.95	RT(2)	A	Hull	L	18-56	Laurence, Gascoigne, Marson	Precious (3)	–	–
19.11.95	SD	A	Doncaster D.	L	8-31	Hopcutt, Tichener	–	–	–
26.11.95	SD	A	Bramley	L	15-17	Ball, Hill, Laurence	Precious, Dobson (dg)	–	–
29.11.95	SD	A	Carlisle	L	8-40	Smirk	Smirk (2)	–	–
3.12.95	SD	H	Chorley	W	18-14	Ball, Smirk, Forsyth	Smirk (3)	494	Oddy
10.12.95	SD	A	Highfield	D	24-24	Smith (2), Johnson, Mawer	Smirk (4)	–	–
13.12.95	SD	H	Bramley	W	24-12	Pallister, Smirk, Smith, Walsh	Precious (4)	405	Ganson
17.12.95	SD	H	Barrow B.	W	42-6	Walsh (2), Smirk (2), Hopcutt (2), Ball, Laurence	Precious (5)	525	Gilmour
19.12.95	SD	A	Hunslet H.	W	26-22	Laurence (3), Hopcutt, Johnson	Precious (3)	–	–
2.1.96	SD	A	Hull K.R.	L	2-26	–	Precious	–	–
7.1.96	SD	A	Leigh C.	L	24-36	Laurence (3), Mountain	Precious (4)	–	–
10.1.96	SD	H	Swinton	W	36-20	Laurence (2), Cain, Kettlestring, Pallister, Smirk	Precious (6)	460	Owram

*Martin Offiah, of Wigan, the 1995-96 joint leading try
scorer – a record sixth time at top of the chart – also
equalling a Division One record of touching down in
11 successive league matches.*

RECORDS

LEADING SCORERS FOR 1995-96
● Club and representative matches

TOP TEN TRIES
1. Martin Offiah (Wigan)..28
   David Plange (Hull K.R.) 28
3. Anthony Sullivan (St. Helens)................................24
4. Va'aiga Tuigamala (Wigan) 22
5. Jason Robinson (Wigan) 21
6. Simon Ashcroft (Swinton) 20
7. Joey Hayes (St. Helens) 18
   Jason Viller (Hunslet H.) 18
   Gary Atkins (Hull K.R.) 18
10. Jason Roach (Swinton) 17
    Nathan McAvoy (Salford R.) 17

TOP TEN GOALS
● Including drop goals
1. Bobbie Goulding (St. Helens) 135
2. Mike Fletcher (Hull K.R.) 117
3. Steve McNamara (Hull) 101
4. Paul Cook (Bradford B.)...99
5. Willie Richardson (Carlisle) 96
6. Steve Blakeley (Salford R.) 93
7. Andrew Farrell (Wigan)...92
8. Martin Pearson (Featherstone R.) 86
9. Simon Irving (Keighley C.)....................................81
   Chris Wilkinson (Leigh C.)......................................81

TOP FIVE DROP GOALS
1. Carl Briggs (Halifax) 9
2. David Close (Hunslet H.)...7
   Steve Hampson (Salford R.) 7
   Chris Wilkinson (Leigh C.)..7
5. Greg Mackey (Warrington)......................................6

TOP TEN POINTS

		T	G	DG	Pts
1.	Bobbie Goulding (St. Helens)	4	134	1	285
2.	Mike Fletcher (Hull K.R.)	5	116	1	253
3.	Paul Cook (Bradford B.)	12	99	0	246
4.	Steve McNamara (Hull)	10	100	1	241
5.	Martin Pearson (Featherstone R.)	16	83	3	233
6.	Steve Blakeley (Salford R.)	9	93	0	222
7.	Willie Richardson (Carlisle)	6	96	0	216
8.	Andrew Farrell (Wigan)	7	92	0	212
9.	Simon Irving (Keighley C.)	9	81	0	198
10.	Henry Paul (Wigan)	15	65	0	190

Key:
SBC .... Stones Bitter Centenary Championship
FD .... First Division
SD .... Second Division
PT .... Premiership Trophy
SDP .... Second Division Premiership
RT .... Regal Trophy
CC .... Challenge Cup
N .... Neutral venue
NA .... Non-appearance
WC .... World Cup

138

OUTSTANDING FEATS IN 1995-96
INDIVIDUAL
Most tries in a match:
7 by Brad Davis (York) v. Highfield........................... SD
5 by Damien Pickles (Bramley) v. Chorley C. .... SD
   Martin Offiah (Wigan) v. Whitehaven .... RT

Most goals in a match:
12 by Martin Pearson (Featherstone R.) v. Whitehaven FD
    Bobbie Goulding (St. Helens) v. Warrington ..... RT
11 by Andrew Johns (Australia) v. South Africa .... WC
    Paul Cook (Leeds) v. Halifax .... SBC
    Bobbie Goulding (St. Helens) v. Sheffield E. ..... SBC
    Dean Creasser (Bramley) v. Chorley C.............. SD
    Simon Wilson (Hunslet H.) v. Highfield............ SD
10 by Phil Atkinson (Barrow B.) v. Highfield .... SD
    Andrew Farrell (Wigan) at St. Helens.............. SBC
    Mike Smith (Chorley C.) v. Nottingham C........ RT
    Greg Pearce (Huddersfield) v. Batley................ FD

Most points in a match:
40 by Martin Pearson (Featherstone R.) v. Whitehaven FD
30 by Andrew Johns (Australia) v. South Africa .... WC
    Simon Wilson (Hunslet H.) v. Highfield............ SD

TEAM
Highest score:
Chorley C. 92 v. Nottingham C. 0............................ RT
● There was a total of 52 matches in which a team scored 50 points or more, including four World Cup matches. Other 60-plus score in 1995-96 were:

Home:
Australia 86 v. South Africa 6.................................... WC
Hunslet H. 82 v. Highfield 0 .... RT
London B. 82 v. Highfield 0 .... RT
St. Helens 80 v. Warrington 0 .... RT
Bramley 74 v. Chorley C. 0 .... SD
York 74 v. Highfield 14.. RT
Hull K.R. 72 v. Blackpool G. 6 .... RT
Carlisle 70 v. Highfield 0.. SD
Wigan 68 v. Whitehaven 26...................................... RT
Australia 66 v. Fiji 0.. WC
Barrow B. 64 v. Highfield 10.................................... SD
Carlisle 62 v. Chorley C. 10 .... SD
St. Helens 62 v. Sheffield E. 20 .... SBC
Featherstone R. 60 v. Whitehaven 10 .... FD
Hull K.R. 60 v. Highfield 6 .... SD
Leeds 60 v. Halifax 27 .... SBC

Away:
Chorley C. 10 v. Warrington 68 .... RT
Highfield 2 v. Swinton 66... SD
Highfield 5 v. Leigh C. 66.. SD
Workington T. 22 v. St. Helens 66 .... SBC

Highest score by a losing team:
London B. 44 v. Castleford 50 .... SBC
● There was a total of 77 matches in which the losing side scored 20 points or more, including three World Cup games.

High-scoring draws:

Castleford 26 v. Halifax 26 .... SBC
Highfield 24 v. York 24 .... SD
Chorley C. 20 v. Bramley 20 .... SD

● From the start of the 1983-84 season, the value of a try was raised from three to four points. It was decided officially that records for most points in a match, season or career would subsequently include the four-point try and that no attempt would be made to adjust existing records featuring the three-point try. This rule applies to all changes in pointscoring values.
● Substitute appearances do not count towards players' full appearance records.
● Points and appearances in abandoned matches are included in records, except in League matches which are replayed. Although abandoned League match points and appearances are included in players' overall totals they do not count towards League records.
● The 1995-96 season ended with the completion of the League programme on 21 January and does not include the Silk Cut Challenge Cup which preceded the 1996 Super League season.

RECORD FEATS IN 1995-96

AT A GLANCE

MARTIN OFFIAH of Wigan finished as the top tryscorer for a record sixth time and equalled a top division record of scoring at least one try in 11 successive matches.

BRAD DAVIS of York achieved club records of seven tries and 28 points in a match.

RICHARD HENARE of Carlisle scored a club record-equalling four tries in a match.

EVAN COCHRANE, PAUL HAUFF and SHANE VINCENT of London Broncos all equalled the club record of four tries in a match.

MARTIN HOLDEN of Chorley Chieftains scored a club record four tries in a match and equalled the record of 10 in a season.

MIKE SMITH of Chorley Chieftains achieved club match records of 18 goals and 24 points.

DEAN CREASSER of Bramley kicked a club record-equalling 11 goals in a match.

MARTIN PEARSON of Featherstone Rovers scored a club record 40 points in a match.

SIMON WILSON of Hunslet Hawks scored a club match record of 30 points.

ANDREW FARRELL achieved Charity Shield match records of eight goals and 20 points.

ANDREW JOHNS of Australia equalled international match records of 11 goals and 30 points.

MIKE FLETCHER of Hull Kingston Rovers scored in all of his club's matches throughout the season.

CHORLEY CHIEFTAINS gained a club record 92-0 victory.

HUNSLET HAWKS scored a club record 82-0 victory.

LONDON BRONCOS had a club record 82-0 victory.

BRAMLEY scored a club record 74-0 victory.

CARLISLE rattled up a club record 70-0 victory.

WARRINGTON suffered a club record 80-0 defeat.

WIGAN ran up a Charity Shield record score with their 45-20 defeat of Leeds.

AUSTRALIA scored a world record 86-6 international victory.

NEW RECORDS IN DETAIL . . .

MARTIN OFFIAH of Wigan finished as the leading tryscorer for a record sixth time and equalled a Division One record of touching down in 11 successive League matches.

The winger shared the top tryscoring spot with David Plange of Hull Kingston Rovers, both scoring 28. While at Widnes, Offiah had been the clear leader with 44 in 1987-88, 60 in 1988-89, 45 in 1989-90 and 49 in 1990-91. He first headed the chart as a Wigan player with 53 in 1994-95.

The previous record of five seasons at the top was shared by Australian winger Eric Harris of Leeds in the 1930s and Warrington's Brian Bevan over 40 years ago.

Offiah equalled the record of scoring a try in 11 successive "major" League matches. He touched down in Wigan's last match of the old Division One in 1994-95 and in the first 10 Stones Bitter Centenary Championship matches.

His scoring sequence brought him a total of 12 tries compared with 16 when he scored in 11 successive Division One matches for Widnes in 1987-88.

New Zealand centre Gary Prohm had set the record with Hull Kingston Rovers when he totalled 13 touching down in the last nine League matches of 1984-85 and the first two of the following season.

BRAD DAVIS of York scored club match records of seven tries and 28 points in the 74-14 Division Two home defeat of Highfield on 17 September. Playing at stand off, it was to be the Australian's last match for York as he was transferred to Wakefield Trinity shortly after.

The previous record of six tries had been shared by wingers Roy Hardgrave in a 40-11 League home defeat of Bramley on 5 January 1935 and David Kettlestring in a 70-8 League win at Keighley on 11 March 1990.

Davis' 28 points equalled the record set by stand off Gary Pearce with 12 goals and a try in an 84-0 Division Three win at Nottingham City on 4 October 1992.

RICHARD HENARE of Carlisle scored a club record-equalling four tries in the 42-4 Division Two home defeat of Doncaster on 3 January. It was only the New Zealand winger's second full game for the club after starting with a substitute appearance.

He shares the record with centres Gary Peacham, who scored four in a 42-6 home League defeat of Workington

139

Town on 25 January 1987, and Kevin Pape, who matched it in a 30-22 Silk Cut Challenge Cup first round home replay win over Rochdale Hornets on 11 February the same year.

EVAN COCHRANE, PAUL HAUFF and SHANE VINCENT of London Broncos all equalled the club record of four tries in a match.

Winger Cochrane became the first of the Australian trio to achieve the feat in the 42-10 Stones Bitter Centenary Championship win at Sheffield Eagles on 24 September.

Former Test full back Paul Hauff followed up with four in the next match, a 44-8 home League defeat of Workington Town on 1 October.

Winger Shane Vincent then scored four tries in the 82-0 home defeat of Highfield in the Regal Trophy second round tie on 12 November.

Players to have scored four tries before last season were: Mark Riley (v. Highfield, 17 October 1993), Mark Johnson (at Highfield, 1 April 1994) and Scott Roskell (at Bramley, 19 March 1995).

MARTIN HOLDEN and MIKE SMITH of Chorley Chieftains combined to achieve all three club match records when the team scored their biggest win with a 92-0 Regal Trophy first round home defeat of Nottingham on 1 October.

Winger Holden became the first Chorley player to score four tries in a match, while full back Mike Smith beat two records he had set himself with 10 goals and 24 points, including a try.

Smith's old records were also set against Nottingham when he scored 17 points from nine goals, including a drop goal, in a 57-20 Division Three home victory on 28 March 1993.

Holden went on to equal the club record of 10 tries in a season set by winger David Bacon in 1989-90 and hooker Joe Walsh in 1992-93.

DEAN CREASSER of Bramley kicked a club record-equalling 11 goals in the 74-0 Division Two home defeat of Chorley on 17 September.

The full back equalled the record set by Bernard Ward in a 52-17 Yorkshire Cup first round home defeat of Doncaster on 1 September 1974.

MARTIN PEARSON of Featherstone Rovers scored a club record 40 points with four tries and 12 goals in a 60-10 Division One home defeat of Whitehaven on 26 November.

The stand off beat the 30 points by centre Mark Knapper, who scored a try and 13 goals in the 86-18 Yorkshire Cup first round home defeat of Keighley on 17 September 1989.

SIMON WILSON of Hunslet Hawks scored a club record 30 points with 11 goals and a two tries in the club's record 82-0 Division Two home defeat of Highfield on 21 January.

The centre's tally beat the 28 points by half back Tim Lumb (3t, 8g) in a 52-12 home League defeat of Runcorn Highfield on 7 October 1990 and forward Richard Pell (2t, 10g) in a 64-4 Silk Cut Challenge Cup third round home defeat of Wigan St. Patricks amateurs on 22 January 1995.

Wilson also holds the Batley match records of 13 goals and 30 points.

ANDREW FARRELL of Wigan broke a Charity Shield record with 20 points, including a try and record-equalling eight goals, in the 45-20 Charity Shield defeat of Leeds at Dublin.

The loose forward's points tally beat the 16 (8g) by Wigan winger David Stephenson in the 44-12 defeat of Halifax in 1987 and centre Jonathan Davies' 16 (3t, 2g) for Widnes when they beat Wigan 24-8 in 1990.

Farrell's eight goals equalled Stephenson's 1987 total.

ANDREW JOHNS equalled world international match records with 11 goals and 30 points, including two tries, in the 86-6 World Cup defeat of South Africa at Gateshead on 10 October.

On his international debut, the 21-year-old scrum half equalled the 11 goals by Australia's Rod Wishart in a 1994 Test against France and New Zealand's Des White in a 1952 Test against Australia.

Johns' 30 points equalled the international record set by winger Michael O'Connor with four tries and seven goals for Australia against Papua New Guinea in 1988.

MIKE FLETCHER of Hull Kingston Rovers became only the third player to have twice scored in all matches for his club during the season, having first achieved the feat in 1989-90.

Others to have done the double are David Watkins with Salford in 1972-73 and 1973-74 plus Mick Parrish for Hunslet in 1979-80 and for Oldham in 1981-82.

Fletcher played centre, full back and stand off during 1995-96 when his match-by-match figures were:

	T	G	DG	Pts
Doncaster D. ....(A)	0	7	0	14
Leigh C. ....(H)	0	6	0	12
York....................................(A)	1	3	0	10
Bramley................................(H)	2	9	0	26
Barrow B. ....(A)	0	4	0	8
Hunslet H.............................(H)	0	5	0	10
Swinton ....(A)	0	3	0	6
Blackpool G. (RT) ....(H)	0	4	0	8
Carlisle ....(H)	0	2	0	4
Chorley C. ....(A)	0	8	0	16
Rochdale H. (RT) ....(H)	0	1	0	2
Leigh C. ....(A)	0	4	1	9
Barrow B. ....(H)	0	6	0	12
Highfield.............................(H)	1	6	0	16
Doncaster D. ....(H)	0	8	0	16
Hunslet H. ....(A)	0	4	0	8
Highfield ....(A)	0	7	0	14
Swinton ....(H)	0	7	0	14
York....................................(H)	0	3	0	6
Carlisle ....(A)	1	4	0	12
Bramley...............................(A)	0	6	0	12
Chorley C. ....(H)	0	9	0	18
Totals				
22 appearances........................	**5**	**116**	**1**	**253**

CHORLEY CHIEFTAINS ran up their highest ever score with a 92-0 Regal Trophy first round home defeat of Nottingham City on 1 October during their first season back as a senior club after two years in the National Conference League.

Their previous highest score was also against Nottingham, whom they beat 57-20 in a Division Three home game on 28 March 1993.

LONDON BRONCOS raced to a club record 82-0 home victory at the expense of visiting Highfield in a Regal Trophy second round tie on 12 November when they scored 15 tries.

They had set the previous record as London Crusaders with a 12-try 66-12 Division Two Premiership first round home defeat of Keighley Cougars on 8 May 1994.

BRAMLEY gained a club record 74-0 victory at home to Chorley in a Division Two match on 17 October. They scored 13 tries, one more than in their previous record win of 62-14 at home to Dewsbury in a Division Two match on 30 October 1988.

CARLISLE rattled up a club record 70-0 victory at home to Highfield in a Division Two match on 23 August, when they scored 14 tries. The Cumbrians' previous highest score was a ten-try 60-0 Division Two win at Nottingham City on 11 March 1990.

WARRINGTON suffered a club record defeat when they crashed 80-0 at St. Helens in the Regal Trophy semi-final on 4 January. The 14-try hammering surpassed a record defeat that had stood since 10 April 1928 when Warrington conceded 16 tries in a 68-14 League loss at Hunslet.

WIGAN ran up the highest Charity Shield score with their 45-20 defeat of Leeds at Dublin. The champions scored seven tries, as they did when setting the old record with a 44-12 defeat of Halifax in the Isle of Man in 1987, which remains the widest winning margin.

AUSTRALIA scored a world international record victory with their 16-try 86-6 defeat of South Africa in a World Cup match at Gateshead on 10 October. It beat the record they themselves set with a 74-0 Test win in France on 4 December 1994 when they scored 13 tries.

MILESTONES . . .

MARTIN OFFIAH of Wigan took his career try total to 401 with four in a 42-10 Stones Bitter Centenary Championship away win against London Broncos at Brentford's soccer ground on 3 December. At the end of the season he had totalled 406 tries in 345 matches and only nine years as a rugby league player.

The former Rosslyn Park RU winger's try total consisted of 174 for Wigan, 181 for Widnes and 51 in representative matches including 27 in Test and World Cup matches for Great Britain.

Offiah's 406 tries put him eighth in the all-time list but still well behind former Warrington winger Brian Bevan's record total of 796 tries between 1945 and 1964.

He raced to the fastest century of Division One tries when reaching the milestone in only his 70th match, no other player having achieved the feat in fewer than 100 matches. Offiah has also twice equalled the top division record sequence of 11 successive tryscoring matches.

Last season he headed the try chart for a record-breaking sixth time.

Offiah still holds the Widnes record for most tries in a season with 58 in 1988-89, having set the record with 42 the previous term — his first in rugby league. He is also the joint holder of the Widnes match record with five against Warrington on 15 March 1989.

Offiah continued his record-breaking at Wigan after being signed for a world record cash transfer fee of £440,000. He shattered the club match record with 10 in a home Stones Bitter Premiership semi-final defeat of Leeds on 10 May 1992.

He also holds the Great Britain Test match record with five against France at Leeds on 16 February 1991.

His total of 46 hat-tricks includes one 10-try feat, six five-try feats and nine four-try feats.

Offiah made his senior rugby league debut for Widnes on 30 August 1987 when he failed to score in a 28-6 Division One home defeat of Halifax. He also failed to score on his debut for Wigan in a 20-2 home League defeat of Wakefield Trinity on 5 January 1992.

Offiah's season-by-season tryscoring figures are as follows:

	App.	Tries
Widnes		
1987-88	35	42 + 1t GB, 1t RL XIII
1988-89	41	58 + 2t GB (inc 1 non-Test)
1989-90	32	40 + 5t GB
1990-91	37	41 + 8t GB
Wigan		
1991-92	15+1	30
1992-93	38	30 + 2t England
1993-94	34	35 + 2t GB
1994-95	38	53
1995-96	23	26 + 2t England
Totals		
Widnes	145	181
Wigan	148+1	174
Britain	34	27 Inc 1t in non-Test
3 tours	9+2	19 Not inc 9 Test tries
England	4	4
RL XIII	1	1
Lancashire	1	0
GRAND TOTALS	**342+3**	**406**

GARRY SCHOFIELD of Leeds scored the 300th try of his career with one in the 23-11 Stones Bitter Centenary Championship home defeat of Wigan on 3 November. At the end of the League season Schofield had totalled 304 tries in 445 matches with 147 for Leeds, 107 Hull and 50 in representative games.

The half back or centre's 31 tries for Great Britain in Test and World Cup matches put him second to Mick Sullivan's record 41 touchdowns, having equalled the former winger's record 46 caps.

Schofield equalled the British match record for tries with four as a centre in the 25-8 defeat of New Zealand at Wigan in 1985. He also scored four for the British Lions in a match on the 1984 tour and has one other hat-trick in a Test for Britain. His total of nine hat-tricks in club matches includes four four-try feats.

A former Hunslet Parkside Junior, Schofield signed for Hull after captaining the Great Britain youth squad to New Zealand in 1983. He made his debut for Hull in a 22-22 Division One home draw against Warrington on 21 August 1983 and finished as the game's top tryscorer in his first season with 38.

Hull transferred Schofield to Leeds in a then world record £155,000 deal and he scored two tries on his debut in a 25-29 defeat by Auckland on 25 October 1987.

Schofield's season-by-season tryscoring figures are as follows:

	App.	Tries
Hull		
1983-84....................	30+3	37 + 1t GB Under-21s
1984-85....................	32+2	23
1985-86....................	23	15 + 5t GB
1986-87....................	31+1	32 + 5t GB
Leeds		
1987-88....................	27	22 + 3t GB
1988-89....................	30	20 + 1t GB*, 1t Yorkshire
1989-90....................	29	20 + 1t Yorkshire
1990-91....................	30	20 + 5t GB
1991-92....................	32+1	13 + 1t GB
1992-93....................	25	14 + 3t GB, 1t England
1993-94....................	23+1	9 + 1t GB
1994-95....................	33+3	19
1995-96....................	13+2	10
Totals		
Hull	116+6	107
Leeds	242+7	147
Great Britain	47*	32*
England....................	3	1
Yorkshire.................	4	2
GB U-21/24	2+2	1
Chairman's XIII	1	0
Tours (4).................	15	14 Not inc Tests
GRAND TOTALS ..	**430+15**	**304**

* Including a try in a non-Test against a World XIII

PAUL NEWLOVE scored the 200th try of his career with one in Bradford Bulls' 20-10 Stones Bitter Centenary Championship defeat at Halifax on 27 August. The centre's total had moved on to 212 in 263 matches by the end of the season, having scored 66 for Bradford, 122 for Featherstone Rovers and three after his mid-season move to St. Helens, plus 21 in representative matches.

Newlove is the joint holder of most tries by a centre in a season with 52, including a club record 48 for Featherstone

plus four international touchdowns in 1992-93.

His best match feat is four tries each for Featherstone and Bradford. He has scored 12 other hat-tricks, including one for Great Britain.

Signed by Featherstone from local amateur club Travellers, Newlove made his senior debut on the wing seven weeks after his 17th birthday in an 18-0 Yorkshire Cup tie defeat at Hull on 27 September 1988.

He moved to Bradford for £245,000 – a record for both clubs and the highest fee set by the transfer tribunal – in August 1993. Newlove scored a try on his debut at centre in Bradford's 32-18 Division One home defeat of Widnes on 29 August 1993.

Over two years later he was transferred to St. Helens in a world record £500,000 deal with Bradford receiving £250,000 plus Sonny Nickle, Paul Loughlin and Bernard Dwyer. Newlove made a tryscoring debut in a 58-10 Stones Bitter Centenary Championship home defeat of Workington Town on 3 December 1995.

Newlove's season-by-season tryscoring figures are as follows:

	App.	Tries
Featherstone R.		
1988-89....................	30	18 + GB U21s 1t
1989-90....................	30	18 + GB U21s 1t, Yorkshire 2t
1990-91....................	23	13
1991-92....................	32	25 + GB U21s 2t, GB 1t
1992-93....................	35	48 + GB 3t, England 1t
Bradford B.		
1993-94....................	34+2	35 + GB 2t
1994-95....................	27+1	25 + GB 1t
1995-96....................	6	6 + England 4t
St. Helens		
1995-96....................	5	3
Totals		
Featherstone R	150	122
Bradford B	67+3	66
St. Helens.................	5	3
Gt Britain	12+4	8
1992 Tour...............	6+1	2 Not inc 1t in 3+2 Tests.
England....................	6	5
Yorkshire.................	1	2
GB Under-21s	8	4
GRAND TOTALS ..	**255+8**	**212**

GARY CONNOLLY of Wigan scored the 100th try of his career with one in the 44-20 Stones Bitter Centenary Championship home defeat of Workington Town on 19 November. At the end of the League season Connolly's total stood at 107 tries in 273 matches with 56 for Wigan, 46 St. Helens and five in representative games.

The centre or full back's most prolific tryscoring season was 1994-95 when he scored 30 for Wigan to finish seventh in the try chart, his only top ten placing. The total included the only three hat-tricks of his career.

A former Blackbrook (St. Helens) amateur, Connolly

signed for St. Helens in December 1988 and made his debut as a 17-year-old full back in a 29-0 Division One home defeat of Hull Kingston Rovers on 22 January 1989. He made 133 appearances for the Saints before being transferred to Wigan for £250,000 in August 1993.

Connolly made a tryscoring centre debut for Wigan in a 32-2 Division One home defeat of Widnes on 24 September 1993.

His season-by-season tryscoring figures are as follows:

	App.	Tries
St. Helens		
1988-89....................	13	1
1989-90....................	24+1	3
1990-91....................	22+2	4
1991-92....................	34+2	22 + 2t GB Under-21s
1992-93....................	35	16
Wigan		
1993-94....................	41	10
1994-95....................	43+2	30
1995-96....................	22	16
Totals		
St. Helens.................	128+5	46
Wigan	106+2	56
Great Britain	14+3	0
England....................	2	0
Tour	6+3	3 Not inc 2+2 Test app.
Gt Britain U-21s.......	4	2
GRAND TOTALS ..	**260+13**	**107**

TONY MARCHANT of Castleford scored his 100th try for the club with the first of two touchdowns in the 34-25 Stones Bitter Centenary Championship home defeat of Warrington on 24 September. At the end of the season Marchant's club total was 101 in 267 matches during two spells at Castleford.

After gaining international youth honours, Marchant first signed for Castleford over 14 years ago and less than two months later made his debut at centre in a 25-7 home League defeat against Hull on 17 March 1982.

Marchant moved to Bradford after eight seasons and scored 53 tries before leaving for Dewsbury in 1994. He scored 17 tries in two seasons at Dewsbury and then returned to Castleford for the start of the 1995-96 season.

He has scored three hat-tricks for Castleford, including one four-try feat.

His season-by-season tryscoring totals for Castleford are as follows:

	App.	Tries
1981-82....................	9+1	2
1982-83....................	35+1	16
1983-84	36	16
1984-85	32	12
1985-86....................	37	21
1986-87....................	29	8
1987-88....................	31	10
1988-89....................	35	13
1989-90	9+3	0

1995-96....................	8+1	3
Totals....................	**261+6**	**101**

ALAN TAIT of Leeds scored the 100th try of his career with one in the 50-12 Stones Bitter Centenary Championship home defeat of Workington Town on 27 September. His total of 106 in 272 matches at the end of the season consisted of 42 for Leeds, 55 Widnes and nine in representative matches, including six Test tries for Great Britain.

A former Scotland RU international, Tait switched codes with Widnes and made his debut as a substitute in a 36-26 Premiership first round home win over Halifax on 24 April 1988. He made two other substitute appearances in the Premiership, including the final when he scored his first try in the 38-14 defeat of St. Helens at Old Trafford.

Tait's full debut came in the Charity Shield the following season when he was full back in the 20-14 defeat of Wigan at Douglas, Isle of Man, on 21 August 1988.

Leeds signed him five years later in exchange for Bobbie Goulding plus a cash sum of less than £10,000 and he made his debut in a 14-27 Division One home defeat against St. Helens on 30 August 1992.

He has scored only one hat-trick, at full back for Widnes in 1989-90 when he finished with his season's best total of 20, including three for Britain.

Tait's season-by-season tryscoring figures are as follows:

	App.	Tries
Widnes		
1987-88....................	0+3	1
1988-89....................	39	16 + 1t GB
1989-90....................	36	17 + 3t GB
1990-91....................	28	12
1991-92....................	29+1	9 + 2t Cumbria
Leeds		
1992-93....................	32	9 + 2t GB
1993-94....................	34	11
1994-95....................	37	13
1995-96....................	13+3	9
Totals		
Widnes.....................	132+4	55
Leeds	116+3	42
Great Britain	10+4	6
Tour	1+1	1 Not inc 2 Test app
Cumbria...................	1	2
GRAND TOTALS ..	**260+12**	**106**

DARREN WRIGHT of Widnes scored the 100th try of his career with two in the 22-18 Division One win at Batley on 13 December. At the end of the season his total stood at 101, having scored 100 for Widnes and one for Great Britain Under-21s. He had made a total of 337 appearances.

The centre reached his century of touchdowns for Widnes with one in the 24-22 home League defeat of Salford on 4 January.

A former Leigh Miners Welfare amateur, Wright made his senior debut for Widnes as a substitute in a 14-12 Division One home defeat of York on 12 December 1985. Three days

143

later he was in the centre when Widnes lost 8-15 at home to Hull Kingston Rovers.

Wright has scored three hat-tricks, with the last at home to Featherstone Rovers in October 1991.

His season-by-season tryscoring figures are as follows:

	App.	Tries
Widnes		
1985-86....................	23+2	5
1986-87....................	40	15 + 1t GB Under-21s
1987-88....................	33	11
1988-89....................	37+1	18
1989-90....................	31+1	8
1990-91....................	26+6	9
1991-92....................	35	12
1992-93....................	29+2	7
1993-94....................	7+1	1
1994-95....................	29+1	7
1995-96....................	22	7
Totals		
Widnes.....................	312+14	100
Great Britain	0+1	0
Tour	7	0 Not inc 1 Test sub app
GB Under-21s.........	2	1
Lancashire..............	1	0
GRAND TOTALS..	**322+15**	**101**

PAUL LOUGHLIN scored the 2,000th point of his St. Helens career with a try in the 50-34 Stones Bitter Centenary Championship win away to London Broncos on 1 November. The centre scored only one other try to finish with 2,004 points for the Saints before being transferred to Bradford Bulls as part of the record £500,000 exchange deal for Paul Newlove.

His points total was made up of 80 tries and 842 goals in 297 matches, including 11 as a substitute.

Loughlin left with two club match records of 16 goals and 40 points in a 112-0 Lancashire Cup first round home defeat of Carlisle on 14 September 1986. His most prolific season was 1986-87 when he headed two scoring lists with 190 goals and 424 points.

Signed from St. Helens Colts, Loughlin made his senior debut as a substitute and kicked a goal in the 31-20 Division One home win against Oldham on 1 April 1984. He made one other substitute appearance before his full debut in the centre 20 days later, kicking another goal in a 28-28 League draw at Widnes.

Loughlin's season-by-season totals for St. Helens:

	App.	T	G	Pts
1983-84....................	1+2	0	2	4
1984-85....................	2+2	0	5	10
1985-86....................	24+3	4	43	102
1986-87....................	39	9	178	392
1987-88....................	37+1	8	111	254
1988-89....................	33	5	109	238
1989-90....................	32	17	135	338
1990-91....................	27	8	94	220

1991-92....................	11	5	40	100
1992-93	19+1	5	65	150
1993-94	29	3	58	128
1994-95....................	19+2	10	2	44
1995-96....................	13	6	0	24
Totals...................	**286+11**	**80**	**842**	**2,004**

MARTIN PEARSON of Featherstone Rovers passed the 1,000 points mark in club and representative matches with a try and six goals in the 27-18 Division One win at Whitehaven on 10 September. The full back went on to surpass 1,000 points for Featherstone alone with a try and seven goals in the 34-18 home League defeat of Hull on 19 November.

At the end of the season his overall points total stood at 1,175, including 1,107 for Featherstone plus 68 for Great Britain Under-21s.

The stand off smashed the Featherstone match points record during the season with 40 from 12 goals and four tries in a 60-10 home League defeat of Whitehaven on 26 November. He also holds the club points in a season record with 391 from 28 tries and 140 goals, including a drop goal, in 1992-93.

Great Britain Under-21s records held by Pearson are: most tries (3) and points (24) playing stand off against France at Halifax on 6 March 1991 and most goals (8) in a 58-0 defeat of Papua New Guinea at Leeds on 30 October 1991.

A former local amateur from Travellers, Pearson signed for Featherstone in November 1988 and made his debut as a substitute in a 19-24 Division One home defeat by Wigan on 1 March 1989. His full debut followed four days later when he was stand off in an 18-40 League defeat at Oldham.

Pearson's season-by-season scoring figures are as follows:

	App.	T	G	Pts
Featherstone R.				
1988-89....................	1+1	0	0	0
1989-90....................	0+2	0	0	0
1990-91....................	15+6	10	47	134
1991-92....................	22+6	9	1	38 +
			19g, 4t GB U-21s	
1992-93....................	33+2	28	140 (1)	391 +
				5g, 1t GB U-21s
1993-94....................	31+1	21	92 (1)	267
1994-95....................	5	1	20	44
1995-96....................	21	16	86(3)	233
Totals				
Featherstone R.	128+18	85	386(5)	1,107
Gt Britain U-21s.......	4	5	24	68
GRAND TOTALS..	**132+18**	**90**	**410(5)**	**1,175**

( ) denotes drop goals included in main total.

BOBBIE GOULDING of St. Helens scored the 1,000th point of his career with the second of 12 goals in the 80-0 Regal Trophy semi-final home defeat of Warrington on 4 January.

The scrum half's total at the end of the season was 1,052 made up of 601 for St. Helens, 114 Wigan, 61 Leeds, 218 Widnes and 58 in representative matches. In a total of 227 matches he has scored 46 tries and 445 goals, including 22 drop goals.

A former Widnes St. Maries amateur, Goulding turned professional with Wigan and made a tryscoring debut as a 16-year-old scrum half in a 20-16 Division One win at Halifax on 11 December 1988.

After failing to gain a regular first team spot, he moved to Leeds for £90,000 and made his debut for them in a 12-10 Division One defeat at Widnes on 1 September 1991.

A year later Goulding was transferred to Widnes in exchange for Alan Tait, with Leeds also paying a cash adjustment of under £10,000. He made a tryscoring debut for his home town club in a 16-6 Division One home defeat of Castleford on 30 August 1992.

Another two years and Goulding moved on to St. Helens for a transfer tribunal-fixed fee of £160,000. They ordered an immediate payment of £135,000 plus £25,000 if he played four times for Great Britain and/or England while at St. Helens, which he did. Goulding kicked five goals on his St. Helens debut in a 34-28 Division One home defeat of Salford on 4 September 1994.

His season-by-seasons figures are as follows:

	App.	T	G	Pts
Wigan				
1988-89	2	1	0	4
1989-90	14+11	7	29 (1)	85 + 1g GB U-21s
1990-91	12+6	3	8 (3)	25 + 1t GB U-21s
Leeds				
1991-92	32+3	7	19 (5)	61 + 1t, 1g GB U-21s
Widnes				
1992-93	31+2	3	16 (2)	42
1993-94	34	6	77 (2)	176
St. Helens				
1994-95	36	11	155 (7)	347 + 3g GB
1995-96	21	3	121	254 + 1t, 14(1)g England
Totals				
Wigan	28+17	11	37 (4)	114
Leeds	32 +3	7	19 (5)	61
Widnes	65+2	9	93 (4)	218
St. Helens	57	14	276 (7)	601
Great Britain	7+2	2	3	14
Tour	3+1	0	1 (1)	1
				Not inc 2t in 5 Tests
England	4	1	14 (1)	31
GB Under-21s	5	2	2	12
Lancashire	1	0	0	0
GRAND TOTALS..	**202+25**	**46**	**445(22)**	**1,052**

( ) Denotes drop goals included in main total

DEAN MARWOOD of Workington Town took his points total for the club past 1,000 with 16 in the 32-10 home League defeat of London Broncos on 7 January. At the end of the season the scrum half had totalled 1,026 points in 127 matches with 31 tries and 455 goals, including eight drop goals.

Marwood holds two club match records of 13 goals and 42 points, which he has achieved on two occasions. He set the records against Highfield on 1 November 1992 and equalled them against Leigh on 25 February 1995, scoring four tries each time.

A former Barrow Island amateur, Marwood turned professional with Barrow in February 1988 and scored 510 points for them before moving to Workington and making his debut in a 26-5 Division Two defeat at Carlisle on 26 December 1991.

Marwood's most prolific season was 1992-93 when he finished third in the points chart with 418 from 179 goals and 15 tries.

Marwood's season-by-season scoring figures for Workington are as follows:

	App.	T	G	Pts
1991-92	13+1	1	15 (3)	31
1992-93	34	15	179	418
1993-94	27	4	100 (1)	215
1994-95	33	7	114 (2)	254
1995-96	18+1	4	47 (2)	108
Totals	**125+2**	**31**	**455 (8)**	**1,026**

( ) denotes drop goals included in total.

Workington Town scrum half Dean Marwood.

LEADING SCORERS

	TRIES	GOALS	POINTS
1895-96	Hurst (Oldham) 28	Lorimer (Manningham).........35	Cooper (Bradford) 106
			Lorimer (Manningham).......106
1896-97	Hannah (Hunslet) 19	Goldthorpe (Hunslet) 26	Rigg (Halifax) 112
		Sharpe (Liversedge)...............26	
1897-98	Hoskins (Salford) 30	Goldthorpe (Hunslet) 66	Goldthorpe (Hunslet)..........135
1898-99	Williams (Oldham)................39	Goldthorpe (Hunslet) 67	Jaques (Hull) 169
1899-00	Williams (Oldham)................36	Cooper (Bradford) 39	Williams (Oldham)..............108
1900-01	Williams (Oldham)................47	Goldthorpe (Hunslet) 44	Williams (Oldham)..............141
1901-02	Wilson (Broughton R.) 38	James (Broughton R.).............75	Lomas (Salford) 172
1902-03	Evans (Leeds) 27	Goldthorpe (Hunslet) 48	Davies (Batley)....................136
1903-04	Hogg (Broughton R.) 34	Lomas (Salford) 66	Lomas (Salford) 222
1904-05	Dechan (Bradford) 31	Ferguson (Oldham) 50	Lomas (Salford) 146
1905-06	Leytham (Wigan) 40	Ferguson (Oldham) 49	Leytham (Wigan) 160
1906-07	Eccles (Halifax)....................41	Lomas (Salford) 86	Lomas (Salford) 280
1907-08	Leytham (Wigan) 44	Goldthorpe (Hunslet) 101	Goldthorpe (Hunslet)..........217
1908-09	Miller (Wigan) 49	Lomas (Salford) 88	Lomas (Salford) 272
	Williams (Halifax) 49		
1909-10	Leytham (Wigan) 48	Carmichael (Hull K.R.) 78	Leytham (Wigan) 232
1910-11	Kitchen (Huddersfield)..........41	Carmichael (Hull K.R.) 129	Carmichael (Hull K.R.).......261
1911-12	Rosenfeld (Huddersfield).......78	Carmichael (Hull K.R.) 127	Carmichael (Hull K.R.).......254
1912-13	Rosenfeld (Huddersfield).......56	Carmichael (Hull K.R.) 93	Thomas (Wigan) 198
1913-14	Rosenfeld (Huddersfield).......80	Holland (Huddersfield) 131	Holland (Huddersfield) 268
1914-15	Rosenfeld (Huddersfield).......56	Gronow (Huddersfield) 136	Gronow (Huddersfield) 284
● Competitive matches suspended during war years			
1918-19	Francis (Hull) 25	Kennedy (Hull)......................54	Kennedy (Hull)....................135
1919-20	Moorhouse (Huddersfield) 39	Gronow (Huddersfield) 148	Gronow (Huddersfield) 332
1920-21	Stone (Hull)...........................41	Kennedy (Hull) 108	Kennedy (Hull)....................264
1921-22	Farrar (Oldham) 49	Sullivan (Wigan) 100	Farrar (Oldham) 213
1922-23	Ring (Wigan) 41	Sullivan (Wigan) 161	Sullivan (Wigan) 349
1923-24	Ring (Wigan) 49	Sullivan (Wigan) 158	Sullivan (Wigan) 319
1924-25	Ring (Wigan) 54	Sullivan (Wigan) 138	Sullivan (Wigan) 282
1925-26	Ring (Wigan) 63	Sullivan (Wigan) 131	Sullivan (Wigan) 274
1926-27	Ellaby (St. Helens) 55	Sullivan (Wigan) 149	Sullivan (Wigan) 322
1927-28	Ellaby (St. Helens) 37	Thompson (Leeds) 106	Thompson (Leeds)...............233
1928-29	Brown (Wigan) 44	Sullivan (Wigan) 107	Sullivan (Wigan) 226
	Mills (Huddersfield) 44		
1929-30	Ellaby (St. Helens) 39	Thompson (Leeds) 111	Thompson (Leeds)...............243
1930-31	Harris, E. (Leeds)..................58	Sullivan (Wigan) 133	Sullivan (Wigan) 278
1931-32	Mills (Huddersfield) 50	Sullivan (Wigan) 117	Sullivan (Wigan) 249
1932-33	Harris, E. (Leeds)..................57	Sullivan (Wigan) 146	Sullivan (Wigan) 307
1933-34	Brown (Salford) 45	Sullivan (Wigan) 194	Sullivan (Wigan) 406
1934-35	Morley (Wigan)....................49	Sullivan (Wigan) 165	Sullivan (Wigan) 348
1935-36	Harris, E. (Leeds)..................63	Sullivan (Wigan) 117	Sullivan (Wigan) 246
1936-37	Harris, E. (Leeds)..................40	Sullivan (Wigan) 120	Sullivan (Wigan) 258
1937-38	Harris, E. (Leeds)..................45	Sullivan (Wigan) 135	Sullivan (Wigan) 285
1938-39	Markham (Huddersfield).......39	Sullivan (Wigan) 124	Risman (Salford).................267

● For the next six seasons emergency war-time competitions resulted in a reduction of matches and players were allowed to "guest" for other clubs

1939-40 Batten (Hunslet) 38	Hodgson (Swinton) 98	Hodgson (Swinton) 208
1940-41 Walters (Bradford N.) 32	Lockwood (Halifax)...............70	Belshaw (Warrington) 174
1941-42 Francis (Barrow) 30	Lockwood (Halifax)...............91	Lockwood (Halifax) 185
1942-43 Batten (Hunslet) 24	Lockwood (Halifax)...............65	Lockwood (Halifax) 136
1943-44 Lawrenson (Wigan) 21	Horne (Barrow)....................57	Horne (Barrow) 144
1944-45 Batten (Bradford N.) 41	Stott (Wakefield T.) 51	Stott (Wakefield T.) 129
● Normal peace-time rugby resumed		
1945-46 Batten (Bradford N.) 35	Ledgard (Dewsbury) 89	Bawden (Huddersfield) 239
1946-47 Bevan (Warrington)...............48	Miller (Hull) 103	Bawden (Huddersfield) 243
1947-48 Bevan (Warrington)...............57	Ward (Wigan) 141	Ward (Wigan) 312
1948-49 Cooper (Huddersfield) 60	Ward (Wigan) 155	Ward (Wigan) 361
1949-50 Nordgren (Wigan).................57	Gee (Wigan) 133	Palin (Warrington) 290
	Palin (Warrington) 133	
1950-51 Bevan (Warrington)...............68	Cook (Leeds) 155	Cook (Leeds) 332
1951-52 Cooper (Huddersfield) 71	Ledgard (Leigh) 142	Horne (Barrow) 313
1952-53 Bevan (Warrington)...............72	Bath (Warrington) 170	Bath (Warrington)................379
1953-54 Bevan (Warrington)...............67	Metcalfe (St. Helens)...........153	Metcalfe (St. Helens) 369
	Bath (Warrington) 153	
1954-55 Cooper (Huddersfield) 66	Ledgard (Leigh) 178	Ledgard (Leigh) 374
1955-56 McLean (Bradford N.) 61	Ledgard (Leigh) 155	Bath (Warrington) 344
1956-57 Boston (Wigan)....................60	Jones (Leeds) 194	Jones (Leeds) 496
1957-58 Sullivan (Wigan) 50	Ganley (Oldham) 219	Ganley (Oldham) 453
1958-59 Vollenhoven (St. Helens).......62	Ganley (Oldham) 190	Griffiths (Wigan) 394
1959-60 Vollenhoven (St. Helens).......54	Rhodes (St. Helens) 171	Fox (Wakefield T.)...............453
	Fox (Wakefield T.) 171	
1960-61 Vollenhoven (St. Helens).......59	Rhodes (St. Helens) 145	Rhodes (St. Helens) 338
1961-62 Boston (Wigan)....................51	Fox (Wakefield T.) 183	Fox (Wakefield T.)...............456
1962-63 Glastonbury (Work'ton T.)....41	Coslett (St. Helens) 156	Coslett (St. Helens).............321
1963-64 Stopford (Swinton)...............45	Coslett (St. Helens) 138	Fox (Wakefield T.) 313
1964-65 Lake (Wigan) 40	Kellett (Hull K.R.) 150	Killeen (St. Helens).............360
1965-66 Killeen (St. Helens) 32	Killeen (St. Helens) 120	Killeen (St. Helens).............336
Lake (Wigan) 32		
1966-67 Young (Hull K.R.) 34	Risman (Leeds) 163	Killeen (St. Helens).............353
Howe (Castleford)..................34		
1967-68 Millward (Hull K.R.).............38	Risman (Leeds) 154	Risman (Leeds)....................332
1968-69 Francis (Wigan) 40	Risman (Leeds) 165	Risman (Leeds)....................345
1969-70 Atkinson (Leeds)...................38	Tyrer (Wigan) 167	Tyrer (Wigan) 385
1970-71 Haigh (Leeds) 40	Coslett (St. Helens) 193	Coslett (St. Helens).............395
Jones (St. Helens)..................40		
1971-72 Atkinson (Leeds)...................36	Coslett (St. Helens) 214	Watkins (Salford) 473
Lamb (Bradford N.) 36		
1972-73 Atkinson (Leeds)...................39	Watkins (Salford) 221	Watkins (Salford) 493
1973-74 Fielding (Salford) 49	Watkins (Salford) 183	Watkins (Salford) 438
1974-75 Dunn (Hull K.R.) 42	Fox (Hull K.R.) 146	Fox (Hull K.R.) 333
1975-76 Richards (Salford) 37	Watkins (Salford) 175	Watkins (Salford) 385
1976-77 Wright (Widnes) 31	Lloyd (Castleford) 163	Lloyd (Castleford)...............341
1977-78 Wright (Widnes) 33	Pimblett (St. Helens) 178	Pimblett (St. Helens)...........381
1978-79 Hartley (Hull K.R.) 35	Lloyd (Hull) 172	Lloyd (Hull) 373
1979-80 Fielding (Salford) 30	Quinn (Featherstone R.)......163	Quinn (Featherstone R.)......375
Hubbard (Hull K.R.)..............30		
1980-81 Crossley (York) 35	Hesford (Warrington) 147	Hesford (Warrington)..........310

1981-82	Jones (Workington T.)...........31	Hopkins (Workington T.) 190	Hopkins (Workington T.)....446
1982-83	Eccles (Warrington) 37	Diamond (Fulham) 136	Diamond (Fulham) 308
1983-84	Schofield (Hull) 38	Hesford (Warrington).........142	Woods (Leigh) 355
1984-85	Hanley (Bradford N.) 55	Day (St. Helens) 157	Day (St. Helens) 362
1985-86	Halliwell (Leigh) 49	Johnson, C. (Leigh) 173	Johnson, C. (Leigh).............400
1986-87	Hanley (Wigan).....................63	Loughlin (St. Helens) 190	Loughlin (St. Helens)..........424
1987-88	Offiah (Widnes) 44	Woods (Warrington)............152	Woods (Warrington) 351
1988-89	Offiah (Widnes) 60	Aston (Sheffield E.) 148	Aston (Sheffield E).............307
1989-90	Offiah (Widnes) 45	Fletcher, M. (Hull K.R.)......199	Fletcher, M. (Hull K.R.) 450
1990-91	Offiah (Widnes) 49	Kerry (Salford) 177	Kerry (Salford)....................427
1991-92	Edwards (Wigan) 40	Botica (Wigan) 161	Botica (Wigan)....................364
1992-93	Newlove (Featherstone R.) 52	Wasyliw (Keighley C.) 187	Wasyliw (Keighley C.).........490
1993-94	Johnson (London B.).............43	Botica (Wigan) 188	Botica (Wigan)....................422
1994-95	Offiah (Wigan) 53	Botica (Wigan) 186	Botica (Wigan)....................408
1995-96	Offiah (Wigan) 28	Goulding (St. Helens) 135	Goulding (St. Helens) 285
	Plange (Hull K.R.) 28		

Shaun Edwards, top try scorer in 1991-92.

Frano Botica, top goals and points scorer in 1991-92, 1993-94 and 1994-95.

ALL-TIME RECORDS

Most goals in a match:
22 by JIM SULLIVAN (Wigan) v. Flimby & Fothergill (Challenge Cup), 14 February 1925

Most goals in a season:
DAVID WATKINS holds the record for most goals in a season with 221 — all for Salford — in 1972-73. Watkins played and scored a goal in every match that season as follows:

1972

Aug.	19	Leeds ....(H)	5
	23	Featherstone R. ....(A)	3
	26	Whitehaven.................................(A)	4
	28	Swinton.................................(H)	4
Sep.	1	Oldham ....(LC) (H)	10
	9	Leeds.................................(A)	2
	15	Rochdale H. ....(LC) (H)	11
	17	Leigh ....(A)	6
	24	Barrow ....(JP) (A)	4
	29	Huyton ....(H)	10
Oct.	3	Oldham.................................(FT) (A)	4
	6	Wigan ....(LC)(A)	4
	8	Blackpool B. ....(A)	5
	13	Blackpool B. ....(H)	8
	21	Swinton.............(Warrington, LC Final)	5
Nov.	5	Huyton ....(A)	8
	10	Rochdale H. ....(H)	6
	17	Warrington ....(A)	4
	19	New Zealand ....(H)	10
	24	Dewsbury.................................(JP) (H)	4
	26	Workington T. ....(H)	6
Dec.	1	Barrow ....(H)	9
	10	Bradford N. ....(JP) (H)	9
	13	Oldham ....(A)	4
	15	Leigh ....(H)	3
	24	Bradford N. ....(A)	5
	26	Workington T. ....(A)	3
	30	Hull K.R. ....(JP) (A)	5

1973

Jan.	3	Bradford N. ....(H)	6
	7	Rochdale H. ....(A)	2
	12	Featherstone R. ....(H)	4
	28	Featherstone R. ....(RL Cup) (A)	4
Feb.	2	Whitehaven ....(H)	4
	11	Barrow ....(A)	5
	23	St. Helens ....(H)	3
Mar.	7	Widnes ....(A)	3
	9	Dewsbury.................................(H)	3
	16	St. Helens ....(A)	2
	24	Leeds ....(Huddersfield, JP Final)	3
	30	Warrington ....(H)	1
Apr.	6	Widnes ....(H)	4
	13	Oldham.................................(H)	3
	15	Dewsbury ....(A)	2
	17	Wigan ....(A)	3

	20	Swinton ....(A)	7
	23	Wigan ....(H)	3
	29	Rochdale H. ....(top 16) (H)	2

	App	Goals
League	34	147
Lancs Cup.....................................	4	30
John Player	5	24
Tour match	1	10
RL Cup	1	4
Floodlit Cup.....................................	1	4
Top 16.....................................	1	2
Totals.....................................	**47**	**221**

Fastest goals century:
Four players share the record of scoring the fastest 100 goals from the start of a season in terms of number of matches played. They are BERNARD GANLEY, DAVID WATKINS, STEVE QUINN and JOHN WASYLIW, who achieved the century in 18 matches.

Ganley reached 100 goals on 16 November 1957, after playing 17 matches for Oldham and one for Great Britain.

Watkins scored his 100th goal on 17 November 1972, all for Salford.

Quinn scored his 100th goal on 16 December 1979, all for Featherstone Rovers.

Wasyliw equalled the record with his 100th goal for Keighley Cougars on 31 January 1993.

Most goals in a career:
JIM SULLIVAN holds the record for most goals in a career with 2,867 between 1921-22 and 1945-46. He scored a century of goals in every season after leaving Welsh Rugby Union for Wigan until the war interrupted the 1939-40 campaign. The Test full back played all of his club rugby for Wigan apart from war-time appearances with Bradford Northern, Dewsbury and Keighley.

Sullivan's total includes 441 in representative matches, including three tours of Australasia. These figures are accepted by the Record Keepers' Club following research by James Carter and Malcolm Bentley.

Most one-point drop goals in a match:
5 by DANNY WILSON (Swinton) v. Hunslet (John Player Special), 6 November 1983
PETER WOOD (Runcorn H.) v. Batley, 21 October 1984
PAUL BISHOP (Warrington) at Wigan (Premiership semi-final), 11 May 1986

Most one-point drop goals in a season:
29 by LYN HALLETT (Cardiff C.) 1983-84

Most one-point drop goals in a career:
97 by NORMAN TURLEY (Warrington, Runcorn H., Swinton, Blackpool B., Rochdale H., Barrow, Workington T., Trafford B., Whitehaven)...............................1974-91

149

Longest successful goal kick:

ARTHUR ATKINSON of Castleford is credited with the longest successful goal kick, covering 75 yards (68.5 metres) to the posts. The centre's wind-assisted penalty kick was taken during Castleford's 20-10 League win at St. Helens on 26 October 1929.

Martin Hodgson of Swinton has often been credited with the longest successful kick, but his goal at Rochdale Hornets on 13 April 1940 was measured at 77¾ yards (71.06m) to beyond the posts where the ball landed. Reports at the time referred to a 58-yard (53m) goal.

● Details of the record kick were discovered following research by Graham Morris.

Most tries in a match:

11 by GEORGE WEST (Hull K.R.) v. Brookland Rovers (Challenge Cup), 4 March 1905

Most tries in a career:

BRIAN BEVAN holds the record for most tries in a career with 796 between 1946 and 1964. His season-by-season record is:

1946-47	48
1947-48	57
1948-49	56
1949-50	33
1950-51	68
1951-52	51
1952-53	72
1953-54	67
1954-55	63
1955-56	57
1956-57	17
1957-58	46
1958-59	54
1959-60	40
1960-61	35
1961-62	15
1962-63	10
1963-64	7

Totals

Warrington	740
Blackpool Borough	17
Other Nationalities	26
Other representative matches	13
Grand Total	**796**

The Australian winger played his first game for Warrington on 17 November 1945 and his last on 23 April 1962 before having two seasons at Blackpool Borough. His last match for Borough was on 22 February 1964.

Most tries in a season:

ALBERT ROSENFELD holds the record for most tries in a season with 80 — all for Huddersfield — in 1913-14.

Rosenfeld's match-by-match record:

1913

Sep.	6	York	(A)	4
	8	Warrington	(H)	2
	13	Leeds	(H)	5
	20	Halifax	(A)	1
	27	Batley	(A)	0
Oct.	4	Oldham	(H)	2
	11	Rochdale H.	(A)	0
	18	Bramley	(YC) (H)	2
	25	Dewsbury	(A)	4
Nov.	1	Halifax	(YC) (A)	2
	8	Wigan	(A)	1
	15	Dewsbury	(YC) (H)	3
	19	Bradford N.	(H)	3
	22	Leeds	(A)	3
	29	Bradford N.	(Halifax, YCF)	1
Dec.	3	Halifax	(H)	3
	6	Hunslet	(A)	2
	13	Rochdale H.	(H)	3
	20	Hull K.R.	(A)	2
	25	Hull	(A)	1
	26	Wakefield T.	(H)	3
	27	Hunslet	(H)	0

1914

Jan.	1	St. Helens	(A)	0
	3	Warrington	(A)	0
	10	York	(H)	3
	17	Keighley	(A)	2
	24	Dewsbury	(H)	1
	31	Batley	(H)	0
Feb.	7	Oldham	(A)	0
	14	Bramley	(H)	5
	21	Wigan	(H)	3
	28	Swinton Park R.	(RL Cup) (H)	7
Mar.	7	Wakefield T.	(A)	2
	14	Hull K.R.	(RL Cup) (A)	2
	18	Bramley	(A)	3
	21	Widnes	(RL Cup) (H)	0
	25	Keighley	(H)	3
	28	Hull K.R.	(H)	1
	30	Bradford N.	(A)	1
Apr.	4	Hull	(Leeds, RL Cup SF)	0
	11	Hull	(H) did not play	
	13	St. Helens	(H)	0
	20	Hull	(Play-off) (H) did not play	
	25	Salford	(Leeds, Championship Final)	0

	App	Tries
League	33	63
Yorks Cup	4	8
RL Cup	4	9
Play-off	1	0
Totals	**42**	**80**

Most points in a season:
LEWIS JONES holds the record for most points in a season with 496 from 194 goals and 36 tries for Leeds and representative teams in 1956-57.

Jones's match-by-match record:

For Leeds

1956			G	T	Pts
Aug.	17	Halifax ....(H)	3	0	6
	22	Bradford N. ....(A)	11	3	31
	25	Wigan..............................(A)	4	0	8
	27	Featherstone R. ....(H)	4	1	11
Sep.	1	Wakefield T. ....(YC) (A)	3	1	9
	8	Dewsbury..........................(A)	6	0	12
	15	Warrington ....(H)	7	0	14
	22	Huddersfield ....(A)	3	0	6
	29	York.................................(H)	6	0	12
Oct.	6	Batley ....(A)	4	2	14
	13	Australia..........................(H)	Did not play		
	20	Hull K.R. ....(A)	Did not play		
	27	Wigan..............................(H)	2	0	4
Nov.	3	Hunslet............................(A)	1	0	2
	10	Barrow ....(H)	3	2	12
	17	Halifax.............................(A)	4	0	8
	24	Keighley ....(H)	3	3	15
Dec.	1	Barrow.............................(A)	4	0	8
	8	Bramley...........................(A)	5	0	10
	15	Doncaster.........................(H)	1	2	8
	22	Bradford N. ..(abandoned) (H)	1	1	5
	25	Batley...............................(H)	8	1	19
	29	Keighley............................(A)	3	0	6
1957					
Jan.	5	Hull ....(H)	5	2	16
	12	Warrington........................(A)	0	3	9
	19	St. Helens ....(H)	5	1	13
	26	Doncaster ....(A)	Did not play		
Feb.	2	Huddersfield......................(H)	6	0	12
	9	Wigan...............(RL Cup) (H)	2	1	7
	16	York ....(A)	7	1	17
	23	Warrington ....(RL Cup) (H)	5	1	13
	27	Castleford..........................(H)	4	1	11
Mar.	9	Halifax............(RL Cup) (A)	5	0	10
	16	Wakefield T. ....(H)	5	1	13
	20	Bradford N. ....(H)	5	1	13
	23	Hull ....(A)	2	0	4
	30	Whitehaven			
		................(Odsal, RL Cup SF)	1	0	2
Apr.	3	Wakefield T. ....(A)	3	0	6
	6	St. Helens ....(A)	0	0	0
	12	Hull K.R. ....(H)	Did not play		
	13	Dewsbury..........................(A)	6	2	18
	19	Hunslet ....(H)	5	2	16
	20	Featherstone R. ....(A)	2	0	4
	22	Castleford ....(A)	2	0	4
	23	Bramley............................(H)	7	1	17
May	4	Oldham ....(Play-off) (A)	3	0	6

			G	T	Pts
	11	Barrow			
		........(Wembley, RL Cup final)	0	0	0

Representative matches
For Great Britain:

			G	T	Pts
Jan.	26	France ....(at Leeds)	9	1	21
Mar.	3	France ....(at Toulouse)	5	1	13
Apr.	10	France..............(at St. Helens)	7	1	17

For The Rest:

Oct.	3	Britain XIII ....(at Bradford)	4	0	8

For RL XIII:

Oct.	29	Australia ....(Leigh)	3	0	6

	App	G	T	Pts
League	36	147	30	384
RL Cup.............................	5	13	2	32
Yorks Cup	1	3	1	9
Play-off	1	3	0	6
Representative	5	28	3	65
Totals.............................	**48**	**194**	**36**	**496**

Most points in a match:
53 (11t,10g) by GEORGE WEST (Hull K.R.) v. Brookland Rovers (RL Cup), 4 March 1905

Most points in a career:
NEIL FOX holds the record for most points in a career with 6,220 between 1956 and 1979. This total does not include points scored during a spell of club rugby in New Zealand.

Fox was a month short of his 17th birthday when he made his debut for Wakefield Trinity on 10 April 1956. Apart from a brief time at Bradford Northern, Fox had 19 seasons at Wakefield before moving to a succession of clubs in later years.

After a long career as an international centre Fox moved into the forwards and played his last professional match for Bradford in their opening fixture of the 1979-80 season, on 19 August. That match enabled him to join the elite few who have played first team rugby at 40 years of age.

Fox's season-by-season tally is as follows:

	G	T	Pts
1955-56	6	0	12
1956-57	54	10	138
1957-58	124	32	344
1958-59	148	28	380
1959-60	171	37	453
1960-61	94	20	248
1961-62	183	30	456
1962 Tour			
Australasia	85	19	227
South Africa...........................	19	4	50
1962-63	125	14	292
1963-64	125	21	313
1964-65	121	13	281
1965-66	98	11	229
1966-67	144	16	336

1967-68	98	18	250
1968-69	95	9	217
1969-70	17	5	49
1970-71	110	12	256
1971-72	84	6	186
1972-73	138	8	300
1973-74	62	8	148
1974-75	146(1)	14	333
1975-76	102(1)	4	215
1976-77	79(1)	6	175
1977-78	95(1)	9	216
1978-79	50	4	112
1979-80	2	0	4

A breakdown of Fox's club and representative totals is as follows:

	App	G	T	Pts
Wakefield T.	574	1,836	272	4,488
Bradford N.	70	85(1)	12	205
Hull K.R........................	59	212(2)	16	470
York	13	42	2	90
Bramley	23	73	6	164
Huddersfield	21	73(1)	5	160
Club Totals	**760**	**2,321(4)**	**313**	**5,577**
Yorkshire	17	60	9	147
Britain v. Australia..........	8	26	3	61
New Zealand.................	4	11	1	25
France	17	56	10	142
Other representative games including tour ...	22	101	22	268
Representative Totals...	**68**	**254**	**45**	**643**
Grand Totals................	**828**	**2,575(4)**	**358**	**6,220**

( ) Figures in brackets are one-point drop goals included in total.

Score-a-match:

The following players have appeared and scored in all of their club's matches in one season:

Jim Hoey (Widnes)	1932-33
Billy Langton (Hunslet)	1958-59
Stuart Ferguson (Leigh).............................	1970-71
David Watkins (Salford)	1972-73
David Watkins (Salford)	1973-74
John Woods (Leigh)...................................	1977-78
Steve Quinn (Featherstone R.)	1979-80
Mick Parrish (Hunslet)	1979-80
John Gorton (Swinton)	1980-81
Mick Parrish (Oldham)	1981-82
Peter Wood (Runcorn H.)..........................	1984-85
David Noble (Doncaster)	1986-87
Mark Aston (Sheffield E.)	1988-89
Mike Fletcher (Hull K.R.)	1989-90
Steve Carroll (Bramley)	1991-92
Paul Bishop (Halifax)	1992-93
John Wasyliw (Keighley C.)	1992-93
John Schuster (Halifax)	1994–95
Mike Fletcher (Hull K.R.)	1995–96

Longest scoring run:

DAVID WATKINS holds the record for the longest scoring run, playing and scoring in 92 consecutive matches for Salford from 19 August 1972 to 25 April 1974. He totalled 403 goals, 41 tries and 929 points.

Longest run of appearances:

KEITH ELWELL holds the record for the longest run of appearances with one club with a total of 239 for Widnes. The consecutive run started at Wembley in the 1977 Challenge Cup final against Leeds on 7 May, and ended after he played in a Lancashire Cup tie at home to St. Helens on 5 September 1982. He was dropped for the match at Featherstone Rovers a week later. Although he went on as a substitute the record refers to full appearances only. Elwell played as a substitute in the nex* match and then made a full appearance before his run of all appearances ended at 242.

TEAM
Highest score:

Huddersfield 142 v. Blackpool Gladiators 4 (Regal Trophy)
..... 26 November 1994

Widest margin:

As above and
Barrow 138 v. Nottingham City 0 (Regal Trophy)
..... 27 November 1994

Highest score away:

Highfield 4 v. Keighley Cougars 104 (Division Two, played at Rochdale Hornets) ....23 April 1995

● The highest score on an opponent's ground is:
Blackpool Gladiators 5 v. Dewsbury 90 (Division Three)
.... 4 April 1993

Widest margin:

Runcorn Highfield 2 v. Leigh 88 (Division Two)
..... 15 January 1989

Most points in all matches in a season:

1,735 by Wigan from 45 matches in 1994-95 as follows:

30 Division One matches	1,148
6 Challenge Cup	230
5 Regal Trophy...	170
3 Premiership	167
1 Australia	20

Most League points in a season:

1,156 by Leigh from 34 Division Two matches in 1985-86.

Longest winning run:

29 by Wigan from February to October 1987, as follows:
20 Division One, 3 Premiership, 4 Lancashire Cup, 1 Charity Shield and 1 World Club Challenge.

Longest unbeaten run:

43 Cup and League matches, including two draws, by Huddersfield in 1914-19.

They were unbeaten in the last 38 matches of 1914-15 and after the interruption of the First World War won their next five competitive matches — four Yorkshire Cup ties in 1918-19 and the first League match of 1919-20.

Longest winning run in the League:
31 matches by Wigan. Last 8 matches of 1969-70 and first 23 of 1970-71.
● In 1978-79 Hull won all of their 26 Division Two matches, the only time a club has won all its League matches in one season.

Longest losing run:
61 Cup and League matches by Runcorn Highfield from January 1989 to February 1991. Made up of 55 Division Two, 2 Challenge Cup, 2 Regal Trophy and 2 Lancs Cup.

Longest run without a win:
75 Cup and League matches by Runcorn Highfield from October 1988 to March 1991. Made up of 67 Division Two, 3 Challenge Cup, 3 Regal Trophy and 2 Lancs Cup.

Longest League losing run and run without a win:
Included in the above.
● Only three teams have lost all their matches in a season: Liverpool City (1906-07)*, Runcorn Highfield (1989-90) and Nottingham City (1991-92).
*Liverpool drew a League match against Bramley but this was expunged from the records as the return fixture was cancelled.

TOP SCORING AND APPEARANCE CHARTS
The following are extended charts of outstanding scoring and appearance records established by British-based players.

*Denotes amateur or non-league team

EIGHT OR MORE TRIES IN A MATCH
11	George West (Hull K.R.) v. Brookland R.*	4 Mar. 1905
10	Lionel Cooper (Huddersfield) v. Keighley	17 Nov. 1951
	Martin Offiah (Wigan) v. Leeds	10 May 1992
	Shaun Edwards (Wigan) at Swinton	29 Sep. 1992
9	Ray Markham (Huddersfield) v. Featherstone R.	21 Sep. 1935
	Greg Austin (Huddersfield) v. Blackpool G.*	26 Nov. 1994
8	Dai Thomas (Dewsbury) v. Liverpool C.	13 Apr. 1907
	Albert Rosenfeld (Huddersfield) v. Wakefield T.	26 Dec. 1911
	Fred Webster (Leeds) v. Coventry	12 Apr. 1913
	Eric Harris (Leeds) v. Bradford N.	14 Sep. 1931
	Lionel Cooper (Huddersfield) v. Yorkshire Amateurs*	11 Sep. 1948
	Keith Williams (Halifax) v. Dewsbury	9 Nov. 1957

14 OR MORE GOALS IN A MATCH
22	Jim Sullivan (Wigan) v. Flimby & Fothergill*	14 Feb. 1925
18	Major Holland (Huddersfield) v. Swinton Park*	28 Feb. 1914
17	Geoff "Sammy" Lloyd (Castleford) v. Millom*	16 Sep. 1973
	Darren Carter (Barrow) v. Nottingham C.*	27 Nov. 1994
16	Paul Loughlin (St. Helens) v. Carlisle	14 Sep. 1986
15	Mick Stacey (Leigh) v. Doncaster	28 Mar. 1976
	John Wasyliw (Keighley C.) v. Nottingham C.	1 Nov. 1992

14	Alf Carmichael (Hull K.R.) v. Merthyr Tydfil	8 Oct. 1910
	Jim Kennedy (Hull) v. Rochdale H.	7 Apr. 1921
	Harold Palin (Warrington) v. Liverpool S.	13 Sep. 1950
	Joe Phillips (Bradford N.) v. Batley	6 Sep. 1952
	Bernard Ganley (Oldham) v. Liverpool C.	4 Apr. 1959
	Bruce Burton (Halifax) v. Hunslet	27 Aug. 1972
	Geoff "Sammy" Lloyd (Hull) v. Oldham	10 Sep. 1978
	Chris Johnson (Leigh) v. Keighley	30 Apr. 1986
	Steve Turner (Rochdale H.) v. Runcorn H.	5 Nov. 1989
	Mike Fletcher (Hull K.R.) v. Whitehaven	18 Mar. 1990
	Colin Armstrong (Hull K.R.) at Nottingham C.	19 Aug. 1990

On tour with Great Britain:

17	Ernest Ward v. Mackay (Australia)	2 Jul. 1946
15	Alf Wood v. South Australia	23 May 1914
	Jim Ledgard v. Wide Bay (Australia)	28 Jun. 1950
	Lewis Jones v. Southern New South Wales (Australia)	21 Aug. 1954
	Eric Fraser v. North Queensland (Australia)	29 Jun. 1958

35 POINTS OR MORE IN A MATCH

53	George West (Hull K.R.) v. Brookland R.*	4 Mar. 1905
44	Jim Sullivan (Wigan) v. Flimby & Fothergill*	14 Feb. 1925
43	Geoff "Sammy" Lloyd (Castleford) v. Millom*	16 Sep. 1973
42	Dean Marwood (Workington T.) v. Highfield	1 Nov. 1992
	Darren Carter (Barrow) v. Nottingham C.*	27 Nov. 1994
	Dean Marwood (Workington T.) v. Leigh	26 Feb. 1995
40	Paul Loughlin (St. Helens) v. Carlisle	14 Sep. 1986
	Martin Offiah (Wigan) v. Leeds	10 May 1992
	Shaun Edwards (Wigan) at Swinton	29 Sep. 1992
	Martin Pearson (Featherstone R.) v. Whitehaven	26 Nov. 1995
39	James Lomas (Salford) v. Liverpool C.	2 Feb. 1907
	Major Holland (Huddersfield) v. Swinton Park*	28 Feb. 1914
38	John Woods (Leigh) v. Blackpool B.	11 Sep. 1977
	Bob Beardmore (Castleford) v. Barrow	22 Mar. 1987
	John Woods (Leigh) v. Ryedale-York	12 Jan. 1992
36	Jim Kennedy (Hull) v. Keighley	29 Jan. 1921
	Mick Stacey (Leigh) v. Doncaster	28 Mar. 1976
	John Woods (Bradford N.) v. Swinton	13 Oct. 1985
	Graham Steadman (Castleford) v. Salford	1 Apr. 1990
	John Wasyliw (Keighley C.) v. Nottingham C.*	31 Oct. 1993
	Greg Austin (Huddersfield) v. Blackpool G.*	26 Nov. 1994
35	Jim Bawden (Huddersfield) v. Swinton	20 Apr. 1946

50 TRIES OR MORE IN A SEASON

80 Albert Rosenfeld (Huddersfield)............1913-14
78 Albert Rosenfeld (Huddersfield).............1911-12
72 Brian Bevan (Warrington)......................1952-53
71 Lionel Cooper (Huddersfield) 1951-52
68 Brian Bevan (Warrington)......................1950-51
67 Brian Bevan (Warrington)......................1953-54
66 Lionel Cooper (Huddersfield) 1954-55
63 Johnny Ring (Wigan) 1925-26
     Eric Harris (Leeds) 1935-36
     Jack McLean (Bradford N.) 1951-52
     Brian Bevan (Warrington)......................1954-55
     Ellery Hanley (Wigan) 1986-87
62 Tom Van Vollenhoven (St. Helens)........1958-59
61 Jack McLean (Bradford N.) 1955-56
60 Lionel Cooper (Huddersfield) 1948-49
     Billy Boston (Wigan) 1956-57
     Martin Offiah (Widnes) 1988-89
59 Lionel Cooper (Huddersfield) 1950-51
     Jack McLean (Bradford N.) 1952-53
     Tom Van Vollenhoven (St. Helens)........1960-61
58 Eric Harris (Leeds) 1930-31
57 Eric Harris (Leeds) 1932-33
     Brian Bevan (Warrington)......................1947-48
     Brian Nordgren (Wigan) 1949-50
     Brian Bevan (Warrington)......................1955-56
56 Albert Rosenfeld (Huddersfield).............1912-13
     Albert Rosenfeld (Huddersfield).............1914-15
     Brian Bevan (Warrington)......................1948-49
55 Alf Ellaby (St. Helens) 1926-27
     Ellery Hanley (Bradford N.)...................1984-85
54 Stan Moorhouse (Huddersfield) 1911-12
     Johnny Ring (Wigan) 1924-25
     Brian Bevan (Warrington)......................1958-59
     Billy Boston (Wigan) 1958-59
     Tom Van Vollenhoven (St. Helens)........1959-60
53 Ray Markham (Huddersfield) 1935-36
     Martin Offiah (Wigan)...........................1994-95
52 Jack Harrison (Hull) 1914-15
     Frank Castle (Barrow) 1951-52
     Jack McLean (Bradford N.) 1953-54
     Paul Newlove (Featherstone R.) 1992-93
     Greg Austin (Huddersfield)....................1994-95
51 Brian Bevan (Warrington)......................1951-52
     Jim Lewthwaite (Barrow) 1956-57
     Billy Boston (Wigan) 1961-62
50 Ernest Mills (Huddersfield)...................1931-32
     Lionel Cooper (Huddersfield) 1952-53
     Mick Sullivan (H'field and Wigan) 1957-58

170 GOALS OR MORE IN A SEASON

●   Including drop goals
221 David Watkins (Salford) 1972-73
219 Bernard Ganley (Oldham)...................1957-58
214 Kel Coslett (St. Helens) 1971-72
199 Mike Fletcher (Hull K.R.)...................1989-90
194 Jim Sullivan (Wigan)...........................1933-34
      Lewis Jones (Leeds) 1956-57
193 Kel Coslett (St. Helens) 1970-71
      David Watkins (Salford) 1971-72
190 Bernard Ganley (Oldham)...................1958-59
      Lyn Hopkins (Workington T.) 1981-82
      Paul Loughlin (St. Helens)..................1986-87
189 Bernard Ganley (Oldham)...................1956-57
188 Frano Botica (Wigan) 1993-94
187 John Wasyliw (Keighley C.) 1992-93
186 Frano Botica (Wigan) 1994-95
184 Frano Botica (Wigan) 1992-93
183 Fred Griffiths (Wigan) 1961-62
      Neil Fox (Wakefield T.) 1961-62
      David Watkins (Salford) 1973-74
181 Billy Langton (Hunslet) 1958-59
179 Dean Marwood (Workington T.) 1992-93
178 Jim Ledgard (Leigh) 1954-55
      Geoff Pimblett (St. Helens)................1977-78
177 Steve Kerry (Salford) 1990-91
176 Fred Griffiths (Wigan) 1958-59
175 David Watkins (Salford) 1975-76
173 Eddie Tees (Bradford N.) 1971-72
      Chris Johnson (Leigh).........................1985-86
172 Geoff "Sammy" Lloyd (Hull) 1978-79
171 Austin Rhodes (St. Helens) 1959-60
      Neil Fox (Wakefield T.) 1959-60
170 Harry Bath (Warrington) 1952-53
      Steve Hesford (Warrington) 1978-79

370 OR MORE POINTS IN A SEASON

496	Lewis Jones (Leeds)	1956-57
493	David Watkins (Salford)	1972-73
490	John Wasyliw (Keighley C.)	1992-93
476	David Watkins (Salford)	1971-72
456	Neil Fox (Wakefield T.)	1961-62
453	Bernard Ganley (Oldham)	1957-58
	Neil Fox (Wakefield T.)	1959-60
452	Kel Coslett (St. Helens)	1971-72
450	Mike Fletcher (Hull K.R.)	1989-90
446	Lyn Hopkins (Workington T.)	1981-82
438	David Watkins (Salford)	1973-74
427	Steve Kerry (Salford)	1990-91
424	Paul Loughlin (St. Helens)	1986-87
423	Frano Botica (Wigan)	1992-93
422	Frano Botica (Wigan)	1993-94
418	Dean Marwood (Workington T.)	1992-93
408	Frano Botica (Wigan)	1994-95
406	Jim Sullivan (Wigan)	1933-34
405	Martin Pearson (Featherstone R.)	1992-93
400	Chris Johnson (Leigh)	1985-86
399	Austin Rhodes (St. Helens)	1959-60
395	Kel Coslett (St. Helens)	1970-71
394	Fred Griffiths (Wigan)	1958-59
392	Simon Irving (Keighley C.)	1994-95
390	Fred Griffiths (Wigan)	1961-62
385	Colin Tyrer (Wigan)	1969-70
	David Watkins (Salford)	1975-76
384	Bernard Ganley (Oldham)	1956-57
	John Gallagher (London C.)	1993-94
383	Bernard Ganley (Oldham)	1958-59
381	Geoff Pimblett (St. Helens)	1977-78
380	Neil Fox (Wakefield T.)	1958-59
	Billy Langton (Hunslet)	1958-59
379	Harry Bath (Warrington)	1952-53
	Mick Parrish (Oldham)	1981-82
376	Nigel Stephenson (Dewsbury)	1972-73
375	Steve Quinn (Featherstone R.)	1979-80
374	Jim Ledgard (Leigh)	1954-55
373	Geoff "Sammy" Lloyd (Hull)	1978-79
372	John Woods (Leigh)	1981-82

300 TRIES OR MORE IN A CAREER

796	Brian Bevan (Warrington, Blackpool B.)	1945-1964
571	Billy Boston (Wigan, Blackpool B.)	1953-1970
446	Alf Ellaby (St. Helens, Wigan)	1926-1939
443	Eric Batten (Wakefield T., Hunslet, Bradford N., Featherstone R.)	1933-1954
441	Lionel Cooper (Huddersfield)	1947-1955
428	Ellery Hanley (Bradford N., Wigan, Leeds)	1978-
415	Johnny Ring (Wigan, Rochdale H.)	1922-1933
406	Clive Sullivan (Hull, Hull K.R., Oldham, Doncaster)	1961-1985
406	Martin Offiah (Widnes, Wigan)	1987-
401	John Atkinson (Leeds, Carlisle)	1966-1983
399	Eric Harris (Leeds)	1930-1939
395	Tom Van Vollenhoven (St. Helens)	1957-1968
386	Albert Rosenfeld (Huddersfield, Wakefield T., Bradford N.)	1909-1924
383	Jim Lewthwaite (Barrow)	1943-1957
374	Ike Southward (Workington T., Oldham, Whitehaven)	1952-1969
372	Barney Hudson (Salford)	1928-1946
358	Neil Fox (Wakefield T., Bradford N., Hull K.R., York, Bramley, Huddersfield)	1956-1979
342	Mick Sullivan (Huddersfield, Wigan, St. Helens, York, Dewsbury)	1952-1966
321	Johnny Lawrenson (Wigan, Workington T., Swinton)	1939-1954
319	Eric Ashton (Wigan)	1955-1969
314	Jim Leytham (Wigan)	1901-1912
312	Brian Nordgren (Wigan)	1946-1955
311	Alan Smith (Leeds)	1962-1983
310	Jim Lomas (Bramley, Salford, Oldham, York)	1902-1923
304	Alan Hardisty (Castleford, Leeds)	1958-1974
304	Garry Schofield (Hull, Leeds)	1983-
302	Maurice Richards (Salford)	1969-1983

1,000 OR MORE GOALS IN A CAREER

2,867	Jim Sullivan (Wigan)	1921-1946
2,575	Neil Fox (Wakefield T., Bradford N., Hull K.R., York, Bramley, Huddersfield)	1956-1979
1,768	Cyril Kellett (Hull K.R., Featherstone R.)	1956-1974
1,698	Kel Coslett (St. Helens, Rochdale H.)	1962-1979
1,677	Gus Risman (Salford, Workington T., Batley)	1929-1954
1,591	John Woods (Leigh, Bradford N., Warrington, Rochdale H.)	1976-1992
1,578	Steve Quinn (York, Featherstone R.)	1970-1988
1,560	Jim Ledgard (Leeds, Dewsbury, Leigh)	1944-1961
1,478	Lewis Jones (Leeds)	1952-1964
1,398	Bernard Ganley (Oldham)	1951-1961
1,376	Ray Dutton (Widnes, Whitehaven)	1966-1981
1,342	David Watkins (Salford, Swinton, Cardiff C.)	1967-1983
1,306	George Fairbairn (Wigan, Hull K.R.)	1974-1990
1,272	Colin Tyrer (Leigh, Wigan, Barrow, Hull K.R.)	1962-1978
1,189	Frank Dyson (Huddersfield, Oldham)	1949-1965
1,179	Terry Clawson (Featherstone R., Bradford N., Hull K.R., Leeds, Oldham, York, Wakefield T., Huddersfield, Hull)	1957-1980
1,169	Steve Hesford (Warrington, Huddersfield B.)	1975-1986
1,154	Derek Whitehead (Swinton, Oldham, Warrington)	1964-1979
1,127	Geoff "Sammy" Lloyd (Castleford, Hull)	1970-1983
1,092	John McKeown (Whitehaven)	1948-1961
1,081	Vic Yorke (York)	1954-1967
1,075	Ken Gowers (Swinton)	1954-1973
1,046	Lee Crooks (Hull, Leeds, Castleford)	1980-
1,044	Billy Langton (Hunslet)	1955-1966
1,030	Ron James (Halifax)	1961-1971
1,016	Iain MacCorquodale (Salford, Workington T., Fulham, Blackpool B., Rochdale H.)	1970-1982

Lee Crooks, scorer of 1,046 goals in a 16-year career.

2,500 OR MORE POINTS IN A CAREER

6,220	Neil Fox (Wakefield T., Bradford N., Hull K.R., York, Bramley, Huddersfield)	1956-1979
6,022	Jim Sullivan (Wigan)	1921-1946
4,050	Gus Risman (Salford, Workington T., Batley)	1929-1954
3,985	John Woods (Leigh, Bradford N., Warrington, Rochdale H.)	1976-1992
3,686	Cyril Kellett (Hull K.R., Featherstone R.)	1956-1974
3,545	Kel Coslett (St. Helens, Rochdale H.)	1962-1979
3,445	Lewis Jones (Leeds)	1952-1964
3,438	Steve Quinn (York, Featherstone R.)	1970-1988
3,279	Jim Ledgard (Leeds, Dewsbury, Leigh)	1944-1961
3,117	David Watkins (Salford, Swinton, Cardiff C.)	1967-1982
2,902	Colin Tyrer (Leigh, Wigan, Barrow, Hull K.R.)	1962-1978
2,894	George Fairbairn (Wigan, Hull K.R.)	1974-1990
2,844	Bernard Ganley (Oldham)	1951-1961
2,786	Ray Dutton (Widnes, Whitehaven)	1966-1981
2,574	Terry Clawson (Featherstone R., Bradford N., Hull K.R., Leeds, Oldham, York, Wakefield T., Huddersfield, Hull)	1957-1980
2,561	Frank Dyson (Huddersfield, Oldham)	1949-1965

650 APPEARANCES OR MORE IN A CAREER

● Figures in brackets denote substitute appearances included in main total.

928	Jim Sullivan (Wigan)	1921-1946
873	Gus Risman (Salford, Workington T., Batley)	1929-1954
828 (28)	Neil Fox (Wakefield T., Bradford N., Hull K.R., York, Bramley, Huddersfield)	1956-1979
776 (57)	Jeff Grayshon (Dewsbury, Bradford N., Leeds, Featherstone R., Batley)	1969-
740 (46)	Graham Idle (Bramley, Wakefield T., Bradford N., Hunslet, Rochdale H., Sheffield E., Doncaster, Nottingham C., Highfield)	1969-1993
738 (25)	Colin Dixon (Halifax, Salford, Hull K.R.)	1961-1981
727 (9)	Paul Charlton (Workington T., Salford, Blackpool B.)	1961-1981
695 (26)	Keith Mumby (Bradford N., Sheffield E., Keighley C., Ryedale-York, Wakefield T.)	1973-1995
691 (1)	Ernie Ashcroft (Wigan, Huddersfield, Warrington)	1942-1962
688	Brian Bevan (Warrington, Blackpool B.)	1945-1964
683 (24)	John Wolford (Bramley, Bradford N., Dewsbury, Hunslet)	1962-1985
682	Joe Ferguson (Oldham)	1899-1923
679	Joe Oliver (Huddersfield, Batley, Hull, Hull K.R.)	1923-1945
669 (33)	John Joyner (Castleford)	1973-1992
665	George Carmichael (Hull K.R., Bradford N.)	1929-1950
663 (25)	John Holmes (Leeds)	1968-1989
662 (28)	Mal Aspey (Widnes, Fulham, Wigan, Salford)	1964-1983
651	Jack Miller (Warrington, Leigh)	1926-1947

Wigan skipper Shaun Edwards, extending his record number of appearances in a final to 29, lifts the 1995-96 Regal Trophy.

CUPS

CUPS

CHALLENGE CUP ROLL OF HONOUR

Year	Winners		Runners-up		Venue	Attendance	Receipts
1897	Batley	10	St. Helens	3	Leeds	13,492	£624.17.7
1898	Batley	7	Bradford	0	Leeds	27,941	£1,586.3.0
1899	Oldham	19	Hunslet	9	Manchester	15,763	£946.16.0
1900	Swinton	16	Salford	8	Manchester	17,864	£1,100.0.0
1901	Batley	6	Warrington	0	Leeds	29,563	£1,644.16.0
1902	Broughton R.	25	Salford	0	Rochdale	15,006	£846.11.0
1903	Halifax	7	Salford	0	Leeds	32,507	£1,834.8.6
1904	Halifax	8	Warrington	3	Salford	17,041	£936.5.6
1905	Warrington	6	Hull K.R.	0	Leeds	19,638	£1,271.18.0
1906	Bradford	5	Salford	0	Leeds	15,834	£920.0.0
1907	Warrington	17	Oldham	3	Broughton	18,500	£1,010.0.0
1908	Hunslet	14	Hull	0	Huddersfield	18,000	£903.0.0
1909	Wakefield T.	17	Hull	0	Leeds	23,587	£1,490.0.0
1910	Leeds	7	Hull	7	Huddersfield	19,413	£1,102.0.0
Replay	Leeds	26	Hull	12	Huddersfield	11,608	£657.0.0
1911	Broughton R.	4	Wigan	0	Salford	8,000	£376.0.0
1912	Dewsbury	8	Oldham	5	Leeds	15,271	£853.0.0
1913	Huddersfield	9	Warrington	5	Leeds	22,754	£1,446.9.6
1914	Hull	6	Wakefield T.	0	Halifax	19,000	£1,035.5.0
1915	Huddersfield	37	St. Helens	3	Oldham	8,000	£472.0.0
1920	Huddersfield	21	Wigan	10	Leeds	14,000	£1,936.0.0
1921	Leigh	13	Halifax	0	Broughton	25,000	£2,700.0.0
1922	Rochdale H.	10	Hull	9	Leeds	32,596	£2,964.0.0
1923	Leeds	28	Hull	3	Wakefield	29,335	£2,390.0.0
1924	Wigan	21	Oldham	4	Rochdale	41,831	£3,712.0.0
1925	Oldham	16	Hull K.R.	3	Leeds	28,335	£2,879.0.0
1926	Swinton	9	Oldham	3	Rochdale	27,000	£2,551.0.0
1927	Oldham	26	Swinton	7	Wigan	33,448	£3,170.0.0
1928	Swinton	5	Warrington	3	Wigan	33,909	£3,158.1.11
1929	Wigan	13	Dewsbury	2	Wembley	41,500	£5,614.0.0
1930	Widnes	10	St. Helens	3	Wembley	36,544	£3,102.0.0
1931	Halifax	22	York	8	Wembley	40,368	£3,908.0.0
1932	Leeds	11	Swinton	8	Wigan	29,000	£2,479.0.0
1933	Huddersfield	21	Warrington	17	Wembley	41,874	£6,465.0.0
1934	Hunslet	11	Widnes	5	Wembley	41,280	£6,686.0.0
1935	Castleford	11	Huddersfield	8	Wembley	39,000	£5,533.0.0
1936	Leeds	18	Warrington	2	Wembley	51,250	£7,070.0.0
1937	Widnes	18	Keighley	5	Wembley	47,699	£6,704.0.0
1938	Salford	7	Barrow	4	Wembley	51,243	£7,174.0.0
1939	Halifax	20	Salford	3	Wembley	55,453	£7,681.0.0
1940	*No competition*						
1941	Leeds	19	Halifax	2	Bradford	28,500	£1,703.0.0
1942	Leeds	15	Halifax	10	Bradford	15,250	£1,276.0.0
1943	Dewsbury	16	Leeds	9	Dewsbury	10,470	£823.0.0
	Dewsbury	0	Leeds	6	Leeds	16,000	£1,521.0.0
	Dewsbury won on aggregate 16-15						
1944	Bradford N.	0	Wigan	3	Wigan	22,000	£1,640.0.0
	Bradford N.	8	Wigan	0	Bradford	30,000	£2,200.0.0
	Bradford won on aggregate 8-3						
1945	Huddersfield	7	Bradford N.	4	Huddersfield	9,041	£1,184.3.7
	Huddersfield	6	Bradford N.	5	Bradford	17,500	£2,050.0.0
	Huddersfield won on aggregate 13-9						

Year	Winners		Runners-up		Venue	Attendance	Receipts
1946	Wakefield T.	13	Wigan	12	Wembley	54,730	£12,013.13.6
1947	Bradford N.	8	Leeds	4	Wembley	77,605	£17,434.5.0
1948	Wigan	8	Bradford N.	3	Wembley	91,465	£21,121.9.9
1949	Bradford N.	12	Halifax	0	Wembley	*95,050	£21,930.5.0
1950	Warrington	19	Widnes	0	Wembley	94,249	£24,782.13.0
1951	Wigan	10	Barrow	0	Wembley	94,262	£24,797.19.0
1952	Workington T.	18	Featherstone R.	10	Wembley	72,093	£22,374.2.0
1953	Huddersfield	15	St. Helens	10	Wembley	89,588	£30,865.12.3
1954	Warrington	4	Halifax	4	Wembley	81,841	£29,706.7.3
Replay	Warrington	8	Halifax	4	Bradford	102,569	£18,623.7.0
1955	Barrow	21	Workington T.	12	Wembley	66,513	£27,453.16.0
1956	St. Helens	13	Halifax	2	Wembley	79,341	£29,424.7.6
1957	Leeds	9	Barrow	7	Wembley	76,318	£32,671.14.3
1958	Wigan	13	Workington T.	9	Wembley	66,109	£33,175.17.6
1959	Wigan	30	Hull	13	Wembley	79,811	£35,718.19.9
1960	Wakefield T.	38	Hull	5	Wembley	79,773	£35,754.16.0
1961	St. Helens	12	Wigan	6	Wembley	94,672	£38,479.11.9
1962	Wakefield T.	12	Huddersfield	6	Wembley	81,263	£33,390.18.4
1963	Wakefield T.	25	Wigan	10	Wembley	84,492	£44,521.17.0
1964	Widnes	13	Hull K.R.	5	Wembley	84,488	£44,840.19.0
1965	Wigan	20	Hunslet	16	Wembley	89,016	£48,080.4.0
1966	St. Helens	21	Wigan	2	Wembley	*98,536	£50,409.0.0
1967	Featherstone R.	17	Barrow	12	Wembley	76,290	£53,465.14.0
1968	Leeds	11	Wakefield T.	10	Wembley	87,100	£56,171.16.6
1969	Castleford	11	Salford	6	Wembley	*97,939	£58,848.1.0
1970	Castleford	7	Wigan	2	Wembley	95,255	£89,262.2.0
1971	Leigh	24	Leeds	7	Wembley	85,514	£84,452.15
1972	St. Helens	16	Leeds	13	Wembley	89,495	£86,414.30
1973	Featherstone R.	33	Bradford N.	14	Wembley	72,395	£125,826.40
1974	Warrington	24	Featherstone R.	9	Wembley	77,400	£132,021.05
1975	Widnes	14	Warrington	7	Wembley	85,098	£140,684.45
1976	St. Helens	20	Widnes	5	Wembley	89,982	£190,129.40
1977	Leeds	16	Widnes	7	Wembley	80,871	£241,488.00
1978	Leeds	14	St. Helens	12	Wembley	*96,000	£330,575.00
1979	Widnes	12	Wakefield T.	3	Wembley	94,218	£383,157.00
1980	Hull K.R.	10	Hull	5	Wembley	*95,000	£448,202.90
1981	Widnes	18	Hull K.R.	9	Wembley	92,496	£591,117.00
1982	Hull	14	Widnes	14	Wembley	92,147	£684,500.00
Replay	Hull	18	Widnes	9	Elland Rd, L'ds	41,171	£180,525.00
1983	Featherstone R.	14	Hull	12	Wembley	84,969	£655,510.00
1984	Widnes	19	Wigan	6	Wembley	80,116	£686,171.00
1985	Wigan	28	Hull	24	Wembley	*97,801	£760,322.00
1986	Castleford	15	Hull K.R.	14	Wembley	82,134	£806,676.00
1987	Halifax	19	St. Helens	18	Wembley	91,267	£1,009,206.00
1988	Wigan	32	Halifax	12	Wembley	*94,273	£1,102,247.00
1989	Wigan	27	St. Helens	0	Wembley	*78,000	£1,121,293.00
1990	Wigan	36	Warrington	14	Wembley	*77,729	£1,360,000.00
1991	Wigan	13	St. Helens	8	Wembley	75,532	£1,610,447.00
1992	Wigan	28	Castleford	12	Wembley	77,286	£1,877,564.00
1993	Wigan	20	Widnes	14	Wembley	*77,684	£1,981,591.00
1994	Wigan	26	Leeds	16	Wembley	*78,348	£2,032,839.00
1995	Wigan	30	Leeds	10	Wembley	*78,550	£2,040,000.00

*Indicates a capacity attendance, the limit being fixed annually taking into account variable factors.

RUGBY LEAGUE CHALLENGE CUP FINAL PLAYERS' REGISTER

The following is an index of players who have appeared in the Rugby League Challenge Cup final in the last 20 seasons. It also includes the pre-1975 record of any listed player. W — winners, L — losers, D — draw. Substitute appearances in lower case letters. The year denotes the second half of the season. *denotes replay.

ADAMS, Mick: Widnes 75W, 76L, 77L, 79W, 81W, 82DL*, 84W
AGAR, Allan: Hull K.R. 80W
AH KUOI, Fred: Hull 85L
ANDERSON, Chris: Widnes 75W; Halifax 87W
ANDERSON, Grant: Castleford 92L
ANDERSON, Tony: Halifax 88L
ARKWRIGHT, Chris: St. Helens 87L
ASHCROFT, Kevin: Leigh 71W; Warrington 74W, 75L
ASHURST, Bill: Wigan 70L; Wakefield T. 79L
ASPEY, Malcolm: Widnes 75W, 77L, 79W
ATCHESON, Paul: Wigan 95w
ATKINSON, John: Leeds 68W, 71L, 72L, 77W, 78W

BANKS, Alan: Featherstone R. 83W
BARKER, Nigel: Featherstone R. 83W
BASNETT, John: Widnes 82DL*, 84W
BEARDMORE, Kevin: Castleford 86W
BEARDMORE, Bob: Castleford 86W
BEEVERS, Graham: Halifax 87W
BELL, Dean: Wigan 88W, 89W, 90W, 91W, 92W, 93W, 94W
BENTLEY, Keith: Widnes 81W
BENYON, Billy: St. Helens 66W, 72W, 76W
BETTS, Denis: Wigan 89W, 90W, 91W, 92W, 93W, 94W, 95W
BEVAN, John: Warrington 74W, 75L
BIRDSALL, Charlie: Hull 80L
BISHOP, Paul: Warrington 90L; St. Helens 91L
BLACKMORE, Richard: Castleford 92L
BLOOR, Darren: St. Helens 89l
BOTICA, Frano: Wigan 91W, 92W, 93W, 94W, 95W
BOWDEN, Reg: Widnes 75W, 76L, 77L, 79W
BRADLEY, Graeme: Castleford 92L
BRAY, Graham: Featherstone R. 74L; Hull 80L
BRIDGES, John "Keith": Featherstone R. 73W, 74L; Hull 83L
BRIGGS, Wilf: Warrington 75l
BURKE, John: Leeds 71L; Wakefield T. 79L
BURKE, Mick: Widnes 79W, 81W, 82DL*, 84W
BURKE, Tony: St. Helens 87L, 89L; Warrington 90L
BURTON, Chris: Hull K.R. 81L
BYRNE, Ged: Wigan 88w

CAMPBELL, Danny: Wigan 85w
CANNON, Mark: Wigan 84L
CASE, Brian: Wigan 84L, 85W, 88W
CASEY, Len: Hull K.R. 80W, 81L
CASSIDY, Mick: Wigan 94w, 95W
CHISNALL, Dave: Warrington 74W, 75L; St. Helens 78L
CHISNALL, Eric: St. Helens 72W, 76W
CLARK, Brett: St. Helens 87L
CLARK, Garry: Hull K.R. 86L
CLARKE, Phil: Wigan 91W, 92W, 93W, 94W, 95W
CONNOLLY, Gary: St. Helens 89L, 91l; Wigan 94W, 95W
CONROY, Tom: Warrington 75L
COOKSON, Phil: Leeds 72L, 77W, 78W
COOPER, Shane: St. Helens 89L, 91L
COSLETT, Kel: St. Helens 72W, 76W
COURTNEY, Neil: Wigan 85W

COWIE, Neil: Wigan 92w, 95W
CRANE, Mick: Leeds 78W; Hull 82Dw*, 83l
CROMPTON, Martin: Warrington 90L
CROOKS, Lee: Hull 82dW*, 83L, 85L; Castleford 92L
CROOKS, Steve: Hull K.R. 81L
CUMMINS, Francis: Leeds 94L, 95L
CUNNINGHAM, Eddie: St. Helens 76W, 78L; Widnes 81W, 82DL*
CURRIER, Andy: Widnes 93L

DARBYSHIRE, Paul: Warrington 90L
DAVIES, Jonathan: Widnes 93L
DAY, Terry: Hull 82D, 83l
DEAN, Tony: Hull 82W*
DEARDEN, Alan: Widnes 77L, 79W
DERMOTT, Martin: Wigan 90W, 91W, 92W, 93W, 94W
DEVEREUX, John: Widnes 93L
DIAMOND, Steve: Wakefield T. 79L
DICK, Kevin: Leeds 77W, 78w
DICKINSON, Roy: Leeds 77w, 78w
DIVORTY, Gary: Hull 85l
DIXON, Paul: Halifax 87W, 88L
DONLAN, Steve: Wigan 85W
DORAHY, John: Hull K.R. 86L
DRUMMOND, Des: Warrington 90L
DUKE, Tony: Hull 82W*
DUNN, Brian: Wigan 85W
DUTTON, Ray: Widnes 75W, 76L, 77L
DWYER, Bernard: St. Helens 89L, 91L
DYL, Les: Leeds 71l, 72L, 77W, 78W

EADIE, Graham: Halifax 87W, 88L
ECCLES, Graham, Leeds 77W, 78W
ECKERSLEY, David: Leigh 71W; Widnes 76L, 77L, 79W
EDWARDS, Shaun: Wigan 84L, 85W, 88W, 89W, 90W, 91W, 92W, 93W, 94W, 95W
ELIA, Mark: St. Helens 87L
ELLIS, St. John: Castleford 92L
ELVIN, Wayne: Wigan 84l
ELWELL, Keith: Widnes 75W, 76L, 77L, 79W, 81W, 82DL*, 84W
EMA, Asuquo: Hull K.R. 86L
ENGLAND, Keith: Castleford 86W, 92L
EVANS, Steve: Hull 82DW*, 83L, 85L
EVANS, Stuart: St. Helens 89l
EYRES, Richard: Widnes 93L; Leeds 94L, 95L

FAIMALO, Esene: Widnes 93L; Leeds 95L
FAIRBAIRN, George: Hull K.R. 86L
FAIRBANK, Dick: Halifax 88l
FALLON, Jim: Leeds 94L, 95L
FARRAR, Andrew: Wigan 93W
FARRAR, Vince: Featherstone R. 73W; Hull 80l
FARRELL, Andrew: Wigan 93w, 94W, 95w
FEARNLEY, Stan: Bradford N. 73L; Leeds 77W
FERGUSON, John: Wigan 85W
FIELDHOUSE, John: St. Helens 87L
FLETCHER, Andrew: Wakefield T. 79L
FORAN, John: Widnes 75W, 76L, 77l
FORBER, Paul: St. Helens 89L

FORD, Mike: Wigan 85W, Castleford 92L
FORSTER, Mark: Warrington 90L
FRANCIS, Bill: Wigan 70L; St. Helens 78L
FRENCH, Ian: Castleford 86W

GEORGE, Derek "Mick": Widnes 75W, 76L, 77l, 79W, 81W
GEORGE, Wilf: Halifax 87W
GIBBINS, Mick: Featherstone R. 83W
GILBERT, John: Featherstone R. 83W
GILDART, Ian: Wigan 90w
GILL, Henderson: Wigan 84L, 85W, 88W
GLYNN, Peter: St. Helens 76w, 78L
GOODWAY, Andy: Wigan 88W, 89w, 90W, 91w
GORDON, Parry: Warrington 74W, 75L
GORLEY, Les: Widnes 81W, 82DL*, 84W
GOULDING, Bobbie: Wigan 90w, 91w; Widnes 93L
GREGORY, Andy: Widnes 81W, 82DL*, 84W; Wigan 88W, 89W, 90W, 91W, 92W
GREGORY, Mike: Warrington 90L
GRIFFITHS, Jonathan: St. Helens 91L
GROGAN, Bob: Halifax 88L
GROVES, Paul: St. Helens 89L, 91l
GWILLIAM, Ken: Salford 69L; St. Helens 78L

HAGGERTY, Roy: St. Helens 87L, 89L
HAGUE, Neil: Leeds 77W, 78W
HALL, David: Hull K.R. 80W, 81L
HALL, Martin: Wigan 95W
HAMPSON, Steve: Wigan 89W, 90W, 91W, 92w, 93W
HANCOCK, Brian: Hull 80l
HANDSCOMBE, Ray: Featherstone R. 83W
HANKINS, Steve: Featherstone R. 83W
HANLEY, Ellery: Wigan 88W, 89W, 90W, 91W; Leeds 94L, 95L
HARKIN, Kevin: Hull 82D, 83L
HARKIN, Paul: Hull K.R. 81L, 86L
HARMON, Neil: Warrington 90L; Leeds 94L, 95l
HARRISON, Des: Hull K.R. 86L
HARRISON, John: St. Helens 91L
HARRISON, Mick: Leeds 77W, 78W
HARTLEY, Steve: Hull K.R. 80W, 81L
HEATON, Jeff: St. Helens 72W, 76W
HEMSLEY, Kerry: Wigan 84L
HOBBS, David: Featherstone R. 83W
HOGAN, Phil: Hull K.R. 80w, 81L
HOLDING, Neil: St. Helens 87L, 89L
HOLDSTOCK, Roy: Hull K.R. 80W, 81L
HOLLIDAY, Les: Halifax 88L
HOLMES, John: Leeds 71L, 72L, 77W, 78W
HOLROYD, Graham: Leeds 94L, 95L
HORTON, Stuart: Castleford 86w
HOWARD, Harvey: Widnes 93L; Leeds 94L, 95L
HUBBARD, Steve: Hull K.R. 80W, 81L
HUDSON, Terry: Featherstone R. 83W
HUGHES, Eric: Widnes 75W, 76L, 77L, 79W, 81W, 82DL*, 84W
HULL, David: St. Helens 76W; Widnes 79w
HULME, David: Widnes 84w, 93L
HULME, Paul: Widnes 93L
HUNTE, Alan: St. Helens 91L
HYDE, Gary: Castleford 86W

IDLE, Graham: Wakefield T. 79L
INNES, Craig: Leeds 94L, 95L
IRO, Kevin: Wigan 88W, 89W, 90W, 91W; Leeds 94L, 95L

IRO, Tony: Wigan 88W, 89W

JACKSON, Bob: Warrington 90L
JAMES, Kevin: Hull 85L
JAMES, Mel: St. Helens 76w, 78L
JAMES, Neil: Halifax 87w, 88L
JENKINS, David: Widnes 76L
JOHNSON, Barry: Castleford 86W
JOHNSTON, Peter: Hull K.R. 86L
JONES, Les: St. Helens 72W, 76W, 78L
JOYNER, John: Castleford 86W
JULIFF, Brian: Wakefield T. 79L; Wigan 84l; Halifax 87w

KARALIUS, Tony: St. Helens 76W
KELLETT, Ken: Featherstone R. 73W, 83W
KELLY, Andy: Hull K.R. 86L
KEMBLE, Gary: Hull 82DW*, 83L, 85L
KENNY, Brett: Wigan 85W
KETTERIDGE, Martin: Castleford 86W, 92L
KISS, Nicky: Wigan 85W, 88W, 89W

LAMPKOWSKI, Mike: Wakefield T. 79L
LAUGHTON, Doug: Wigan 70L; Widnes 75W, 76L, 77L, 79W
LAWS, David: Hull K.R. 86L
LEDGER, Barry: St. Helens 87L
LEULUAI, James: Hull 82W*, 83L, 85L
LIPTROT, Graham: St. Helens 78L, 87L
LLOYD, Geoff "Sammy": Hull 80L, 82D
LOCKWOOD, Brian: Castleford 69W, 70W; Hull K.R. 80W; Widnes 81W, 82DL*
LORD, Gary: Castleford 86W
LOUGHLIN, Paul: St. Helens 87L, 89L, 91L
LOWE, Phil: Hull K.R. 80W, 81L
LOWES, James: Leeds 94L, 95L
LUCAS, Ian: Wigan 89W, 91W
LYDIAT, John: Hull K.R. 86l
LYDON, Joe: Widnes 84W; Wigan 88W, 89W, 90W, 92W, 93W
LYMAN, Paul: Featherstone R. 83w
LYON, David: Warrington 90L

McCALLION, Seamus: Halifax 87W, 88L
McCORMACK, Kevin: St. Helens 87L
McCURRIE, Alan: Wakefield T. 79L
McCURRIE, Steve: Widnes 93l
McGINTY, Billy: Warrington 90l; Wigan 92W
MANN, Duane: Warrington 90L
MANN, George: St. Helens 91L; Leeds 95l
MANTLE, John: St. Helens 66W, 72W, 76W
MARCHANT, Tony: Castleford 86W
MARSDEN, John: Featherstone R. 83W
MARTYN, Tommy: Warrington 75L
MATHER, Barrie-Jon: Wigan 94W
MATHIAS, Roy: St. Helens 76W, 78L
MERCER, Gary: Warrington 90L; Leeds 94L, 95L
MEREDITH, Martin: Halifax 88L
MILES, Gene: Wigan 92W
MILLER, Gavin: Hull K.R. 86L
MILLINGTON, John: Hull K.R. 80w, 81l
MILLS, Jim: Widnes 75W, 77L, 79W
MILLWARD, Roger: Hull K.R. 80W
MUGGLETON, John: Hull 85L
MURRELL, Brian: Leeds 77W

163

MUSCROFT, Peter: Hull K.R. 81L
MYERS, David: Wigan 91W; Widnes 93L
MYLER, John: Widnes 81w
MYLER, Tony: Widnes 82d

NEILL, Jonathan: St. Helens 91L
NELLER, Keith: Halifax 87W, 88L
NELSON, David: Castleford 92L
NELSON, Nick: Widnes 76L
NEWLOVE, John: Featherstone R. 73W, 74L; Hull 80L
NICHOLAS, Mike: Warrington 74W, 75l
NICHOLLS, George: St. Helens 76W, 78L
NIKAU, Tawera: Castleford 92L
NOONAN, Derek: Warrington 74W, 75L; St. Helens 76W, 78L
NORTON, Steve: Hull 80L, 82DW*, 83L, 85L

O'CONNOR, Michael: St. Helens 89L
OFFIAH, Martin: Wigan 92W, 93W, 94W, 95W
O'HARA, Dane: Hull 82D, 83L, 85L
O'LOUGHLIN, Keiron: Widnes 82DL*, 84W
O'NEILL, Dennis: Widnes 76l, 77L
O'NEILL, Julian: Widnes 93l
O'NEILL, Mike: Widnes 79w, 81W, 82DL*, 84W; Leeds 94l
O'NEILL, Steve: Widnes 82d, 84W
OULTON, Willie: Leeds 78W

PANAPA, Sam: Wigan 93w, 94w
PATRICK, Shaun: Hull 85L
PAUL, Henry: Wigan 95W
PENDLEBURY, John: Wigan 84L; Halifax 87W, 88L
PHILBIN, Barry: Warrington 74W, 75L
PHILBIN, Mike: Warrington 74W, 75L
PICKERILL, Clive: Hull 80L
PIMBLETT, Geoff: St. Helens 72W, 76W, 78L
PINNER, Harry: St. Helens 78L
PITCHFORD, Steve: Leeds 77W, 78W
PLANGE, David: Castleford 86W
PLATT, Andy: St. Helens 87L; Wigan 89W, 90W, 91W, 92W, 93W, 94W
POTTER, Ian: Wigan 85W, 88W, 89W
PRENDIVILLE, Paul: Hull 80L, 82DW*, 83L
PRESCOTT, Alan: Widnes 75W, 76L
PRESCOTT, Eric: Widnes 81W, 82DL*
PRESTON, Mark: Wigan 90W
PROCTOR, Paul: Hull K.R. 81l
PROHM, Gary: Hull K.R. 86L
PUCKERING, Neil: Hull 85L

QUINN, Steve: Featherstone R. 83W
QUIRK, Les: St. Helens 89L, 91L

RAMSDALE, Denis: Wigan 84L
RAMSEY, Bill: Hunslet 65L; Leeds 68W, 71L, 72L; Widnes 77L
RAYNE, Keith: Wakefield T. 79L
REYNOLDS, Frank: Warrington 75L
RIX, Grant: Halifax 87W
ROBINSON, Jason: Wigan 93W, 95W
ROBINSON, Steve: Halifax 88L
ROOCKLEY, David: Castleford 86w
ROPATI, Tea: St. Helens 91L
ROSE, Paul: Hull K.R. 80W; Hull 83L, 85L
ROUND, Paul: St. Helens 87l

SAMPSON, Dean: Castleford 92l
SANDERSON, Gary: Warrington 90L
SANDERSON, John "Sammy": Leeds 78W
SANDY, Jamie: Castleford 86W
SCHOFIELD, Garry: Hull 85l; Leeds 94L, 95L
SCOTT, Mick: Wigan 84L; Halifax 87W, 88l
SHAW, Glyn: Widnes 79W, 81w
SHEARD, Les: Wakefield T. 79L
SHELFORD, Adrian: Wigan 88W, 89W, 90W
SHERIDAN, Barry: Widnes 75W, 76l
SIDDALL, Gary: Featherstone R. 83w
SKERRETT, Kelvin: Wigan 92W, 93W, 94W, 95W
SKERRETT, Trevor: Wakefield T. 79L; Hull 82DW*, 83L
SLATTER, Tim: Featherstone R. 83W
SMITH, Alan: Leeds 68W, 72L, 77W
SMITH, David: Leeds 77w, 78W
SMITH, Gordon: Hull K.R. 86l
SMITH, Keith: Wakefield T. 79L
SMITH, Mike: Hull K.R. 80W, 81L, 86L
SMITH, Peter: Featherstone R. 83W
SMITH, Tony: Castleford 92l
SORENSEN, Kurt: Widnes 93L
SOUTHERNWOOD, Graham: Castleford 92L
SPRUCE, Stuart: Widnes 93L
STEADMAN, Graham: Castleford 92L
STEPHENS, Gary: Wigan 84L; Halifax 87W
STEPHENSON, David: Wigan 84L, 85W
STERLING, Peter: Hull 85L
STONE, Richard "Charlie": Featherstone R. 73W, 74l; Hull 80L, 82DW*, 83L
SULLIVAN, Clive: Hull K.R. 80W; Hull 82W*

TAIT, Alan: Leeds 94L, 95L
TAMATI, Howie: Wigan 84L
TAMATI, Kevin: Widnes 84W
THOMAS, Mark: Warrington 90l
TINDALL, Keith: Hull 80L, 82W*
TOPLISS, David: Wakefield T. 79L; Hull 82DW*, 83L
TUIGAMALA, Va'aiga: Wigan 94W, 95W

VASSILAKOPOULOS, Marcus: Leeds 94l
VAUTIN, Paul: St. Helens 89L
VEIVERS, Phil: St. Helens 87L, 89L, 91L

WALTERS, Graham: Hull 80L
WANBON, Bobby: Warrington 74w, 75L
WANE, Shaun: Wigan 88w
WARD, David: Leeds 77W, 78W
WARD, Kevin: Castleford 86W; St. Helens 91L
WATKINSON, David: Hull K.R. 80W, 81L, 86L
WEST, Graeme: Wigan 84L, 85W
WHITEHEAD, Derek: Warrington 74W, 75L
WHITFIELD, Colin: Wigan 84L; Halifax 87W, 88L
WHITFIELD, Fred: Widnes 84w
WHITTLE, Alan: Warrington 74W, 75L
WILBY, Tim: Hull 80L
WILEMAN, Ron: Hull 80L, 82D
WILKINSON, Ian: Halifax 88L
WILSON, Scott: Halifax 87W
WOOD, John: Widnes 76L
WOODS, Paul: Hull 80L
WRAY, Jon: Castleford 92L
WRIGHT, Darren: Widnes 93L
WRIGHT, Stuart: Widnes 77L, 79W, 81W, 82DL*, 84W

THE LANCE TODD TROPHY

The Lance Todd Trophy is presented to the Man of the Match in the Rugby League Challenge Cup final, the decision being reached by a ballot of members of the Rugby League Writers' Association present at the game.

Lance Todd made his name in Britain as a player with Wigan and as manager of Salford. His untimely death in a road accident on the return journey from a game at Oldham was commemorated by the introduction of the Lance Todd Trophy.

The award was instituted by Australian-born Harry Sunderland, Warrington director Bob Anderton and Yorkshire journalist John Bapty.

Around 1950, the Red Devils' Association at Salford, comprising players and officials who had worked with Todd, raised sufficient funds to provide a trophy and replica for each winner.

Hull's Tommy Harris is the only hooker to earn the title; and Ray Ashby and Brian Gabbitas the only players to share the honour.

Following the 1954 replay, it was decided by the Red Devils that in the future the trophy would be awarded for the Wembley game. In 1954, Gerry Helme had received the trophy for his performance in the Odsal replay. In the 1982 replay at Elland Road, Leeds, the Man of the Match award went to Hull skipper David Topliss, the Lance Todd Trophy having been awarded to Eddie Cunningham, of Widnes, in the drawn Wembley tie.

In 1990 Andy Gregory, of Wigan, became the first player to win the trophy twice at Wembley, having also won it two years earlier, a feat emulated by Martin Offiah in 1992 and 1994.

Eddie Cunningham, the 1982 recipient of the Lance Todd Trophy.

The Lance Todd Trophy Roll of Honour

Year	Winner	Team	Position
1946	Billy Stott	Wakefield Trinity (v Wigan)	Centre
1947	Willie Davies	Bradford Northern (v Leeds)	Stand off
1948	Frank Whitcombe	Bradford Northern (v Wigan)	Prop
1949	Ernest Ward	Bradford Northern (v Halifax)	Centre
1950	Gerry Helme	Warrington (v Widnes)	Scrum half

1951	Cec Mountford	Wigan (v Barrow)	Stand off
1952	Billy Ivison	Workington T. (v Featherstone R.)	Loose forward
1953	Peter Ramsden	Huddersfield (v St. Helens)	Stand off
1954	Gerry Helme	Warrington (v Halifax)	Scrum half
1955	Jack Grundy	Barrow (v Workington Town)	Second row
1956	Alan Prescott	St. Helens (v Halifax)	Prop
1957	Jeff Stevenson	Leeds (v Barrow)	Scrum half
1958	Rees Thomas	Wigan (v Workington Town)	Scrum half
1959	Brian McTigue	Wigan (v Hull)	Second row
1960	Tommy Harris	Hull (v Wakefield Trinity)	Hooker
1961	Dick Huddart	St. Helens (v Wigan)	Second row
1962	Neil Fox	Wakefield Trinity (v Huddersfield)	Centre
1963	Harold Poynton	Wakefield Trinity (v Wigan)	Stand off
1964	Frank Collier	Widnes (v Hull K.R.)	Prop
1965	Ray Ashby	Wigan	Full back
	Brian Gabbitas	Hunslet	Stand off
1966	Len Killeen	St. Helens (v Wigan)	Winger
1967	Carl Dooler	Featherstone Rovers (v Barrow)	Scrum half
1968	Don Fox	Wakefield Trinity (v Leeds)	Prop
1969	Malcolm Reilly	Castleford (v Salford)	Loose forward
1970	Bill Kirkbride	Castleford (v Wigan)	Second row
1971	Alex Murphy	Leigh (v Leeds)	Scrum half
1972	Kel Coslett	St. Helens (v Leeds)	Loose forward
1973	Steve Nash	Featherstone R. (v Bradford N.)	Scrum half
1974	Derek Whitehead	Warrington (v Featherstone Rovers)	Full back
1975	Ray Dutton	Widnes (v Warrington)	Full back
1976	Geoff Pimblett	St. Helens (v Widnes)	Full back
1977	Steve Pitchford	Leeds (v Widnes)	Prop
1978	George Nicholls	St. Helens (v Leeds)	Second row
1979	David Topliss	Wakefield Trinity (v Widnes)	Stand off
1980	Brian Lockwood	Hull K.R. (v Hull)	Prop
1981	Mick Burke	Widnes (v Hull K.R.)	Full back
1982	Eddie Cunningham	Widnes (v. Hull)	Centre
1983	David Hobbs	Featherstone Rovers (v Hull)	Second row
1984	Joe Lydon	Widnes (v Wigan)	Centre
1985	Brett Kenny	Wigan (v Hull)	Stand off
1986	Bob Beardmore	Castleford (v Hull K.R.)	Scrum half
1987	Graham Eadie	Halifax (v St. Helens)	Full back
1988	Andy Gregory	Wigan (v Halifax)	Scrum half
1989	Ellery Hanley	Wigan (v St. Helens)	Loose forward
1990	Andy Gregory	Wigan (v Warrington)	Scrum half
1991	Denis Betts	Wigan (v St. Helens)	Second row
1992	Martin Offiah	Wigan (v Castleford)	Winger
1993	Dean Bell	Wigan (v Widnes)	Loose forward
1994	Martin Offiah	Wigan (v Leeds)	Winger
1995	Jason Robinson	Wigan (v Leeds)	Winger

CHALLENGE CUP RECORDS

ALL ROUNDS

TEAM
Highest score:
Huddersfield 119 v. *Swinton Park 2 1914

INDIVIDUAL

Most goals in a match:
22 by Jim Sullivan (Wigan) v. *Flimby and Fothergill
.... 1925

Most tries in a match:
11 by George West (Hull K.R.) v. *Brookland Rovers
.... 1905

Most points in a match:
53 (11t,10g) by George West (Hull K.R.) as above.

*Amateur teams

FINAL RECORDS

TEAM

Most wins: 16 by Wigan

Most finals: 25 by Wigan

Highest score:
Wakefield T. 38 v. Hull 5 1960

Widest margin:
Huddersfield 37 v. St. Helens 3 1915

Biggest attendance:
102,569 Warrington v. Halifax (Replay) at Bradford
.... 1954

*Hull full back Gary Kemble, one of a record 10 overseas players
in the 1985 Wembley final.*

INDIVIDUAL

Most goals:
8 by Cyril Kellett (Featherstone R.) v. Bradford N.
.... 1973

Most tries:
3 by Bob Wilson (Broughton R.) v. Salford 1902
Stan Moorhouse (Huddersfield) v. Warrington 1913
Tom Holliday (Oldham) v. Swinton 1927

Most points:
20 (2t,7g) by Neil Fox (Wakefield T.) v. Hull 1960

WEMBLEY FACTS
WIGAN have made a record 21 appearances at Wembley and won there a record 15 times, including a record eight successive appearances from 1988.

A RECORD 10 overseas players trod the Wembley turf in 1985. Hull fielded six — a record for one club. The Airlie Birds sextet were Australians Peter Sterling and John Muggleton, plus New Zealanders Gary Kemble, James Leuluai, Dane O'Hara and Fred Ah Kuoi. Wigan added Australians John Ferguson and Brett Kenny together with New Zealanders Graeme West and Danny Campbell, who went on as substitute. South African Nick Du Toit was substitute back but did not play.

THE 1985 aggregates of 10 tries and 52 points were both record totals for a Challenge Cup final with Hull's 24 points the most by a losing side. There were also 10 tries in the 1915 final when Huddersfield beat St. Helens 37-3, which is the widest margin. Wakefield Trinity ran up the highest Cup final score when they beat Hull 38-5 in 1960.

WORLD RECORD receipts of £2,040,000 were taken at the 1995 final between Wigan and Leeds from a capacity crowd of 78,550.

SHAUN EDWARDS holds the record for most Cup-winning appearances at Wembley with nine from a record 10 appearances.
Edwards made his debut in Wigan's losing side of 1984, earning winners' medals in 1985 and from 1988-95 inclusive.

ERIC ASHTON captained a record six teams at Wembley — Wigan in 1958, 1959, 1961, 1963, 1965 and 1966. His record of three wins (in 1958, 1959, 1965) is shared with Derek Turner (Wakefield Trinity 1960, 1962, 1963), Alex Murphy (St. Helens 1966, Leigh 1971 and Warrington 1974), Ellery Hanley (Wigan 1989, 1990, 1991) and Dean Bell (Wigan 1992, 1993 and 1994), Hanley's and Bell's being the only three successive wins.

THE YOUNGEST player to appear in a Wembley Cup final was Francis Cummins who was 17 years and 200 days when he played on the wing for Leeds against Wigan in 1994. Shaun Edwards was the youngest captain at Wembley, leading Wigan to success in the 1988 final against Halifax at the age of 21 years, 6 months and 14 days. The youngest winner at Wembley was Wigan's Andrew Farrell, a substitute in the 1993 final against Widnes at 17 years, 11 months. The youngest forward to play at Wembley is Marcus Vassilakopoulos of Leeds who went on as a substitute against Wigan in 1994 at 17 years and seven months.

ALEX MURPHY has been a record six times to Wembley as a coach. He was a winner as player-coach with Leigh (1971) and Warrington (1974), but losing each time when confined to the bench with Warrington (1975), Wigan (1984) and St. Helens (1987 and 1989). Murphy also went twice solely as a player, with St. Helens in 1961 and 1966.

MOST WINS as a coach at Wembley is four, by John Monie (Wigan 1990, 1991, 1992 and 1993).

THE OLDEST player at Wembley was Gus Risman, who at 41 years, 29 days led Workington Town to victory over Featherstone Rovers in 1952. He played full back.

THE TALLEST players at Wembley were St. Helens second row man John Harrison who appeared in the 1991 final, and Barrie-Jon Mather who was at centre for Wigan in 1994. Both were 6ft 7in.

SCHOOLBOYS who have appeared in an Under-11 curtain-raiser at Wembley and gone on to play in the major final at the stadium are Joe Lydon, David Hulme, Mike Ford, Neil Puckering, David Plange, Denis Betts, Bobby Goulding and Phil Clarke. Lydon became the first to achieve the feat with Widnes in the 1984 final against Wigan, followed by teammate Hulme who went on as a 72nd-minute substitute. Both had played in the first schoolboys' curtain-raiser in 1975 — Lydon for Wigan, and Hulme for Widnes.

CYRIL KELLETT holds the record for most goals in a Challenge Cup final with his eight for Featherstone Rovers in 1973.

In the most remarkable exhibition of kicking seen at Wembley, the veteran full back was successful with every one of his attempts as Bradford Northern crashed 33-14.

Nine years earlier he scored only one for Hull Kingston Rovers in the 13-5 defeat by Widnes.

NEIL FOX piled up the most points in a Challenge Cup final in 1960. His 20 points helped Wakefield Trinity to a 38-5 defeat of Hull. Fox's points came from two tries and seven goals.

His three drop goals for Trinity in the 12-6 victory over Huddersfield two years later was another extraordinary feat in the days when the drop goal was a rarity.

NO player has scored a hat-trick of tries at Wembley, the feat being achieved only three times in the preceding era.

The last to do it was Oldham winger Tom Holliday in the 26-7 defeat of Swinton in 1927.

Bob Wilson, the Broughton Rangers centre and captain, was the first to score three tries, in the 25-0 victory over

Salford in 1902.

In between, Stan Moorhouse's three-try feat accounted for all of Huddersfield's points when they beat Warrington 9-5 in 1913.

MANY great players have gone through an entire career without achieving their ambition of playing at Wembley. Hull's Mike Smith achieved it in his first senior game.

Smith made one of the most remarkable debuts in sporting history when he played in the second row of an injury-hit Boulevard side against Wakefield Trinity in 1960.

In contrast, Freddie Miller signed for Hull in 1932 and did not play at Wembley until 1952 . . . two years after joining Featherstone Rovers.

A NOTABLE Wembley captain was Gus Risman who led two clubs to victory . . . 14 years apart. He was captain of Salford when they beat Barrow in 1938. At 41, he led Workington Town to their triumph over Featherstone Rovers in 1952.

Mike O'Neill holds the record for the longest playing span at Wembley of 15 years. He was a playing substitute for Widnes in 1979 and had the same role with Leeds in 1994. He played in five finals.

PROBABLY the unluckiest Challenge Cup finalist was Dai Davies who appeared in four finals and was on the losing side each time. Three of those occasions were at Wembley with different clubs. He was a loser with Warrington (1933), Huddersfield (1935) and Keighley (1937). Before the Wembley era he was also in Warrington's beaten team of 1928.

Steve Norton and Lee Crooks played at Wembley four times and were never on the winning side. Norton was in the beaten Hull teams of 1980, 1983 and 1985 in addition to playing in the 1982 drawn final. In 1970 he was a non-playing substitute for Castleford, who won the Cup.

Crooks was in the beaten Hull sides of 1983 and 1985 plus the drawn final of 1982. He was then in Castleford's beaten 1992 team.

Norton and Crooks both won winners' medals in the 1982 replay.

Bill Ramsey was on the losing side in four Wembley finals but gained a winners' medal with Leeds in 1968. He picked up losers' medals with Hunslet (1965), Leeds (1971 and 1972) and Widnes (1977).

TWELVE of last season's clubs have never appeared at Wembley. They are: Batley, Bramley, Carlisle, Chorley Chieftains, Doncaster Dragons, Highfield, London Broncos, Oldham Bears, Rochdale Hornets, Sheffield Eagles, Swinton and Whitehaven.

Fate seems to be against Swinton and Oldham. In the five years preceding the move to Wembley, one or the other appeared in the final, twice meeting each other. Oldham played in four successive finals in that period. Swinton's run of three finals ended when the first Wembley took place in 1929. They got through to the final three years later . . . only for it to be played at Wigan!

CHALLENGE CUP PROGRESS CHART

A 20-year review . . . .

Key: W — Winners. F — Beaten finalists. SF — Semi-final. P — Preliminary round.

	1994-95	1993-94*	1992-93	1991-92	1990-91	1989-90	1988-89	1987-88	1986-87	1985-86	1984-85	1983-84	1982-83	1981-82	1980-81	1979-80	1978-79	1977-78	1976-77	1975-76
BARROW B.	4	4	1	2	2	1	2	1	2	2	P	1	2	2	1	2	3	1	2	1
BATLEY	5	4	2	1	1	1	1	1	1	1	1	1	1	2	1	1	1	1	1	1
BLACKPOOL G.	(2)	(1)	P	1	1	2	2	2	1	2	1	1	1	1	1	1	1	1	1	1
BRADFORD B.	4	6	SF	SF	3	3	2	1	2	3	3	3	SF	3	1	3	SF	3	3	2
BRAMLEY	4	4	1	P	1	1	P	P	1	2	3	1	1	1	1	1	2	1	1	1
CARLISLE	4	4	1	P	P	1	2	1	2	1	1	P	1	1						
CASTLEFORD	4	SF	3	F	1	P	2	1	1	W	SF	3	SF	SF	2	2	3	3	3	1
CHORLEY C.	(3)	(2)	1	P	1	1														
DEWSBURY	4	4	1	2	1	2	1	1	1	1	1	1	1	2	1	2	1	3	1	
DONCASTER D.	4	6	1	2	1	P	1	3	1	2	P	2	1	1	1	1	1	1	1	2
FEATHERSTONE R.	SF	6	1	3	1	1	3	2	1	1	P	1	W	P	3	1	1	SF	2	SF
HALIFAX	4	4	3	3	3	1	1	F	W	1	2	1	2	3	2	SF	1	1	1	1
HIGHFIELD	3	4	1	1	1	1	1	1	1	1	2	1	2	1	1	1	1	1	1	1
HUDDERSFIELD	6	4	2	P	P	P	1	P	1	1	1	1	1	1	1	2	3	3	1	1
HULL	4	5	P	SF	P	2	1	SF	3	1	F	2	F	W	2	F	3	2	2	1
HULL K.R.	5	5	3	1	1	1	3	3	3	F	SF	3	1	2	F	W	2	1	SF	2
HUNSLET H.	4	4	2	2	1	1	P	1	2	1	3	2	3	1	1	1	1	2	1	2
KEIGHLEY C.	5	5	2	1	2	2	2	2	2	1	1	1	1	1	2	1	2	1	1	SF
LEEDS	F	F	SF	2	2	P	3	2	3	SF	1	SF	2	SF	1	2	1	W	W	3
LEIGH C.	5	4	1	1	1	1	1	1	SF	3	2	1	1	3	2	1	2	1	1	3
LONDON B.	4	4	1	2	1	2	1	1	1	1	1	2	2	2	1					
NOTTINGHAM C.	(1)	(1)	1	P	1	1	1	2	2	P	1									
OLDHAM B.	SF	5	3	1	SF	SF	3	1	2	SF	1	2	1	2	3	2	2	2	1	3
ROCHDALE H.	4	4	2	1	2	2	1	2	1	2	2	1	1	2	1	2	2	1	2	1
ST. HELENS	4	SF	2	3	F	SF	F	3	F	2	1	3	3	1	SF	2	SF	F	SF	W
SALFORD R.	5	4	1	1	3	2	1	SF	1	1	2	1	2	1	3	3	1	2	2	2
SHEFFIELD E.	5	5	2	2	2	2	2	2	1	1										
SWINTON	4	4	P	1	1	1	1	1	P	P	1	P	2	1	1	1	1	2	2	1
WAKEFIELD T.	4	4	2	1	2	3	2	1	2	1	2	2	2	3	3	3	F	2	2	1
WARRINGTON	5	5	1	2	3	F	SF	2	1	2	2	2	3	1	SF	3	1	SF	1	3
WHITEHAVEN	6	5	1	1	2	3	1	P	3	1	1	1	1	1	1	1	1	1	1	1
WIDNES	6	6	F	1	SF	3	SF	3	SF	3	3	W	1	F	W	SF	W	3	F	F
WIGAN	W	W	W	W	W	W	W	W	1	3	W	F	1	2	1	1	2	2	2	2
WORKINGTON T.	6	5	1	3	2	1	P	1	P	1	2	2	3	2	2	1	1	2	3	2
YORK	5	4	1	1	1	1	1	1	P	2	1	SF	1	1	2	2	1	1	1	2

* From 1993-94, Second Division clubs entered the new-style tournament in the third round, First Division clubs being exempt until the fourth round, there being six rounds before the semi-finals.

( ) Entered as non-League side.

169

PREMIERSHIP ROLL OF HONOUR

Year	Winners	Runners-up	Venue	Attendance	Receipts
1975	Leeds (3)...............26	St. Helens (1) 11	Wigan.................................14,531		£7,795
1976	St. Helens (4) 15	Salford (1)............... 2	Swinton 18,082		£13,138
1977	St. Helens (2).........32	Warrington (5) 20	Swinton 11,178		£11,626
1978	Bradford N. (2) 17	Widnes (1) 8	Swinton 16,813		£18,677
1979	Leeds (4)................24	Bradford N. (8) 2	Huddersfield......................19,486		£21,291
1980	Widnes (2) 19	Bradford N. (1) 5	Swinton 10,215		£13,665
1981	Hull K.R. (3).........11	Hull (7)................. 7	Leeds 29,448		£47,529
1982	Widnes (3) 23	Hull (2)................. 8	Leeds 12,100		£23,749
1983	Widnes (5) 22	Hull (1).................10	Leeds 17,813		£34,145
1984	Hull K.R. (1).........18	Castleford (4).........10	Leeds 12,515		£31,769
1985	St. Helens (2).........36	Hull K.R. (1).........16	Elland Rd, Leeds 15,518		£46,950
1986	Warrington (4) 38	Halifax (1)..............10	Elland Rd, Leeds 13,683		£50,879
1987	Wigan (1)............... 8	Warrington (3) 0	Old Trafford, Man'r...........38,756		£165,166
1988	Widnes (1) 38	St. Helens (2).........14	Old Trafford, Man'r...........35,252		£202,616
1989	Widnes (1) 18	Hull (4).................10	Old Trafford, Man'r...........40,194		£264,242
1990	Widnes (3) 28	Bradford N. (4) 6	Old Trafford, Man'r...........40,796		£273,877
1991	Hull (3).................14	Widnes (2) 4	Old Trafford, Man'r...........42,043		£384,300
1992	Wigan (1)...............48	St. Helens (2).........16	Old Trafford, Man'r...........33,157		£389,988
1993	St. Helens (2).........10	Wigan (1)............... 4	Old Trafford, Man'r...........36,598		£454,013
1994	Wigan (1)...............24	Castleford (4).........20	Old Trafford, Man'r...........35,644		£475,000
1995	Wigan (1)...............69	Leeds (2)................24	Old Trafford, Man'r...........30,160		£351,038

( ) denotes final League position

PREMIERSHIP TROPHY FINAL PLAYERS' REGISTER

The following is an index of players who have appeared in the Premiership final since the first in 1975. W — winners, L — losers. Substitute appearances in lower case letters. The year denotes the second half of the season.

ADAMS, Bryan: Leeds 79w
ADAMS, Mick: Widnes 78L, 80W, 82W, 83W
AINSWORTH, Gary: St. Helens 85W
ALLEN, Shaun: St. Helens 85w, 88l
ANDERSON, Chris: Halifax 86L
ANDERSON, Tony: Halifax 86L
ARKWRIGHT, Chris: St. Helens 85W
ASHTON, Alan: St. Helens 77l
ASPEY, Malcolm: Widnes 78L, 80W
ATCHESON, Paul: Wigan 93L, 94W
ATKINS, Brett: Castleford 84L
ATKINSON, John: Leeds 75W, 79W
AUSTIN, Jack: Bradford N. 78W

BAILEY, Mark: St. Helens 88L
BANKS, Barry: Hull 81L
BARENDS, David: Bradford N. 78W
BASNETT, John: Widnes 82W, 83W
BATTEN, Ray: Leeds 75W
BEARDMORE, Bob: Castleford 84L
BELL, Dean: Wigan 87W, 92W
BENTLEY, Keith: Widnes 80W

BENYON, Billy: St. Helens 76W, 77W
BETTS, Denis: Wigan 92W, 94W, 95W
BEVAN, John: Warrington 77L
BISHOP, Paul: Warrington 86W, 87L; St. Helens 92L
BLACKER, Brian: Hull 89L
BLACKMORE, Richard: Castleford 94L
BOND, Steve: Halifax 86l
BOTICA, Frano: Wigan 92W, 93L, 94W, 95W
BOWDEN, Reg: Widnes 78L, 80W
BOYD, Les: Warrington 86W
BRIDGES, John "Keith": Bradford N. 79L, 80L; Hull 83L
BROADHURST, Mark: Hull K.R. 84W, 85L
BURKE, Mick: Widnes 80W, 82W, 83W
BURKE, Tony: St. Helens 85W, 88L
BURTON, Chris: Hull K.R. 81w, 84W
BUSBY, Dean: Hull 91w
BUTLER, John: Salford 76L

CARBERT, Brian: Warrington 86W
CASE, Brian: Warrington 77L; Wigan 87W
CASEY, Len: Bradford N. 79L; Hull K.R. 81W
CASSIDY, Mick: Wigan 93L, 94w, 95w
CHISNALL, Dave: St. Helens 77W
CHISNALL, Eric: St. Helens 75L, 76W, 77W
CLARK, Garry: Hull K.R. 84W, 85L
CLARKE, Phil: Wigan 92W, 93L, 94W, 95W
CLARKSON, Geoff: Bradford N. 80L
COEN, Darren: Castleford 84L
CONNELL, Gary: Castleford 84L

CONNOLLY, Gary: St. Helens 92L, 93W; Wigan 94W, 95W
COOKSON, Phil: Leeds 75W, 79W
COOPER, David: Bradford N. 90l
COOPER, Shane: St. Helens 92L, 93W
CORDLE, Gerald: Bradford N. 90L
COSLETT, Kel: St. Helens 75L, 76W
COULMAN, Mike: Salford 76L
COWIE, Neil: Wigan 92W, 93L, 94W, 95W
CRAMPTON, Jimmy: Castleford 84L
CRANE, Mick: Hull 81L, 83l
CROOKS, Lee: Hull 82L, 83L; Castleford 94L
CROOKS, Steve: Hull 89L
CROSSLEY, John: Halifax 86L
CULLEN, Paul: Warrington 86W, 87L
CUMMINS, Francis: Leeds 95L
CUNLIFFE, Dave: Warrington 77l
CUNNINGHAM, Eddie: St. Helens 75l, 77W; Widnes 82W
CURLING, Denis: Warrington 77L
CURRIER, Andy: Widnes 88W, 89W, 90W, 91L

DANNATT, Andy: Hull 89L, 91W
DAVIES, Jonathan: Widnes 89W, 90W, 91L
DAY, Sean: St. Helens 85W
DAY, Terry: Hull 82l, 83L
DEAN, Tony: Hull 81L, 83L
DERMOTT, Martin: Wigan 92W, 93L
DEVEREUX, John: Widnes 91L
DICK, Kevin: Leeds 79W
DICKINSON, Roy: Leeds 75W
DIVORTY, Gary: Hull 89L
DIXON, Colin: Salford 76L
DIXON, Paul: Halifax 86L
DORAHY, John: Hull K.R. 84W
DOWD, Barry: Widnes 88W, 91L
DRUMMOND, Des: Warrington 87L
DUANE, Ronnie: Warrington 86W, 87L
DWYER, Bernard: St. Helens 88l, 92L, 93W
DYL, Les: Leeds 75W, 79W

EASTWOOD, Paul: Hull 89L, 91W
ECCLES, Bob: Warrington 87l
ECCLES, Graham: Leeds 75w, 79W
ECKERSLEY, David: Widnes 78L, 80W
EDWARDS, Shaun: Wigan 87W, 92W, 93L, 94W, 95W
ELIA, Mark: St. Helens 88L
ELLIOTT, David: Hull 81L
ELLIS, St. John: Castleford 94L
ELWELL, Keith: Widnes 78L, 80W, 82W, 83W
EMA, Asuquo: Hull K.R. 85L
ENTAT, Patrick: Hull 91W
EVANS, Steve: Hull 82L, 83L
EVANS, Stuart: St. Helens 88L
EYRES, Richard: Widnes 88W, 89W, 90W; Leeds 95L

FAIMALO, Esene: Leeds 95L
FAIRBAIRN, George: Hull K.R. 84W, 85L
FAIRBANK, Karl: Bradford N. 90L
FALLON, Jim: Leeds 95L
FARRAR, Andrew: Wigan 93L
FARRELL, Andrew: Wigan 93L, 94W, 95W
FERRES, Steve: Bradford N. 79L, 80l
FIELDHOUSE, John: St. Helens 88L
FIELDING, Keith: Salford 76L
FINNEGAN, Derek: Warrington 77L
FLETCHER, Paul: Hull 89L
FLETCHER, Paul: Leeds 79w
FORBER, Paul: St. Helens 85w, 88L
FORD, Mike: Castleford 94L
FORD, Paul: Warrington 86W
FORSHAW, Mike: Wigan 93l
FORSTER, Mark: Warrington 86W, 87L
FORSYTH, Colin: Bradford N. 78w, 79L, 80L
FOX, Neil: Bradford N. 78w
FRANCIS, Richard: Bradford N. 90L

GANT, Les: Bradford N. 79L, 80L
GAY, Richard: Hull 91W
GEORGE, Derek "Mick": Widnes 78l, 80W
GILDART, Ian: Wigan 93l
GILL, Henderson: Wigan 87W
GILL, Ken: Widnes 78L
GLYNN, Peter: St. Helens 76W, 77W
GOODWAY, Andy: Wigan 87W
GORDON, Parry: Warrington 77L
GORLEY, Les: Widnes 80W, 82W, 83W
GORLEY, Peter: St. Helens 85W
GRAHAM, Gordon: Salford 76L
GRAYSHON, Jeff: Bradford N. 79L, 80L
GREGORY, Andy: Widnes 82W, 83W; Warrington 86W; Wigan 87W
GREGORY, Mike: Warrington 86W, 87l
GRIFFITHS, Jonathan: St. Helens 92l, 93w
GRIMA, Joe: Widnes 88W, 89W, 90w, 91L
GROVES, Paul: St. Helens 88L, 92l
GWILLIAM, Alan: Warrington 77L
GWILLIAM, Ken: St. Helens 75l, 76w, 77W

HAGGERTY, Roy: St. Helens 85W, 88L
HAGUE, Neil: Leeds 79W
HAIGH, Bob: Leeds 75W; Bradford N. 78W
HALE, Gary: Bradford N. 80L
HALL, David: Hull K.R. 81W, 84W, 85L
HALL, Martin: Wigan 94W, 95W
HAMPSON, Steve: Wigan 87W, 92W
HANLEY, Ellery: Wigan 87W
HARKIN, Kevin: Hull 82L
HARKIN, Paul: Hull K.R. 81W, 84W, 85l; Bradford N. 90L
HARMON, Neil: Leeds 95l
HARRISON, Karl: Hull 91W
HARRISON, Mick: Leeds 79W

HARTLEY, Steve: Hull K.R. 81W
HASSAN, Phil: Leeds 95L
HAUGHTON, Simon: Wigan 95w
HAY, Andy: Castleford 94L
HEATON, Jeff: St. Helens 75L, 76W
HEPWORTH, Keith: Leeds 75W
HESFORD, Steve: Warrington 77L
HESKETH, Chris: Salford 76L
HOBBS, David: Bradford N. 90L
HOGAN, Brian: Widnes 80w
HOGAN, Phil: Hull K.R. 81W, 85L
HOLDING, Neil: St. Helens 85W, 88L
HOLDSTOCK, Roy: Hull K.R. 81W, 84W
HOLLIDAY, Les: Widnes 90W
HOLROYD, Graham: Leeds 95L
HOLMES, John: Leeds 75W
HORTON, Stuart: Castleford 84L
HOWARD, Harvey: Widnes 91l; Leeds 95L
HUBBARD, Steve: Hull K.R. 81W
HUGHES, Eric: Widnes 78L, 82W, 83W
HULL, David: St. Helens 75L; Widnes 78L, 80W
HULME, David: Widnes 83w, 88W, 89W, 90W, 91L
HULME, Paul: Widnes 88W, 89W, 90W, 91L
HUMPHRIES, Tony: Warrington 87L
HUNTE, Alan: St. Helens 92L, 93W
HYDE, Gary: Castleford 84L
HYNES, Syd: Leeds 75W

INNES, Craig: Leeds 95L
IRO, Kevin: Leeds 95L

JACKSON, Bob: Warrington 86W, 87L
JACKSON, Lee: Hull 89L, 91W
JAMES, Mel: St. Helens 76W, 77W
JAMES, Neil: Halifax 86L
JOHNSON, Brian: Warrington 86w, 87L
JONES, Les: St. Helens 75L, 76W, 77W
JOYCE, Graham: Bradford N. 78W; Leeds 79W
JOYNER, John: Castleford 84L
JOYNT, Chris: St. Helens 93W
JULIFF, Brian: Halifax 86L

KARALIUS, Tony: St. Helens 75L, 76W, 77w
KEAR, John: Castleford 84L
KELLY, Andy: Hull K.R. 85L
KELLY, Mike: Warrington 77L
KEMBLE, Gary: Hull 82L, 83L
KETTERIDGE, Martin: Castleford 94L
KISS, Nicky: Wigan 87W
KNIGHTON, John: Salford 76L
KOLOTO, Emosi: Widnes 89W, 90W, 91L

LAUGHTON, Doug: Widnes 78L
LAWS, David: Hull K.R. 84W, 85L
LEDGER, Barry: St. Helens 85W, 88L
LESTER, Roy: Warrington 77L

LEULUAI, James: Hull 82L, 83L
LINTON, Ralph: Widnes 83W
LIPTROT, Graham: St. Helens 77W
LLOYD, Geoff "Sammy": Hull 82l
LOCKWOOD, Brian: Widnes 82W
LOUGHLIN, Paul: St. Helens 88L, 92L, 93W
LOWE, Phil: Hull K.R. 81W
LOWES, James: Leeds 95L
LYDIAT, John: Hull K.R. 84w 85l
LYDON, Joe: Widnes 83W; Wigan 87W, 92W, 94w
LYON, David: St. Helens 93W

McCALLION, Seamus: Halifax 86L
McCURRIE, Steve: Widnes 91L
McGARRY, Damien: Hull 91W
McGINTY, Billy: Warrington 86w; Wigan 92W
McGOWAN, Steve: Bradford N. 90L
McKENZIE, Phil: Widnes 88W, 89W, 90W, 91L
MACKEY, Greg: Hull 91W
MacLEAN, Ian: Bradford N. 80L
MADLEY, Ian: Hull 81l
MANN, George: St. Helens 92L, 93W; Leeds 95L
MANTLE, John: St. Helens 75L, 76W
MARCHANT, Tony: Castleford 84L; Bradford N. 90L
MARLOW, Ian: Hull 91W
MARSHALL, David: Leeds 75w
MARTYN, Tommy: Warrington 77L
MASON, Mel: Leeds 75W
MATHIAS, Roy: St. Helens 75L, 76W, 77W
MEDLEY, Paul: Bradford N. 90L
MENINGA, Mal: St. Helens 85W
MERCER, Gary: Leeds 95L
MIDDLETON, Simon: Castleford 94L
MILES, Gene: Wigan 92W
MILLINGTON, John: Hull K.R. 81W, 84W
MILLS, Jim: Widnes 78L
MORDUE, David: Bradford N. 79l
MUMBY, Keith: Bradford N. 78W, 79L, 80L, 90L
MUSCROFT, Peter: Hull K.R. 81W
MYERS, David: Wigan 92w
MYLER, Tony: Widnes 82w, 83W, 89w, 90w

NASH, Steve: Salford 76L
NEILL, Jonathan: St. Helens 92L, 93W
NICHOLLS, George: St. Helens 75L, 76W, 77W
NICKLE, Sonny: St. Helens 92L, 93W
NIKAU, Tawera: Castleford 94L
NOBLE, Brian: Bradford N. 90L
NOLAN, Gary: Hull 91w
NOLAN, Rob: Hull 89l
NOONAN, Derek: St. Helens 76W
NORTON, Steve: Hull 81L, 82L, 83L

O'DONNELL, Gus: St. Helens 93W
OFFIAH, Martin: Widnes 88W, 89W, 90W, 91L; Wigan 92W, 93L, 94W, 95W

O'HARA, Dane: Hull 82L, 83L, 89L
OKULICZ, Eddie: Bradford N. 79L
O'LOUGHLIN, Kieron: Widnes 82W
O'NEILL, Mike: Widnes 80W, 82W, 83W, 88W, 89W, 90W
O'NEILL, Steve: Widnes 83w, 88w

PANAPA, Sam: Wigan 92w, 93L, 94W
PARKER, Derek: Bradford N. 79L, 80L
PAUL, Henry: Wigan 95W
PEACHAM, Gary: Hull 81L
PEARCE, Gary: Hull 89L
PEERS, Mike: Warrington 77l
PETERS, Barry: Warrington 87L
PETERS, Steve: St. Helens 85W
PHILBIN, Barry: Warrington 77L
PIMBLETT, Geoff: St. Helens 75L, 76W, 77W
PINNER, Harry: St. Helens 77W, 85W
PITCHFORD, Steve: Leeds 75W, 79W
PLATT, Andy: St. Helens 85W; Wigan 92W
PLATT, Duncan: Widnes 88W
POTTER, Ian: Wigan 87W
PRENDIVILLE, Paul: Hull 81L, 82L
PRESCOTT, Eric: Salford 76L; Widnes 82W, 83W
PRICE, Joe: Warrington 77L
PRICE, Richard; Hull 89L
PROCTOR, Paul: Hull K.R. 81W
PROHM, Gary: Hull K.R. 84W, 85L
PYKE, Derek: Widnes 89w

QUIRK, Les: St. Helens 88L

RADLINSKI, Kris: Wigan 95W
RAISTRICK, Dean: Salford 76L; Bradford N. 78W
RAMSEY, Bill: Widnes 78l
REDFEARN, Alan: Bradford N. 78W, 79L, 80L
REDFEARN, David: Bradford N. 78W, 80L
RICHARDS, Craig: Bradford N. 90l
RICHARDS, Maurice: Salford 76L
RIDDLESDEN, Eddie: Halifax 86L
RILEY, Mike: St. Helens 93W
ROBERTS, Mark: Warrington 86W, 87L
ROBINSON, Geoff: Halifax 86L
ROBINSON, Ian: Hull K.R. 84w, 85L
ROBINSON, Jason: Wigan 93L, 94W, 95W
ROBINSON, Steve: Castleford 84L
ROE, Peter: Bradford N. 78W
ROOCKLEY, David: Castleford 84L
ROPATI, Joe: Warrington 87L
ROPATI, Tea: St. Helens 92L, 93W
ROSE, Paul: Hull 83L
RUDD, Chris: Hull K.R. 84W
RUSSELL, Richard: Wigan 87w; Castleford 94L

SAMPSON, Dean: Castleford 94L
SANDERSON, Gary: Warrington 86W, 87L
SANDERSON, John "Sammy": Leeds 79W

SCOTT, Mick: Halifax 86L
SHARP, Jon: Hull 89L, 91W
SHAW, Glyn: Widnes 78L, 80W
SHEFFIELD, Bill: Salford 76L
SIMPSON, Roger: Bradford N. 90L
SKERRETT, Kelvin: Bradford N. 90L; Wigan 93L, 94W, 95W
SKERRETT, Trevor: Hull 81L, 82L, 83L
SMALES, Ian: Castleford 94l
SMITH, Alan: Leeds 75W, 79W
SMITH, Chris: Castleford 94L
SMITH, David: Leeds 79W
SMITH, Gordon: Hull K.R. 85L
SMITH, Mike: Hull K.R. 81W, 84W, 85L
SMITH, Steve: Halifax 86l
SMITH, Tony: Castleford 94L
SOLAL, Patrick: Hull 83l
SORENSEN, Kurt: Widnes 88W, 89W, 90W, 91L
SPENCER, Alan: Bradford N. 79L
STEADMAN, Graham: Castleford 94L
STEPHENS, Gary: Halifax 86L
STEPHENSON, David: Wigan 87W
STEPHENSON, Nigel: Bradford N. 80L
STONE, Richard "Charlie": Hull 81L, 82L, 83L
SULLIVAN, Anthony: St. Helens 92L
SYKES, Nathan: Castleford 94l

TAIT, Alan: Widnes 88w, 89W, 90W, 91L; Leeds 95L
TAMATI, Kevin: Warrington 86W, 87L
TANNER, David: St. Helens 88L
THACKRAY, Rick: Widnes 88W
THOMPSON, Jimmy: Bradford N. 78W, 79L, 80L
TINDALL, Keith: Hull 81L, 82L
TOPLISS, David: Hull 82L, 83L
TROTTER, Dennis: Bradford N. 78W, 79L
TURNBULL, Sam: Salford 76l
TURNER, Neil: Hull 91W

VAN BELLEN, Gary: Bradford N. 80l
VAN BELLEN, Ian: Bradford N. 78W, 79l
VASSILAKOPOULOS, Marcus: Leeds 95l
VEIVERS, Phil: St. Helens 85W, 92L

WALKER, Russ: Hull 91W
WALSH, John: St. Helens 75L
WANE, Shaun: Wigan 87W
WARD, David: Leeds 75W, 79W
WARD, Kevin: Castleford 84L; St. Helens 92L
WARLOW, John: St. Helens 75L
WATKINS, David: Salford 76L
WATKINSON, David: Hull K.R. 81W, 85L
WEAVILL, Dave: Warrington 77L
WEBB, Brad: Hull 91W
WELHAM, Paul: Hull 89L
WEST, Graeme: Wigan 87w
WHITFIELD, Colin: Halifax 86L

173

WHITFIELD, Fred: Widnes 82w, 83W
WILBY, Tim: Hull 81L, 89l
WILEMAN, Ronnie: Hull 81L, 82L
WILKINSON, Ian: Bradford N. 90L
WILSON, Frank: St. Helens 75L
WILSON, Scott: Halifax 86L
WINDLEY, Phil: Hull 89L
WOLFORD, John: Bradford N. 78W
WOODS, Paul: Widnes 78L; Hull 81L
WRIGHT, Darren: Widnes 88W, 89W, 90W, 91l
WRIGHT, Stuart: Widnes 78L, 80W, 82W

THE HARRY SUNDERLAND TROPHY

The trophy, in memory of the famous Queenslander, a former Australian tour manager, broadcaster and journalist, is presented to the Man of the Match in the end-of-season Championship or Premiership final. The award is donated and judged by the Rugby League Writers' Association and is sponsored by Stones Bitter. The roll of honour is:

Year	Winner	Team	Position
1965	Terry Fogerty	Halifax (v. St. Helens)	Second row
1966	Albert Halsall	St. Helens (v. Halifax)	Prop
1967	Ray Owen	Wakefield T. (v. St. Helens)	Scrum half
1968	Gary Cooper	Wakefield T. (v. Hull K.R.)	Full back
1969	Bev Risman	Leeds (v. Castleford)	Full back
1970	Frank Myler	St. Helens (v. Leeds)	Stand off
1971	Bill Ashurst	Wigan (v. St. Helens)	Second row
1972	Terry Clawson	Leeds (v. St. Helens)	Prop
1973	Mick Stephenson	Dewsbury (v. Leeds)	Hooker
1974	Barry Philbin	Warrington (v. St. Helens)	Loose forward
1975	Mel Mason	Leeds (v. St. Helens)	Stand off
1976	George Nicholls	St. Helens (v. Salford)	Second row
1977	Geoff Pimblett	St. Helens (v. Warrington)	Full back
1978	Bob Haigh	Bradford N. (v. Widnes)	Loose forward
1979	Kevin Dick	Leeds (v. Bradford N.)	Stand off
1980	Mal Aspey	Widnes (v. Bradford N.)	Centre
1981	Len Casey	Hull K.R. (v. Hull)	Second row
1982	Mick Burke	Widnes (v. Hull)	Full back
1983	Tony Myler	Widnes (v. Hull)	Stand off
1984	John Dorahy	Hull K.R. (v. Castleford)	Stand off
1985	Harry Pinner	St. Helens (v. Hull K.R.)	Loose forward
1986	Les Boyd	Warrington (v. Halifax)	Prop
1987	Joe Lydon	Wigan (v. Warrington)	Winger
1988	David Hulme	Widnes (v. St. Helens)	Scrum half
1989	Alan Tait	Widnes (v. Hull)	Full back
1990	Alan Tait	Widnes (v. Bradford N.)	Full back
1991	Greg Mackey	Hull (v. Widnes)	Stand off
1992	Andy Platt	Wigan (v. St. Helens)	Prop
1993	Chris Joynt	St. Helens (v. Wigan)	Second row
1994	Sam Panapa	Wigan (v. Castleford)	Centre
1995	Kris Radlinski	Wigan (v. Leeds)	Centre

PREMIERSHIP RECORDS   First staged 1975

ALL ROUNDS
TEAM
Highest score: Wigan 74 v. Leeds 6 ....Semi-final 1992
(Also widest margin)
Biggest attendance: 42,043 Hull v. Widnes
(at Old Trafford, Manchester) ....Final 1991

INDIVIDUAL
Most goals:
10 by Frano Botica (Wigan) v. St. Helens ....Final 1992
     Frano Botica (Wigan) v. Leeds ....Final 1995
Most tries:
10 by Martin Offiah (Wigan) v. Leeds ....Semi-final 1992
Most points:
40 (10t) by Martin Offiah (Wigan) v. Leeds..Semi-final 1992

PREMIERSHIP FINAL
TEAM
Most appearances: 8 by Widnes
Most wins: 6 by Widnes
Highest score:
Wigan 69 v. Leeds 12 (also widest margin) 1995
Biggest attendance:
42,043 Hull v. Widnes
     (at Old Trafford, Manchester).........................1991

INDIVIDUAL
Most tries: 3 by Kris Radlinski (Wigan) v. Leeds 1995
     Gary Connolly (Wigan) v. Leeds..........1995
Most goals:
10 by Frano Botica (Wigan) v. St. Helens 1992
     Frano Botica (Wigan) v. Leeds............................1995
Most points:
20 (10g) by Frano Botica (Wigan) v. St. Helens............1992
     Frano Botica (Wigan) v. Leeds..................1995

SECOND DIVISION PREMIERSHIP
ROLL OF HONOUR

Year	Winners		Runners-up		Venue
1987	Swinton (2)	27	Hunslet (1)	10	Old Trafford, Manchester
1988	Oldham (1)	28	Featherstone R. (2)	26	Old Trafford, Manchester
1989	Sheffield E. (3)	43	Swinton (5)	18	Old Trafford, Manchester
1990	Oldham (3)	30	Hull K.R. (1)	29	Old Trafford, Manchester
1991	Salford (1)	27	Halifax (2)	20	Old Trafford, Manchester
† 1992	Sheffield E. (1)	34	Oldham (3)	20	Old Trafford, Manchester
† 1993	Featherstone R. (1)	20	Workington T. (★2)	16	Old Trafford, Manchester
1994	Workington T. (1)	30	London C. (3)	22	Old Trafford, Manchester
1995	Keighley C. (1)	26	Huddersfield (3)	6	Old Trafford, Manchester

( ) Denotes Second Division position...   (★) Denotes Third Division position
† Divisional Premiership, three-division era

THE TOM BERGIN TROPHY

The trophy, in honour of the late president of the Rugby League Writers' Association and former editor of the *Salford City Reporter*, is presented to the Man of the Match in the end-of-season Second Division, later Divisional Premiership final. The award is donated and judged by the Association and sponsored by Stones Bitter.

Year	Winner	Team	Position
1987	Gary Ainsworth	Swinton (v. Hunslet)	Hooker
1988	Des Foy	Oldham (v. Featherstone R.)	Centre
1989	Mark Aston	Sheffield E. (v. Swinton)	Stand off
1990	Mike Ford	Oldham (v. Hull K.R.)	Scrum half
1991	Steve Kerry	Salford (v. Halifax)	Scrum half
1992	Daryl Powell	Sheffield E. (v. Oldham)	Centre
1993	Paul Newlove	Featherstone R. (v. Workington T.)	Centre
1994	Dean Marwood	Workington T. (v. London C.)	Scrum half
1995	Martin Wood	Keighley C. (v. Huddersfield)	Loose forward

SECOND DIVISION/DIVISIONAL PREMIERSHIP TROPHY FINAL PLAYERS' REGISTER

The following is an index of players who have appeared in the Second Division Premiership final since the first in 1987. It also includes the Divisional finals of 1992 and 1993 when Third Division clubs were included in the competition. W — winners, L — losers. Substitute appearances in lower case letters. The year denotes the second half of the season.

AINSWORTH, Gary: Swinton 87W, 89L
ALLEN, John: Swinton 87w, 89L
APPLEBY, Darren: Keighley C. 95W
ARMSTRONG, Colin: Hull K.R. 90l; Workington T. 93L, 94W
ASTON, Mark: Sheffield E. 89W, 92W
AUSTIN, Greg: Hull K.R. 90L; Halifax 91L; Huddersfield 95L

BANKS, Alan: Featherstone R. 88L
BANNISTER, Andy: Featherstone R. 88L
BARTON, Ben: Huddersfield 95L
BASTIAN, John: Featherstone R. 88l
BATE, Derek: Swinton 87W, 89L
BATEMAN, Andy: Hunslet 87L
BELL, Keith: Featherstone R. 88L
BELL, Peter: Halifax 91L
BIRKETT, Martin: Salford 91W
BISHOP, David: Hull K.R. 90L
BLEASE, Ian: Salford 91W
BOWDEN, Chris: Hunslet 87L
BRADSHAW, Arthur: Salford 91W
BROADBENT, Paul: Sheffield E. 89W, 92W
BROWN, Jeff: Swinton 87W
BROWN, Peter: Halifax 91L
BURGESS, Andy: Salford 91W
BURKE, Mick: Oldham 88W
BURNS, Paul: Workington T. 94W
BUTT, Ikram: Featherstone R. 93W
BYRNE, Ged: Oldham 92L; Workington T. 93L, 94W

CAMPBELL, Logan: London C. 94L
CARTER, Scott: London C. 94L
CARTWRIGHT, Phil: Sheffield E. 89W
CASEY, Leo: Oldham 90W; Featherstone R. 93W
CASSIDY, Frank: Salford 91W
CLARK, Brett: Oldham 90W
CLARK, Garry: Hull K.R. 90L
CLOSE, David: Sheffield E. 89W
COATES, Ged: Hunslet 87L
COCHRANE, Gareth: Keighley C. 95W
COCKER, Stuart: Workington T. 94W
COOK, Mick: Sheffield E. 89W, 92W
COULTER, Gary: Huddersfield 95l
CROSSLEY, John: Featherstone R. 88l

DAUNT, Brett: Featherstone R. 93W
DEAN, Mick: Salford 91w
DERBYSHIRE, Alan: Swinton 87W
DICKINSON, Andy: Sheffield E. 89W
DIXON, Keith: Keighley C. 95W
DRUMMOND, Des: Workington T. 93L, 94W

EMA, Asuquo: Hull K.R. 90L
EVANS, Steve: Sheffield E. 89w
EVANS, Tex: Salford 91W
EYRES, Andy: Keighley C. 95W

FARRELL, Anthony: Sheffield E. 92W
FIELDHOUSE, John: Oldham 90W
FLANAGAN, Terry: Oldham 88W
FLEARY, Darren: Keighley C. 95W
FLEMING, Mark: Sheffield E. 89W
FLETCHER, Mike: Hull K.R. 90L
FORD, Mike: Oldham 88W, 90W
FOX, Deryck: Featherstone R. 88L
FOY, Des: Oldham 88W
FRODSHAM, Tommy: Swinton 89L

GALLAGHER, John: London C. 94L
GAMSON, Mark: Sheffield E. 89W, 92W
GATELY, Ian: Keighley C. 95W
GIBSON, Phil: Hunslet 87L
GIBSON, Steve: Salford 91W
GILFILLAN, John: Salford 91W
GRAHAM, Mal: Oldham 88W
GRIMA, Joe: Swinton 87W
GUNN, Richard: Featherstone R. 93w

HADLEY, Adrian: Salford 91W
HANSEN, Shane: Salford 91W
HANGER, Dean: Huddersfield 95L
HARRISON, Des: Hull K.R. 90L
HARRISON, Karl: Featherstone R. 88L
HAWKYARD, Colin: Oldham 88W
HELLEWELL, Phil: Huddersfield 95L
HENDERSON, John: Oldham 90W
HEPI, Brad: Workington T. 93L, 94W
HEWITT, Tony: Swinton 89L
HILL, Brendan: Halifax 91L; Keighley C. 95W
HOLLIDAY, Les: Swinton 87W
HOLLIDAY, Mike: Swinton 87W
HORROCKS, John: Swinton 89l
HUGHES, Ian: Sheffield E. 92W
HUGHES, Paul: Featherstone R. 88L
HYDE, Gary: Oldham 90W

IRVINE, Jimmy: Hunslet 87L; Hull K.R. 90l
IRVING, Richard: Oldham 88w, 90W
IRVING, Simon: Keighley C. 95W

JENNINGS, Graeme: Hunslet 87L
JOHNSON, Mark: London C. 94L

JOYNT, Chris: Oldham 92L

KAY, Andy: Hunslet 87L
KAY, Tony: Workington T. 93L, 94W
KING, Graham: Hunslet 87L
KING, Dave: Huddersfield 95L
KEEBLES, Mick: Halifax 91L
KERRY, Steve: Salford 91W; Huddersfield 95L
KITCHIN, Wayne: Workington T. 93L, 94W

LAUGHTON, Dale: Sheffield E. 92W
LARDER, David: Keighley C. 95w
LEE, Mark: Salford 91W
LEE, Martin: Swinton 87W
LORD, Paul: Oldham 90W
LIGHTFOOT, David: Hull K.R. 90L
LUMB, Tim: Sheffield E. 92w
LUXON, Geoff: London C. 94l
LYMAN, Paul: Featherstone R. 88L; Hull K.R. 90L
LYONS, John: Halifax 91L

McALISTER, Charlie: Oldham 88W, 90W; Sheffield E. 92W
McDERMOTT, Paul: Sheffield E. 89w
McIVOR, Dixon: London C. 94L
McKENZIE, Phil: Workington T. 93L, 94W
MALONEY, Dave: Swinton 89l
MALONEY, Francis: Featherstone R. 93W
MANNING, Terry: Featherstone R. 93W
MARSH, Richard: Featherstone R. 88L
MARTYN, Tommy: Oldham 90w, 92L
MARWOOD, Dean: Workington T. 93L, 94W
MASON, Keith: Hunslet 87l
MEADOWS, Kevin: Oldham 88W
MELLING, Alex: Swinton 89L
MILNER, Richard: Halifax 91L
MOONEY, Frank: Swinton 89L
MULLER, Roby: Swinton 87W
MULLIGAN, Mark: Workington T. 93L, 94W
MUMBY, Keith: Sheffield E. 92w
MYCOE, David: Sheffield E. 92W
MYLER, John: Swinton 89L

NEWLOVE, Paul: Featherstone R. 93W
NEWTON, Keith: Oldham 90w, 92L
NICKLE, Sonny: Sheffield E. 89W
NICKLIN, Vince: Oldham 92L
NIEBLING, Bryan: Hull K.R. 90L

OGLANBY, Martin: Workington T. 93l, 94W
O'NEILL, Steve: Swinton 89L

PACHNIUK, Richard: Oldham 92L
PARKER, Wayne: Hull K.R. 90L
PEARCE, Greg: Huddersfield 95L
PEARSON, Martin: Featherstone R. 93W
PENOLA, Colin: Hunslet 87L

PENRICE, Paul: Workington T. 94w
PICKERING, James: Workington T. 93L, 94W
PINKNEY, Nick: Keighley C. 95W
PLANGE, David: Sheffield E. 92W
PLATT, Alan: Hunslet 87L; Halifax 91l
PLATT, Duncan: Oldham 90W, 92L
POWELL, Daryl: Sheffield E. 89W, 92W; Keighley C. 95W
PRICE, Gary S.: Featherstone R. 93W
PRICE, Richard: Sheffield E. 92W
PUCILL, Andy: Huddersfield 95L

QUINN, Steve: Featherstone R. 88L

RAMSEY, Neville: London C. 94L
RAMSHAW, Jason: Halifax 91L; Keighley C. 95W
RANSON, Scott: Swinton 89L; Oldham 92L
RATCLIFFE, Alan: Swinton 87w
REYNOLDS, Simon: Huddersfield 95L
RICHARDS, Basil: Huddersfield 95L
RILEY, Mark: London C. 94L
RILEY, Peter: Workington T. 93L, 94w
RIPPON, Andy: Swinton 87W
ROEBUCK, Neil: Featherstone R. 93w
ROPATI, Iva: Oldham 92L
ROSKELL, Scott: London C. 94L
ROSOLEN, Steve: London C. 94L
ROTHERAM, Dave: London C. 94L
ROUND, Paul: Oldham 88W, 90W
RUANE, Andy: Oldham 90W
RUDD, Chris: Hull K.R. 90L
RUSSELL, Richard: Oldham 90W, 92L

ST. HILAIRE, Lee: Huddersfield 95L
SANDERSON, Ian: Oldham 88W
SCHUBERT, Gary: Workington T. 93l
SCOTT, Ian: Workington T. 93L
SCOTT, Mick: Halifax 91l
SENIOR, Gary: Hunslet 87l; Huddersfield 95L
SHERRATT, Ian: Oldham 88W, 92L; Salford 91w
SHELFORD, Darrall: Huddersfield 95L
SIDDALL, Gary: Featherstone R. 88L
SILVA, Matthew: Halifax 91L
SIMPSON, Owen: Featherstone R. 93W
SMALES, Ian: Featherstone R. 93W
SMILES, Warren: Sheffield E. 89W
SMITH, Gary: Workington T. 93L
SMITH, Kris: London C. 94l
SMITH, Peter: Featherstone R. 88L
SMITH, Steve: Halifax 91L
SNAPE, Steve: Swinton 87W, 89L
SOUTHERNWOOD, Roy: Halifax 91L
STEADMAN, Graham: Featherstone R. 93W
STEWART, Sam: London C. 94L
STOOP, Andre: London C. 94L; Keighley C. 95W
STREET, Tim: Oldham 92l
SULLIVAN, Anthony: Hull K.R. 90L
SYKES, Andy: Hunslet 87L

SYKES, David: Featherstone R. 88L

TAEKATA, Wayne: Featherstone R. 93W
TATE, Phil: Hunslet 87L
TAYLOR, Mick: Huddersfield 95l
THOMPSON, Andy: Hull K.R. 90L
TOPPING, Paul: Swinton 87W, 89L
TUPAEA, Shane: Oldham 92L; Keighley C. 95w
TUUTA, Brendon: Featherstone R. 93W
TYRER, Sean: Oldham 92L

VAN BELLEN, Gary: Sheffield E. 89W
VILLER, Mark: Swinton 87W, 89L

WADDELL, Hugh: Oldham 88W; Sheffield E. 92W
WALSH, Peter: Oldham 88W
WARBURTON, Steve: Oldham 92l
WARNECKE, Gary: Oldham 88w
WHITELEY, Chris: London C. 94L
WILSON, Mark: Featherstone R. 93W
WILSON, Warren: Hunslet 87L; Halifax 91L
WOOD, Martin: Halifax 91L; Keighley C. 95W
WORRALL, Mick: Salford 91W

YOUNG, Andy: Sheffield E. 89W

SECOND DIVISION/DIVISIONAL PREMIERSHIP RECORDS
First staged 1987
ALL ROUNDS
TEAM
Highest score: Sheffield E. 72 v. Keighley C. 14............1992
(Also widest margin)
Biggest attendance: 5,885 Halifax v. Leigh..................1991
(Not including final)

INDIVIDUAL
Most goals:
12 by Mark Aston (Sheffield E.) v. Keighley C. 1992
Most tries:
4 by Martin Wood (Halifax) v. Fulham 1991
Most points:
26 (3t, 7g) by Martin Pearson (Featherstone R.) v.
Ryedale-York 1993

FINAL ONLY
TEAM
Most appearances: 3 by Oldham
Most wins: 2 by Oldham, Sheffield E.
Highest score:
Sheffield E. 43 v. Swinton 18 1989
(Also widest margin)

INDIVIDUAL
Most goals:
8 by Mark Aston (Sheffield E.) v. Swinton 1989
Most tries:
3 by Daryl Powell (Sheffield E.) v. Swinton 1989
Daryl Powell (Sheffield E.) v. Oldham..................1992
Mark Johnson (London C.) v. Workington T. 1994
Most points:
19 (1t,7g,1dg) by Mark Aston (Sheffield E. v. Swinton) 1989

*Featherstone Rovers' Martin Pearson, holder of the record for
most points in a Second Division Premiership match.*

REGAL TROPHY

1995-96 Final

St. Helens pushed Wigan all the way before succumbing to the individual brilliance of Henry Paul, who scored two superb solo tries and kicked four goals in a magnificent 25th Regal Trophy final at Huddersfield's Alfred McAlpine Stadium.

Wigan's 25-16 victory made it a record-extending eighth win in nine finals to complete their domination of a competition whose future was in some doubt with the advent of Super League.

After St. Helens' 80-0 semi-final thrashing of Warrington, Wigan captain Shaun Edwards tried to take the pressure off his side by suggesting the Saints would be now be favourites to lift the trophy. But the bookmakers thought otherwise and installed the holders as 1-4 favourites.

The odds seemed justified when Va'aiga Tuigamala powered over after only 15 minutes with Paul adding the goal, but St. Helens powered back to take an 8-6 interval lead with tries from Joey Hayes and Paul Newlove. Hayes' try followed a bewildering bout of eight passes back and forth across the field.

Wigan needed to pull out something extra in the second half. And they did with a little help from the unfortunate Saints centre Scott Gibbs, who lost the ball on his own line and Kris Radlinski snapped it up for a soft 46th minute try goaled by Paul. Gibbs's misery was deepened when the former Welsh Rugby Union international was sent off in the 79th minute for illegal use of the elbow against a tackler.

Before then Wigan still had a tough battle on their hands and they owed much to the wiz-ardry of Paul, who conjured up two spellbinding tries out of nothing to clinch victory. The first came in the 52nd minute when the young New Zealand international tricked his way past three defenders on a meandering 30-metre run to the line.

The titanic battle still had to be won going into the last minute with Wigan under immense pressure as they hung on to a 19-16 lead. Then Paul struck again, picking his way through a mass of defenders for a try between the posts to which he added the final points.

The standoff's last-minute try would surely have clinched him the man of the match award had the press votes not already been collected in favour of St. Helens hooker Keiron Cunningham, who had staked his claim with several dashing runs and a 70th minute try that left Saints only three points behind. Cunningham's try was an extraordinary effort as he somehow managed to stretch his arm through two or three tacklers to plant the ball down.

A Bobbie Goulding penalty had edged St. Helens nearer to an upset midway through the second half and Edwards was quick to give Wigan a little more breathing space with a 64th minute drop goal as the game soared to its tremendous climax

Edwards was playing in his 29th final of all competitions and Wigan's captain admitted this was one of the toughest after picking up a seventh Regal Trophy winners' medal.

The closeness of the encounter extended to the penalty count, which finished at 7-7, and the overall tackling statistics of 267 by Wigan and 262 by St. Helens with the victors' Mick Cassidy heading the individual honours after making 40 tackles in an all-action second row performance.

179

REGAL TROPHY FINAL

13 January 1996   **Huddersfield**

WIGAN 25   ST. HELENS 16

Wigan		St. Helens
Gary Connolly	1.	Steve Prescott
Jason Robinson	2.	Joey Hayes
Va'aiga Tuigamala	3.	Scott Gibbs
Kris Radlinski	4.	Paul Newlove
Martin Offiah	5.	Anthony Sullivan
Henry Paul	6.	Karle Hammond
Shaun Edwards, Capt.	7.	Bobbie Goulding, Capt.
Neil Cowie	8.	Apollo Perelini
Martin Hall	9.	Keiron Cunningham
Terry O'Connor	10.	Ian Pickavance
Scott Quinnell	11.	Chris Joynt
Mick Cassidy	12.	Simon Booth
Simon Haughton	13.	Dean Busby

Substitutes   Substitutes

Rob Smyth for Connolly (42 min., blood bin)	14.	Andy Northey for Sullivan (47 min.)
Martin Dermott for Quinnell (69 min.)	15.	Vila Matautia for Pickavance (22 min.)

T: Paul (2), Tuigamala, Radlinski   T: Hayes, Newlove, Cunningham
G: Paul (4), Edwards (dg)   G: Goulding (2)
Half-time: 6-8   Attendance: 17,590
Referee: Russell Smith (Castleford)   Sent off: Gibbs (79 min.)

Wigan celebrate a record-extending eighth Regal Trophy triumph, having defeated arch rivals St. Helens 25-16 at Huddersfield.

1995-96 Round by Round

The first round involved the 11 clubs from the lowest of the three senior divisions, seven non-League sides plus the two leading French clubs. All the senior English clubs were given home advantage except for Doncaster Dragons, who had not been fully re-admitted after financial problems caused them to close down for a brief period during the summer. They were drawn away to Carlisle and lost 38-10.

Beaten French Championship finalists St. Esteve followed up their success at Hunslet a year earlier with a 19-16 defeat of the joint Division Two leaders Leigh Centurions. Pia almost made it a Gallic double as the French champions went down 24-22 after leading 16-8 at half-time. Chorley ran up their highest ever score with a 92-0 thrashing of Nottingham City in which club match records fell to Martin Holden (four tries) and Mike Smith (10 goals and 24 points). Woolston went nearest to a non-League victory before losing 20-17 at Bramley.

St. Esteve were drawn at home to Workington Town in the second round but the competition rules do not allow matches in France and they went down 30-14 at Derwent Park. The Frenchmen were always struggling after Bernard Cartier was sent off early on. All the clubs from the top two divisions entered the second round and first grade Castleford suffered a major embarrassment as they crashed 19-18 at third based Carlisle. The Cumbrians pulled back from being 10-18 down and snatched victory with Mike Kavanagh's drop goal in the 72nd minute. London Broncos had a club record 82-0 victory at home to Highfield with Shane Vincent equalling their best try feat of four before going off injured in the 64th minute. Jim Fallon powered in for four tries as Leeds gained a 46-22 home win

over Salford. Keighley Cougars' hopes of enhancing their Super League claims were sunk at a rain-lashed Cougar Park where St. Helens cruised to a 42-14 victory. The televised encounter was virtually over by half-time with the Saints 20-4 ahead. Widnes pushed their Super League claims with a 32-8 home victory over Stones Bitter Championship strugglers Oldham. The visitors never recovered after Chris Parr was sent off in the 27th minute and they finished with only 11 men as Paul Davidson ended the game in the sin bin. A strong defensive effort by Bradford Bulls laid the foundations for a 22-0 home victory against a disappointing Sheffield Eagles. Martin Offiah raced back to top scoring form with five tries, while Jason Robinson grabbed a hat-trick on the other wing in Wigan's 68-26 home thrashing of Whitehaven. Greg Pearce added a superb touchline goal to Brimah Kebbie's last minute try to snatch Huddersfield a 22-21 home win over Featherstone Rovers. It was an unhappy return for Featherstone centre Matt Calland, who was sent off for a high tackle on Kebbie only 25 minutes into his first game since completing a six-match suspension. Rochdale Hornets pulled off a surprise 14-10 win at Hull Kingston Rovers in a game of missed opportunities by both sides. There was almost a major shock at Halifax where the Stones Bitter Championship outfit just held on for a 20-18 victory over third grade side Swinton. Chorley took a shock lead at home to Warrington with a Jeff Robinson try after ten minutes but then crashed to a 68-10 defeat. Steve McNamara collected 24 points from two tries and eight goals leading Hull to a 56-18 home defeat of York. The all-Leeds derby encounter brought Hunslet a 22-4 win at Bramley, who trailed by only four points at the interval but faded away in the second half. A brilliant solo try by Australian scrum half Glen

181

Tomlinson inspired Batley to a hard-earned 21-14 victory at home to Wakefield Trinity. South African international Kobus van Deventer kicked five goals, including a drop goal, to play a big part in Dewsbury's 17-6 defeat of visiting Barrow Braves.

The televised third round game was staged at the Harlequins Rugby Union ground, The Stoop, where London Broncos were hoping to increase their Super League profile. But Halifax dashed those plans with a 22-18 away victory after being 14 points down in the early stages. Hull put up a mighty battle at home to St. Helens before going down 26-38, the visitors only clinching victory with two late tries. Widnes stepped up a division and gained an outstanding 32-8 away victory over Stones Bitter Championship opponents Workington Town. South African international Guy Coombe made his debut for Dewsbury, who went out 14-26 to visiting Rochdale Hornets. Teenage scrum half Steve Booth was given a tough full Huddersfield first team debut against visiting Wigan and came through with plenty of credit despite a 32-0 defeat. Batley kept snapping away at Warrington before going down 22-35. An 11th successive victory swept Carlisle into the last eight for only the second time in their brief history, overcoming a strong challenge from Hunslet to hang on for a 22-17 away win. Leeds seemed to be coasting to a comfortable home victory over Bradford Bulls as they led 40-12 going into the last 25 minutes, but were almost caught out as the visitors stormed back to equal their tally of six tries. Paul Cook's nine goals made all the difference as St. John Ellis landed only two for Bradford in their 42-28 defeat.

An epic televised battle was the outstanding tie of the fourth round with Wigan coming out on top 28-23 at Widnes after 30 tension-packed minutes of extra time. The trophy holders had fought back from being 16-4 down to snatch two converted tries in the last ten minutes while Widnes loose forward Steve McCurrie was in the sin bin to make it 16-16 and force the tie into extra time. Widnes regained the lead early in the extra period before Wigan finished the marathon with a sprint finish that produced three tries. Even without record signing Paul Newlove, who was Cup-tied, St. Helens had too much power for Halifax as they charged to a 46-18 home victory. Carlisle took a surprise early lead at Leeds when Phil Manning touched down but the Cumbrians failed to maintain the pace and went down 44-22. It was a similar story at Warrington where Rochdale Hornets went ahead with a third minute try by Chris Churm before being eventually worn down and losing 38-20.

St. Helens scored an astonishing 80-0 record semi-final victory over Warrington in a home tie postponed to a Thursday night because of frost. They swept past the previous highest semi-final score set by Wigan in a 36-8 defeat of Leigh 10 years earlier with a brilliant 14-try exhibition of attacking rugby. It was also a record defeat for Warrington, beating the 68-14 loss suffered at Hunslet back in 1928. Coach Brian Johnson was so upset by the thrashing that he resigned the following day.

Wigan cruised into a record-breaking ninth final with a 38-18 home defeat of Leeds. The trophy holders were 38-6 ahead before Leeds hit back with three tries in the last 12 minutes. Henry Paul had an outstanding game at stand off with seven goals and a try, while Gary Connolly raced in for two touchdowns including a great 80-metre solo effort. But the man of the match award went to hard-working hooker Martin Hall.

1995-96 RESULTS

First Round

Barrow B.	29	Park Amateurs	11
Bramley	20	Woolston R.	17
Carlisle	38	Doncaster	10
Chorley	92	Nottingham C.	0
Highfield	48	Hemel Hempstead	18
Hull K.R.	72	Blackpool G.	6
Hunslet H.	34	Ellenborough R.	24
Leigh C.	16	St. Esteve	19
Swinton	44	West Hull	20
York	24	Pia	22

Second Round

Batley	21	Wakefield T.	14
Bradford B.	22	Sheffield E.	0
Bramley	4	Hunslet H.	22
Carlisle	19	Castleford	18
Chorley	10	Warrington	68
Dewsbury	17	Barrow B.	6
Halifax	20	Swinton	18
Huddersfield	22	Featherstone R.	21
Hull	56	York	18
Hull K.R.	10	Rochdale H.	14
Keighley C.	14	St. Helens	42
Leeds	46	Salford R.	22
London B.	82	Highfield	0
Widnes	32	Oldham B.	8
Wigan	68	Whitehaven	26
Workington T.	30	St. Esteve	14

Third Round

Batley	22	Warrington	35
Dewsbury	14	Rochdale H.	26
Huddersfield	0	Wigan	32
Hull	26	St. Helens	38
Hunslet	17	Carlisle	22
Leeds	42	Bradford B.	28
London B.	18	Halifax	22
Workington T.	8	Widnes	32

Fourth Round

Leeds	44	Carlisle	22
St. Helens	46	Halifax	18
Warrington	38	Rochdale H.	20
Widnes	23	Wigan	28

(30 min. extra time. 16-16 at normal time)

Semi-finals

St. Helens	80	Warrington	0
Wigan	38	Leeds	18

Final

Wigan	25	St. Helens	16

(at Huddersfield)

1995-96 PRIZES

First Round .... £3,500 to each RFL club and two
French clubs £1,000 to each amateur club
Second Round................ £3,500 to losers
Third Round................. £6,000 to losers
Quarter-finals .... £9,000 to losers
Semi-finals .... £12,500 to losers
Runners-up £35,000
Winners £60,000

Total Prize Money	£315,000
Capital Development Fund	£135,000
Grand Total	£450,000

REGAL TROPHY ROLL OF HONOUR

Season	Winners		Runners-up		Venue	Attendance	Receipts
1971-72	Halifax	22	Wakefield T.	11	Bradford	7,975	£2,545
1972-73	Leeds	12	Salford	7	Fartown, Huddersfield	10,102	£4,563
1973-74	Warrington	27	Rochdale H.	16	Wigan	9,347	£4,380
1974-75	Bradford N.	3	Widnes	2	Warrington	5,935	£3,305
1975-76	Widnes	19	Hull	13	Leeds	9,035	£6,275
1976-77	Castleford	25	Blackpool B.	15	Salford	4,512	£2,919

(Continued)

183

1977-78	Warrington	9	Widnes	4	St. Helens	10,258	£8,429
1978-79	Widnes	16	Warrington	4	St. Helens	10,743	£11,709
1979-80	Bradford N.	6	Widnes	0	Leeds	9,909	£11,560
1980-81	Warrington	12	Barrow	5	Wigan	12,820	£21,020
1981-82	Hull	12	Hull K.R.	4	Leeds	25,245	£42,987
1982-83	Wigan	15	Leeds	4	Elland Rd, Leeds	19,553	£49,027
1983-84	Leeds	18	Widnes	10	Wigan	9,510	£19,824
1984-85	Hull K.R.	12	Hull	0	Hull City FC	25,326	£69,555
1985-86	Wigan	11	Hull K.R.	8	Elland Rd, Leeds	17,573	£66,714
1986-87	Wigan	18	Warrington	4	Bolton W. FC	21,144	£86,041
1987-88	St. Helens	15	Leeds	14	Wigan	16,669	£62,232
1988-89	Wigan	12	Widnes	6	Bolton W. FC	20,709	£94,874
1989-90	Wigan	24	Halifax	12	Leeds	17,810	£73,688
1990-91	Warrington	12	Bradford N.	2	Leeds	11,154	£57,652
1991-92	Widnes	24	Leeds	0	Wigan	15,070	£90,453
1992-93	Wigan	15	Bradford N.	8	Elland Rd, Leeds	13,221	£90,204
1993-94	Castleford	33	Wigan	2	Leeds	15,626	£99,804
1994-95	Wigan	40	Warrington	10	McAlpine St'm, Hudd'd	19,636	£161,976
1995–96	Wigan	25	St. Helens	16	McAlpine St'm, Hudd'd	17,590	

REGAL TROPHY MAN OF THE MATCH

Season	Winner	Team	Position
1971-72	Bruce Burton	Halifax (v. Wakefield T.)	Stand off
1972-73	Keith Hepworth	Leeds (v. Salford)	Scrum half
1973-74	Kevin Ashcroft	Warrington (v. Rochdale H.)	Hooker
1974-75	Barry Seabourne	Bradford N. (v. Widnes)	Scrum half
1975-76	Reg Bowden	Widnes (v. Hull)	Scrum half
1976-77	Gary Stephens	Castleford	Scrum half
	Howard Allen	Blackpool B.	Hooker
1977-78	Steve Hesford	Warrington (v. Widnes)	Winger
1978-79	David Eckersley	Widnes (v. Warrington)	Full back
1979-80	Len Casey	Bradford N. (v. Widnes)	Loose forward
1980-81	Tommy Martyn	Warrington (v. Barrow)	Second row
1981-82	Trevor Skerrett	Hull (v. Hull K.R.)	Prop
1982-83	Martin Foy	Wigan (v. Leeds)	Stand off
1983-84	Mark Laurie	Leeds (v. Widnes)	Second row
1984-85	Paul Harkin	Hull K.R. (v. Hull)	Scrum half
1985-86	Paul Harkin	Hull K.R. (v. Wigan)	Scrum half
1986-87	Andy Goodway	Wigan (v. Warrington)	Loose forward
1987-88	Paul Loughlin	St. Helens (v. Leeds)	Centre
1988-89	Ellery Hanley	Wigan (v. Widnes)	Loose forward
1989-90	Ellery Hanley	Wigan (v. Halifax)	Loose forward
1990-91	Billy McGinty	Warrington (v. Bradford N.)	Second row
1991-92	Les Holliday	Widnes (v. Leeds)	Loose forward
1992-93	Shaun Edwards	Wigan (v. Bradford N.)	Scrum half
1993-94	Martin Ketteridge	Castleford (v. Wigan)	Prop
1994-95	Phil Clarke	Wigan (v. Warrington)	Loose forward
1995–96	Keiron Cunningham	St. Helens (v. Wigan)	Hooker

REGAL TROPHY FINAL PLAYERS' REGISTER

The following is an index of players who have appeared in the Regal Trophy final since its inauguration as the Player's No. 6 Trophy in 1971-72.
W — winners, L — losers. Substitute appearances in lower case letters. The year denotes the second half of the season.

ADAMS, Mick: Widnes 75L, 76W, 78L, 79W, 80L, 84L
AH KUOI, Fred: Hull 85L
ALLEN, Howard: Blackpool B. 77L; Barrow 81L
ANDERSON, Chris: Widnes 75L
ANDERSON, Grant: Castleford 94W
ANDERSON, Tony: Halifax 90L; Bradford N. 93L
ASHCROFT, Kevin: Warrington 74W
ASHTON, Ray: Leeds 88L
ASPEY, Mal: Widnes 75L, 76W, 78L, 79W, 80L
ASPINALL, Willie: Rochdale H. 74L
ATCHESON, Paul: Widnes 92w; Wigan 95w
ATKINSON, John: Leeds 73W

BAKER, Gordon: Halifax 72W
BALL, Ian: Barrow 81L
BANKS, Barry: Hull 82W
BANNER, Peter: Salford 73L
BARENDS, David: Bradford N. 80W
BARLOW, Tukere: Warrington 95L
BASNETT, John: Leeds 88L
BATEMAN, Allan: Warrington 91W, 95L
BELL, Dean: Leeds 84W; Wigan 87W, 89W, 90W, 93W
BELL, Peter: Halifax 90L
BENNETT, Andrew: Warrington 95l
BENTLEY, John: Leeds 92L
BENYON, Billy: Warrington 78W, 79L
BETTS, Denis: Wigan 89W, 90W, 93W, 95W
BEVAN, John: Warrington 74W, 78W, 81W
BLACKER, Mick: Bradford N. 75W
BLACKMORE, Richard: Castleford 94W
BLACKWOOD, Bob: Widnes 75L
BOOTH, Simon: St. Helens 96L
BOTICA, Frano: Wigan 93W, 94L, 95W
BOWDEN, Reg: Widnes 75L, 76W, 78L, 79W, 80L
BOXALL, Keith: Hull 76L
BOYD, Les: Warrington 87L
BRADY, Brian: Warrington 74W
BRELSFORD, Norman: Rochdale H. 74L
BRIDGES, John "Keith": Bradford N. 80W
BRIGGS, Trevor: Castleford 77W
BROADHURST, Mark: Hull K.R. 85W
BROPHY, Tom: Rochdale H. 74L
BURKE, Mick: Widnes 79W, 80L, 84L
BURKE, Tony: Leeds 83L; St. Helens 88W
BURTON, Bruce: Halifax 72W; Castleford 77W
BURTON, Chris: Hull K.R. 82l, 85W, 86L
BUSBY, Dean: St. Helens 96L
BUTLER, John: Rochdale H. 74L
BYRNE, Ged: Wigan 89W

CAIRNS, David: Barrow 81L
CALLON, David: Halifax 72W
CAMPBELL, Danny: Wigan 83W
CAMPBELL, Mark: Leeds 83l
CARLTON, Stuart: Bradford N. 75W
CASE, Brian: Warrington 79L, 81W; Wigan 83w, 87W
CASEY, Len: Bradford N. 80W; Hull K.R. 82L
CASSIDY, Mick: Wigan 94l, 95W, 96W
CHAMBERS, Gary: Warrington 91W
CHARLTON, Paul: Salford 73L
CHISNALL, Dave: Warrington 74W; Barrow 81L
CLARK, Garry: Hull K.R. 85W, 86L
CLARK, George: Hull 76L
CLARK, Trevor: Bradford N. 93l
CLARKE, Phil: Wigan 93W, 94L, 95W
CLAWSON, Terry: Leeds 73W
COLLOBY, Tony: Salford 73L
CONNOLLY, Gary: Wigan 94L, 95W, 96W
COOKSON, Phil: Leeds 73W
COOPER, Shane: St. Helens 88W
CORDLE, Gerald: Bradford N. 91L
COURTNEY, Neil: Warrington 81W
COWIE, Neil: Wigan 93W, 94L, 95W, 96W
CRANE, Mick: Hull 76L, 82W
CREASSER, David: Leeds 84W, 88L, 92L
CRELLIN, Jim: Rochdale H. 74L
CROFT, David: Bradford N. 91L
CROOKS, Lee: Hull 82W, 85L; Castleford 94W
CROOKS, Steve: Hull K.R. 82L
CULLEN, Paul: Warrington 87L, 91W, 95L
CUNNINGHAM, Keiron: St. Helens 96L
CURRIER, Andy: Widnes 89L, 92W

DALGREEN, John: Warrington 78W
DANNATT, Andy: Hull 85l
DARBYSHIRE, Paul: Warrington 95L
DAVIDSON, Chris: Hull 76l
DAVIES, Doug: Salford 73l
DAVIES, Jonathan: Widnes 92W; Warrington 95L
DAVIES, Phil: Halifax 72W
DAY, Terry: Hull 82W
DEAN, Tony: Hull 82W
DEARDEN, Alan: Widnes 78l, 79W
DERMOTT, Martin: Wigan 87W, 89W, 90W, 93W, 94L, 96w
DEVEREUX, John: Widnes 92W
DEWHIRST, Terry: Halifax 72W
DICK, Kevin: Leeds 83L, 84W
DICKINSON, Alan: Castleford 77W
DICKINSON, Roy: Leeds 83L

185

DIVORTY, Gary: Hull 85L; Leeds 92L
DIXON, Colin: Salford 73L
DIXON, Paul: Leeds 92L
DORAHY, John: Hull K.R. 86L; Halifax 90L
DOWD, Barry: Widnes 92W
DOWLING, Greg: Wigan 86W
DRUMMOND, Des: Warrington 91W
DUANE, Ian: Warrington 81W
DUANE, Ronnie: Warrington 87L
DU TOIT, Nick: Wigan 86w
DUTTON, Ray: Widnes 75L, 76W
DYL, Les: Leeds 73W, 83L

EARL, Kelvin: Bradford N. 75W
ECCLES, Bob: Warrington 81w
ECCLES, Graham: Leeds 73W
ECKERSLEY, David: Widnes 78L, 79W, 80L
EDMONDS, Phil: Hull 85L
EDWARDS, Morvin: Leeds 92L
EDWARDS, Shaun: Wigan 86W, 87W, 89W, 90W, 93W, 94L, 95W, 96W
EGAN, Joe: Blackpool B. 77L
ELIA, Mark: St. Helens 88W
ELLA, Steve: Wigan 86W
ELLIOTT, David: Barrow 81L
ELLIS, Kevin: Warrington 91W
ELLIS, St. John; Castleford 94W
ELWELL, Keith: Widnes 75L, 76W, 78L, 79W, 80L, 84L
EMA, Asuquo: Hull K.R. 85W, 86L
EVANS, Steve: Hull 85L
EVANS, Stuart: St. Helens 88w
EYRES, Richard: Widnes 89L, 92W

FAIRBAIRN, George: Hull K.R. 82L, 85W
FAIRBANK, John: Leeds 88l
FAIRBANK, Karl: Bradford N. 93L
FAIRHURST, Jimmy: Wigan 83W
FARRAR, Andrew: Wigan 93W
FARRELL, Andrew: Wigan 94L
FEARNLEY, Stan: Bradford N. 75W
FENTON, Steve: Castleford 77W
FERRES, Steve: Bradford N. 80w
FINNIGAN, Derek: Warrington 78W, 79L
FISHER, Tony: Leeds 73W
FLANAGAN, Peter: Hull 76L
FLYNN, Malcolm: Barrow 81L
FOGERTY, Terry: Halifax 72W; Rochdale H. 74L
FORAN, John: Widnes 76W
FORBER, Paul: St. Helens 88W
FORD, Mike: Wigan 86W; Castleford 94W
FORD, Phil: Leeds 92L
FORSTER, Mark: Warrington 87L, 91W, 95L
FORSYTH, Colin: Bradford N. 80W
FOULKES, Kenny: Hull 76L
FOX, Deryck: Bradford N. 93L
FOX, Neil: Wakefield T. 72L

FOY, Martin: Wigan 83W
FRANCIS, Rudi: Bradford N. 75W
FRENCH, Nigel: Barrow 81L

GAMBLE, Paul: Blackpool B. 77L
GANT, Les: Bradford N. 75W, 80W
GARTLAND, Peter: Rochdale H. 74L
GEORGE, Derek "Mick": Widnes 76W, 78L, 80L
GEORGE, Wilf: Halifax 90L
GIBBS, Scott: St. Helens 96L
GIBSON, Carl: Leeds 88L, 92l
GILDART, Ian: Wigan 90W
GILL, Henderson: Wigan 83W, 86W, 87W
GILL, Ken: Salford 73L
GOODWAY, Andy: Wigan 86W, 87W, 89w, 90w
GORDON, Parry: Warrington 74W, 78W, 79L
GORLEY, Les: Widnes 80L, 84L
GOULDING, Bobbie: Leeds 92L; St Helens 96L
GRAYSHON, Jeff: Bradford N. 80W
GREGORY, Andy: Widnes 84L; Wigan 89w, 90W
GREGORY, Mike: Warrington 87L
GRICE, Alan: Salford 73L
GRIMA, Joe: Widnes 89L, 92w
GROVES, Ken: Blackpool B. 77L
GROVES, Paul: St. Helens 88W
GUNN, Richard: Leeds 92L
GURR, Marty: Leeds 88L
GWILLIAM, Alan: Warrington 79L, 81W

HADLEY, Derek: Barrow 81L
HAGGERTY, Roy: St. Helens 88W
HAGUE, Neil: Leeds 83l
HAIGH, Bob: Leeds 73W
HALL, David: Hull K.R. 82L
HALL, Martin: Wigan 95W, 96W
HALMSHAW, Tony: Halifax 72W; Rochdale H. 74L
HAMER, Jon: Bradford N. 91L
HAMILTON, Jim: Blackpool B. 77L
HAMMOND, Karle: St. Helens 96L
HAMPSON, Steve: Wigan 86W, 87W, 89W, 93W
HANCOCK, Brian: Hull 76L
HANLEY, Ellery: Wigan 86W, 87W, 89W, 90W
HARDISTY, Alan: Leeds 73W
HARKIN, Kevin: Wakefield T. 72L; Hull 82w
HARKIN, Paul: Hull K.R. 82L, 85W, 86L
HARMON, Neil: Warrington 91W
HARRIS, Iestyn: Warrington 95L
HARRIS, Ray: Rochdale H. 74L
HARRISON, Chris: Hull 82W
HARRISON, Peter: Wakefield T. 72L
HARTLEY, Steve: Hull K.R. 82L
HAUGHTON, Simon: Wigan 96W
HAWKSLEY, Roy: Halifax 72W
HAY, Andy: Castleford 94w
HAYES, Joey: St. Helens 96L
HEGARTY, John: Wakefield T. 72L

HELLEWELL, Phil: Bradford N. 911
HEPWORTH, Keith: Leeds 73W
HEPWORTH, Tony: Halifax 72W
HERITAGE, John: Blackpool B. 77L
HERON, David: Leeds 83L, 88L; Bradford N. 93L
HERON, Wayne: Leeds 83L
HESFORD, Steve: Warrington 78W, 79L, 81W
HESKETH, Chris: Salford 73L
HETHERINGTON, Brian: Halifax 90L
HILL, Brendan: Halifax 90L
HOBBS, David: Bradford N. 91L, 93L
HOGAN, Brian: Widnes 80L
HOGAN, Phil: Hull K.R. 82L, 85W
HOLDING, Neil: St. Helens 88W
HOLDSTOCK, Roy: Hull K.R. 82L
HOLLIDAY, Bill: Rochdale H. 74L
HOLLIDAY, Les: Halifax 90L; Widnes 92W
HOLMES, John: Leeds 73W, 83L, 84W
HOWARD, Harvey: Widnes 92W
HUBBARD, Steve: Hull K.R. 82L
HUGHES, Eric: Widnes 75L, 76W, 78L, 79W, 80L, 84L
HULL, David: Widnes 78L, 79W, 80L
HULME, David: Widnes 89L
HULME, Paul: Widnes 89l, 92W
HUNTER, Eddie: Warrington 79l, 81W
HUNTER, Paul: Hull 76L
HURST, Phil: Blackpool B. 77l
HYNES, Syd: Leeds 73W

IRO, Kevin: Wigan 89W, 90W
IRO, Tony: Wigan 89W
IRVING, Simon: Leeds 92L
ITI, Brett: Bradford N. 91L

JACKSON, Bob: Warrington 87L
JACKSON, Peter: Leeds 88L
JACKSON, Phil: Bradford N. 75W
JAMES, Kevin: Barrow 81L
JARVIS, Francis: Bradford N. 75W
JEANES, David: Wakefield T. 72L; Leeds 73W
JENKINS, David: Widnes 76W
JOHNSON, Brian: Warrington 87L
JOHNSON, Phil: Castleford 77W
JOHNSTON, Lindsay: Halifax 90L
JOHNSTON, Peter: Hull K.R. 86L
JOYCE, Graham: Bradford N. 75W
JOYNER, John: Castleford 77W
JOYNT, Chris: St. Helens 96l
JULIFF, Brian: Wigan 83w

KAHN, Paul: Castleford 77W
KELLY, Andy: Hull K.R. 86L
KELLY, Ken: Warrington 78W, 79L, 81W, 87L
KELLY, Mike: Halifax 72W
KELLY, Mike: Warrington 79L, 81W
KEMBLE, Gary: Hull 85L

KEMP, Tony: Castleford 94W
KETTERIDGE, Martin: Castleford 94W
KIRKBRIDE, Bill: Salford 73L
KIRKBY, Steve: Barrow 81L
KISS, Nicky: Wigan 83W, 86W
KOLOTO, Emosi: Widnes 89L

LAMB, Cliff: Blackpool B. 77l
LAUGHTON, Doug: Widnes 75L, 78L
LAURIE, Mark: Leeds 84W
LAWS, David: Hull K.R. 85W, 86L
LESTER, Roy: Warrington 78W, 79L
LEULUAI, James: Hull 82W, 85L
LINTON, Ralph: Widnes 84L
LLOYD, Geoff "Sammy": Castleford 77W
LOUGHLIN, Paul: St. Helens 88W
LOWE, Phil: Hull K.R. 82L
LUCAS, Ian: Wigan 90W
LYDIAT, John: Hull K.R. 86L
LYDON, Joe: Widnes 84L; Wigan 87W, 89W, 90W, 93w, 94L
LYON, David: Warrington 91W
LYONS, John: Halifax 90L
LYONS, Steve: Wakefield T. 72L

McCALLION, Seamus: Halifax 90L
McCONNELL, Ralph: Barrow 81L
McDERMOTT, Barrie: Wigan 95w
McGINTY, Billy: Warrington 91W; Wigan 93W
McGOWAN, Steve: Bradford N. 93W
McGUIRE, Bruce: Warrington 95L
MACKAY, Graham: Salford 73L
McKENZIE, Phil: Widnes 89L
MACHEN, Paul: Blackpool B. 77L
MACKEY, Greg: Warrington 95L
MACKLIN, Alf: Hull 76L
MAJOR, Mick: Wakefield T. 72L
MALONEY, Francis: Warrington 95L
MANN, Duane: Warrington 91W
MARCHANT, Tony: Bradford N. 91L, 93L
MARSH, Ged: Blackpool B. 77L
MARSHALL, David: Wigan 90W
MARSTON, Jack: Wakefield T. 72L
MARTIN, John: Halifax 72W
MARTYN, Tommy: Warrington 78W, 79L, 81W
MASKILL, Colin: Leeds 88L
MASON, Mel: Barrow 81L
MATAUTIA, Vila: St. Helens 96l
MATHER, Barrie-Jon: Wigan 94L
MEADOWS, Kevin: Warrington 87L
MEDLEY, Paul: Leeds 88L; Bradford N. 91L, 93L
MERCER, Gary: Warrington 91W
MIDDLETON, Simon: Castleford 94W
MILLER, Gavin: Hull K.R. 85W, 86L
MILLINGTON, John: Hull K.R. 82l
MILLS, Jim: Widnes 75L, 76W, 79W, 80l
MILNER, Richard: Halifax 90L

MOLLOY, Steve: Leeds 92l
MOORBY, Gary: Leeds 84W
MORAN, Dave: Widnes 79W
MORDT, Ray: Wigan 86W
MORGAN, Mick: Wakefield T. 72L
MORRIS, Steve: Leeds 88L
MORRISON, Tony: Castleford 94W
MUMBY, Keith: Bradford N. 80W, 93l
MUSCROFT, Peter: Hull K.R. 82L
MYLER, Rob: Warrington 95L
MYLER, Tony: Widnes 89L

NEWALL, Jackie: Blackpool B. 77L
NEWLOVE, Paul: St. Helens 96L
NICHOLAS, Mike: Warrington 74w, 78W, 79L
NIKAU, Tawera: Castleford 94W
NOBLE, Brian: Bradford N. 91L, 93L
NOONAN, Derek: Warrington 74W
NORTHEY, Andy: St. Helens 96l
NORTON, Steve: Castleford 77W; Hull 82W

O'CONNOR, Terry: Wigan 96W
OFFIAH, Martin: Widnes 89L; Wigan 93W, 94L, 95W
O'HARA, Dane: Hull 82W, 85L
O'LOUGHLIN, Keiron: Widnes 84L
O'NEILL, Dennis: Widnes 75L
O'NEILL, Mike: Widnes 89L; Leeds 92L
O'NEILL, Steve: Widnes 84L
O'SULLIVAN, Chris: Warrington 91W

PANAPA, Sam: Wigan 93w, 94l
PARKER, Derek: Bradford N. 80W
PATRICK, Shaun: Hull 85L
PATTINSON, Malcolm: Blackpool B. 77L
PAUL, Henry: Wigan 95W, 96W
PENDLEBURY, John: Wigan 83W; Bradford N. 91L
PERELINI, Apollo: St. Helens 96L
PETERS, Steve: Warrington 87L
PHILBIN, Barry: Warrington 74W, 78W
PHILBIN, Mike: Warrington 74W
PHILLIPS, Rowland: Warrington 91w
PICKAVANCE, Ian: St. Helens 96L
PICKUP, Bill: Warrington 74w
PICKUP, Fred: Leeds 73w
PITMAN, Phil: Blackpool B. 77L
PLATT, Andy: St. Helens 88W; Wigan 90W, 93W, 94L
PORTZ, Steve: Hull 76L
POTTER, Ian: Warrington 78W, 81W; Wigan 86W, 87W, 89W
POWELL, Roy: Leeds 88L, 92L; Bradford N. 93L
PRENDIVILLE, Paul: Hull 82W; Leeds 84W
PRESCOTT, Alan: Widnes 75L, 76L
PRESCOTT, Steve: St. Helens 96L

PRESTON, Mark: Wigan 90W
PROCTOR, Wayne: Hull 85L
PROHM, GARY: Hull K.R. 85W

QUINNELL, Scott: Wigan 96W
QUIRK, Les: St. Helens 88W

RADLINSKI, Kris: Wigan 96W
RAMSDALE, Denis: Wigan 83W
RAMSEY, Bill: Hull 76L; Widnes 78L
RAMSHAW, Terry: Salford 73L
RATHBONE, Alan: Warrington 87l
RAYNE, Keith: Leeds 84W
RAYNE, Kevin: Leeds 84W, 88L
RAYNER, David: Halifax 72W
REDFEARN, Alan: Bradford N. 80W
REDFEARN, David: Bradford N. 75W, 80W
REEVES, Derek: Halifax 72w
REILLY, Malcolm: Castleford 77W
REYNOLDS, Doug: Blackpool B. 77L
REYNOLDS, Frank: Warrington 74W
RICHARDS, Maurice: Salford 73L
RIDDLESDEN, Eddie: Halifax 90L
ROBERTS, Ian: Wigan 87W
ROBERTS, Mark: Warrington 87L
ROBINSON, Doug: Blackpool B. 77L
ROBINSON, Ian: Hull K.R. 85W, 86l
ROBINSON, Jason: Wigan 93W, 94L, 95W, 96W
ROPATI, Joe: Warrington 87L
ROSE, Paul: Hull 85L
RUSSELL, Richard: Castleford 94W

SAMPSON, Dean: Castleford 94w
SANDERSON, Gary: Warrington 87L, 95l
SANDERSON, John "Sammy": Halifax 72w
SARSFIELD, Mark: Widnes 92W
SCHOFIELD, Garry: Hull 85l; Leeds 88L, 92L
SCOTT, Mick: Wigan 83W; Halifax 90l
SEABOURNE, BARRY: Bradford N. 75W
SHAW, Glyn: Widnes 78L, 79W, 80L; Wigan 83W
SHEFFIELD, Bill: Rochdale H. 74L
SHELFORD, Adrian: Wigan 89W
SHELFORD, Darrall: Bradford N. 91L
SHELFORD, Kelly: Warrington 95L
SHERIDAN, Barry: Widnes 75L, 76W
SIMPSON, Roger: Bradford N. 91L, 93L
SKERRETT, Kelvin: Wigan 94L, 95W
SKERRETT, Trevor: Hull 82W
SLATER, Keith: Wakefield T. 72L
SMALES, Ian: Castleford 94W
SMITH, Alan: Leeds 73W
SMITH, Andy: Leeds 83L, 84W
SMITH, David: Widnes 92W
SMITH, Gordon: Hull K.R. 86L
SMITH, Mike: Hull K.R. 82L, 85W, 86L
SMITH, Steve: Halifax 90l
SMYTH, Rob: Wigan 96w

SORENSEN, Kurt: Widnes 89L, 92W
SOUTO, Peter: St. Helens 88W
SPENCER, Ray: Wakefield T. 72l
SPURR, Bob: Castleford 77W
SQUIRE, Kevin: Leeds 84w
STEADMAN, Graham: Castleford 94W
STEPHENS, Gary: Castleford 77W
STEPHENSON, David: Wigan 83W, 86W, 87W
STEPHENSON, Mike: Hull 76L
STEPHENSON, Nigel: Bradford N. 80W
STERLING, Peter: Hull 85L
STONE, Richard "Charlie": Hull 82W
SULLIVAN, Anthony: St. Helens 96L
SUMMERS, Neil: Bradford N. 91L, 93L
SUTTON, Dave: Warrington 79L
SYKES, Andy: Leeds 83L
SZYMALA, Eddie: Barrow 81l

TAIT, Alan: Widnes 89L, 92W
TAMATI, Kevin: Widnes 84L; Warrington 87L
TANNER, David: St. Helens 88W
TAYLOR, David: Rochdale H. 74L
TEES, Gary: Warrington 95L
THACKRAY, Rick: Warrington 81W; Widnes 89L
THOMAS, Mark: Warrington 91w
THOMPSON, Jimmy: Bradford N. 80W
THORNILEY, Tony: Warrington 91W
TOPLISS, David: Wakefield T. 72L; Hull 85L
TROTTER, Dennis: Bradford N. 75W
TUIGAMALA, Va'aiga: Wigan 95W, 96W
TUNKS, Peter: Leeds 88L

VALENTINE, Rob: Wakefield T. 72L
VAN BELLEN, Gary: Bradford N. 80W
VAN BELLEN, Ian: Bradford N. 80w
VEIVERS, Phil: St. Helens 88W

WAINWRIGHT, Tony: Barrow 81L
WALKER, Malcolm: Hull 76L
WALLER, Tony: Warrington 79L, 81W
WANBON, Bobby: Warrington 74W
WANE, Shaun: Wigan 86W, 89W, 90w; Leeds 92L
WARD, Bernard: Wakefield T. 72l
WARD, David: Leeds 73w, 83L, 84W
WARD, Johnny: Salford 73L
WARD, Phil: Salford 73l; Bradford N. 75W
WARDELL, Alan: Hull 76L
WATKINS, David: Salford 73L
WATKINSON, David: Hull K.R. 82L, 85W, 86L
WATSON, David: Bradford N. 93L
WEBB, Terry: Leeds 84W
WEST, Graeme: Wigan 83W, 86W, 87W
WHITEHEAD, Derek: Warrington 74W
WHITEHEAD, Stuart: Rochdale H. 74L
WHITFIELD, Colin: Wigan 83W; Halifax 90L
WHITFIELD, Fred: Widnes 84L
WHITTLE, Alan: Warrington 74W

WILEMAN, Ron: Hull 82W
WILKINSON, Ian: Leeds 83L, 84W; Bradford N. 91L
WILLIAMS, Barry: Wigan 83W
WILLICOMBE, David: Halifax 72W
WILSON, Frank: Warrington 78W
WOOD, Harry: Rochdale H. 74l
WOOD, John: Widnes 76W
WOODS, Paul: Widnes 78L
WRAITH, Geoff: Wakefield T. 72L; Castleford 77W
WRIGHT, Darren: Widnes 89L, 92W
WRIGHT, Dave: Warrington 74W
WRIGHT, Stuart: Widnes 78L, 79W, 80L, 84L

REGAL TROPHY RECORDS

ALL ROUNDS

TEAM
Highest score: Huddersfield 142 v. Blackpool G. 4 (1994-95)
  Also widest margin win with Barrow 138 v. Nottingham C. 0 (1994-95)
Biggest attendance: 25,326 Hull v. Hull K.R.
  (at Hull C. FC) ....Final 1984-85

INDIVIDUAL
Most tries: 9 by Greg Austin (Huddersfield) v. Blackpool G. (1994-95)
Most goals: 17 by Sammy Lloyd (Castleford) v. Millom (1973-74)
  17 by Darren Carter (Barrow) v. Nottingham C. (1994-95)
Most points: 43 (3t,17g) by Sammy Lloyd (Castleford) v. Millom (1973-74)

REGAL TROPHY FINAL RECORDS

TEAM
Most final appearances: 9 by Wigan
Most wins: 8 by Wigan
Highest score: Wigan 40 v. Warrington 10 1994-95
Widest margin win: Castleford 33 v. Wigan 2 1993-94
Biggest attendance: 25,326 Hull v. Hull K.R. (at Hull
  C. FC) 1984-85
Biggest receipts: £161,976 Warrington v. Wigan (at
  McAlpine Stad'm, Hudd'd) 1994-95

INDIVIDUAL
Most tries: 3 by Ellery Hanley (Wigan) v. Halifax.....1989-90
Most goals: 8 by Frano Botica (Wigan) v. Warrington
 1994-95
Most points: 20 (1t, 8g) by Frano Botica (Wigan) v.
  Warrington 1994-95

189

REGAL TROPHY PROGRESS CHART

Key: W — Winners. F — Beaten finalists. SF — Semi-final. P — Preliminary round.

	1995-96	1994-95	1993-94	1992-93	1991-92	1990-91	1989-90	1988-89	1987-88	1986-87	1985-86	1984-85	1983-84	1982-83	1981-82	1980-81	1979-80	1978-79	1977-78	1976-77	1975-76	1974-75	1973-74	1972-73	1971-72
BARROW B.	2	2	2	1	1	1	1	1	1	3	2	1	2	3	3	F	1	1	1	1	2	1	1	1	3
BATLEY	3	3	3	1	1	3	1	1	2	P	1	1	P	1	1	1	1	1	1	2	1	1	1	2	1
BLACKPOOL G.	(1)	(1)	(1)	P	1	1	1	2	3	2	1	1	1	2	P	2	2	1	1	F	1	1	1	1	3
BRADFORD B.	3	4	SF	F	3	F	2	SF	1	3	2	2	1	3	2	1	W	SF	SF	2	1	W	1	3	1
BRAMLEY	2	2	3	1	1	2	1	2	P	1	1	3	*	1	1	1	2	1	1	2	1	2	SF	2	2
CARLISLE	4	2	4	2	2	P	1	1	1	2	P	P	2	2	2										
CASTLEFORD	2	SF	W	SF	3	3	SF	2	2	2	1	2	1	1	2	SF	3	3	2	W	SF	1	2	1	2
CHORLEY C.	2	(1)	(1)	P	P	1	1																		
DEWSBURY	3	3	2	1	P	1	2	1	2	1	1	3	1	1	1	1	1	2	1	1	1	1	3	2	1
DONCASTER D.	1	2	2	1	2	2	1	2	1	2	2	1	1	1	1	1	1	1	1	2	1	1	1	1	1
FEATHERSTONE R.	2	2	2	2	3	2	3	1	1	2	P	2	3	1	2	2	2	2	3	2	1	1	1	2	1
HALIFAX	4	2	3	2	2	P	F	2	2	2	1	SF	1	1	1	3	1	2	1	2	1	1	2	1	W
HIGHFIELD	2	2	2	P	1	1	1	1	1	1	1	2	2	P	1	1	1	1	1	1	1	2	1	1	1
HUDDERSFIELD	3	2	2	P	1	1	2	1	1	P	1	1	1	2	2	2	1	1	3	1	3	1	1	2	2
HULL	3	3	4	SF	2	1	1	2	3	SF	3	F	2	2	W	SF	1	2	1	3	F	1	1	3	3
HULL K.R.	2	2	2	2	1	1	1	3	2	1	F	W	2	3	F	2	1	SF	1	1	3	SF	1	SF	2
HUNSLET	3	1	2	2	1	1	2	P	1	1	2	P	1	1	2	1	1	2	1	2	1	1	1	1	
KEIGHLEY C.	2	4	2	1	2	2	1	1	1	1	2	1	2	1	2	3	2	1	1	2	3	1	2		
LEEDS	SF	4	2	1	F	2	3	1	F	1	1	SF	W	F	3	1	2	1	1	3	2	3	3	W	SF
LEIGH C.	1	2	3	3	P	2	1	3	2	3	SF	1	SF	2	1	3	3	3	3	SF	2	1	2	2	1
LONDON B.	3	2	4	2	1	1	1	P	P	1	1	1	1	1	1	2									
NOTTINGHAM C.	(1)	(1)	(1)	1	1	1	1	2	1	1	1														
OLDHAM	2	3	3	1	2	2	3	1	SF	1	2	2	1	1	SF	1	1	2	2	2	2	1	1	1	
ROCHDALE H.	4	2	2	2	P	SF	1	2	1	1	1	2	1	2	1	1	1	1	1	1	1	F	1	2	
ST. HELENS	F	4	3	3	SF	3	SF	SF	W	3	SF	3	SF	2	1	1	2	2	2	2	3	1	SF	SF	SF
SALFORD R.	2	3	SF	1	SF	1	2	1	3	1	2	1	2	3	3	2	SF	2	2	2	SF	3	2	F	1
SCARBOROUGH P.				P																					
SHEFFIELD E.	2	3	2	1	2	P	3	2	1	2	1	1													
SWINTON	2	2	2	P	1	1	2	1	1	2	1	1	3	1	SF	1	1	1	1	1	1	3	1	3	1
WAKEFIELD T.	2	2	2	1	2	2	P	3	2	1	2	P	1	1	1	1	SF	3	SF	1	2	2	3	2	F
WARRINGTON	SF	F	4	2	1	W	P	3	3	F	3	1	2	SF	2	W	3	F	W	1	3	W	1	1	
WHITEHAVEN	2	3	2	1	1	1	2	1	1	1	1	2	P	1	1	3	1	1	1	1	SF	2	1	3	1
WIDNES	4	SF	3	3	W	SF	2	F	1	SF	3	3	F	SF	3	3	F	W	F	SF	W	F	1	3	1
WIGAN	W	W	F	W	3	3	W	W	SF	W	W	2	3	W	1	1	2	2	3	2	2	2	2	1	3
WORKINGTON T.	3	3	2	3	1	1	1	P	1	1	1	1	1	1	2	1	3	2	2	3	3	1	2	1	1
YORK	2	2	3	1	P	P	1	1	P	3	1	1	2	1	2	2	1	1	3	1	2	2	2	2	

* Bramley withdrew from the Trophy while in liquidation, opponents Hull K.R. receiving a bye.
( ) Entrant as non-League side

CHARITY SHIELD

Wigan completed a hat-trick of devastating defeats of Leeds with a Charity Shield record 45-20 victory at the Royal Dublin Showground. It followed their 30-10 Silk Cut Challenge Cup success at Wembley and Premiership final record 69-12 thrashing of Leeds a few months earlier. The previous highest Charity Shield score was Wigan's 44-12 defeat of Halifax in 1987, which remains the widest winning margin.

The victory in Dublin was also an individual triumph for Andrew Farrell, who achieved two Charity Shield records with eight goals and 20 points including a try. The loose forward's goals tally equalled the eight by Wigan's David Stephenson against Halifax in 1987, while his 20 points beat the 16 by Stephenson, and Jonathan Davies for Widnes against Wigan in 1990. Farrell, who was made captain in the absence of injured Shaun Edwards, completed an outstanding performance by winning the man of the match award.

Leeds were struggling from the moment they were reduced to 12 men with the ninth-minute dismissal of scrum half Marcus Vassilakopoulos for tripping Nigel Wright as the Wigan stand off scored the opening try. Farrell added the goal to an earlier penalty to make it 8-0.

Tony Kemp, a pre-season signing from Castleford, marked his Leeds debut with a 30th-minute try but Wigan were well on the way to victory by half-time when they led 23-8.

Wigan carried off the Waterford Crystal Bowl to add to their 1994-95 Grand Slam haul of all four domestic trophies plus the World Club Championship held since 1994.

The Charity Shield was revived for the first time since 1992 and played in Dublin to test development plans in Ireland. Unfortunately, the match clashed with the televised All Ireland Gaelic Football semi-final and that kept the crowd down to 5,716.

CHARITY SHIELD

13 August 1995   **Royal Showground, Dublin**

WIGAN   45   **LEEDS   20**

Henry Paul	1.	Alan Tait
Jason Robinson	2.	Jim Fallon
Va'aiga Tuigamala	3.	Kevin Iro
Gary Connolly	4.	Francis Cummins
Kris Radlinski	5.	Paul Cook
Nigel Wright	6.	Tony Kemp
Craig Murdock	7.	Marcus Vassilakopoulos
Kelvin Skerrett	8.	Neil Harmon
Martin Hall	9.	James Lowes, Capt.
Neil Cowie	10.	Esene Faimalo
Simon Haughton	11.	Gary Mercer
Mick Cassidy	12.	George Mann
Andrew Farrell, Capt.	13.	Mike Forshaw

Substitutions:
Terry O'Connor for Skerrett (47 min.)
Rob Smyth for Wright (54 min.)
Andy Johnson for Cowie (67 min.)
Matthew Knowles for Haughton (70 min.)

Substitutions:
Adrian Morley for Mercer (48 min.)
David Gibbons for Faimalo (50 min.)
Nick Fozzard for Mann (63 min.)
Marvin Golden for Fallon (70 min.)

T: Wright (2), Connolly, Haughton, Farrell, Cassidy, O'Connor
G: Farrell (8), Wright (dg)
Referee: Russell Smith (Castleford)
Attendance: 5,716

T: Kemp, Faimalo, Forshaw
G: Cook (4)

Half-time: 23-8
Sent off: Vassilakopoulos (9 min.)

191

CHARITY SHIELD HISTORY
● From 1985-86 to 1992-93 and again in 1995-96, the Charity Shield was scheduled to be contested between the previous season's Challenge Cup winners and Division One Champions. When Wigan won both trophies in 1990 and 1991 they met the previous season's Premiership final winners. When Wigan won the Championship, Challenge Cup and Premiership in 1992 and 1995, they met the previous season's Division One title runners-up.

CHARITY SHIELD ROLL OF HONOUR

Year	Winners		Runners-up		Venue	Attendance
1985-86	Wigan	34	*Hull K.R.	6	Isle of Man	4,066
1986-87	*Halifax	9	Castleford	8	Isle of Man	3,276
1987-88	*Wigan	44	Halifax	12	Isle of Man	4,804
1988-89	*Widnes	20	Wigan	14	Isle of Man	5,044
1989-90	*Widnes	27	Wigan	22	Liverpool FC	17,263
1990-91	†Widnes	24	*Wigan	8	Swansea C. FC	11,178
1991-92	*Wigan	22	†Hull	8	Gateshead	10,248
1992-93	#St. Helens	17	*Wigan	0	Gateshead	7,364
1995-96	*Wigan	45	#Leeds	20	Dublin	5,716

*Denotes previous season's Champions; †Premiership winners; unmarked, Challenge Cup winners; #Championship runner-up

CHARITY SHIELD . . . . A REVIEW

1985-86
Wigan 34 Hampson; P. Ford, Stephenson (7g), Donlan (2t), Gill (2t); Edwards, M. Ford (1t); Courtney (Mayo), Kiss, Campbell, West (Lucas), Du Toit, Wane
Hull K.R. 6 Fairbairn (Lydiat 1g); Clark (1t), Robinson, Prohm, Laws; M. Smith, G. Smith; Des Harrison, Watkinson, Ema, Kelly (Rudd), Burton, Hogan
Referee: R. Campbell (Widnes)

1986-87
Halifax 9 Smith (Wilson); Riddlesden, Whitfield (1t), Hague (1dg), George (1t); C. Anderson, Stephens; Dickinson, McCallion, Juliff, Scott (James), Bell, Dixon
Castleford 8 Roockley; Plange, Lord (1t), Irwin (R. Southernwood), Spears; Joyner (Fletcher), R. Beardmore; Ward, K. Beardmore, Johnson, Ketteridge (2g), Mountain, England
Referee: G.F. Lindop (Wakefield)

1987-88
Wigan 44 Hampson (2t); Stephenson (8g), Byrne (Russell), Bell (2t), Gill (1t); Edwards (2t), Gregory; West, Kiss, Case, Gildart (Wane), Potter, Goodway
Halifax 12 Eadie (2g); Taylor, Wilson, T. Anderson, George; Simpson (Juliff 1t), Stephens; Dickinson, Pendlebury, Beevers, James, Scott (Bell), Dixon (1t)
Referee: J. Holdsworth (Kippax)

1988-89
Widnes 20 Tait; Thackray, Currier (4g), D. Wright (1t), Offiah (1t); Dowd, D. Hulme; Sorensen, McKenzie (1t), Grima (Pyke), M. O'Neill, P. Hulme, R. Eyres
Wigan 14 Hampson; Gill, Lydon (1t, 1g), Bell, Preston (Lucas); Byrne, Gregory; Shelford (Betts), Kiss, Case, T. Iro (2t), Wane, Goodway
Referee: R. Tennant (Castleford)

1989-90
Widnes 27 Tait (1dg); Kebbie (1t), Davies (1t, 5g), D. Wright, Offiah (1t); A. Myler, D. Hulme (1t); Sorensen, P. Hulme, Grima (Pyke), M. O'Neill, Koloto, R. Eyres
Wigan 22 Hampson; Bell (Gilfillan), K. Iro (1t), Lydon (1t, 5g), Preston; Byrne, Gregory; Lucas, Kiss, Platt (1t) (Stazicker), Betts, Gildart, Goodway
Referee: J. Holdsworth (Kippax)

1990-91
Widnes 24 Tait; Devereux (1t), Currier, Davies (3t, 2g), Offiah (1t); A. Myler, D. Hulme; Ashurst (D. Wright), McKenzie, Grima, P. Hulme (Sorensen), Koloto, Holliday
Wigan 8 Gilfillan; Myers, Bell, Byrne, Preston; Botica (1t, 2g) (Edwards), Goulding; Skerrett, Bridge, Wane, Gildart (Forshaw), Platt, Betts
Referee: C. Morris (Huddersfield)

1991-92
Wigan 22 Hampson; Myers (1t), Bell (2t), Lydon, Botica (3g); Edwards (1t), Gregory; Lucas (Gildart), Dermott, Skerrett, Betts, Platt (Forshaw), Goodway
Hull 8 Feather; Eastwood (2g), Blacker, G. Nolan (1t), Turner; Hanlan, Mackey; Durham (Dixon), L. Jackson, Marlow, McNamara (Jones), Walker, Busby
Referee: R. Whitfield (Widnes)

1992-93
St. Helens 17 Hunte; Riley, Connolly, Ropati (1t, 2g), Sullivan (1t); Griffiths, O'Donnell (1dg) (Quirk); Neill, Dwyer, Ward, Harrison, Mann (Forber), Cooper (1t)
Wigan 0 Hampson; Panapa, Bell, Lydon (Myers), Offiah; Botica, Crompton; Lucas, Cassidy, Skerrett (Goodway), Betts, McGinty, Clarke
Referee: S. Cummings (Widnes)

CHARITY SHIELD RECORDS

TEAM
Most appearances: 8 Wigan
Most wins: 4 Wigan
Highest score: Wigan 45 v. Leeds 20 1995
Widest margin: Wigan 44 v. Halifax 12 1987
Biggest attendance:
17,263 Widnes v. Wigan (at Liverpool FC) 1989

INDIVIDUAL
Most tries:
3 by Jonathan Davies (Widnes) v. Wigan 1990
Most goals:
8 by David Stephenson (Wigan) v. Halifax 1987
     Andrew Farrell (Wigan) v. Leeds 1995
Most points:
20 (1t, 8g) by Andrew Farrell (Wigan) v. Leeds 1995

MAN OF THE MATCH AWARDS

Season	Winner	Team	Position
1985-86	Shaun Edwards	Wigan (v. Hull K.R.)	Stand off
1986-87	Chris Anderson	Halifax (v. Castleford)	Stand off
1987-88	Shaun Edwards	Wigan (v. Halifax)	Stand off
1988-89	Phil McKenzie	Widnes (v. Wigan)	Hooker
1989-90	Denis Betts	Wigan (v. Widnes)	Second row
1990-91	Jonathan Davies	Widnes (v. Wigan)	Centre
1991-92	Dean Bell	Wigan (v. Hull)	Centre
1992-93	Alan Hunte	St. Helens (v. Wigan)	Full back
1995-96	Andrew Farrell	Wigan (v. Leeds)	Loose forward

● From 1987 it became the Jack Bentley Trophy in memory of the former *Daily Express* Rugby League journalist.

Alan Hunte, man of the match at Gateshead in 1992-93.

Andrew Farrell, man of the match and victorious skipper in Dublin in 1995-96.

WORLD CLUB CHALLENGE
ROLL OF HONOUR

Year	Winners		Runners-up		Venue	Attendance	Receipts
1987	Wigan	8	Manly-Warringah	2	Wigan	36,895	£131,000
1989	Widnes	30	Canberra	18	Old Trafford, Man'r	30,786	£207,764
1991	Wigan	21	Penrith	4	Anfield, Liverpool	20,152	£179,797
1992	Brisbane B.	22	Wigan	8	Wigan	17,746	£170,911
1994	Wigan	20	Brisbane B.	14	Brisbane	54,220	$448,041

A REVIEW . . .
1987-88
Wigan 8 Hampson; Russell, Stephenson (4g), Lydon, Gill; Edwards, Gregory; Case (Lucas), Kiss, Wane, Goodway, Potter, Hanley
Manly 2 Shearer; Ronson, Williams (Ticehurst), O'Connor (1g), Davis; Lyons, Hasler; Daley, Cochrane, Gately (Brokenshire), Gibbs, Cunningham (Shaw), Vautin
Referee: J. Holdsworth (Kippax)
1989-90
Widnes 30 Tait; Currier, Davies (1t, 3g), D. Wright (1t), Offiah (2t); A. Myler (Dowd), D. Hulme; Grima (Moriarty), McKenzie, Pyke, Sorensen, P. Hulme (1t), R. Eyres (1t)
Canberra 18 Belcher; Wood (2g), Meninga (1t) (Martin), Daley, Ferguson; O'Sullivan (1t, 1g), Stuart; Jackson (Lowry), Walters (1t), Lazarus, Lance, Coyne, Clyde
Referee: F. Desplas (France)
1991-92
Wigan 21 Hampson; Myers (1t), Panapa (1t), Lydon (1dg), Botica (6g); Edwards, Gregory; Skerrett (Cowie) (Lucas), Dermott, Platt, Betts, McGinty (Gildart), Clarke (Forshaw)
Penrith 4 Barwick (B. Alexander); Willis (1t) (Smith), Bradley, B. Izzard, Mackay; Carter, G. Alexander; Lee (G. Izzard), Simmons, Dunn, Clarke, Cartwright, Van Der Voort (Xuereb)
Referee: A. Sablayrolles (France)

1992-93
Brisbane B. 22 O'Neill (1t) (Plowman); Carne, Renouf, Johns (Currie), Hancock (2t); Kevin Walters, Langer (Plath); Lazarus, Kerrod Walters (1t), Gee (Ryan), Gillmeister, Hohn, Matterson (3g)
Wigan 8 Stoop (Crompton); Robinson, Bell, Farrar, Offiah; Botica (2g), Edwards (1t); Skerrett (Lucas), Dermott, Platt (Cowie), Betts, McGinty (Panapa), Clarke
Referee: D. Hale (New Zealand)
1993-94
Wigan 20 Connolly; Robinson (1t), Panapa, Mather (1t) (Atcheson), Offiah; Botica (4g), Edwards; Cowie, Dermott (Hall), McGinty (Cassidy), Betts (1t), Farrell, Clarke
Brisbane B. 14 Carne; Sailor (1t), Renouf (Ryan), Johns, Hancock (1t); Kevin Walters (Plath) (McKenna), Langer; Lazarus, Kerrod Walters, Gee (Gonea), Hohn, Carn, O'Neill (1t,1g)
Referee: Greg McCallum (Australia)

MAN OF THE MATCH AWARDS

1987: Shaun Wane (Wigan)
1989: David Hulme (Widnes)
1991: Frano Botica (Wigan)
1992: Terry Matterson (Brisbane B.)
1994: Shaun Edwards (Wigan)

Seventh heaven . . .
Wigan celebrate lifting the 1995-96 Centenary
Championship Trophy for a record extending seventh
consecutive season. Skipper Shaun Edwards holds the trophy,
which carried a prize cheque for £75,000.

LEAGUE

LEAGUE

The last winter season before the switch to summer rugby lasted from 18 August to 21 January, with a four-week break for the World Cup in October. It brought much criticism as clubs in all three divisions had to play regular midweek games to cram in their 20-match League programme.

But they deemed it necessary to maintain a cash flow before the start of the summer season, which would also herald the Super League era. The format for the interim season was a Stones Bitter Centenary Championship of 11 clubs, with a First and Second Division of equal number. There was no promotion or relegation and only the winners of each division received prize money.

An extra incentive for the Centenary Championship clubs was that, in addition to the winners receiving a record £75,000, they would also keep the historic Championship Cup which was to be replaced by a new Super League trophy. Many felt the old trophy should not become the property of any club, but with Wigan lifting it for a record-extending seventh successive season it seemed to have already found a permanent home.

Wigan again began as odds-on favourites and led all the way after winning 48-6 in the opening match at Workington Town. By late September nine successive wins had taken them eight points clear of St. Helens, who had played only one match fewer, and many felt the race was already over before the October break for the World Cup.

But Leeds gave themselves and the chasing pack renewed hope when club rugby resumed by beating Wigan 23-11 in a magnificent encounter at Headingley. It moved them to within two points of the champions after both had played 10 matches. Leeds were unable to maintain the pressure in the second half of the season, however, and virtually handed Wigan the title by crashing 27-22 at home to Sheffield

Eagles and 47-14 at Warrington in successive matches.

There was no stopping Wigan now, although second-off-bottom Oldham embarrassed them with a shock 28-26 home victory. Wigan looked to be heading for the expected runaway win when they led 20-6 inside half an hour before Oldham battled back to snatch a late victory.

It was to be Wigan's last defeat and when injury-hit St. Helens gave up the title chase by fielding a virtual reserve side to concentrate on the Regal Trophy, the champions hammered them 58-4 at home on the last traditional Boxing Day clash between the two arch rivals.

Wigan made certain of winning the title in their 18th match with a 32-18 home victory over Bradford Bulls to complete another triumphant season for coach Graeme West and captain Shaun Edwards.

The new-styled First Division title and £30,000 prize money went to Salford Reds, who collected 35 points to finish seven ahead of second-placed Keighley Cougars. The final margin was a surprise for it had been a close race until Keighley collapsed and lost five of their last eight matches, including a 34-6 home defeat against Salford.

Keighley had won 22-14 at Salford in the middle of an opening sequence of 12 matches without defeat which raised the possibility of them going through the season unbeaten. But a 16-4 loss at Wakefield Trinity started the rot as Salford began their charge for the title to complete a successful first full season as coach for Andy Gregory.

Hull Kingston Rovers won their last 12 matches to finish four points clear of Leigh Centurions at the top of the new-styled Second Division and walk away with the £15,000 prize money. Coach Steve Crooks brought Rovers through some early season inconsistency to weld them into a side clearly in a class above the rest.

Results to 21 January 1996

STONES BITTER CENTENARY CHAMPIONSHIP

	P.	W.	D.	L.	Dg.	FOR Gls.	FOR Trs.	FOR Pts.	Dg.	AGAINST Gls.	AGAINST Trs.	AGAINST Pts.	Pts.
Wigan	20	18	0	2	2	124	140	810	2	47	55	316	36
Leeds	20	14	0	6	4	82	96	552	7	61	69	405	28
Halifax	20	12	1	7	10	65	79	456	3	74	78	463	25
St. Helens	20	12	0	8	2	109	128	732	2	79	87	508	24
Sheffield E.	20	10	0	10	4	71	84	482	4	70	96	528	20
Castleford	20	9	1	10	0	70	77	448	8	81	99	566	19
Bradford B.	20	8	0	12	0	65	72	418	4	68	84	476	16
Oldham B.	20	8	0	12	2	58	66	382	3	88	89	535	16
Warrington	20	7	0	13	11	68	74	443	6	88	83	514	14
London B.	20	7	0	13	4	61	85	466	5	86	102	585	14
Workington T.	20	4	0	16	5	50	53	317	0	81	112	610	8

STONES BITTER CENTENARY FIRST DIVISION

	P.	W.	D.	L.	Dg.	FOR Gls.	FOR Trs.	FOR Pts.	Dg.	AGAINST Gls.	AGAINST Trs.	AGAINST Pts.	Pts.
Salford R.	20	17	1	2	11	111	107	661	2	44	47	278	35
Keighley C.	20	13	2	5	7	84	79	491	3	46	40	255	28
Widnes	20	13	1	6	1	73	82	475	4	59	53	334	27
Hull	20	11	0	9	3	94	95	571	2	69	70	420	22
Featherstone R.	20	11	0	9	2	79	65	420	5	69	72	431	22
Whitehaven	20	10	2	8	3	49	61	345	1	71	73	435	22
Wakefield T.	20	10	0	10	2	42	65	346	0	71	70	422	20
Rochdale H.	20	8	1	11	7	57	61	365	1	77	82	483	17
Huddersfield	20	6	0	14	3	64	66	395	5	68	86	485	12
Batley	20	5	1	14	0	43	54	302	10	81	80	492	11
Dewsbury	20	2	0	18	1	42	44	261	7	83	106	597	4

STONES BITTER CENTENARY SECOND DIVISION

	P.	W.	D.	L.	Dg.	FOR Gls.	FOR Trs.	FOR Pts.	Dg.	AGAINST Gls.	AGAINST Trs.	AGAINST Pts.	Pts.
Hull K.R.	20	18	0	2	4	114	128	744	5	31	41	231	36
Leigh C.	20	16	0	4	8	82	105	592	7	52	56	335	32
Hunslet H.	20	14	0	6	8	73	90	514	7	46	54	315	28
Swinton	20	13	0	7	3	67	96	521	3	44	60	331	26
Carlisle	20	12	0	8	0	82	109	600	5	56	48	309	24
York	20	10	1	9	8	69	74	442	5	65	70	415	21
Bramley	20	9	1	10	2	55	72	400	6	72	71	434	19
Barrow B.	20	6	0	14	8	55	56	342	6	77	82	488	12
Chorley C.	20	5	1	14	8	54	52	324	4	96	103	608	11
Doncaster D.	20	5	0	15	4	52	60	348	6	86	117	646	10
Highfield	20	0	1	19	5	44	39	249	4	122	179	964	1

TWO DIVISION CHAMPIONSHIP ROLL OF HONOUR

	FIRST DIVISION	SECOND DIVISION
1902-03	Halifax	Keighley
1903-04	Bradford	Wakefield Trinity
1904-05	Oldham	Dewsbury
1962-63	Swinton	Hunslet
1963-64	Swinton	Oldham
1973-74	Salford	Bradford Northern
1974-75	St. Helens	Huddersfield
1975-76	Salford	Barrow
1976-77	Featherstone Rovers	Hull
1977-78	Widnes	Leigh
1978-79	Hull Kingston Rovers	Hull
1979-80	Bradford Northern	Featherstone Rovers
1980-81	Bradford Northern	York
1981-82	Leigh	Oldham
1982-83	Hull	Fulham
1983-84	Hull Kingston Rovers	Barrow
1984-85	Hull Kingston Rovers	Swinton
1985-86	Halifax	Leigh
1986-87	Wigan	Hunslet
1987-88	Widnes	Oldham
1988-89	Widnes	Leigh
1989-90	Wigan	Hull Kingston Rovers
1990-91	Wigan	Salford
1991-92	Wigan	Sheffield Eagles
1992-93	Wigan	Featherstone Rovers
1993-94	Wigan	Workington Town
1994-95	Wigan	Keighley Cougars

1995-96 Wigan won Centenary Championship, Salford won new First Division Championship and Hull Kingston Rovers took the new Second Division Championship

THIRD DIVISION CHAMPIONS

| 1991-92 | Huddersfield |
| 1992-93 | Keighley Cougars |

RELEGATION AND PROMOTION
Since reintroduction of two divisions in 1973-74.

● Figure in brackets indicates position in division.

	RELEGATED	PROMOTED
1973-74	Oldham (13) Hull K.R. (14) Leigh (15) Whitehaven (16)	Bradford Northern (1) York (2) Keighley (3) Halifax (4)
1974-75	York (13) Bramley (14) Rochdale Hornets (15) Halifax (16)	Huddersfield (1) Hull K.R. (2) Oldham (3) Swinton (4)
1975-76	Dewsbury (13) Keighley (14) Huddersfield (15) Swinton (16)	Barrow (1) Rochdale Hornets (2) Workington Town (3) Leigh (4)
1976-77	Rochdale Hornets (13) Leigh (14) Barrow (15) Oldham (16)	Hull (1) Dewsbury (2) Bramley (3) New Hunslet (4)
1977-78	Hull (13) New Hunslet (14) Bramley (15) Dewsbury (16)	Leigh (1) Barrow (2) Rochdale Hornets (3) Huddersfield (4)
1978-79	Barrow (13) Featherstone Rovers (14) Rochdale Hornets (15) Huddersfield (16)	Hull (1) New Hunslet (2) York (3) Blackpool Borough (4)
1979-80	Wigan (13) Hunslet (14) York (15) Blackpool Borough (16)	Featherstone Rovers (1) Halifax (2) Oldham (3) Barrow (4)
1980-81	Halifax (13) Salford (14) Workington Town (15) Oldham (16)	York (1) Wigan (2) Fulham (3) Whitehaven (4)
1981-82	Fulham (13) Wakefield Trinity (14) York (15) Whitehaven (16)	Oldham (1) Carlisle (2) Workington Town (3) Halifax (4)
1982-83	Barrow (13) Workington Town (14) Halifax (15) Carlisle (16)	Fulham (1) Wakefield Trinity (2) Salford (3) Whitehaven (4)

1983-84	Fulham (13)	Barrow (1)
	Wakefield Trinity (14)	Workington Town (2)
	Salford (15)	Hunslet (3)
	Whitehaven (16)	Halifax (4)
1984-85	Barrow (13)	Swinton (1)
	Leigh (14)	Salford (2)
	Hunslet (15)	York (3)
	Workington Town (16)	Dewsbury (4)
1985-86	York (14)	Leigh (1)
	Swinton (15)	Barrow (2)
	Dewsbury (16)	Wakefield Trinity (3)
1986-87	Oldham (13)	Hunslet (1)
	Featherstone Rovers (14)	Swinton (2)
	Barrow (15)	
	Wakefield Trinity (16)	
1987-88	Leigh (12)	Oldham (1)
	Swinton (13)	Featherstone Rovers (2)
	Hunslet (14)	Wakefield Trinity (3)
1988-89	Oldham (12)	Leigh (1)
	Halifax (13)	Barrow (2)
	Hull K.R. (14)	Sheffield Eagles (3)
1989-90	Leigh (12)	Hull K.R. (1)
	Salford (13)	Rochdale Hornets (2)
	Barrow (14)	Oldham (3)
1990-91	Oldham (12)	Salford (1)
	Sheffield Eagles (13)	Halifax (2)
	Rochdale Hornets (14)	Swinton (3)

	FIRST DIVISION	SECOND DIVISION	THIRD DIVISION
1991-92	Down: Featherstone R. (13)	Up: Sheffield E. (1)	Up: Huddersfield (1)
	Swinton (14)	Leigh (2)	Bramley (2)
		Down: Ryedale-York (7)	
		Workington Town (8)	
1992-93	Salford (13)	Up: Featherstone R. (1)	Keighley C. (1)
	Hull K.R. (14)	Oldham (2)	Workington T. (2)

● Reverted to two divisions with only Featherstone and Oldham moving divisions.

	RELEGATED	PROMOTED
1993-94	Hull K.R. (15)	Workington Town (1)
	Leigh (16)	Doncaster (2)
1994-95	Hull (15)	Keighley Cougars (1)
	Doncaster (16)	Batley (2)

● Promotion and relegation not carried out following formation of Super League and two other divisions.

● League match records do not include scores in abandoned matches that were replayed.

FIRST DIVISION RECORDS
(Records refer to the old-style First Division and the 1995-96 Stones Bitter Centenary Championship season)

INDIVIDUAL
Match records
Most tries:
6 Shane Cooper (St. Helens) v. Hull, 17 February 1988
Most goals: 13 Geoff Pimblett (St. Helens) v. Bramley, 5 March 1978
Most points: 38 (4t,11g) Bob Beardmore (Castleford) v. Barrow, 22 March 1987

Season records
Most tries: 44 Ellery Hanley (Wigan)   1986-87
Most goals: 130 Steve Hesford (Warrington)   1978-79
Most points: 326 (18t,126g,2dg) John Schuster (Halifax)   1994-95

The inimitable Ellery Hanley, holder of the First Division records for most tries in a career and a season.

TEAM
Highest score and widest margin: Leeds 90 v. Barrow 0, 11 February 1990
Highest away score: Rochdale H. 12 v. Castleford 76, 3 March 1991
Widest away margin: Doncaster 0 v. Halifax 72, 9 October 1994
Most points by losing team: London B. 44 v. Castleford 50, 21 January 1996
Scoreless draw: Wigan 0 v. Castleford 0, 26 January 1974
Highest score draw: Leeds 46 v. Sheffield E. 46, 10 April 1994
Best opening sequence: 13 wins then a draw by Widnes 1981-82; 13 wins by Wigan 1994-95
Longest winning run: 25 by St. Helens. Won last 13 of 1985-86 and first 12 of 1986-87 (Also longest unbeaten run)
Longest losing run: 20 by Whitehaven   1983-84; Rochdale H. 1990-91
Longest run without a win: 23, including 3 draws, by Whitehaven 1981-82 (Also worst opening sequence)
Biggest attendance: 29,839 Wigan v. St. Helens, 9 April 1993

Top ten Division One career tries
279 Ellery Hanley (Bradford N., Wigan, Leeds)
227 Martin Offiah (Widnes, Wigan)
178 Phil Ford (Warrington, Wigan, Bradford N., Leeds, Salford)
175 Garry Schofield (Hull, Leeds)
165 Keith Fielding (Salford)
164 Shaun Edwards (Wigan)
144 David Smith (Wakefield T., Leeds, Bradford N.)
139 Stuart Wright (Wigan, Widnes)
136 Roy Mathias (St. Helens)
134 Des Drummond (Leigh, Warrington, Workington T.)

Most Division One career goals
862 John Woods (Leigh, Bradford N., Warrington)

Most Division One career points
2,150 John Woods (Leigh, Bradford N., Warrington)

20 Division One tries in a season
1973-74	36	Keith Fielding (Salford)
	29	Roy Mathias (St. Helens)
	21	David Smith (Wakefield T.)
1974-75	21	Maurice Richards (Salford)
	21	Roy Mathias (St. Helens)
1975-76	26	Maurice Richards (Salford)
	20	David Smith (Wakefield T.)
1976-77	22	David Topliss (Wakefield T.)
	21	Keith Fielding (Salford)
	21	Ged Dunn (Hull K.R.)
	20	David Smith (Leeds)
	20	Stuart Wright (Widnes)
1977-78	26	Keith Fielding (Salford)
	25	Steve Fenton (Castleford)
	24	Stuart Wright (Widnes)
	20	David Smith (Leeds)
	20	Bruce Burton (Castleford)
	20	John Bevan (Warrington)
1978-79	28	Steve Hartley (Hull K.R.)
1979-80	24	Keith Fielding (Salford)
	21	Roy Mathias (St. Helens)
	21	Steve Hubbard (Hull K.R.)
	20	David Smith (Leeds)

1980-81	20	Steve Hubbard (Hull K.R.)
1981-82		David Hobbs (Featherstone R.) was top scorer with 19 tries.
1982-83	22	Bob Eccles (Warrington)
	20	Steve Evans (Hull)
1983-84	28	Garry Schofield (Hull)
	23	John Woods (Leigh)
	20	James Leuluai (Hull)
1984-85	40	Ellery Hanley (Bradford N.)
	34	Gary Prohm (Hull K.R.)
	23	Henderson Gill (Wigan)
	22	Barry Ledger (St. Helens)
	22	Mal Meninga (St. Helens)
1985-86	22	Ellery Hanley (Wigan)
1986-87	44	Ellery Hanley (Wigan)
	24	Phil Ford (Bradford N.)
	24	Henderson Gill (Wigan)
	23	Garry Schofield (Hull)
	21	John Henderson (Leigh)
1987-88	33	Martin Offiah (Widnes)
	22	Ellery Hanley (Wigan)
1988-89	37	Martin Offiah (Widnes)
	20	Grant Anderson (Castleford)
1989-90	28	Martin Offiah (Widnes)
	25	Mark Preston (Wigan)
	20	Steve Larder (Castleford)
1990-91	22	Martin Offiah (Widnes)
	22	Les Quirk (St. Helens)
	20	Ellery Hanley (Wigan)
1991-92	31	John Devereux (Widnes)
	27	Greg Austin (Halifax)
	25	Shaun Edwards (Wigan)
	23	Mark Preston (Halifax)
1992-93	24	Shaun Edwards (Wigan)
	23	Ellery Hanley (Leeds)
	20	Martin Offiah (Wigan)
	20	Alan Hunte (St. Helens)
1993-94	30	St. John Ellis (Castleford)
	26	Martin Offiah (Wigan)
	24	Jason Critchley (Salford)
	23	Paul Newlove (Bradford N.)
	21	John Bentley (Halifax)
	20	Anthony Sullivan (St. Helens)
1994-95	33	Martin Offiah (Wigan)
	29	Ellery Hanley (Leeds)
	26	John Bentley (Halifax)
	25	Alan Hunte (St. Helens)
	23	Paul Newlove (Bradford N.)
	21	Mark Preston (Halifax)
1995-96	20	Martin Offiah (Wigan)

Top Division One goalscorers

1973-74	126	David Watkins (Salford)
1974-75	96	Sammy Lloyd (Castleford)
1975-76	118	Sammy Lloyd (Castleford)
1976-77	113	Steve Quinn (Featherstone R.)
1977-78	116	Steve Hesford (Warrington)
1978-79	130	Steve Hesford (Warrington)
1979-80	104	Steve Hubbard (Hull K.R.)
1980-81	96	Steve Diamond (Wakefield T.)
1981-82	110	Steve Quinn (Featherstone R.)
		John Woods (Leigh)
1982-83	105	Bob Beardmore (Castleford)
1983-84	106	Steve Hesford (Warrington)
1984-85	114	Sean Day (St. Helens)
1985-86	85	David Stephenson (Wigan)
1986-87	120	Paul Loughlin (St. Helens)
1987-88	95	John Woods (Warrington)
1988-89	95	David Hobbs (Bradford N.)
1989-90	96	Paul Loughlin (St. Helens)
1990-91	85	Paul Eastwood (Hull)
1991-92	86	Frano Botica (Wigan)
1992-93	107	Frano Botica (Wigan)
1993-94	123	Frano Botica (Wigan)
1994-95	128	John Schuster (Halifax)
1995-96	90	Bobbie Goulding (St. Helens)

Top Division One points-scorer 1995–96

198 (11t, 77g) Paul Cook (Bradford B.)

New Zealander Dean Bell, given his first head coaching post by Leeds in September 1995.

COACHES

COACHES

Robin Dewhurst (Leeds)
Bakary Diabira (Blackpool B., Keighley)
Tommy Dickens (Blackpool B., Leigh)
Roy Dickinson (Bramley)
Colin Dixon (Halifax, Keighley, Salford)
Mal Dixon (York)
John Dorahy (Halifax, Warrington, Wigan)
David Doyle-Davidson (Hull, York)
Ray Dutton (Whitehaven)

Graham Eadie (Halifax)
Bob Eccles (Blackpool G., Chorley)
Derek Edwards (Doncaster)
Joe Egan Jnr. (Blackpool B.)

George Fairbairn (Huddersfield, Hull K.R., Wigan)
Vince Farrar (Featherstone R.)
Albert Fearnely (Batley, Blackpool B., Keighley)
Steve Ferres (Hunslet)
John Fieldhouse (Oldham)
Tony Fisher (Bramley, Dewsbury, Doncaster,
    Keighley)
Eric Fitzsimons (Oldham, Rochdale H., Whitehaven)
Bob Fleet (Swinton)
Geoff Fletcher (Huyton, Runcorn H.)
Terry Fogerty (Rochdale H.)
Chris Forster (Bramley, Huddersfield B.)
Derek Foster (Ryedale-York)
Frank Foster (Barrow, Whitehaven)
Kenny Foulkes (Hull)
Don Fox (Batley)
Harry Fox (Halifax)
Neil Fox (Huddersfield)
Peter Fox (Bradford N., Bramley, Featherstone R.,
    Leeds, Wakefield T.)
Bill Francis (Oldham)
Roy Francis (Bradford N., Leeds)
Tommy Frodsham (Highfield)

Paul Gamble (Blackpool G.)
Bill Gardner (Sheffield E.)
Brian Gartland (Oldham)
Andy Gascoigne (Doncaster D.)
Steve Gibson (Rochdale H.)
Stan Gittins (Blackpool B., Chorley, Rochdale H.,
    Springfield B.)
Andy Goodway (Oldham)
Bill Goodwin (Fulham, Kent Invicta)
Tony Gordon (Hull, London C.)
Terry Gorman (Huyton, Swinton)
Keith Goulding (Featherstone R., Huddersfield,
    York)

Mal Graham (Oldham)
Tom Grainey (Leigh, Swinton)
Jeff Grayshon (Batley, Dewsbury)
Lee Greenwood (Keighley, Mansfield
    M./Nottingham C.)
Andy Gregory (Salford)
Gary Grienke (London B.)
Geoff Gunney (Wakefield T.)

Bob Haigh (Wakefield T.)
Derek Hallas (Halifax)
Ken Halliwell (Swinton)
Alan Hardisty (Dewsbury, Halifax, York)
Paul Harkin (Wakefield T.)
Arnold Hema (Nottingham C.)
Graham Heptinstall (Doncaster)
Alan Hepworth (Batley)
Keith Hepworth (Bramley, Hull)
Gary Hetherington (Sheffield E.)
Ron Hill (Dewsbury)
David Hobbs (Bradford N., Wakefield T.)
Neil Holding (Rochdale H.)
Bill Holliday (Swinton)
Stewart Horton (Ryedale-York)
Eric Hughes (Rochdale H., St. Helens, Widnes)
Syd Hynes (Leeds)

Bob Irving (Blackpool B.)
Keith Irving (Workington T.)

Garry Jack (Salford)
Dennis Jackson (Barrow)
Francis Jarvis (Huddersfield)
Peter Jarvis (Bramley, Hunslet)
Graeme Jennings (Hunslet)
Barry Johnson (Bramley)
Brian Johnson (Warrington)
Willie Johnson (Highfield)
Allen Jones (Huddersfield B.)
Lewis Jones (Dewsbury)
John Joyner (Castleford)

Vince Karalius (Widnes, Wigan)
Paul Kavanagh (Barrow)
John Kear (Bramley)
Arthur Keegan (Bramley)
Ivor Kelland (Barrow)
Alan Kellett (Carlisle, Halifax, Keighley)
Andy Kelly (Wakefield T.)
Bill Kenny (Doncaster)
Bill Kindon (Leigh)

COACHES

Bill Kirkbride (Mansfield M., Rochdale H.,
  Wakefield T., York)
Phil Kitchin (Whitehaven, Workington T.)

Dave Lamming (Wakefield T.)
Steve Lane (Kent Invicta)
Phil Larder (Keighley C., Widnes)
Doug Laughton (Leeds, Widnes)
Roy Lester (Carlisle, Fulham)
Bob Lindner (Oldham)
Alan Lockwood (Dewsbury)
Brian Lockwood (Batley, Huddersfield,
  Wakefield T.)
Paul Longstaff (Rochdale H.)
Graham Lowe (Wigan)
Phil Lowe (York)
Trevor Lowe (Batley, Doncaster)
Ken Loxton (Bramley)
Ian Lucas (Leigh)
Geoff Lyon (Blackpool B.)

Mike McClennan (St. Helens)
Stan McCormick (Salford)
John McFarlane (Whitehaven)
Alan McInnes (Salford, Wigan)
Shaun McRae (St. Helens)
John Mantle (Blackpool B., Cardiff C., Leigh)
Stan Martin (Whitehaven)
Steve Martin (Featherstone R.)
Jack Melling (Blackpool G.)
Roger Millward (Halifax, Hull K.R., Ryedale-York)
John Monie (Wigan)
Mick Morgan (Carlisle)
Geoff Morris (Doncaster)
David Mortimer (Huddersfield)
Alex Murphy (Huddersfield, Leigh, St. Helens,
  Salford, Warrington, Wigan)
Frank Myler (Oldham, Rochdale H., Swinton,
  Widnes)
Tony Myler (Widnes)

Steve Nash (Mansfield M.)
Steve Norton (Barrow)

Chris O'Sullivan (Swinton)

Les Pearce (Bramley, Halifax)
Mike Peers (Blackpool G., Chorley B./Trafford B.,
  Highfield, Swinton)
Geoff Peggs (Keighley)
George Pieniazek (Batley, Featherstone R.)

Billy Platt (Mansfield M.)
Harry Poole (Hull K.R.)

Denis Ramsdale (Barrow, Leigh)
Bill Ramsey (Hunslet)
Terry Ramshaw (Oldham)
Keith Rayne (Batley)
Rod Reddy (Barrow)
Graham Rees (Blackpool B.)
Peter Regan (Doncaster D., Rochdale H.)
Malcolm Reilly (Castleford, Halifax, Leeds)
Alan Rhodes (Doncaster, Sheffield E.)
Austin Rhodes (Swinton)
Bev Risman (Fulham)
Ken Roberts (Halifax)
Don Robinson (Bramley)
Don Robson (Doncaster)
Peter Roe (Barrow, Halifax, Keighley, Swinton)
Sol Roper (Workington T.)

Roy Sabine (Keighley)
Dave Sampson (Castleford, Doncaster,
  Nottingham C.)
Barry Seabourne (Bradford N., Huddersfield,
  Keighley)
Les Sheard (Huddersfield)
Danny Sheehan (York)
John Sheridan (Doncaster)
Phil Sigsworth (Hull)
Royce Simmons (Hull)
Steve Simms (Halifax, Leigh)
Tommy Smales [Scrum half] (Featherstone R.)
Tommy Smales [Forward] (Batley, Bramley,
  Dewsbury, Doncaster, Featherstone R.)
Peter Smethurst (Leigh, Oldham)
Barry Smith (Whitehaven)
Bill Smith (Whitehaven, Workington T.)
Brian Smith (Huddersfield)
Brian Smith [Australian] (Bradford B., Hull)
Norman Smith (Dewsbury)
Kurt Sorensen (Whitehaven, Workington T.)
Ike Southward (Whitehaven, Workington T.)
Graham Starkey (Oldham, Rochdale H.)
Gary Stephens (York)
Nigel Stephenson (Huddersfield, Hunslet)
Dave Stockwell (Batley, Bramley)
John Stopford (Swinton)
Ted Strawbridge (Doncaster)
Ross Strudwick (Fulham/London C., Halifax)
Clive Sullivan (Doncaster, Hull)
Phil Sullivan (Fulham)

Kevin Tamati (Salford)
John Taylor (Chorley B.)
Bob Tomlinson (Huddersfield)
Ted Toohey (Wigan)
David Topliss (Wakefield T.)
Peter Tunks (Oldham)
Norman Turley (Trafford B., Whitehaven,
   Workington T.)
Derek Turner (Wakefield T.)
Colin Tyrer (Widnes)

Darryl Van de Velde (Castleford, Huddersfield)
Don Vines (Doncaster)

Hugh Waddell (Carlisle)
Arnold Walker (Whitehaven)
Russ Walker (Hull)
Trevor Walker (Batley)
Peter Walsh (Workington T.)
David Ward (Batley, Featherstone R., Hunslet,
   Leeds)

John Warlow (Bridgend)
David Watkins (Cardiff C.)
Bernard Watson (Dewsbury)
Graeme West (Wigan)
Neil Whittaker (Huddersfield B.)
Mel Wibberley (Nottingham C.)
Ron Willey (Bradford N.)
Dean Williams (Workington T.)
Frank Wilson (Runcorn H.)
Phil Windley (Hull)
John Wolford (Hunslet)
Jeff Woods (Bridgend)
John Woods (Leigh)
Paul Woods (Runcorn H.)
Geoff Worrall (Barrow)
Geoff Wraith (Wakefield T.)

Billy Yates (Doncaster)

Mirror image . . . Darryl Van de Velde (left), former coach of Castleford and in charge of Huddersfield in 1995-96 and Mick Morgan, ex-coach of Carlisle.

207

DOSSIER OF 1995–96 COACHES

The following is a dossier of the British coaching and playing careers of coaches holding first team posts from 1 June 1995 to 31 January 1996. Overseas details are not included.

● BF — beaten finalist.

CHRIS ARKWRIGHT
Highfield:	Apr. 91 - Aug. 91
Highfield:	Sep. 94 - July 95

Played for: St. Helens, Highfield

RAY ASHTON
Workington T:	June 90 - Dec. 91
Bramley:	Sep. 93 -
Lancashire	1991 - 92

Played for: Oldham, Leeds, Workington T., Bramley

PETER ASTBURY
Doncaster: July 95 - Sep. 95
Played for: Bramley, Bradford N., Doncaster, Halifax, Keighley, Leeds, Wakefield T.

TONY BARROW
Warrington:	Mar. 86 - Nov. 88 (Premier winners & BF, John Player BF, Lancs. Cup BF)
Oldham:	Nov. 88 - Jan. 91 (Promotion, Lancs. Cup BF, Div. 2 Premier winners)
Swinton:	Jan. 92 - Jan. 96

Played for: St. Helens, Leigh

DEAN BELL (New Zealander)
Leeds: Sep. 95 -
Played for: Carlisle, Leeds, Wigan

Tony Barrow, who stepped down as coach of Swinton in January 1996 to concentrate on his duties as general manager.

PAUL CHARLTON
Workington T.:	June 75 - June 76 (Promotion)
Workington T.:	July 82 - Dec. 82
Carlisle:	Dec. 94 -

Played for: Workington T., Salford

JIM CRELLIN
Blackpool B.:	May 76 - Mar. 77 (John Player BF)
Halifax:	June 77 - Oct. 77
Swinton:	Nov. 83 - May 86 (Div. 2 champs)
Mansfield M.:	Dec. 86 - June 88
Rochdale H.:	June 88 - June 89
Swinton:	July 89 - July 91 (Promotion)
Leigh:	July 92 - Sep. 92
Highfield:	Jan. 96 -

Played for: Workington T., Oldham, Rochdale H.

STEVE CROOKS
Ryedale-York	Nov. 92 - May 94
Hull K.R.	May 94 - (Div. 2 champs - new division)

Played for: Hull K.R., Hull, York

TONY CURRIE (Australian)
London B.: Jan. 96 -
Played for: Leeds

JOHN DORAHY (Australian)
Halifax:	June 89 - Aug. 90 (Regal Trophy BF)
Wigan:	June 93 - May 94 (Div. 1 champs, RL Cup winners, Regal Trophy BF)
Warrington:	Jan. 96 -

Played for: Leigh, Hull K.R., Halifax

BOB ECCLES
Chorley B.:	May 90 - Sep. 91
Blackpool G.:	Nov. 92 - Jan. 93
Chorley C.:	Aug. 95 -

Played for: Warrington, Springfield B./Chorley B./ Trafford B., Chorley C.

GEORGE FAIRBAIRN
Wigan:	Apr. 80 - May 81 (Promotion)
Hull K.R.:	May 91 - May 94
Huddersfield:	June 94 - Oct 95 (Div. 2 Premier BF)

Played for: Wigan, Hull K.R.

STEVE FERRES
Hunslet: Jan. 94 -
Played for: Bramley, York, Dewsbury, Bradford N.,
Carlisle, Kent I., Keighley, Batley, Sheffield E.

TONY FISHER
Bramley: Nov. 87 - Feb. 89
Keighley: June 90 - Sep. 91
Doncaster: Nov. 92 - Dec. 94 (Promotion)
Dewsbury: Apr. 95 -
Played for: Bradford N., Leeds, Castleford

PETER FOX
Featherstone R.: Jan. 71 - May 74
                  (RL Cup winners & BF)
Wakefield T.:   June 74 - May 76
                  (Yorks. Cup BF)
Bramley: Sep. 76 - Apr. 77 (Promotion)
Bradford N.:   Apr. 77 - May 85 (Div. 1 champs
                  (2), Yorks. Cup winners & BF
                  (2), Premier winners & BF (2),
                  John Player winners)
Leeds: May 85 - Dec. 86
Featherstone R.: May 87 - Oct. 91 (Promotion,
                  Div. 2 Premier BF, Yorks. Cup
                  BF)
Bradford N.:   Oct. 91 - June 95 (Regal Trophy
                  BF)
England: 1977 (2 matches)
Great Britain: 1978 (3 Tests v. Australia)
Yorkshire: 1985-86 to 1991-92
Played for: Featherstone R., Batley, Hull K.R.,
Wakefield T.

TOMMY FRODSHAM
Highfield: July 95 - Jan. 96
Played for: Blackpool G., Trafford B., Swinton, St.
Helens, Highfield, Chorley C.

ANDY GASCOIGNE
Doncaster: July 95 - Sep. 95
Played for: Hunslet, Bramley, Leeds, Hull, York,
Keighley C., Doncaster

STEVE GIBSON (Australian)
Rochdale H.:   Oct. 93 -
Played for: Salford, Rochdale H.

ANDY GOODWAY
Oldham: May 94 -
Played for: Oldham, Wigan, Leeds

Australian Steve Gibson, appointed player-coach of Rochdale Hornets in October 1993.

JEFF GRAYSHON
Dewsbury: May 78 - Oct. 78
Batley: Oct. 94 - (Promotion)
Played for: Dewsbury, Bradford N., Leeds,
Featherstone R., Batley

ANDY GREGORY
Salford: Mar. 95 - (Div. 1 champs - new
                  division)
Played for: Widnes, Warrington, Wigan, Leeds,
Salford

GARY GRIENKE (Australian)
London B.:   May 94 - Jan. 96
Played for: St. Helens

PAUL HARKIN
Wakefield T.:   Jan. 95 -
Played for: Hull K.R., Bradford N., Featherstone R.,
Leeds, Halifax, Hunslet

GARY HETHERINGTON
Sheffield E.:   July 86 - May 93 (Div. 2 champs,
                  Promotion (2),
                  Div. 2 Premier winners,
                  Divisional Premier winners,
                  Yorks. Cup BF)
Sheffield E.:   Dec. 93 -
Great Britain
   Under-21s: 1994-95
Played for: York, Leeds, Kent I., Sheffield E.

STEWART HORTON
Ryedale-York: Jan. 95 -
Played for: Castleford, Ryedale-York

ERIC HUGHES
Widnes: June 84 - Jan. 86
Rochdale H.:   June 87 - June 88
St. Helens: Jan. 94 - Jan. 96 (Regal Trophy
                  BF)
Played for: Widnes, St. Helens, Rochdale H.

BRIAN JOHNSON (Australian)
Warrington: Nov. 88 - Jan. 96 (Lancs. Cup
                  winners, RL Cup BF, Regal
                  winners & BF)
Played for: Warrington

JOHN JOYNER
Castleford: May 93 - (Regal Trophy winners,
                  Premier BF)
Played for: Castleford

ANDY KELLY
Wakefield T.:   Jan. 95 -
Played for: Wakefield T., Huddersfield, Hull K.R.

PHIL LARDER
Widnes: May 92 - May 94 (RL Cup BF)
Keighley C.:   May 94 - (Div. 2 champs, Div. 2
                  Premier winners)
England: 1995-96
Great Britain
   Under-21s: 1990-91, 1991-92, 1995-96
Played for: Oldham, Whitehaven

Gary Hetherington, who resumed the coaching role at Sheffield Eagles in December 1993.

Brian Johnson, who resigned as coach of Warrington in January 1996 after a reign of over seven years.

DOUG LAUGHTON
Widnes:	May 78 - Mar. 83
	(RL Cup winners (2) & BF,
	Lancs. Cup winners (2) & BF,
	John Player winners & BF,
	Premier winners (2), Floodlit
	Trophy winners)
Widnes:	Jan. 86 - May 91 (Div. 1 champs
	(2), Premier winners (3) & BF,
	Charity Shield winners (3), John
	Player BF, Lancs. Cup winners,
	World Club Challenge winners)
Leeds:	May 91 - June 95(Regal Trophy
	BF, RL Cup BF (2), Premier BF)
Lancashire:	1982-83, 1988-89, 1989-90
Widnes:	Aug. 95 -

Played for: Wigan, St. Helens, Widnes

IAN LUCAS
Leigh:	Dec. 94 -

Played for: Wigan

SHAUN McRAE (Australian)
St. Helens:	Jan. 96 -

STAN MARTIN (New Zealander)
Whitehaven:	Oct. 95 -

TONY MYLER
Widnes:	May 94 - Aug. 95

Played for: Widnes

PETER REGAN (Australian)
Rochdale H.:	Jan. 93 - Oct. 93
Doncaster D.:	Sep. 95 -

PETER ROE
Keighley:	Sep. 85 - July 86
Halifax:	Aug. 90 - May 91 (Promotion,
	Div. 2 Premier BF)
Keighley C.:	Sep. 91 - Apr. 94 (Div. 3 champs)
Barrow:	Sep. 94 - Jan. 96
Swinton:	Jan. 96 -

Played for: Keighley, Bradford N., York, Hunslet

PHIL SIGSWORTH (Australian)
Hull:	Jan. 96 -

STEVE SIMMS (Australian)
Leigh:	Nov. 92 - Sep. 94
Halifax:	Sep. 94 -

BRIAN SMITH (Australian)
Hull:	July 88 - Jan. 91 (Premier BF)
Bradford B.:	June 95 -

NORMAN SMITH
Dewsbury:	Aug. 93 - Apr. 95

Played for: Bramley, Dewsbury

KURT SORENSEN (New Zealander)
Whitehaven:	May 93 - Aug. 95
Cumbria:	1994-95
Workington T.:	Aug. 95 -

Played for: Widnes, Wigan, Whitehaven

DARRYL VAN DE VELDE (Australian)
Castleford:	July 88 - May 93 (Yorks. Cup
	winners (2) & BF, Challenge Cup
	(BF)
Huddersfield:	Dec. 95 -

PETER WALSH (Australian)
Workington T.:	Apr. 92 - July 95 (Div. 2 champs,
	Div. 2 Premier winners,
	Divisional Premier BF)
Cumbria:	1994-95

Played for: Oldham

DAVID WARD
Hunslet:	July 86 - Apr. 88 (Div. 2 champs,
	Div. 2 Premier BF)
Hunslet:	Jan. 89 - May 89
Leeds:	Sep. 89 - May 91
Batley:	May 91 - Oct. 94
Featherstone R.:	Oct. 94 -

Played for: Leeds, Workington T.

GRAEME WEST (New Zealander)
Wigan:	May 94 - (Premier winners (2),
	World Club Challenge winners,
	Div. 1 champs (2*), Regal Trophy
	winners (2), RL Cup winners,
	Charity Shield winners)
	Including Centenary Championship

Played for: Wigan

PHIL WINDLEY
Hull:	Dec. 94 - Nov. 95

Played for: Hull

REPRESENTATIVE REGISTER

The following is a list of international and county coaches since 1974-75.

GREAT BRITAIN

Jim Challinor	Dec. 71 - Aug. 74 (Inc. tours)
David Watkins	1977 World Championship
Peter Fox	1978
Eric Ashton	1979 tour
Johnny Whiteley	Aug. 80 - Nov. 82
Frank Myler	Dec. 82 - Aug. 84 (Inc. tour)
Maurice Bamford	Oct. 84 - Dec. 86
Malcolm Reilly	Jan. 87 - Aug. 94 (Inc. tours)
Ellery Hanley	Aug. 94 - May 95

ENGLAND

Alex Murphy	Jan. 75 - Nov. 75 (Inc. World Championship tour)
Peter Fox	1976-77
Frank Myler	1977-78
Eric Ashton	1978-79, 1979-80
Johnny Whiteley	1980-81, 1981-82
Reg Parker (Mgr)	1984-85
Malcolm Reilly	1992-93
Ellery Hanley	1994-95
Phil Larder	1995-96

WALES

Les Pearce	Jan. 75 - Nov. 75 (Inc. World Championship tour)
David Watkins } Bill Francis	1976-77
Kel Coslett } Bill Francis	1977-78
Kel Coslett	1978-79 to 1981-82
David Watkins	1982-83, 1984-85
Clive Griffiths	1991-92, 1992-93, 1993-94, 1994-95, 1995-96

GREAT BRITAIN UNDER-24s

Johnny Whiteley	1976-82
Frank Myler	1983-84

GREAT BRITAIN UNDER-21s

Maurice Bamford	Oct. 84 - Dec. 86
Malcolm Reilly	1986-87, 1987-88, 1989-90, 1991-92, 1992-93, 1993-94
David Topliss	1988-89
Phil Larder	1990-91, 1991-92
Gary Hetherington	1994-95
Phil Larder	1995-96

CUMBRIA

Ike Southward	1975-76
Frank Foster	1976-77 to 1977-78
Sol Roper	1978-79
Frank Foster	1979-80
Phil Kitchin	1980-81 to 1981-82
Frank Foster	1982-83
Jackie Davidson	1985-86
Phil Kitchin	1986-87 to 1991-92
Gordon Cottier	1992-93
Peter Walsh } Kurt Sorensen	1994-95

LANCASHIRE

Alex Murphy	1973-74 to 1977-78
Eric Ashton	1978-79 to 1979-80
Tom Grainey	1980-81 to 1981-82
Doug Laughton	1982-83
Alex Murphy	1985-86 to 1987-88
Doug Laughton	1988-89 to 1989-90
Ray Ashton	1991-92

YORKSHIRE

Johnny Whiteley	1970-71 to 1979-80
Arthur Keegan	1980-81
Johnny Whiteley	1981-82 to 1982-83
Peter Fox	1985-86 to 1991-92

OTHER NATIONALITIES

Dave Cox	1974-75 to 1975-76

Australia captain Brad Fittler shows off the Halifax Centenary World Cup, watched by chief guest HRH Prince Edward.

1995 WORLD CUP

1995 WORLD CUP

THE HALIFAX RUGBY LEAGUE CENTENARY WORLD CUP 1995

After several months of doubts and general public pessimism, the Halifax Rugby League Centenary World Cup was soon being widely acclaimed as a huge success once the competition got underway.

Maurice Lindsay, the RFL chief executive and tournament director, had parried pre-World Cup criticism by insisting that the players would make it a success by their performances on the field and he was to be proved right.

Although the final, in which Australia beat England 16-8, was disappointing, most of the group matches and semi-finals were highly entertaining, with the South Pacific countries adding an exotic touch of colour with their war dances and exciting brand of open rugby.

England got the tournament off to a magnificent start by beating Australia 20-16 in the opening match at Wembley before a 41,271 crowd that was much higher than expected only a week earlier when poor publicity resulted in low advance ticket sales.

It also answered criticism of taking the opening match to Wembley, which was scheduled to stage the final three weeks later when another 66,540 sent the tournament's aggregate attendance to 265,619.

England's matches against Fiji (26,263) and South Africa (14,041) also produced much higher than expected attendances, while Wales played before packed stadiums at Cardiff and Swansea.

The tournament marked the game's centenary and was sponsored by the Halifax Building Society, who were reluctant to disclose their exact financial involvement which was generally estimated at over £1 million.

Bookmakers William Hill made Australia 2-5 favourites to retain the world title they had held since 1975, even though the Australian RL did not select any players who had signed for the new Super League.

They kept faith with those who had beaten New Zealand 3-0 in the mid-year Test series, including Brad Fittler as captain. This meant leaving out such great players as Laurie Daley, Steve Renouf, Ricky Stuart and Bradley Clyde. In fact, their Cup final starting line-up contained only three or four players who might have been selected in a full strength side. One was Fittler, who again led them in great style at stand-off.

England were made 11-4 second favourites, enticing odds for a side that was tipped by many to lift the new £10,000 silver trophy designed and manufactured by world famous jewellers Tiffany's. The Rugby Football League also offered England – and Wales – a record international bonus of £250,000 to become the first side to bring the world title back to Europe since Great Britain in 1972.

Both home countries did well to head their respective groups which led to an eagerly awaited semi-final showdown at a packed Old Trafford where England triumphed 25-10.

The other semi-final produced a much closer encounter with Australia beating New Zealand 30-20 in extra time of a thriller at Huddersfield's Alfred McAlpine Stadium.

Discipline throughout the tournament was excellent and reflected in the fact that not one player was sent off, though there were a few trips to the sin bin.

The major blot on the tournament was the banning of three players who failed drugs tests – South Africa's Pierre Grobbelaar, Syd Eru of New Zealand and France's Stephan Millet.

Only Eru had played in the tournament before they were kicked out. The hooker tested positive for pseudoephedrine, a stimulant commonly found in cough and cold medicines. Millet's sample contained traces of cannabis, while Grobbelaar was found guilty of the most serious offence of using anabolic steroids.

WORLD CUP FACTS AND FIGURES AT A GLANCE

Group One

Date	Team	Score	v	Team	Score	Venue	Attendance
7 Oct	England	20	v	Australia	16	Wembley	41,271
8 Oct	Fiji	52	v	South Africa	6	Keighley	4,845
10 Oct	Australia	86	v	South Africa	6	Gateshead	9,191
11 Oct	England	46	v	Fiji	0	Wigan	26,263
14 Oct	Australia	66	v	Fiji	0	Huddersfield	7,127
14 Oct	England	46	v	South Africa	0	Leeds	14,041

Group One Table

	P	W	D	L	F	A	Pts
England	3	3	0	0	112	16	6
Australia	3	2	0	1	168	26	4
Fiji	3	1	0	2	52	118	2
South Africa	3	0	0	3	12	184	0

Group Two

Date	Team	Score	v	Team	Score	Venue	Attendance
8 Oct	New Zealand	25	v	Tonga	24	Warrington	8,083
10 Oct	Papua New Guinea	28	v	Tonga	28	Hull	5,121
13 Oct	New Zealand	22	v	Papua New Guinea	6	St. Helens	8,679

Group Two Table

	P	W	D	L	F	A	Pts
New Zealand	2	2	0	0	47	30	4
Tonga	2	0	1	1	52	53	1
Papua New Guinea	2	0	1	1	34	50	1

Group Three

Date	Team	Score	v	Team	Score	Venue	Attendance
9 Oct	Wales	28	v	France	6	Cardiff	10,250
12 Oct	Western Samoa	56	v	France	10	Cardiff	2,173
15 Oct	Wales	22	v	Western Samoa	10	Swansea	15,385

Group Three Table

	P	W	D	L	F	A	Pts
Wales	2	2	0	0	50	16	4
Western Samoa	2	1	0	1	66	32	2
France	2	0	0	2	16	84	0

Semi-finals

Date	Team	Score	v	Team	Score	Venue	Attendance
21 Oct	England	25	v	Wales	10	Man. U.FC	30,042
22 Oct	Australia	30	v	New Zealand	20	Huddersfield	16,608

(After extra time. Normal time 20-20)

Final

Date	Team	Score	v	Team	Score	Venue	Attendance
28 Oct	England	8	v	Australia	16	Wembley	66,540

OUTSTANDING FEATS

ALL MATCHES
Tries: 6 by Steve Menzies (Australia)
Goals: 27 by Andrew Johns (Australia)
Points: 62 (2t, 27g) by Andrew Johns (Australia)

ONE MATCH
Tries: 3 by John Hopoate (Australia) v South Africa
Brett Dallas (Australia) v Fiji
Robbie O'Davis (Australia) v Fiji
Anthony Sullivan (Wales) v France
Goals: 11 by Andrew Johns (Australia) v South Africa
Points: 30 (2t, 11g) by Andrew Johns (Australia) v South Africa

HIGHEST SCORE
Australia 86 v South Africa 6 (Also widest margin)

BIGGEST ATTENDANCE
66,540 England v Australia at Wembley (Final)
Total: 265,619

THE HALIFAX MAN OF THE MATCH WINNERS
Andrew Johns (Australia) v South Africa
v Fiji
v England (Final)
Bobbie Goulding (England)
v Fiji
v Wales (Semi-final)
Adrian Lam (Papua New Guinea)
v Tonga
v New Zealand
Andrew Farrell (England) v Australia
Iliesa Toga (Fiji) v South Africa
Nick Pinkney (England) v South Africa
Duane Mann (Tonga) v New Zealand
Iestyn Harris (Wales) v France
Vila Matautia (Western Samoa) v France
Scott Quinnell (Wales) v Western Samoa
Steve Menzies (Australia) v New Zealand (Semi-final)

MAN OF THE TOURNAMENT
Andrew Johns (Australia)

TEAM OF THE TOURNAMENT
A panel of coaches and journalists selected a best World XIII based solely on performances in the World Cup. A surprise omission was Andrew Johns, who picked up three man of the match awards including the final and was named as the outstanding player of the tournament, but it was explained that the Australian had played at both hooker and scrum-half without confirming he was the best in either position.

WORLD XIII
1. Iestyn Harris (Wales)
2. Jason Robinson (England)
3. Paul Newlove (England)
4. Richard Blackmore (New Zealand)
5. Anthony Sullivan (Wales)
6. Brad Fittler (Australia)
7. Adrian Lam (Papua New Guinea)
8. Mark Carroll (Australia)
9. Lee Jackson (England)
10. David Westley (Papua New Guinea)
11. Denis Betts (England)
12. Steve Menzies (Australia)
13. Andrew Farrell (England)

PRE-TOURNAMENT ODDS TO WIN THE CUP
Bookmakers William Hill offered the following odds before the start of tournament:

2-5	Australia	100-1	France
11-4	England	500-1	Tonga
6-1	New Zealand		Papua New Guinea
20-1	Wales	750-1	Fiji
66-1	Western Samoa		South Africa

Australia's manager Geoff Carr leads out his team for the opening match against England at Wembley, acclaimed by pre-match entertainer Diana Ross

England scrum half Bobbie Goulding faces opposite number Geoff Toovy of Austrailia at Wembley.

Australian centre Terry Hill dives in for a try in extra time of the semi-final against New Zealand.

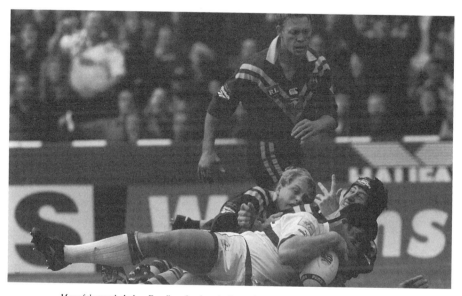

Man of the match Andrew Farrell touches down in the opening encounter against Australia at Wembley.

AUSTRALIA DASH ENGLAND'S HOPES

England's high hopes of ending Australia's 20-year reign as world champions were soon deflated as they failed to rise to the occasion and went down 16-8 in the final of the Halifax Rugby League Centenary World Cup. They disappointed their supporters in the 66,540 crowd at Wembley and the choice of veteran pop group Status Quo for the pre-match entertainment could not have been more appropriate as Australia proved that little has changed.

Yet, many had felt that England would never have a better chance of becoming world champions as they faced an Australian side minus many of their greatest players because of the Super League dispute. That view seemed to be confirmed when England beat Australia 20-16 in the opening match – also at Wembley, where the Kangaroos had suffered shock defeats against Great Britain on their two previous tours to foster the belief that they never played well at the stadium.

But Australia had beaten Britain in the 1992 final at Wembley and built a reputation of always coming out on top when it mattered most. They were to do so again.

Australia's coach Bob Fulton was always confident that his squad would improve with each game as many of the players had not played since the end of their season several weeks earlier; and that is what happened, although they had a narrow escape in the semi-final before beating New Zealand in extra time.

Bookmakers William Hill also remained convinced of Australia's superiority and made them 8-13 favourites in the final although giving England only two points' start on the handicap coupons.

Australia made four changes from the starting line-up that had lost to England with the most significant being Andrew Johns at hooker for Wayne Bartim. Johns had arrived as an out standing scrum-half prospect but after excelling in that position on his international debut against South Africa, when he scored a World Cup record 30 points, he was switched to hooker and went on to become the official player of the tournament.

But though Johns packed down and wore the number nine jersey he reverted to his normal half-back play in the loose where he was a constant threat to England in the final. In addition to kicking four goals, Johns was involved in both of Australia's tries.

It was the half-back's perfectly judged kick which led to Australia's stunning sixth-minute try as Rod Wishart dived to get the faintest of touchdowns just ahead of England winger Jason Robinson.

Johns was also involved in the move that brought the 67th-minute try by Tim Brasher which finished off England, combining with Mark Carroll before slipping a tackle and getting the ball away. There was then a bit of loose play which ended with Brasher kicking ahead and winning the scramble to touch down.

Australia were well led by Brad Fittler throughout the tournament and the stand-off earned his reward when he went up to receive the trophy from Prince Edward, who was attending his first rugby league match.

England's only try went to Paul Newlove after a typical short, powerful charge from a play-the-ball, which brought them back into the game at 8-10 in the 44th minute. But they rarely put the opposition under sustained pressure and Australia finished well on top.

Gary Connolly was one of the few England players to come off with credit as the centre completed a remarkable recovery from pneumonia, which had ruled him out of all the previous Cup matches.

HALIFAX CENTENARY WORLD CUP FINAL
Saturday 28 October 1995   Wembley

ENGLAND	8			AUSTRALIA	16
Kris Radlinski		1.		Tim Brasher	
Jason Robinson		2.		Rod Wishart	
Gary Connolly		3.		Mark Coyne	
Paul Newlove		4.		Terry Hill	
Martin Offiah		5.		Brett Dallas	
Tony Smith		6.		Brad Fittler, Capt.	
Bobbie Goulding		7.		Geoff Toovey	
Karl Harrison		8.		Dean Pay	
Lee Jackson		9.		Andrew Johns	
Andy Platt		10.		Mark Carroll	
Denis Betts, Capt.		11.		Steve Menzies	
Phil Clarke		12.		Gary Larson	
Andrew Farrell		13.		Jim Dymock	

Substitutes
Mick Cassidy for Harrison (31 min.)
Harrison for Platt (61 min.)
Chris Joynt for Cassidy (69 min.)
Platt for Harrison (70 min.)
Barrie-Jon Mather not used
Nick Pinkney not used

Substitutes
Jason Smith for Carroll (50 min.)
Carroll for Smith (61 min.)
Smith for Pay (75 min.)
Robbie O'Davis not used
Matthew Johns not used
Nik Kosef not used
Sin bin: Carroll (78 min.)

T: Newlove

G: Goulding (2)

T: Wishart, Brasher

G: Johns (4)

Half-time: 4-10
Attendance: 66,540
Referee: Stuart Cummings (England)

Score chart

Minute	Score	Eng	Aus
4:	Goulding (P)	2	0
7:	Wishart (T)		
	Johns (G)	2	6
16:	Goulding (P)	4	6
25:	Johns (P)	4	8
30	Johns (P)	4	10
44	Newlove (T)	8	10
67	Brasher (T)		
	Johns (G)	8	16
	Scrums	8	7
	Penalties	12	9

England prop Andy Platt.

GROUP ONE
Saturday 7 October 1995 **Wembley**
ENGLAND 20 AUSTRALIA 16

Kris Radlinski	1.	Tim Brasher
Jason Robinson	2.	Rod Wishart
Barrie-Jon Mather	3.	Mark Coyne
Paul Newlove	4.	Terry Hill
John Bentley	5.	John Hopoate
Daryl Powell	6.	Brad Fittler, Capt.
Shaun Edwards, Capt.	7.	Geoff Toovey
Karl Harrison	8.	David Gillespie
Lee Jackson	9.	Wayne Bartim
Andy Platt	10.	Mark Carroll
Denis Betts	11.	Steve Menzies
Phil Clarke	12.	Dean Pay
Andrew Farrell	13.	Jim Dymock

Substitutes
Bobby Goulding not used
Nick Pinkney not used
Chris Joynt played
Simon Haughton played

T: Farrell, Joynt, Robinson, Newlove

G: Farrell (2)

Half-time: 4-6
Penalties: 6-5

Substitutes
Robbie O'Davis not used
Matthew Johns played
Jason Smith played
Paul Harragon played

T: Menzies (2), Coyne

G: Wishart (2)

Attendance: 41,271
Referee: Stuart Cummings
(England)

ENGLAND'S SUPREMACY
American singing star Diana Ross provided the pre-match entertainment, but it was England who hit the top notes as they upset the World Cup favourites in the opening match to give the tournament a tremendous start.

Australia, fielding several players who had not played for a number of weeks, were caught cold by an England side whose four tries followed mistakes by Australia.

The first came in the 35th minute after Australian full back Tim Brasher dropped Shaun Edwards' high kick. England loose forward Andrew Farrell broke quickly from the following scrum to power 10 metres through two tackles and crash over. It left England only

4-6 behind at half-time, Steve Menzies having opened the tryscoring for Australia five minutes earlier and Rod Wishart added the goal.

Brasher made another handling error over his own line soon after the interval and Chris Joynt pounced to get a disputed touchdown. A Mark Coyne try put Australia level at 10-10 before another blunder cost them dearly.

When John Hopoate tried to run the ball clear after fielding a kick the winger spilled it in a double tackle and opposite number Jason Robinson snapped it up to scamper in for a gift try. Man of the match Farrell added a magnificent touchline goal and then Paul Newlove intercepted Jim Dymock's pass to race 40 metres for a try that made victory certain.

GROUP ONE
Sunday 8 October 1995   **Cougar Park, Keighley**
FIJI   52
SOUTH AFRICA   6

Waisale Sovatabua	1.	Pierre van Wyk
Joe Dakuitoga	2.	Guy Coombe
Livai Nalagilagi, Capt.	3.	Andrew Ballot
Filemoni Seru	4.	Willem Boshoff
Noa Nadruku	5.	Mark Johnson
Noa Nayacakalou	6.	Francois Cloete
Save Taga	7.	Berend Alkema
Malakai Yasa	8.	Gideon Watts
Iane Sagaitu	9.	Kobus van Deventer
Pio Nakubuwai	10.	Jaco Booysen, Capt.
Apisalome Degei	11.	Gerald Williams
Iliesa Toga	12.	Tim Fourie
Sam Marayawa	13.	Jaco Alberts

Substitutes
Kajava Salusalu played
George Vatubua played
Ulaiasi Wainidroa played
Kalaveti Naisoro played

Substitutes
Ernest Ludick played
Eugene Powell not used
Koot Human played
Jaco van Niekerk played

T: Sovatabua (2), Seru (2),
Nadruku, Taga, Sagaitu,
Marayawa, Naisoro,
Dakuitoga

G: van Wyk (3)

G: Nayacakalou (3),
Taga (3)

Half-time: 16-6
Penalties: 5-10

Attendance: 4,845
Referee: David Manson
(Australia)

FIJIANS THRILL AT COUGAR PARK

Fiji became an instant hit with Cougar Park fans as they brought a touch of South Sea sparkle to Keighley with a brilliant display of all-action rugby that swept aside a disappointing South Africa side.

Both countries were playing their first full international match but it was soon clear that Fiji were far from novices as they produced several high-speed attacks while preventing their limited opponents from touching down.

Powerful second row Iliesa Toga was the crowd's favourite and they cheered his line-clearing runs as South Africa repeatedly kicked towards him on the restarts. The announcement that he had won the man of the match award brought another roar of approval but a share should have gone to Waisale Sovatabua, who had an outstanding game at full back.

Sovatabua slipped through for two tries, had a hand in three more and produced several other touches of class in a brilliant display.

Although Noa Nadruku had already made a big impression in Australia it was Fiji's other winger, Joe Dakuitoga, who made the bigger impression on the day and scored the game's best solo try after a 60-metre run.

What South Africa lacked in class they made up for in determination as they followed the example of hard-working captain Jaco Booysen. But they had to settle for three penalty goals by Pierre van Wyk for their only points.

GROUP ONE
Tuesday 10 October 1995   Gateshead International Stadium

AUSTRALIA 86		SOUTH AFRICA 6
Robbie O'Davis	1.	Pierre van Wyk
Brett Dallas	2.	Guy Coombe
Danny Moore	3.	Andrew Ballot
Paul McGregor	4.	Willem Boshoff
John Hopoate	5.	Mark Johnson
Matthew Johns	6.	Berend Alkema
Andrew Johns	7.	Kobus van Deventer
Adam Muir	8.	Gideon Watts
Aaron Raper	9.	Francois Cloete
Paul Harragon, Capt.	10.	Jaco Booysen, Capt.
Billy Moore	11.	Gerald Williams
Jason Smith	12.	Koot Human
Nik Kosef	13.	Tim Fourie

Substitutes
Tim Brasher played
Jim Dymock played
Wayne Bartrim played
Mark Carroll played

Substitutes
Ernest Ludick played
Eugene Powell played
Nico Serfontein played
Jaco van Niekerk played

T: Hopoate (3), McGregor (2),
A. Johns (2), D. Moore (2),
O'Davis (2), Kosef, Raper,
Dymock, Smith, Brasher

T: Watts

G: van Wyk

G: A. Johns (11)

Half-time: 52-0
Penalties: 4-9

Attendance: 9,191
Referee: Russell Smith (England)

AUSTRALIA'S RECORD SPREE
The clash of world champions Australia and rugby league newcomers South Africa brought the inevitable result with the Kangaroos running up a record international score and Andrew Johns equalling two individual records.

Australia's 16-try 86-6 victory beat the previous record they had themselves set with a 74-0 away win against France a year earlier.

And 21-year-old scrum half Andrew Johns made a memorable international debut with world best scoring figures of 11 goals and 30 points, including two tries. His goals tally equalled the 11 by Australia's Rod Wishart against France in 1994 and New Zealand's Des

White against Australia in 1952.

Johns' 30 points equalled the international record set by winger Michael O'Connor with four tries and seven goals in Australia's 70-8 home defeat of Papua New Guinea in 1988.

The youngster was an obvious choice as man of the match and his performance put him on the way to capturing a World Cup final place after being switched to hooker.

Paul Harragon defied a fractured cheekbone, sustained in the defeat against England a few days earlier, to captain Australia for the first time but lasted for only 15 minutes before taking another blow to the injury, which ruled him out for the rest of the tournament.

GROUP ONE

Wednesday 11 October 1995   **Central Park, Wigan**

ENGLAND   46   **FIJI   0**

Kris Radlinski	1.	Waisale Sovatabua
Jason Robinson	2.	Joe Dakuitoga
Nick Pinkney	3.	Livai Nalagilagi, Capt.
Paul Newlove	4.	Filemoni Seru
John Bentley	5.	Noa Nadruku
Tony Smith	6.	Noa Nayacakalou
Bobbie Goulding	7.	Save Taga
Paul Broadbent	8.	Malakai Yasa
Lee Jackson	9.	Iane Sagaitu
Dean Sampson	10.	Pio Nakubuwai
Denis Betts, Capt.	11.	Apisalome Degei
Mick Cassidy	12.	Iliesa Toga
Andrew Farrell	13.	Sam Marayawa

Substitutes
Shaun Edwards not used
Paul Cook played
Simon Haughton played
Steve McCurrie played

Substitutes
Niumaia Korovata played
Ulaiasi Wainidroa played
George Vatubua played
Kalaveti Naisoro played
Sin bin: Sagaitu (79 min.)

T: Robinson (2), Radlinski,
Bentley, Broadbent,
Haughton, Smith, Newlove

G: Farrell (4), Goulding (3)

Half-time: 30-0
Penalties: 9-10
Attendance: 26,263
Referee: Dennis Hale
(New Zealand)

ENGLAND COAST INTO SEMI-FINALS

England made certain of a semi-final place with an impressive performance that raised hopes of them going on to lift the trophy. Even allowing for a disappointing display by Fiji, who seemed to be overawed by an unexpectedly large crowd of 26,263 mainly partisan home supporters, it was an impressive display by England.

Bobbie Goulding was brought in as a late replacement for Shaun Edwards, who remained on the bench after suffering a stomach upset, and made a strong claim to be retained as scrum half with a man of the match game.

The St. Helens captain had a hand or foot in four of England's eight tries, with Jason Robinson touching down two of Goulding's perfectly placed kicks.

Castleford's Tony Smith also made a strong claim to be retained after a confident full England debut at stand off which included a 49th-minute try.

It was all over by half-time as England raced to a 30-0 interval lead, with the Fijians unable to hold back the onslaught of attacks. The visitors fared a little better in the second half when England eased up on attack although delighting coach Phil Larder by remaining tight on defence to nil the opposition.

Fiji rarely threatened England's line. Iane Sagaitu was an exception as the hooker with a lively display until he was sent to the sin bin in the last minute for a high tackle.

GROUP ONE
Saturday 14 October 1995 Alfred McAlpine Stadium, Huddersfield

AUSTRALIA 66		FIJI 0
Tim Brasher	1.	Waisale Sovatabua
Brett Dallas	2.	Orisi Cavuilati
Mark Coyne	3.	Livai Nalagilagi, Capt.
Terry Hill	4.	Filemoni Seru
Robbie O'Davis	5.	Noa Nadruku
Brad Fittler, Capt.	6.	Noa Nayacakalou
Geoff Toovey	7.	Save Taga
Dean Pay	8.	Malakai Yasa
Andrew Johns	9.	Iane Sagaitu
Mark Carroll	10.	Pio Nakubuwai
Steve Menzies	11.	Joe Dakuitoga
Gary Larson	12.	Samuela Davetawalu
Jim Dymock	13.	Niumaia Korovata

Substitutes
Paul McGregor played
Matthew Johns played
Jason Smith played
Nik Kosef played

Substitutes
Kalaveti Naisoro played
George Vatubua played
Waisake Vatubua not used
Kini Koroibuleka played

T: Dallas (3), O'Davis (3),
Menzies (2), Hill (2),
Brasher, Larson

G: A. Johns (9)

Half-time: 32-0
Penalties: 4-5
Attendance: 7,127
Referee: Eddie Ward (Australia)

LARSON MAKES A FLYING START

Gary Larson wasted no time making an impact for Australia only a few days after flying in as a replacement for the injured Paul Harragon. The hard-working forward had been a late withdrawal from Australia's squad for domestic reasons, but he jumped at the chance of finally joining the party and was pitched straight in against Fiji.

He did his usual big tackling stint and chipped in with a try to put himself right in line for a semi-final call-up as he made the perfect second row pairing alongside Steve Menzies, whose superb attacking play brought him two more tries.

Coach Bob Fulton sprang a surprise by switching Andrew Johns from scrum half to hooker for the first time and the youngster made the most of it with another man of the match performance and nine more goals.

Brad Fittler pushed him close for match honours with Australia's captain sparking off several tryscoring moves, while wingers Robbie O'Davis and Brett Dallas both collected well-taken hat-tricks, with the latter impressing enough to gain a starting place in the semi-final line-up.

The supposedly neutral crowd soon took sides to get behind the underdogs but failed to inspire the Fijians, whose first-match promise had now evaporated and they looked a well-beaten side long before the finish.

Fijian Halifax Centenary World Cup star Noa Nayacakalou.

GROUP ONE
Saturday 14 October 1995   **Headingley, Leeds**

ENGLAND 46		SOUTH AFRICA 0
Paul Cook	1.	Pierre van Wyk
John Bentley	2.	Guy Coombe
Nick Pinkney	3.	Tim Fourie
Barrie-Jon Mather	4.	Willem Boshoff
Martin Offiah	5.	Andrew Ballot
Daryl Powell	6.	Mark Johnson
Bobbie Goulding	7.	Berend Alkema
Karl Harrison	8.	Gideon Watts
Mick Cassidy	9.	Kobus van Deventer
Andy Platt	10.	Jaco Booysen, Capt.
Simon Haughton	11.	Gerald Williams
Chris Joynt	12.	Jaco Alberts
Phil Clarke, Capt.	13.	John Mudgeway

Substitutes
Kris Radlinski played
Paul Broadbent played
Tony Smith played
Dean Sampson played

Substitutes
Justin Jennings played
Elmar Lubbe played
Francois Cloete played
Jaco Visser played

T: Pinkney (2), Haughton,
Goulding, Sampson,
Broadbent, Radlinski,
Smith

G: Goulding (7)

Half-time: 16-0
Penalties: 3-4
Attendance: 14,041
Referee: David Manson (Australia)

BATTLING SA PREVENT MASSACRE

After conceding a total of 138 points in their previous two World Cup matches, South Africa were expected to be on the receiving end of another massacre and the record books had been well checked before the kick-off. But they restricted England to a modest 46 points and prevented Martin Offiah from scoring even one try when many were predicting the winger would grab a record haul of half a dozen or more.

It was Offiah's first match in the tournament after recovering from injury but he looked far from match fit and could not shake off the eager South African defence.

Although coach Phil Larder was disappointed with England's overall performance he expressed delight with the form of man of the match Nick Pinkney, from his Keighley Cougars side, and gave a strong hint that he would be in the semi-final starting line-up. Pinkney gave a first-class centre display that brought him two tries, including an 85-metre solo effort that must rank as one of the outstanding scores of the tournament.

Paul Broadbent and Dean Sampson both made a quick impact after going on as second-half substitutes, with the props each charging through for an early try that dashed any hopes of South Africa building on a creditable first 40 minutes, which left them only 16-0 down.

Fijian winger Noa Nadruku on the attack against South Africa at Keighley.

England second row Simon Haughton on his way to a try against South Africa at Leeds.

GROUP TWO
Sunday 8 October 1995 Wilderspool Stadium, Warrington

NEW ZEALAND 25		TONGA 24
Matthew Ridge, Capt.	1.	Asa Amone
Sean Hoppe	2.	Una Taufa
Richard Blackmore	3.	Tevita Vaikona
Ruben Wiki	4.	Phil Howlett
Richard Barnett	5.	Jimmy Veikoso
Gene Ngamu	6.	Angelo Dymock
Stacey Jones	7.	Willie Wolfgramm
Quentin Pongia	8.	Martin Masella
Syd Eru	9.	Duane Mann, Capt.
Jason Lowrie	10.	Lee Hansen
Tony Iro	11.	George Mann
Stephen Kearney	12.	Solomon Haumono
Tony Kemp	13.	Awen Guttenbeil

Substitutes
Henry Paul played
Hitro Okesene played
Kevin Iro played
Mark Horo played

Substitutes
Salesi Finau played
Talite Liava'a played
Luke Leilua not used
Taukolo Tonga not used

T: Blackmore (2), Hoppe, Kemp, Okesene

T: Wolfgramm, Taufa, Veikoso, Finau

G: Ridge (2), Ridge (dg)

G: Amone (4)

Half-time: 12-6
Penalties: 1-6

Attendance: 8,083
Referee: David Campbell (England)

TONGA NEAR SHOCK WIN

A last-minute drop goal by New Zealand captain Matthew Ridge denied Tonga a well-deserved draw after they seemed to be heading for one of the biggest international shocks in the game's history. Roared on by most of the spectators in Wilderspool's biggest crowd of the season, the Tongans led 24-12 going into the last ten minutes before New Zealand produced a storming finish.

The Kiwis stepped up the pace for Hitro Okesene and Richard Blackmore to rip in for tries, both goaled by Ridge who then got into position to land the vital drop goal from close range. But their late surge was aided by referee David Campbell's tackle-count blunder at a crucial stage of the game.

With Tonga in possession and leading 24-18, the referee signalled five instead of four tackles and the ball was kicked to New Zealand who set up the equalising try and goal. Campbell's apology for the mistake was taken in good spirit by the Tongans after the match.

Tonga's own fightback began after they had trailed 12-6 at the interval and was led by captain Duane Mann, the man of the match. It was Mann's kick to the corner which led to Tonga going ahead in the 49th minute when Jimmy Veikoso scooped up the ball and dived over all in one amazing movement. Salesi Finau snapped up a loose ball to race through for another touchdown and goals from Asa Amone took Tonga's lead to 12 points before New Zealand's rally completed a match to remember.

231

GROUP TWO

Tuesday 10 October 1995   **The Boulevard, Hull**

PAPUA NEW GUINEA   28   **TONGA   28**

David Buko	1.	Asa Amone
James Kops	2.	Una Taufa
David Gomia	3.	Tevita Vaikona
John Okul	4.	Phil Howlett
Joshua Kouoru	5.	Jimmy Veikoso
Stanley Gene	6.	Angelo Dymock
Adrian Lam, Capt.	7.	Willie Wolfgramm
Tuiyo Evei	8.	Martin Masella
Elias Paiyo	9.	Duane Mann, Capt.
David Westley	10.	Lee Hansen
Max Tiri	11.	George Mann
Nande Yer	12.	Solomon Haumono
Bruce Mamando	13.	Awen Guttenbeil

Substitutes
Robert Tela played
Lucas Solbat played
Marcus Bai played
David Reeka played

Substitutes
Salesi Finau played
Tau'alupe Liku played
Luke Leilua not used
Taukolo Tonga played
Sin bin: Haumono (15 min.)

T: Lam, Paiyo, Buko, Gene, Solbat

T: Guttenbeil (2), Howlett, Wolfgramm, Liku, Taufa

G: Paiyo (4)

G: Amone (2)

Half-time: 0-20
Penalties: 15-4

Attendance: 5,121
Referee: Claude Alba (France)

LAM INSPIRES KUMULS COMEBACK

Australia-based scrum half Adrian Lam inspired a remarkable Papua New Guinea comeback that produced a last-minute equaliser after Tonga had raced to an impressive 20-0 interval lead. It was the first time they had avoided defeat in a full international match outside their own country.

Man of the match Lam had received little support in the first 40 minutes but the second-half response was magnificent as he touched down and was involved in all but one of the Kumuls' five tries, including the last-minute match-saver from Lucas Solbat.

Elias Paiyo added the simple equalising goal for a match tally of four, which proved all-important as Tonga scored six tries to five. The busy hooker also scored a try to complete a large contribution to Papua's rousing rally that thrilled The Boulevard's biggest crowd of the season.

It was all so different in the first half when Tonga played some spectacular rugby to run in four tries, including a brilliant solo effort by former Australian Schoolboy international Phil Howlett. There were several other clever touches by the 20-year-old centre in an outstanding display.

GROUP TWO
Friday 13 October 1995   **Knowsley Road, St. Helens**

NEW ZEALAND   22   PAPUA NEW GUINEA   6

New Zealand	No.	Papua New Guinea
Matthew Ridge, Capt.	1.	David Buko
Sean Hoppe	2.	James Kops
Richard Blackmore	3.	David Gomia
Ruben Wiki	4.	John Okul
Jason Williams	5.	Joshua Kouoru
Henry Paul	6.	Stanley Gene
Stacey Jones	7.	Adrian Lam, Capt.
Quentin Pongia	8.	Nande Yer
Gary Freeman	9.	Elias Paiyo
Jason Lowrie	10.	David Westley
Stephen Kearney	11.	Max Tiri
Mark Horo	12.	Michael Angra
Tony Kemp	13.	Bruce Mamando

Substitutes
Gene Ngamu played
Hitro Okesene played
Kevin Iro played
Tony Iro played

T: Ridge, Blackmore, Hoppe

G: Ridge (4), Ngamu

Half-time: 16-2
Penalties: 11-13

Substitutes
Robert Tela played
Lucas Solbat played
Marcus Bai played
Ben Biri played

T: Bai

G: Paiyo

Attendance: 8,679
Referee: Stuart Cummings
(England)

NEW ZEALAND ONTO SEMI-FINAL

New Zealand were far from convincing despite setting up a semi-final showdown against Australia with a hard-won victory over Papua New Guinea, who did much better than the scoreline suggests.

Once again a supposedly neutral crowd got wholeheartedly behind the underdogs and Papua did not let them down, rocking back New Zealand repeatedly with their all-out efforts which deserved greater reward.

Adrian Lam picked up his second man of the match award with another outstanding scrum-half display that confirmed him as one of the stars of the World Cup.

Elias Paiyo was one of the smallest players in the tournament, but the Papua New Guinea hooker again played well above his weight to at least match any of the much bigger Kiwi forwards.

New Zealand coach Frank Endacott sprang a pre-match surprise by selecting Gary Freeman, the most capped Kiwi of all time, at hooker after a long career as one of the world's greatest half backs. He replaced the squad's only regular hooker Syd Eru, who had been banned from the tournament a few hours earlier after failing a drugs test.

Tonga in full war cry before their tremendous battle against New Zealand at Warrington.

France stop this Western Samoa attacking raid but crash 56-10 at Cardiff.

GROUP THREE
Monday 9 October 1995   **Ninian Park, Cardiff**

WALES 28   **FRANCE 6**

Wales		France
Iestyn Harris	1.	David Despin
John Devereux	2.	Frederic Banquet
Allan Bateman	3.	David Fraisse
Scott Gibbs	4.	Pierre Chamorin
Anthony Sullivan	5.	Jean-Marc Garcia
Jonathan Davies, Capt.	6.	Pascal Fages
Kevin Ellis	7.	Patrick Entat, Capt.
Kelvin Skerrett	8.	Didier Cabestany
Martin Hall	9.	Patrick Torreilles
David Young	10.	Frederic Teixido
Paul Moriarty	11.	Gael Tallec
Mark Perrett	12.	Pascal Jampy
Richie Eyres	13.	Thierry Valero

Substitutes
Mark Jones played
Adrian Hadley played
Keiron Cunningham played
Rowland Phillips played

Substitutes
Vincent Banet played
Karl Jaavuo played
Brian Coles played
Lilian Hebert played

T: Sullivan (3), Harris, Devereux

G: Davies (3), Harris

Half-time: 12-0
Penalties: 6-8

T: Torreilles

G: Banquet

Attendance: 10,250
Referee: Eddie Ward (Australia)

HARRIS THE RISING STAR

Iestyn Harris confirmed his status as Wales's fastest rising star with a superb display that earned him the man of the match award despite a hat-trick of tries from Anthony Sullivan.

The 19-year-old utility back began at full back and did well enough there but it was when he moved to stand off after injured Jonathan Davies departed in the 57th minute that the youngster really shone. Within minutes he slipped effortlessly through from a scrum near halfway and flew away for a superb try.

Sullivan earned his hat-trick with some superb finishing as the St. Helens winger revived memories of his late father, Clive Sullivan, who led Great Britain to the World Cup in 1972.

Former Wales rugby union international Davies was involved in the build-up to all three of Sullivan's tries and it was a blow when he went off with concussion after going awkwardly into a tackle.

After some early promise, France rarely put the Welsh line under sustained pressure although they scored a splendid try when Pierre Chamorin's curving run set up a touchdown for Patrick Torreilles.

Wales were reported for using one more than the permitted four substitutes, but after an investigation by the tournament referees' director Greg McCallum it was decided the extra replacement was a genuine mistake and no action was taken.

GROUP THREE

Thursday 12 October 1995 **Ninian Park, Cardiff**

WESTERN SAMOA   56   FRANCE   10

Paki Tuimavave	1.	Frederic Banquet
Brian Laumatia	2.	Brian Coles
John Schuster, Capt.	3.	Jean-Marc Garcia
Va'aiga Tuigamala	4.	Pierre Chamorin
Lolani Koko	5.	Pascal Mons
Tea Ropati	6.	Pascal Fages
Willie Swann	7.	Patrick Entat, Capt.
Se'e Solomona	8.	Hadj Boudebza
Willie Poching	9.	Patrick Torreilles
Fa'ausu Afoa	10.	Karl Jaavuo
Tony Tatupu	11.	Cyril Baudouin
Vila Matautia	12.	Didier Cabestany
Tony Tuimavave	13.	Thierry Valero

Substitutes
Mark Elia played
Sam Panapa played
Apollo Perelini played
Joe Vagana played

Substitutes
Vincent Banet not used
Pascal Jampy played
Frederic Teixido played
Marc Tisseyre played

T: Tuigamala (2), Swann,
Matautia (2), Tatupu (2),
P. Tuimavave, Laumatia,
Perelini

T: Chamorin, Cabestany

G: Schuster (8)

G: Banquet

Half-time: 26-4
Attendance: 2,173
Referee: Kelvin Jeffs (Australia)

SAMOA MAKE IMPRESSIVE ENTRY

Western Samoa were the last of the ten countries to get into action and they made up for the long wait with a devastating destruction of a poor French side that must have thought they had been hit by a South Sea hurricane.

The lowest crowd of the tournament – a mere 2,173 – saw a runaway victory that ensured a packed house for the Swansea showdown between Wales and the Samoans to decide who went through to the semi-finals.

A powerful Samoan side that included several players with British and Australian League experience brushed aside some weak French tackling to charge in for ten tries. St. Helens forward Vila Matautia grabbed two of them on his way to lifting the man of the match award, while Wigan superstar Va'aiga Tuigamala also blasted in for two touchdowns.

Although Halifax centre John Schuster did not get among the tries, Samoa's captain boosted the total with eight goals. Such was the strength of the islanders' squad, they could afford to have such outstanding players as Sam Panapa and Apollo Perelini as substitutes.

France were already 26-4 down by half-time and did not score their second try until the 72nd minute when Didier Cabestany found a way through.

237

GROUP THREE

Sunday 15 October 1995   **Vetch Field, Swansea**

WALES 22		WESTERN SAMOA 10
Iestyn Harris	1.	Paki Tuimavave
Anthony Sullivan	2.	John Schuster, Capt.
Allan Bateman	3.	Tea Ropati
John Devereux	4.	Va'aiga Tuigamala
Adrian Hadley	5.	Brian Laumatia
Jonathan Davies, Capt.	6.	Sam Panapa
Kevin Ellis	7.	Willie Swann
Kelvin Skerrett	8.	Se'e Solomona
Martin Hall	9.	Willie Poching
David Young	10.	Fa'ausu Afoa
Paul Moriarty	11.	Tony Tatupu
Scott Quinnell	12.	Vila Matautia
Richie Eyres	13.	Tony Tuimavave

Substitutes
Neil Cowie played
Keiron Cunningham
   played
Rowland Phillips played
Paul Atcheson played

Substitutes
Mark Elia played
Des Maea played
Apollo Perelini played
Joe Vagana played
Sin bin: Ropati (5 min.)
   Maea (58 min.)

T: Harris, Sullivan, Ellis

T: Matautia

G: Davies (4), Davies (dg),
Harris (dg)

G: Schuster (3)

Half-time: 14-10
Penalties: 14-9

Attendance: 15,385
Referee: Russell Smith (England)

WALES BATTERED BUT UNBOWED

Wales withstood a tremendous battering from a highly physical Western Samoan side to earn a well-deserved semi-final clash with England after one of the most memorable nights in Welsh rugby league history.

A capacity crowd of 15,385 packed into the Swansea soccer ground and their vociferous partisan support provided an electric atmosphere that inspired Wales to give a mighty performance packed with passion.

It was also an emotional farewell for Jonathan Davies, who was playing his last match in Wales before making a return to his rugby union roots. The Welsh captain did not have an outstanding game as an individual but he led his side in great style.

But the game also marked the emergence of another former rugby union international as a future league star as Scott Quinnell took the man of the match award.

And Iestyn Harris confirmed his rating as one of the most outstanding players of the tournament, cutting through for the first try and adding a drop goal at a crucial stage late in the game.

Western Samoa were a disappointment as they tried to batter the Welsh into submission instead of relying on the talents of their more skilful players.

New Zealand's Sean Hoppe on the attack against Australia in the semi-final at Huddersfield.

Welsh forwards Martin Hall (9) and Kelvin Skerrett up-end an English player in the semi-final at Old Trafford, Manchester.

SEMI-FINAL

Saturday 21 October 1995   **Old Trafford, Manchester**

ENGLAND 25		WALES 10
Kris Radlinski	1.	Iestyn Harris
Jason Robinson	2.	John Devereux
Nick Pinkney	3.	Allan Bateman
Paul Newlove	4.	Scott Gibbs
Martin Offiah	5.	Anthony Sullivan
Tony Smith	6.	Jonathan Davies, Capt.
Bobbie Goulding	7.	Kevin Ellis
Karl Harrison	8.	Kelvin Skerrett
Lee Jackson	9.	Martin Hall
Andy Platt	10.	David Young
Denis Betts, Capt.	11.	Paul Moriarty
Phil Clarke	12.	Scott Quinnell
Andrew Farrell	13.	Richie Eyres

Substitutes
Barrie-Jon Mather not used
Mick Cassidy played
Simon Haughton played
Dean Sampson played

Substitutes
Mark Jones played
Keiron Cunningham played
Rowland Phillips played
Adrian Hadley not used
Sin bin: Moriarty (42 min.)

T: Offiah (2), Newlove, Betts,
Clarke

T: Phillips

G: Farrell, Goulding,
Goulding (dg)

G: Davies (3)

Penalties: 5-8
Half-time: 11-4

Attendance: 30,042
Referee: Eddie Ward (Australia)

ENGLAND ROAR BACK TO WEMBLEY

A well-drilled England carried out coach Phil Larder's game plan almost to perfection to break down a spirited Welsh side and book themselves a return trip to Wembley for the final. Five tries to one reflected England's superiority with Bobbie Goulding virtually making certain of a final place with a man of the match performance.

The St. Helens scrum half's pin-point kicking produced two tries in the corner for Martin Offiah and he drew aside the Welsh defence like a curtain to send in Phil Clarke for the final touchdown. Goulding also landed two goals, including a drop goal, in an impressive all-round display.

With Tony Smith doing enough at stand-off to retain his place after replacing injured Daryl Powell it looked as if England would go into the final with a completely different half-back combination to the one that started the competition.

No one was more upset over Wales's defeat than their captain Jonathan Davies, who had already said he would retire from the international scene after the World Cup and gave a strong indication at the post-match press conference that he had played his last rugby league match before returning to his Welsh rugby union roots.

SEMI-FINAL

Sunday 22 October 1995   Alfred McAlpine Stadium, Huddersfield

AUSTRALIA 30   **NEW ZEALAND 20**

(After extra time. Normal time score 20-20)

Australia		New Zealand
Tim Brasher	1.	Matthew Ridge, Capt.
Rod Wishart	2.	Sean Hoppe
Mark Coyne	3.	Kevin Iro
Terry Hill	4.	Richard Blackmore
Brett Dallas	5.	Richard Barnett
Brad Fittler, Capt.	6.	Tony Kemp
Geoff Toovey	7.	Stacey Jones
Dean Pay	8.	John Lomax
Andrew Johns	9.	Henry Paul
Mark Carroll	10.	Jason Lowrie
Steve Menzies	11.	Stephen Kearney
Gary Larson	12.	Quentin Pongia
Jim Dymock	13.	Mark Horo

Substitutes
Robbie O'Davis played
Matthew Johns played
Jason Smith played
Nik Kosef played
Sin bin: Hill (76 min.)

Substitutes
Gene Ngamu played
Ruben Wiki played
Tony Iro played
Hitro Okesene played

T: Menzies (2), Brasher,
Coyne, Hill, Fittler

T: Barnett, T. Iro, K. Iro

G: A. Johns (3)

G: Ridge (4)

Half-time: 14-4
Penalties: 7-13

Attendance: 16,608
Referee: Russell Smith (England)

AUSTRALIA TRIUMPH IN EXTRA TIME

New Zealand went within inches of snatching a dramatic last-minute victory before Australia recovered in extra time to force a final showdown with England. Australia seemed to be coasting to a comfortable victory when they led 20-6 going into the last 20 minutes, but New Zealand hit back with a three-try blast plus a goal to level the scores just two minutes from the end of normal time.

Matthew Ridge missed the chance of glory when he failed with his touchline kick and then saw his towering drop goal attempt from 40 metres brush past the wrong side of an upright.

It was breathtaking stuff and there was more to come as the game went into extra time. Australia began it with only 12 men as Terry Hill still had six minutes to complete in the sin bin. The rest seemed to benefit the centre as he returned to finish off a sweeping 60-metre raid that put Australia on the way to victory.

Captain Brad Fittler made certain when he sidestepped through for a try to give his side a convincing six tries to three advantage.

There had been little sign of the thrills to come as Australia dominated the first half and began the second in similar style when Steve Menzies beat three players on an 80-metre dash to the line for probably the best solo try of the tournament.

Australia's Steve Menzies finds his path blocked by New Zealander Richard Blackmore in the semi-final.

Scott Gibbs of Wales in determined mood against France at Cardiff.

ENGLAND

Coach: Phil Larder
Manager: Phil Lowe
Captain: Shaun Edwards

	App	T	G	Pts
John Bentley (Halifax)	3	1	0	4
Denis Betts (Auckland Warriors)	4	1	0	4
Paul Broadbent (Sheffield Eagles)	1+1	2	0	8
Mick Cassidy (Wigan)	2+2	0	0	0
Phil Clarke	4	1	0	4
(Sydney City Roosters)				
Gary Connolly (Wigan)	1	0	0	0
Paul Cook (Leeds)	1+1	0	0	0
Shaun Edwards (Wigan)	1	0	0	0
Andrew Farrell (Wigan)	4	1	7	18
Bobbie Goulding (St. Helens)	4	1	14 (1)	31
Karl Harrison (Halifax)	4	0	0	0
Simon Haughton (Wigan)	1+3	2	0	8
Lee Jackson (Sheffield Eagles)	4	0	0	0
Chris Joynt (St. Helens)	1+2	1	0	4
Barrie-Jon Mather (Wigan)	2	0	0	0
Steve McCurrie (Widnes)	0+1	0	0	0
Paul Newlove (Bradford Bulls)	4	4	0	16
Martin Offiah (Wigan)	3	2	0	8
Nick Pinkney (Keighley Cougars)	3	2	0	8
Andy Platt (Auckland W./Widnes)	4	0	0	0
Daryl Powell (Keighley Cougars)	2	0	0	0
Kris Radlinski (Wigan)	4+1	2	0	8
Jason Robinson (Wigan)	4	3	0	12
Dean Sampson (Castleford)	1+2	1	0	4
Tony Smith (Castleford)	3+1	2	0	8
Totals		26	21(1)	145

( ) drop goals included in total

England coach Phil Larder had named a 40-man squad in mid-July before reducing it to the World Cup maximum of 25. The players omitted were:

Grant Anderson (Halifax), Martin Crompton (Oldham), Francis Cummins (Leeds), Anthony Farrell (Sheffield E.), Vince Fawcett (Workington T.), Richard Goddard (Castleford), Neil Harmon (Leeds), Andy Hay (Sheffield E.), Stephen Holgate (Workington T.), Alan Hunte (St. Helens), Barrie McDermott (Wigan), Steve Molloy (Featherstone R.), Sonny Nickle (St. Helens), Martin Pearson (Featherstone R.), Steve Prescott (St. Helens), Stuart Spruce (Widnes), Mike Wainwright (Warrington), Nigel Wright (Wigan).

Broadbent, Cook and Haughton were the only players not in the 40-man squad who were chosen for the final 25.

WALES

Coach: Clive Griffiths
Manager: Mike Nicholas
Captain: Jonathan Davies

	App	T	G	Pts
Paul Atcheson (Oldham)	0+1	0	0	0
Allan Bateman (Warrington)	3	0	0	0
Dean Busby (St. Helens)	0	0	0	0
Neil Cowie (Wigan)	0+1	0	0	0
Keiron Cunningham (St. Helens)	0+3	0	0	0
Jonathan Davies (Warrington)	3	0	11(1)	21
John Devereux (Widnes)	3	1	0	4
Kevin Ellis (Warrington)	3	1	0	4
Richie Eyres (Leeds)	3	0	0	0
Phil Ford (Salford)	0	0	0	0
Scott Gibbs (St. Helens)	2	0	0	0
Jonathan Griffiths (St. Helens)	0	0	0	0
Adrian Hadley (Widnes)	1+1	0	0	0
Martin Hall (Wigan)	3	0	0	0
Iestyn Harris (Warrington)	3	2	2(1)	11
Mark Jones (Warrington)	0+2	0	0	0
Paul Moriarty (Halifax)	3	0	0	0
Mark Perrett (Halifax)	1	0	0	0
Rowland Phillips (Workington T.)	0+3	1	0	4
Scott Quinnell (Wigan)	2	0	0	0
Kelvin Skerrett (Wigan)	3	0	0	0
Gareth Stephens (Castleford)	0	0	0	0
Anthony Sullivan (St. Helens)	3	4	0	16
Richard Webster (Salford)	0	0	0	0
David Young (Salford)	3	0	0	0
Totals		9	13(2)	60

( ) drop goals included in total

Wales Coach Clive Griffiths had named a 40-man squad in July before reducing it to the World Cup maximum of 25. The players omitted were:

Gareth Cochrane (Keighley C.), Gerald Cordle (Bradford N.), Jason Critchley (Keighley C.), Gareth Davies (Sir John Moores University), Craig Dean (Halifax), Mike Edwards (Oldham), Andy Eyres (Keighley C.), Jason Lee (Warrington), Ian Marlow (Wakefield T.), Daio Powell (Wakefield T.), Gareth Price-Jones (Swinton), Mark Sheals (Wakefield T.), Ian Watson (Salford), Barry Williams (Workington T.), David Williams (Cardiff Sea Eagles).

AUSTRALIA

Coach: Bob Fulton
Manager: Geoff Carr
Captain: Brad Fittler

	App	T	G	Pts
Wayne Bartrim (St. George)	1+1	0	0	0
Tim Brasher (Sydney Tigers)	4+1	4	0	16
Mark Carroll (Manly)	4+1	0	0	0
Mark Coyne (St. George)	4	2	0	8
Brett Dallas (Sydney Bulldogs)	4	3	0	12
Jim Dymock (Sydney Bulldogs)	4+1	1	0	4
Brad Fittler (Penrith)	4	1	0	4
David Gillespie (Manly)	1	0	0	0
Paul Harragon	1+1	0	0	0
(Newcastle Knights)				
Terry Hill (Manly)	4	3	0	12
John Hopoate (Manly)	2	3	0	12
Andrew Johns	4	2	27	62
(Newcastle Knights)				
Matthew Johns	1+3	0	0	0
(Newcastle Knights)				
Nik Kosef (Manly)	1+2	1	0	4
Gary Larson* (North Sydney)	3	1	0	4
Paul McGregor (Illawarra)	1+1	2	0	8
Steve Menzies (Manly)	4	6	0	24
Billy Moore (North Sydney)	1	0	0	0
Danny Moore (Manly)	1	2	0	8
Adam Muir (Newcastle Knights)	1	0	0	0
Robbie O'Davis	2+1	5	0	20
(Newcastle Knights)				
Dean Pay (Sydney Bulldogs)	4	0	0	0
Aaron Raper (Cronulla)	1	1	0	4
Jason Smith (Sydney Bulldogs)	1+4	1	0	4
Geoff Toovey (Manly)	4	0	0	0
Rod Wishart (Illawarra)	3	1	2	8
Totals		39	29	214

* Larson replaced injured Harragon after two matches.

FIJI

Coach: Graham Murray
Manager: Epell Lagiloaloa
Captain: Livai Nalagilagi

	App	T	G	Pts
Orisi Cavuilati (Bulldogs)	1	0	0	0
Joe Dakuitoga (Penrith)	3	1	0	4
Samuela Davetawalu	1	0	0	0
(Fiji Fish Nadi)				
Apisalome Degei (Parramatta)	2	0	0	0
Kini Koroibuleka	0+1	0	0	0
Niumaia Korovata	1+1	0	0	0
(Yanco Wamoon)				
Sam Marayawa (Tumbarumba)	2	1	0	4
Noa Nadruku (Canberra Raiders)	3	1	0	4
Kalaveti Naisoro	0+3	1	0	4
(Lautoka Foodtown)				
Pio Nakubuwai (Yanco Wamoon)	3	0	0	0
Livai Nalagilagi (Penrith)	3	0	0	0
Noa Nayacakalou (Penrith)	3	0	3	6
Inoke Ratudina	0	0	0	0
(Carpenters Motors)				
Kiniviliame Ratukana	0	0	0	0
(Fiji Bitter Army)				
Freddie Robarts	0	0	0	0
(Waitakere Raiders)				
Iane Sagaitu (North Sydney)	3	1	0	4
Kaiava Salusalu	0+1	0	0	0
(Lautoka Foodtown)				
Filemoni Seru	3	2	0	8
(S. Queensland Crushers)				
Waisale Sovatabua	3	2	0	8
(Carpenters Motors)				
Save Taga (Fiji Fish Nadi)	3	1	3	10
Iliesa Toga (Narrabeean)	2	0	0	0
Vonivate Toga (Fiji Fish Nadi)	0	0	0	0
George Vatubua	0+3	0	0	0
(Lautoka Foodtown)				
Waisake Vatubua	0	0	0	0
(Hyundai Bulldogs)				
Ulaiasi Wainidroa (Fiji Fish Nadi)	0+2	0	0	0
Malakai Yasa	3	0	0	0
(Lautoka Foodtown)				
Totals		10	6	52

FRANCE

Coach: Ivan Greseque
Manager: Tas Baitieri
Captain: Patrick Entat

	App	T	G	Pts
Patrick Acroue (Avignon)	0	0	0	0
Ezzedine Attia (Cannes)	0	0	0	0
Vincent Banet (Limoux)	0+1	0	0	0
Frederic Banquet (Sheffield Eagles)	2	0	2	4
Cyril Baudouin (Carpentras)	1	0	0	0
Hadj Boudebza (St. Esteve)	1	0	0	0
Didier Cabestany (Catalan)	2	1	0	4
Pierre Chamorin (St. Esteve)	2	1	0	4
Brian Coles (Catalan)	1+1	0	0	0
David Despin (Villeneuve-sur-Lot)	1	0	0	0
Patrick Entat (Avignon)	2	0	0	0
Pascal Fages (Pia)	2	0	0	0
David Fraisse (Workington Town)	1	0	0	0
Jean-Marc Garcia (St. Esteve)	2	0	0	0
Lilian Hebert (Pia)	0+1	0	0	0
Karl Jaavuo (Pia)	1+1	0	0	0
Pascal Jampy (St. Esteve)	1+1	0	0	0
Stephan Millet (St. Gaudens)	0	0	0	0
Pascal Mons (Carcassonne)	1	0	0	0
Gael Tallec (Wigan)	1	0	0	0
Frederic Teixido (Limoux)	1+1	0	0	0
Marc Tisseyre (Limoux)	0+1	0	0	0
Patrick Torreilles (Pia)	2	1	0	4
Thierry Valero (FC Lezignan)	2	0	0	0
Totals		**3**	**2**	**16**

NEW ZEALAND

Coach: Frank Endacott
Manager: Bevan Olsen
Captain: Matthew Ridge

	App	T	G	Pts
Richard Barnett (Cronulla)	2	1	0	4
Richard Blackmore (Auckland Warriors)	3	3	0	12
Syd Eru (Auckland Warriors)	1	0	0	0
Gary Freeman (Penrith)	1	0	0	0
Daryl Halligan (Sydney Bulldogs)	0	0	0	0
Sean Hoppe (Auckland Warriors)	3	2	0	8
Mark Horo (Western Suburbs)	2+1	0	0	0
Kevin Iro (Leeds)	1+2	1	0	4
Tony Iro (Sydney City Roosters)	1+2	1	0	4
Stacey Jones (Auckland Warriors)	3	0	0	0
Stephen Kearney (Auckland W.)	3	0	0	0
Tony Kemp (Leeds)	3	1	0	4
John Lomax (Canberra Raiders)	1	0	0	0
Jason Lowrie (Sydney City Roosters)	3	0	0	0
Gene Ngamu (Auckland Warriors)	1+2	0	1	2
Hitro Okesene (Auckland Warriors)	0+3	1	0	4
Henry Paul (Wigan)	2+1	0	0	0
Quentin Pongia (Canberra Raiders)	3	0	0	0
Matthew Ridge (Manly)	3	1	11(1)	25
Brent Stuart (Western Suburbs)	0	0	0	0
John Timu (Sydney Bulldogs)	0	0	0	0
Brendon Tuuta (Castleford)	0	0	0	0
Ruben Wiki (Canberra Raiders)	2+1	0	0	0
Jason Williams (Sydney Bulldogs)	1	0	0	0
Totals		**11**	**12(1)**	**67**

( ) denotes drop goals included in total

One appearance for David Fraisse.

PAPUA NEW GUINEA

Coach: Joe Tokam
Managers: Bob Robertson, James Korarome
Captain: Adrian Lam

	App	T	G	Pts
Michael Angra (Hagen Eagles)	1	0	0	0
Marcus Bai	0+2	1	0	4
(Port Moresby Vipers)				
Ben Biri (Port Moresby Vipers)	0+1	0	0	0
David Buko (Goroka Lahanis)	2	1	0	4
Aquila Emil	0	0	0	0
(Port Moresby Vipers)				
Tuiyo Evei (Goroka Lahanis)	1	0	0	0
Stanley Gene (Goroka Lahanis)	2	1	0	4
David Gomia (Goroka Lahanis)	2	0	0	0
August Joseph (Rabaul Gurias)	0	0	0	0
James Kops (Hagen Eagles)	2	0	0	0
Joshua Kouoru (Rabaul Gurias)	2	0	0	0
Adrian Lam	2	1	0	4
(Sydney City Roosters)				
Bruce Mamando	2	0	0	0
(Canberra Raiders)				
Billy Noi Jnr. (Hagen Eagles)	0	0	0	0
John Okul (Moorebank Bulldogs)	2	0	0	0
Elias Paiyo (Port Moresby Vipers)	2	1	5	14
Samuel Pinpin (Mendi Muruks)	0	0	0	0
David Reeka (Lae Bombers)	0+1	0	0	0
Lucas Solbat (Rabaul Gurias)	0+2	1	0	4
Robert Tela (Lae Bombers)	0+2	0	0	0
Petrus Thomas (Mendi Muruks)	0	0	0	0
Max Tiri (Hagen Eagles)	2	0	0	0
David Westley (Canberra Raiders)	2	0	0	0
Nande Yer (Mendi Muruks)	2	0	0	0
Totals		6	5	34

SOUTH AFRICA

Coach: Tony Fisher
Manager: Ockie Oosthuizen
Captain: Jaco Booysen

	App	T	G	Pts
Jaco Alberts	2	0	0	0
(S. Queensland Crushers)				
Berend Alkema	3	0	0	0
Andrew Ballot (Bay of Plenty)	3	0	0	0
Jaco Booysen (St. Helens Devils)	3	0	0	0
Willem Boshoff (Eastern Reds)	3	0	0	0
Francois Cloete (Barea Students)	2+1	0	0	0
Guy Coombe (Durban Sharks)	3	0	0	0
Tim Fourie (City Scorpions)	3	0	0	0
Pierre Grobbelaar	0	0	0	0
(Vaal Buffaloes)				
Koot Human	1+1	0	0	0
(S. Queensland Crushers)				
Justin Jennings	0+1	0	0	0
(S. Queensland Crushers)				
Mark Johnson	3	0	0	0
(Workington Town)				
Elmar Lubbe (Eastern Reds)	0+1	0	0	0
Ernest Ludick	0+2	0	0	0
Warren McCann	0	0	0	0
John Mudgeway (Durban Sharks)	1	0	0	0
Eugene Powell (City Scorpions)	0+1	0	0	0
Nico Serfontein	0+1	0	0	0
Kobus van Deventer	3	0	0	0
(Genniston Warriors)				
Jaco van Niekerk (Eastern Reds)	0+2	0	0	0
Pierre van Wyk (Eastern Reds)	3	0	4	8
Jaco Visser	0+1	0	0	0
Gideon Watts	3	1	0	4
Gerald Williams (Durban Sharks)	3	0	0	0
Totals		1	4	12

TONGA

Coach: Mike McClennan
Manager: Graham Mattson
Captain: Duane Mann

	App	T	G	Pts
Peri Amato (Mua Saints)	0	0	0	0
Asa Amone (Halifax)	2	0	6	12
Angelo Dymock (Moorepark)	2	0	0	0
Salesi Finau (Canberra Raiders)	0+2	1	0	4
Awen Guttenbeil (Manly)	2	2	0	8
Lee Hansen (Widnes)	2	0	0	0
Solomon Haumono (Manly)	2	0	0	0
Phil Howlett (Parramatta)	2	1	0	4
Luke Leilua (Otahuhu)	0	0	0	0
Talite Liava'a (Litchfield)	0+1	0	0	0
Tau'alupe Liku (Leigh)	0+1	1	0	4
Mateaki Mafi (Kolomua)	0	0	0	0
Duane Mann (Auckland Warriors)	2	0	0	0
George Mann (Leeds)	2	0	0	0
Martin Masella (Illawarra)	2	0	0	0
Andrew Tangata-Toa (Newcastle Knights)	0	0	0	0
Una Taufa (Canberra Raiders)	2	2	0	8
Taukolo Tonga (Kolomua Warriors)	0+1	0	0	0
Tevita Vaikona (Hull)	2	0	0	0
Jimmy Veikoso (Belconen)	2	1	0	4
Frank Watene (Auckland Warriors)	0	0	0	0
Willie Wolfgramm (Narrandera)	2	2	0	8
Totals		**10**	**6**	**52**

WESTERN SAMOA

Coach: Graham Lowe
Manager: Fou Solomona
Captain: John Schuster

	App	T	G	Pts
Fa'ausu Afoa (Penrith)	2	0	0	0
Mark Elia (Albi)	0+2	0	0	0
Lolani Koko (Narrendera)	1	0	0	0
Brian Laumatia (Cronulla)	2	1	0	4
Des Maea (Auckland Warriors)	0+1	0	0	0
Gus Maieta-Brown (Auckland Warriors)	0	0	0	0
Vila Matautia (St. Helens)	2	3	0	12
Sam Panapa (Salford)	1+1	0	0	0
Apollo Perelini (St. Helens)	0+2	1	0	4
Robert Piva (Queensland Cowboys)	0	0	0	0
Willie Poching (Auckland Warriors)	2	0	0	0
Tea Ropati (Auckland Warriors)	2	0	0	0
John Schuster (Halifax)	2	0	11	22
Mike Setefano (North Harbour)	0	0	0	0
Se'e Solomona (Auckland Warriors)	2	0	0	0
Henry Suluvale (Sydney City Roosters)	0	0	0	0
Willie Swann (Auckland Warriors)	2	1	0	4
Tony Tatupu (Auckland Warriors)	2	2	0	8
Setu Tuilaepa (Narrendera)	0	0	0	0
Va'aiga Tuigamala (Wigan)	2	2	0	8
Paki Tuimavave (North Harbour)	2	1	0	4
Tony Tuimavave (Auckland Warriors)	2	0	0	0
Earl Va'a (Wellington Dukes)	0	0	0	0
Joe Vagana (Auckland Warriors)	0+2	0	0	0
Nigel Vagana (Auckland Warriors)	0	0	0	0
Totals		**11**	**11**	**66**

Post-defeat condolences for Tongan hooker Duane Mann (left).

HALIFAX EMERGING NATIONS TOURNAMENT

The first Emerging Nations tournament was introduced to give the increasing number of countries who have only recently started playing rugby league to test their development against each other and to assess their potential for being promoted to the senior international scene.

Seven nations took part in the event played in England over an eight-day period during the major World Cup and had the same sponsors – the Halifax Building Society. Given a low-key send-off, the tournament became a bigger success than expected with the attendances many more than the few hundred that was forecast. Although the tournament was highly competitive, the matches do not have full international match status and are not included in the players' senior records.

Among the professional players from senior clubs who played in the tournament was full back Martin Crompton, who had been chosen in England's original squad of 40 for the major World Cup, but opted to play for Ireland under the grandparent qualification rule.

Leeds full back Alan Tait asked not to be considered for the senior England squad and was later chosen to lead his native Scotland.

Each nation was restricted to three professional players in a match. The full list of players from English professional clubs was:

Cook Islands: Jason Temu (Oldham)
Ireland: Leo Casey (Featherstone Rovers), Richard Smith and George Slicker (Halifax), Martin Crompton and Paul Topping (Oldham)
Scotland: Martin Ketteridge (Halifax), Darren Shaw (London Broncos), Darrall Shelford (Huddersfield), Alan Tait and Steve Tait (Leeds).

In addition former professionals Des Foy and Seamus McCallion (Ireland) plus Hugh Waddell (Scotland) also played in the tournament.

Cook Islands justified their ranking as pre-tournament favourites by winning all three of their group matches and then beating Ireland in the final at Swinton's home venue Gigg Lane, Bury, which attracted the ground's biggest rugby attendance of 4,147 despite being played in heavy rain.

Ali Davys took the man of the match award, with the Brisbane Broncos reserve grade scrum half a key figure behind the Cook Islands' victory and regarded as the outstanding player of the tournament.

HALIFAX EMERGING NATIONS FINAL
Tuesday 24 October 1995   Gigg Lane, Bury
COOK ISLANDS 22   IRELAND 6

Tiri Toa	1.	Gavin Gordon
Sonny Shepherd	2.	Phelim Comerford
Andrew Paita	3.	Richard Smith
Allan Tuaru	4.	Ricky Smith
Ngere Tariu	5.	Eugene McEntaggert
Craig Bowen, Capt.	6.	Craig McElhatton
Ali Davys	7.	Martin Crompton
Bob Hunter	8.	Bryan Smyth
James Cuthers	9.	Seamus McCallion
Jason Temu	10.	Leo Casey
Alex Kermode	11.	Gary Grainey
Tama Henry	12.	Tony Nuttall
Meti Noovao	13.	Paul Owens, Capt.

Substitutes
Tangi Tangimeta played
Tungane Tini played
Lloyd Matapo not used
Lefou Jack not used

Substitutes
Conor O'Sullivan played
Des Foy played
Sean Casey played
Eric Boyle not used

T: Cuthers, Bowen, Kermode, Shepherd

T: Comerford

G: Noovao (3)

G: Comerford

Half-time: 10-4
Penalties: 7-6

Attendance: 4,147
Referee: Dennis Hale (NZ)

GROUP ONE
First round

Date					Venue	Attendance
Mon 16 Oct.	**Cook Islands**	64	**USA**	6	**Featherstone**	3,133

T: Cuthers (3), Hunter (2),   T: Preston
Noovao (2), Johnston (2),   G: Niu
Bowen, Toa
G: Noovao (10)

Scotland 34 **Russia** 9 **Followed above**
T: Blee (2), Tait (2), How,   T: Netchaev, Otradnov
Waddell   G: Scheglov (dg)
G: McAlister (4),
Thompson

Second round

Wed. 18 Oct.	**Cook Islands**	58	**Russia**	20	**Leigh**	1,921

T: Tariu (4), Cuthers (2),   T: Kiryakov (2), Sirgeev,
Tuaru (2), Shepherd,   Romanov
Noovao, Bowen, Toa   G: Kozlov, Vinokhodov
G: Noovao (4), Piakura

Wed. 18 Oct.	**Scotland**	38	**USA**	16	**Northampton**	2,088*

T: Shelford (3), Thompson,   T: Niu (2), Lewis
Ketteridge, How, M. Smith   G: Niu (2)
G: Thompson (5)

Third round

Fri. 20 Oct.	**Cook Islands**	21	**Scotland**	10	**Castleford**	2,889

T: Tariu (2), Shepherd (2)   T: A. Tait (2)
G: Noovao (2), Davys (dg)   G: Thompson

Fri. 20 Oct.	**Russia**	28	**USA**	26	**Warrington**	1,950

T: Gavrilin (3), Kiryakov,   T: Preston (2), Maffie,
Romanov, Netchaev   Wallace, Broussard
G: Scheglov, Netchaev   G: Niu (3)

GROUP TWO

Mon. 16 Oct.	**Ireland**	48	**Moldova**	26	**Rochdale**	1,235

T: Gordon (3), Crompton,   T: Piskunov (2), Olar,
Foy, Casey, Grainey, Smith,   Krivtsov, Benkovskiy
McElhatton   G: Olar (3)
G: Comerford (6)

Wed. 18 Oct.	**Moldova**	24	**Morocco**	19	**Northampton**	2,088*

T: Piskunov (3), Strakh,   T: Katir (2), Mahabi
V. Sapega   G: Echalouki (2), Mahabi,
G: Olar, Piskunov   Katir (dg)

251

| Fri. 20 Oct. | **Ireland** | 42 | **Morocco** | 6 | **Dewsbury** | 1,756 |

T: Ricky Smith, Horrigan, Grainey, Gordon, Comerford, Foy, Browne, Sullivan
G: Comerford (5)

T: Bibarss
G: Amar

* double-header

GROUP ONE FINAL TABLE

	P	W	D	L	F	A	Pts
Cook Islands	3	3	0	0	143	36	6
Scotland	3	2	0	1	82	46	2
Russia	3	1	0	2	57	118	2
USA	3	0	0	3	48	130	0

GROUP TWO FINAL TABLE

	P	W	D	L	F	A	Pts
Ireland	2	2	0	0	90	32	4
Moldova	2	1	0	1	50	67	2
Morocco	2	0	0	2	25	66	0

LEADING SCORERS
Most tries: 6 by James Cuthers (Cook Islands)
Ngere Tariu (Cook Islands)
Most goals: 19 by Meti Noovao (Cook Islands)
Most points: 50 (3t, 19g) by Meti Noovao (Cook Islands)

Stand-off
Brad Fittler, captain of Australia in the victorious 1995
three-match Test series against New Zealand.

DOWN UNDER

WINFIELD CUP
1995 Premiership Grand Final

The last Winfield Cup Grand Final was a fitting triumph for Sydney Bulldogs captain Terry Lamb, who carried off the trophy after a 17-4 victory over league leaders Manly-Warringah brought down the curtain on his record-breaking career of 328 first grade games.

The former Australian Test stand off went out in style with an inspiring performance that completed a remarkable end-of-season flourish by the former Canterbury-Bankstown club. They became the lowest placed team – they finished sixth – to lift the trophy after the play-offs were extended to the top eight for the first time following the expansion of the league to 20 clubs with the introduction of Auckland Warriors, Perth Western Reds, South Queensland Crushers and North Queensland Cowboys.

Man of the Match Jim Dymock's biggest single contribution to victory was his superb pass round a defender that enabled Simon Gillies to put in Steve Price for the first of the Bulldogs' three tries in the 21st minute. Although Dymock's pass appeared to be forward on the TV replays it proved to be the breakthrough and Manly struggled to get back into the game.

There was also controversy about the second touchdown as it came after a sixth tackle but referee Eddie Ward allowed it and Glen Hughes claimed the quickest try in Grand Final history — just 15 seconds after going on as a 60th minute substitute.

Chris Anderson had an additional claim to fame as he became the first to achieve the triple of being a winner of the English Challenge Cup and Championship plus Australia's Grand Final as both a player and coach. He had won Challenge Cup medals with Widnes and Halifax and also steered the latter to Cup and Championship triumphs as a player-coach.

Winfield's involvement with the competition ended after 14 years because of Australia's new, stringent laws governing the sponsorship of sport. The advent of Super League also meant things would never be the same again as Manly stayed with the Australian RL and the Bulldogs joined Rupert Murdoch's breakaway group.

1995 WINFIELD CUP

	P	W	D	L	F	A	Pts
Manly-Warringah	22	20	0	2	687	248	40
Canberra	22	20	0	2	634	255	40
Brisbane Broncos	22	17	0	5	600	364	34
Cronulla-Sutherland	22	16	0	6	516	287	32
Newcastle	22	15	0	7	549	396	28
Sydney Bulldogs	22	14	0	8	468	352	28
St. George	22	13	0	9	583	382	26
North Sydney	22	11	2	9	542	331	24
Sydney City Roosters	22	12	0	10	466	406	24
Auckland Warriors	22	13	0	9	544	493	24*
Western Reds	22	11	0	11	361	549	22
Illawarra	22	10	1	11	519	431	21
Western Suburbs	22	10	0	12	459	534	20
Penrith	22	9	0	13	481	484	18
Sydney Tigers	22	7	0	15	309	591	14
Sth. Queensland Crushers	22	6	1	15	303	502	13
Gold Coast	22	4	1	17	350	628	9
South Sydney	22	4	1	17	319	686	9
Parramatta	22	3	0	19	310	690	6
Nth. Queensland Cowboys	22	2	0	20	269	660	4

* Two points deducted for breach of substitute rule

WINFIELD CUP GRAND FINAL

Sunday 24 September 1995   **Sydney Football Stadium**

SYDNEY BULLDOGS 17		**MANLY-WARRINGAH 4**
Rod Silva	1.	Matthew Ridge
Jason Williams	2.	Craig Hancock
John Timu	3.	Danny Moore
Matthew Ryan	4.	Terry Hill
Darryl Halligan	5.	John Hopoate
Terry Lamb, Capt.	6.	Cliff Lyons
Craig Polla-Mounter	7.	Geoff Toovey, Capt.
Darren Britt	8.	David Gillespie
Jason Hetherington	9.	Des Hasler
Dean Pay	10.	Mark Carroll
Steven Price	11.	Steve Menzies
Simon Gillies	12.	Ian Roberts
Jim Dymock	13.	Nik Kosef

Substitutes:
Mitch Newton for Britt (28 min.)
Jason Smith for Pay (34 min.)
Glen Hughes for Smith (60 min.)

Substitutes:
Owen Cunningham for Carroll (25 min.)
Solomon Haumono for Gillespie (49 min.)
Daniel Gartner for Kosef (67 min.)

T: Price, Hughes, Silva
G: Halligan (2), Lamb (dg)
Sin bin: Lamb (6 min.)
Coach: Chris Anderson
Attendance: 41,127

G: Ridge (2)

Coach: Bob Fulton
Referee: Eddie Ward
Half-time: 6-4
Clive Churchill Medal for Man of the Match: Jim Dymock (Sydney Bulldogs)

WINFIELD CUP PLAY-OFF

Quarter-finals
Brisbane Broncos 8 v. Canberra 14
(At Suncorp Stadium, Brisbane)
North Sydney 12 v. Newcastle 20
(At Parramatta Stadium)
Sydney Bulldogs 12 v. St. George 8
(At Sydney Football Stadium)
Manly 24 v. Cronulla 20
(At Sydney Football Stadium)
Semi-finals
Cronulla 18 v. Newcastle 19
Sydney Bulldogs 24 v. Brisbane Broncos 10
(Both at Sydney Football Stadium)

Preliminary finals
Sydney Bulldogs 25 v. Canberra 6
Manly 12 v. Newcastle 4
(Both at Sydney Football Stadium)
Grand Final
Sydney Bulldogs 17 v. Manly 4
(At Sydney Football Stadium)
LEADING SCORERS
(Not including play-offs)
Tries
21 Steve Menzies (Manly)
Goals (Including drop goals)
100 Matthew Ridge (Manly)
Points
239 Matthew Ridge (Manly)

255

BRITISH PLAYERS IN 1995 WINFIELD CUP

A total of 14 British players appeared in the Winfield Cup during the 1995 season, equalling the record of 1989. They included five players who were transferred from their British clubs — Wigan's Andy Platt, Denis Betts and Phil Clarke plus St. John Ellis and Mike Ford of Castleford. The others signed just for a few months before returning home.

Ford was the most active of the British players as he appeared in 15 matches for the South Queensland Crushers, including one as a substitute. Betts was the top tryscorer with five, while Jonathan Davies was the top pointscorer with 43 from a try and 20 goals including one drop goal.

No British players appeared in the Grand Final for a sixth successive year.

British players' records in the 1995 Winfield Cup, including play-off matches:

	App	T	G	Pts
Allan Bateman (Warrington-Cronulla)	7+2	1	0	4
Denis Betts (Wigan-Auckland Warriors)	11	5	0	20
Phil Clarke (Wigan-Eastern Suburbs)	10	2	0	8
Jonathan Davies (Warrington-N. Queensland Cowboys)	9	1	20(1)	43
St. John Ellis (Castleford-S. Queensland Crushers)	8+2	1	13	30
Vince Fawcett (Workington T.-Parramatta)	5+1	2	0	8
Mike Ford (Castleford-S. Queensland Crushers)	14+1	3	0	12
Lee Jackson (Sheffield E.-South Sydney)	8	2	0	8
Chris Joynt (St. Helens-Newcastle)	4+3	1	0	4
Barrie-Jon Mather (Wigan-Western Reds)	10	4	0	16
David Myers (Bradford B.-Western Suburbs)	1	0	0	0
Andy Platt (Wigan-Auckland Warriors)	13+1	0	0	0
Daio Powell (Wakefield T.-Western Reds)	0+1	0	0	0
Dean Sampson (Castleford-Parramatta)	3+3	2	0	8

( ) denotes drop goal included in total

Great Britain loose forward Phil Clarke, who made 10 appearances for new club Eastern Suburbs in 1995.

STATE OF ORIGIN MATCHES * Denotes captain

15 May
Sydney
New South Wales 0
Tim Brasher (Sydney Tigers)
Rod Wishart (Illawarra)
Terry Hill (Manly)
Paul McGregor (Illawarra)
Craig Hancock (Manly)
Matthew Johns (Newcastle)
Andrew Johns (Newcastle)
Paul Harragon (Newcastle)
Jim Serdaris (Western Suburbs)
Mark Carroll (Manly)
Brad Mackay (Western Reds)
Steve Menzies (Manly)
*Brad Fittler (Penrith)
Subs: David Fairleigh (N. Sydney)
    Greg Florimo (N. Sydney)
    Matt Seers (N. Sydney)
    Adam Muir (Newcastle)

31 May
Melbourne
New South Wales 12
Tim Brasher (Sydney Tigers)
Rod Wishart (Illawarra) 2g
Terry Hill (Manly)
Paul McGregor (Illawarra)
John Hopoate (Manly)
*Brad Fittler (Penrith)
Andrew Johns (Newcastle)
Paul Harragon (Newcastle)
Jim Serdaris (Western Suburbs) 1t
Dean Pay (Sydney Bulldogs)
David Barnhill (St. George)
Brad Mackay (St. George)
Greg Florimo (N. Sydney)
Subs: Steve Menzies (Manly)
    Brett Rodwell (Illawarra) 1t
    David Fairleigh (N. Sydney)
    Adam Muir (Newcastle)

12 June
Brisbane
New South Wales 16
Tim Brasher (Sydney Tigers) 1t
Rod Wishart (Illawarra) 1t, 2g
Terry Hill (Manly)
Paul McGregor (Illawarra)
David Hall (North Sydney)
Matthew Johns (Newcastle)
Geoff Toovey (Manly)
Paul Harragon (Newcastle)
Jim Serdaris (Western Suburbs)
Mark Carroll (Manly)
Steve Menzies (Manly)
Adam Muir (Newcastle) 1t
*Brad Fittler (Penrith)
Subs: David Barnhill (St. George)
    David Fairleigh (N. Sydney)
    Greg Florimo (N. Sydney)
    Matt Seers (N. Sydney)

Queensland 2
Robbie O'Davis (Newcastle)
Brett Dallas (Sydney Bulldogs)
Mark Coyne (St. George)
Danny Moore (Manly)
Matt Sing (Penrith)
Dale Shearers (S.Q. Crushers)
Adrian Lam (Eastern Suburbs)
Gavin Allen (Brisbane Broncos)
Wayne Bartrim (St. George) 1g
Tony Hearn (North Sydney)
*Trevor Gillmeister (S.Q. Crushers)
Gary Larson (North Sydney)
Billy Moore (North Sydney)
Subs: Mark Hohn (S.Q. Crushers)
    Terry Cook (S.Q. Crushers)
    Craig Teevan (S.Q. Crushers)
    Ben Ikin (Gold Coast)
Referee: Eddie Ward
Man of the Match: Larson

Queensland 20
Robbie O'Davis (Newcastle)
Brett Dallas (Sydney Bulldogs) 1t
Mark Coyne (St. George) 1t
Danny Moore (Manly)
Matt Sing (Penrith)
Jason Smith (Sydney Bulldogs)
Adrian Lam (Eastern Suburbs) 1t
Gavin Allen (Brisbane Broncos)
Wayne Bartrim (St. George) 4g
Tony Hearn (North Sydney)
*Trevor Gillmeister (S.Q. Crushers)
Gary Larson (North Sydney)
Billy Moore (North Sydney)
Subs: Mark Hohn (S.Q. Crushers)
    Terry Cook (S.Q. Crushers)
    Craig Teevan (S.Q. Crushers)
    Ben Ikin (Gold Coast)
Referee: Eddie Ward
Man of the Match: Smith

Queensland 24
Robbie O'Davis (Newcastle)
Brett Dallas (Sydney Bulldogs) 1t
Mark Coyne (St. George)
Danny Moore (Manly) 1t
Matt Sing (Penrith)
Jason Smith (Sydney Bulldogs) 1t
Adrian Lam (Eastern Suburbs)
Gavin Allen (Brisbane Broncos)
Wayne Bartrim (St. George) 4g
Tony Hearn (North Sydney)
*Trevor Gillmeister (S.Q. Crushers)
Gary Larson (North Sydney)
Billy Moore (North Sydney)
Subs: Mark Hohn (S.Q. Crushers)
    Terry Cook (S.Q. Crushers)
    Craig Teevan (S.Q. Crushers)
    Ben Ikin (Gold Coast) 1t
Referee: David Manson
Man of the Match: Larson

AUSTRALIA v. NEW ZEALAND 1995 TEST SERIES *Denotes captain

23 June	7 July	14 July
Brisbane	**Sydney**	**Brisbane**
Australia 26	**Australia 20**	**Australia 46**
Tim Brasher	Tim Brasher	Tim Brasher
Brett Dallas 2t	Matt Sing	Robbie O'Davis 1t
Mark Coyne	Mark Coyne	Greg Florimo
Terry Hill 1t	Danny Moore	Danny Moore 1t
Rod Wishart 5g	Rod Wishart 5g	Rod Wishart 1t, 7g
*Brad Fittler	*Brad Fittler 1dg	*Brad Fittler
Geoff Toovey	Geoff Toovey	Geoff Toovey
David Gillespie	David Gillespie	David Gillespie 1t
Wayne Bartrim	Wayne Bartrim 1t	Jim Serdaris
Mark Carroll	Mark Carroll	Mark Carroll
Steve Menzies	Steve Menzies 1t	Steve Menzies 2t
Gary Larson	Gary Larson	Gary Larson
Jason Smith	Jason Smith	Jason Smith
Subs: Trevor Gillmeister	Subs: Trevor Gillmeister	Subs: Trevor Gillmeister
Adam Muir 1t	Greg Florimo 1dg	Jamie Ainscough 1t
Danny Moore	Paul Harragon	Paul Harragon 1t
Robbie O'Davis	Matthew Johns	Matthew Johns

New Zealand 8	**New Zealand 10**	**New Zealand 10**
Matthew Ridge 2g	Matthew Ridge 3g	Matthew Ridge 1g
Sean Hoppe	Sean Hoppe 1t	Sean Hoppe
Jarrod McCracken	Jarrod McCracken	Jarrod McCracken
Richard Blackmore	Ruben Wiki	Ruben Wiki
Jason Williams	Henry Paul	Henry Paul
Gene Ngamu	Gene Ngamu	Gene Ngamu 1t
Gary Freeman	*Gary Freeman	*Gary Freeman
*John Lomax	Quentin Pongia	Quentin Pongia
Syd Eru	Syd Eru	Syd Eru
Brent Stuart	Jason Lowrie	Jason Lowrie
Quentin Pongia	Tony Tatupu	Stephen Kearney
Stephen Kearney 1t	Tony Iro	Tony Iro
Brendon Tuuta	Brendon Tuuta	Tony Tatupu
Subs: Jason Lowrie	Subs: Brent Stuart	Subs: Brent Stuart
Henry Paul	Tony Tuimavave	Brendon Tuuta
Logan Edwards	John Timu	John Timu
Darryl Halligan		Darryl Halligan 2g
Referee: Dennis Hale (NZ)	Referee: Phil Houston (NZ)	Referee: Phil Houston (NZ)
Att: 25,304	Att: 27,568	Att: 20,803

FRANCE TOUR OF NEW ZEALAND 1995

Date	Result	Score	Opposition	Venue	Attendance
6 June	Won	24-2	**Waikato** T: Banquet (2), Millet, Sirvent G: Millet (2), Banquet (2)	Huntly	

Date	Result	Score	Opposition	Venue	Attendance
9 June	Lost	6-22	**NEW ZEALAND**	Auckland	15,000

New Zealand:
Matthew Ridge (1g); Sean Hoppe (1t), Jarrod McCracken, Richard Blackmore (1t), Jason Williams; Gene Ngamu (2t), Gary Freeman; John Lomax (Capt.), Syd Eru, Brent Stuart, Stephen Kearney, Quentin Pongia, Brendon Tuuta.
Subs: Darryl Halligan (2g), Logan Edwards, Henry Paul, Jason Lowrie.

France:
Stephane Millet (1g); Jean-Marc Garcia, Frederic Banquet, David Despin, Pascal Bomati; Jacques Pech, Patrick Entat (Capt.); Henry Boudebza, Patrick Torreilles, Frederic Texeido, Frederic Sana, Didier Cabestany (1t), Thierry Valero.
Subs: Stephane Tena, Claude Sirvent, Pascal Jampy, Gael Tallec.
Referee: Marcel Chanfreau (France)

Date	Result	Score	Opposition	Venue	Attendance
13 June	Lost	10-40	**North Harbour** T: Bomati, Sirvent G: Dulac	Takapuna	

Date	Result	Score	Opposition	Venue	Attendance
16 June	Drew	16-16	**NEW ZEALAND**	Palmerston North	10,400

New Zealand:
Matthew Ridge (1t); Sean Hoppe, Jarrod McCracken (1t), Richard Blackmore, Darryl Halligan (2g); Gene Ngamu, Gary Freeman; John Lomax (Capt.), Syd Eru (1t), Brent Stuart, Stephen Kearney, Quentin Pongia, Brendon Tuuta.
Subs: Henry Paul, Logan Edwards, Jason Lowrie.

France:
Stephane Millet; Brian Coles (1t), Jean-Marc Garcia, Frederic Banquet (2t, 2g), Pascal Bomati; Jacques Pech, Patrick Entat (Capt.); Didier Cabestany, Patrick Torreilles, Frederic Texeido, Frederic Sana, Pascal Jampy, Thierry Valero.
Subs: Arnaud Dulac, Lilian Hebert, Gael Tallec, Claude Sirvent.
Referee: Marcel Chanfreau (France)

TOUR SUMMARY

P	W	D	L	F	A
4	1	1	1	56	80

TOUR REGISTER
Manager: Tas Baitieri
Coach: Ivan Greseque
Captain: Patrick Entat

Player	Club	App	T	G	Pts
BANET, Vincent	XIII Catalan	1+1	0	0	0
BANQUET, Frederic	Featherstone R.	3	4	4	24
BOMATI, Pascal	XIII Catalan	2+1	1	0	4
BOUDEBZA, Hadj	St. Esteve	2	0	0	0
CABESTANY, Didier	XIII Catalan	3	1	0	4
CHAMORIN, Pierre	St. Esteve	1	0	0	0
COLES, Brian	XIII Catalan	2	1	0	4
DESPIN, David	Limoux	2	0	0	0
DEVECCHI, Fabien	Lezignan	2	0	0	0
DEVERGIE, Thierry	Lyon Villeurbanne	0+2	0	0	0
DULAC, Arnaud	St. Gaudens	1+1	0	1	2
ENTAT, Patrick	Leeds	2	0	0	0
FRAISSE, David	Bradford N.	2	0	0	0
GARCIA, Jean-Marc	St. Esteve	2	0	0	0
HEBERT, Lilian	Pia	2+1	0	0	0
JAMPY, Pascal	St. Esteve	3+1	0	0	0
MILLET, Stephane	St. Gaudens	3+1	1	3	10
PECH, Jacques	Pia	2	0	0	0
SANA, Frederic	St. Esteve	3	0	0	0
SIRVENT, Claude	St. Gaudens	2+2	2	0	8
TALLEC, Gael	Wigan	1+3	0	0	0
TEIXIDO, Frederic	Limoux	2+1	0	0	0
TENA, Stephane	XIII Catalan	2+1	0	0	0
TORREILLES, Patrick	Pia	2	0	0	0
VALERO, Thierry	Lezignan	3	0	0	0
VERGES, Bruno	St. Esteve	2	0	0	0
			10	8	56

● On the way home from New Zealand, France played a match against Canada in Montreal on 18 June and won 72-32, but it did not have full international status and is not included in their tour records.

Great Britain scrum half Bobbie Goulding on the attack in the second John Smith's Test against Australia in 1994, with teammate Daryl Powell in support.

GREAT BRITAIN

GREAT BRITAIN

TESTS

● Although early Tests were played under the titles of Northern Union or England, it is acceptable to regard them as Great Britain.
W - Won, D - Drawn, L - Lost refer to Great Britain.

GREAT BRITAIN v. AUSTRALIA

Date	Result	Score	Venue	Attendance
12 Dec. 1908	D	22-22	QPR, London	2,000
23 Jan. 1909	W	15-5	Newcastle	22,000
15 Feb. 1909	W	6-5	Birmingham	9,000
18 Jun. 1910	W	27-20	Sydney	42,000
2 Jul. 1910	W	22-17	Brisbane	18,000
8 Nov. 1911	L	10-19	Newcastle	6,500
16 Dec. 1911	D	11-11	Edinburgh	6,000
1 Jan. 1912	L	8-33	Birmingham	4,000
27 Jun. 1914	W	23-5	Sydney	40,000
29 Jun. 1914	L	7-12	Sydney	55,000
4 Jul. 1914	W	14-6	Sydney	34,420
26 Jun. 1920	L	4-8	Brisbane	28,000
3 Jul. 1920	L	8-21	Sydney	40,000
10 Jul. 1920	W	23-13	Sydney	32,000
1 Oct. 1921	W	6-5	Leeds	32,000
5 Nov. 1921	L	2-16	Hull	21,504
14 Jan. 1922	W	6-0	Salford	21,000
23 Jun. 1924	W	22-3	Sydney	50,000
28 Jun. 1924	W	5-3	Sydney	33,842
12 Jul. 1924	L	11-21	Brisbane	36,000
23 Jun. 1928	W	15-12	Brisbane	39,200
14 Jul. 1928	W	8-0	Sydney	44,548
21 Jul. 1928	L	14-21	Sydney	37,000
5 Oct. 1929	L	8-31	Hull K.R.	20,000
9 Nov. 1929	W	9-3	Leeds	31,402
4 Jan. 1930	D	0-0	Swinton	34,709
15 Jan. 1930	W	3-0	Rochdale	16,743
6 Jun. 1932	W	8-6	Sydney	70,204
18 Jun. 1932	L	6-15	Brisbane	26,500
16 Jul. 1932	W	18-13	Sydney	50,053
7 Oct. 1933	W	4-0	Belle Vue, Manchester	34,000
11 Nov. 1933	W	7-5	Leeds	29,618
16 Dec. 1933	W	19-16	Swinton	10,990
29 Jun. 1936	L	8-24	Sydney	63,920
4 Jul. 1936	W	12-7	Brisbane	29,486
18 Jul. 1936	W	12-7	Sydney	53,546
16 Oct. 1937	W	5-4	Leeds	31,949
13 Nov. 1937	W	13-3	Swinton	31,724
18 Dec. 1937	L	3-13	Huddersfield	9,093
17 Jun. 1946	D	8-8	Sydney	64,527
6 Jul. 1946	W	14-5	Brisbane	40,500
20 Jul. 1946	W	20-7	Sydney	35,294
9 Oct. 1948	W	23-21	Leeds	36,529
6 Nov. 1948	W	16-7	Swinton	36,354
29 Jan. 1949	W	23-9	Bradford	42,000
12 Jun. 1950	W	6-4	Sydney	47,215
1 Jul. 1950	L	3-15	Brisbane	35,000
22 Jul. 1950	L	2-5	Sydney	47,178
4 Oct. 1952	W	19-6	Leeds	34,505
8 Nov. 1952	W	21-5	Swinton	32,421
13 Dec. 1952	L	7-27	Bradford	30,509
12 Jun. 1954	L	12-37	Sydney	65,884
3 Jul. 1954	W	38-21	Brisbane	46,355
17 Jul. 1954	L	16-20	Sydney	67,577
17 Nov. 1956	W	21-10	Wigan	22,473
1 Dec. 1956	L	9-22	Bradford	23,634
15 Dec. 1956	W	19-0	Swinton	17,542
14 Jun. 1958	L	8-25	Sydney	68,777
5 Jul. 1958	W	25-18	Brisbane	32,965
19 Jul. 1958	W	40-17	Sydney	68,720
17 Oct. 1959	L	14-22	Swinton	35,224
21 Nov. 1959	W	11-10	Leeds	30,184
12 Dec. 1959	W	18-12	Wigan	26,089
9 Jun. 1962	W	31-12	Sydney	70,174
30 Jun. 1962	W	17-10	Brisbane	34,766
14 Jul. 1962	L	17-18	Sydney	42,104
16 Oct. 1963	L	2-28	Wembley	13,946
9 Nov. 1963	L	12-50	Swinton	30,833
30 Nov. 1963	W	16-5	Leeds	20,497
25 Jun. 1966	W	17-13	Sydney	57,962
16 Jul. 1966	L	4-6	Brisbane	45,057
23 Jul. 1966	L	14-19	Sydney	63,503
21 Oct. 1967	W	16-11	Leeds	22,293
3 Nov. 1967	L	11-17	White City, London	17,445
9 Dec. 1967	L	3-11	Swinton	13,615
6 Jun. 1970	L	15-37	Brisbane	42,807
20 Jun. 1970	W	28-7	Sydney	60,962
4 Jul. 1970	W	21-17	Sydney	61,258
3 Nov. 1973	W	21-12	Wembley	9,874
24 Nov. 1973	L	6-14	Leeds	16,674
1 Dec. 1973	L	5-15	Warrington	10,019
15 Jun. 1974	L	6-12	Brisbane	30,280
6 Jul. 1974	W	16-11	Sydney	48,006
20 Jul. 1974	L	18-22	Sydney	55,505
21 Oct. 1978	L	9-15	Wigan	17,644
5 Nov. 1978	W	18-14	Bradford	26,447
18 Nov. 1978	L	6-23	Leeds	29,627
16 Jun. 1979	L	0-35	Sydney	23,051
30 Jun. 1979	L	16-24	Sydney	26,837
14 Jul. 1979	L	2-28	Sydney	16,844
30 Oct. 1982	L	4-40	Hull C. FC	26,771
20 Nov. 1982	L	6-27	Wigan	23,216
28 Nov. 1982	L	8-32	Leeds	17,318
9 Jun. 1984	L	8-25	Sydney	30,190
26 Jun. 1984	L	6-18	Brisbane	26,534
7 Jul. 1984	L	7-20	Sydney	18,756

25 Oct. 1986	L	16-38	Man U. FC	50,583	* 24 Nov. 1990	L	0-14	Elland Rd,	
8 Nov. 1986	L	4-34	Elland Rd,					Leeds	32,500
			Leeds	30,808	12 Jun. 1992	L	6-22	Sydney	40,141
* 22 Nov. 1986	L	15-24	Wigan	20,169	26 Jun. 1992	W	33-10	Melbourne	30,257
11 Jun. 1988	L	6-17	Sydney	24,202	* 3 Jul. 1992	L	10-16	Brisbane	32,313
28 Jun. 1988	L	14-34	Brisbane	27,103	22 Oct. 1994	W	8-4	Wembley	57,034
* 9 Jul. 1988	W	26-12	Sydney	15,994	5 Nov. 1994	L	8-38	Man U. FC	43,930
27 Oct. 1990	W	19-12	Wembley	54,569	20 Nov. 1994	L	4-23	Elland Rd,	
10 Nov. 1990	L	10-14	Man U. FC	46,615				Leeds	39,468

* Also World Cup match.

	Played	Won	Drawn	Lost	Tries	Goals	Dr	Pts for
Great Britain	111	53	4	54	264	276	7	1382
Australia	111	54	4	53	320	343	7	1718

GREAT BRITAIN-AUSTRALIA TEST MATCH RECORDS

Britain

Highest score:	40-17 Third Test at Sydney, 19 July 1958
Widest margin win:	As above and
	33-10 Second Test at Melbourne, 26 June 1992
Most tries in a match:	4 by Jim Leytham (Wigan) Second Test at Brisbane, 2 July 1910
Most goals in a match:	10 by Lewis Jones (Leeds) Second Test at Brisbane, 3 July 1954
Most points in a match:	20 by Lewis Jones (as above)
	20 (2t, 7g) by Roger Millward (Hull K.R.) Second Test at Sydney, 20 June 1970
Biggest attendance:	57,034 First Test at Wembley, London, 22 October 1994

● For the World Cup final at Wembley on 24 October 1992, there was an attendance of 73,631

Australia

Highest score:	50-12 Second Test at Swinton, 9 Nov 1963 (Also widest margin win)
Most tries in a match:	3 by Jimmy Devereux, First Test at QPR, London, 12 December 1908
	3 by Reg Gasnier, First Test at Swinton, 17 October 1959
	3 by Reg Gasnier, First Test at Wembley, 16 October 1963
	3 by Ken Irvine, Second Test at Swinton, 9 November 1963
	3 by Ken Irvine, Third Test at Sydney, 23 July 1966
	3 by Gene Miles, First Test at Old Trafford, Manchester, 25 October 1986
	3 by Michael O'Connor, First Test at Old Trafford, Manchester, 25 October 1986
Most goals in a match:	10 by Mick Cronin, First Test at Brisbane, 16 June 1979
Most points in a match:	22 (3t, 5g) by Michael O'Connor, First Test at Old Trafford, Manchester, 25 October 1986
Biggest attendance:	70,204 First Test at Sydney, 6 June 1932

● In a World Cup match at Perpignan, France, on 29 October 1972, Bobby Fulton scored 3 tries

GREAT BRITAIN v. NEW ZEALAND

Date		Result	Venue	Attendance
25 Jan.	1908	W 14-6	Leeds	8,182
8 Feb.	1908	L 6-18	Chelsea	14,000
15 Feb.	1908	L 5-8	Cheltenham	4,000
30 Jul.	1910	W 52-20	Auckland	16,000
1 Aug.	1914	W 16-13	Auckland	15,000
31 Jul.	1920	W 31-7	Auckland	34,000
7 Aug.	1920	W 19-3	Christchurch	10,000
14 Aug.	1920	W 11-10	Wellington	4,000
2 Aug.	1924	L 8-16	Auckland	22,000
6 Aug.	1924	L 11-13	Wellington	6,000
9 Aug.	1924	W 31-18	Dunedin	14,000
2 Oct.	1926	W 28-20	Wigan	14,500
13 Nov.	1926	W 21-11	Hull	7,000
15 Jan.	1927	W 32-17	Leeds	6,000
4 Aug.	1928	L 13-17	Auckland	28,000
18 Aug.	1928	W 13-5	Dunedin	12,000
25 Aug.	1928	W 6-5	Christchurch	21,000
30 Jul.	1932	W 24-9	Auckland	25,000
13 Aug.	1932	W 25-14	Christchurch	5,000
20 Aug.	1932	W 20-18	Auckland	6,500
8 Aug.	1936	W 10-8	Auckland	25,000
15 Aug.	1936	W 23-11	Auckland	17,000
10 Aug.	1946	L 8-13	Auckland	10,000
4 Oct.	1947	W 11-10	Leeds	28,445
8 Nov.	1947	L 7-10	Swinton	29,031
20 Dec.	1947	W 25-9	Bradford	42,680
29 Jul.	1950	L 10-16	Christchurch	10,000
12 Aug.	1950	L 13-20	Auckland	20,000
6 Oct.	1951	W 21-15	Bradford	37,475
10 Nov.	1951	W 20-19	Swinton	29,938
15 Dec.	1951	W 16-12	Leeds	18,649
24 Jul.	1954	W 27-7	Auckland	22,097
31 Jul.	1954	L 14-20	Greymouth	4,240
14 Aug.	1954	W 12-6	Auckland	6,186
8 Oct.	1955	W 25-6	Swinton	21,937
12 Nov.	1955	W 27-12	Bradford	24,443
17 Dec.	1955	L 13-28	Leeds	10,438
26 Jul.	1958	L 10-15	Auckland	25,000
9 Aug.	1958	W 32-15	Auckland	25,000
30 Sep.	1961	L 11-29	Leeds	16,540
21 Oct.	1961	W 23-10	Bradford	19,980
4 Nov.	1961	W 35-19	Swinton	22,536
28 Jul.	1962	L 0-19	Auckland	14,976
11 Aug.	1962	L 8-27	Auckland	16,411
25 Sep.	1965	W 7-2	Swinton	8,541
23 Oct.	1965	W 15-9	Bradford	15,740
6 Nov.	1965	D 9-9	Wigan	7,919
6 Aug.	1966	W 25-8	Auckland	14,494
20 Aug.	1966	W 22-14	Auckland	10,657
11 Jul.	1970	W 19-15	Auckland	15,948
19 Jul.	1970	W 23-9	Christchurch	8,600
25 Jul.	1970	W 33-16	Auckland	13,137
25 Sep.	1971	L 13-18	Salford	3,764
16 Oct.	1971	L 14-17	Castleford	4,108
6 Nov.	1971	W 12-3	Leeds	5,479
27 Jul.	1974	L 8-13	Auckland	10,466
4 Aug.	1974	W 17-8	Christchurch	6,316
10 Aug.	1974	W 20-0	Auckland	11,574
21 Jul.	1979	W 16-8	Auckland	9,000
5 Aug.	1979	W 22-7	Christchurch	8,500
11 Aug.	1979	L 11-18	Auckland	7,000
18 Oct.	1980	D 14-14	Wigan	7,031
2 Nov.	1980	L 8-12	Bradford	10,946
15 Nov.	1980	W 10-2	Leeds	8,210
14 Jul.	1984	L 0-12	Auckland	10,238
22 Jul.	1984	L 12-28	Christchurch	3,824
28 Jul.	1984	L 16-32	Auckland	7,967
19 Oct.	1985	L 22-24	Leeds	12,591
2 Nov.	1985	W 25-8	Wigan	15,506
* 9 Nov.	1985	D 6-6	Elland Rd, Leeds	22,209
* 17 Jul.	1988	L 10-12	Christchurch	8,525
21 Oct.	1989	L 16-24	Man U. FC	18,273
28 Oct.	1989	W 26-6	Elland Rd, Leeds	13,073
* 11 Nov.	1989	W 10-6	Wigan	20,346
24 Jun.	1990	W 11-10	Palmerston N.	8,073
8 Jul.	1990	W 16-14	Auckland	7,843
* 15 Jul.	1990	L 18-21	Christchurch	3,133
12 Jul.	1992	L 14-15	Palmerston N.	11,548
19 Jul.	1992	W 16-14	Auckland	10,223
16 Oct.	1993	W 17-0	Wembley	36,131
30 Oct.	1993	W 29-12	Wigan	16,502
6 Nov.	1993	W 29-10	Leeds	15,139

* Also World Cup match.

	Played	Won	Drawn	Lost	Tries	Goals	Dr	Pts for
Great Britain	82	51	3	28	291	236	8	1401
New Zealand	82	28	3	51	185	232	2	1062

GREAT BRITAIN-NEW ZEALAND TEST MATCH RECORDS

Britain

Highest score:	52-20 First Test at Auckland, 30 July 1910 (Also widest margin win)
Most tries in a match:	4 by Billy Boston (Wigan) First Test at Auckland, 24 July 1954
	4 by Garry Schofield (Hull) Second Test at Wigan, 2 November 1985
Most goals in a match:	7 by Eric Fraser (Warrington) Second Test at Auckland, 9 August 1958
	7 by Neil Fox (Wakefield T.) Third Test at Swinton, 4 November 1961
Most points in a match:	16 (4t) by Garry Schofield (Hull) Second Test at Wigan, 2 November 1985
Biggest attendance:	42,680 Third Test at Bradford, 20 December 1947

● In a World Cup Match at Pau, France, on 4 November 1972, Britain won 53-19 with John Holmes (Leeds) scoring 26 points from 10 goals and two tries.
In a World Cup match at Sydney on 8 June 1968, Bev Risman scored seven goals.

New Zealand

Highest score:	32-16 Third Test at Auckland, 28 July 1984
Widest margin win:	19-0 First Test at Auckland, 28 July 1962
	27-8 Second Test at Auckland, 11 August 1962

No player has scored three tries or more in a Test.

Most goals and points:	7g-14pts by Des White, Second Test at Greymouth, 31 July 1954
	Jack Fagan, First Test at Headingley, 30 September 1961
	Ernie Wiggs, Second Test at Auckland, 20 August 1966
Biggest attendance:	34,000 First Test at Auckland, 31 July 1920

● In a World Cup match at Sydney, Australia, on 25 June 1957, Bill Sorensen also scored seven goals, 14 points.

GREAT BRITAIN v. FRANCE

● **Results since France were given Test match status.**

Date		Res		Venue	Att
26 Jan. 1957	W	45-12	Leeds		20,221
3 Mar. 1957	D	19-19	Toulouse		16,000
10 Apr. 1957	W	29-14	St. Helens		23,250
3 Nov. 1957	W	25-14	Toulouse		15,000
23 Nov. 1957	W	44-15	Wigan		19,152
2 Mar. 1958	W	23-9	Grenoble		20,000
14 Mar. 1959	W	50-15	Leeds		22,000
5 Apr. 1959	L	15-24	Grenoble		8,500
6 Mar. 1960	L	18-20	Toulouse		15,308
26 Mar. 1960	D	17-17	St. Helens		14,000
11 Dec. 1960	W	21-10	Bordeaux		8,000
28 Jan. 1961	W	27-8	St. Helens		18,000
17 Feb. 1962	L	15-20	Wigan		17,277
11 Mar. 1962	L	13-23	Perpignan		14,000
2 Dec. 1962	L	12-17	Perpignan		5,000
3 Apr. 1963	W	42-4	Wigan		19,487
8 Mar. 1964	W	11-5	Perpignan		4,326
18 Mar. 1964	W	39-0	Leigh		4,750
6 Dec. 1964	L	8-18	Perpignan		15,000
23 Jan. 1965	W	17-7	Swinton		9,959
16 Jan. 1966	L	13-18	Perpignan		6,000
5 Mar. 1966	L	4-8	Wigan		14,004
22 Jan. 1967	W	16-13	Carcassonne		10,650
4 Mar. 1967	L	13-23	Wigan		7,448
11 Feb. 1968	W	22-13	Paris		8,000
2 Mar. 1968	W	19-8	Bradford		14,196
30 Nov. 1968	W	34-10	St. Helens		6,080
2 Feb. 1969	L	9-13	Toulouse		10,000
7 Feb. 1971	L	8-16	Toulouse		14,960
17 Mar. 1971	W	24-2	St. Helens		7,783
6 Feb. 1972	W	10-9	Toulouse		11,508
12 Mar. 1972	W	45-10	Bradford		7,313
20 Jan. 1974	W	24-5	Grenoble		5,500
17 Feb. 1974	W	29-0	Wigan		10,105
6 Dec. 1981	W	37-0	Hull		13,173

20 Dec. 1981	L	2-19	Marseilles	6,500	21 Jan. 1989	W	26-10	Wigan	8,266
20 Feb. 1983	W	20-5	Carcassonne	3,826	5 Feb. 1989	W	30-8	Avignon	6,500
6 Mar. 1983	W	17-5	Hull	6,055	18 Mar. 1990	W	8-4	Perpignan	6,000
29 Jan. 1984	W	12-0	Avignon	4,000	7 Apr. 1990	L	18-25	Leeds	6,554
17 Feb. 1984	W	10-0	Leeds	7,646	* 27 Jan. 1991	W	45-10	Perpignan	3,965
1 Mar. 1985	W	50-4	Leeds	6,491	16 Feb. 1991	W	60-4	Leeds	5,284
17 Mar. 1985	L	16-24	Perpignan	5,000	16 Feb. 1992	W	30-12	Perpignan	5,688
* 16 Feb. 1986	D	10-10	Avignon	4,000	* 7 Mar. 1992	W	36-0	Hull	5,250
1 Mar. 1986	W	24-10	Wigan	8,112	7 Mar. 1993	W	48-6	Carcassonne	5,500
* 24 Jan. 1987	W	52-4	Leeds	6,567	2 Apr. 1993	W	72-6	Leeds	8,196
8 Feb. 1987	W	20-10	Carcassonne	2,000	20 Mar. 1994	W	12-4	Carcassonne	7,000
24 Jan. 1988	W	28-14	Avignon	6,500	* Also World Cup match.				
6 Feb. 1988	W	30-12	Leeds	7,007					

	Played	Won	Drawn	Lost	Tries	Goals	Dr	Pts for
Great Britain	59	42	3	14	282	258	1	1473
France	59	14	3	42	106	137	4	625

GREAT BRITAIN-FRANCE TEST MATCH RECORDS

Britain

Highest score:	72-6 at Leeds, 2 April 1993 (Also widest margin win)
Most tries in a match:	5 by Martin Offiah (Widnes) at Leeds, 16 February 1991
Most goals in a match:	10 by Bernard Ganley (Oldham) at Wigan, 23 November 1957
	10 by Jonathan Davies (Widnes) at Leeds, 2 April 1993
Most points in a match:	21 (1t, 9g) by Lewis Jones (Leeds) at Leeds, 26 January 1957
	21 (1t, 9g) by Neil Fox (Wakefield T.) at Wigan, 3 April 1963
	21 (1t, 9g) by Neil Fox (Wakefield T.) at Leigh, 18 March 1964
Biggest attendance:	23,250 at St. Helens, 10 April 1957

France

Highest score:	25-18 at Leeds, 7 April 1990
Widest margin win:	19-2 at Marseilles, 20 December 1981
Most tries in a match:	3 by Didier Couston at Perpignan, 17 March 1985
Most goals in a match:	7 by Pierre Lacaze at Wigan, 4 March 1967
Most points in a match:	14 by Pierre Lacaze (as above)
	14 (2t, 4g) by Gilbert Benausse at Wigan, 17 February 1962
Biggest attendance:	20,000 at Grenoble, 2 March 1958

● In a World Cup match at Toulouse on 7 November 1954, there were 37,471

Additional Great Britain v. France

Pre-Test status

22 May 1952	L	12-22	Paris	16,466
24 May 1953	L	17-28	Lyons	
27 Apr. 1954	W	17-8	Bradford	14,153
11 Dec 1955	L	5-17	Paris	18,000
11 Apr. 1956	W	18-10	Bradford	10,453

Other match

31 July 1982	L	7-8	Venice	1,500

GREAT BRITAIN v. PAPUA NEW GUINEA

5 Aug. 1984	W	38-20	Mt. Hagen	7,510
* 24 Oct. 1987	W	42-0	Wigan	9,121
* 22 May 1988	W	42-22	Port Moresby	12,107

27 May 1990	L	18-20	Goroka	11,598
* 2 Jun. 1990	W	40-8	Port Moresby	5,969
* 9 Nov. 1991	W	56-4	Wigan	4,193
31 May 1992	W	20-14	Port Moresby	7,294

*Also World Cup match.

	Played	Won	Lost	Tries	Goals	Dr	Pts for
Great Britain	7	6	1	45	38	0	256
Papua New Guinea	7	1	6	14	15	2	88

GREAT BRITAIN-PAPUA NEW GUINEA TEST MATCH RECORDS

Britain
Highest score: 56-4 at Wigan, 9 November 1991 (Also widest margin win)
Most tries in a match: No player has scored 3 or more
Most goals in a match: 8 by Jonathan Davies (Widnes) at Wigan, 9 November 1991
Most points in a match: 16 by Jonathan Davies (Widnes) as above
Biggest attendance: 9,121 at Wigan, 24 October 1987

Papua New Guinea
Highest score: 22-42 at Port Moresby, 22 May 1988
Only win: 20-18 at Goroka, 27 May 1990
Most tries in a match: No player has scored 3 or more
Most goals in a match: 6 by Bal Numapo at Goroka, 27 May 1990
Most points in a match: 11 (5g, 1dg) by Bal Numapo as above
Biggest attendance: 12,107 at Port Moresby, 22 May 1988

Great Britain coaching duo Ellery Hanley (right) and assistant Gary Hetherington, at the helm for the 1994 John Smith's Test series with Australia

GREAT BRITAIN REGISTER

The following is a record of the 617 players who have appeared for Great Britain in 285 Test and World Cup matches.

It does not include matches against France before 1957, the year they were given official Test match status.

Figures in brackets are the total of appearances, with the plus sign indicating substitute appearances, e.g. (7+3).

For matches against touring teams, the year given is for the first half of the season.

World Cup matches are in bold letters except when also classified as Test matches. Substitute appearances are in lower case letters.

A - Australia, F - France, NZ - New Zealand, P - Papua New Guinea.

ACKERLEY, Alvin (2) Halifax: 1952 A; 1958 NZ
ADAMS, Les (1) Leeds: 1932 A
ADAMS, Mick (11+2) Widnes: 1979 Aa,NZ3; 1980 NZ; 1984 A2a,NZ3,P
ARKWRIGHT, Chris (+2) St. Helens: 1985 nz2
ARKWRIGHT, Jack (6) Warrington: 1936 A2,NZ; 1937 A3
ARMITT, Tom (8) Swinton: 1933 A; 1936 A2,NZ2; 1937 A3
ASHBY, Ray (2) Liverpool: 1964 F; Wigan: 1965 F
ASHCROFT, Ernest (11) Wigan: 1947 NZ2; 1950 A3,NZ; 1954 A3,NZ2
ASHCROFT, Kevin (5+1) Leigh: **1968 A**; 1968 F; 1969 F; **1970 F,NZ**; Warrington: 1974 nz
ASHTON, Eric (26) Wigan: **1957 A,NZ**; 1958 A2,NZ2; 1959 F,A3; 1960 F2; **1960 NZ,A**; 1961 NZ3; 1962 F3,A3; 1963 F,A2
ASHURST, Bill (3) Wigan: 1971 NZ; 1972 F2
ASKIN, Tom (6) Featherstone R: 1928 A3,NZ3
ASPINALL, Willie (1) Warrington: 1966 NZ
ASTON, Len (3) St. Helens: 1947 NZ3
ASTON, Mark (+1) Sheffield E: 1991 f
ATKINSON, Arthur (7) Castleford: 1929 A3; 1932 A3,NZ3; 1933 A; 1936 A
ATKINSON, John (26) Leeds: **1968 F,NZ**; 1970 A3,NZ3; **1970 A2,F,NZ**; 1971 F2,NZ; 1972 F2; **1972 A2,F,NZ**; 1973 A2; 1978 A2; 1980 NZ
AVERY, Albert (4) Oldham: 1910 A,NZ; 1911 A2

BACON, Jim (11) Leeds: 1920 A3,NZ3; 1921 A3; 1924 A; 1926 NZ
BARENDS, David (2) Bradford N: 1979 A2
BARTON, Frank (1) Wigan: 1951 NZ
BARTON, John (2) Wigan: 1960 F; 1961 NZ
BASNETT, John (2) Widnes: 1984 F; 1986 A

BASSETT, Arthur (2) Halifax: 1946 A2
BATEMAN, Allan (1+2) Warrington: 1992 F; 1993 f; 1994 a
BATES, Alan (2+2) Dewsbury: 1974 F2, nz2
BATTEN, Billy (10) Hunslet: 1907 NZ; 1908 A3; 1910 A2, NZ; 1911 A2; Hull: 1921 A
BATTEN, Eric (4) Bradford N: 1946 A2,NZ; 1947 NZ
BATTEN, Ray (3) Leeds: 1969 F; 1973 A2
BAXTER, Johnnie (1) Rochdale H: 1907 NZ
BEAMES, Jack (2) Halifax: 1921 A2
BEARDMORE, Kevin (13+1) Castleford: 1984 nz; 1987 F2; 1988 F2,P,A2,NZ; 1989 F2,NZ; 1990 F2
BELSHAW, Billy (8) Liverpool S: 1936 A3,NZ2; 1937 A; Warrington: 1937 A2
BENNETT, Jack (7) Rochdale H: 1924 A3,NZ3; Wigan: 1926 NZ
BENTHAM, Billy (2) Broughton R: 1924 NZ2
BENTHAM, Nat (10) Wigan H: 1928 A3,NZ3; Halifax: 1929 A2; Warrington: 1929 A2
BENTLEY, John (2) Leeds: 1992 F; Halifax: 1994 F
BENTLEY, Keith (1) Widnes: 1980 NZ
BENYON, Billy (5+1) St. Helens: 1971 F2,NZnz; 1972 F2
BETTS, Denis (24+1) Wigan: 1990 fF,P2,NZ3,A3; 1991 F,P; 1992 F,P,A3,NZ2, **A**; 1993 F,NZ; 1994 A3
BEVAN, Dai (1) Wigan: 1952 A
BEVAN, John (6) Warrington: 1974 A2,NZ2; 1978 A2
BEVERLEY, Harry (6) Hunslet: 1936 A3; 1937 A; Halifax: 1937 A2
BIBB, Chris (1) Featherstone R: 1990 NZ
BIRCH, Jim (1) Leeds: 1907 NZ
BISHOP, David (+1) Hull KR: 1990 f
BISHOP, Tommy (15) St. Helens: 1966 A3,NZ2; 1967 A3; 1968 F3; **1968 A,F,NZ**; 1969 F
BLAN, Billy (3) Wigan: 1951 NZ3
BLINKHORN, Tom (1) Warrington: 1929 A
BOLTON, Dave (23) Wigan: 1957 F3; 1958 F,A2; 1959 F,A3; 1960 F2; 1961 NZ3; 1962 F2,A,NZ2; 1963 F,A2
BOSTON, Billy (31) Wigan: 1954 A2,NZ3; 1955 NZ; 1956 A3; 1957 F5; **1957 F,A**; 1958 F; 1959 A; 1960 F; **1960 A**; 1961 F,NZ3; 1962 F2,A3,NZ; 1963 F
BOTT, Charlie (1) Oldham: 1966 F
BOWDEN, Jim (3) Huddersfield: 1954 A2,NZ
BOWEN, Frank (3) St. Helens Recs: 1928 NZ3
BOWERS, Joe (1) Rochdale H: 1920 NZ
BOWMAN, Eddie (4) Workington T: **1977 F,NZ,A2**
BOWMAN, Harold (8) Hull: 1924 NZ2; 1926 NZ2; 1928 A2,NZ; 1929 A
BOWMAN, Ken (3) Huddersfield: 1962 F; 1963 F,A
BOYLEN, Frank (1) Hull: 1908 A
BRADSHAW, Tommy (6) Wigan: 1947 NZ2; 1950 A3,NZ
BRIDGES, John "Keith" (3) Featherstone R: 1974 F2,A
BRIGGS, Brian (1) Huddersfield: 1954 NZ
BROGDEN, Stan (16) Huddersfield: 1929 A; 1932 A3,NZ3; 1933 A2; Leeds: 1936 A3,NZ2; 1937 A2
BROOKE, Ian (13) Bradford N: 1966 A3, NZ2; Wakefield T: 1967 A3; 1968 F2; **1968 A,F,NZ**
BROOKS, Ernie (3) Warrington: 1908 A3

BROUGH, Albert (2) Oldham: 1924 A,NZ
BROUGH, Jim (5) Leeds: 1928 A2,NZ2; 1936 A
BROWN, Gordon (6) Leeds: **1954 F2,NZ,A**; 1955 NZ2
BRYANT, Bill (4+1) Castleford: 1964 F2; 1966 Aa; 1967 F
BUCKLEY, Alan (7) Swinton: 1963 A; 1964 F; 1965 NZ; 1966 F,A2,NZ
BURGESS, Bill (16) Barrow: 1924 A3,NZ3; 1926 NZ3; 1928 A3,NZ2; 1929 A2
BURGESS, Bill (14) Barrow: 1962 F; 1963 A; 1965 NZ2; 1966 F,A3,NZ2; 1967 F,A; 1968 F; Salford: 1969 F
BURGHAM, Oliver (1) Halifax: 1911 A
BURKE, Mick (14+1) Widnes: 1980 NZ; 1981 fF; 1983 F; 1984 A3,NZ3,P; 1985 NZ3; 1986 F
BURNELL, Alf (3) Hunslet: 1951 NZ2; 1954 NZ
BURTON, Chris (8+1) Hull KR: 1982 A; 1984 A3,NZ2; 1985 nz; 1986 A; 1987 F
BURWELL, Alan (7+1) Hull KR: 1967 a; 1968 F3; **1968 A,F,NZ**; 1969 F
BUTTERS, Fred (2) Swinton: 1929 A2

CAIRNS, David (2) Barrow: 1984 F2
CAMILLERI, Chris (2) Barrow: 1980 NZ2
CARLTON, Frank (2) St. Helens: 1958 NZ; Wigan: 1962 NZ
CARR, Charlie (7) Barrow: 1924 A2,NZ2; 1926 NZ3
CARTWRIGHT, Joe (7) Leigh: 1920 A,NZ3; 1921 A3
CASE, Brian (6+1) Wigan: 1984 A,NZ3; 1987 P; 1988 P,a
CASEY, Len (12+2) Hull KR: **1977 f,nz,A**; 1978 A; Bradford N: 1979 A2,NZ3; Hull KR: 1980 NZ3; 1983 F2
CASSIDY, Mick (+2) Wigan: 1994 a2
CASTLE, Frank (4) Barrow: 1952 A3; 1954 A
CHALLINOR, Jim (3) Warrington: 1958 A,NZ; **1960 F**
CHARLTON, Paul (18+1) Workington T: 1965 NZ; Salford: **1970 nz**; 1972 F2; **1972 A2,F,NZ**; 1973 A3; 1974 F2,A3,NZ3
CHERRINGTON, Norman (1) Wigan: 1960 F
CHILCOTT, Jack (3) Huddersfield: 1914 A3
CHISNALL, Dave (2) Leigh: 1970 A; **1970 NZ**
CHISNALL, Eric (4) St. Helens: 1974 A2,NZ2
CLAMPITT, Jim (3) Broughton R: 1907 NZ; 1911 A; 1914 NZ
CLARK, Doug (11) Huddersfield: 1911 A2; 1914 A3; 1920 A3,NZ3
CLARK, Garry (3) Hull KR: 1984 F2; 1985 F
CLARK, Mick (5) Leeds: 1968 F2; **1968 A,F,NZ**
CLARKE, Colin (7) Wigan: 1965 NZ; 1966 F,NZ; 1967 F; 1973 A3
CLARKE, Phil (15+1) Wigan: 1990 p; 1992 P,A3,NZ2, **A**; 1993 F2,NZ3; 1994 A3
CLAWSON, Terry (14) Featherstone R: 1962 F2; Leeds: **1972 A2,F**; Oldham: 1973 A3; 1974 F2,A2,NZ2
CLOSE, Don (1) Huddersfield: 1967 F
COLDRICK, Percy (4) Wigan: 1914 A3,NZ
COLLIER, Frank (2) Wigan: 1963 A; Widnes: 1964 F
CONNOLLY, Gary (14+3) St. Helens: 1991 p; 1992 F2,a2,NZ2,**A**; 1993 F2; Wigan: 1993 NZ3; 1994 F,A3

CORDLE, Gerald (1) Bradford N: 1990 F
COULMAN, Mike (2+1) Salford: 1971 f,NZ2
COURTNEY, Neil (+1) Warrington: 1982 a
COVERDALE, Bob (4) Hull: **1954 F2,NZ,A**
COWIE, Neil (1) Wigan: 1993 F
CRACKNELL, Dick (2) Huddersfield: 1951 NZ2
CRANE, Mick (1) Hull: 1982 A
CREASSER, David (2+2) Leeds: 1985 F2; 1987 f; 1988 f
CROOKS, Lee (17+2) Hull: 1982 A2; 1984 f,A2; 1985 NZnz; 1986 F2,A3; 1987 F; Leeds: 1989 F; Castleford: 1992 F2,P,A; 1994 F
CROSTON, Jim (1) Castleford: 1937 A
CROWTHER, Hector (1) Hunslet: 1929 A
CUNLIFFE, Billy (11) Warrington: 1920 A,NZ2; 1921 A3; 1924 A3,NZ; 1926 NZ
CUNLIFFE, Jack (4) Wigan: 1950 A,NZ; 1951 NZ; 1954 A
CUNNIFFE, Bernard (1) Castleford: 1937 A
CUNNINGHAM, Eddie (1) St. Helens: 1978 A
CURRAN, George (6) Salford: 1946 A,NZ; 1947 NZ; 1948 A3
CURRIER, Andy (2) Widnes: 1989 NZ; 1993 F
CURZON, Ephraim (1) Salford: 1910 A

DAGNALL, Bob (4) St. Helens: 1961 NZ2; 1964 F; 1965 F
DALGREEN, John (1) Fulham: 1982 A
DANBY, Tom (3) Salford: 1950 A2,NZ
DANIELS, Arthur (3) Halifax: 1952 A2; 1955 NZ
DANNATT, Andy (3) Hull: 1985 F2; 1991 F
DARWELL, Joe (5) Leigh: 1924 A3,NZ2
DAVIES, Alan (20) Oldham: 1955 NZ; 1956 A3; **1957 F,A**; 1957 F2; 1958 F,A2,NZ2; 1959 F,A; **1960 NZ,F,A**; 1960 F
DAVIES, Billy (1) Swinton: 1968 F
DAVIES, Billy J (1) Castleford: 1933 A
DAVIES, Evan (3) Oldham: 1920 NZ3
DAVIES, Jim (2) Huddersfield: 1911 A2
DAVIES, Jonathan (12+1) Widnes: 1990 P2,NZ3,a; 1991 P; 1992 F; 1993 F; Warrington: 1993 NZ3; 1994 A
DAVIES, Will T (1) Halifax: 1911 A
DAVIES, Willie A (2) Leeds: 1914 A,NZ
DAVIES, Willie T.H. (3) Bradford N: 1946 NZ; 1947 NZ2
DAWSON, Edgar (1) York: 1956 A
DERMOTT, Martin (11) Wigan: 1990 NZ2; 1991 P; 1992 F,P,A3,**A**; 1993 F,NZ
DEVEREUX, John (6+2) Widnes: 1992 F,nz,**a**; 1993 F2,NZ3
DICK, Kevin (2) Leeds: 1980 NZ2
DICKENSON, George (1) Warrington: 1908 A
DICKINSON, Roy (2) Leeds: 1985 F2
DINGSDALE, Billy (3) Warrington: 1929 A2; 1933 A
DIVORTY, Gary (2) Hull: 1985 F2
DIXON, Colin (12+2) Halifax: 1968 F; Salford: 1969 F; 1971 NZ; **1972 F**; 1973 a2; 1974 F2,A3,NZ3
DIXON, Malcolm (2) Featherstone R: 1962 F; 1964 F
DIXON, Paul (11+4) Halifax: 1987 f; 1988 fF,p,A2; Leeds: 1990 P2,NZ2nz,A3; 1992 F
DOCKAR, Alec (1) Hull KR: 1947 NZ

DONLAN, Steve (+2) Leigh: 1984 nz,p
DRAKE, Bill (1) Hull: 1962 F
DRAKE, Jim (1) Hull: 1960 F
DRUMMOND, Des (24) Leigh: 1980 NZ2; 1981 F2; 1982 A3; 1983 F2; 1984 F,A3,NZ3,P; 1985 NZ3; 1986 F2; Warrington: 1987 P; 1988 F
DUANE, Ronnie (3) Warrington: 1983 F2; 1984 F
DUTTON, Ray (6) Widnes: 1970 NZ2; **1970 A2,F,NZ**
DYL, Les (11) Leeds: 1974 A2,NZ3; **1977 F,NZ,A2**; 1978 A; 1982 A
DYSON, Frank (1) Huddersfield: 1959 A

EASTWOOD, Paul (13) Hull: 1990 P2,A3; 1991 F2; 1992 F,P,A2,NZ2
ECCLES, Bob (1) Warrington: 1982 A
ECCLES, Percy (1) Halifax: 1907 NZ
ECKERSLEY, David (2+2) St. Helens: 1973 Aa; 1974 Aa
EDGAR, Brian (11) Workington T: 1958 A,NZ; 1961 NZ; 1962 A3,NZ; 1965 NZ; 1966 A3
EDWARDS, Alan (7) Salford: 1936 A3,NZ2; 1937 A2
EDWARDS, Derek (3+2) Castleford: 1968 f; 1970 A; 1971 NZ2nz
EDWARDS, Shaun (32+4) Wigan: 1985 F,nzNZ; 1986 a; 1987 F2,P; 1988 F2,P; 1989 F2,nzNZ2; 1990 F2; 1991 F2,P; 1992 F,P,aA2,NZ2,**A**; 1993 F2,NZ3; 1994 F,A2
EGAN, Joe (14) Wigan: 1946 A3; 1947 NZ3; 1948 A3; 1950 A3,NZ2
ELLABY, Alf (13) St. Helens: 1928 A3,NZ2; 1929 A2; 1932 A3,NZ2; 1933 A
ELLIS, Kevin (+1) Warrington: 1991 f
ELLIS, St. John (+3) Castleford: 1991 f2; 1994 f
ELWELL, Keith (3) Widnes: **1977 A**; 1980 NZ2
ENGLAND, Keith (6+5) Castleford: 1987 fF; 1989 f,nz; 1990 F,pP,NZ3; 1991 f
EVANS, Bryn (10) Swinton: 1926 NZ; 1928 NZ; 1929 A; 1932 A2,NZ3; 1933 A2
EVANS, Frank (4) Swinton: 1924 A2,NZ2
EVANS, Jack (4) Hunslet: 1951 NZ; 1952 A3
EVANS, Jack (3) Swinton: 1926 NZ3
EVANS, Roy (4) Wigan: 1961 NZ2; 1962 F,NZ
EVANS, Steve (7+3) Featherstone R: 1979 Aa2,NZ3; 1980 NZnz; Hull: 1982 A2
EYRE, Ken (1) Hunslet: 1965 NZ
EYRES, Richard (3+6) Widnes: 1989 f; 1991 fF; 1992 f,**a**; 1993 F2; Leeds: 1993 nz2

FAIRBAIRN, George (17) Wigan: **1977 F,NZ,A2**; 1978 A3; 1979 A2,NZ3; 1980 NZ2; Hull KR: 1981 F; 1982 A2
FAIRBANK, Karl (10+6) Bradford N: 1987 p; 1990 F,P,a; 1991 fF,p2; 1992 F2,P,nz; 1993 f,NZ3; 1994 F
FAIRCLOUGH, Les (6) St. Helens: 1926 NZ; 1928 A2,NZ2; 1929 A
FARRAR, Vince (1) Hull: 1978 A
FARRELL, Andrew (5) Wigan: 1993 NZ; 1994 F, A3
FEATHERSTONE, Jim (6) Warrington: 1948 A; 1950 NZ2; 1952 A3

FEETHAM, Jack (8) Hull KR: 1929 A; Salford: 1932 A2,NZ2; 1933 A3
FIELD, Harry (3) York: 1936, A,NZ2
FIELD, Norman (1) Batley: 1963 A
FIELDHOUSE, John (7) Widnes: 1985 NZ3; 1986 F2,A; St. Helens: 1986 A
FIELDING, Keith (3) Salford: 1974 F2; **1977 F**
FILDES, Alec (15) St. Helens Recs: 1926 NZ2; 1928 A3,NZ3; 1929 A3; St. Helens: 1932, A,NZ3
FISHER, Tony (11) Bradford N: 1970 A2,NZ3; **1970 A**; Leeds: **1970 A**; 1971 F2; Bradford N: 1978 A2
FLANAGAN, Peter (14) Hull KR: 1962 F; 1963 F; 1966 A3,NZ; 1967 A3; 1968 F2; **1968 F,NZ**; 1970 A
FLANAGAN, Terry (4) Oldham: 1983 F2; 1984 NZ,P
FOGERTY, Terry (2+1) Halifax: 1966 nz; Wigan: 1967 F; Rochdale H: 1974 F
FORD, Mike (+2) Castleford: 1993 f2
FORD, Phil (13) Wigan: 1985 F; Bradford N: 1987 P; 1988 F,P,A3, NZ; Leeds: 1989 F2,NZ3
FORSTER, Mark (2) Warrington: 1987 F2
FOSTER, Frank (1) Hull KR: 1967 A
FOSTER, Peter (3) Leigh: 1955 NZ2
FOSTER, Trevor (3) Bradford N: 1946 NZ; 1948 A2
FOX, Deryck (10+4) Featherstone R: 1985 F2, NZ3; 1986 F2,A2; 1989 nz; 1990 p; 1991 p; 1992 f; Bradford N: 1992 **A**
FOX, Don (1) Featherstone R: 1963 A
FOX, Neil (29) Wakefield T: 1959 F,A2; 1960 F3; 1961 NZ2; 1962 F3,A3,NZ2; 1963 A2,F; 1964 F; 1965 F; 1966 F; 1967 F2,A; 1968 F3; 1969 F
FOY, Des (3) Oldham: 1984 F,A; 1985 F
FRANCIS, Bill (4) Wigan: 1967 A; **1977 NZ,A2**
FRANCIS, Roy (1) Barrow: 1947 NZ
FRASER, Eric (16) Warrington: 1958 A3,NZ2; 1959 F2,A; 1960 F3; **1960 F,NZ**; 1961 F,NZ2
FRENCH, Ray (4) Widnes: 1968 F2; **1968 A,NZ**
FRODSHAM, Alf (3) St. Helens: 1928 NZ2; 1929 A

GABBITAS, Brian (1) Hunslet: 1959 F
GALLAGHER, Frank (12) Dewsbury: 1920 A3; 1921 A; Batley: 1924 A3,NZ3; 1926 NZ2
GANLEY, Bernard (3) Oldham: 1957 F2; 1958 F
GARDINER, Danny (1) Wigan: 1965 NZ
GEE, Ken (17) Wigan: 1946 A3,NZ; 1947 NZ3; 1948 A3; 1950 A3,NZ2; 1951 NZ2
GEMMELL, Dick (3) Leeds: 1964 F; Hull: 1968 F; 1969 F
GIBSON, Carl (10+1) Batley: 1985 f; Leeds: 1990 F,P2,NZ3,A3; 1991 F
GIFFORD, Harry (2) Barrow: 1908 A2
GILFEDDER, Laurie (5) Warrington: 1962 A,NZ2,F; 1963 F
GILL, Henderson (14+1) Wigan: 1981 F2; 1982 A; 1985 F; 1986 F,A3; 1987 F2; 1988 P,A2a,NZ
GILL, Ken (5+2) Salford: 1974 F2,A2,NZ; **1977 f,a**
GOODWAY, Andy (23) Oldham: 1983 F2; 1984 F,A3,NZ3,P; 1985 F; Wigan: 1985 NZ3; 1986 A3; 1987 F,P; 1989 NZ3; 1990 F
GOODWIN, Dennis (5) Barrow: 1957 F2; 1958 F,NZ2

GORE, Jack (1) Salford: 1926 NZ
GORLEY, Les (4+1) Widnes: 1980 NZnz; 1981 F2; 1982 A
GORLEY, Peter (2+1) St. Helens: 1980 NZ; 1981 Ff
GOULDING, Bobbie (7+2) Wigan: 1990 P2,NZ3; Leeds: 1992 F; St. Helens: 1994 Aa2
GOWERS, Ken (14) Swinton: 1962 F; 1963 F,A3; 1964 F2; 1965 NZ2; 1966 F2,A,NZ2
GRAY, John (5+3) Wigan: 1974 f2,A2a,NZ3
GRAYSHON, Jeff (13) Bradford N: 1979 A2, NZ3; 1980 NZ2; 1981 F2; 1982 A2; Leeds: 1985 NZ2
GREENALL, Doug (6) St. Helens: 1951 NZ3; 1952 A2; 1954 NZ
GREENALL, Johnny (1) St. Helens Recs: 1921 A
GREENOUGH, Bobby (1) Warrington: **1960 NZ**
GREGORY, Andy (25+1) Widnes: 1981 F2; 1982 A; 1983 F2; 1984 a,NZ2,P; Warrington: 1986 A; Wigan: 1987 F,P; 1988 F,P,A3,NZ; 1989 F2,NZ; 1990 F,A3; 1992 A
GREGORY, Mike (19+1) Warrington: 1987 F2; 1988 P,A3,NZ; 1989 F2,NZ3; 1990 F2,P2,NZ3,a
GRIBBIN, Vince (1) Whitehaven: 1985 F
GRIFFITHS, Jonathan (1) St. Helens: 1992 F
GRONOW, Ben (7) Huddersfield: 1911 A2; 1920 A2,NZ3
GROVES, Paul (1) St. Helens: 1987 P
GRUNDY, Jack (12) Barrow: 1955 NZ3; 1956 A3; 1957 F3; **1957 F,A,NZ**
GUNNEY, Geoff (11) Hunslet: 1954 NZ3; 1956 A; 1957 F3; **1957 F,NZ**; 1964 F; 1965 F
GWYNNE, Emlyn (3) Hull: 1928 A,NZ; 1929 A
GWYTHER, Elwyn (6) Belle Vue R: 1947 NZ2; 1950 A3; 1951 NZ

HAGGERTY, Roy (2) St. Helens: 1987 F2
HAIGH, Bob (5+1) Wakefield T: **1968 A,F**; Leeds: **1970 NZ,a**; 1971 F,NZ
HALL, Billy (4) Oldham: 1914 A3,NZ
HALL, Dave (2) Hull KR: 1984 F2
HALLAS, Derek (2) Leeds: 1961 F,NZ
HALMSHAW, Tony (1) Halifax: 1971 NZ
HALSALL, Hector (1) Swinton: 1929 A
HAMPSON, Steve (11+1) Wigan: 1987 P; 1988 F2; 1989 f,NZ; 1990 A3; 1991 F2,P; 1992 P
HANLEY, Ellery (35+1) Bradford N: 1984 fF,A3,NZ3,P; 1985 F2; Wigan: 1985 NZ3; 1986 F,A; 1987 F2,P; 1988 F2,P,A3,NZ; 1989 F2; 1990 F,A3; 1991 F2; Leeds: 1992 **A**; 1993 F
HARDISTY, Alan (12) Castleford: 1964 F3; 1965 F,NZ; 1966 A3,NZ; 1967 F2; 1970 A
HARE, Ian (1) Widnes: 1967 F
HARKIN, Paul (+1) Hull KR: 1985 f
HARRIS, Tommy (25) Hull: 1954 NZ2; 1956 A3; 1957 F5; **1957 F,A**; 1958 A3,NZ,F; 1959 F2,A3; 1960 F2; **1960 NZ**
HARRISON, Fred (3) Leeds: 1911 A3
HARRISON, Karl (11+3) Hull: 1990 A3; Halifax: 1991 P; 1992 a2,nzNZ; 1993 F,NZ2; 1994 A3
HARRISON, Mick (7) Hull: 1967 F2; 1971 NZ2; 1972 F2; 1973 A

HARTLEY, Dennis (11) Hunslet: 1964 F2; Castleford: 1968 F; 1969 F; 1970 A2,NZ2; **1970 A2,F**
HARTLEY, Steve (3) Hull KR: 1980 NZ; 1981 F2
HELME, Gerry (12) Warrington: 1948 A3; 1954 A3,NZ2; **1954 F2,A,NZ**
HEPWORTH, Keith (11) Castleford: 1967 F2; 1970 A3,NZ2; **1970 A2,F,NZ**
HERBERT, Norman (6) Workington T: 1961 NZ; 1962 F,A3,NZ
HERON, David (1+1) Leeds: 1982 aA
HESKETH, Chris (21+2) Salford: 1970 NZ; **1970 NZ,a**; 1971 Ff,NZ3; **1972 A2,F,NZ**; 1973 A3; 1974 F2,A3,NZ3
HICKS, Mervyn (1) St. Helens: 1965 NZ
HIGGINS, Fred (6) Widnes: 1950 A3,NZ2; 1951 NZ
HIGGINS, Harold (2) Widnes: 1937 A2
HIGSON, John (2) Hunslet: 1908 A2
HILL, Cliff (1) Wigan: 1966 F
HILL, David (1) Wigan: 1971 F
HILTON, Herman (7) Oldham: 1920 A3,NZ3; 1921 A
HILTON, Jack (4) Wigan: 1950 A2,NZ2
HOBBS, David (10+2) Featherstone R: 1984 F2,Aa,NZ3,P; Oldham: 1987 F2; Bradford N: 1989 NZnz
HODGSON, Martin (16) Swinton: 1929 A2; 1932 A3,NZ3; 1933 A3; 1936 A3,NZ; 1937 A
HOGAN, Phil (6+3) Barrow: **1977 F,NZ,A2**; 1978 a; Hull KR: 1979 Aa,NZnz
HOGG, Andrew (1) Broughton R: 1907 NZ
HOLDEN, Keith (1) Warrington: 1963 A
HOLDER, Billy (1) Hull: 1907 NZ
HOLDING, Neil (4) St. Helens: 1984 A3,NZ
HOLDSTOCK, Roy (2) Hull KR: 1980 NZ2
HOLLAND, Dave (4) Oldham: 1914 A3,NZ
HOLLIDAY, Bill (9+1) Whitehaven: 1964 F; Hull KR: 1965 F,NZ3; 1966 Ff; 1967 A3
HOLLIDAY, Les (3) Widnes: 1991 F; 1992 F2
HOLLINDRAKE, Terry (1) Keighley: 1955 NZ
HOLMES, John (14+6) Leeds: 1971 NZ; 1972 F2; **1972 Aa,NZ**; **1977 F,NZ,Aa**; 1978 a3; 1979 A2a,NZ3; 1982 A
HORNE, Willie (8) Barrow: 1946 A3; 1947 NZ; 1948 A; 1952 A3
HORTON, Bill (14) Wakefield T: 1928 A3,NZ3; 1929 A; 1932 A3,NZ; 1933 A3
HOWLEY, Tommy (6) Wigan: 1924 A3,NZ3
HUDDART, Dick (16) Whitehaven: 1958 A2,NZ2; St. Helens: 1959 A; 1961 NZ3; 1962 F2,A3,NZ2; 1963 A
HUDSON, Barney (8) Salford: 1932 NZ, 1933 A2; 1936 A,NZ2; 1937 A2
HUDSON, Bill (1) Wigan: 1948 A
HUGHES, Eric (8) Widnes: 1978 A; 1979 A3,NZ3; 1982 A
HULME, David (7+1) Widnes: 1988 p,A3,NZ; 1989 NZ3
HULME, Paul (3+5) Widnes: 1988 aA,nz; 1989 NZ2; 1992 a2,nz
HUNTE, Alan (7) St. Helens: 1992 F,**A**; 1993 F2; 1994 A3
HURCOMBE, Danny (8) Wigan: 1920 A2,NZ; 1921 A; 1924 A2,NZ2

271

HYNES, Syd (12+1) Leeds: 1970 A2,NZ2nz; **1970 A2,F,NZ**; 1971 F; 1973 A3

IRVING, Bob (8+3) Oldham: 1967 F2,A3; 1970 a,NZ; 1971 NZ; 1972 f; **1972 NZ,a**
IRWIN, Shaun (+4) Castleford: 1990 f,p,nz2

JACKSON, Ken (2) Oldham: 1957 F2
JACKSON, Lee (17) Hull: 1990 P2,NZ,A3; 1991 F2; 1992 F,NZ2; Sheffield E: 1993 NZ2; 1994 F,A3
JACKSON, Michael (2+4) Wakefield T: 1991 P; 1992 F,a,nz; Halifax: 1993 nz2
JACKSON, Phil (27) Barrow: 1954 A3,NZ3; **1954 F2,A,NZ**; 1955 NZ3; 1956 A3; **1957 F,NZ**; 1957 F5; 1958 F,A2,NZ
JAMES, Neil (1) Halifax: 1986 F
JARMAN, Billy (2) Leeds: 1914 A2
JASIEWICZ, Dick (1) Bradford N: 1984 F
JEANES, David (8) Wakefield T: 1971 F,NZ2; 1972 F2; Leeds: **1972 A2,NZ**
JENKINS, Bert (12) Wigan: 1907 NZ3; 1908 A3; 1910 A,NZ; 1911 A2; 1914 A,NZ
JENKINS, Dai (1) Hunslet: 1929 A
JENKINS, Dai (1) Leeds: 1947 NZ
JENKINS, Emlyn (9) Salford: 1933 A; 1936 A3,NZ2; 1937 A3
JENKINSON, Albert (2) Hunslet: 1911 A2
JOHNSON, Albert (4) Widnes: 1914 A,NZ; 1920 A2
JOHNSON, Albert (6) Warrington: 1946 A2,NZ; 1947 NZ3
JOHNSON, Chris (1) Leigh: 1985 F
JOLLEY, Jim (3) Runcorn: 1907 NZ3
JONES, Berwyn (3) Wakefield T: 1964 F; 1965 F; 1966 F
JONES, Dai (2) Merthyr: 1907 NZ2
JONES, Ernest (4) Rochdale H: 1920 A,NZ3
JONES, Joe (1) Barrow: 1946 NZ
JONES, Keri (2) Wigan: **1970 F,NZ**
JONES, Les (1) St. Helens: 1971 NZ
JONES, Lewis (15) Leeds: 1954 A3,NZ3; 1955 NZ3; 1957 F3; **1957 F,A,NZ**
JONES, Mark (+1) Hull: 1992 f
JORDAN, Gary (2) Featherstone R: 1964 F; 1967 A
JOYNER, John (14+2) Castleford: 1978 A2; 1979 A3,NZ3; 1980 NZ3; 1983 F2; 1984 F,nz2
JOYNT, Chris (7+1) St. Helens: 1993 f,NZ3; 1994 F,A3
JUBB, Ken (2) Leeds: 1937 A2
JUKES, Bill (6) Hunslet: 1908 A3; 1910 A2,NZ

KARALIUS, Tony (4+1) St. Helens: 1971 NZ3; 1972 F; **1972 nz**
KARALIUS, Vince (12) St. Helens: 1958 A2,NZ2; 1959 F; **1960 NZ,F,A**; 1960 F; 1961 F; Widnes: 1963 A2
KEEGAN, Arthur (9) Hull: 1966 A2; 1967 F2,A3; 1968 F; 1969 F
KELLY, Ken (4) St. Helens: 1972 F2; Warrington: 1980 NZ; 1982 A
KEMEL, George (2) Widnes: 1965 NZ2
KERSHAW, Herbert (2) Wakefield T: 1910 A,NZ
KINNEAR, Roy (1) Wigan: 1929 A

KISS, Nicky (1) Wigan: 1985 F
KITCHEN, Frank (2) Leigh: **1954 A,NZ**
KITCHIN, Phil (1) Whitehaven: 1965 NZ
KITCHING, Jack (1) Bradford N: 1946 A
KNAPMAN, Ernest (1) Oldham: 1924 NZ
KNOWELDEN, Bryn (1) Barrow: 1946 NZ

LAUGHTON, Doug (15) Wigan: 1970 A3,NZ2; **1970 A2,F,NZ**; 1971 F2; Widnes: 1973 A; 1974 F2; 1979 A
LAWRENSON, John (3) Wigan: 1948 A3
LAWS, David (1) Hull KR: 1986 F
LEDGARD, Jim (11) Dewsbury: 1947 NZ2; Leigh: 1948 A; 1950 A2,NZ; 1951 NZ; **1954 F2,A,NZ**
LEDGER, Barry (2) St. Helens: 1985 F; 1986 A
LEWIS, Gordon (1) Leigh: 1965 NZ
LEYTHAM, Jim (5) Wigan: 1907 NZ2; 1910 A2,NZ
LITTLE, Syd (10) Oldham: 1956 A; 1957 F5; **1957 F,A,NZ**; 1958 F
LLEWELLYN, Tom (2) Oldham: 1907 NZ2
LLOYD, Robbie (1) Halifax: 1920 A
LOCKWOOD, Brian (8+1) Castleford: **1972 A2,F,NZ**; 1973 A2; 1974 F; Hull KR: 1978 A; 1979 nz
LOMAS, Jim (7) Salford: 1908 A2; 1910 A2,NZ; Oldham: 1911 A2
LONGSTAFF, Fred (2) Huddersfield: 1914 A,NZ
LONGWORTH, Bill (3) Oldham: 1908 A3
LOUGHLIN, Paul (14+1) St. Helens: 1988 F,P,A3,NZ; 1989 F,NZ3; 1990 F,a; 1991 F; 1992 P,A
LOWE, John (1) Leeds: 1932 NZ
LOWE, Phil (12) Hull KR: 1970 NZ; 1972 F2; **1972 A2,F,NZ**; 1973 A3; 1978 A2
LOXTON, Ken (1) Huddersfield: 1971 NZ
LUCAS, Ian (1+1) Wigan: 1991 F; 1992 a
LYDON, Joe (23+7) Widnes: 1983 F2; 1984 F,a,NZ2,P; 1985 NZ3; Wigan: 1986 F,A3; 1987 F2,P; 1989 F2,nz; 1990 F,NZ3; 1992 p,a3,nz,**A**

McCORMICK, Stan (3) Belle Vue R: 1948 A2; St. Helens: 1948 A
McCUE, Tommy (6) Widnes: 1936 A; 1937 A; 1946 A3,NZ
McCURRIE, Steve (1) Widnes: 1993 F
McDERMOTT, Barrie (1+2) Wigan: 1994 A,a2
McGINTY, Billy (4) Wigan: 1992 A2,NZ2
McINTYRE, Len (1) Oldham: 1963 A
McKEATING, Vince (2) Workington T: 1951 NZ2
McKINNEY, Tom (11) Salford: 1951 NZ; 1952 A2; 1954 A3,NZ; Warrington: 1955 NZ3; St. Helens: **1957 NZ**
McNAMARA, Steve (+2) Hull: 1992 f; 1993 f
McTIGUE, Brian (25) Wigan: 1958 A2,NZ2; 1959 F2,A3; 1960 F2; **1960 NZ,F,A**; 1961 F,NZ3; 1962 F,A3,NZ2; 1963 F
MANN, Arthur (2) Bradford N: 1908 A2
MANTLE, John (13) St. Helens: 1966 F2,A3; 1967 A2; 1969 F; 1971 F2,NZ2; 1973 A
MARCHANT, Tony (3) Castleford: 1986 F,A2
MARTIN, Billy (1) Workington T: 1962 F

MARTYN, Mick (2) Leigh: 1958 A; 1959 A
MATHER, Barrie-Jon (+1) Wigan: 1994f
MATHIAS, Roy (1) St. Helens: 1979 A
MEASURES, Jim (2) Widnes: 1963 A2
MEDLEY, Paul (3+1) Leeds: 1987 P; 1988 Ff,P
MIDDLETON, Alf (1) Salford: 1929 A
MILLER, Joe (1) Wigan: 1911 A
MILLER, Joe "Jack" (6) Warrington: 1933 A3; 1936 A,NZ2
MILLS, Jim (6) Widnes: 1974 A2,NZ; 1978 A2; 1979 A
MILLWARD, Roger (28+1) Castleford: 1966 F; Hull KR: 1967 A3; 1968 F2; **1968 A,F,NZ**; 1970 A2,NZ3; 1971 F,NZ3; 1973 A; 1974 A2a; **1977 F,NZ,A2**; 1978 A3
MILNES, Alf (2) Halifax: 1920 A2
MOLLOY, Steve (2) Leeds: 1993 F; Featherstone R: 1994 F
MOONEY, Walter (2) Leigh: 1924 NZ2
MOORHOUSE, Stan (2) Huddersfield: 1914 A,NZ
MORGAN, Arnold (4) Featherstone R: 1968 F2; **1968 F,NZ**
MORGAN, Edgar (2) Hull: 1921 A2
MORGAN, Ron (2) Swinton: 1963 F,A
MORIARTY, Paul (1+1) Widnes: 1991 P; 1994 f
MORLEY, Jack (2) Wigan: 1936 A; 1937 A
MORTIMER, Frank (2) Wakefield T: 1956 A2
MOSES, Glyn (9) St. Helens: 1955 NZ2; 1956 A; 1957 F3; **1957 F,A,NZ**
MUMBY, Keith (11) Bradford N: 1982 A; 1983 F; 1984 F2,A3,NZ3,P
MURPHY, Alex (27) St. Helens: 1958 A3,NZ; 1959 F2,A; **1960 NZ,F,A**; 1960 F; 1961 F,NZ3; 1962 F,A3; 1963 A2; 1964 F; 1965 F,NZ; 1966 F2; Warrington: 1971 NZ
MURPHY, Harry (1) Wakefield T: 1950 A
MYLER, Frank (23+1) Widnes: **1960 NZ,F,A**; 1960 F; 1961 F; 1962 F; 1963 A; 1964 F; 1965 F,NZ; 1966 A,NZnz; 1967 F2; St. Helens: 1970 A3,NZ3; **1970 A2,F**
MYLER, Tony (14) Widnes: 1983 F2; 1984 A2,NZ2,P; 1985 NZ2; 1986 F2,A3

NASH, Steve (24) Featherstone R: 1971 F,NZ; 1972 F2; **1972 A2,F,NZ**; 1973 A2; 1974 A3,NZ3; Salford: **1977 F,NZ,A2**; 1978 A3; 1982 A
NAUGHTON, Albert (2) Warrington: **1954 F2**
NEWBOULD, Tommy (1) Wakefield T: 1910 A
NEWLOVE, Paul (12+4) Featherstone R: 1989 nzNZ2; 1991 P; 1992 p,A3,nz; 1993 F; Bradford N: 1993 NZ3; 1994 F,Aa
NICHOLLS, George (29) Widnes: 1971 NZ; 1972 F2; **1972 A2,F,NZ**; St. Helens: 1973 A2; 1974 F2,A3,NZ3; **1977 F,NZ,A**; 1978 A3; 1979 A3,NZ3
NICHOLSON, Bob (3) Huddersfield: 1946 NZ; 1948 A2
NICKLE, Sonny (1+5) St. Helens: 1992 p; 1993 f,NZnz2; 1994 a
NOBLE, Brian (11) Bradford N: 1982 A; 1983 F2; 1984 F,A3,NZ3,P

NORTON, Steve (11+1) Castleford: 1974 a,NZ2; Hull: 1978 A3; 1979 A2; 1980 NZ; 1981 F2; 1982 A

OFFIAH, Martin (33) Widnes: 1988 F,A3,NZ; 1989 F2,NZ3; 1990 F2,NZ3,A3; 1991 F2; Wigan: 1992 P,A3,NZ2,**A**; 1993 NZ2; 1994 F,A3
O'GRADY, Terry (6) Oldham: 1954 A2,NZ3; Warrington: 1961 NZ
OLIVER, Joe (4) Batley: 1928 A3,NZ
O'NEILL, Dennis (2+1) Widnes: 1971 nz; **1972 A,F**
O'NEILL, Mike (3) Widnes: 1982 A; 1983 F2
OSTER, Jack (1) Oldham: 1929 A
OWEN, Jim (1) St. Helens Recs: 1921 A
OWEN, Stan (1) Leigh: 1958 F
OWENS, Ike (4) Leeds: 1946 A3,NZ

PADBURY, Dick (1) Runcorn: 1908 A
PALIN, Harold (2) Warrington: 1947 NZ2
PARKER, Dave (2) Oldham: 1964 F2
PARKIN, Jonty (17) Wakefield T: 1920 A2,NZ3; 1921 A2; 1924 A3,NZ; 1926 NZ2; 1928 A,NZ; 1929 A2
PARR, Ken (1) Warrington: 1968 F
PAWSEY, Charlie (7) Leigh: 1952 A3; 1954 A2,NZ2
PEPPERELL, Albert (2) Workington T: 1950 NZ; 1951 NZ
PHILLIPS, Doug (4) Oldham: 1946 A3; Belle Vue R: 1950 A
PIMBLETT, Albert (3) Warrington: 1948 A3
PINNER, Harry (6+1) St. Helens: 1980 nzNZ; 1985 NZ3; 1986 F; Widnes: 1986 A
PITCHFORD, Frank (2) Oldham: 1958 NZ; 1962 F
PITCHFORD, Steve (4) Leeds: **1977 F,NZ,A2**
PLANGE, David (1) Castleford: 1988 F
PLATT, Andy (21+4) St. Helens: 1985 f; 1986 f,a; 1988 F2,A2; Wigan: 1989 NZ3; 1990 F,A2; 1991 F2,P; 1992 f,P,A3,NZ2,**A**; 1993 F
POLLARD, Charlie (1) Wakefield T: 1924 NZ
POLLARD, Ernest (2) Wakefield T: 1932 A2
POLLARD, Roy (1) Dewsbury: 1950 NZ
POOLE, Harry (3) Hull KR: 1964 F; Leeds: 1966 NZ2
POTTER, Ian (7+1) Wigan: 1985 NZ3; 1986 F2,A2a
POWELL, Daryl (19+9) Sheffield E: 1990 f,P2,nzNZ2,A3; 1991 F2,P; 1992 fF,P,A3,NZ2; 1993 f,nz3; 1994 f,A2a
POWELL, Roy (13+6) Leeds: 1985 f; 1988 F2,A2a,NZ; 1989 F2,NZ2; 1990 P2,nz2NZ,Aa; 1991 f
POYNTON, Harold (3) Wakefield T: 1962 A2,NZ
PRESCOTT, Alan (28) St. Helens: 1951 NZ2; 1952 A3; 1954 A3,NZ3; 1955 NZ3; 1956 A3; 1957 F5; **1957 F,A,NZ**; 1958 F,A2
PRICE, Gary H (+1) Wakefield T: 1991 p
PRICE, Jack (6) Broughton R: 1921 A2; Wigan: 1924 A2,NZ2
PRICE, Malcolm (2) Rochdale H: 1967 A2
PRICE, Ray (9) Warrington: 1954 A,NZ2; 1955 NZ; 1956 A3; 1957 F2
PRICE, Terry (1) Bradford N: 1970 A
PRIOR, Bernard (1) Hunslet: 1966 F
PROCTOR, Wayne (+1) Hull: 1984 p

PROSSER, Dai (1) Leeds: 1937 A
PROSSER, Stuart (1) Halifax: 1914 A

RAE, Johnny (1) Bradford N: 1965 NZ
RAMSDALE, Dick (8) Wigan: 1910 A2; 1911 A2; 1914 A3,NZ
RAMSEY, Bill (7+1) Hunslet: 1965 NZ2; 1966 F,A2,NZ2; Bradford N; 1974 nz
RATCLIFFE, Gordon (3) Wigan: 1947 NZ; 1950 A2
RATHBONE, Alan (4+1) Bradford N: 1982 a; 1983 F2; 1985 F2
RAYNE, Keith (4) Leeds: 1984 F2,A,P
RAYNE, Kevin (1) Leeds: 1986 F
REDFEARN, Alan (1) Bradford N: 1979 A
REDFEARN, David (6+1) Bradford N: **1972 nz**; 1974 F2,A,NZ3
REES, Billo (11) Swinton: 1926 NZ2; 1928 A3,NZ3; 1929 A3
REES, Dai (1) Halifax: 1926 NZ
REES, Tom (1) Oldham: 1929 A
REILLY, Malcolm (9) Castleford: 1970 A3,NZ3; **1970 A2,F**
RENILSON, Charlie (7+1) Halifax: 1965 NZ; 1967 a; 1968 F3; **1968 A,F,NZ**
RHODES, Austin (4) St. Helens: **1957 NZ; 1960 F,A**; 1961 NZ
RICHARDS, Maurice (2) Salford: 1974 A,NZ
RILEY, Joe (1) Halifax: 1910 A
RING, Johnny (2) Wigan: 1924 A; 1926 NZ
RISMAN, Bev (5) Leeds: 1968 F2; **1968 A,F,NZ**
RISMAN, Gus (17) Salford: 1932 A,NZ3; 1933 A3; 1936 A2,NZ2; 1937 A3; 1946 A3
RIX, Sid (9) Oldham: 1924 A3,NZ3; 1926 NZ3
ROBERTS, Ken (10) Halifax: 1963 A; 1964 F2; 1965 F,NZ3; 1966 F,NZ2
ROBINSON, Asa (3) Halifax: 1907 NZ; 1908 A2
ROBINSON, Bill (2) Leigh: 1963 F,A
ROBINSON, Dave (13) Swinton: 1965 NZ; 1966 F2,A3,NZ2; 1967 F2,A2; Wigan: 1970 A
ROBINSON, Don (10) Wakefield T: **1954 F2,NZ,A**; 1955 NZ; Leeds: 1956 A2; 1959 A2; 1960 F
ROBINSON, Jack (2) Rochdale H: 1914 A2
ROBINSON, Jason (4) Wigan: 1993 NZ; 1994 A3
ROGERS, Johnny (7) Huddersfield: 1914 A; 1920 A3; 1921 A3
ROSE, David (4) Leeds: **1954 F2,A,NZ**
ROSE, Paul (2+3) Hull KR: 1974 a; 1978 Aa2; Hull: 1982 A
ROUND, Gerry (8) Wakefield T: 1959 A; 1962 F2,A3,NZ2
RUDDICK, George (3) Broughton R: 1907 NZ2; 1910 A
RYAN, Bob (5) Warrington: 1950 A,NZ2; 1951 NZ; 1952 A
RYAN, Martin (4) Wigan: 1947 NZ; 1948 A2; 1950 A
RYDER, Ron (1) Warrington: 1952 A

SAYER, Bill (7) Wigan: 1961 NZ; 1962 F,A3,NZ; 1963 A

SCHOFIELD, Derrick (1) Halifax: 1955 NZ
SCHOFIELD, Garry (44+2) Hull: 1984 F,A3,NZ; 1985 NZ3; 1986 F2,A3; 1987 F2; Leeds: 1988 F2,P,A; 1990 F2,P2,NZ3,A3; 1991 F2,P; 1992 P,A3,NZ2,**A**; 1993 F,NZ3; 1994 F,a2
SEABOURNE, Barry (1) Leeds: 1970 NZ
SENIOR, Ken (2) Huddersfield: 1965 NZ; 1967 F
SHARROCK, Jim (4) Wigan: 1910 A2,NZ; 1911 A
SHAW, Brian (6) Hunslet: 1956 A2; **1960 F,A**; 1960 F; Leeds: 1961 F
SHAW, Glyn (1) Widnes: 1980 NZ
SHAW, John (5) Halifax: **1960 F,A**; 1960 F; 1961 F; 1962 NZ
SHELTON, Geoff (7) Hunslet: 1964 F2; 1965 NZ3; 1966 F2
SHOEBOTTOM, Mick (10+2) Leeds: **1968 A,nz**; 1969 F; 1970 A2a,NZ; **1970 A2,F,NZ**; 1971 F
SHUGARS, Frank (1) Warrington: 1910 NZ
SILCOCK, Dick (1) Wigan: 1908 A
SILCOCK, Nat (12) Widnes: 1932 A2,NZ2; 1933 A3; 1936 A3; 1937 A2
SILCOCK, Nat (3) Wigan: 1954 A3
SIMMS, Barry (1) Leeds: 1962 F
SKELHORNE, George "Jack" (7) Warrington: 1920 A,NZ3; 1921 A3
SKERRETT, Kelvin (14+2) Bradford N: 1989 NZ3; 1990 F2,NZ3; Wigan: 1992 F,p,A3,NZ,**a**; 1993 NZ
SKERRETT, Trevor (4) Wakefield T: 1979 A2, NZ2; Hull: 1980 NZ2; 1981 F2; 1982 A2
SLOMAN, Bob (5) Oldham: 1928 A3,NZ2
SMALES, Tommy (8) Huddersfield: 1962 F; 1963 F,A; 1964 F2; Bradford N: 1965 NZ3
SMALL, Peter (1) Castleford: 1962 NZ
SMITH, Alan (10) Leeds: 1970 A2,NZ3; **1970 A2**; 1971 F2; 1973 A
SMITH, Arthur (6) Oldham: 1907 NZ3; 1908 A3
SMITH, Bert (2) Bradford N: 1926 NZ2
SMITH, Fred (9) Hunslet: 1910 A,NZ; 1911 A3; 1914 A3,NZ
SMITH, Geoff (3) York: 1963 A; 1964 F2
SMITH, Mike (10+1) Hull KR: 1979 NZ3; 1980 NZ2; 1981 F2; 1982 A2; 1984 f,NZ
SMITH, Peter (1+5) Featherstone R: **1977 a2**; 1982 A; 1983 f2; 1984 f
SMITH, Sam (4) Hunslet: **1954 A,NZ,F2**
SMITH, Stanley (11) Wakefield T: 1929 A; Leeds: 1929 A2; 1932 A3,NZ3; 1933 A2
SOUTHWARD, Ike (11) Workington T: 1958 A3,NZ; Oldham: 1959 F2,A2; 1960 F2; 1962 NZ
SPENCER, Jack (1) Salford: 1907 NZ
SPRUCE, Stuart (1) Widnes: 1993 F
STACEY, Cyril (1) Halifax: 1920 NZ
STEADMAN, Graham (9+1) Castleford: 1990 F; 1992 fF,A3,NZ2; 1994 F,A
STEPHENS, Gary (5) Castleford: 1979 A2,NZ3
STEPHENSON, David (9+1) Wigan: 1982 A2; 1986 A; 1987 F,P; Leeds: 1988 f,P,A2,NZ

STEPHENSON, Mick (5+1) Dewsbury: 1971 nz; 1972 F; **1972 A2,F,NZ**
STEVENSON, Jeff (19) Leeds: 1955 NZ3; 1956 A3; 1957 F5; **1957 F,A,NZ**; 1958 F; York: 1959 A2; 1960 F2
STOCKWELL, Squire (3) Leeds: 1920 A; 1921 A2
STONE, Billy (8) Hull: 1920 A3,NZ3; 1921 A2
STOPFORD, John (12) Swinton: 1961 F; 1963 F,A2; 1964 F2; 1965 F,NZ2; 1966 F2,A
STOTT, Jim (1) St. Helens: 1947 NZ
STREET, Harry (4) Dewsbury: 1950 A3,NZ
SULLIVAN, Anthony (1) St. Helens: 1991 P
SULLIVAN, Clive (17) Hull: 1967 F; **1968 A,F,NZ**; 1970 A; 1971 NZ3; 1972 F2; **1972 A2,F,NZ**; 1973 A3
SULLIVAN, Jim (25) Wigan: 1924 A3,NZ; 1926 NZ3; 1928 A3,NZ3; 1929 A3; 1932 A3,NZ3; 1933 A3
SULLIVAN, Mick (46) Huddersfield: **1954 F2,NZ,A**; 1955 NZ3; 1956 A3; 1957 F3; **1957 F,A,NZ**; Wigan: 1957 F2; 1958 F,A3,NZ2; 1959 F2,A3; 1960 F3; **1960 F,NZ,A**; St. Helens: 1961 F,NZ2; 1962 F3,A3,NZ; York: 1963 A
SZYMALA, Eddie (1+1) Barrow: 1981 fF

TAIT, Alan (10+4) Widnes: 1989 F2,NZ2; 1990 F2,P2; 1992 F; Leeds: 1992 **a**; 1993 F,nz3
TAYLOR, Bob (2) Hull: 1921 A; 1926 NZ
TAYLOR, Harry (3) Hull: 1907 NZ3
TEMBEY, John (2) St. Helens: 1963 A; 1964 F
TERRY, Abe (11) St. Helens: 1958 A2; 1959 F2,A3; 1960 F; 1961 F,NZ; Leeds: 1962 F
THOMAS, Arthur "Ginger" (4) Leeds: 1926 NZ2; 1929 A2
THOMAS, George (1) Warrington: 1907 NZ
THOMAS, Gwyn (9) Wigan: 1914 A; Huddersfield: 1920 A3,NZ2; 1921 A3
THOMAS, Johnny (8) Wigan: 1907 NZ; 1908 A3; 1910 A2,NZ; 1911 A
THOMAS, Les (1) Oldham: 1947 NZ
THOMAS, Phil (1) Leeds: 1907 NZ
THOMPSON, Cecil (2) Hunslet: 1951 NZ2
THOMPSON, Jim (20+1) Featherstone R: 1970 A2,NZ2; **1970 A2,F,NZ**; 1971 Ff; 1974 A3,NZ3; **1977 F,NZ,A2**; Bradford N: 1978 A
THOMPSON, Joe (12) Leeds: 1924 A,NZ2; 1928 A,NZ; 1929 A; 1932 A3,NZ3
THORLEY, John (4) Halifax: **1954 F2,NZ,A**
TOOHEY, Ted (3) Barrow: 1952 A3
TOPLISS, David (4) Wakefield T: 1973 A2; 1979 A; Hull: 1982 A
TRAILL, Ken (8) Bradford N: 1950 NZ2; 1951 NZ; 1952 A3; 1954 A,NZ
TROUP, Alec (2) Barrow: 1936 NZ2
TURNBULL, Andrew (1) Leeds: 1951 NZ
TURNER, Derek (24) Oldham: 1956 A2; 1957 F5; **1957 F,A,NZ**; 1958 F; Wakefield T: 1959 A; 1960 F3; **1960 NZ,A**; 1961 F,NZ; 1962 A2,NZ2,F
TYSON, Brian (3) Hull KR: 1963 A; 1965 F; 1967 F
TYSON, George (4) Oldham: 1907 NZ; 1908 A3

VALENTINE, Bob (1) Huddersfield: 1967 A
VALENTINE, Dave (15) Huddersfield: 1948 A3; 1951 NZ; 1952 A2; 1954 A3, NZ2; **1954 F2,NZ,A**
VINES, Don (3) Wakefield T: 1959 F2,A

WADDELL, Hugh (5) Oldham: 1988 F2,A,NZ; Leeds: 1989 F
WAGSTAFF, Harold (12) Huddersfield: 1911 A2; 1914 A3,NZ; 1920 A2,NZ2; 1921 A2
WALKER, Arnold (1) Whitehaven: 1980 NZ
WALLACE, Jim (1) St. Helens Recs: 1926 NZ
WALSH, Joe (1) Leigh: 1971 NZ
WALSH, John (4+1) St. Helens: 1972 f; **1972 A2,F,NZ**
WALTON, Doug (1) Castleford: 1965 F
WANE, Shaun (2) Wigan: 1985 F; 1986 F
WARD, Billy (1) Leeds: 1910 A
WARD, David (12) Leeds: **1977 F,NZ,A**; 1978 A; 1979 A3,NZ3; 1981 F; 1982 A
WARD, Edward (3) Wigan: 1946 A2; 1947 NZ
WARD, Ernest (20) Bradford N: 1946 A3,NZ; 1947 NZ2; 1948 A3; 1950 A3,NZ2; 1951 NZ3; 1952 A3
WARD, Johnny (4) Castleford: 1963 A; 1964 F2; Salford: 1970 NZ
WARD, Kevin (15+2) Castleford: 1984 F; 1986 A3; 1987 P; 1988 F2,P,A3,NZ; 1989 F2; St. Helens: 1990 a2; 1992 **A**
WARLOW, John (6+1) St. Helens: 1964 F; **1968 f,NZ**; 1968 F; Widnes: 1971 F2,NZ
WARWICK, Silas (2) Salford: 1907 NZ2
WATKINS, Billy (7) Salford: 1933 A; 1936 A2,NZ2; 1937 A2
WATKINS, David (2+4) Salford: 1971 f,NZ; 1973 a; 1974 f2,A
WATKINSON, David (12+1) Hull KR: 1979 a; 1980 NZ; 1981 F; 1984 F; 1985 F,NZ3; 1986 F2,A3
WATSON, Cliff (29+1) St. Helens: 1963 A2; 1966 F2,A3,NZ2; 1967 F,A3; 1968 F2; **1968 A,F,nz**; 1969 F; 1970 A3,NZ3; **1970 A2,F,NZ**; 1971 F
WATTS, Basil (5) York: **1954 F2,NZ,A**; 1955 NZ
WEBSTER, Fred (3) Leeds: 1910 A2,NZ
WHITCOMBE, Frank (2) Bradford N: 1946 A2
WHITE, Les (7) Hunslet: 1932 A3,NZ2; 1933 A2
WHITE, Les (6) York: 1946 A3,NZ; Wigan: 1947 NZ2
WHITE, Tommy (1) Oldham: 1907 NZ
WHITEHEAD, Derek (3) Warrington: 1971 F2,NZ
WHITELEY, Johnny (15) Hull: **1957 A**; 1958 A3,NZ; 1959 F2,A2; 1960 F; **1960 NZ,F**; 1961 NZ2; 1962 F
WILKINSON, Jack (13) Halifax: 1954 A,NZ2; 1955 NZ3; Wakefield T: 1959 A; 1960 F2; **1960 NZ,F,A**; 1962 NZ
WILLIAMS, Billy (2) Salford: 1929 A; 1932 A
WILLIAMS, Dickie (12) Leeds: 1948 A2; 1950 A2,NZ2; 1951 NZ3; Hunslet: 1954 F2,NZ
WILLIAMS, Frank (2) Halifax: 1914 A2
WILLIAMS, Peter (1+1) Salford: 1989 fF
WILLICOMBE, David (3) Halifax: 1974 F; Wigan: 1974 F,NZ

275

WILSON, George (3) Workington T: 1951 NZ3
WILSON, Harry (3) Hunslet: 1907 NZ3
WINSLADE, Charlie (1) Oldham: 1959 F
WINSTANLEY, Billy (5) Leigh: 1910 A,NZ; Wigan: 1911 A3
WOOD, Alf (4) Oldham: 1911 A2; 1914 A,NZ
WOODS, Harry (6) Liverpool S: 1936 A3,NZ2; Leeds: 1937 A
WOODS, Jack (1) Barrow: 1933 A
WOODS, John (7+4) Leigh: 1979 A3,nz; 1980 NZ; 1981 F2; 1982 Aa; 1983 f; Warrington: 1987 p

WOODS, Tommy (2) Rochdale H: 1911 A2
WORRALL, Mick (3) Oldham: 1984 F,A2
WRIGHT, Darren (+1) Widnes: 1988 a
WRIGHT, Joe (1) Swinton: 1932 NZ
WRIGHT, Stuart (7) Widnes: **1977 F,NZ,A2**; 1978 A3
WRIGLESWORTH, Geoff (5) Leeds: 1965 NZ; 1966 A2,NZ2

YOUNG, Chris (5) Hull KR: 1967 A3; 1968 F2
YOUNG, Frank (1) Leeds: 1908 A
YOUNG, Harold (1) Huddersfield: 1929 A

Tryscoring full back Jonathan Davies (centre) leads the celebrations after the first John Smith's Test victory over Australia in 1994, flanked by Jason Robinson (left) and Andrew Farrell.

GREAT BRITAIN TOUR SUMMARIES

	P	W	D	L	T	G	For Pts	T	G	Against Pts
1910										
In Australia	14	9	1	4	76	56	340	51	47	247
In New Zealand	4	4	0	0	43	29	187	11	7	47
TOTAL	18	13	1	4	119	85	527	62	54	294
1914										
In Australia	12	9	0	3	77	55	341	24	31	134
In New Zealand	6	6	0	0	46	28	194	12	13	62
TOTAL	18	15	0	3	123	83	535	36	44	196
1920										
In Australia	15	12	0	3	83	64	377	48	42	228
In New Zealand	10	9	0	1	89	47	361	24	16	104
TOTAL	25	21	0	4	172	111	738	72	58	332
1924										
In Australia	18	14	0	4	104	77	466	56	45	258
In New Zealand	9	7	0	2	64	40	272	25	21	117
TOTAL	27	21	0	6	168	117	738	81	66	375
1928										
In Australia	16	11	1	4	67	60	321	43	45	219
In New Zealand	8	7	0	1	55	36	237	16	12	72
TOTAL	24	18	1	5	122	96	558	59	57	291
1932										
In Australia	18	15	1	2	105	84	483	32	38	172
In New Zealand	8	8	0	0	65	52	299	17	18	87
TOTAL	26	23	1	2	170	136	782	49	56	259
1936										
In Australia	17	14	0	3	79	82	401	38	45	204
In New Zealand	8	8	0	0	52	27	210	8	16	56
TOTAL	25	22	0	3	131	109	611	46	61	260
1946										
In Australia	20	16	1	3	146	100	638	36	45	198
In New Zealand	7	5	0	2	35	20	145	12	21	78
TOTAL	27	21	1	5	181	120	783	48	66	276
1950										
In Australia	19	15	0	4	133	102	603	22	56	178
In New Zealand	6	4	0	2	37	25	161	16	20	88
TOTAL	25	19	0	6	170	127	764	38	76	266

	P	W	D	L	T	G	Pts (For)	T	G	Pts (Against)
1954										
In Australia	*22	13	1	7	133	114	627	78	96	426
In New Zealand	10	8	0	2	60	56	292	14	32	106
TOTAL	*32	21	1	9	193	170	919	92	128	532

*One match abandoned. Scores included in points total.

	P	W	D	L	T	G	Pts (For)	T	G	Pts (Against)
1958										
In Australia	21	19	1	1	184	129	810	64	93	378
In New Zealand	9	8	0	1	88	61	386	18	27	108
TOTAL	30	27	1	2	272	190	1,196	82	120	486
1962										
In Australia	21	18	0	3	151	113	679	61	60	303
In New Zealand	9	6	0	3	73	50	319	35	28	161
TOTAL	30	24	0	6	224	163	998	96	88	464
1966										
In Australia	22	13	0	9	112	85	506	47	83	307
In New Zealand	8	8	0	0	57	47	265	10	24	78
TOTAL	30	21	0	9	169	132	771	57	107	385
1970										
In Australia	17	15	1	1	104	92	496	27	66	213
In New Zealand	7	7	0	0	61	37	257	9	24	75
TOTAL	24	22	1	1	165	129	753	36	90	288

	P	W	D	L	T	G	DG	Pts (For)	T	G	DG	Pts (Against)
1974												
In Australia	20	15	0	5	104	93	2	500	38	59	3	235
In New Zealand	8	6	0	2	37	32	0	175	8	27	0	78
TOTAL	28	21	0	7	141	125	2	675	46	86	3	313
1979												
In Australia	18	13	1	4	66	73	3	347	39	68		253
In New Zealand	9	8	0	1	48	34	0	212	15	12		69
TOTAL	27	21	1	5	114	107	3	559	54	80		322
1984												
In Australia	15	11	0	4	70	59	1	399	40	46	2	254
In New Zealand	8	4	0	4	32	25	1	179	21	21	0	126
In Papua New Guinea	1	1	0	0	7	5	0	38	4	2	0	20
TOTAL	24	16	0	8	109	89	2	616	65	69	2	400
1988												
In Papua New Guinea	2	2	0	0	13	13	0	78	7	6	0	40
In Australia	13	8	0	5	59	47	0	330	42	36	1	241
In New Zealand	3	1	0	2	8	8	0	48	10	10	0	60
TOTAL	18	11	0	7	80	68	0	456	59	52	1	341

1990	P	W	D	L	T	G	DG	For Pts	T	G	DG	Against Pts
In Papua New Guinea	5	4	0	1	31	24	0	172	7	15	2	60
In New Zealand	10	6	0	4	30	28	3	179	24	32	1	161
TOTAL	15	10	0	5	61	52	3	351	31	47	3	221

1992	P	W	D	L	T	G	DG	Pts	T	G	DG	Pts
In Papua New Guinea	3	3	0	0	15	11	0	82	8	8	1	49
In Australia	10	7	0	3	32	29	2	188	20	19	0	118
In New Zealand	4	3	0	1	10	11	2	64	7	8	1	45
TOTAL	17	13	0	4	57	51	4	334	35	35	2	212

GREAT BRITAIN TOUR SQUADS TO AUSTRALIA AND NEW ZEALAND

Captains in bold

1910 Tour

J. Lomas (Salford)
A. Avery (Oldham)
J. Bartholomew (Huddersfield)
W. Batten (Hunslet)
F. Boylen (Hull)
E. Curzon (Salford)
J. Davies (Huddersfield)
F. Farrar (Hunslet)
T. Helm (Oldham)
B. Jenkins (Wigan)
T. Jenkins (Ebbw Vale)
W. Jukes (Hunslet)
H. Kershaw (Wakefield T.)
J. Leytham (Wigan)
T. Newbould (Wakefield T.)
R. Ramsdale (Wigan)
J. Riley (Halifax)
G. Ruddick (Broughton R.)
J. Sharrock (Wigan)
F. Shugars (Warrington)
F. Smith (Hunslet)
J. Thomas (Wigan)
W. Ward (Leeds)
F. Webster (Leeds)
W. Winstanley (Leigh)
F. Young (Leeds)

Managers: J. Clifford
(Huddersfield) and
J. Houghton (St. Helens)

1914 Tour

H. Wagstaff (Huddersfield)
J. Chilcott (Huddersfield)
J. Clampitt (Broughton R.)
D. Clark (Huddersfield)
A. Coldrick (Wigan)
W. A. Davies (Leeds)
A. Francis (Hull)
J. Guerin (Hunslet)
W. Hall (Oldham)
D. Holland (Oldham)
J. Jarman (Leeds)
B. Jenkins (Wigan)
A. Johnson (Widnes)
F. Longstaff (Huddersfield)
S. Moorhouse (Huddersfield)
J. O'Garra (Widnes)
W. Prosser (Halifax)
R. Ramsdale (Wigan)
J. Robinson (Rochdale H.)
J. Rogers (Huddersfield)
W. Roman (Rochdale H.)
J. Smales (Hunslet)
F. Smith (Hunslet)
G. Thomas (Wigan)
F. Williams (Halifax)
A. Wood (Oldham)

Managers: J. Clifford
(Huddersfield) and
J. Houghton (St. Helens)

1920 Tour

H. Wagstaff (Huddersfield)
J. Bacon (Leeds)
J. Bowers (Rochdale H.)
J. Cartwright (Leigh)
D. Clark (Huddersfield)
W. Cunliffe (Warrington)
E. Davies (Oldham)
J. Doyle (Barrow)
F. Gallagher (Dewsbury)
B. Gronow (Huddersfield)
H. Hilton (Oldham)
D. Hurcombe (Wigan)
A. Johnson (Widnes)
E. Jones (Rochdale H.)
R. Lloyd (Halifax)
A. Milnes (Halifax)
J. Parkin (Wakefield T.)
G. Rees (Leeds)
W. Reid (Widnes)
J. Rogers (Huddersfield)
G. Skelhorne (Warrington)
J. Stacey (Halifax)
S. Stockwell (Leeds)
W. Stone (Hull)
G. Thomas (Huddersfield)
A. Wood (Oldham)

Managers: S. Foster (Halifax)
and J. Wilson (Hull K.R.)

1924 Tour

J. Parkin (Wakefield T.)
J. Bacon (Leeds)
J. Bennett (Rochdale H.)
W. Bentham (Broughton R.)
H. Bowman (Hull)
A. Brough (Oldham)
W. Burgess (Barrow)
C. Carr (Barrow)
W. Cunliffe (Warrington)
J. Darwell (Leigh)
F. Evans (Swinton)
F. Gallagher (Batley)
B. Gronow (Huddersfield)
T. Howley (Wigan)
D. Hurcombe (Wigan)
E. Knapman (Oldham)
W. Mooney (Leigh)
C. Pollard (Wakefield T.)
J. Price (Wigan)
D. Rees (Halifax)
J. Ring (Wigan)
S. Rix (Oldham)
R. Sloman (Oldham)
J. Sullivan (Wigan)
J. Thompson (Leeds)
S. Whitty (Hull)

Managers: J.H. Dannatt
(Hull) and E. Osborne
(Warrington)

1928 Tour

J. Parkin (Wakefield T.)
T. Askin (Featherstone R.)
N. Bentham (Wigan Highfield)
F. Bowen (St. Helens Recs)
H. Bowman (Hull)
J. Brough (Leeds)
W. Burgess (Barrow)
O. Dolan (St. Helens Recs)
A. Ellaby (St. Helens)
B. Evans (Swinton)
J. Evans (Swinton)
L. Fairclough (St. Helens)
A. Fildes (St. Helens Recs)
A. Frodsham (St. Helens)
W. Gowers (Rochdale H.)
E. Gwynne (Hull)
B. Halfpenny (St. Helens)
W. Horton (Wakefield T.)
J. Oliver (Batley)
W. Rees (Swinton)
M. Rosser (Leeds)
R. Sloman (Oldham)
J. Sullivan (Wigan)
J. Thompson (Leeds)
W. Williams (Salford)
H. Young (Bradford N.)

Managers: G. Hutchins
(Oldham) and E. Osborne
(Warrington)

1932 Tour

J. Sullivan (Wigan)
L. Adams (Leeds)
A. Atkinson (Castleford)
S. Brogden (Huddersfield)
F. Butters (Swinton)
I. Davies (Halifax)
W. Dingsdale (Warrington)
A. Ellaby (St. Helens)
B. Evans (Swinton)
J. Feetham (Salford)
N. Fender (York)
A. Fildes (St. Helens)
M. Hodgson (Swinton)
W. Horton (Wakefield T.)
B. Hudson (Salford)
J. Lowe (Leeds)
E. Pollard (Wakefield T.)
A. Risman (Salford)
G. Robinson (Wakefield T.)
N. Silcock (Widnes)
S. Smith (Leeds)
J. Thompson (Leeds)
L. White (Hunslet)
W. Williams (Salford)
J. Woods (Barrow)
J. Wright (Swinton)

Managers: R. Anderton
(Warrington) and G. Hutchins
(Oldham)

1936 Tour

J. Brough (Leeds)
J. Arkwright (Warrington)
T. Armitt (Swinton)
A. Atkinson (Castleford)
W. Belshaw (Liverpool S.)
H. Beverley (Hunslet)
S. Brogden (Leeds)
E. Davies (Wigan)
A. Edwards (Salford)
H. Ellerington (Hull)
G. Exley (Wakefield T.)
H. Field (York)
F. Harris (Leeds)
M. Hodgson (Swinton)

B. Hudson (Salford)
E. Jenkins (Salford)
H. Jones (Keighley)
T. McCue (Widnes)
J. Miller (Warrington)
J. Morley (Wigan)
A. Risman (Salford)
N. Silcock (Widnes)
S. Smith (Leeds)
L. Troup (Barrow)
W. Watkins (Salford)
H. Woods (Liverpool S.)

Managers: R. Anderton
(Warrington) and
W. Popplewell (Bramley)

1946 Tour

A. Risman (Salford)
A. Bassett (Halifax)
E. Batten (Bradford N.)
G. Curran (Salford)
W.T.H. Davies (Bradford N.)
J. Egan (Wigan)
T. Foster (Bradford N.)
K. Gee (Wigan)
W. Horne (Barrow)
F. Hughes (Workington T.)
D. Jenkins (Leeds)
A. Johnson (Warrington)
J. Jones (Barrow)
J. Kitching (Bradford N.)

280

B. Knowelden (Barrow)
J. Lewthwaite (Barrow)
T. McCue (Widnes)
H. Murphy (Wakefield T.)
R. Nicholson (Huddersfield)
I. Owens (Leeds)
D. Phillips (Oldham)
M. Ryan (Wigan)
Edward Ward (Wigan)
Ernest Ward (Bradford N.)
F. Whitcombe (Bradford N.)
L. White (York)

Managers: W. Popplewell
(Bramley) and W. Gabbatt
(Barrow)

1950 Tour

E. Ward (Bradford N.)
E. Ashcroft (Wigan)
T. Bradshaw (Wigan)
J. Cunliffe (Wigan)
T. Danby (Salford)
A. Daniels (Halifax)
J. Egan (Wigan)
J. Featherstone (Warrington)
K. Gee (Wigan)
E. Gwyther (Belle Vue R.)
F. Higgins (Widnes)
J. Hilton (Wigan)
W. Horne (Barrow)
J. Ledgard (Leigh)
H. Murphy (Wakefield T.)
D. Naughton (Widnes)
F. Osmond (Swinton)
A. Pepperell (Workington T.)
D. Phillips (Belle Vue R.)
R. Pollard (Dewsbury)
G. Ratcliffe (Wigan)
M. Ryan (Wigan)
R. Ryan (Warrington)
H. Street (Dewsbury)
K. Traill (Bradford N.)
R. Williams (Leeds)

Managers: G. Oldroyd
(Dewsbury) and T. Spedding
(Belle Vue R.)

1954 Tour

R. Williams (Hunslet)
E. Ashcroft (Wigan)
W. Boston (Wigan)
J. Bowden (Huddersfield)
B. Briggs (Huddersfield)
A. Burnell (Hunslet)
E. Cahill (Rochdale H.)
F. Castle (Barrow)
J. Cunliffe (Wigan)
D. Greenall (St. Helens)
G. Gunney (Hunslet)
T. Harris (Hull)
G. Helme (Warrington)
J. Henderson (Workington T.)
P. Jackson (Barrow)
B.L. Jones (Leeds)
T. McKinney (Salford)
T. O'Grady (Oldham)
C. Pawsey (Leigh)
A. Prescott (St. Helens)
R. Price (Warrington)
N. Silcock (Wigan)
K. Traill (Bradford N.)
A. Turnbull (Leeds)
D. Valentine (Huddersfield)
J. Wilkinson (Halifax)

Managers: T. Hesketh
(Wigan) and H. Rawson
(Hunslet)

1958 Tour

A. Prescott (St. Helens)
A. Ackerley (Halifax)
H. Archer (Workington T.)
E. Ashton (Wigan)
D. Bolton (Wigan)
F. Carlton (St. Helens)
J. Challinor (Warrington)
A. Davies (Oldham)
B. Edgar (Workington T.)
E. Fraser (Warrington)
D. Goodwin (Barrow)
T. Harris (Hull)
R. Huddart (Whitehaven)
K. Jackson (Oldham)
P. Jackson (Barrow)
V. Karalius (St. Helens)

B. McTigue (Wigan)
M. Martyn (Leigh)
G. Moses (St. Helens)
A. Murphy (St. Helens)
F. Pitchford (Oldham)
I. Southward (Workington T.)
M. Sullivan (Wigan)
A. Terry (St. Helens)
J. Whiteley (Hull)
W. Wookey (Workington T.)

Managers: B. Manson
(Swinton) and T. Mitchell
(Workington T.)
Coach: J. Brough
(Workington T.)

1962 Tour

E. Ashton (Wigan)
D. Bolton (Wigan)
W. Boston (Wigan)
F. Carlton (Wigan)
G. Cooper (Featherstone R.)
B. Edgar (Workington T.)
R. Evans (Wigan)
D. Fox (Featherstone R.)
N. Fox (Wakefield T.)
E. Fraser (Warrington)
L. Gilfedder (Warrington)
N. Herbert (Workington T.)
R. Huddart (St. Helens)
B. McTigue (Wigan)
A. Murphy (St. Helens)
K. Noble (Huddersfield)
H. Poynton (Wakefield T.)
G. Round (Wakefield T.)
W. Sayer (Wigan)
J. Shaw (Halifax)
P. Small (Castleford)
I. Southward (Workington T.)
M. Sullivan (St. Helens)
J. Taylor (Hull K.R.)
D. Turner (Wakefield T.)
J. Wilkinson (Wakefield T.)

Managers: S. Hadfield
(Wakefield T.) and A. Walker
(Rochdale H.)
Coach: C. Hutton (Hull K.R.)

1966 Tour

H. Poole (Leeds)
W. Aspinall (Warrington)
T. Bishop (St. Helens)
I. Brooke (Bradford N.)
W. Bryant (Castleford)
A. Buckley (Swinton)
W. Burgess (Barrow)
C. Clarke (Wigan)
G. Crewdson (Keighley)
C. Dooler (Featherstone R.)
B. Edgar (Workington T.)
P. Flanagan (Hull K.R.)
T. Fogerty (Halifax)
K. Gowers (Swinton)
A. Hardisty (Castleford)
B. Jones (Wakefield T.)
A. Keegan (Hull)
J. Mantle (St. Helens)
F. Myler (Widnes)
W. Ramsey (Hunslet)
K. Roberts (Halifax)
D. Robinson (Swinton)
G. Shelton (Hunslet)
J. Stopford (Swinton)
C. Watson (St. Helens)
G. Wriglesworth (Leeds)

Managers: W. Spaven (Hull
K.R.) and J. Errock (Oldham)

1970 Tour

F. Myler (St. Helens)
J. Atkinson (Leeds)
D. Chisnall (Leigh)
R. Dutton (Widnes)
D. Edwards (Castleford)
A. Fisher (Bradford N.)
P. Flanagan (Hull K.R.)
A. Hardisty (Castleford)
D. Hartley (Castleford)
K. Hepworth (Castleford)
C. Hesketh (Salford)
S. Hynes (Leeds)
R. Irving (Oldham)
D. Laughton (Wigan)
P. Lowe (Hull K.R.)
R. Millward (Hull K.R.)
T. Price (Bradford N.)

M. Reilly (Castleford)
D. Robinson (Wigan)
B. Seabourne (Leeds)
M. Shoebottom (Leeds)
A. Smith (Leeds)
C. Sullivan (Hull)
J. Thompson (Featherstone R.)
J. Ward (Salford)
C. Watson (St. Helens)

Manager: J. Harding (Leigh)
Coach: J. Whiteley (Hull)

1974 Tour

C. Hesketh (Salford)
K. Ashcroft (Warrington)
J. Atkinson (Leeds)
A. Bates (Dewsbury)
J. Bates (Dewsbury)
J. Bevan (Warrington)
J. Bridges (Featherstone R.)
J. Butler (Rochdale H.)
P. Charlton (Salford)
E. Chisnall (St. Helens)
T. Clawson (Oldham)
C. Dixon (Salford)
L. Dyl (Leeds)
D. Eckersley (St. Helens)
K. Gill (Salford)
J. Gray (Wigan)
J. Mills (Widnes)
R. Millward (Hull K.R.)
S. Nash (Featherstone R.)
G. Nicholls (St. Helens)
S. Norton (Castleford)
D. Redfearn (Bradford N.)
P. Rose (Hull K.R.)
J. Thompson (Featherstone R.)
D. Watkins (Salford)
D. Willicombe (Wigan)

Replacements during tour
W. Ramsey (Bradford N.) for
J. Bates; M. Richards
(Salford) for Atkinson

Manager: R. Parker
(Blackpool B.)
Coach: J. Challinor
(St. Helens)

1979 Tour

D. Laughton (Widnes)
M. Adams (Widnes)
D. Barends (Bradford N.)
L. Casey (Bradford N.)
S. Evans (Featherstone R.)
P. Glynn (St. Helens)
J. Grayshon (Bradford N.)
P. Hogan (Hull K.R.)
J. Holmes (Leeds)
E. Hughes (Widnes)
M. James (St. Helens)
J. Joyner (Castleford)
G. Liptrot (St. Helens)
B. Lockwood (Hull K.R.)
T. Martyn (Warrington)
R. Mathias (St. Helens)
J. Mills (Widnes)
R. Millward (Hull K.R.)
K. Mumby (Bradford N.)
S. Nash (Salford)
G. Nicholls (St. Helens)
S. Norton (Hull)
A. Redfearn (Bradford N.)
T. Skerrett (Wakefield T.)
M. Smith (Hull K.R.)
G. Stephens (Castleford)
C. Stone (Hull)
D. Ward (Leeds)
D. Watkinson (Hull K.R.)
J. Woods (Leigh)

Replacements during tour
J. Burke (Wakefield T.) for
Mills; G. Fairbairn (Wigan)
for Martyn; D. Topliss
(Wakefield T.) for Millward

Managers: H. Womersley
(Bradford N.) and
R. Gemmell (Hull)
Coach: E. Ashton (St. Helens)

1984 Tour*

B. Noble (Bradford N.)
M. Adams (Widnes)
R. Ashton (Oldham)
K. Beardmore (Castleford)
M. Burke (Widnes)
C. Burton (Hull K.R.)
B. Case (Wigan)
G. Clark (Hull K.R.)
L. Crooks (Hull)
S. Donlan (Leigh)
D. Drummond (Leigh)
R. Duane (Warrington)
T. Flanagan (Oldham)
D. Foy (Oldham)
A. Goodway (Oldham)
A. Gregory (Widnes)
E. Hanley (Bradford N.)
D. Hobbs (Featherstone R.)
N. Holding (St. Helens)
J. Joyner (Castleford)
J. Lydon (Widnes)
K. Mumby (Bradford N.)
A. Myler (Widnes)
M. O'Neill (Widnes)
H. Pinner (St. Helens)
W. Proctor (Hull)
Keith Rayne (Leeds)
G. Schofield (Hull)
M. Smith (Hull K.R.)
M. Worrall (Oldham)

Replacement during tour
J. Basnett (Widnes) for Duane

Managers: R. Gemmell (Hull)
and R. Davis (RLHQ)
Coach: Frank Myler (Oldham)

*One match in Papua New
 Guinea

1988 Tour*

E. Hanley (Wigan)
K. Beardmore (Castleford)
B. Case (Wigan)
L. Crooks (Leeds)
P. Dixon (Halifax)
S. Edwards (Wigan)
K. Fairbank (Bradford N.)
M. Ford (Oldham)
P. Ford (Bradford N.)
C. Gibson (Leeds)
H. Gill (Wigan)
A. Gregory (Wigan)
M. Gregory (Warrington)
P. Groves (St. Helens)
R. Haggerty (St. Helens)
D. Hulme (Widnes)
P. Loughlin (St. Helens)
P. Medley (Leeds)
M. Offiah (Widnes)
A. Platt (St. Helens)
R. Powell (Leeds)
G. Schofield (Leeds)
D. Stephenson (Leeds)
H. Waddell (Oldham)
K. Ward (Castleford)
I. Wilkinson (Halifax)

Replacements during tour
D. Wright (Widnes) for
Edwards; A. Currier (Widnes)
and P. Hulme (Widnes) for
Schofield and Medley; R. Eyres
(Widnes) and J. Joyner
(Castleford) for Crooks, Dixon
and Platt

Managers: L. Bettinson
(Salford) and D. Howes
(RLHQ)
Coach: M. Reilly

*Including Papua New Guinea

1990 Tour*

M. Gregory (Warrington)
D. Betts (Wigan)
C. Bibb (Featherstone R.)
D. Bishop (Hull K.R.)
P. Clarke (Wigan)
J. Davies (Widnes)
M. Dermott (Wigan)
P. Dixon (Leeds)
P. Eastwood (Hull)
K. England (Castleford)
K. Fairbank (Bradford N.)
D. Fox (Featherstone R.)
C. Gibson (Leeds)
R. Goulding (Wigan)
S. Irwin (Castleford)
L. Jackson (Hull)
I. Lucas (Wigan)
J. Lydon (Wigan)
M. Offiah (Widnes)
D. Powell (Sheffield E.)
R. Powell (Leeds)
G. H. Price (Wakefield T.)
G. Schofield (Leeds)
R. Simpson (Bradford N.)
K. Skerrett (Bradford N.)
I. Smales (Featherstone R.)
G. Steadman (Castleford)
A. Sullivan (Hull K.R.)
A. Tait (Widnes)

Replacements during tour
J. Devereux (Widnes) for
Sullivan; D. Lyon
(Warrington) for Tait

Manager: M. Lindsay (Wigan)
Coach: M. Reilly

*Papua New Guinea and
 New Zealand only

1992 Tour*

E. Hanley (Leeds)
D. Betts (Wigan)
P. Clarke (Wigan)
G. Connolly (St. Helens)
N. Cowie (Wigan)
L. Crooks (Castleford)
M. Dermott (Wigan)
J. Devereux (Widnes)
P. Eastwood (Hull)
S. Edwards (Wigan)
K. Ellis (Warrington)
K. Fairbank (Bradford N.)
D. Fox (Featherstone R.)
A. Gregory (Wigan)
G. Hallas (Hull K.R.)

S. Hampson (Wigan)
L. Holliday (Widnes)
A. Hunte (St. Helens)
L. Jackson (Hull)
M. Jackson (Wakefield T.)
P. Loughlin (St. Helens)
I. Lucas (Wigan)
J. Lydon (Wigan)
W. McGinty (Wigan)
P. Newlove (Featherstone R.)
S. Nickle (St. Helens)
M. Offiah (Wigan)
A. Platt (Wigan)
D. Powell (Sheffield E.)
G. Schofield (Leeds)

K. Skerrett (Wigan)
G. Steadman (Castleford)

Replacements during tour
P. Hulme (Widnes) for Nickle
K. Harrison (Halifax),
S. McNamara (Hull), D. Myers
(Wigan), M. Aston (Sheffield E.)
and P. Broadbent (Sheffield E.)
for Gregory, Holliday, Loughlin,
Hanley and Lucas; D. Sampson
(Castleford) for Cowie

Manager: M. Lindsay (Wigan)
Coach: M. Reilly

*Including Papua New Guinea

ALL TIME TOUR RECORDS

IN AUSTRALIA
Highest score: 101-0 v. South Australia in 1914

Biggest defeat: 42-6 v. New South Wales in 1920 (Also *widest margin*)

Fewest defeats: 1 (and 1 draw) from 21 matches in 1958 and from 17 matches in 1970

Most defeats: 9 from 22 matches in 1966

Biggest attendances: 70,419 v. New South Wales (Sydney) in 1950

IN NEW ZEALAND
Highest score: 81-14 v. Bay of Plenty in 1962

Widest margin win: 72-3 v. Buller in 1928
72-3 v. North Island in 1958

Biggest defeat: 46-13 v. Auckland in 1962 (Also *widest margin*)

Fewest defeats: The tourists have won all their matches in the following years: 1910 (4 matches), 1914 (6), 1932 (8), 1936 (8), 1966 (8), 1970 (7).

Most defeats: 4 from 8 matches in 1984

Biggest attendance: 35,000 v. Auckland in 1920

PLAYERS' FULL TOUR RECORDS
Most full appearances: 24 by Dick Huddart in 1958

Most tries: 38 by Mick Sullivan in 1958

Most goals and points: 127g, 278 pts by Lewis Jones in 1954

Most tours: 4 by Garry Schofield (1984, 1988, 1990, 1992)

Biggest club representation: 13+1 replacement by Wigan in 1992 — Denis Betts, Phil Clarke, Neil Cowie, Martin Dermott, Shaun Edwards, Andy Gregory, Steve Hampson, Ian Lucas, Joe Lydon, Billy McGinty, Martin Offiah, Andy Platt, Kelvin Skerrett, plus David Myers as a replacement

Brothers touring together: Bryn and Jack Evans (1928), Don and Neil Fox (1962), Alan and John Bates (1974), David and Paul Hulme (1988, Paul as replacement)

Paul Newlove, the youngest-ever Great Britain debutant, at 18 years 72 days, in 1989.

GREAT BRITAIN RECORDS

● In Test and World Cup matches.

MOST TRIES IN CAREER

*41	Mick Sullivan (Huddersfield, Wigan, St. Helens, York)	1954-63
31	Garry Schofield (Hull, Leeds)	1984-
26	Martin Offiah (Widnes, Wigan)	1988-
24	Billy Boston (Wigan)	1954-63
20	Ellery Hanley (Bradford N., Wigan, Leeds)	1984-93
17	Roger Millward (Cas'd, Hull K.R.)	1966-78
16	Alex Murphy (St. Helens, Warrington)	1958-71
15	Shaun Edwards (Wigan)	1985-
14	Eric Ashton (Wigan)	1957-63
14	Neil Fox (Wakefield T.)	1959-69
13	Clive Sullivan (Hull)	1967-73
12	John Atkinson (Leeds)	1968-80
10	Jim Leytham (Wigan)	1907-10

* Mick Sullivan also scored two tries for Great Britain against France before the matches were given Test status.

● Most tries by a forward is eight by Derek Turner (Oldham, Wakefield T.) 1956-62; and Phil Lowe (Hull K.R.) 1970-78.

MOST GOALS IN CAREER

93	Neil Fox (Wakefield T.)	1959-69
66	Lewis Jones (Leeds)	1954-57
64	Jim Sullivan (Wigan)	1924-33
53	Eric Fraser (Warrington)	1958-61
49	Jonathan Davies (Widnes, Warrington)	1990-94
44	George Fairbairn (Wigan, Hull K.R.)	1977-82
39	Paul Eastwood (Hull)	1990-
31	Paul Loughlin (St. Helens)	1988-
26	Joe Lydon (Widnes, Wigan)	1983-92
25	Terry Clawson (Featherstone R., Leeds, Oldham)	1962-74
22	Ray Dutton (Widnes)	1970
22	John Holmes (Leeds)	1971-82
22	Ernest Ward (Bradford N.)	1946-52
21	Mick Burke (Widnes)	1980-86
21	Ken Gowers (Swinton)	1962-66

MOST POINTS IN CAREER

228	Neil Fox (Wakefield T.)	1959-69
149	Garry Schofield (Hull, Leeds)	1984-
147	Lewis Jones (Leeds)	1954-57
128	Jim Sullivan (Wigan)	1924-33
123	Mick Sullivan (Huddersfield, Wigan, St. Helens, York)	1954-63
112	Jonathan Davies (Widnes, Warrington)	1990-94
109	Eric Fraser (Warrington)	1958-61
106	Paul Eastwood (Hull)	1990-
104	Martin Offiah (Widnes, Wigan)	1988-
91	George Fairbairn (Wigan, Hull K.R.)	1977-82
81	Roger Millward (Castleford, Hull K.R.)	1966-78
80	Ellery Hanley (Bradford N., Wigan, Leeds)	1984-93
79	Joe Lydon (Widnes, Wigan)	1983-92

MOST TRIES IN A MATCH

5 by Martin Offiah (Widnes) v. France at Leeds
16 February, 1991

4 by Jim Leytham (Wigan) v. Australia at Brisbane
2 July, 1910
Billy Boston (Wigan) v. New Zealand at Auckland
24 July, 1954
Alex Murphy (St. Helens) v. France at Leeds
14 March, 1959
Garry Schofield (Hull) v. New Zealand at Wigan
2 November, 1985

3 by Bill Jukes (Hunslet) v. Australia at Sydney
18 June, 1910
Bert Avery (Oldham) v. New Zealand at Auckland
30 July, 1910
Billy Stone (Hull) v. New Zealand at Auckland
31 July, 1920
Jonty Parkin (Wakefield T.) v. New Zealand at Auckland 31 July, 1920
Charlie Carr (Barrow) v. New Zealand at Leeds
15 January, 1927
Stan Smith (Leeds) v. Australia at Sydney
16 July, 1932
Arthur Bassett (Halifax) v. Australia at Brisbane
6 July, 1946
George Wilson (Workington T.) v. New Zealand at Bradford 6 October, 1951
Mick Sullivan (Huddersfield) v. New Zealand at Bradford 12 November, 1955
Dave Bolton (Wigan) v. France at Wigan
23 November, 1957
Mick Sullivan (Wigan) v. Australia at Sydney
19 July, 1958
Mick Sullivan (Wigan) v. New Zealand at Auckland
9 August, 1958
Mick Sullivan (Wigan) v. France at Leeds
14 March, 1959
Clive Sullivan (Hull) v. New Zealand at Sydney
(World Cup) 8 June, 1968
Bill Burgess (Barrow) v. France at St. Helens
30 November, 1968
Keith Fielding (Salford) v. France at Grenoble
20 January, 1974
Henderson Gill (Wigan) v. France at Hull
6 December, 1981
Garry Schofield (Leeds) v. France at Leeds
16 February, 1991
Garry Schofield (Leeds) v. France at Carcassonne
7 March, 1993
Paul Newlove (Featherstone R.) v. France at Leeds
2 April, 1993

● Bill Jukes and Bert Avery are the only forwards to have scored hat-tricks for Great Britain, both on tour in 1910.

MOST GOALS IN A MATCH

10 by Lewis Jones (Leeds) v. Australia at Brisbane
3 July, 1954
Bernard Ganley (Oldham) v. France at Wigan
23 November, 1957
John Holmes (Leeds) v. New Zealand at Pau
(World Cup) 4 November, 1972
Jonathan Davies (Widnes) v. France at Leeds
2 April, 1993

9 by Lewis Jones (Leeds) v. France at Leeds
26 January, 1957
Neil Fox (Wakefield T.) v. France at Wigan
3 April, 1963
Neil Fox (Wakefield T.) v. France at Leigh
18 March, 1964

8 by Eric Fraser (Warrington) v. Australia at Sydney
19 July, 1958
David Creasser (Leeds) v. France at Leeds
1 March, 1985
Joe Lydon (Wigan) v. France at Leeds
24 January, 1987
Paul Eastwood (Hull) v. France at Leeds
16 February, 1991
Jonathan Davies (Widnes) v. Papua New Guinea at
Wigan 9 November, 1991

7 by Lewis Jones (Leeds) v. France at St. Helens
10 April, 1957
Eric Fraser (Warrington) v. New Zealand at Auckland
9 August, 1958
Eric Fraser (Warrington) v. France at Leeds
14 March, 1959
Neil Fox (Wakefield T.) v. New Zealand at Swinton
4 November, 1961
Neil Fox (Wakefield T.) v. France at Swinton
23 January, 1965
Bev Risman (Leeds) v. New Zealand at Sydney
(World Cup) 8 June, 1968
Roger Millward (Hull K.R.) v. Australia at Sydney
20 June, 1970
George Fairbairn (Wigan) v. France at Auckland
(World Cup) 5 June, 1977
John Woods (Leigh) v. France at Hull
6 December, 1981
David Stephenson (Wigan) v. Papua New Guinea at
Wigan 24 October, 1987
Paul Loughlin (St. Helens) v. Papua New Guinea at
Port Moresby 22 May, 1988

MOST POINTS IN A MATCH

26 (2t, 10g) by John Holmes (Leeds) v. New Zealand at
Pau (World Cup) 4 November, 1972
21 (1t, 9g) by Lewis Jones (Leeds) v. France at Leeds
26 January, 1957
Neil Fox (Wakefield T.) v. France at
Wigan 3 April, 1963
Neil Fox (Wakefield T.) v. France at Leigh
18 March, 1964

20 (10g) by Lewis Jones (Leeds) v. Australia at
Brisbane 3 July, 1954
(10g) Bernard Ganley (Oldham) v.
France at Wigan 23 November,
1957
(2t, 7g) Roger Millward (Hull K.R.) v.
Australia at Sydney 20 June, 1970
(1t, 8g) Joe Lydon (Wigan) v. France at
Leeds 24 February, 1987
(5t) Martin Offiah (Widnes) v. France
at Leeds 16 February, 1991
(1t, 8g) Paul Eastwood (Hull) v. France at
Leeds 16 February, 1991
(10g) Jonathan Davies (Widnes) v.
France at Leeds 2 April, 1993

MOST APPEARANCES

46   Mick Sullivan*
46(2)   Garry Schofield
36(1)   Ellery Hanley
36(4)   Shaun Edwards
33   Martin Offiah
31   Billy Boston
30(1)   Cliff Watson
30(7)   Joe Lydon
29   George Nicholls
29   Neil Fox
29(1)   Roger Millward
28   Alan Prescott
28(9)   Daryl Powell
27   Phil Jackson
27   Alex Murphy
26   Eric Ashton
26   John Atkinson
26(1)   Andy Gregory
25   Brian McTigue
25   Jim Sullivan
25   Tommy Harris
25(1)   Denis Betts
25(4)   Andy Platt

( ) Indicates substitute appearance included in total

* Mick Sullivan's joint record number of appearances includes a record run of 36 successive matches. In addition he played in two matches against France before they were given Test status.

LONGEST TEST CAREERS

14 years — Gus Risman
1932 to 1946 (17 appearances)

13 years 9 months — Billy Batten
1908 to 1921 (10 appearances)

13 years 6 months — Alex Murphy
1958 to 1971 (27 appearances)

12 years 9 months — Roger Millward
1966 to 1978 (28+1 appearances)

12 years 6 months — John Atkinson
1968 to 1980 (26 appearances)

12 years 6 months — Terry Clawson
1962 to 1974 (14 appearances)

YOUNGEST TEST PLAYER

Paul Newlove was 18 years 72 days old when he made his Great Britain Test debut as a 76th-minute substitute in the first Test against New Zealand at Old Trafford, Manchester, on 21 October 1989, making his full debut a week later. Born on 10 August 1971, he beat the previous record held by Shaun Edwards (born 17 October 1966) who was 18 years 135 days old when capped against France at Leeds on 1 March 1985.

Roger Millward (born 16 September 1947) was 18 years 37 days old when he was a non-playing substitute for the second Test against New Zealand at Bradford on 23 October 1965.

OLDEST TEST PLAYER

Jeff Grayshon (born 4 March 1949) was 36 years 8 months when he played in his last Test for Britain, against New Zealand at Elland Road, Leeds, on 9 November 1985.

RECORD TEAM CHANGES

The record number of team changes made by the Great Britain selectors is 10, on three occasions, all against Australia.

In 1929, Britain crashed 31-8 to Australia in the first Test at Hull KR and retained only three players for the second Test at Leeds, where they won 9-3.

After their biggest ever defeat of 50-12 in the 1963 second Test at Swinton, Britain dropped nine players and were forced to make another change when Vince Karalius was injured and replaced by Don Fox. Britain stopped Australia making a clean sweep of the series by winning 16-5 at Leeds in the last Test.

Following the 40-4 first Test defeat at Hull City's soccer ground in 1982, the selectors again made 10 changes, not including substitutes, Britain going down 27-6 in the second Test at Wigan.

Britain have never fielded the same team for three or more successive Tests.

Wales centre Allan Bateman, an ever present in the 1995 Halifax Centenary World Cup, taking his tally of caps to 11.

ENGLAND AND WALES

ENGLAND AND WALES

ENGLAND REGISTER
● Since reintroduction in 1975

The following is a register of England appearances since the reintroduction of European and World Championship matches in 1975, but does not include the challenge match against Australia played after the 1975 World Championship.

Figures in brackets are the total appearances for England since 1975, with the plus sign indicating substitute appearances, e.g. (7+3).

A few players also played in the 1969-70 European Championship and this is shown as an additional total outside bracket, e.g. (11)2.

World Championship matches are in bold letters. Substitute appearances are in lower case letters.

A - Australia, Fi - Fiji, F - France,
NZ - New Zealand, SA - South Africa
W - Wales.

ADAMS, Mick (3+2) Widnes: 1975 **NZ**, a; 1978 F; 1979 W; 1981 w
ARKWRIGHT, Chris (+1) St. Helens: 1984 w
ATKINSON, John (7)4 Leeds: 1975 W, **F, W, NZ, W**; 1978 F, W

BALDWIN, Simon (1+1) Halifax: 1995 w, F
BANKS, Barry (+1) York: 1979 f
BEARDMORE, Kevin (1) Castleford: 1984 W
BENTLEY, John (4) Halifax: 1995 F, **A, Fi, SA**
BETTS, Denis (4) Auckland W.: 1995 **A, A, Fi, W**
BEVERLEY, Harry (1) Workington T: 1979 W
BRIDGES, John "Keith" (7) Featherstone R: 1975 **NZ, A, W, F, NZ, A**; 1977 W
BROADBENT, Paul (2+1) Sheffield E.: 1995 F, **Fi, sa**
BURKE, Mick (1) Widnes: 1984 W
BUSBY, Dean (+1) Hull: 1992 w
BUTT, Ikram (1) Featherstone R.: 1995 W

CAIRNS, David (1) Barrow: 1984 W
CASE, Brian (1) Warrington: 1981 F
CASEY, Len (5) Hull KR: 1978 F, W; 1980 W; 1981 F, W
CASSIDY, Mick (2+3) Wigan: 1995 w, a, **Fi, SA, w**
CHARLTON, Paul (1) Salford: 1975 F
CHISNALL, Dave (3+1) Warrington: 1975 w, **F, W, NZ**
CHISNALL, Eric (3+1) St. Helens: 1975 F, **W, NZ, a**
CLARK, Garry (1) Hull KR: 1984 W
CLARKE, Phil (6) Wigan: 1992 W; 1995 W; Sydney C.R.: **A, A, SA, W**
CONNOLLY, Gary (1) St. Helens: 1992 W

COOK, Paul (1+1) Leeds: 1995 **fi, SA**
COOKSON, Phil (2) Leeds: 1975 **NZ, A**
COULMAN, Mike (5) Salford: 1975 F, W, **W, A**; 1977 F
CRITCHLEY, Jason (+1) Salford: 1992 w
CROOKS, Lee (1) Castleford: 1992 W
CUMMINS, Francis (1) Leeds: 1995 F
CUNNINGHAM, John (2) Barrow: 1975 F, W

DONLAN, Steve (1) Leigh: 1984 W
DRUMMOND, Des (5) Leigh: 1980 W, F; 1981 F, W; 1984 W
DUNN, Ged (6) Hull KR: 1975 W, **A, F, NZ, A**; 1977 F
DYL, Les (12+1) Leeds: 1975 F, W, **F, W, NZ, A, nz, A**; 1977 W, F; 1978 F, W; 1981 W

ECKERSLEY, Dave (+5) St. Helens: 1975 f, w, **f**; Widnes: 1977 w; 1978 w
EDWARDS, Shaun (1) Wigan: 1995 **A**
ELWELL, Keith (2) Widnes: 1978 F, W
EVANS, Steve (3) Featherstone R: 1979 F; 1980 W, F
EYRES, Richard (1) Widnes: 1992 W

FAIRBAIRN, George (15) Wigan: 1975 **W, NZ, A, W, F, NZ, A**; 1977 W, F; 1978 F; 1980 W, F; 1981 F, W; Hull KR: 1981 W
FARRAR, Vince (1) Featherstone R: 1977 F
FARRELL, Andrew (4) Wigan: 1995 **A, A, Fi, W**
FARRELL, Anthony (1) Sheffield E.: 1995 W
FENTON, Steve (2) Castleford: 1981 F, W
FIELDING, Keith (7) Salford: 1975 F, **W, NZ, A, W, F**
FORD, Mike (1) Castleford: 1992 W
FORSYTH, Colin (3) Bradford N: 1975 **W, F, NZ**
FOX, Deryck (2) Bradford N.: 1995 W, F

GAY, Richard (2) Hull: 1995 W, F
GILL, Henderson (1) Wigan: 1981 W
GILL, Ken (9+2) Salford: 1975 W, **F, w, NZ, a, W, F, NZ, A**; 1977 W, F
GLYNN, Peter (2) St. Helens: 1979 W, F
GODDARD, Richard (1) Castleford: 1995 F
GOODWAY, Andy (1) Oldham: 1984 W
GORLEY, Les (1+1) Workington T: 1977 W; Widnes: 1981 w
GORLEY, Peter (2+1) St. Helens: 1980 W, f; 1981 W
GOULDING, Bobbie (4) St. Helens: 1995 **A, Fi, SA, W**
GRAY, John (3) Wigan: 1975 F, W, F
GRAYSHON, Jeff (9+1) Dewsbury: 1975 **W, F, NZ, A**; 1977 W; Bradford N: 1979 W, F; 1980 w, F; 1981 W

HANLEY, Ellery (2) Bradford N: 1984 W; Leeds: 1992 W
HARRISON, Karl (5) Halifax: 1995 W, **A, A, SA, W**
HARRISON, Mick (2) Leeds: 1978 F, W
HAUGHTON, Simon (1+3) Wigan: 1995 **a, fi, SA, w**
HILTON, Mark (+1) Warrington, 1995 f
HOBBS, David (1) Featherstone R: 1984 W
HOGAN, Brian (5) Wigan: 1975 **W, F, NZ, A**; 1977 W
HOGAN, Phil (1) Hull KR: 1979 F

HOLDING, Neil (1) St. Helens: 1980 W
HOLDSTOCK, Roy (3) Hull KR: 1980 W, F; 1981 W
HOLGATE, Stephen (1) Workington T.: 1995 F
HOLMES, John (5+2) Leeds: 1975 **W, F, NZ, A**; 1977 W, f; 1978 f
HOWARD, Harvey (1) Leeds: 1995 W
HUDDART, Milton (1) Whitehaven: 1984 W
HUGHES, Eric (8+1) Widnes: 1975 **W, F, NZ, a**; 1977 F; 1978 F, W; 1979 W, F
HUNTE, Alan (1) St. Helens: 1992 W

IRVING, Bob (3) Wigan: 1975 **W, F, A**

JACKSON, Lee (6) Hull: 1992 W; Sheffield E.: 1995 F, **A, A, Fi, W**
JACKSON, Phil (2) Bradford N: 1975 W, **F**
JONES, Les (1) St. Helens: 1977 W
JOYNER, John (4) Castleford: 1980 W, F; 1981 F, W
JOYNT, Chris (1+3) St. Helens: 1992 w; 1995 **a, a, SA**

KELLY, Andy (1) Hull KR: 1984 W
KELLY, Ken (3) Warrington: 1979 W; 1981 F, W

LAUGHTON, Doug (1) Widnes: 1977 W
LEDGER, Barry (+1) St. Helens: 1984 w
LIPTROT, Graham (2) St. Helens: 1979 W, F
LOCKWOOD, Brian (2)+1 Hull KR: 1979 W, F
LOWE, Phil (3)2 Hull KR: 1977 F; 1978 F; 1981 W

McCURRIE, Steve (+3) Widnes: 1995 w, f, **fi**
McNAMARA Steve (1+1) Hull: 1995, w, F
MARTYN, Tommy (4+1) Warrington: 1975 W, **F, w**; 1979 W, F
MATHER, Barrie-Jon (2) Wigan: 1995 **A, SA**
MILLINGTON, John (2) Hull KR: 1975 F; 1981 W
MILLWARD, Roger (13)3+1 Hull KR: 1975 F, W, **F, W, A, W, F, NZ, A**; 1977 W, F; 1978 F, W
MOLLOY, Steve (1) Leeds: 1992 W
MORGAN, Mick (3+3) Wakefield T: 1975 f, W, **f, W, nz, A**
MUMBY, Keith (2) Bradford N: 1979 W, F
MURPHY, Martin (1) Oldham: 1975 F

NASH, Steve (7) Featherstone R: 1975 **W, NZ, A**; Salford: 1978 F, W; 1981 W, W
NEWLOVE, Paul (6) Featherstone R: 1992 W; Bradford N.: 1995 W, **A, A, Fi, W**
NICHOLLS, George (7+4) St. Helens: 1975 F, **W, NZ, A, w, nz, f**; 1977 f; 1978 F, W
NICKLE, Sonny (1) St. Helens: 1995 W
NOONAN, Derek (3) Warrington: 1975 W, **F, W**
NORTON, Steve (11) Castleford: 1975 **W, NZ, A, W, F, NZ, A**; 1977 F; Hull: 1978 W; 1981 W, W

OFFIAH, Martin (4) Wigan: 1992 W; 1995 **A, SA, W**
O'NEILL, Steve (1) Wigan: 1981 F

PATTINSON, Bill (1+1) Workington T: 1981 f, **W**
PHILBIN, Barry (1) Warrington: 1975 **F**
PIMBLETT, Geoff (1) St. Helens: 1978 W
PINKNEY, Nick (4) Keighley C.: 1995 F, **Fi, SA, W**
PINNER, Harry (3) St. Helens: 1980 W, F; 1981 F
PLATT, Andy (4) Widnes/Auckland W.: 1995 **A, A, SA, W**
POTTER, Ian (2) Warrington: 1981 F, W
POWELL, Daryl (4+1) Sheffield E: 1992 w; 1995 W, F, **A, SA**

RADLINSKI, Kris (4+1) Wigan: 1995 **A, A, sa, W, Fi**
RAYNE, Keith (2) Wakefield T: 1980 W, F
REDFEARN, Alan (2) Bradford N: 1979 F; 1980 F
REDFEARN, Dave (2) Bradford N: 1975 F, **A**
REILLY, Malcolm (+1)2 Castleford: 1977 w
RICHARDSON, Terry (1) Castleford: 1981 W
ROBINSON, Jason (5) Wigan: 1995 W, **A, A, Fi, W**
ROSE, Paul (2) Hull KR: 1977 F; 1978 W
RUSSELL, Richard (1) Castleford: 1995 W

SAMPSON, Dean (1+2) Castleford: **Fi, sa, w**
SCHOFIELD, Garry (3) Hull: 1984 W; Leeds: 1992 W; 1995 W
SHEARD, Les (1) Wakefield T: 1975 W
SIMPSON, Roger (+1) Bradford N.: 1995 f
SMITH, David (1) Leeds: 1977 F
SMITH, Keith (1) Wakefield T: 1979 W
SMITH, Mike (5) Hull KR: 1980 W, F; 1981 F, W, W
SMITH, Peter (1) Featherstone R: 1980 F
SMITH, Tony (3+2) Castleford: 1995 f, **A, Fi, sa, W**
SPRUCE, Stuart (1) Widnes: 1992 W
STEPHENS, Gary (1) Castleford: 1979 W
SZYMALA, Eddie (+1) Barrow: 1979 f

THOMPSON, Jimmy (2+1)1 Featherstone R: 1975 **A**; 1977 W; Bradford N: 1978 w
TINDALL, Keith (1) Hull: 1979 F
TOPLISS, David (1) Wakefield T: 1975 F

WADDELL, Hugh (1) Blackpool B: 1984 W
WALKER, Arnold (1) Whitehaven: 1981 F
WALSH, John (3) St. Helens: 1975 F, **NZ, A**
WARD, David (6) Leeds: 1977 F; 1980 W, F; 1981 F, W, W
WATKINSON, David (+1) Hull KR: 1977 w
WOODS, John (3+4) Leigh: 1979 w, F; 1980 w, F; 1981 f, w, **W**
WRIGHT, Nigel (1) Wakefield T.: 1995 F
WRIGHT, Stuart (7) Wigan: 1975 **NZ**; Widnes: 1977 W; 1978 F, W; 1979 W, F; 1980 W

WALES REGISTER

● Since 1975

Figures in brackets are the total appearances for Wales since 1975, with the plus sign indicating substitute appearances, e.g. (7+3).

A few players also played in the 1969-70 European Championship and this is shown as an additional total outside bracket, e.g. (11)2.

World Championship matches are in bold letters. Substitute appearances are in lower case letters. A - Australia, E - England, F - France, NZ - New Zealand, P - Papua New Guinea, WS - Western Samoa.

ACKERMAN, Rob (4+1) Carlisle: 1991 P; 1992 F; Salford: 1992 E, F; Cardiff I. ARL: 1993 nz
ATCHESON, Paul (2+1) Wigan: 1995 E, F; Oldham: **ws**

BANNER, Peter (9) Salford: 1975 F, E, **F, E, NZ**; Featherstone R: 1975 **E, A, NZ, F**
BATEMAN, Allan (11) Warrington: 1991 P; 1992 F, E; 1993 NZ; 1994 F; 1995 E, F, **F, WS, E**
BAYLISS, Steve (1) St. Helens: 1981 E
BEVAN, John (17) Warrington: 1975 F, E, **E, A, NZ, F**; 1977 E, F; 1978 A; 1979 F, E; 1980 F, E; 1981 F, E, E; 1982 A
BISHOP, David (4) Hull KR: 1991 P; 1992 F; London C: 1992 E, F
BOX, Harold (5) Featherstone R: 1979 F, E; 1980 F, E; Wakefield T: 1981 F
BUTLER, Brian (2+2) Swinton: 1975 **F, nz**; Warrington: 1975 f; 1977 F

CAMBRIANI, Adrian (3) Fulham: 1981 F, E, E
CAMILLERI, Chris (3) Barrow: 1980 F; Widnes: 1982 A; Bridgend: 1984 E
CORDLE, Gerald (3+2) Bradford N: 1991 p; 1992 E; 1993 NZ; 1994 F, a
COSLETT, Kel (8)2 St. Helens: 1975 F, E, **F, E, A, NZ, E, A**
COWIE, Neil (+3) Wigan: 1995 e, f, **ws**
CUNNINGHAM, Eddie (8) St. Helens: 1975 **E, A, E, A**; 1977 E; 1978 F, E, A
CUNNINGHAM, Keiron (+3) St. Helens: 1995 **f, ws, e**
CUNNINGHAM, Tommy (2) Warrington: 1979 F, E
CURLING, Dennis (+1) Warrington: 1977 f

DAVID, Tommy (2) Cardiff C: 1981 E; 1982 A
DAVIES, Frank (1) New Hunslet: 1978 E
DAVIES, Jonathan (9) Widnes: 1991 P; 1992 F; Warrington: 1993 NZ; 1994 F; 1995 E, F, **F, WS, E**
DAVIES, Mike (1) Bridgend: 1984 E

DEVEREUX, John (10) Widnes: 1991 P; 1992 F, E, F; 1993 NZ; 1994 A; 1995 F, **F, WS, E**
DIAMOND, Steve (2+1) Wakefield T: 1980 F, e; 1981 F
DIXON, Colin (10)3 Salford: 1975 F, E, **F, E, NZ, A**; 1977 E, F; 1978 F; Hull KR: 1981 E

ELLIS, Kevin (12) Warrington: 1991 P; 1992 F, E, F; 1993 NZ; 1994 F, A; 1995 **F, WS, E**; Workington T.: 1995 E, F
EVANS, Richard (5) Swinton: 1975 E, **F**; 1978 F; Salford: 1978 E
EYRES, Richard (5) Leeds: 1995 E, F, **F, WS, E**

FENWICK, Steve (2) Cardiff C: 1981 E; 1982 A
FISHER, Tony (10)4 Leeds: 1975 F, **E, A, NZ**; Castleford: 1975 **E, A, NZ**; 1977 E, F; Bradford N: 1978 A
FLOWERS, Ness (4) Wigan: 1980 F, E; 1981 E; Bridgend: 1984 E
FORD, Phil (9+1) Warrington: 1984 E; Leeds: 1991 P; 1992 F; Salford: 1992 E, F; 1993 NZ; 1994 F, A; 1995 E, f
FRANCIS, Bill (19) Wigan: 1975 F, E, **F, E, A, NZ, E, A, NZ, F**; 1977 E, F; St. Helens: 1978 F, E, A; 1979 F, E; Oldham: 1980 F, E

GALLACHER, Stuart (3+1) Keighley: 1975 f, E, **NZ, F**
GIBBS, Scott (3) St. Helens: 1994 A, 1995 **F, E**
GREGORY, Brian (3) Wigan: 1975 **E, NZ, F**
GRIFFITHS, Clive (+2) St. Helens: 1980 f; 1981 f
GRIFFITHS, Jonathan (6) St. Helens: 1991 P; 1992 F, E; 1993 NZ; 1994 F, A

HADLEY, Adrian (3+6) Salford: 1991 p; 1992 f; Widnes: 1992 e, F; 1993 nz; 1994 A; 1995 f, **f, WS**
HALL, Martin (5) Wigan: 1995 E, F, **F, WS, E**
HALLETT, Lynn (2) Cardiff C: 1982 A; Bridgend: 1984 E
HARRIS, Iestyn (6) Warrington: 1994 A, 1995 E, F, **F, WS, E**
HERDMAN, Martin (2+1) Fulham: 1981 e, E; 1982 A
HOPKINS, Lyn (1) Workington T: 1982 A

JAMES, Mel (11) St. Helens: 1975 **E**; 1978 F, E, A; 1979 F, E; 1980 F, E; 1981 F, E, E
JOHNS, Graeme (+2) Salford: 1979 f; Blackpool B: 1984 e
JONES, Clive (1+3) Leigh: 1975 **nz, F**; 1978 f, e
JONES, Mark (5+2) Hull: 1991 P; 1992 F, E; 1993 NZ; 1994 F; Warrington: **f, e**
JULIFF, Brian (8) Wakefield T: 1979 F, E; 1980 F, E; 1981 F, E; Wigan: 1982 A; 1984 E

KENNETT, Paul (+1) Swinton: 1992 f

LEE, Jason (+1) Warrington: 1994 a

McJENNETT, Mark (2+1) Barrow: 1980 F; 1982 a; 1984 E
MANTLE, John (11+1)3 St. Helens: 1975 F, E, **F, e, A, NZ, E, A, NZ, F**; 1977 E; 1978 E

MARLOW, Ian (5+1) Hull: 1992 F, E, F; Wakefield T: 1993 NZ; 1994 f, A

MATHIAS, Roy (20) St. Helens: 1975 F, E, **F, E, A, NZ, A, NZ, F**; 1977 E, F; 1978 F, E, A; 1979 F, E; 1980 F, E; 1981 F, E

MILLS, Jim (13)4 Widnes: 1975 F, E, **E, A, NZ, A, NZ**; 1977 E, F; 1978 F, E, A; 1979 F

MORAN, Mark (+2) Leigh: 1992 e, f

MORIARTY, Paul (10) Widnes: 1991 P; 1992 E, F; 1994 F; Halifax: 1994 A; 1995 E, **F, WS, E**

MURPHY, Mick (4+1) Bradford N: 1975 **F, NZ, F**; 1977 f; St. Jacques, France: 1979 F

NICHOLAS, Mike (4+2) Warrington: 1975 F, e; 1977 E, F; 1978 F; 1979 e

O'BRIEN, Chris (1) Bridgend: 1984 E

OWEN, Gareth (2) Oldham: 1981 E, F

OWEN, Roger (+2) St. Helens: 1981 f, e

PARRY, Donald (6) Blackpool B: 1980 F, E; 1981 F, E, E; 1982 A

PEARCE, Gary (1+3) Scarborough P: 1991 p; Ryedale-York: 1992 f, e, F

PERRETT, Mark (5) Halifax: 1994 F, A; 1995 E, F, **F**

PHILLIPS, Rowland (4+8) Warrington: 1991 p; 1992 f, e, F; 1993 NZ; 1994 F, A; Workington T.: 1995 e, f, **f, ws, e**

POWELL, Daio (+2) Bradford N: 1994 f, a

PREECE, Chris (1) Bradford N: 1984 E

PRENDIVILLE, Paul (4+2) Hull: 1979 e; 1980 E; 1981 F, e; 1982 A; 1984 E

PRITCHARD, Gordon (1+2) Barrow: 1978 f, e; Cardiff C: 1981 E

QUINNELL, Scott (2) Wigan: 1995 **WS, E**

RICHARDS, Maurice (2)1 Salford: 1975 **F**; 1977 E

RINGER, Paul (2) Cardiff C: 1981 E; 1982 A

RISMAN, John (2+1) Workington T: 1978 F; 1979 f, E

ROWE, Peter (4+3)2 Blackpool B: 1975 **a, e, a**; Huddersfield: 1977 E, F; 1979 F, E

RULE, Steve (1) Salford: 1981 E

SELDON, Chris (1+1) St. Helens: 1980 f, E

SHAW, Glyn (7) Widnes: 1978 F, A; 1980 F, E; 1981 E; Wigan: 1982 A; 1984 E

SILVA, Matthew (+1) Halifax: 1991 p

SKERRETT, Kelvin (5) Wigan: 1995 E, F, **F, WS, E**

SKERRETT, Trevor (7) Wakefield T: 1978 A; 1979 F, E; 1980 F; Hull: 1981 F, E; 1984 E

STEVENS, Ian (+1) Hull: 1992 f

SULLIVAN, Anthony (12) St. Helens: 1991 P; 1992 F, E, F; 1993 NZ; 1994 F, A: 1995 E, F, **F, WS, E**

SULLIVAN, Clive (10)4 Hull KR: 1975 **E, A, NZ, E**; 1977 F; 1978 F, E, A; 1979 F, E

TREASURE, David (5) Oldham: 1975 **E, A, NZ, E**; 1977 F

TURNER, Glyn (3+3) Hull KR: 1975 **e, A, e, A, f**; Hull: 1978 E

WALLACE, Richard (+1) York: 1975 **f**

WALTERS, Graham (2+1) Hull: 1980 E; 1981 E; Bridgend 1984 e

WANBON, Bobby (3)3+1 Warrington: 1975 **E, A, NZ**

WATKINS, David (14) Salford: 1975 F, E, **F, E, A, NZ, E, A, NZ, F**; 1977 E; 1978 E, A; 1979 F

WEBSTER, Richard (+2) Salford: 1994 f, a

WILKINS, Ray (+1) Workington T: 1977 e, F

WILLIAMS, Barry (4) Carlisle: 1991 P; 1992 F; 1993 NZ; 1994 F

WILLIAMS, Brynmor (1) Cardiff C: 1982 A

WILLIAMS, Peter (+1) Salford: 1992 f

WILLICOMBE, David (11)+2 Wigan: 1975 F, E, **F, E, A, NZ, NZ, F**; 1978 F, E, A

WILSON, Danny (4) Swinton: 1981 F, E, E; 1984 E

WILSON, Frank (7+2)4 St. Helens: 1975 F, E, **F, e, a, E, A, NZ, F**

WOODS, Paul (10) Widnes: 1977 E, F; 1978 F, E, A; Rochdale H: 1979 F, E; Hull: 1980 E; 1981 F, E

YOUNG, David (12) Salford: 1991 P; 1992 F, E, F; 1993 NZ; 1994 F, A; 1995 E, F, **F, WS, E**

Five-cap Wales prop Kelvin Skerrett, one of a crop of Anglo-Welshmen to qualify by grandparentage during 1995.

ENGLAND SYNOPSIS

	P	W	D	L	F	A
v. FRANCE						
Euro'n Championship	27	18	2	7	341	307
World Cup	2	2	0	0	68	4
Other matches	1	1	0	0	18	6
Totals	30	21	2	7	427	317
v. WALES						
Euro'n Championship	26	16	0	10	459	249
World Championship	3	2	0	1	54	38
Other matches	32	25	2	5	670	429
Totals	61	43	2	16	1,183	716
v. AUSTRALIA						
World Championship	4	2	1	1	54	55
Other matches	9	5	1	3	93	153
Totals	13	7	2	4	147	208
v. NEW ZEALAND						
World Championship	2	1	1	0	44	29
Others	1	1	0	0	18	16
Totals	3	2	1	0	62	45
v. PAPUA NEW GUINEA						
Other matches	1	1	0	0	40	12
v. FIJI						
World Championship	1	1	0	0	46	0
v. SOUTH AFRICA						
World Championship	1	1	0	0	46	0
v. OTHER NATIONALITIES						
Euro'n Championship	6	2	0	4	106	152
Other matches	10	6	1	3	230	173
Totals	16	8	1	7	336	325
GRAND TOTALS	126	84	8	34	2,287	1,623

WALES SYNOPSIS

	P	W	D	L	F	A
v. ENGLAND						
Euro'n Championship	26	10	0	16	249	459
World Championship	3	1	0	2	38	54
Other matches	32	5	2	25	429	670
Totals	61	16	2	43	716	1,183
v. FRANCE						
Euro'n Championship	26	10	0	16	356	377
World Championship	3	2	0	1	58	22
Other matches	6	3	0	3	91	101
Totals	35	15	0	20	505	500
v. AUSTRALIA						
World Championship	2	0	0	2	19	48
Other matches	8	0	0	8	84	229
Totals	10	0	0	10	103	277
v. NEW ZEALAND						
World Championship	2	1	0	1	33	37
Other matches	5	2	0	3	85	83
Totals	7	3	0	4	118	120
v. PAPUA NEW GUINEA						
Other matches	1	1	0	0	68	0
v. WESTERN SAMOA						
World Championship	1	1	0	0	22	10
v. OTHER NATIONALITIES						
Euro'n Championship	5	1	0	4	60	101
GRAND TOTALS	120	37	2	81	1,592	2,191

Hull K.R. hooker Richard Chamberlain, capped twice by Great Britain under-21s in 1993.

UNDER-21s

GREAT BRITAIN UNDER-21s REGISTER

The following is a register of appearances for Great Britain Under-21s from this classification of match was introduced in 1984 until 1995.

Figures in brackets are the total appearances, with the plus sign indicating substitute appearances, e.g. (3+1).

Away matches are in bold letters. Substitute appearances are in lower case letters.

ALLEN, Shaun (1) St. Helens: 1984 F
ANDERSON, Grant (4) Castleford: 1989 F, **F**; 1990 **F**, F
ANDERSON, Paul (2) Leeds: 1992 **F**, 1993 F
ATCHESON, Paul (1) Wigan: 1993 F

BALDWIN, Simon (1) Halifax: 1995 **F**
BECKWITH, Mark (1+1) Whitehaven: 1986 **f**, F
BETTS, Denis (4) Wigan: 1989 F, **F**; 1990 **F**, F
BIBB, Chris (5) Featherstone R.: 1987 **F**, F; 1988 F; 1989 F, **F**
BISHOP, Paul (1+1) Warrington: 1987 **F**, f
BONSON, Paul (2) Featherstone R.: 1992 F, **F**
BOOTHROYD, Giles (1) Castleford: 1989 F
BURGESS, Andy (+1) Salford: 1991 f
BUSBY, Dean (2+1) Hull: 1991 P; 1992 F, **f**

CARBERT, Brian (3) Warrington: 1985 NZ; 1986 **F**, F
CASSIDY, Frank (1+1) Swinton: 1988 **f**, F
CASSIDY, Jez (+3) Hull: 1993 nz, f; 1994a
CASSIDY, Mick (2+1) Wigan: 1993 f, NZ, F
CHAMBERLAIN, Richard (1+1) Hull K.R.: 1993 f, F
CHAMBERS, Gary (2) Warrington: 1991 **F**, F
CHRISTIE, Gary (1) Oldham: 1993 F
CLARK, Garry (2) Hull K.R.: 1984 F, **F**
CLARKE, John (1) Oldham: 1984 A
CLARKE, Phil (5) Wigan: 1990 **F**; 1991 **F**, F; 1992 F, **F**
COCHRANE, Gareth (+1) Keighley C.: 1995 **f**
CONNOLLY, Gary (4) St. Helens: 1990 F; 1991 F, P; 1992 **F**
CONWAY, Mark (1) Leeds: 1984 F
CREASSER, David (5) Leeds: 1984 F, **F**; 1985 NZ; 1986 **F**, F
CRITCHLEY, Jason (+1) Widnes: 1990 **f**
CROOKS, Lee (2) Hull: 1984 F, **F**
CUMMINS, Francis (2) Leeds: 1994 A, 1995 **F**
CURRIER, Andy (2) Widnes: 1984, F, **F**

DALTON, James (3) Whitehaven: 1985 NZ; 1986 **F**, F
DANBY, Rob (2) Hull: 1993 NZ, F
DANNATT, Andy (6) Hull: 1984 F, **F**; 1985 NZ; 1986 **F**; 1987 **F**, F
DARBYSHIRE, Paul (1+1) Warrington: 1991 **f**, F
DELANEY, Paul (+2) Leeds: 1990 **f**, f

DERMOTT, Martin (5) Wigan: 1987 **F**, F; 1988 **F**, F; 1989 F
DISLEY, Gary (+1) Salford: 1987 f
DIVORTY, Gary (6) Hull: 1984 F; 1985 NZ; 1986 **F**, F; 1987 **F**, F
DIXON, Mike (1) Hull: 1991 P
DONOHUE, Jason (+2) Leigh: 1992 f; 1993 f

EASTWOOD, Paul (2) Hull: 1987 **F**, F
EDWARDS, Shaun (4) Wigan: 1984 F; 1985 NZ; 1987 F, **F**

FARRELL, Andrew (1) Wigan: 1993 NZ
FARRELL, Anthony (1+1) Huddersfield: 1989 f, **F**
FAWCETT, Vince (3) Leeds: 1990 **F**, F; 1991 **F**
FLETCHER, Mike (2) Hull K.R.: 1988 **F**, F
FLYNN, Adrian (1) Wakefield T.: 1995 **F**
FORD, Mike (3+1) Wigan: 1985 NZ; 1986 **F**; Leigh: 1987 **f**, F
FORSHAW, Michael (+2) Wigan: 1991 **f**, f
FORSTER, Mark (3) Warrington: 1985 NZ; 1986 **F**, F
FOX, Deryck (1) Featherstone R.: 1984 **F**

GILDART, Ian (6) Wigan: 1988 **F**, F; 1989 F, **F**; 1990 **F**, F
GODDARD, Richard (4) Wakefield T.: 1993 NZ, F; Castleford: 1994 A; 1995 **F**
GOULDING, Bobbie (5) Wigan: 1990 **F**, F; 1991 **F**, F; Leeds: 1991 P
GREGORY, Mike (1) Warrington: 1984 **F**
GRIBBIN, Vince (1+1) Whitehaven: 1984 f, **F**
GROVES, Paul (3) Salford: 1984 F, **F**; 1985 NZ

HALLAS, Graeme (1+2) Hull K.R.: 1991 P; 1992 f, **f**
HAMMOND, Karle (1+1) Widnes: 1994 A; 1995 **f**
HARCOMBE, Kevin (1) Rochdale H.: 1986 F
HARLAND, Lee (2 +1) Halifax: 1993 NZ, f; 1994 A
HARMON, Neil (1+3) Warrington: 1988 **f**, F; 1989 f, **f**
HARRIS, Iestyn (2) Warrington: 1993 NZ, F
HAY, Andy (1) Castleford: 1995 **F**
HEWITT, Mark (1+1) Hull: 1994 a; 1995 **F**
HILL, Brendan (+1) Leeds: 1986 f
HILL, Kenny (3) Castleford: 1988 F, **F**; 1989 **F**
HILTON, Mark (2) Warrington: 1994 A; 1995 **F**
HOLROYD, Graham (+1) Leeds: 1993 f
HUGHES, Gary (1) Leigh: 1986 F
HUGHES, Ian (1) Sheffield E.: 1993 F
HULME, David (2+1) Widnes: 1985 nz; 1986 **F**, F
HUNTE, Alan (2) St. Helens: 1990 F; 1991 F

IRWIN, Shaun (4) Castleford: 1988 **F**; 1989 F, **F**; 1990 **F**

JACKSON, Michael (+1) Hunslet: 1991 **f**
JOHNSON, Errol (2) Leeds: 1988 **F**, F
JOYNT, Chris (4) Oldham: 1991 P; 1992 F, **F**; St. Helens: 1993 F

LAY, Steve (+1) Hunslet: 1989 **f**

LEATHAM, Jim (+1) Leeds: 1994 **f**
LORD, Gary (1) Castleford: 1988 **F**
LOUGHLIN, Paul (2) St. Helens: 1987 **F**, F
LUCAS, Ian (4) Wigan: 1988 **F**, F; 1989 F, **F**
LUMB, Tim (+1) Hunslet: 1991 **f**
LYMAN, Paul (3) Featherstone R.: 1985 NZ; 1986 F, **F**
LYON, David (2) Widnes: 1985 NZ; 1986 **F**

McAVOY, Nathan (+1) Salford: 1994 a
McCORMACK, Kevin (2) St. Helens: 1987 **F**, F
McCURRIE, Steve (4+1) Widnes: 1991 P; 1992 f; 1993 F, NZ, F
McNAMARA, Steve (5) Hull: 1991 **F**, F, P; 1992 **F**; 1993 F
MAKIN, Craig (+1) Widnes: 1993 nz
MALONEY, Francis (2) Featherstone R.: 1993 NZ, F
MARTIN, Scott (2+2) Leigh: 1993 nz, f, Sheffield E.: 1994 A; Leigh: 1995 **F**
MARTYN, Tommy (1+3) Oldham: 1991 **F**, f, p; 1992 **f**
MATHER, Barrie-Jon (3+1) Wigan: 1992 f; 1993 F, NZ, F
MEDLEY, Paul (2) Leeds: 1987 **F**, F
MOLLOY, Steve (2) Warrington: 1990 **F**, F
MOSLEY, James (1) Wakefield T.: 1993 F
MOUNTAIN, Dean (+1) Castleford: 1987 **f**
MOXON, Darren (1) Bradford N.: 1991 **F**
MYCOE, David (4) Sheffield E.: 1990 **F**; 1991 P; 1992 F, **F**
MYERS, David (5) Wigan: 1991 **F**, F, P; 1992 F, **F**

NEWLOVE, Paul (8) Featherstone R.: 1989 F, **F**; 1990 **F**, F; 1991 **F**, P; 1992 F, **F**
NICKLE, Sonny (1) Sheffield E.: 1990 **F**

O'DONNELL, Gus (2) Wigan: 1992 F, **F**

PARKER, Wayne (2) Hull K.R.: 1988 **F**, F
PARR, Chris (1) Huddersfield: 1991 P
PEARSON, Martin (4) Featherstone R.: 1991 P; 1992 F, **F**; 1993 F
PENNY, Lee (3) Warrington: 1993 F, NZ, F
PERRETT, Mark (2) Halifax: 1993 F, 1994 A
PICKSLEY, Richard (1) Sheffield E.: 1992 F
PINKNEY, Nick (+1) Ryedale-York: 1991 p
POWELL, Daio (2) Bradford N.: 1993 NZ, F
POWELL, Roy (5) Leeds: 1984 F, **F**; 1985 NZ; 1986 **F**, F
PRATT, Richard (2) Leeds: 1988 **F**, F
PRECIOUS, Andy (+1) Hunslet: 1991 p
PRESCOTT, Steve (2) St. Helens: 1994 A; 1995 **F**
PRICE, Gary H. (5+1) Wakefield T.: 1988 f; 1989 F, **F**; 1990 F; 1991 **F**, F
PRICE, Richard (2) Hull: 1989 F, **F**
PROCTOR, Wayne (+1) Hull: 1984 f
PUCKERING, Neil (4) Hull: 1986 **F**, F; 1987 **F**, F

REYNOLDS, Simon (+1) Huddersfield: 1995 **f**
RICHARDS, Craig (2) Bradford N.: 1991 **F**, F
RILEY, Mike (2) St. Helens: 1992 F, **F**
RIPPON, Andy (1) Swinton: 1984 **F**
ROBINSON, Jason (1) Wigan: 1993 F

ROBINSON, Steve (1) Halifax: 1988 F
ROEBUCK, Neil (+1) Castleford: 1990 f
ROUND, Paul (1+1) St. Helens: 1984 F, **f**
ROWLEY, Paul (1) Halifax: 1995 **F**
RUDD, Chris (2) Warrington: 1991 **F**, F
RUSSELL, Richard (1+1) Wigan: 1987 **F**; 1988 f

SAMPSON, Dean (1) Castleford: 1988 **F**
SANDERSON, Gary (4) Warrington: 1987 **F**, F; 1988 **F**, F
SCHOFIELD, Garry (2) Hull: 1984 **F**, F
SHERIDAN, Ryan (1) Sheffield E.: 1994 A
SLATER, Richard (+1) Wakefield T.: 1992 **f**
SMITH, Chris (2) Castleford: 1994 A; 1995 **F**
SMITH, Tony (1) Castleford: 1991 **F**
SOUTHERNWOOD, Graham (6) Castleford: 1990 **F**, F; 1991 **F**, F; 1992 F, **F**
SOUTHERNWOOD, Roy (2) Castleford: 1989 F, **F**
SPRUCE, Stuart (+1) Widnes: 1991 f
STEPHENS, Gareth (2+1) Leeds: 1993 f, NZ, F
STREET, Tim (2) Leigh: 1989 F, **F**
SULLIVAN, Anthony (1) Hull K.R.: 1990 F
SUMNER, Phil (3) Warrington: 1990 F; 1991 P; 1992 F
SYKES, Nathan (1+1) Castleford: 1993 F; 1994 a

THOMPSON, Alex (3) Sheffield E.: 1993 NZ; 1994 A; 1995 **F**
TURNER, Robert (1) Warrington: 1990 F

WANE, Shaun (3) Wigan: 1984 **F**; 1985 NZ; 1986 **F**
WESTHEAD, John (1+2) Leigh: 1985 nz; 1986 **f**, F
WRIGHT, Darren (2) Widnes: 1987 **F**; 1988 **F**
WRIGHT, Nigel (3+1) Wakefield T.: 1993 F; Wigan 1993 nz; Wakefield T.: 1994 A, 1995 **F**

Twin Under-21 cap, St. Helens full back Steve Prescott.

UNDER-21s RECORDS

Highest score:	58-0 v. Papua New Guinea at Leeds, 30 October 1991
Highest against:	10-54 v. Australia at Gateshead 15 November 1994
Most tries in a match:	3 by Neil Puckering (Hull) v. France at St. Helens, 21 March 1987 David Myers (Wigan) v. PNG at Leeds, 30 October 1991 David Myers (Wigan) v. France at Halifax, 6 March 1992 Martin Pearson (Featherstone R.) v. France at Halifax, 6 March 1992 David Myers (Wigan) v. France at Albi, 20 March 1992
Most goals in a match:	8 by Chris Rudd (Warrington) v. France at Limoux, 26 January 1991 Martin Pearson (Featherstone R.) v. PNG at Leeds, 30 October 1991
Most points in a match:	24 (3t,6g) by Martin Pearson (Featherstone R.) v. France at Halifax, 6 March 1992
Biggest attendance:	4,596 v. France at Doncaster, 16 February 1990

UNDER-24s RESULTS

3 Apr.	1965	W	17-9	v.	F	Toulouse
20 Oct.	1965	W	12-5	v.	F	Oldham
26 Nov.	1966	L	4-7	v.	F	Bayonne
17 Apr.	1969	W	42-2	v.	F	Castleford
14 Nov.	1976	W	19-2	v.	F	Hull K.R.
5 Dec.	1976	W	11-9	v.	F	Albi
12 Nov.	1977	W	27-9	v.	F	Hull
18 Dec.	1977	W	8-4	v.	F	Tonneins
4 Oct.	1978	L	8-30	v.	A	Hull K.R.
14 Jan.	1979	W	15-3	v.	F	Limoux
24 Nov.	1979	W	14-2	v.	F	Leigh
13 Jan.	1980	W	11-7	v.	F	Carcassonne
5 Nov.	1980	L	14-18	v.	NZ	Fulham
10 Jan.	1981	W	9-2	v.	F	Villeneuve
16 Jan.	1982	W	19-16	v.	F	Leeds
21 Feb.	1982	W	24-12	v.	F	Tonneins
16 Jan.	1983	W	19-5	v.	F	Carpentras
11 Nov.	1983	W	28-23	v.	F	Villeneuve
4 Dec.	1983	W	48-1	v.	F	Oldham

GREAT BRITAIN UNDER-24s REGISTER

The following is a register of appearances by current players, who played at least one club game in 1995-96, for Great Britain Under-24s since this classification of match was reintroduced in 1976, until it was replaced by the new Under-21 level in 1984.

Figures in brackets are the total appearances, with the plus sign indicating substitute appearances, e.g. (7+3).

Away matches are in bold letters. Substitute appearances are in lower case letters.

ASHTON, Ray (3) Oldham: 1983 **F**, **F**, F

CROOKS, Lee (1) Hull: 1983 F

ECCLES, Bob (2) Warrington: 1978 A; 1979 F
ENGLAND, Keith (+1) Castleford: 1983 **f**

FIELDHOUSE, John (1+1) Warrington: 1983 **F**, f
FORD, Phil (1) Warrington: 1982 **F**

GREGORY, Andy (1) Widnes: 1982 F

MASKILL, Colin (1) Wakefield T.: 1983 **F**
MUMBY, Keith (6) Bradford N.: 1976 F, **F**; 1977 F, **F**; 1978 A; 1981 **F**

SCHOFIELD, Garry (+2) Hull: 1983 **f**, f

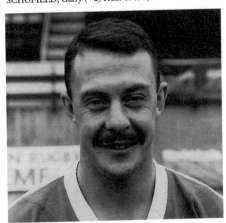

Garry Schofield, who made two appearances for Great Britain Under-21s in 1983 while serving Hull.

New world record transfer Paul Newlove celebrates his £500,000-rated move from Bradford Bulls to St. Helens in November 1995.

TRANSFERS

RECORD TRANSFERS

The first £1,000 transfer came in 1921 when Harold Buck joined Leeds from Hunslet, although there were reports at the time that another player was involved in the deal to make up the four-figure transfer. Other claims for the first £1,000 transfer are attached to Stan Brogden's move from Bradford Northern to Huddersfield in 1929. The following list shows how transfer fees have grown this century in straight cash deals only:

Season	Player	Position	From	To	Fee
1901-02	Jim Lomas	Centre	Bramley	Salford	£100
1910-11	Jim Lomas	Centre	Salford	Oldham	£300
1912-13	Billy Batten	Centre	Hunslet	Hull	£600
1921-22	Harold Buck	Wing	Hunslet	Leeds	£1,000
1929-30	Stanley Smith	Wing	Wakefield T.	Leeds	£1,075
1933-34	Stanley Brogden	Wing/Centre	Huddersfield	Leeds	£1,200
1937-38	Billy Belshaw	Full back	Liverpool S.	Warrington	£1,450
1946-47	Bill Davies	Full back/Centre	Huddersfield	Dewsbury	£1,650
1947-48	Bill Hudson	Forward	Batley	Wigan	£2,000
1947-48	Jim Ledgard	Full back	Dewsbury	Leigh	£2,650
1948-49	Ike Owens	Forward	Leeds	Castleford	£2,750
1948-49	Ike Owens	Forward	Castleford	Huddersfield	£2,750
1948-49	Stan McCormick	Wing	Belle Vue R.	St. Helens	£4,000
1949-50	Albert Naughton	Centre	Widnes	Warrington	£4,600
1950-51	Bruce Ryan	Wing	Hull	Leeds	£4,750
1950-51	Joe Egan	Hooker	Wigan	Leigh	£5,000
1950-51	Harry Street	Forward	Dewsbury	Wigan	£5,000
1957-58	Mick Sullivan	Wing	Huddersfield	Wigan	£9,500
1958-59	Ike Southward	Wing	Workington T.	Oldham	£10,650
1960-61	Mick Sullivan	Wing	Wigan	St. Helens	£11,000
1960-61	Ike Southward	Wing	Oldham	Workington T.	£11,002 10s
1968-69	Colin Dixon	Forward	Halifax	Salford	£12,000
1969-70	Paul Charlton	Full back	Workington T.	Salford	£12,500
1972-73	Eric Prescott	Forward	St. Helens	Salford	£13,000
1975-76	Steve Nash	Scrum half	Featherstone R.	Salford	£15,000
1977-78	Bill Ashurst	Forward	Wigan	Wakefield T.	£18,000
1978-79	Clive Pickerill	Scrum half	Castleford	Hull	£20,000
1978-79	Phil Hogan	Forward	Barrow	Hull K.R.	£35,000
1979-80	Len Casey	Forward	Bradford N.	Hull K.R.	£38,000
1980-81	Trevor Skerrett	Forward	Wakefield T.	Hull	£40,000
1980-81	George Fairbairn	Full back	Wigan	Hull K.R.	£72,500
1985-86	Ellery Hanley	Centre/Stand off	Bradford N.	Wigan	£85,000
1985-86	Joe Lydon	Centre	Widnes	Wigan	£100,000
1986-87	Andy Gregory	Scrum half	Warrington	Wigan	£130,000
1987-88	Lee Crooks	Forward	Hull	Leeds	£150,000
1987-88	Garry Schofield	Centre	Hull	Leeds	£155,000
1989-90	Graham Steadman	Stand off	Featherstone R.	Castleford	£170,000
1991-92	Ellery Hanley	Forward	Wigan	Leeds	£250,000
1991-92	Martin Offiah	Winger	Widnes	Wigan	£440,000

TRANSFER REVIEW
1 June 1995 to 31 January 1996

Paul Newlove was involved in a world record transfer deal when he moved from Bradford Bulls to St. Helens in a cash-plus-players move reckoned to be worth £500,000. The Great Britain Test centre signed for St. Helens on 29 November for £250,000 plus Saints trio Sonny Nickle, Bernard Dwyer and Paul Loughlin, who moved to Odsal.

The previous record deal was Test winger Martin Offiah's move from Widnes to Wigan in January 1992 for £440,000, which remains the highest cash-only transfer.

Bradford had signed Newlove from Featherstone in July 1993 for a transfer tribunal record fixed fee of £245,000. He became unsettled two years later when Bradford sacked Peter Fox as coach and the club valued him at £750,000 as St. Helens, Leeds and Wigan began to show an interest.

The only six-figure straight cash deal during the centenary season involved Wigan Test forward Barrie McDermott's transfer to Leeds for £100,000 in September.

There were other big exchange deals with one of the most debated being Paul Cook's surprise departure from Leeds to Bradford Bulls in December, only two months after the 19-year-old utility back made his debut for England in the Centenary World Cup. Bradford signed Cook in exchange for centre Carl Hall plus a cash balance variably reported between £50,000 and £75,000.

Earlier in the season, promising young Wakefield Trinity centre Adrian Flynn moved to Castleford for about £70,000 plus £40,000-rated winger Jon Wray. Batley also rated Australian scrum half Glen Tomlinson at £100,000 when he moved to Bradford Bulls in part-exchange for Roger Simpson, David Turpin and Phil Hardwick.

Towards the end of the season League officials were watching closely the developments of soccer's "Bosman Case" in which the European Court ruling appeared to indicate that the Belgian and other sportsmen could move freely between European countries at the end of their contract without a transfer fee being paid.

RUGBY UNION SIGNINGS

There were no major signings among only four home-based Rugby Union players to switch to Rugby League as the top stars received big cash incentives not to exchange codes in the wake of the revolutionary decision by the 15-a-side game to go professional. But a few Rugby Union internationals from the South Pacific countries were lured into Rugby League during the season.

OVERSEAS PLAYERS

A big increase in the recruitment of South Pacific players was the most significant development during the period with many of them being snapped up following outstanding performances in the Centenary World Cup. The signings also included a number of Rugby Union internationals, resulting in a total of almost 30 players from the Cook Islands, Fiji, Tonga, and Western Samoa playing first-team rugby during the season, compared with around a dozen the previous year.

Five of the South African World Cup squad also made their senior English club debuts with Dewsbury. Frenchmen and a Kenyan added to the cosmopolitan mixture but the biggest overseas presence again came from Australia (65 players) and New Zealand (42). There was a total of 149 overseas players making at least one first-team appearance during the season compared with 127 the previous year, but still down on the peak of 168 in 1990-91.

301

At the end of the season the League's Board of Directors recommended an increase in the overseas quota from three to five players per club, including players from emerging nations who had previously been exempt from the quota. London Broncos, who relied almost entirely on Australians plus a few New Zealanders in 1995-96, would continue to be exempt from the quota ruling.

The following is a list of overseas players who made at least one first team appearance during the 1995-96 season:

OVERSEAS REGISTER 1995-96
*Test or World Cup players as at 1 February 1996

AUSTRALIA (65)

Sean Alvarez	(Rochdale H.)
Darren Appleby	(Keighley C.)
Greg Austin	(Huddersfield)
Glen Barber	(Barrow B.)
Russell Bawden	(London B.)
Graeme Bradley	(Bradford B.)
Justin Bryant	(London B.)
Logan Campbell	(Workington T.)
Paul Carr	(Sheffield E)
Evan Cochrane	(London B.)
Brad Davis	(Wakefield T., York)
Scott Donnelly	(Dewsbury)
Jeremy Donougher	(Bradford B.)
Grant Doorey	(Keighley C.)
Leo Dynevor	(London B.)
Mick Francis	(London B.)
Ian Gateley	(Keighley C.)
Steve Georgallis	(Wakefield T.)
Steve Gibson	(Rochdale H.)
Wally Gibson	(Oldham B.)
Peter Gill	(London B.)
Craig Green	(London B.)
Dean Hanger	(Huddersfield)
*Paul Hauff	(London B.)
Cavill Heugh	(London B., Wakefield T.)
Rod Hill	(York)
Trent Jordan	(Dewsbury)
Shaun Keating	(London B.)
Dave King	(Warrington)
Kevin Langer	(London B.)
Jason Laurence	(York)
Andrew Leeds	(Wakefield T.)
Greg Mackey	(Warrington)
Terry Matterson	(London B.)
Danny McAllister	(Sheffield E.)
*Bruce McGuire	(Warrington)
Danny McKelvie	(Dewsbury)
Chris McKenna	(London B.)
Phil McKenzie	(Workington T.)
Duncan McRae	(London B.)
Tony Mestrov	(London B.)
Kieran Meyer	(London B.)
Paul Mills	(London B.)
David O'Donnell	(London B.)
Julian O'Neill	(London B.)
Greg Pearce	(Huddersfield)
Mike Pechey	(Widnes)
John Perigo	(Leigh C.)
Darryll Pitt	(London B.)
Brett Plowman	(Widnes)
Darren Pollinger	(Doncaster D.)
Tony Rea	(London B.)
Scott Roskell	(London B.)
Steve Rosolen	(London B.)
Danny Russell	(Carlisle)
Matthew Ryan	(Rochdale H.)
Andrew Schick	(Castleford)
Gary Schubert	(Workington T.)
Darren Shaw	(London B.)
Glen Tomlinson	(Batley)
Adrian Toole	(Huddersfield)
Phil Veivers	(St. Helens)
Shane Vincent	(London B.)
Ben Walker	(London B.)
Alan Wilson	(Bradford B., Huddersfield)

NEW ZEALAND (42)

*Simon Angell	(Featherstone R.)
Glen Bell	(Dewsbury)
Eugene Bourneville	(Bradford B.)
Bernard Carroll	(London B.)
*Shane Cooper	(Widnes)
Maea David	(Hull)
Casino Doyle	(Whitehaven)
*Peter Edwards	(Salford R.)
Shane Edwards	(Whitehaven)
*Esene Faimalo	(Leeds)
Joe Faimalo	(Oldham B.)
Neil Felton	(London B.)
Carl Hall	(Bradford B., Leeds)
Richard Henare	(Carlisle)
Darren Hogg	(London B.)
Craig Innes	(Leeds)
*Kevin Iro	(Leeds)
*Tony Kemp	(Leeds)
Brett Kingham	(Whitehaven)
*Mike Kuiti	(Wakefield T.)
Matt Levien	(Doncaster D., Hunslet H.)
Damien Mackie	(Featherstone R.)
Tane Manihera	(Carlisle)
**George Mann	(Leeds)
*Gary Mercer	(Leeds)
Martin Moana	(Halifax)
*Tawera Nikau	(Castleford)
Jason Palmada	(Workington T.)
**Sam Panapa	(Salford R.)
*Henry Paul	(Wigan)
Robbie Paul	(Bradford B.)
Jason Penny	(Doncaster D.)
Mark Riley	(London B.)
Brett Rodger	(Featherstone R.)
*Kelly Shelford	(Warrington)
Darrall Shelford	(Huddersfield)
*Sam Stewart	(Hull K.R.)
Jason Temu	(Oldham B.)
Shane Tupaea	(Keighley C.)
*Brendon Tuuta	(Castleford, Featherstone R.)
Sonny Whakarau	(Sheffield E., Wakefield T.)
Christian Wilson	(Leigh C.)

**Mann also played for Tonga
**Panapa also played for W. Samoa

New Zealander Tony Kemp, who made 16 appearances for Leeds in the 1995-96 Centenary season, having moved from Castleford in June 1995.

COOK ISLANDS (1)
Ali Davys   (Salford R.)

FIJI (5)
*Josaia "Joe"   (Sheffield E.)
  Dakuitoga
Carlos Hassan   (Bradford B.)
*Waisale Sovatabua   (Sheffield E.)
Manoa Thompson   (Warrington)
*Malakai Yasa   (Sheffield E.)
(Also known as Kaunaivalu)

FRANCE (5)
*Frederic Banquet   (Sheffield E., Wakefield T.)
*David Fraisse   (Workington T.)
*Jean-Marc Garcia   (Sheffield E.)
*Gael Tallec   (Wigan)
Jerome Vincent   (Sheffield E.)

KENYA (1)
Eddie Rombo   (Featherstone R.)

SOUTH AFRICA (7)
*Jaco Booyson   (Dewsbury)
*Guy Coombe   (Dewsbury)
*Tim Fourie   (Dewsbury)
*Mark Johnson   (Workington T.)
Andre Stoop   (Keighley C.)
*Kobus van Deventer   (Dewsbury)
*Pierre van Wyk   (Dewsbury)

TONGA (12)
*Asa Amone   (Halifax)
*Salesi Finau   (Warrington)
*Liuaki "Lee"   (Leigh C.)
  Hansen
Peaufai "Afi" Leuila   (Oldham B.)
*Talite Liava'a   (Swinton)
*Tau'alupe Liku   (Leigh C.)
Mateaki Mafi   (Warrington)
*Taukolo Tonga   (Workington T.)
Hamoni Tuavoa   (Leigh C.)
*Tevita Vaikona   (Hull)

*Jimmy Veikoso   (Leigh C.)
*Willie Wolfgramm   (Swinton)

WESTERN SAMOA (11)
Lafaele Filipo   (Workington T.)
*Des Maea   (Hunslet H.)
*Vila Matautia   (St. Helens)
*Apollo Perelini   (St. Helens)
Lokeni Savelino   (Salford R.)
*John Schuster   (Halifax)
Iefata "Fata" Sini   (Salford R.)
**Shem Tatupu   (Wigan)
*Va'aiga Tuigamala   (Wigan)
Fereti Tuilagi   (Halifax)
Mike Umaga   (Halifax)
**Tatupu also played for New Zealand

Western Samoan Vila Matautia scorer of 10 tries in 18 appearances for St. Helens in the 1995-96 Centenary season.

AWARDS

JOHN SMITH'S INTERNATIONAL PLAYER OF THE YEAR 1995

Wales' teenage utility back Iestyn Harris was crowned John Smith's International Player of the Year 1995.

Nineteen-year-old Harris was an ever-present in the Welsh side which won the John Smith's European Championship in the March – for the first time in 57 years – and reached the semi-finals of October's Halifax Centenary World Cup.

The Warrington star received a cheque for £1,000 and an engraved decanter and glasses. He is the second annual winner of the prestigious title of John Smith's International Player of the Year, Great Britain hooker Lee Jackson, then with Sheffield Eagles, taking the inaugural honour 12 months earlier.

Oldham-born Harris, who qualifies for Wales by parentage, made his debut for the Dragons against Australia in October 1994 at the age of 18 years, four months.

Harris figured at centre in Wales' memorable 18-16 victory over England in the opening game of the 1995 John Smith's European Championship in Cardiff, scoring a try from the wing in the 22-10 success over France in Carcassonne which clinched the title for the first time since 1936-37.

Harris, who celebrated his 19th birthday in June 1995, was switched to full back for the Centenary World Cup campaign.

He earned Man of the Match rating in the opening fixture against France at Cardiff, scoring a try in the 28-6 triumph. Six days later at Swansea, Harris contributed a try and a drop goal as the Welsh disposed of highly rated Western Samoa by 22-10 in front of a capacity Vetch Field crowd. He was then the outstanding Welsh player in the 25-10 semi-final defeat by England at Manchester United's Old Trafford.

Harris' new-found stature on the international scene was confirmed by his selection at full back in the official World Cup XIII chosen by a panel of specialist judges at the end of the 10-nation tournament.

Wales teenage star Iestyn Harris, John Smith's International Player of the Year 1995.

MAN OF STEEL ROLL OF HONOUR

	Man of Steel	1st Division Player	2nd Division Player	Young Player	Coach	Referee
1977	David Ward (Leeds)	Malcolm Reilly (Castleford)	Ged Marsh (Blackpool B.)	David Ward (Leeds)	Eric Ashton (St. Helens)	Billy Thompson (Huddersfield)
1978	George Nicholls (St. Helens)	George Nicholls (St. Helens)	John Woods (Leigh)	John Woods (Leigh)	Frank Myler (Widnes)	Billy Thompson (Huddersfield)
1979	Doug Laughton (Widnes)	Mick Adams (Widnes)	Steve Norton (Hull)	Steve Evans (Featherstone R.)	Doug Laughton (Widnes)	Mick Naughton (Widnes)
1980	George Fairbairn (Wigan)	Mick Adams (Widnes)	Steve Quinn (Featherstone R.)	Roy Holdstock (Hull K.R.)	Peter Fox (Bradford N.)	Fred Lindop (Wakefield)
1981	Ken Kelly (Warrington)	Ken Kelly (Warrington)	John Crossley (York)	Des Drummond (Leigh)	Billy Benyon (Warrington)	John Holdsworth (Kippax)
1982	Mick Morgan (Carlisle)	Steve Norton (Hull)	Mick Morgan (Carlisle)	Des Drummond (Leigh)	Arthur Bunting (Hull)	Fred Lindop (Wakefield)
1983	Allan Agar (Featherstone R.)	Keith Mumby (Bradford N.)	Steve Nash (Salford)	Brian Noble (Bradford N.)	Arthur Bunting (Hull)	Robin Whitfield (Widnes)
1984	Joe Lydon (Widnes)	Joe Lydon (Widnes)	David Cairns (Barrow)	Joe Lydon (Widnes)	Tommy Dawes (Barrow)	Billy Thompson (Huddersfield)
1985	Ellery Hanley (Bradford N.)	Ellery Hanley (Bradford N.)	Graham Steadman (York)	Lee Crooks (Hull)	Roger Millward (Hull K.R.)	Ron Campbell (Widnes)
1986	Gavin Miller (Hull K.R.)	Gavin Miller (Hull K.R.)	Derek Pyke (Leigh)	Shaun Edwards (Wigan)	Chris Anderson (Halifax)	Fred Lindop (Wakefield)
1987	Ellery Hanley (Wigan)	Andy Gregory (Wigan)	John Cogger (Runcorn H.)	Shaun Edwards (Wigan)	Graham Lowe (Wigan)	John Holdsworth (Kippax)
1988	Martin Offiah (Widnes)	Steve Hampson (Wigan)	Peter Smith (Featherstone R.)	Shaun Edwards (Wigan)	Doug Laughton (Widnes)	Fred Lindop (Wakefield)
1989	Ellery Hanley (Wigan)	David Hulme (Widnes)	Daryl Powell (Sheffield E.)	Paul Newlove (Featherstone R.)	Graham Lowe (Wigan)	John Holdsworth (Kippax)
1990	Shaun Edwards (Wigan)	Andy Goodway (Wigan)	John Woods (Rochdale H.)	Bobbie Goulding (Wigan)	John Monie (Wigan)	Robin Whitfield (Widnes)

	Man of Steel	1st Division Player	2nd Division Player	3rd Division Player	Young Player	Coach	Referee
1991	Garry Schofield (Leeds)	Jonathan Davies (Widnes)	Tawera Nikau (Ryedale-York)	—	Denis Betts (Wigan)	John Monie (Wigan)	John Holdsworth (Kippax)
1992	Dean Bell (Wigan)	Graham Steadman (Castleford)	Iva Ropati (Oldham)	Wally Gibson (Huddersfield)	Gary Connolly (St. Helens)	John Monie (Wigan)	Robin Whitfield (Widnes)
1993	Andy Platt (Wigan)	Tea Ropati (St. Helens)	Paul Newlove (Featherstone R.)	Martin Wood (Keighley C.)	Jason Robinson (Wigan)	John Monie (Wigan)	John Connolly (Wigan)
1994	Jonathan Davies (Warrington)	Jonathan Davies (Warrington)	Martin Oglanby (Workington T.)	—	Andrew Farrell (Wigan)	John Joyner (Castleford)	John Connolly (Wigan)
1995	Denis Betts (Wigan)	Bobbie Goulding (St. Helens)	Nick Pinkney (Keighley C.)	—	Andrew Farrell (Wigan)	Graeme West (Wigan)	Russell Smith (Castleford)

NOMINEES:

1977 *1st Division Player:* Bruce Burton (Castleford), Vince Farrar (Featherstone R.). *2nd Division Player:* Jeff Grayshon (Dewsbury), Keith Hepworth (Hull). *Young Player:* Jimmy Crampton (Hull), Harry Pinner (St. Helens). *Coach:* Keith Cotton (Featherstone R.), Mal Reilly (Castleford). *Referee:* Joe Jackson (Pudsey), Mick Naughton (Widnes).

1978 *1st Division Player:* Roger Millward (Hull K.R.), Harry Pinner (St. Helens). *2nd Division Player:* Phil Hogan (Barrow), Mick Morgan (York). *Young Player:* Neil Hague (Leeds), Keith Mumby (Bradford N.). *Coach:* Eric Ashton MBE (St. Helens), John Mantle (Leigh). *Referee:* Ron Campbell (Widnes), Fred Lindop (Wakefield).

1979 *1st Division Player:* Brian Lockwood (Hull K.R.), Tommy Martyn (Warrington). *2nd Division Player:* Barry Banks (York), John Wolford (Dewsbury). *Young Player:* Mick Burke (Widnes), John Woods (Leigh). *Coach:* Billy Benyon (Warrington), Arthur Bunting (Hull). *Referee:* Fred Lindop (Wakefield), Billy Thompson (Huddersfield).

1980 *1st Division Player:* Len Casey (Hull K.R.), George Fairbairn (Wigan). *2nd Division Player:* Mick Blacker (Halifax), John Wolford (Dewsbury). *Young Player:* Steve Hubbard (Hull K.R.), Harry Pinner (St. Helens). *Coach:* Maurice Bamford (Halifax), Arthur Bunting (Hull). *Referee:* Ron Campbell (Widnes), Billy Thompson (Huddersfield).

1981 *1st Division Player:* Mick Adams (Widnes), Tommy Martyn (Warrington). *2nd Division Player:* Arnie Walker (Whitehaven), Danny Wilson (Swinton). *Young Player:* Paul Harkin (Hull K.R.), Keith Mumby (Bradford N.). *Coach:* Reg Bowden (Fulham), Peter Fox (Bradford N.). *Referee:* Ron Campbell (Widnes), Fred Lindop (Wakefield).

1982 *1st Division Player:* Jeff Grayshon (Bradford N.), Andy Gregory (Widnes). *2nd Division Player:* Denis Boyd (Carlisle), Alan Fairhurst (Swinton). *Young Player:* Lee Crooks (Hull), Andy Gregory (Widnes). *Coach:* Doug Laughton (Widnes), Alex Murphy/Colin Clarke (Leigh). *Referee:* Gerry Kershaw (York), Billy Thompson (Huddersfield).

1983 *1st Division Player:* Bob Eccles (Warrington), David Topliss (Hull). *2nd Division Player:* Tommy David (Cardiff C.), Mike Lampkowski (Wakefield T.). *Young Player:* Ronnie Duane (Warrington), Andy Goodway (Oldham). *Coach:* Alex Murphy (Wigan), Frank Myler (Oldham). *Referee:* John Holdsworth (Leeds), Fred Lindop (Wakefield).

1984 *1st Division Player:* Garry Schofield (Hull), John Woods (Leigh). *2nd Division Player:* Lyn Hopkins (Workington T.), John Wolford (Hunslet). *Young Player:* Gary Divorty (Hull), Garry Schofield (Hull). *Coach:* Arthur Bunting (Hull), Roger Millward (Hull). *Referee:* Derek Fox (Wakefield), Fred Lindop (Wakefield).

1985 *1st Division Player:* Harry Pinner (St. Helens), Gary Prohm (Hull K.R.). *2nd Division Player:* Terry Langton (Mansfield M.), Peter Wood (Runcorn H.). *Young Player:* Deryck Fox (Featherstone R.), Andy Platt (St. Helens). *Coach:* Arthur Bunting (Hull), Colin Clarke/Alan McInnes (Wigan). *Referee:* Fred Lindop (Wakefield), Stan Wall (Leigh).

1986 *1st Division Player:* Steve Ella (Wigan), John Fieldhouse (Widnes). *2nd Division Player:* John Henderson (Leigh), Graham King (Hunslet). *Young Player:* Paul Lyman (Featherstone R.), Roy Powell (Leeds). *Coach:* Roger Millward (Hull K.R.), John Sheridan (Doncaster). *Referee:* John Holdsworth (Kippax), Robin Whitfield (Widnes).

1987 *1st Division Player:* Lee Crooks (Hull), Ellery Hanley (Wigan). *2nd Division Player:* Andy Bateman (Hunslet), Les Holliday (Swinton). *Young Player:* Paul Loughlin (St. Helens), Kevin McCormack (St. Helens). *Coach:* Chris Anderson (Halifax), Alex Murphy (St. Helens). *Referee:* Kevin Allatt (Southport), Fred Lindop (Wakefield).

1988 *1st Division Player:* Martin Offiah (Widnes), Kurt Sorensen (Widnes). *2nd Division Player:* Deryck Fox (Featherstone R.), Hugh Waddell (Oldham). *Young Player:* Paul Medley (Leeds), Steve Robinson (Halifax). *Coach:* Alex Murphy (St. Helens), Barry Seabourne (Bradford N.). *Referee:* John Holdsworth (Kippax), Ray Tennant (Castleford).

1989 *1st Division Player:* Andy Gregory (Wigan), Kelvin Skerrett (Bradford N.). *2nd Division Player:* Cavill Heugh (Barrow), Chris Johnson (Leigh). *Young Player:* Grant Anderson (Castleford), Denis Betts (Wigan). *Coach:* Peter Fox (Featherstone R.), Brian Smith (Hull). *Referee:* Ray Tennant (Castleford), Robin Whitfield (Widnes).

1990 *1st Division Player:* Deryck Fox (Featherstone R.), Andy Platt (Wigan). *2nd Division Player:* Cavill Heugh (Hull K.R.), John Cogger (Oldham). *Young Player:* Denis Betts (Wigan), Anthony Sullivan (Hull K.R.). *Coach:* Tony Barrow (Oldham), Brian Johnson (Warrington). *Referee:* John Holdsworth (Kippax), Colin Morris (Huddersfield).

1991 *1st Division Player:* Andy Gregory (Wigan), George Mann (St. Helens). *2nd Division Player:* Steve Kerry (Salford), Peter Ropati (Leigh). *Young Player:* Phil Clarke (Wigan), Craig Richards (Bradford N.). *Coach:* Ray Ashton (Workington T.), Doug Laughton (Widnes). *Referee:* Brian Galtress (Bradford), Jim Smith (Halifax).

1992 *1st Division Player:* Dean Bell (Wigan), John Devereux (Widnes). *2nd Division Player:* Clayton Friend (Carlisle), Paul Topping (Leigh). *3rd Division Player:* Steve Carroll (Bramley), Paul Delaney (Dewsbury). *Young Player:* Paul Newlove (Featherstone R.), David Myers (Wigan). *Coach:* Alex Murphy (Huddersfield), Darryl Van de Velde (Castleford). *Referee:* Stuart Cummings (Widnes), John Holdsworth (Kippax).

1993 *1st Division Player:* Phil Clarke (Wigan), Andy Platt (Wigan). *2nd Division Player:* Neil Flanagan (Huddersfield), Brendon Tuuta (Featherstone R.). *3rd Division Player:* Clayton Friend (Whitehaven), Brad Hepi (Workington T.). *Young Player:* Chris Joynt (St. Helens), Nigel Wright (Wakefield T.). *Coach:* Peter Fox (Bradford N.), Mike McClennan (St. Helens). *Referee:* John Holdsworth (Kippax), Russell Smith (Castleford).

1994 *1st Division Player:* Lee Crooks (Castleford). *2nd Division Player:* Glen Tomlinson (Batley).

1995 *1st Division Player:* Denis Betts (Wigan), Va'aiga Tuigamala (Wigan). *2nd Division Player:* Steve Hall (Keighley C.), Glen Tomlinson (Batley). *Young Player:* Keiron Cunningham (St. Helens), Iestyn Harris (Warrington). *Coach:* Andy Goodway (Oldham), Phil Larder (Keighley C.). *Referee:* David Campbell (St. Helens), Stuart Cummings (Widnes).

POT POURRI

DISCIPLINARY RECORDS

This is a compilation of sendings off and disciplinary verdicts for first team players.

The following information is based on the workings of the League's Disciplinary Committee which meets weekly during a season.

– club not in existence	1995-96	1994-95	1993-94	1992-93	1991-92	1990-91
Barrow B.	1	4	2	3	6	5
Batley	1	5	3	4	7	4
Blackpool G.	–	–	–	0	6	2
Bradford B.	1	2	2	0	4	3
Bramley	2	8	3	4	2	5
Carlisle	2	1	9	6	2	4
Castleford	0	3	1	3	3	4
Chorley C.	1	–	–	0	5	7
Dewsbury	1	4	4	1	1	5
Doncaster D.	2	5	3	2	3	4
Featherstone R.	4	6	3	3	7	1
Halifax	3	1	1	1	2	3
Highfield	5	5	3	7	7	3
Huddersfield	4	1	3	6	2	1
Hull	1	3	1	3	2	1
Hull K.R.	1	3	0	0	1	3
Hunslet H.	2	7	5	3	2	6
Keighley C.	0	3	3	2	4	5
Leeds	3	1	2	1	2	5
Leigh C.	0	3	3	1	3	1
London B.	0	2	1	5	2	1
Nottingham C.	–	–	–	2	2	2
Oldham B.	4	6	2	6	5	3
Rochdale H.	1	5	1	2	4	5
St. Helens	6	4	3	1	6	1
Salford R.	3	1	1	0	0	5
Scarborough P.	–	–	–	–	1	–
Sheffield E.	1	2	1	4	7	2
Swinton	0	6	2	3	4	1
Wakefield T.	1	1	3	1	3	2
Warrington	4	3	0	2	6	2
Whitehaven	1	7	4	1	5	3
Widnes	1	5	0	5	2	2
Wigan	1	3	1	2	2	7
Workington T.	0	2	2	4	6	4
York	2	4	4	2	1	3
Totals	**59**	**116**	**76**	**90**	**127**	**115**

DISCIPLINARY ANALYSIS 1995-96

The following is a club-by-club disciplinary record for 1995-96, showing the players sent off in first team matches and the findings of the League's Disciplinary Committee.

The committee's verdict is featured in the brackets after the player's name, each number indicating the match ban imposed. SOS stands for sending off sufficient and NG for not guilty. A suspension reduced or increased on appeal is shown as follows, 6 to 4.

During 1988-89 the totting-up system for sin-bin suspensions was abandoned. Previously two points were issued for a 10-minute temporary dismissal, a one-match ban being imposed when the total reached six. Instead, the sin bins were recorded and taken into account when considering a full dismissal.

The 1984-85 season was the first time video action other than official BBC or ITV tapes could be offered in evidence.

Towards the end of the 1994-95 season, new Referees' Coaching Director Greg McCallum introduced on-field reporting, with the alleged offenders being reported to the League's Board of Directors for them to decide whether there was a charge to answer.

Halifax skipper Karl Harrison, suspended for two matches in 1995-96.

Club	Total sent off	Dismissed Player	Number of sin bins
Barrow B.	1	Sam Hansen (SOS)	8
Batley	1	Graham Middleton (3)	9
Bradford B.	1	Matt Calland (To 1 March 1996)	4
Bramley	2	Ray Ashton (2), Dean Hall (2)	7
Carlisle	2	Gary Charlton (NG), Jason Thurlow (SOS)	6
Castleford	0	–	12
Chorley C.	1	John Costello (2)	5
Dewsbury	1	Jaco Booyson (1)	9
Doncaster D.	2	Ian Fletcher (NG), Howard Roberts (2)	7
Featherstone R.	4	Matt Calland (6,2), Joe Naidole (NG), Jason Sims (1)	13
Halifax	3	Asa Amone (1), Karl Harrison (2), Wayne Jackson (NG)	8
Highfield	5	Darren Chisnall (6,2), Roy Litherland (3), Neil Measures (4), Tony Pennington (SOS)	6
Huddersfield	4	Dean Hanger (2), Lee St. Hilaire (SOS), Andy Pucill (3), Adrian Toole (2 to 1)	11
Hull	1	Andy Fisher (1)	6
Hull K.R.	1	Andy Dannatt (2)	4
Hunslet H.	2	Lee Hanlan (SOS), Chris Watson (1)	8
Keighley C.	0	–	6
Leeds	3	Harvey Howard (2), Barrie McDermott (SOS), Marcus Vassilakopoulos (1)	12
Leigh C.	0	–	5
London B.	0	–	6
Oldham B.	4	Iyan Green (2), Chris Parr (1), Ian Sherratt (5), Jason Temu (NG)	8
Rochdale H.	1	Mark Meadows (2)	9
St. Helens	6	Bernard Dwyer (SOS), Scott Gibbs (2), Vila Matautia (Fined £300, 3), Sonny Nickle (3), Andy Northey (1)	4
Salford R.	3	Cliff Eccles (NG), Peter Edwards (SOS), Ian Watson (SOS)	11
Sheffield E.	1	Paul Dixon (1)	6
Swinton	0	–	6
Wakefield T.	1	Wayne McDonald (3)	9
Warrington	4	Gary Chambers (2), Salesi Finau (2), Lee Penny (SOS)	5
Whitehaven	1	Paul Lancaster (SOS)	11
Widnes	1	David Hulme (SOS)	12
Wigan	1	Neil Cowie (1)	8
Workington T.	0	–	6
York	2	Andy Gascoigne (SOS), Lee Tichener (SOS)	10

In addition, the following players were dealt with by the Disciplinary Committee after either being referred by the League's Board of Directors or placed on report by the match referee:

Referrals
Bramley: Ray Ashton (Fined £350)
Carlisle: Stuart Rhodes (5)
Castleford: Adrian Flynn (2), Colin Maskill (2)
Hull: Anthony Jackson (2)
Hunslet H.: Martin Rowse (6)
Oldham B.: Peaufai Leuila (4)
St. Helens: Bobbie Goulding (3)
Wigan: Shaun Edwards (1 & fined £50 – quashed on appeal)

On report
Bradford B.: Eugene Bourneville (4)
Castleford: Tony Smith (1)
Halifax: Paul Moriarty (NG), Paul Rowley (3)
Leeds: Craig Innes (NG)
Warrington: Mark Jones (2)

REFEREES HONOURS 1995–96
Regal Trophy Final:
Russell Smith
Charity Shield:
Russell Smith
Centenary World Cup:
Stuart Cummings
Australia v. England
Australia v. England (F)
Russell Smith
Australia v. S. Africa
New Zealand v. PNG
Wales v. Western Samoa
Australia v. New Zealand
David Campbell
New Zealand v. Tonga

SENIOR REFEREES 1996
Premier Division

Alan Bates	Karl Kirkpatrick
Dave Campbell	Colin Morris
John Connolly	Steve Presley
Robert Connolly	Russell Smith
Stuart Cummings	

Grade One

Dave Asquith	Paul Lee
Dave Atkin	Ian McGregor
Alan Burke	Nick Oddy
Steve Cross	Gary Owram
Steve Ganson	Steve Nicholson
Peter Gilmour	Graham Shaw
Paul Grimshaw	Pete Taberner

Grade Two

Martin Ashcroft	Mark Kennedy
James Benson	Ron Laughton
Steven Bright	Lenny Lockton
Paul Byrne	Steve Lowe
Steve Chestney	Andy Pedder
Ray Cornish	Alan Perris
Ian Devany	Martin Phillips
Robert Ellis	Steve Royle
Darren Gillespie	Steve Sharp
Steve Greenhalgh	Bob Stokes
Dave Griffiths	Howard Underwood
Paul Grundill	Gordon Wallace
Gerry Hodgson	Pete Wharton
Colin Johnson	

QUEEN'S HONOURS

Ten Rugby League players have been awarded the MBE and three others the OBE by Her Majesty the Queen for their services to the game. Former Castleford player-coach Malcolm Reilly was awarded the OBE in June 1991, while Great Britain's full-time coach.

Player	Awarded MBE	GB Caps	Career	Clubs
Eric Ashton	June 1966	26	1955-69	Wigan
Geoff Gunney	June 1970	11	1951-73	Hunslet
Clive Sullivan	January 1974	17	1961-85	Hull, Hull K.R., Oldham, Doncaster
Chris Hesketh	January 1976	21+2	1963-79	Wigan, Salford
Roger Millward	January 1983	28+1	1963-80	Castleford, Hull K.R.
Neil Fox	June 1983	29	1956-79	Wakefield T., Bradford N., Hull K.R., York, Bramley, Huddersfield
David Watkins	January 1986	2+4	1967-82	Salford, Swinton, Cardiff C.
Ellery Hanley	January 1990	33+1	1978-	Bradford N., Wigan, Leeds
Jeff Grayshon	June 1992	13	1970-	Dewsbury, Bradford N., Leeds, Featherstone R., Batley
Jonathan Davies	January 1995	12+1	1989-	Widnes, Warrington
	Awarded OBE			
Malcolm Reilly	June 1991	9	1967-87	Castleford
Garry Schofield	June 1994	44+2	1983-	Hull, Leeds
Shaun Edwards	January 1996	32+4	1983-	Wigan

FINAL TABLES 1995-96

ALLIANCE CHAMPIONSHIP

	P.	W.	D.	L.	Dg.	FOR Gls.	Trs.	Pts.	Dg.	AGAINST Gls.	Trs.	Pts.	Pts.
St. Helens	18	14	1	3	4	53	79	426	2	46	46	278	29
Leeds	18	13	0	5	1	59	88	471	2	35	48	264	26
Castleford T.	18	11	0	7	0	48	71	380	2	35	54	288	22
Bradford B.	18	10	0	8	7	57	68	393	0	67	79	450	20
Wigan	18	9	0	9	2	53	91	472	0	52	73	396	18
Hull	18	9	0	9	0	51	54	318	3	52	71	391	18
Salford R.	18	6	1	11	3	48	65	359	3	59	79	437	13
Warrington	18	6	0	12	1	62	69	401	6	53	76	416	12
Oldham B.	18	6	0	12	3	41	55	305	5	61	76	431	12
Dewsbury	18	5	0	13	4	42	52	296	2	54	90	470	10

ALLIANCE FIRST DIVISION

	P.	W.	D.	L.	Dg.	FOR Gls.	Trs.	Pts.	Dg.	AGAINST Gls.	Trs.	Pts.	Pts.
Halifax	18	15	0	3	7	77	97	549	1	47	64	351	30
Hull K.R.	18	13	1	4	3	90	111	627	1	36	40	233	27
Featherstone R.	18	12	1	5	1	65	91	495	4	49	53	314	25
Sheffield E.	18	10	0	8	3	93	119	665	2	54	77	418	20
Workington T.	18	9	0	9	3	49	78	413	5	48	69	377	18
Wakefield T.	18	8	1	9	6	47	58	332	5	55	76	419	17
Widnes	18	7	1	10	3	57	75	417	3	61	68	397	15
York	18	6	0	12	5	44	60	333	3	70	99	539	12
Leigh C.	18	3	2	13	0	27	55	274	5	83	106	595	8
Keighley C.	18	4	0	14	3	32	48	259	5	78	140	721	8

ALLIANCE SECOND DIVISION

	P.	W.	D.	L.	Dg.	FOR Gls.	Trs.	Pts.	Dg.	AGAINST Gls.	Trs.	Pts.	Pts.
London B.	18	12	2	4	1	88	105	597	5	36	49	273	26
Batley	18	13	0	5	2	68	80	458	5	40	55	305	26
Swinton	18	12	1	5	3	72	95	527	1	34	57	297	25
Huddersfield	18	12	0	6	5	54	77	421	2	53	68	380	24
Whitehaven	18	11	0	7	6	55	76	420	4	60	76	428	22
Rochdale H.	18	9	0	9	0	58	81	440	9	60	71	413	18
Hunslet H.	18	6	0	12	6	41	72	376	2	59	82	448	12
Blackpool G.	18	6	0	12	6	49	62	352	3	73	94	525	12
Barrow B.	18	5	0	13	8	44	51	300	3	68	100	539	10
Carlisle	18	2	1	15	1	36	52	281	4	82	99	564	5

ATTENDANCES

CLUB ATTENDANCE REVIEW

The following is a review of clubs' home attendances for League matches from 1987-88.

The main figure is the individual club's average gate for League games during that season. The figure in brackets indicates an upward or downward trend compared with the previous season.

Also indicated is the division the club competed in that season, i.e.,

1 — First Division/Centenary Championship
2 — Second Division/Centenary First Division,
3 — Third Division/Centenary Second Division

Club	87-88	88-89	89-90	90-91	91-92	92-93	93-94	94-95	95-96
Barrow B.	2 1624 (−1040)	2 1594 (−30)	1 1997 (+403)	2 962 (−1035)	3 1003 (+41)	3 786 (−217)	2 1318 (+532)	2 957 (−361)	3 666 (−291)
Batley	2 859 (+115)	2 924 (+65)	2 1506 (+582)	2 1188 (−318)	3 1145 (−43)	3 925 (−220)	2 1227 (+302)	2 1509 (+282)	2 1305 (−204)
Blackpool G.	2 922 (+447)	2 512 (−410)	2 780 (+258)	2 638 (−142)	3 309 (−329)	3 475 (+166)	—	—	—
Bradford B.	1 4723 (+411)	1 4969 (+246)	1 5584 (+615)	1 5274 (−310)	1 4725 (−549)	1 5082 (+357)	1 6513 (+1431)	1 5654 (−859)	1 4593 (−1061)
Bramley	2 858 (+121)	2 1004 (+146)	2 982 (−22)	2 805 (−177)	3 870 (+65)	2 980 (+110)	2 729 (−251)	2 758 (+29)	3 446 (−312)
Carlisle	2 763 (−26)	2 678 (−85)	2 574 (−104)	2 781 (+207)	2 800 (+19)	2 648 (−152)	2 603 (−45)	2 375 (−228)	3 495 (+120)
Castleford	1 4520 (−238)	1 6580 (+2060)	1 6428 (−152)	1 6019 (−409)	1 6465 (+446)	1 5658 (−807)	1 5555 (−103)	1 5090 (−465)	1 4072 (−1018)
Chorley C.	—	—	2 806	2 690 (−116)	3 394 (−296)	3 434 (+40)	—	—	3 501
Dewsbury	2 658 (−11)	2 772 (+114)	2 1227 (+455)	2 955 (−272)	3 1140 (+185)	3 1108 (−32)	2 1366 (+258)	2 1859 (+493)	2 1324 (−535)
Doncaster D.	2 1450 (−93)	2 1906 (+456)	2 1965 (+59)	2 1458 (−507)	3 1158 (−300)	3 997 (−161)	2 1648 (+651)	1 3495 (+1847)	3 1026 (−2469)
Featherstone R.	2 1879 (−727)	1 4379 (+2500)	1 4269 (−110)	1 4722 (+453)	1 4001 (−721)	2 2670 (−1331)	1 4030 (+1360)	1 3683 (−347)	2 2097 (−1586)
Halifax	1 6521 (+1630)	1 8022 (+1501)	2 5921 (−2101)	2 4458 (−1463)	1 7181 (+2723)	1 6452 (−729)	1 6608 (+156)	1 5600 (−1008)	1 4657 (−943)
Highfield	2 515 (+184)	2 298 (−217)	2 453 (+155)	2 632 (+179)	3 319 (−313)	3 378 (+59)	2 403 (+25)	2 550 (+147)	3 338 (−212)
Huddersfield	2 601 (+77)	2 1114 (+513)	2 1634 (+520)	2 1306 (−328)	3 2271 (+965)	2 1985 (−286)	2 2227 (+242)	2 2904 (+677)	2 2427 (−477)
Hull	1 5111 (−427)	1 6804 (+1693)	1 6218 (−586)	1 6699 (+481)	1 5892 (−807)	1 4860 (−1032)	1 4314 (−546)	1 4165 (−149)	2 2824 (−1341)
Hull K.R.	1 4186 (−465)	1 5298 (+1112)	2 4851 (−447)	1 4952 (+101)	1 4752 (−200)	1 3609 (−1143)	1 3403 (−206)	2 1900 (−1503)	3 1638 (−262)
Hunslet H.	1 2678 (+1628)	2 947 (−1731)	2 1046 (+99)	2 767 (−279)	3 770 (+3)	3 724 (−46)	2 740 (+16)	2 852 (+112)	3 870 (+18)

(continued)

ATTENDANCES

Club	87-88	88-89	89-90	90-91	91-92	92-93	93-94	94-95	95-96
Keighley C.	2 958 (+513)	2 961 (+3)	2 936 (−25)	2 985 (+49)	3 1196 (+211)	3 2060 (+864)	2 3032 (+972)	2 3723 (+691)	2 3787 (+64)
Leeds	1 9911 (+3518)	1 12060 (+2149)	1 12251 (+191)	1 11102 (−1149)	1 12164 (+1062)	1 11527 (−637)	1 9545 (−1982)	1 12516 (+2971)	1 11594 (−922)
Leigh C.	1 4516 (+284)	2 2346 (−2170)	1 4568 (+2222)	2 1719 (−2849)	2 3014 (+1295)	1 3967 (+953)	1 3385 (−582)	2 1550 (−1855)	3 1195 (−355)
London C.	2 615 (−69)	2 588 (−27)	2 841 (+253)	2 557 (−284)	2 724 (+167)	2 554 (−170)	2 734 (+180)	2 814 (+80)	1 2386 (+1572)
Nottingham C.	2 368	2 560 (+192)	2 577 (+17)	2 255 (−322)	3 270 (+15)	3 270	—	—	—
Oldham B.	2 3790 (−125)	1 5759 (+1969)	2 4401 (−1358)	1 5094 (+693)	2 3149 (−1945)	2 2809 (−340)	1 4062 (+1253)	1 3889 (−173)	1 3187 (−702)
Rochdale H.	2 1106 (+229)	2 1027 (−79)	2 2510 (+1483)	1 2542 (+32)	2 1415 (−1127)	2 1308 (−107)	2 1063 (−245)	2 1089 (+26)	2 1298 (+209)
St. Helens	1 8417 (+1076)	1 9514 (+1097)	1 8555 (−959)	1 7391 (−1164)	1 8456 (+1065)	1 8908 (+452)	1 7264 (−1644)	1 7467 (+203)	1 7143 (−324)
Salford R.	1 3747 (+921)	1 5470 (+1723)	1 3720 (−1750)	2 2314 (−1406)	1 3785 (+1471)	1 4098 (+313)	1 4106 (+8)	1 3600 (−506)	2 2610 (−990)
Scarborough P.	—	—	—	—	3 777	—	—	—	—
Sheffield E.	2 847 (+139)	2 838 (−9)	1 4038 (+3200)	1 4031 (−7)	2 2435 (−1596)	1 3069 (+634)	1 3050 (−19)	1 2661 (−389)	1 3106 (+445)
Swinton	1 2987 (+1365)	2 1435 (−1552)	2 1678 (+243)	2 1737 (+59)	1 2702 (+965)	2 1051 (−1651)	2 788 (−263)	2 776 (−12)	3 757 (−19)
Wakefield T.	2 2416 (−221)	1 5151 (+2735)	1 5428 (+277)	1 4848 (−580)	1 5022 (+174)	1 4505 (−517)	1 3822 (−683)	1 3438 (−384)	2 1824 (−1614)
Warrington	1 4974 (+802)	1 4893 (−81)	1 5412 (+519)	1 5915 (+503)	1 5204 (−711)	1 4550 (−754)	1 6188 (+1638)	1 5380 (−808)	1 4922 (−458)
Whitehaven	2 1772 (−28)	2 1310 (−462)	2 961 (−349)	2 1035 (+74)	3 632 (−403)	3 1462 (+830)	2 1257 (−205)	2 1149 (−108)	2 1205 (+56)
Widnes	1 6262 (+2422)	1 8648 (+2386)	1 7858 (−790)	1 6793 (−1065)	1 6291 (−502)	1 5540 (−751)	1 4525 (−1015)	1 4086 (−439)	2 2908 (−1178)
Wigan	1 13021 (+289)	1 14543 (+1522)	1 13973 (−570)	1 14493 (+520)	1 14040 (−453)	1 14553 (+513)	1 14561 (+8)	1 14195 (−366)	1 11947 (−2248)
Workington T.	2 737 (+84)	2 774 (+37)	2 691 (−83)	2 1426 (+735)	2 1884 (+458)	3 2040 (+156)	2 2603 (+563)	1 3776 (+1173)	1 3061 (−715)
York	2 1406 (−114)	2 2021 (+615)	2 2495 (+474)	2 1857 (−638)	2 1181 (−676)	3 1701 (+520)	2 1311 (−390)	2 1120 (−191)	3 642 (−478)

COMPETITION ATTENDANCE REVIEW

		87-88	88-89	89-90	90-91	91-92	92-93	93-94	94-95	95-96
FIRST DIVISION	Total	1,060,296	1,327,192	1,173,815	1,168,407	1,185,117	1,122,955	1,364,056	1,330,538	606,728[1]
	Av.	5,826	7,292	6,450	6,420	6,511	6,170	5,683	5,543	5,515
SECOND DIVISION	Total	381,825	298,776	515,687	371,398	204,304	168,069	315,841	328,377	236,132[2]
	Av.	1,364	1,067	1,754	1,263	1,824	1,501	1,316	1,368	2,146
THIRD DIVISION	Total	—	—	—	—	159,209	160,348	—	—	85,772[3]
	Av.					875	1,027			780
LEAGUE TOTALS (1st & 2nd) *plus 3rd	Total	1,442,121	1,625,968	1,689,502	1,539,805	1,548,630*	1,451,372*	1,679,897	1,658,915	928,632
	Av.	3,121	3,519	3,549	3,235	3,253*	3,225*	3,499	3,456	2,814*
CHALLENGE CUP	Av.	8,764	8,666	7,339	6,748	6,899	7,771	5,907	5,821	—
REGAL	Av.	3,570	4,987	4,876	3,515	4,007	3,624	2,690	3,627	3,200
PREMIER	Av.	13,462	15,856	16,796	12,483	13,513	12,788	13,165	11,425	—
10,000+ (No. of)		46	59	54	43	49	38	41	51	20

[1]Centenary Championship   [2]Centenary First Division   [3]Centenary Second Division

20,000-plus crowds . . . A 10-year review

All matches except the Rugby League Challenge Cup final at Wembley

23,866	Hull K.R. v. Leeds	RL Cup semi-final	Elland Rd, Leeds	29 Mar. 1986
32,485	Hull K.R. v. Leeds	RL Cup semi-final replay	Elland Rd, Leeds	3 Apr. 1986
28,252	Wigan v. St. Helens	Lancs Cup semi-final	Wigan	1 Oct. 1986
30,622	Wigan v. Australia	Tour	Wigan	12 Oct. 1986
20,180	Oldham v. Wigan	Lancs Cup final	St. Helens	19 Oct. 1986
50,583	Britain v. Australia	First Test	Manchester U. FC	25 Oct. 1986
30,808	Britain v. Australia	Second Test	Elland Rd, Leeds	8 Nov. 1986
20,169	Britain v. Australia	Third Test	Wigan	22 Nov. 1986
21,214	St. Helens v. Wigan	Division One	St. Helens	26 Dec. 1986
21,144	Warrington v. Wigan	John Player final	Bolton W. FC	10 Jan. 1987
20,355	Wigan v. St. Helens	Division One	Wigan	17 Apr. 1987
22,457	Wigan v. Halifax	Premiership semi-final	Wigan	10 May 1987
38,756	Warrington v. Wigan	Premiership final	Manchester U. FC	17 May 1987
36,895	Wigan v. Manly	World Club Challenge	Wigan	7 Oct. 1987
20,234	Wigan v. Warrington	Lancs Cup final	St. Helens	11 Oct. 1987
23,809	Wigan v. St. Helens	Division One	Wigan	27 Dec. 1987
25,110	Wigan v. Leeds	RL Cup round 2	Wigan	14 Feb. 1988
20,783	Salford v. Wigan	RL Cup semi-final	Bolton W. FC	12 Mar. 1988
20,534	Halifax v. Hull	RL Cup semi-final	Leeds	26 Mar. 1988
25,117	Halifax v. Hull	RL Cup semi-final replay	Elland Rd, Leeds	30 Mar. 1988
21,812	St. Helens v. Wigan	Division One	St. Helens	1 Apr. 1988
35,252	St. Helens v. Widnes	Premiership final	Manchester U. FC	15 May 1988
22,968	Castleford v. Leeds	Yorks Cup final	Elland Rd, Leeds	16 Oct. 1988

(continued)

315

20,709	Widnes v. Wigan	John Player final	Bolton W. FC	7 Jan. 1989
26,080	Leeds v. Widnes	RL Cup round 2	Leeds	26 Feb. 1989
26,529	Warrington v. Wigan	RL Cup semi-final	Manchester C. FC	25 Mar. 1989
21,076	Wigan v. St. Helens	Division One	Wigan	12 Apr. 1989
40,194	Hull v. Widnes	Premiership final	Manchester U. FC	14 May 1989
30,786	Widnes v. Canberra	World Club Challenge	Manchester U. FC	4 Oct. 1989
20,346	Britain v. New Zealand	Third Test	Wigan	11 Nov. 1989
27,075	Wigan v. St. Helens	Division One	Wigan	26 Dec. 1989
23,570	Leeds v. Wigan	Division One	Leeds	4 Mar. 1990
26,489	St. Helens v. Wigan	RL Cup semi-final	Manchester U. FC	10 Mar. 1990
24,462	Wigan v. Leeds	Division One	Wigan	10 Apr. 1990
40,796	Bradford N. v. Widnes	Premiership final	Manchester U. FC	13 May 1990
24,814	Wigan v. Australia	Tour	Wigan	14 Oct. 1990
54,569	Britain v. Australia	First Test	Wembley	27 Oct. 1990
46,615	Britain v. Australia	Second Test	Manchester U. FC	10 Nov. 1990
32,500	Britain v. Australia	Third Test	Elland Rd, Leeds	24 Nov. 1990
29,763	Wigan v. Widnes	Division One	Wigan	9 Apr. 1991
42,043	Hull v. Widnes	Premiership final	Manchester U. FC	12 May 1991
20,152	Wigan v. Penrith	World Club Challenge	Liverpool FC	2 Oct. 1991
26,307	Wigan v. St. Helens	Division One	Wigan	26 Dec. 1991
21,736	Wigan v. Warrington	RL Cup round 2	Wigan	16 Feb. 1992
20,821	Leeds v. Wigan	Division One	Leeds	15 Mar. 1992
33,157	St. Helens v. Wigan	Premiership final	Manchester U. FC	17 May 1992
20,534	St. Helens v. Wigan	Lancs Cup final	St. Helens	18 Oct. 1992
73,631	Britain v. Australia	World Cup final	Wembley	24 Oct. 1992
20,258	Leeds v. Castleford	Division One	Leeds	26 Dec. 1992
21,191	Wigan v. St. Helens	RL Cup round 2	Wigan	13 Feb. 1993
20,057	Leeds v. Wigan	Division One	Leeds	3 Mar. 1993
20,085	Bradford N. v. Wigan	RL Cup semi-final	Elland Rd, Leeds	27 Mar. 1993
29,839	Wigan v. St. Helens	Division One	Wigan	9 Apr. 1993
36,598	St. Helens v. Wigan	Premiership final	Manchester U. FC	16 May 1993
36,131	Britain v. New Zealand	First Test	Wembley	16 Oct. 1993
29,100	Wigan v. St. Helens	Division One	Wigan	26 Dec. 1993
22,615	Leeds v. Bradford N.	RL Cup quarter-final	Leeds	27 Feb. 1994
20,771	St. Helens v. Leeds	RL Cup semi-final	Wigan	26 Mar. 1994
35,644	Castleford v. Wigan	Premiership final	Manchester U. FC	22 May 1994
20,057	Wigan v. Australia	Tour	Wigan	8 Oct. 1994
57,034	Britain v. Australia	First Test	Wembley	22 Oct. 1994
43,930	Britain v. Australia	Second Test	Manchester U. FC	5 Nov. 1994
39,468	Britain v. Australia	Third Test	Elland Rd, Leeds	20 Nov. 1994
20,053	Leeds v. Wigan	Division One	Leeds	11 Dec. 1994
23,278	Wigan v. St. Helens	Regal Trophy quarter-final	Wigan	8 Jan. 1995
21,485	Featherstone R. v. Leeds	RL Cup semi-final	Elland Rd, Leeds	1 Apr. 1995
26,314	Wigan v. St. Helens	Division One	Wigan	14 Apr. 1995
30,160	Leeds v. Wigan	Premiership Final	Manchester U. FC	21 May 1995
41,271	England v. Australia	World Cup	Wembley	7 Oct 1995
26,263	England v. Fiji	World Cup	Wigan	11 Oct 1995
30,042	England v. Wales	World Cup	Manchester U. FC	21 Oct 1995
66,540	England v. Australia	World Cup Final	Wembley	28 Oct 1995

FIXTURES

● Fixtures listed below for June, July and August subject to change for screening by BSkyB

STONES SUPER LEAGUE 1996

FRIDAY, 29 MARCH 1996

Paris	v.	Sheffield E.	7.30

SATURDAY, 30 MARCH 1996

Halifax	v.	London B.	5.30
Oldham B.	v.	Wigan	6.00

SUNDAY, 31 MARCH 1996

Bradford B.	v.	Castleford	6.00
Leeds	v.	Warrington	3.00
Workington T.	v.	St. Helens	3.00

THURSDAY, 4 APRIL 1996

London B.	v.	Paris	T.B.A.

FRIDAY, 5 APRIL 1996

Castleford	v.	Leeds	6.00
Oldham B.	v.	Halifax	3.00
Sheffield E.	v.	Bradford B.	7.30
St. Helens	v.	Wigan	T.B.A.
Warrington	v.	Workington T.	3.00

MONDAY, 8 APRIL 1996

Bradford B.	v.	London B.	6.00
Leeds	v.	St. Helens	3.00
Paris	v.	Oldham B.	8.00
Wigan	v.	Warrington	6.30
Workington T.	v.	Sheffield E.	3.00

TUESDAY, 9 APRIL 1996

Halifax	v.	Castleford	7.30

FRIDAY, 12 APRIL 1996

Warrington	v.	Halifax	7.30

SATURDAY, 13 APRIL 1996

Oldham B.	v.	Leeds	6.00
Paris	v.	Workington T.	8.00

SUNDAY, 14 APRIL 1996

Castleford	v.	Wigan	6.00
Sheffield E.	v.	London B.	6.00
St. Helens	v.	Bradford B.	3.00

FRIDAY, 19 APRIL 1996

Wigan	v.	Bradford B.	7.30

SATURDAY, 20 APRIL 1996

Castleford	v.	Oldham B.	6.00

SUNDAY, 21 APRIL 1996

Halifax	v.	St. Helens	6.30
Leeds	v.	Sheffield E.	3.00
London B.	v.	Workington T.	3.00
Warrington	v.	Paris	3.00

FRIDAY, 3 MAY 1996

Sheffield E.	v.	Castleford	7.30

SATURDAY, 4 MAY 1996

Workington T.	v.	Halifax	6.00

SUNDAY, 5 MAY 1996

Bradford B.	v.	Warrington	6.00
Leeds	v.	London B.	3.00
St. Helens	v.	Oldham B.	3.00
Wigan	v.	Paris	6.30

FRIDAY, 10 MAY 1996

Oldham B.	v.	Bradford B.	7.30
Paris	v.	Leeds	7.30

SUNDAY, 12 MAY 1996

Castleford	v.	Workington T.	6.00
London B.	v.	St. Helens	T.B.A.
Warrington	v.	Sheffield E.	3.00

WEDNESDAY, 15 MAY 1996

Halifax	v.	Wigan	7.30

FRIDAY, 17 MAY 1996

Warrington	v.	St. Helens	7.30

SATURDAY, 18 MAY 1996

Workington T.	v.	Wigan	6.00

SUNDAY, 19 MAY 1996

Bradford B.	v.	Paris	6.00
Castleford	v.	London B.	6.00
Leeds	v.	Halifax	3.00
Sheffield E.	v.	Oldham B.	6.00

FRIDAY, 24 MAY 1996

Bradford B.	v.	Leeds	7.30

SATURDAY, 25 MAY 1996

Paris	v.	Halifax	8.00
Warrington	v.	London B.	6.00

SUNDAY, 26 MAY 1996

Oldham B.	v.	Workington T.	3.00
St. Helens	v.	Castleford	7.00
Wigan	v.	Sheffield E.	6.30

FRIDAY, 31 MAY 1996

Castleford	v.	Warrington	7.30

SATURDAY, 1 JUNE 1996

Leeds	v.	Wigan	6.00

SUNDAY, 2 JUNE 1996

Bradford B.	v.	Workington T.	6.00
Halifax	v.	Sheffield E.	6.30
London B.	v.	Oldham B.	7.30
St. Helens	v.	Paris	7.00

SATURDAY, 8 JUNE 1996

Paris	v.	Castleford	8.00
Sheffield E.	v.	St. Helens	6.00

SUNDAY, 9 JUNE 1996

Halifax	v.	Bradford B.	6.30
Oldham B.	v.	Warrington	6.00
Wigan	v.	London B.	6.30
Workington T.	v.	Leeds	3.00

SATURDAY, 15 JUNE 1996

Sheffield E.	v.	Paris	6.00

SUNDAY, 16 JUNE 1996

Castleford	v.	Bradford B.	6.00
London B.	v.	Halifax	7.30
St. Helens	v.	Workington T.	7.00
Warrington	v.	Leeds	3.00
Wigan	v.	Oldham B.	6.30

FRIDAY, 21 JUNE 1996

Wigan	v.	St. Helens	7.30

SATURDAY, 22 JUNE 1996

Paris	v.	Warrington	8.00

SUNDAY, 23 JUNE 1996

Bradford B.	v.	Sheffield E.	6.00
Halifax	v.	Oldham B.	6.30

Leeds	v.	Castleford	3.00
Workington T.	v.	London B.	3.00

SATURDAY, 29 JUNE 1996

Sheffield E.	v.	Workington T.	6.00

SUNDAY, 30 JUNE 1996

Castleford	v.	Halifax	6.00
London B.	v.	Bradford B.	7.30
Oldham B.	v.	Paris	6.00
St. Helens	v.	Leeds	7.00
Warrington	v.	Wigan	3.00

SUNDAY, 7 JULY 1996

Bradford B.	v.	St. Helens	6.00
Halifax	v.	Warrington	6.30
Leeds	v.	Oldham B.	3.00
London B.	v.	Sheffield E.	7.30
Wigan	v.	Castleford	6.30
Workington T.	v.	Paris	3.00

SUNDAY, 14 JULY 1996

Bradford B.	v.	Wigan	6.00
Oldham B.	v.	Castleford	6.00
Paris	v.	London B.	3.00
Sheffield E.	v.	Leeds	6.00
St. Helens	v.	Halifax	7.00
Workington T.	v.	Warrington	3.00

SATURDAY, 20 JULY 1996

Paris	v.	Wigan	8.30

SUNDAY, 21 JULY 1996

Castleford	v.	Sheffield E.	6.00
Halifax	v.	Workington T.	6.30
London B.	v.	Leeds	7.30
Oldham B.	v.	St. Helens	6.00
Warrington	v.	Bradford B.	3.00

SUNDAY, 28 JULY 1996

Bradford B.	v.	Oldham B.	6.00
Leeds	v.	Paris	3.00
Sheffield E.	v.	Warrington	6.00
St. Helens	v.	London B.	7.00
Wigan	v.	Halifax	6.30
Workington T.	v.	Castleford	3.00

SUNDAY, 4 AUGUST 1996

Castleford	v.	St. Helens	6.00
Halifax	v.	Paris	6.30
Leeds	v.	Bradford B.	3.00
London B.	v.	Warrington	7.30
Sheffield E.	v.	Wigan	6.00
Workington T.	v.	Oldham B.	3.00

SATURDAY, 10 AUGUST 1996

Paris	v.	St. Helens	8.00

SUNDAY, 11 AUGUST 1996

Oldham B.	v.	London B.	6.00
Sheffield E.	v.	Halifax	6.00
Warrington	v.	Castleford	3.00
Wigan	v.	Leeds	6.30
Workington T.	v.	Bradford B.	3.00

SUNDAY, 18 AUGUST 1996

Bradford B.	v.	Halifax	6.00
Castleford	v.	Paris	6.00
Leeds	v.	Workington T.	3.00
London B.	v.	Wigan	7.30
St. Helens	v.	Sheffield E.	7.00
Warrington	v.	Oldham B.	3.00

SATURDAY, 24 AUGUST 1996

Paris	v.	Bradford B.	8.00

SUNDAY, 25 AUGUST 1996

Halifax	v.	Leeds	6.30
London B.	v.	Castleford	7.30
Oldham B.	v.	Sheffield E.	6.00
St. Helens	v.	Warrington	7.00
Wigan	v.	Workington T.	6.30

FIRST DIVISION

SUNDAY, 31 MARCH 1996

Batley	v.	Whitehaven	5.30
Featherstone R.	v.	Rochdale H.	6.00
Huddersfield	v.	Salford R.	3.30
Hull	v.	Wakefield T.	3.15
Keighley C.	v.	Dewsbury	3.30

FRIDAY, 5 APRIL 1996

Dewsbury	v.	Batley	3.00
Rochdale H.	v.	Keighley C.	3.00
Salford R.	v.	Widnes	3.00
Wakefield T.	v.	Featherstone R.	7.30
Whitehaven	v.	Huddersfield	7.30

MONDAY, 8 APRIL 1996

Batley	v.	Wakefield T.	5.30
Featherstone R.	v.	Dewsbury	6.00
Huddersfield	v.	Rochdale H.	7.30
Keighley C.	v.	Hull	3.30
Widnes	v.	Whitehaven	3.00

SUNDAY, 14 APRIL 1996

Dewsbury	v.	Hull	3.00
Huddersfield	v.	Keighley C.	3.30
Rochdale H.	v.	Batley	3.00
Whitehaven	v.	Salford R.	3.30
Widnes	v.	Featherstone R.	3.00

SUNDAY, 21 APRIL 1996

Batley	v.	Huddersfield	5.30
Hull	v.	Widnes	3.15
Rochdale H.	v.	Dewsbury	3.00
Wakefield T.	v.	Salford R.	3.30
Whitehaven	v.	Featherstone R.	3.30

SUNDAY, 5 MAY 1996

Featherstone R.	v.	Batley	6.00
Huddersfield	v.	Hull	3.30
Keighley C.	v.	Whitehaven	3.30
Salford R.	v.	Rochdale H.	3.00
Widnes	v.	Wakefield T.	3.00

SUNDAY, 12 MAY 1996

Dewsbury	v.	Whitehaven	3.00
Hull	v.	Salford R.	3.15
Keighley C.	v.	Featherstone R.	3.30
Wakefield T.	v.	Rochdale H.	3.30
Widnes	v.	Huddersfield	3.00

SUNDAY, 19 MAY 1996

Batley	v.	Keighley C.	5.30
Huddersfield	v.	Wakefield T.	3.30
Salford R.	v.	Featherstone R.	3.00
Whitehaven	v.	Hull	3.30
Widnes	v.	Dewsbury	3.00

SUNDAY, 26 MAY 1996

Batley	v.	Widnes	5.30
Featherstone R.	v.	Huddersfield	6.00
Hull	v.	Rochdale H.	3.15
Salford R.	v.	Dewsbury	3.00
Wakefield T.	v.	Keighley C.	3.30

SUNDAY, 2 JUNE 1996

Dewsbury	v.	Huddersfield	5.00
Hull	v.	Batley	3.15
Keighley C.	v.	Salford R.	6.00
Rochdale H.	v.	Widnes	7.30
Whitehaven	v.	Wakefield T.	3.30

SUNDAY, 9 JUNE 1996

Batley	v.	Salford R.	5.30
Featherstone R.	v.	Hull	6.00
Rochdale H.	v.	Whitehaven	7.00
Wakefield T.	v.	Dewsbury	6.00
Widnes	v.	Keighley C.	3.00

SUNDAY, 16 JUNE 1996

Dewsbury	v.	Keighley C.	5.00
Rochdale H.	v.	Featherstone R.	3.00
Salford R.	v.	Huddersfield	3.00
Wakefield T.	v.	Hull	6.00
Whitehaven	v.	Batley	3.30

SUNDAY, 23 JUNE 1996

Batley	v.	Dewsbury	5.30
Featherstone R.	v.	Wakefield T.	6.00
Huddersfield	v.	Whitehaven	3.30
Keighley C.	v.	Rochdale H.	6.00
Widnes	v.	Salford R.	3.00

SUNDAY, 30 JUNE 1996

Dewsbury	v.	Featherstone R.	5.00
Hull	v.	Keighley C.	6.00
Rochdale H.	v.	Huddersfield	7.00
Wakefield T.	v.	Batley	6.00
Whitehaven	v.	Widnes	3.30

SUNDAY, 7 JULY 1996

Batley	v.	Rochdale H.	5.30
Featherstone R.	v.	Widnes	6.00
Hull	v.	Dewsbury	6.00
Keighley C.	v.	Huddersfield	6.00
Salford R.	v.	Whitehaven	3.00

SUNDAY, 14 JULY 1996

Dewsbury	v.	Rochdale H.	5.00
Featherstone R.	v.	Whitehaven	6.00
Huddersfield	v.	Batley	6.30
Salford R.	v.	Wakefield T.	3.00
Widnes	v.	Hull	3.00

FRIDAY, 19 JULY 1996

Rochdale H.	v.	Salford R.	7.30

SUNDAY, 21 JULY 1996

Batley	v.	Featherstone R.	5.30
Hull	v.	Huddersfield	6.00
Wakefield T.	v.	Widnes	6.00
Whitehaven	v.	Keighley C.	3.30

SATURDAY, 27 JULY 1996

Rochdale H.	v.	Wakefield T.	7.00

SUNDAY, 28 JULY 1996

Featherstone R.	v.	Keighley C.	6.00
Huddersfield	v.	Widnes	6.30
Salford R.	v.	Hull	3.00
Whitehaven	v.	Dewsbury	3.30

SUNDAY, 4 AUGUST 1996

Dewsbury	v.	Salford R.	5.00
Huddersfield	v.	Featherstone R.	6.30
Keighley C.	v.	Wakefield T.	6.00
Rochdale H.	v.	Hull	3.00
Widnes	v.	Batley	3.00

SUNDAY, 11 AUGUST 1996

Batley	v.	Hull	5.30
Huddersfield	v.	Dewsbury	6.30
Salford R.	v.	Keighley C.	3.00
Wakefield T.	v.	Whitehaven	3.30
Widnes	v.	Rochdale H.	3.00

SUNDAY, 18 AUGUST 1996

Dewsbury	v.	Wakefield T.	5.00
Hull	v.	Featherstone R.	6.00
Keighley C.	v.	Widnes	6.00
Salford R.	v.	Batley	3.00
Whitehaven	v.	Rochdale H.	3.30

SUNDAY, 25 AUGUST 1996

Dewsbury	v.	Widnes	5.00
Featherstone R.	v.	Salford R.	6.00
Hull	v.	Whitehaven	6.00
Keighley C.	v.	Batley	6.00
Wakefield T.	v.	Huddersfield	3.30

SECOND DIVISION

SUNDAY, 31 MARCH 1996

Bramley	v.	Leigh C.	3.00
Carlisle	v.	Chorley C.	3.00
Doncaster D.	v.	Barrow B.	3.00
Highfield	v.	Hunslet H.	3.00
York	v.	Swinton	3.15

FRIDAY, 5 APRIL 1996

Barrow B.	v.	Carlisle	7.30
Chorley C.	v.	Doncaster D.	3.00
Hunslet H.	v.	Bramley	7.30
Leigh C.	v.	Swinton	3.00
York	v.	Hull K.R.	3.15

MONDAY, 8 APRIL 1996

Carlisle	v.	Leigh C.	3.00
Doncaster D.	v.	York	7.30
Highfield	v.	Barrow B.	3.00
Hull K.R.	v.	Hunslet H.	3.00
Swinton	v.	Chorley C.	6.30

SUNDAY, 14 APRIL 1996

Bramley	v.	Chorley C.	3.00
Hull K.R.	v.	Highfield	3.00
Hunslet H.	v.	Leigh C.	3.30
Swinton	v.	Doncaster D.	6.30
York	v.	Carlisle	3.15

SUNDAY, 21 APRIL 1996

Carlisle	v.	Bramley	3.00
Chorley C.	v.	Hull K.R.	3.00
Hunslet H.	v.	York	3.30
Leigh C.	v.	Highfield	3.00
Swinton	v.	Barrow B.	3.00

FRIDAY, 3 MAY 1996

York	v.	Barrow B.	7.30

FIXTURES

SUNDAY, 5 MAY 1996

Doncaster D.	v.	Carlisle	3.00
Highfield	v.	Chorley C.	3.00
Hull K.R.	v.	Bramley	3.00
Swinton	v.	Hunslet H.	6.30

FRIDAY, 10 MAY 1996

Barrow B.	v.	Hunslet H.	7.30

SUNDAY, 12 MAY 1996

Bramley	v.	Swinton	3.00
Carlisle	v.	Highfield	3.00
Doncaster D.	v.	Hull K.R.	3.00
Leigh C.	v.	York	3.00

SUNDAY, 19 MAY 1996

Bramley	v.	Highfield	3.00
Chorley C.	v.	Leigh C.	3.00
Hull K.R.	v.	Barrow B.	3.00
Hunslet H.	v.	Doncaster D.	3.30
Swinton	v.	Carlisle	6.30

FRIDAY, 24 MAY 1996

Barrow B.	v.	Bramley	7.30
York	v.	Chorley C.	7.30

SUNDAY, 26 MAY 1996

Carlisle	v.	Hull K.R.	3.00
Highfield	v.	Swinton	3.00
Leigh C.	v.	Doncaster D.	3.00

FRIDAY, 31 MAY 1996

York	v.	Highfield	7.30

SUNDAY, 2 JUNE 1996

Carlisle	v.	Hunslet H.	3.00
Chorley C.	v.	Barrow B.	6.00
Doncaster D.	v.	Bramley	3.00
Leigh C.	v.	Hull K.R.	3.00

FRIDAY, 7 JUNE 1996

Barrow B.	v.	Leigh C.	7.30

SUNDAY, 9 JUNE 1996

Bramley	v.	York	3.00
Highfield	v.	Doncaster D.	3.00
Hull K.R.	v.	Swinton	6.30
Hunslet H.	v.	Chorley C.	3.30

FRIDAY, 14 JUNE 1996

Barrow B.	v.	Doncaster D.	7.30

SUNDAY, 16 JUNE 1996

Chorley C.	v.	Carlisle	6.00
Hunslet H.	v.	Highfield	3.30
Leigh C.	v.	Bramley	3.00
Swinton	v.	York	6.30

FRIDAY, 21 JUNE 1996

Doncaster D.	v.	Chorley C.	7.30

SUNDAY, 23 JUNE 1996

Bramley	v.	Hunslet H.	3.00
Carlisle	v.	Barrow B.	3.00
Hull K.R.	v.	York	6.30
Swinton	v.	Leigh C.	6.30

FRIDAY, 28 JUNE 1996

Barrow B.	v.	Highfield	7.30
York	v.	Doncaster D.	7.30

SUNDAY, 30 JUNE 1996

Chorley C.	v.	Swinton	6.00
Hunslet H.	v.	Hull K.R.	3.30
Leigh C.	v.	Carlisle	3.00

SUNDAY, 7 JULY 1996

Carlisle	v.	York	3.00
Chorley C.	v.	Bramley	6.00
Doncaster D.	v.	Swinton	3.00
Highfield	v.	Hull K.R.	3.00
Leigh C.	v.	Hunslet H.	3.00

FRIDAY, 12 JULY 1996

Barrow B.	v.	Swinton	7.30
York	v.	Hunslet H.	7.30

SUNDAY, 14 JULY 1996

Bramley	v.	Carlisle	3.00
Highfield	v.	Leigh C.	3.00
Hull K.R.	v.	Chorley C.	6.30

FRIDAY, 19 JULY 1996

Barrow B.	v.	York	7.30

SUNDAY, 21 JULY 1996

Bramley	v.	Hull K.R.	3.00
Carlisle	v.	Doncaster D.	3.00
Chorley C.	v.	Highfield	6.00
Hunslet H.	v.	Swinton	3.30

FRIDAY, 26 JULY 1996

York	v.	Leigh C.	7.30

SUNDAY, 28 JULY 1996

Highfield	v.	Carlisle	3.00
Hull K.R.	v.	Doncaster D.	6.30
Hunslet H.	v.	Barrow B.	3.30
Swinton	v.	Bramley	6.30

FRIDAY, 2 AUGUST 1996

Barrow B.	v.	Hull K.R.	7.30

SUNDAY, 4 AUGUST 1996

Carlisle	v.	Swinton	3.00
Doncaster D.	v.	Hunslet H.	3.00
Highfield	v.	Bramley	3.00
Leigh C.	v.	Chorley C.	3.00

SUNDAY, 11 AUGUST 1996

Bramley	v.	Barrow B.	3.00
Chorley C.	v.	York	6.00
Doncaster D.	v.	Leigh C.	3.00
Hull K.R.	v.	Carlisle	6.30
Swinton	v.	Highfield	6.30

FRIDAY, 16 AUGUST 1996

Barrow B.	v.	Chorley C.	7.30

SUNDAY, 18 AUGUST 1996

Bramley	v.	Doncaster D.	3.00
Highfield	v.	York	3.00
Hull K.R.	v.	Leigh C.	6.30
Hunslet H.	v.	Carlisle	3.30

FRIDAY, 23 AUGUST 1996

York	v.	Bramley	7.30

SUNDAY, 25 AUGUST 1996

Chorley C.	v.	Hunslet H.	6.00
Doncaster D.	v.	Highfield	3.00
Leigh C.	v.	Barrow B.	3.00
Swinton	v.	Hull K.R.	6.30